HANDBOOK
TO THE
CHURCH HYMNARY
THIRD EDITION

D0001501

HANDBOOK
TO THE
CHURCH HYMNARY
THIRD EDITION

———

Edited by
THE REVEREND PROFESSOR
JOHN M. BARKLEY
M.A., Ph.D., D.D., F.R.Hist.S.

LONDON   OXFORD   GLASGOW
OXFORD UNIVERSITY PRESS
1979

Oxford University Press, Walton Street, Oxford OX2 6DP

OXFORD LONDON GLASGOW
NEW YORK TORONTO MELBOURNE WELLINGTON
KUALA LUMPUR SINGAPORE JAKARTA HONG KONG TOKYO
DELHI BOMBAY CALCUTTA MADRAS KARACHI
NAIROBI DAR ES SALAAM CAPE TOWN

ISBN 0 19 146811 8

*Printed in Great Britain
at the University Press, Oxford
by Eric Buckley
Printer to the University*

CONTENTS

PREFACE

THE first edition of *The Church Hymnary* was published in 1898, the second in 1927, and the third in 1973. Dr. John Brownlie edited *The Hymns and Hymns Writers of the Church Hymnary*, in 1899, as a handbook to the first edition, and Professor James Moffat and Dr. Millar Patrick *The Handbook to the Church Hymnary*, Revised edition, 1927, to the second, to which Dr. Patrick added a *Supplement* in 1935. The present work has been planned as a handbook to the third, and throughout the second and third editions will be referred to as the RCH and CH3.

The handbook and supplement to the RCH are a mine of information and much use has been made of the material they contained. Indeed, in the case of hymns and tunes, authors and composers, common to both the RCH and CH3, the only changes have been by way of abbreviation, correction, and bringing up to date. Much research has taken place since 1935 and I am deeply indebted to many scholars. Names, like Erik Routley, Cecil Northcott, John Telford, A. E. Rushbridge, and E. P. Sharpe, spring easily to mind, never to mention older works by Frere and Dearmer, John Julian's *Dictionary of Hymnology*, 1907, Wilhelm Nelle's *Schlüssel zum Evangelischen Gesangbuch für Rheinland und Westfalen*, 1924, and Grove's *Dictionary of Music and Musicians*, 1954, as well as *The Oxford Companion to Music* and *The New Oxford History of Music*.

When compiling the 'Biographical Notes' and the 'Notes on the Words and Music' I received much assistance from diocesan registrars, the secretaries of societies, and individual scholars on a wide variety of details. Limitation of space forbids a complete list, but three call for particular mention: Miss Joyce Horn (Oxford University Press), Miss J. Woodward Steele (Westminster Press), and Mr. Andrew J. Hayden, Tonbridge, Kent.

Thanks are due to Dr. Thomas H. Keir, Dr. R. Stuart Louden, and the Revd. A. Stewart Todd for writing introductory articles on the history and place of hymnody, psalmody, and the canticles in the Church's worship, and to Professor Ian Pitt-Watson for his presentation of the principles governing the selection of the music in CH3.

While several gave assistance in typing sections of the work, I must thank in particular Mrs. Ruth Davey, who, apart from deciphering my handwriting, must, when she looked at all the 'wee arrows' on a page, have felt that she was at Crewe junction.

Finally, let me thank the representatives of the Oxford University Press for their guidance and help, and the members of the Church Hymnary Trust for inviting me to act as editor of the handbook to CH3. Every effort has been made to find out all the details and avoid errors. Some details proved impossible to obtain and information on these would be welcome. It is almost impossible to avoid errors completely in a work of this kind. Should any have occurred I alone am responsible for this, and if informed of these I will be only too glad to see that they are corrected. My one hope is that this handbook will enable ministers and congregations to follow the apostolic injunction to 'sing with understanding'.

JOHN M. BARKLEY

INTRODUCTION TO THE
CHURCH HYMNARY, THIRD EDITION

Worship and Hymns

A CHURCH hymn-book is essentially designed for Christian worship.

Christ's earthly life and self-giving on the Cross was itself the one offering of perfect worship to the Father whose will he fulfilled. Through Word and Sacrament, as in daily obedience, his faithful disciples are united with him as his Body in the continuing offering of this worship.

Hence each action in Christian worship has a double significance. It is indeed Christ's people who pray and who praise the Father. Nevertheless they do so as the baptized community whose life is so grounded in Christ and bound up with his life that in worship he, as Head, exercises always his authoritative office as Prophet, High Priest, and King.

Through the Church's worship, therefore, Christ fulfils today in the life of his people what he did on earth 'once and for all'. When Scripture is read and preached, it is not the words of the Minister the congregation awaits but the Word of Christ who is the Word of God. Through the rites of initiation, Holy Baptism, and Confirmation together with Holy Communion, Christ calls his people and establishes them in the covenant of grace. In Baptism he makes the person, whether infant or adult, a member of his Body (1 Cor. 12: 13; Gal. 3: 27; Acts 2: 39). In Confirmation he strengthens and blesses the baptized, who profess their faith, as members of his Body with both privileges and responsibilities (1 Cor. 1: 8; 2 Cor. 1: 21; Col. 2: 7). In the Holy Communion Christ's eternal self-giving is present still in and through his Church (1 Cor. 10: 16, 11: 23–6; Mark 14: 22–4). So, in every action of worship, including what is sung, Christ fulfils his ministry as Prophet, Priest, and King in order that through his Church he may be known as Lord by the world he came to save.

Study of the hymns offered in this book will, it is hoped, make these points clear.

The Cultural Context

It has at all times been necessary for the Committee, in the selection of material, to be aware of the special nature of its responsibility:

to provide the means for high and holy worship, and at the same time to recognize the cultural limits within which this can be done.

On the one hand Christ, the Lord of the Church, is active in the midst of his worshipping people. It follows that as the spoken language used in church must be true and faithful to the Word of Christ, so the musical language also must be true to it. The Committee therefore had to take care, with what success only experience will show, to ensure that tunes are true to the words to which they are set. It is hoped, moreover, that in many instances the offer of a different tune to already well-known words will enable the words to yield up their meaning more fully.

On the other hand, this faithfulness to the Divine in worship must be balanced by a concern that the music is appropriate to the variety of emotions involved in the people's worship as well as to their musical ability. The Committee therefore had to keep in view the requirements of a number of somewhat differing communities not only in Britain but overseas. It also found it necessary to include a number of hymns of more or less local provenance or use, to meet the specific needs of some particular branch of the Church. Thus it has tried to ensure that every congregation will find in the Hymnary a sufficient number of tunes it can use.

The Contents and their Order

In selecting the *contents* of the Hymnary every effort has been made to present the essential elements in the Biblical revelation as adequately as liturgical necessity demanded and available resources permitted. Since a Church hymnal is essentially a liturgical book, the Committee, in determining the *order* in which the hymns are arranged, has borne in mind that the Order of Holy Communion is normative for worship in the Reformed Church and that, where there is no regular weekly celebration of Holy Communion, the service should still follow the eucharistic pattern.

The Order of Common Worship

The central act of Christian worship from the beginning was understood as a unity, the structure of which involved a double action: (*a*) the 'Liturgy of the Word' based on the reading and exposition of the Scriptures; and (*b*) the 'Liturgy of the faithful', sometimes called 'the Liturgy of the Upper Room'—that is, the Holy Communion or Lord's Supper.

Part I: The approach to God

In the early centuries, Christian worship seemed normally to have commenced with reading and preaching. Later, however, it became customary to commence the service with brief acts of approach to God. This comprises *the first part of the service* (Part I of the Hymnary).

Part II: The Word of God

Following his people's approach, God speaks to them through his Word in Holy Scripture and sermon. This 'Liturgy of the Word' is *the second part of the service* (Part II of the Hymnary).

Part III: Response to the Word of God

The third part, to which all else leads, is the 'Liturgy of the Upper Room'—the Holy Communion.

Even where the sacramental elements are not present, there follows response to the Word of God in the Church's outpouring of faith, adoration, thanksgiving, dedication, and intercession, culminating in her rejoicing in the communion of saints and the hope of glory (Parts III and IV of the Hymnary). Thus, recommissioned, the Church returns to her work in the world.

Using the Book

It will be noted that there is a certain correspondence both in style and content between the earlier portions of Parts I and III of the Hymnary, the former acknowledging the greatness of God, the latter providing acts of adoration and thanksgiving. Clearly certain hymns in Part III may with perfect propriety be used for the opening of worship, while some in Part I will provide on occasion suitable acts of response to what God has spoken in his Word. Nevertheless the distinction between the two parts of the book remains valid since the hymns in Part III do on the whole express the heightened adoration and thanksgiving which faithful worshippers are more prepared to offer after the Divine Word has been heard. This again is characteristic of the Communion Service.

The Table of Contents indicates the shape of the service both in its broad pattern and in its variable details; while cross-references at the end of the sub-sections in the body of the book point out certain cognate hymns to be found in other parts of the Hymnary.

The value of arranging a hymn-book in this way, both to ministers in selecting a praise list and to congregations at worship, will, the Committee trusts, prove itself in practice.

Psalms and Paraphrases

From the beginning the Psalter had an integral place in Christian worship. Having regard to this and also to the traditional use of metrical versions in the Reformed Church, the Committee hopes, by including a selection of psalms, both prose and metrical, to promote a fuller use of the riches of the Psalter and that the range of selection may be widened.

The selections from the Psalter and Scottish Paraphrases are normally placed first in the appropriate section or sub-section of the Hymnary.

Hymns for Children

In selecting hymns for use by children, it should not be forgotten that in this, as in other fields, it is better that a child's reach should exceed his grasp than that he should be encouraged to sing what is banal or below his best capacity. Many of the great hymns of the Church are admirably suited for children's enjoyment and use, so that their omission from children's worship is a serious lack.

Hymns suitable only for children and for younger children are placed according to the same principle as the other hymns, hymns of approach to God in Part I and so on, except that they are invariably last in the sub-section. These hymns are designated in a distinctive way in the Index of First Lines.

The Contribution of the Centuries

Each age, including our own, has contributed something new and of value to the rich treasury of the Church's hymnody, and this is reflected in the contents of the book, which contains a number of hymns and tunes written this century, as well as a significant corpus of specially commissioned music.

Congregations will gain both in the variety and the devotional fullness of their worship by extending the range of their hymnody.

So far as possible the dates of author, composer, or source are given.

Thus the Church is constantly reminded that her inheritance and her promise are alike ageless, because they are from God the Eternal;

TO WHOM, FATHER, SON, AND HOLY SPIRIT, ONE GOD,
BE GLORY IN THE CHURCH TO THE AGES OF AGES.

CHRISTIAN HYMNODY

THOMAS H. KEIR

To tell the story of Christian hymnody requires the use of a number of technical terms. While the meaning of these should be clear from the context, the reader who desires fuller knowledge should consult a recognized authority, such as *The Oxford Companion to Music* and *The New Oxford History of Music*. It will also be useful for the reader to have at hand a music edition of CH3 since constant illustration is offered from it.

'No liturgical music is fully understood without profound appreciation of the liturgy itself, its structure and ideas.' For this reason the structure and meaning of Christian worship are set out in the 'Introduction' to CH3. Hymnody must be placed in its liturgical setting.

In an article on hymnody, it is necessary right at the beginning to ask the question, 'What is a hymn?' St. Ambrose of Milan (*c.* 339–97) defines a hymn as 'a song with praise of God':

> If you praise God, without singing, you do not have a hymn. If you praise anything, but not to the glory of God, even if you sing it, it is not a hymn. A hymn, therefore, contains the three elements: *song*, and *praise*, it being *praise of God*.

Ambrose clearly did not rule out other elements, and early Christian hymns commonly concluded with a petition as well as a formal *gloria*. His definition, however, does rule out much that has passed for hymnody in more recent times, the pious poem, for instance, or the lyric of social protest, legitimate though these may be on some Christian occasions. In any case it will serve us well to bear Ambrose's definition in mind.

THE FORMATIVE CENTURIES

Hymns in the New Testament

Our earliest clue is to be found in the passage where St. Paul counsels Christians to communicate with each other in 'psalms and hymns and spiritual songs' (Ephesians 5: 19). What was the origin, and what the function of these forms, apparently familiar to Christians thus early in their history?

It is now well understood that the synagogue—whether the Temple Synagogue referred to in Luke 2: 46, Acts 3: 11 and 5: 12, or the ordinary synagogues of Palestine and of the Dispersion—made a major contribution to the initial forms of Christian worship.

The synagogue Sabbath morning service was an expansion of its daily morning service—a service of reading, liturgical prayers, and singing. This was the worship and these were the songs that Jesus knew. It was this, adapted, reinterpreted and filled out, which developed into Christian 'liturgy'.

It is certain therefore that Paul's 'psalms and hymns and spiritual songs' were part of the Church's debt to Jewry, either by direct inheritance or by development from Jewish prototypes.

Psalms

Tertullian mentions the inclusion of psalms in the service because they were so clearly open to Christian reinterpretation. Thus Psalm 133 was used for the *agape* (the Christian 'love-feast'), while Psalm 92 came to be used for the early Lord's Day service precisely because it was the Jewish Sabbath psalm, thus underlining that the Sabbath had given place to the Lord's Day.

Throughout the course of the centuries the enduring song in all Christian liturgies has been the Old Testament psalms. The story of hymnody is so bound up with psalmody that we cannot tell the one story without continual reference to the other.

Hymns

In the New Testament we have a number of quoted fragments, and also substantial portions of two early hymns. The fragments, quoted by St. Paul, take us back to the middle of the first century—for example:

> Awake, sleeper,
> Rise from the dead,
> And Christ will shine upon you . . .   (Eph. 5)

Other passages from St. Paul, sharply etched confessions of faith, clearly given as quotations, have the doctrinal and charismatic characteristics of early hymnody:

> He is the image of the invisible God;
> His is the primacy over all created things . . . etc.
>   (Col. 1, N.E.B.)

Other likely passages suggest themselves, such as Romans 11: 33-6, 1 Timothy 3: 16, and 1 Corinthians 13, as well as the various doxologies in the Book of Revelation.

Very striking is the famous text in Philippians 2: 6–11, which rises abruptly out of a page of pastoral advice and is thought to be a quotation from a contemporary hymn, ending as it does with two of the recognized elements of primitive hymnody—confession of faith and doxology. It is therefore especially satisfactory that this passage has been rendered in English as a hymn for CH3.

399. *Though in God's form he was*

It is also suggested that the Prologue in the first chapter of St. John is a hymn, the original words interrupted here and there by the evangelist's interpolated comments.

This hymn's poetic structure is known as *synthetic parallelism*, or more particularly *climatic parallelism* or *step-parallelism*, so called 'because every line takes up a word of the preceding line, as it were lifting it a step higher' thus:

> In him was *life*
> And the *life* was the *light* of men,
> And the *light* shines in the *darkness*,
> And the *darkness* has not comprehended it.

The evangelist's interpolations, it has been suggested, are verses 6–8, 12b, 13, 15, and perhaps 18.

On the scholarly assumption that this is in fact a Christian hymn, quite possibly written in the last years of the first century, this passage has also been paraphrased for CH3.

162. *Before all time the Word existed*

'Spiritual Songs'

The 'spiritual songs' referred to by St. Paul must have been a different matter altogether. The Greek word here translated 'spiritual' is *pneumatikos*, seeming to imply a movement of the Spirit. We can only guess whether we have here a kind of musical cousin of the 'glossolalia' or 'speaking in tongues' which constituted a problem for the apostle in the Corinthian Church.

After the New Testament

In 1897 at Oxyrynchus a collection of Greek papyri came to light, dating from the late third century. It was found to include, along with hitherto unknown sayings of Jesus and fragments of a lost Gospel, a Christian hymn. The melody is clearly noted by using the letters of the Greek alphabet to represent notes. (Many centuries, of course, were to pass before there was invented a notation even faintly resembling our modern staff.)

The translation of the hymn, incomplete because of damage to the papyrus, is as follows:

... of the assembly shall be silent ... nor shall the light-bringing stars be left behind. All of the roaring rivers shall sing hymns to our Father, and the Son, and the Holy Spirit. All the (heavenly) powers (host) shall respond: 'Amen, Amen'. Power and praise be to the (sole) giver of all good gifts ... Amen, Amen.

It is clear then that there was an important amount of borrowing from Judaism, a good deal of improvisation based on models from the rich store of Jewish hymns, and finally a number of entirely fresh compositions. Where have they all gone?

We do know that the Council of Laodicea (360–81) forbade the use in worship of non-Scriptural texts, and that during other periods of liturgical puritanism in parts of the Eastern Church, when only psalms were held to be admissible, many hymns were either destroyed or forgotten because of inadequate notation.

Fresh harvests of inspiration, however, were to come. In order to follow the story we must look at the Mediterranean world of the early centuries.

The Church was to make her decisive advance during the turbulent centuries before and after the downfall of the Roman imperial government. Her forms of administration, belief, and worship crystallized in a crucible of developing ferment in which she suffered persecution from without and the periods of heresy from within. Often it was out of the womb of tragedy that there sprang the Christian poets whose songs are sung to this day. Certain local differences in the style of hymn and chant are due to the play of history and the genius of race. Against that people moved about a great deal, so that ideas, and liturgical forms such as hymns, were carried far and wide. In that fluid situation there is to be found one especially dominating influence, that of Syria, as we shall see.

The Historical Geography of Hymnody

As the Church spread from Palestine during the early centuries, the Churches fell naturally into a number of independent groupings, each ordering its own worship and mission, and being coloured by its native characteristics. Councils, called by the Emperor, mainly in the Eastern Mediterranean as at Nicaea and Chalcedon, held the whole Church together in a unity of faith and purpose. Musically as well as liturgically there emerged a number of nerve-centres, namely, Syria, Palestine, and Antioch.

Byzantium

From the fourth century Byzantium emerged, her capital, the new city of Constantinople, having become the Eastern capital of the Roman Empire. She too felt the kindling wind that blew from Syria by way of Antioch; and the rich flush of her response is part of musical history. Later, isolated by the Mohammedan conquests, she developed her own distinctive uses, which remain as a living rite in the Eastern Orthodox Church.

> 192. *A great and mighty wonder*
> 267. *The day of resurrection*
> 269. *Come, ye faithful*

Rome

Rome, which enjoyed a special prestige in the West as the metropolitan see, became increasingly influential after the Mohammedan advances had isolated the Churches of the Near East, including the new imperial capital of Constantinople. In the field of music and liturgy, however, it sometimes appeared as if her character-istic role was to borrow, and then to chasten and remodel what she held to be too florid for proper function and good taste.

Spain

Lower Gaul and northern Spain were linked through their conquest by the Visigoths, who governed their Spanish territories theoretically as imperial nominees, but actually as autonomous rulers. Their forms of worship were so similar as sometimes to be referred to as the Hispano-Gallican rites. After the Moslem invasion of the Peninsula, the Spanish Church was described as *Mozarabic*, signifying that it was tolerated under Arab rule.

For lack of a decipherable notation, its rich corpus of Church chant was largely lost, though its forms of prayer are part of the Christian treasury.

One notable Spanish hymn-writer has left us some hymns of great length, portions of which are sung throughout the Churches still— Prudentius (A.D. 348–*c.* 413).

> 198. *Of the Father's love begotten*
> 199. *Bethlehem, of noblest cities*

Gaul—The Gallican Church

The fact that the Rhône valley had commercial links with Syria even before the Christian era may well account for the early spread of Christianity to Gaul and for the enduring imprint there of Syrian forms of worship. From the Gallican Church come such majestic pieces as those written by Fortunatus (*c.* A.D. 535–600) for use on the occasion of the Empress Sophia sending a (supposed) relic of the True Cross to Queen Ragemund.

> 256. *Sing, my tongue, how glorious battle*
> 257. *The royal banners forward go*

The Celtic Churches of Scotland and Ireland

From Gaul the Eastern fire spread to our own islands. The debt of the Columban Church to the Gallican through St. Martin of Tours and others is well known. One is not surprised therefore to find strong affinities between the Celtic liturgies and those of the Eastern Church. The influence of Syria had reached the last outpost.

> 301. *Christ is the world's Redeemer*
> 397. *O God, thou art the Father*
> 398. *Alone with none but thee, my God*

Characteristics of Eastern hymnody

What are the characteristics of these early Syrian hymns and their many derivatives throughout the ancient world?

Originally written in one or other of the two main forms of Aramaic (the tongue Jesus spoke), their poetic quality springs from a highly imaginative use of the Old Testament archetypes.

A good example of this is *The Reproaches*, in which God reminds His people of His care and their ingratitude. 'O my people, what have I done to thee . . . ? I brought thee forth out of the land of Egypt . . . and thou hast prepared a cross for thy Saviour. . . .' (See Hymn 240.)

The liturgical dialogue called *The Reproaches* (with *Trisagion*) had become part of the Gallican rite for Good Friday probably by the end of the sixth century, and was taken into the Roman service many centuries later, the Latin title being *Improperia*.

Again, the Syrian hymns frequently employed metre, thus early providing models for later practice. Considering that ancient chants were not metrical (though they were verbally rhythmic), one is surprised to discover how familiar the ancient poetic metres are. Well taught by the Eastern models, St. Ambrose of Milan wrote four-line verses in iambic tetrameters—that is, with four stresses to a line. And at a stroke we are caught up in a movement which starts with Syria and continues through Milan and the Medieval Sequences, to emerge, now in the various vulgar tongues of Europe, in a sixteenth-century equivalent—long metre (one of the ballad metres).

> 188. *Give heed, my heart*
> 189. *From east to west, from shore to shore*

Again, there is a vivid awareness of the Church Triumphant, the martyr host and other special witnesses. The hymns, whether Byzantine, Mozarabic, Scottish, or Irish, are full of the same awareness.

542. *Sing Alleluia forth*

Promptings of History and of the Spirit

What prompts the writing of such hymns? The answers are almost endless—though the primary one is God's glory.

(1) *The daily services.* Hymns were extensively written for the non-eucharistic offices of the Church—the daily services, for example.

Within the Communion order no one can dogmatize about what was or was not allowed in one place or another. Liturgical history shows that there is almost no claim for the authority of a practice which cannot be countered by some contradictory precedent elsewhere. It can be confidently said, nevertheless, that the normal and official use for the Communion has invariably been the Old Testament psalm. The hymn was admitted later.

(2) *Countering heresy.* We find hymns being written, however, not only for the worshipping community but for the confession of faith outside the sanctuaries.

Bardesanes of Edessa in Syria (born A.D. 154) devised an astute method of spreading his heresy—the writing of heretical hymns, to be sung in the streets where people gathered in the cool of the Syrian evening. Over a century later another citizen of Edessa, the voluminous hymn-writer Ephrem Syrus (born *c.* A.D. 307) described the effect, which had continued to his day (and does to ours!):

> In the resorts of Bardesanes
> There are songs and melodies,
> For seeing that young persons
> Loved sweet music,
> By the harmony of his songs
> He corrupted their minds.

Ephrem's reply to the threat at Edessa was to prepare orthodox hymns, possibly having them sung to the melodies the heretics had popularized.

In other parts of the Church St. Ambrose of Milan and St. John Chrysostom (*c.* A.D. 347–407) were stealing the Arians' thunder in much the same way. Modern hymnaries include only very short excerpts of these older hymns.

56. *O Trinity, O blessed Light*

(3) *As re-interpreting the Old Covenant.* Part of the domestic piety of the Jewish home in our Lord's time embraced the lighting and blessing of the evening lamp; and to this day the lighting of the Sabbath lamp is the special privilege of Jewish mothers.

By the fourth century a Christianized form of this ceremony had spread throughout the Christian world under the Greek name of *Epiluchnion* or, in the Latin-speaking West, *Lucernarium.*

Part of the beautiful hymn for this office is still sung in the translations of Keble and Bridges. Typically Jewish is the 'seal' of the Name of God at the end, without which—in Jewish thought—the validity of the blessing was questionable.

54. *Hail, gladdening Light*

(4) *As response to historic and personal stress.* Incessantly the stress of events has prompted the composition of verses which have come to be treated as hymns. The illustrious and versatile scholar, statesman, bishop, military authority, and patriot Synesius of Cyrene (*c.* A.D. 375–440), when the Goths were now breaching even the inner ramparts of the Empire, pleaded with the Emperor Arcadius to act. According to Gibbon the court 'indulged the zeal, applauded the eloquence, and neglected the advice . . .'. Out of it all came a 'hymn'. When we sing it, the centuries are left behind; and it becomes personal to ourselves. Hymnaries are full of such responses to historic challenge.

80. *Lord Jesus, think on me*

(5) *Spiritual medicine.* Hymns have also been regarded, and indeed designed, as a form of 'spiritual medicine', serving much the same purpose as the maledictory psalms in the Old Testament, though in a more positive way. The Celtic churchmen of Scotland and Ireland, who greatly loved the *Psalter,* used the psalms in this way. The 70th psalm, *Deus in adjutorium*—'O God, unto mine aid incline; O Lord, make haste to help me' was, it is said, 'the favourite prayer of the Scots, as of the monks of the Thebaid'. Once again, the stamp of the Eastern Church!

Like the psalms, hymns were thought of as a *lorica* or breast-plate. We have one of the most famous—St. Patrick's *Breast-plate*—set to a tune commissioned for CH3 with a second rendering set to Irish airs. The first version of the words is the more authentic.

401. *To-day I arise*
402. *I bind unto myself to-day*

(6) *Antiphons as hymns.* A large number of hymns came into being as it were parasitically as antiphons punctuating the course of the psalm. It is impossible to define antiphonal method categorically so varied

were the patterns. Commencing with Jewish practice, the antiphon was developed in the Christian monasteries of Syria and Palestine, before becoming a universal practice. It was in effect a hymnic piece sung, according to the practice of the area or time or occasion, at the beginning and end of the psalm, or between certain groups of verses of the psalm, by a choir answering the solo voice of the psalm-singer, or else by some other arrangement of the resources.

These antiphonal interpolations might take the form of New Testament paraphrases, celebrating the triumph of Easter for instance, thus most thoroughly baptizing the psalm of the Old Covenant into Christ. Or they might commemorate saints and martyrs, or be simply devotional responses to the words of the psalm.

Since it was the antiphons which enjoyed the greatest popularity, the psalm sometimes in course of time was allowed to drop out, leaving the antiphon as a separate hymn. The word *anthem* derives from *antiphona*.

CH3 includes several twentieth-century settings by Gelineau of psalms with short antiphons.

> 67. *Out of the depths*
> 350. *O give thanks to the Lord*
> 389. *The Lord is my shepherd*

(7) *Tropes and sequences.* More curious, and more important for the ultimate development of popular hymnody, is the wedding of words and music in the reverse of the usual order through the centuries-long epidemic of troping.

Repeatedly throughout history we see the artist reacting at the limits imposed on his creative skills by what seem to him the too rigid restrictions of the Church.

Renaissance painters succeeded in bending the rules by handling the biblical scenarios with a thoroughly humanistic brush. What the musicians of the Carolingian period did was to 'trope' the psalmodic 'Alleluia', and later the 'Kyrie' and other parts of the service.

A trope was by definition a turn or figured treatment added to the chant by using the final '-a' of 'Alleluia' as an opportunity for extended melody. The Celtic monastic foundation of St. Gall is sometimes credited with responsibility for the further development; for by the ninth century words were being wedded to the musical trope, which then required syllabic adjustment.

Practical reasons may have prompted the provision of words. In an age of hopelessly primitive notation, the accurate transmission of a long melismatic tune must have been precarious; but it is common experience that an extended melody comes more readily to the tongue if it has come to be associated with familiar words—the words act as a mnemonic. Possibly also the verbalizing of the trope was necessary in order to justify what would otherwise be felt by the guardians of liturgy to be an unwarranted indulgence.

As soon as words were added, however, it became possible, as on occasion with the antiphons, for the trope to be parted from the present psalm. It was now called a sequence, meaning the hymn that followed the 'Alleluia' or, if the psalm had been dropped, followed the lesson preceding 'Alleluia'.

A late metrical sequence for Pentecost is *Veni, Sancte Spiritus*, words for which are still in regular use in most Churches, translated in the original metre. In CH3 it is set to a new, specially commissioned tune.

105. Come, thou Holy Paraclete

The Oldest Music in our Hymnary

What was the first Christian music like? The absence of an accurate notation such as our staff means that much was lost. It is in any case unlikely that general survival would have perpetuated a chant which by the end of the eighth century was already passing into a new phase through an extension and reform of the Church chant.

This should not be dismissed as ancient history, since modal music, even after the modes were superseded by modern scales, did not die. Its legacy remains in the work of practically every major composer. It is still a living if diminished part of the music of every Church that claims historical catholicity, and has even discovered for itself a new validity in the 'folk-song' of the twentieth century. It is closely akin to the music our Lord knew. It therefore asks to be better understood.

What is a mode?

A mode is a particular way of organizing an ascending range of adjacent notes—a way strikingly different from our familiar major and minor scales. When a congregation, having sung 'O worship the King' to the tune HANOVER (35), turns to 'Come Holy Ghost, our souls inspire' to VENI CREATOR (342) or to 'O come, O come, Emmanuel' to VENI EMMANUEL (165), everyone immediately senses a difference in the 'feel' of the music. Why?

If one plays on the piano all the white notes from D to the D an octave higher, it is obvious to the ear that this way of organizing notes has a different flavour—we call it a different tonality—from what is heard in the modern scale of D major. The modern scale would have F and C sharpened. The first mode, however, with D as the starting point, does not.

If one now plays the white notes from E to upper E, this is the third mode. The tonality again is different. This is because the intervals between the different notes come in a different order. In the first mode—the one starting from D—the interval between the first and second notes of the series is a whole tone. In the third mode—the one starting from E—the interval between the first and second notes of the series is a semi-tone. Each series, therefore—that is to say, each mode—is entirely different from all the others. It is in fact as if you had eight different scales to work with (though the term scale is not applied to modes). Yes, eight, not seven, since the eighth is not managed in quite the same way as the first.

The description plain-chant is strictly applicable—as the term implies—only to the more severe, syllabic chants, and not to those that are melismatic or florid.

The reform of the modal system

In the early centuries only four modes had generally been used, nor was there any strict rule about maintaining a uniform tonality in a chant; it would often be difficult to say to which mode a chant really belonged. In short, it could not readily be classified.

The first reform of the system was carried out at Byzantium in the time of St. John Damascene in the eighth century.

Shortly afterwards the European codification—erroneously attributed to the initiative of Gregory the Great, Bishop of Rome, and ever since called 'Gregorian'—was carried out, it seems, in Charlemagne's territory north of Gaul. This resulted in a system of eight psalm *tones*—one tone (a recitative-type of chant) for each mode.

Hymns 63, 158, 231, 232, 239, 262, 284, 310, and 326

The endings were a key feature of the system. Each tone was provided with a selection of endings. Tone eight, for example, had four. This was done, not simply for the sake of variety but so that the proper ending could be chosen to link smoothly with the antiphon which would at certain points follow the psalm-tone.

The antiphons, the hymn-element in the singing, were melodic. These too were re-formed so that they could be confidently classified as in this mode or that.

The long arm of Charlemagne

All this was happening, it now appears, sometime about the year A.D. 800. Later in the ninth century the new system came to be attributed to Gregory the Great, an attribution flagrantly eponymous, since Gregory had died in the year 604. In an illiterate and uncritical age this attribution seems to have been accepted, and this kind of church music has been called 'Gregorian' ever since.

The Western codification of the Church's chant is now believed to have taken place, as we have said, in the Frankish territory. The conjunction of date and place inevitably raises the possibility that the initiative was in some way connected with the Carolingian liturgical reforms.

Charlemagne, king of the Franks, was the towering figure of his age. His aversion from disorder shaped itself into a design and brought a semblance of common purpose across a vast territory stretching from Germany to Spain and North Italy. In fact the old Roman Empire was being reshaped as the Holy Roman Empire. Over the greater part of this area the Gallican Church bore, as we have seen, the imprint of the Eastern forms and developed a chant of striking vitality.

The 'Gregorian' codification—a fusion of Gallican and Romanized forms of chant—resulted in a system thoroughly neat and orderly; and if something of the liveliness of Gallican church music was lost in the process, there emerged a practice which proved serviceable to this day.

Charlemagne's personal interest in these matters (and indeed there was not much he was not interested in) is indicated by his directive that education should be provided (among other things) in psalms, music notation, and chant.

Father Gelineau has suggested that the modal reform was fathered on Gregory in order to give prestige to the new chant. It may be significant, however, that the attribution to Gregory took place at roughly the same period as the fraudulent Donation of Constantine, the False Decretals, and other forgeries, some of which are known to have emanated from Gaul and some from the Lateran Palace itself, all of which were certainly designed for the aggrandisement of the Roman bishop. It does seem possible then that the curious claim for Gregory was part of the same process, part, however, not only of the Roman political aspiration, but of the Carolingian grand design. Charlemagne had sought a unity, not just military and administrative but total and therefore also ecclesiastical. The new chant therefore would be given a Roman provenance. Hence arose the 'Gregorian myth'.

It is fair to add that the ninth century took a less grave view of such things than the historical conscience of today, and indeed consistently used pseudo-history as the readiest instrument of propaganda.

People in the modal ages were naturally more conscious of the differing flavours of the eight modes and of the psalm tones than we are today. Seven centuries later, in Luther's time, when the Epistle and

the Gospel were still being sung to tones, Luther preferred one tone
for the Epistle to suit the personality of Paul and another to express
the graciousness of Christ. More circumstantially, an unpublished
psalter in 1561, ascribed to Archbishop Parker, contains a poem
describing the different moods of the various tones:

> The first is meek, devout to see,
> The second sad, in majesty,
> The third doth rage and roughly brayeth,
> The fourth doth fawn, and flattery playeth;
> The fifth delight'th, and laugh'th the more,
> The sixth bewayleth, it weepeth full sore,
> The seventh treadeth stout, in froward race,
> The eighth goeth mild, in modest pace.

It was the eighth that Luther chose for the Gospel!

The Age of Development

From two events, as insignificant in their beginnings as the
mountain trickles which become at last the Danube and the Rhine,
flowed extraordinary changes in the structures of musical art in
general and ultimately of popular hymnody. They were the discovery
of harmony and the invention of notation.

The discovery of harmony

Who in the time of Charlemagne could have conceived the
consequences of the long-delayed discovery that two or more notes of
different pitch might be sung together at the same moment acceptably
as a recognized musical form; and that this acceptance could open the
door to a future of unimaginable splendour? No one knows the
beginning of the story, except that man stumbles upon discoveries—
sometimes different men at the same time in different places—and
one discovery leads to another.

The awareness of polyphony as an artistic device may have grown
out of the fact that some people have low voices and others high ones.
In the monasteries where, as everywhere else, music was and had
always been monodic, men with lower voices must often have sung
the melody at a lower pitch than the others and, if they were musical,
instinctively pitched their voices an octave or a fifth or a fourth below
the others.

This simple form of harmony, called *organum*, took several forms.
The main body of singers would hold the melody (*canto fermo*) of the
chant, while other voices vocalized, without words, duplicating the
chant at the interval of a fifth or fourth. With modal music, especially

in a Church that itself expresses the mystery of worship, the effect can
be austerely expressive. We need go no further, however, than Dr.
Kenneth Elliott's scholarly setting of VERBUM SUPERNUM to find how
effectively the ancient technique may be developed for modern use.

116. *Come, gracious Spirit*

Once begun, the development of harmony must have received
many a curious impetus. In Byzantium, largely isolated from the
Western Churches by the Mohammedan conquests, the services,
assisted by choirs of trained choristers, were elaborate and long. To
reduce the time, the practice arose of singing certain consecutive parts
of the liturgy concurrently! Even if the result can hardly have failed to
be aurally disastrous, yet the practice (which was not officially banned
until the seventeenth century) must have served as a kind of
polyphonic laboratory.

In the Western Church development was more decorous. By the
thirteenth century—in the *conductus* and the new form called
motet—it was now regarded as allowable for one or two voices to
enter in the middle of another's phrase. The enrichment of interest
must at first have been startling. The age of polyphony had indeed
come, even though a long road lay ahead, until John Dunstable, one
of the great precursors, and others of his time, finally paved the way
for the dramatic advance of the sixteenth century.

Much of today's terminology comes from this period—tenor, alto,
bass, and treble, for instance.

The invention of notation

So long as the Church's song was a single line of music, the tune
could be transmitted orally, allowing for the possibility of distortion.
Many attempts had been made to find a suitable cypher to enable
music to be read, transmitted, and taught. In Egypt and Babylonia the
pitch and duration of notes had been indicated by cheironomy, the
movement of the choirmaster's hand through the air to indicate such
things as the length and pitch of the notes.

In early Byzantine music the words of the Church chant were
pointed by writing above them 'ecphonetic' signs which to the
modern reader look for all the world like shorthand. These early
symbols stood either for single notes or for short conventional
phrases or groups of several notes. A notation which could, so to
speak, be 'sent through the post' and be reliably interpreted at the
receiving end, had yet to be invented. The neumes of the later period
indicate the extent of progress which was still necessary. The solution
is traditionally ascribed to Guido of Arezzo (*c*. 995–1050), who may
well have developed his system from earlier ideas. Certainly the first

recorded stave was a single line representing the note F, drawn in red ink above the words, the notes of the melody being arranged above and below the line. Later, a second line representing C one fifth higher, was drawn in yellow ink. Finally, with the four-stave 'Guidonian' system, it was clear that essentially the way had been found.

As if that were not enough, the development of the sol-fa notation is also associated with the name of Guido who, it is said, lit on the idea while studying an ancient Latin hymn by Paul the Deacon (eighth century) for the festival of St. John the Baptist. Noticing that each line of the hymn began one note higher than the previous line, he used the initial syllable of each line as a symbol for the note it was sung to, thus going up the scale:

> UT queant laxis
> REsonare fibris
> MIra gestorum
> FAmuli tuorum,
> SOlve polluti
> LAbii reatum,
> > Sancte Johannes.

Ut is not a particularly singable syllable and, in Britain, ultimately was changed to Doh. Thus we have Doh-Re-Mi-, etc. Long after Guido's day the symbols Te and upper Doh were added to complete the octave.

A Popular Hymnody becomes Possible

It is obvious that the modern hymn-tune comes from a different world from that of Guido. For many centuries the ordinary worshipper took no active part in the music of the Church's central service, the Holy Communion, nor did the use of Latin or the elaborate melodies of the antiphons (set sometimes for two choirs) in any way encourage him to do so. But things were happening that were in the long run to alter the Church's style.

The contribution of the castle, the tavern, and the street

During the twelfth and thirteenth centuries the aristocratic singers (*troubadours* in Southern France, *trouveres* in Northern)—following the earlier *jongleurs* (the popular singers)—were breaking new ground. By largely using for their songs of love and chivalry the *modus lascivus* (Ionian mode)—the nearest thing to our major scale— they were already preparing the way for the modern scale-system. By the use of F-sharp in addition to the B-flat already allowed in modal composition, they unconsciously hinted at things to come. By using strongly rhythmic melodies dactylic, trochaic, and the like, in a variety of metres—music, that is to say, with a 'beat'—they gave the people the kind of tunes they could sing for themselves. Equally significant, they sang in the various vernaculars which had developed out of vulgar Latin. Inevitably the movement spread throughout Italy, Germany, and Britain. In the long run its influence on Church practice was bound to be great.

Popular music in the churches

Too much has possibly been made of the fact that popular tunes were sometimes used as the *canto fermo* or main theme of a piece of service-music in the later medieval period. The famous instance is John Taverner's *Westron Wynde* Mass. It has been claimed that such tunes were seldom pressed into service unless they had already fallen out of popular use; and in any case, in their liturgical form were usually so elaborated that the tune itself was hardly more than a pretext for holding the polyphonic structure together. If that is so, the precedent here is, if anything, one which advocates good judgement.

There is no questioning the records, which indicate a good deal of irreverence. Yet the effect in the end was the same, the breaking down of the ancient artistic and liturgical rigidities.

Very different were the popular pageant, the outdoor procession, and the religious drama which reached the height of its popularity in the fifteenth century, since all these accustomed ordinary people to a religious song genuinely popular in style.

The carol played an important role in satisfying the demand for a popular hymnody. The charming intermingling of Church Latin with the vernacular in the so-called *macaronic* type of carol was itself a symbol of the new thrusting its way into the old, as in the familiar fourteenth-century German example:

> *In dulci jubilo*   (with sweet rejoicing)
> Now sing with hearts aglow!
> Our delight and pleasure
> Lies *in praesipio*,   (in the manger)
> Like sunshine is our treasure
> *Matris in gremio*.   (in the mother's womb)
> *Alpha es et O!*   (You are alpha and omega)

Such Latin words were already familiar to the people from hearing the Latin Scriptures and liturgy. In CH3 the carol 'Unto us is born a Son' concludes with a phrase 'Benedicamus Domino' (Let us bless the Lord) familiar enough to those who attended Lauds and Vespers.

187. *Unto us is born a Son*

The threads come together

Such things were part of a wider movement. The growing awareness of local and later of national identity hastened the decline of Latin as the accepted means of communication, and encouraged a vernacular literature. Equally important was the creation of a vernacular music in the different parts of Europe.

In the afterlight of history it is easy to see how all this contributed to a situation in which the Reformation became possible, bringing with it at last a true hymnody for the whole people of God.

The whole range of vernacular and regional styles was ultimately to be demonstrated in a spectacular way in the century of the Reformation. The Masses of Palestrina—'it is almost', comments Robert Bridges, 'as if the sacred words had become musical'—are different from the corresponding English works of William Byrd; the Genevan psalm-tune from the German chorale; the German folk-tunes which Luther baptized into Christ from the English or again from the Scottish or the Irish ones. The spectrum was becoming irridescent, ready to be exploited.

The bequests of the old order

The old order, however, had still some bequests to make to the future.

1. The sequences

The sequences had started as proses (the full and correct description is *prosa ad sequentiam*), which continued to be written in an abundance hardly matched by literary merit throughout the medieval period. The important factor for the future of hymnody was the emergence at a quite early date of a strophic type of sequence, with verses, that is to say, with a standard pattern using, moreover, popular metres such as 'long metre' and Sapphic.

Ultimately the Council of Trent (1545–63), as the strong arm of the Counter-Reformation, was to ban all but four of the sequences. Slight as this contribution may appear, these four, and a fifth added later have fermented in the imagination of translators and composers ever since. They are:

Dies irae ('Day of wrath') by Thomas of Celano (thirteenth century);
Lauda Sion Salvatorem ('Praise thy Saviour, O Sion') by Thomas Aquinas;
Veni, Sancte Spiritus ('Come, Holy Spirit');
Victimae Paschali laudes ('To the Paschal Victim offer praise') attributed to Wipo, a chaplain to the Court of Burgundy in the eleventh century;
Stabat Mater dolorosa ('At the Cross the Mother stood'), a thirteenth-century sequence ascribed to Jacopone da Todi, added to the four by the Roman Church in the eighteenth century.

Parts of two of these appear in translation in CH3. One is a free rendering of part of *Stabat Mater*, to the appropriate sixteenth-century melody.

246. *At the cross, her station keeping*

The other is *Veni, Sancte Spiritus*, attributed without certainty to various authors, including Archbishop Stephen Langton. The new tune was commissioned for CH3.

105. *Come, thou Holy Paraclete*

We shall meet a third, *Victimae Paschali*, later.

2. *The monasteries and the schools*

Verses from the monasteries are often cries of the heart in ages of turbulence and misery.

537. *Jerusalem the golden* (Bernard of Cluny, twelfth century)
377. *Jesus, the very thought* (authorship uncertain)

The world of the schools is also represented, not only by Aquinas but by Peter Abelard (1079-1142), who prepared a hymnary for the monastery of his former sweetheart Heloïse.

535. *O what their joy and their glory must be*

3. *The contribution of the Counter-Reformation*

Most great ages make some part of their bequest to posterity almost as an afterthought. So, the modal age lived on in the minds of many, nostalgic for the past. In the seventeenth century it produced in France some fine hymns, by Charles Coffin and others, together with a crop of Church melodies, many in the evergreen Sapphic metre, which enrich our hymnaries still. The poetic quality is there, the objectivity and therefore the reverence. Such tunes, so far from being museum pieces, provide a needful corrective of that introspection which has been a weakness in some Protestant worship throughout its history.

208. *On Jordan's bank* (Tune: SOLEMNIS HAEC FESTIVITAS)
Tunes 504, 568, 491, etc.

THE FULL FLOOD

By any standards the fifteenth and sixteenth centuries in Europe were remarkable. The Englishman John Dunstable (d. 1453) had done as much as any to prepare the way for the polyphonic intricacy of the Flemish school and the melodic mastery of the Italians. In their more limited field it remained for the musicians of the Reformation to exploit the still maturing techniques of the High Renaissance in the interests of a people's praise. Luther was a first-class musician aided by others of high calibre such as Johann Walther.

It is true that at first Luther gave much care to the provision of chants for the traditional liturgy—Kyrie, Gloria in excelsis, the Litany, and the rest—but this was because he wanted the people to take their part in these also. Nevertheless, it was the small but growing collections of hymns, at first printed on leaflets or broadsheets, that sang themselves—and the reform—into the hearts of the people. The pedlar who, at Magdeburg in 1524, sang the new hymns in the market-place and then sold the leaflets to the populace was promptly gaoled by the mayor, but significantly was as quickly freed on the insistence of the burghers.

Luther had already begun to use hymns for services at Wittenberg. A tiny hymnal of eight pieces (four by Luther) called *Achtliederbuch* was followed by two larger books published at Erfurt in 1524 (possibly without his authority). In it sixteen of the hymns, the greater part of the contents, were his. In the same year, but now under his specific direction, there appeared at Wittenberg a collection of motets called *Geistliche Gesangbuchlein*, edited by Johann Walther.

How did Luther come by such hymns and tunes? He did it, and nobly, by his own pen and by commissioning others to write and compose. But he also did it by purloining, by plagiarism, by adaptation of medieval sequences, and by the familiar method of putting bits and pieces together till they made a harmonious whole. It is, indeed, true that he 'pounced upon his own wherever he found it'.

His own melody for EIN' FESTE BURG (A safe stronghold) seems to be largely a mosaic of conventional phrases. Its second and also final phrase is the same as the final phrase of *Vom Himmel hoch*. Such things are characteristic of popular music. See 406 and 188.

The 'Old Hundreth' from the French-Genevan Psalter is a similar kind of pastiche. See 1.

Again, folk-tunes, suitably modified, were pressed into service. Such tunes were presumably already familiar; it was the words that were new. The melody which, in its ironed-out form we call *Soldau*, appeared in the Wittenberg hymnal already mentioned. The tune was borrowed from a sacred-vernacular song in which, not untypically, each verse ended with '*Kyrieoleis*' that is, 'Kyrie eleison'—'Lord, have mercy'. The strongly pentatonic character of the melody would in any case have proclaimed its folk-song origin.

Tune 109

Not until the twentieth century did Luther's way of adapting popular melodies for church use come fully into vogue in the churches of Britain. The impetus came from a general revival of interest as a result of the researches of Cecil Sharp, Ralph Vaughan Williams, and others.

Inevitably the compilers of hymn-books adopted the same methods as Luther, condensing a fairly discursive original into a compact rhythmic pattern, not only to suit the new text but to make it easier for the people to join in.

The way to the goal is usually devious. 'The miller of Dee' starts as an Aeolian melody (which Vaughan Williams recovered); it is later acclimatized to the modern scale structure as an eighteenth-century opera ballad 'Love in a village'; in the nineteenth century it is heard in yet another form sung by a Kilburn street singer; and finally it ends up in CH3 and other hymnals, in the plainest form of all, as *Kingsfold*.

Tune 220

The tune O WALY WALY has suffered somewhat less from the changing weather of the centuries, and carries more clearly the marks of its ancestry.

Tunes 554, 555, and 632

Many other examples from all the countries of Britain and many from the continent of Europe are to be found in CH3.

Not so successful were Luther's first attempts to metricize well-known Church chants such as *O lux beata Trinitas* (for the chant melody see RCH 4) by keeping the general shape of the tune and putting it into a metrical strait-jacket.

When, on the other hand, Luther took the key idea of the traditional words and the leading *motif* of the music—these and nothing else, allowing them to smoulder in the imagination until the tinder caught fire, the result could be marvellously effective.

In the eleventh-century sequence 'Victimae Paschali laudes', for example, the key idea is that Death and Life had been engaged in a dread conflict, with Christ as victor. Linked with this in the sequence is the theme of springtime. When Luther wrote 'Christ lag in Todesbanden' ('Christ Jesus lay in death's strong bands'), the thing is so freely done that the rugged and splendid result is all his own.

In the same way the Luther–Walther tune relies on no more than the first phrase of the traditional proper chant, developing it from there with occasional echoes of the original melody. The result can be seen and heard in what is potentially a great popular hymn even today.

268. Christ Jesus lay in death's strong bands

In these Lutheran tunes there was no bar-line and therefore no indication as to where the rhythmic stress lay. Good marriage of words and tune must have nullified the problem, since the people did sing them. Actually nearly a hundred hymnals of the German Reformation were published between 1524 and 1546.

This was only the beginning of the flood-tide of hymns from the various branches of the reform. Luther had taught the people to sing their part at the Eucharist, and this not as a concession wrung from grudging authority, but as their privilege and right and Christian duty.

Genevan Psalmody

Had Scotland followed the Lutheran pattern, as had seemed possible till Knox, on his return from Geneva, threw the weight of his powerful witness on the side of Calvinist reform, Scottish hymnody would have a longer history. The sung service at Geneva, however, was restricted to psalms, the traditional canticles, and the people's part in the liturgy as revised by Calvin. Biblical puritanism excluded hymns, and the veto was exported wherever the Calvinian influence spread. In Scotland, therefore, hymns were confined to the sphere of private devotion.

Already, through the Lutheran influence, such provision had been made through the publication by the Wedderburn brothers of Dundee—James, John, and Robert—sometime between 1542 and 1546, of *Ane Compendious Buik of Godlie Psalms and Spiritual Sangis*. This volume, commonly called *The Gude and Godlie Ballatis* (Ballads) consisted of translations of 'manie of Luther's dytements into Scottish meeter'—to use Calderwood's description. In hall and cottage in Scotland people continued to use it long after its first appearance. As in Germany such hymns did much to spread the spirit of reform.

The delayed legacy of Geneva—psalm-tunes for hymns

Since the psalm-tunes of the Genevan Reformation proved too sophisticated for the folk of sixteenth-century Scotland, successive Scottish psalters increasingly offered a diet of settings in common or long metre, with a small handful of others. Many of the splendid Genevan tunes associated with the names of Louis Bourgeois and Claude Goudimel had therefore to wait for three centuries and more before finding a new role as tunes for hymns. The tonality of these tunes is distinctive, and invite us to glance at what was happening in the music of that period and of the century which followed.

Transition to modern scales

As the old system gradually gave place to our modern chromatic scales (our keyboard octave of eight white notes interspersed with five black ones), radical changes were taking place in the music of psalms and hymns.

The Consistory at Geneva at first ruled out harmonized settings as a distraction from the pure intention of worship. Luther, on the other hand, thrilled to the sound of part-singing. As early as 1524 his Wittenberg hymnal was arranged for four and sometimes five parts, to engage the interest of the young, who, he wrote, should be 'trained in music and other fine arts'. These first settings were rhythmically complex, using a considerable range of polyphonic devices. In the same way, the harmonized versions of the Genevan psalters—published elsewhere—were a far cry from the featureless versions of later times, with equal notes following each other in a weary grind.

Modern worshippers confronted by certain of the earlier German chorales or Genevan psalm-tunes (so far as they have been allowed basically to retain their original harmonies) find themselves at first somewhat at a loss, like travellers in an unfamiliar land. In their original form some of these sixteenth-century tunes (which we still sing, the Scottish MARTYRS for instance), are unequivocally modal. Others are minor, but in the restricted sense of using only the notes in the descending scale of melodic minor. Many others, and this is part of their charm, are of indeterminate tonality, not having quite cast off modal characteristics, yet being already within the threshold of the new scales.

> Tune 140. OLD 107TH
> 370. PSALM 3 (O SEIGNEUR)
> 107. MARTYRS

The musical question regarding the Church's praise was not solved, however, by the simple expedient of adopting modern scales while retaining ancient chants where these were still acceptable.

The new problem arose through the emergence of two related factors. One was the increasing use of fixed-pitch instruments; the organ was a case in point. The other was the exploitation of the harmonic riches which lay concealed in the new scale of the diatonic octave in which every note could be sharpened or flattened.

The natural voice—and it must be remembered that church music had been essentially vocal—when it sings 'B sharp', does not simply sing C, which on the keyboard is what we would play for 'B sharp'. A true 'B sharp' is approximately a quarter of a semi-tone above C, and that is how in the late sixteenth century a true voice would have sung it.

It is obvious that true pitch for all the possible sharps and flats would have required an unplayable keyboard. Hence the emergence of the 'well-tempered keyboard' which is the compromise we use today—a compromise which was finally sanctioned by Bach who wrote his 'Forty-eight Preludes and Fugues' to demonstrate its practicality and to prove that the ear does adjust and accept it.

The ear has in fact done so. All the same, to be aware of this problem is to realize why musicians prefer the older music, written for the true voice, to be sung without the accompaniment of fixed-pitch instruments.

Once the new compromise was accepted, however, the possibilities of vastly enriched colour in church music were almost unlimited. It was a new world of high promise, and from the viewpoint of worship of much danger. The final centuries were to show how much.

THE MODERN CENTURIES

Luther had not only provided hymns; he had raised the all-important question: What kind of hymnody? The theoretical answer is to be found in his voluminous writings. The practical answer is in the hymns themselves, which are scriptural and churchly, full of praise and also of tenderness. If one were to pick out one quality in them to use as a standard of judgement for all succeeding hymns, it would have to be their objectivity. The eye of the worshipper is kept on the object in view—on God the inspirer and object of worship, on the saving events set forth in Scripture, and on the objective truth of the sacraments.

As things turned out, a harsh turn of events was to conspire with human frailty to betray much that the reform had accomplished.

The first religious pacification—the Peace of Augsburg in 1555— made the religion of the ruler the religion of his people, thereby committing central Europe to a process of transmigration and unrest. More gravely, a spiritual contradiction, daily underlined by the fact of a divided Church, lay across Europe. A question-mark therefore was set against all external claims to religious authority. This was in time to bring forth a bitter harvest. The uneasy peace was broken by the Thirty Years War (1618-48) in which plague followed in the wake of destruction and hunger.

Hymns of high faith were still being written. A little earlier, in 1599, the 'king of chorales'—'Wake, awake, for night is flying'—had been written, both words and music, by a pastor who had buried 1,300 parishioners dead of plague, in six months (Hymn 315).

In other hymns of the Thirty Years War, one detects, lightly masked, the imagery of siege and assault.

> 12. *Lift up your heads, ye mighty gates*
> 491. *Lord of our life, and God of our salvation*

But here the peril is to the reform itself. The conclusion of that terrible period saw the composition of 'the queen of chorales'—'Now thank we all our God' (3, 368).

In Britain also the prolonged political and religious strife was settled, but only formally, by the crowning of William and Mary in 1689.

By the time it was all over, people were free at least to reckon with the implications of a century and a half of turmoil. The traditional world-picture had been destroyed by the discoveries of Galileo (1564–1642), Isaac Newton (1642–1727), and others. The division of the Churches still left unanswered the question of the credibility of religious authority.

Some writers have pinned down the date of the collapse of Christianity in England almost to a year, 1725. In England 'if anyone mentions religion', said Montesquieu in 1730, 'people begin to laugh'. There was a similar crisis of faith and morals in Scotland after 1730.

The Malady of Introspection

It is not surprising that both on the Continent and in Britain people, confronted by the ambiguous face of traditional authority in matters of faith, should increasingly have looked within for reassurance.

Hymns henceforth were to be increasingly introspective. On the Continent hymnody had moved from mysticism through pietism to the 'Enlightenment' with its rejection of orthodox dogma, its faith in the natural perfectability of man and, in hymnody, its polite and polished versification. The sifting of the years has set most of these hymns aside. A few names remain, of men great enough to transcend the frailty of their time, Paul Gerhardt (1607–76) and Gerhard Tersteegen (1697–1769), to mention the greatest.

> 57. *The duteous day*
> 171. *All my heart this night rejoices*
> 253. *O Sacred Head sore wounded*
> 669. *Put thou thy trust in God*
> 96. *Thou hidden Love of God*
> 355. *God reveals his presence*

The evangelical revivals

In England the reaction against Deism, a kind of British counterpart to the German 'Enlightenment', began with the eighteenth-century evangelical revivals. Typically the movement came with singing. Hints of the new life beginning to flow in the dissenting churches and chapels of England and Wales during that 'century of divine songs' had already been given.

The story is that a young man called Isaac Watts, who had complained of the dullness of the hymns then in vogue in the Independent Chapels, was challenged to write something better. His response the following Sunday was to produce the first of what was to prove a long series of famous hymns—'Behold the glories of the Lamb, Amid his Father's throne' (Paraphrase 65; Hymn 532). Watts (1674-1748) is now universally regarded as the father of the modern hymn in English. The list, even of his better-known hymns, is a long one—'When I survey the wondrous cross' (254), 'Jesus shall reign' (413), and 'O God, our help in ages past' (611). The last was written at a time when the death of Queen Anne raised hopes that the laws unfavourable to the Dissenters might at last be repealed, and many, many others.

Philip Doddridge (1702-51), also a non-conformist, used his admirable and fluent talent copiously, often writing a hymn to suit the theme of his Sunday discourse, the precentor presumably 'lining it out', with the congregation repeating the line after him. 'O God of Bethel' (72) is probably his best known, though partly edited after his time.

The Wesleys

The evangelical revivals of the eighteenth and nineteenth centuries owe more than can be assessed not only to the missionary labours of John Wesley but to the pen of his brother, a prince of hymnodists, whose hand it was, in part collaboration with his brother, that 'wak'd to ecstasy the living lyre'.

The output of the two was so voluminous that inevitably much was written—and, astonishingly, printed—which now provokes only a smile. 'I'm only a miserable worm, blowing the gospel trumpet!' Yet their measure, and their monument, is to be seen in every modern hymnal in hymns that have entered into the very language of the English-speaking Churches.

See CH3, *Index*, under Wesley

The Wesleys were theologians and, by instinct and early training, Churchmen. John Newton and 'the stricken deer' William Cowper also wrote some notable hymns in collaboration, for example Newton's 'How sweet the Name of Jesus sounds' (376) or Cowper's 'O for a closer walk with God' (663), among many others.

This collaboration resulted in *Olney Hymns*, 1779, called after Newton's parish. The collection—for all the occasional merits—illustrates forcefully the epidemic sickness of much of the worship of the eighteenth and nineteenth centuries, an extreme introspection, for example:

> The Lord will happiness divine
>   On contrite hearts bestow:
> Then tell me, gracious Lord, is mine
>   A contrite heart or no?
>
> I hear, but seem to hear in vain,
>   Insensible as steel;
> If aught is felt, 'tis only pain
>   To find I cannot feel.

What had happened? One part of the answer, true as far as it goes, is 'The Romantic Movement'. It was an age of fallen idols. Since the long debate about the divine right of kings, external authority was everywhere questioned. In the religious sphere the question provoked by the continuing intransigence of Churches was still unanswered, the question namely, where to look for an objective word of authority in matters of faith.

The Romantic Movement epitomized that total uncertainty in things ultimate. Always the romantic looked back to a lost past. Characteristic therefore was the gentle melancholy inspired by ruins, archetypal symbols of a lost paradise. It was the nostalgic longing that could be safely enjoyed rather than the thing longed for. William Cowper's nostalgia was the symptom of a malady that was general.

No wonder that many, sadly mistrustful of external authorities, should become their own interpreters of the Bible, and having read or listened, should look within for some emotional signal of acceptance with God.

In the hymns of the period, therefore, we hear much about personal emotions and conversion with its emotional seal of acceptance that is the thing. Baptism is on the way to becoming God's response to man's vow, thus reversing the order. In the same way the Communion is valued in no small measure for the impression made upon the participant. It is as if the hymns were intended to reveal the worshipper rather than the worshipped. The objectivity of the reformers had turned to subjectivity.

As always, there are noble exceptions, among them James Montgomery (1771–1854). It is interesting how frequently a writer's sheer good taste, like an extra grace added to the covenanted graces, can preserve him from the distortions of his time. Montgomery with his Moravian background and his writer's fastidiousness was such a one.

> 38. *Songs of praise the angels sang*
> 182. *Angels from the realms of glory*
> 317. *Hail to the Lord's Anointed*

The tunes

From the earlier part of the period come tunes of solid dignity like Clarke's ST. MAGNUS (286), Croft's ST. MATTHEW (214), and HANOVER (35). Some later tunes are surely an unconscious means of emotional release. RICHMOND (371) was in the eighteenth century dressed up in musical furbelows to sound like a Handelian extravaganza. The eminently sober TALLIS' CANON (599) pirouettes in swirling skirts for all the world like a rather charming dance measure. Of course, in CH3 the original melodies have been restored. The so-called repeater tunes—'*He's our best bul-, He's our best bul-, He's our best bulwark still*' achieved a high peak of popularity, without corresponding good taste.

The Church at her wisest has always understood how to canalize emotion in a worship of general modesty, not without variety and vivid colour, expressing the pressures and polarities of Christian faith and experience through preaching, sacraments, and singing at Advent and Christmas, Holy Week and Easter, Pentecost and All Saints, for natural emotion, if over-exploited, has a limited expectation of life. So, indeed, it was to be proved once again.

Rethinking the Church

The evangelical movement had done much to cleanse Britain and disturb complacency. But, deriving largely from various forms of non-conformity both within and outside the establishments, for reasons we have seen they had not come to terms doctrinally with the concept of 'the Church'.

The first years of the nineteenth century found Christian faith once more at a low ebb. The new American-style evangelisms a few years later, with their emotional emphasis, were to prove one of many means of recalling the Church to the awareness of herself.

Thoughtful men were reflecting that the interior, emotional warrant for religious assurance, if that were to be all, had produced a harvest of subjectivities and sects. It was time to look at the objective certainties in Scripture and the Sacraments of the Word. These were to be seen not as a means of creating and receiving religious impressions, but as God's gift of grace to be answered by obedience and on every count to be understood as linked with the meaning of the Church and central to its life as the People of God and the Body of Christ.

The 'Oxford' or 'Tractarian' Movement

The Tractarians were sometimes referred to as the High Church party in the Anglican Church (somewhat misleadingly; Calvin was doctrinally 'High Church'). What is not in doubt is that the Tractarians were, like others, influenced by the Romantic Movement of the time. If it is the characteristic of the idealist to look forward to some romantic future, it is, as we have seen, the characteristic of the romantic to look back to an idealized past. This the Tractarians did very thoroughly, by seeking to recover what they believed to be the best lineaments of the ancient Church, freed only from popery, corruption, and superstition.

Scholarly and devout, they sought to show the true face of the Church with Gothic architecture, 'Gregorian' chant, medieval vestments, monastic-style communities, and a liturgical reconstruction.

It should not be forgotten either that from their ranks marched forth dedicated men to spend sacrificial lives in work of social reclamation in sordid slums and in missions abroad. Their witness did in fact recall some of the most thoughtful and dedicated men in all communions to a new awareness of the meaning of 'the Church'.

Their hymns

Their contribution to hymnody has been enduring. Seeking, as Luther had done, hymns they believed the Church required, their instinct was at first to look back to the older models. They were immensely fortunate in their translators, especially to John Mason Neale, for superb versions of Greek and Latin hymns. The Wesleys had of course produced good translations, while others such as Catherine Winkworth were performing the same service for the choicest of the earlier German hymns.

The hymn as a means of worship had long been knocking at the door of the Anglican Church. The official sanction which came in 1821 opened the way for these new hymnodists.

A glance at the Index of CH3 under Neale reveals a long list of his translations, used throughout all the Churches:

10. *Christ is made the sure foundation*
105. *Come, thou Holy Paraclete*
165. *O come, O come, Emmanuel*

CONCLUSION

Since the mid nineteenth century a stream of modern hymnals has been published. Some of these have been epoch-making, for example, *The Yattendon Hymnal* (1899), *Hymns Ancient and Modern* (1861), and *The English Hymnal* (1906). The same is true, if to a somewhat lesser degree, of the first edition of *The Church Hymnary* (1898).

The worship of the Christian Church is living and dynamic, so the compilation of a hymn-book, setting forth the profound

New Testament understanding of the Gospel, of the Church and Sacraments, of God's dealings with men and His Church, and of His Church's response, is a complex undertaking. It has to satisfy the legitimate demand that it should contain the best in words and music of all the ages as well as contain the best of its own without being an artificial creation. 'Canons of assessment' are necessary but they must never become 'preconceived structures' or be divorced from the living Church in the world, otherwise a hymn-book, like a liturgy, cannot 'become the real worship of any actual congregation of the period'. In CH3 the riches of the ages and of the people of God in all nations have been garnered and also 'a number of hymns and tunes written this century, as well as a significant corpus of specially commissioned music'. In its compilation not only the revision committee, but the Churches also played a significant role.

Here are hymns of all the Christian ages, hymns for the present time, and, we trust, hymns for the future.

Te Deum laudamus

PSALMODY IN THE CHURCH

R. STUART LOUDEN

The Psalter in Christian Worship

THE Christian Church found its first book of praise ready to hand in the Book of Psalms. The Hebrew Psalter is essentially a liturgical and a devotional book, and it has been appropriately described as the 'hymnal of the Second Temple', dating from the sixth century B.C. The oldest of the psalms probably date back to 1000 B.C., originating in the reigns of King David and King Solomon. The *Psalter* as a whole is a composite work from many hands and many periods, embodying the accumulated treasures of the corporate praise and private devotion in the faith of Israel. The Jewish Psalms cover the whole area of man's relations with the Living God, and present Jahweh in the majesty of His power and the tenderness of His mercy, a Holy Personal God and Divine Providence who is active in the world and among His people, and who has revealed His will supremely in the Torah.

Various literary devices such as refrains, acrostics, etc. (cf. the alphabetic beginnings in Ps. 119) are employed in the original Hebrew Psalter. Poetic parallelism is especially characteristic of this Hebrew poetry, which may be described as rhythmical prose rather than any form of rhymed versification. This is illustrated in the arrangement of the material, for example, in the Songs of Degrees (Pss. 120-34: *canticum graduum*), which may have been antiphonal praise for the People of God, sung in the ascent of the pilgrims' way leading to Jerusalem. That in this way the words of the Psalms are never treated apart from their use in worship and their musical settings, and that so many psalms are arranged according to an antiphonal pattern, is internal evidence of their place in a responsive and corporate Hebrew tradition of worship. (Incidentally, it suggests that a church hymnary should always be treated as a unity of words and music, a 'words only' version being a nonsense!)

In New Testament times, the *Psalter* was the supreme source of liturgical and devotional material for the new Israel, and it was deeply precious to our Lord himself who was nurtured in the faith of Israel. We note how Psalm 22 was the devotional vehicle of His spiritual experience as God-made-Man in the agony of His Passion. Again from the observance of the Jewish festivals, Jesus was steeped in the Hallel (praise), Psalms 113-18. This was probably the reference in the hymn sung in the Upper Room at the conclusion of the Last Supper (Matt. 26: 30). The later Christian use of the Great Hallel or Egyptian Hallel affirmed Christian redemption to be prefigured in the Exodus, and thus the terminology of the Jewish Passover (Pascha) was employed to express the Easter Mystery.

The psalm as both a literary and liturgical form was the pattern for such Christian hymns as began to emerge in Apostolic times: devotional in character; addressed to God; and expressive of both personal and corporate faith, viz. the Song of Zacharias, the Song of Mary, and the Song of Simeon, which are essentially New Testament psalms. In the same way as the 'Psalms of David' are vehicles of praise for the corporate worship of the People of God, so these Lucan hymns were formalized as the *Benedictus*, the *Magnificat*, and the *Nunc dimittis* in the new Israel of God. Other doxological passages in the New Testament writings have a like similarity to the psalm-form, e.g. Philippians 2: 6–11 (Hymn 399); Ephesians 1: 3–14; Colossians 1: 15–20; parts of 1 Corinthians 13, etc. The Jewish synagogue was the matrix of what emerged as Christian worship, and there the Psalms were an established element in the services. Moreover, as we have noted, it is clear that from the Psalms, both as a literary and liturgical form, and with devotional echoes of the Psalms in many Apostolic writings, arose those 'imitations' as the first Christian psalmody and hymnody.

The devotional and liturgical place of the *Psalter* in Christian worship was significant from the beginning. The early Church Fathers (Jerome, Ambrose, etc.) recommended the devotional use of the *Psalter*, while St. Augustine saw Christ and the Church prefigured throughout the Psalms. As Christian worship developed its own structures and patterns, the *Psalter* was already there as basic material in the services. Most significantly, as the structure of Christian worship became overtly eucharistic, the celebration in Bread and Wine of the Lord's Body and Blood had the *Psalter* as an intrinsic element. It surely remains regulative for Christian liturgical practice that from the Upper Room onwards there has never been the Christian Eucharist without the *Psalter* as part of its content.

A further point to note is that *portions* of psalmody have been the characteristic eucharistic use of the *Psalter* in the Church. Continuous responsive repetition of the *Psalter* in its entirety arose in the worship of monastic communities. This accounts for the division of the whole *Psalter* into a month of days in the *Book of Common Prayer* usage, for the office-type services of Matins and Evensong. The psalm portion or selection is traditionally correct and liturgically appropriate for normal Christian public worship, which is itself properly eucharistic.

The Psalms in Reformed Worship

The 'Psalms of David' or the *Psalter* was an enriching rediscovery in the Biblical revival of Reformation times. Not only the long tradition of the Latin tongue, but the late medieval elaborations in church music had obscured and even obliterated the *Psalter* as a living part of the *people's* corporate worship. Some saw the cure in a total exclusion of music from the services of the Church but fortunately the Protestant desire to promote the people's part in worship led to a revival in psalmody along the lines familiar in the Reformed Church. Dr. Millar Patrick has remarked in regard to the Counter-Reformation line taken on church music at the Council of Trent, namely the Papacy's 'resolute refusal to allow the people to praise God in the worship of the Church in their own tongue and in music suitable for them', that 'the Reformation became an inescapable necessity. And nowhere was the need for it more imperative than in loosening the tongues of the silenced people by restoring to them the right and the power to use their own understandings and voices in the common praise of God. In words and in music new methods to meet their needs had to be found or created; and metrical materials, to suitably simple tunes, furnished the means required.'

It can be argued that post-Reformation vernacular metrical psalmody is one of the closest possible parallels to the original Hebrew psalmody. Note has already been taken of the simple poetical forms which characterize the original Hebrew psalms, and simple rhyming verses are a not dissimilar treatment of the material in the vernacular tongues of post-medieval Europe. A case can be made for any simple rhythmical treatment of words and music in psalmody which makes for a ready congregational participation.

The Psalms in Metre emerged within the continental Calvinist tradition, with a rich variety of metres and with tunes of great vigour and very considerable musical merit. Strasbourg and Geneva were the creative centres of this new type of psalmody, soon to be especially characteristic of the Reformed tradition in worship. The earliest published material appeared at Strasbourg in 1539. A notable movement in popular and corporate church praise had been launched with the rendering of vernacular psalms in rhymed verses set to readily singable tunes. The original metrical psalm-tunes were astonishingly varied, including melodies of Gregorian tonality along with those in major and minor keys of modern usage.

Behind any Presbyterian and Scottish tradition of metrical psalmody lies the pioneering of *The French Psalter*, 1541–62; *The Anglo-Genevan Psalter*, 1561; and *The English Psalter*, 1562. Indeed, with the musical contribution of such as Louis Bourgeois, these sources are still the richest and most valuable strand in our Scottish metrical psalmody.

It is to be noted that at first along with the 'Psalms of David' were included New Testament psalms such as the *Magnificat*, the *Nunc dimittis*, etc., and other more liturgical material such as the Commandments, the *Veni Creator*, the *Lord's Prayer*, the *Apostles' Creed*, etc., all rendered into vernacular verse for ready singing by congregations. In this way the psalm was acknowledged as the Scriptural prototype of anything admissible as hymnody in the church. The general liturgical use of the psalms, and in particular their place in the eucharist, is illustrated in the *Book of Common Order*, 1564, rubric: 'the action thus ended, the people sing the 103rd psalm, My soul give laud. . . .'

The metrical psalmody tradition was part of Scottish Presbyterianism from John Knox's time, and by the end of the first half century of the Reformed period, a whole corpus of psalms in metre and a rich heritage of metrical psalm-tunes had been absorbed into common worship. Much of this original material appeared in *The Scottish Psalter*, 1615, the main source of our oldest psalm-tunes in Common Metre.

Musically the high-water mark of Reformation psalmody in the Scottish Church was reached in the great *Scottish Psalter*, 1635. The editor was the self-effacing Edward Millar of Edinburgh. The Proper Tunes, attached in the French way to specific psalms, including many of Louis Bourgeois's compositions, had a large place in the edition. The Common Tunes were the 1615 Scottish Tunes, which were directed towards a musically uninstructed community, but many had lasting merit (e.g. Caithness, Martyrs, Wigtown, etc.). Tunes in Reports were also included in the 1635 *Psalter*.

In retrospect, there must be musical as well as liturgical regret that, rejecting the variety and richness of the 1540–1640 century of Metrical Psalmody, the use and wont within the English-speaking Reformed Churches became stultified and restricted following the Westminster Assembly of Divines and the Scottish revision of the *Psalter* in 1650. This was, a 'words only' publication which became normative for the next three centuries. Most of the varied music of earlier metrical psalmody was neglected and forgotten.

The first collection of tunes for use with *The Scottish Psalter*, 1650, was published in Aberdeen in 1666, and its twelve common metre tunes (with Bon Accord in reports as a local extra) 'were canonized as embodying the accepted and inexpansible musical tradition of the Church of Scotland': viz., Common Tune, King's Tune, Duke's Tune, English Tune, French, London (London New), Stilt (York), Dunfermline, Dundee, Abbey, Martyrs, and Elgin. It has taken a very long period of time for the English-speaking Reformed Churches to recover not only their own rich heritage of diverse and exciting metrical psalm music, but also to draw upon other riches in hymnody and church music generally.

Psalmody and Hymnody

The Scriptural orientation of the Reformed tradition, along with its sensitivity to the 'Psalms of David' being the type and pattern for all the praises of the people of God, ensured that highly critical standards of valuation were applied in the period from the early eighteenth century onward when church praise was developed, enlarged, and diversified. Metrical psalmody, albeit in the restricted mould of *The Scottish Psalter*, 1650, set a pattern for what was genuine church praise. It is significant that the first additional material to be permitted in some churches was in fact Holy Scripture rendered into metre after the style of *The Scottish Psalter*, 1650: The Scottish Paraphrases (1781).

Modern hymns were introduced into Scottish Presbyterian worship in the half century between roughly 1825 and 1875, but only very gradually and in teeth of strong and hostile opposition. *The Church Hymnary* was first published in 1898, seventy-five years before the appearance of this new third edition. One of the by-products of the gradual introduction of hymns into Reformed worship has been a revival and rediscovery of many lost treasures of metrical psalmody, both in words and more notably in music.

The metrical psalms in *The Scottish Psalter*, 1650, edition underwent a considerable process of revitalization when a new music edition was published: *The Scottish Psalter*, 1929. The stamp of this publication can be discerned in many of the metrical-psalm portions and their settings now included in the CH3. The Presbyterian Church in Ireland was earlier active in the field of metrical psalm revision, not only musically but in emending the 1650 version of the words and in offering many 'second versions'. This 'Irish Psalter' appeared in 1880 as *The Psalter in Metre: a Revised Version, prepared and published by authority of the Presbyterian Church in Ireland, with Tunes.* This publication has contributed a few items of metrical psalmody in the present hymnary.

Fifty-seven selected portions of metrical psalmody with appropriate tunes set to them, in a few instances the Proper Tune, is a notable feature of the CH3. It is believed that this psalm selection will ensure a wider and better use of this important heritage of Reformed worship in congregations using the new book of praise. From the earliest Christian centuries, the selection of psalm portions suitable for use in the liturgy has been the practice in the Church Catholic. The presentation of metrical psalmody in this form of psalm portions in a hymn-book liturgically arranged is within the most authentic traditions of public worship, Catholic and Reformed.

The Psalms in the Church Hymnary: Third Edition

The fifty-seven selected portions of the metrical psalms, included in the body of the hymn-book along with all the other various items, are spread throughout the various sections of this liturgically arranged book of praise, according to their subject-matter and wherever appropriate to a particular element in public worship. The somewhat bogus tradition of the *gathering psalm* (which arose in an austere Presbyterian epoch when metrical psalms were the only permitted hymnody, and accordingly, of necessity, the opening praise in a service was always a metrical psalm) is thus replaced by a more authentic cherishing of the 'Psalms of David' now made available for congregational use in their metrical version as viable praise in the whole range of Christian worship.

The portions of metrical psalmody in the CH3 are essentially *The Scottish Psalter*, 1650, words, with the music of *The Scottish Psalter*, 1929. The *proper tune* practice has been adopted with the selected tune printed along with each portion of the words. In some cases an alternative tune is offered, either printed as an alternative tune, or referred to by cross-reference. The harmonization of these metrical psalm-tunes does not deviate greatly from the harmonies as revised for *The Scottish Psalter*, 1929, and it follows the conventional Victorian hymn-tune tradition. With reluctance, and in the interests of congregational singing, the revisers of the hymnary had to depart from any hopes of restoring the exciting broken time and rhythm of some of the original Genevan tunes (e.g. OLD 100TH). Some flexibility has been achieved, for instance, by printing 'French' (DUNDEE) with an original gathering note for the 121st Psalm (139), while the later 'straight' version is printed when it is used as a hymn-tune (543). There has also been enrichment by the revival of a forgotten tune like MONTROSE for the 72nd Psalm (167), a tune also used for Hymns 133, 321, and 343. The OLD 124TH, as well as being in its place as the 'proper tune' for its own psalm (392), has found wider currency both for modern hymnody (Clifford Bax: 84; and Laurence Housman: 507), and also for a metrical (English) version of an ancient Christian doxology (640).

What seemed to be the harsher verbal infelicities of the words in *The Scottish Psalter*, 1650, have been removed by editorial work, particularly the seventeenth-century elisions not acceptable in

modern English usage (e.g. Cov'nant, Sp'rit, wat'ring, etc.). Where
the meaning at a particular point in a psalm has been falsified by the
1650 versification, editorial rewording has taken place, for example
in Psalm 102, second version (333):

> 1650   Thou shalt arise, and mercy yet
>   Thou to Mount Zion shalt extend:
>   Her time for favour which was set,
>   Behold, is now come to an end.

> 1973   Thou shalt arise, and mercy yet
>   Thou to Mount Zion shalt extend:
>   The time is come for favour set,
>   The time when thou shalt blessing send.

The tested and proved revision work of *The Irish Metrical Psalter*,
1880, proved very helpful in this examination of the words of the
metrical psalms. In some instances the actual *Irish Metrical Psalter*
version has been introduced as much preferable to *The Scottish
Psalter*, 1650:

> Hymn 75—Psalm 85, second version, verses 1, 2, 5-7.
> Hymn 348—Psalm 98, second version, verses 1-3, 5-9.

Again, better opening verses for two psalm portions have been
obtained from *The Irish Metrical Psalter*, namely for Hymn 25
(Psalm 62, verses 5-8) and Hymn 626 (Psalm 65, verses 9, 11-13):

> 1650   My soul, wait thou with patience
>   upon thy God alone;
>   On him dependeth all my hope
>   and expectation.

> 1880   Only on God do thou, my soul,
>   Still patiently attend;
>   My expectation and my hope
>   On him alone depend.

> 1650   The earth thou visit'st, wat'ring it;
>   thou mak'st it rich to grow
>   With God's full flood; thou corn prepar'st,
>   when thou provid'st it so.

> 1880   Earth thou dost visit, watering it,
> (revised)   Making it rich to grow
>   With thy full flood, providing corn;
>   Thou hast prepared it so.

In the metrical psalmody of the CH3 the doxology or conclusion
(*Gloria Patri*) appropriate to the particular metre of the psalm
portion is included, except where there is already a doxological

conclusion in the text of the psalm (Hymns 101, 167, 566). The doxologies for the metrical psalms had dropped out of use under English Independent and Scottish Covenanting influences in the mid-seventeenth century. Although the seven conclusions were printed together as an appendix in *The Scottish Psalter*, 1929, their use has only been slowly recovered until the present arrangement in this 1973 book of praise. Calderwood's famous appeal in the General Assembly of 1649, when it was proposed to drop the doxology at the close of a psalm portion, may be recalled: 'Moderator, I entreat that the doxology be not laid aside, for I hope to sing it in Heaven.'

In spite of the traditional Reformed reverence for the Holy Scriptures in the Authorized Version, the chanting and the responsive or antiphonal reading of the prose psalms have not been widely practised in Presbyterian worship. *The Prose Psalter* (Authorized Version) pointed for Anglican chanting has been in use in some Church of Scotland congregations since the end of the nineteenth century. A greatly improved version of a prose psalter for chanting was published as *The Scottish Psalter*, 1929: Authorized Version Pointed with Chants. There has been very considerable experiment and development in chanting over recent years, achieving musical settings with more of a speech rhythm, and this improved standard of chanting is represented in the psalmody included in the CH3. (In the Introductory Notes to the Music, a section on Prose Settings describes the musical styles employed for chanting: pp. xiv–xvi.)

Two prose psalms which enjoy what may be termed canticle-status are set to a choice of Anglican single chants: Hymn 3: *Jubilate Deo*: Psalm 100; and Hymn 20: *Venite, exultemus*: Psalm 95, verses 1–7. The words are a version of Coverdale (1535), as found in *The Book of Common Prayer* (1662). Set to Anglican double chants, for use in the Marriage Service, is Hymn 598: Psalm 67; and also for general use Hymn 349: Psalm 98.

A few additional prose psalms in the Authorized Version are included, where the chant is just a short series of chords, repeated for each verse, and intended to be simpler for congregations to sing in unison or in harmony: Hymn 21: Psalm 95, verses 1–7; Hymn 66: Psalm 130. John Currie is the composer.

Plain-chants, referred to in a supplementary selection of the Authorized Version prose psalms in *The Scottish Psalter*, 1929 (prose) as Gregorian Tones, developed from the oldest forms of church music. Originally designed for the psalms in Latin (the Vulgate), they are still in current use in churches. Such plainchant settings are represented in a number of psalm selections (Authorized Version)

offered for antiphonal reading or plain-chant singing in the changing
seasons of the Christian year: for Advent, Hymn 158: Psalm 72,
verses 1, 2, 5, 11, 17-19; Hymn 310: Psalm 50, verses 1-6, 14, 23; for
Christmas, Hymn 166: Psalm 2, verses 1-3, 6-8, 10-12; for Lent,
Hymn 63: Psalm 51, verses 1-4, 6-12; for Passiontide, Hymn 231:
Psalm 42, verses 1-5, 8-11; Hymn 232: Psalm 118, verses 19-29;
Hymn 239: Psalm 22, verses 1-9, 11, 15-19, 22-24, 27, 30, 31; for
Easter, Hymn 262: Psalm 118, verses 15-24; for Ascensiontide, Hymn
284: Psalm 47; and for Pentecost, Hymn 326: Psalm 104, verses 1-5,
30-34. The plain-chant was designed for singing without instrumental
accompaniment, so that these tones are printed in this hymnary as a
single line of modal music: any organ accompaniment would be at the
improvization of the skilled church musician.

Still further variety in psalmody is provided by the inclusion of
three Gelineau Psalms: Hymn 67: Psalm 130, with a choice of two
Antiphons: I place all my trust in you, my God; all my hope is in your
saving word; or, With the Lord there is mercy without end. Hymn
350: Psalm 136, with the Antiphon, Great is his love, love without
end. Hymn 389: Psalm 23, with a choice of three Antiphons: My
shepherd is the Lord, nothing indeed shall I want; or, His goodness
shall follow me always to the end of my days; or, The Lord is my
shepherd, nothing shall I want: he leads me by safe paths, nothing
shall I fear. Joseph Gelineau collaborated with the new translation of
the Scriptures into French in the *Bible de Jérusalem* (2nd edition,
1955), giving special attention to the rhythmic structure of the Psalms
in the original Hebrew, and seeking to develop a simple melodic
musical recitation of the psalms, with congregational antiphon. In the
event this psalmody quickly gained popularity among French Roman
Catholics. The Grail initiated an English version with the collaboration of Dom Gregory Murray, O.S.B., designed for singability
in English. The three Gelineau psalms are chosen because of their
established popularity.

Three psalms from the *New English Bible* have been adapted by Ian
Pitt-Watson and arranged in verses of varied metre, unrhymed,
presenting psalmody in a contemporary mould, the tunes set being
selected from more traditional material: Hymn 64: Psalm 51, verses
1-12; Hymn 68: Psalm 139; Hymn 126: Psalm 19, verses 7-14.

This survey of the variety of psalmody in the CH3 reveals that there
are seventy-nine psalm portions in a hymnary of 695 items. But
further, the following well-known and generally popular hymns are
all based on particular psalms, and in several cases are a virtual
metrical paraphrase of a psalm: Hymn 2: Psalm 100; Hymn 33:
Psalm 136; Hymn 35: Psalm 104; Hymn 37: Psalm 148; Hymn 321:
Psalms 85, 82, 86; Hymn 360: Psalm 103; Hymn 362: Psalm 117;

Hymn 388: Psalm 23; Hymn 404: Psalm 27; and Hymn 611: Psalm 90.

Psalmody emerges ever more clearly as the pattern and model for genuine hymnody. The psalms, however, provided the guide and directive on the true nature of church praise and on the structure and content of any church hymnary.

THE CANTICLES AND THE PEOPLE'S PART IN THE DIVINE SERVICE

A. STEWART TODD

For he lives twice who can at once employ
The present well, and ev'n the past enjoy

ALEXANDER POPE

THE Church in its worship must be contemporary. It must give thanks for salvation in Christ, confess sins and bring within the scope of its intercessory prayer burning issues. It must endeavour earnestly to find contemporary language and thought-forms for the contemporary topics about which it has a mind to sing to God, and it must make use of contemporary musical idioms where they are serviceable as a vehicle both of man's eloquence and of the spiritual eloquence of Christ, the Church's true Choir Master. This is the nature of the Church's life and it is what the Holy Spirit requires of her but He also requires the Church to avoid parochialism either of time or of space. Clearly if the communion of saints means anything Christians in one part of the Church ought to be informed by the fullness of Christian belief and practice as it is preserved fragmented in the separated branches, because these are areas of operation of the Holy Spirit and likewise Christians in one age ought to be informed by the belief and practice of former ages, because these were ages of operation of the Holy Spirit.

In the canticles and in the people's part in Divine Service there is preserved the articulate audible voice of the Church's earliest days, for some of the items come from New Testament times. Those congregations who bring them imaginatively and contextually into their worship do not merely enrich their worship-life, rather as Alexander Pope said, and Martial long before him, they live twice.

Magnificat (163)

The hymn which is ascribed to Mary and which purports to express her joy upon being made certain that she is to be the mother of the Messiah is so-called from the opening words in the Vulgate text: Magnificat anima mea dominum.

In the Eastern Church it was sung at Lauds. This was also the original practice in the West but later it was prescribed for Vespers, whence it came into Anglican Evening Prayer.

Only a foolish liturgical fundamentalism would preclude this fine hymn from the widest possible use in the worship of those who use CH3 and even the briefest exegesis of it demonstrates what an eminently churchly hymn it is. Mary is the eschatological personification of Israel: '... for He hath regarded the low estate of His hand-maiden ... He hath holpen His servant Israel; as He promised to our forefathers, Abraham and his seed for ever.' Mary symbolizes the people of God, thought of here especially as the poor of the Lord, and as in the Beatitudes this language is to be understood spiritually. So understood the *Magnificat* becomes a classic celebration of the fact that God loves the poor in spirit. The birth of the Messiah of a poor virgin is a particular and glorious demonstration of this blessed truth but the truth is for all time and the hymn is proper to any Sunday of the Christian Year.

The likelihood is that Luke found this hymn in a Judean source available to him. The song is, of course, based in large part on the canticle of Hannah in 1 Samuel 2: 1-10. Like the *Magnificat* Hannah's canticle is a song of Messianic expectation, and a celebration of God's glory revealed in the victory of the humble.

Mary is the eschatological personification of Israel. The Church, too, is the handmaid of the Lord. Mary's delight and the joy of her soul are likewise the prefiguring of the eschatological delight and joy of the Church and of all creation, which will one day see the Lord returning in glory.

The mould in which this richness of biblical content and typology are cast is also worthy of comment. The *Magnificat* has all the qualities of good liturgy and good hymnody in that its language and mode of expression possess transparency and detachment and direction towards God. Mary's soul rejoices unquestionably in God, her Saviour. Certainly all generations shall call her blessed but not for any merit of her own but solely because of what God has made possible in her poverty and humility. Without any hint of mariology but simply taking seriously the Incarnation the Church naturally associates herself with Mary's faith and certitude. Karl Barth writes: 'Our calling is to be on the side of Mary. For this joy and this revelation of the soul can also be at any instant our joy.'

Benedictus (161)

The song ascribed to Zacharias (Luke 1: 68-79) has always held a prominent place in the affections of the Church. Because it is a perfect model of a Christian hymn it deserves not only a place in CH3 but also a place in the repertoire of far more congregations. It takes its name from its opening word in the Latin Vulgate.

The reference to John the Baptist makes the *Benedictus* a hymn we should obviously want to sing on the third Sunday in Advent when the Church traditionally recalls that our Lord at His first coming sent His messenger before Him and remembers all who are called to ministry in the Church today, but really this particularity is only one of the more modest of the hymn's attributes. Its real distinction is that it is 'the last prophecy of the Old Dispensation and the first in the New'. Significantly the hymn was for centuries known in the Gallican rite as 'Prophetia' and indeed in Gaul it was sung every Sunday as the normal hymn of the introductory part of the service where other parts of Christendom sang the *Gloria in excelsis.*

The *Benedictus* may have come like the *Magnificat* from a Judean source available to Luke. The language is largely drawn from the *Psalter* but the distinctive voice of the early Christian community is heard in the reference to the child John's becoming the Lord's forerunner and bringing to his people the knowledge of salvation through the remission of their sins.

The sheer spirituality of the hymn is perhaps its chief commendation. The deliverance of which it sings will certainly be deliverance 'out of the hand of our enemies' but the freedom won is freedom for God—that we 'might serve him without fear, in holiness and righteousness before him, all the days of our life'.

The reference to the Messianic era as 'dayspring' or 'sunrise' after the world's night is reminiscent of Isaiah 9: 2 and 60: 1 and especially of Malachi 4: 2. The Fourth Gospel speaks of Christ as 'the true light which lighteth every man that cometh into the world'. The author of the Book of Revelation saw in His vision the countenance of Christ and it was 'as the sun shineth in his strength'.

The wholesome evangelical optimism of the *Benedictus* makes it a characteristic Christian hymn which, whether said or sung, enriches a congregation's devotions.

Nunc dimittis (204)

The *Nunc dimittis* is the most restrained but in some ways the most intense of the biblical canticles. Since the fifth century it has been a feature of the evening devotions of the Church, vespers in the East, compline in the West whence like the *Magnificat* it came into the Anglican Evening Prayer in the 1549 *Book of Common Prayer*. In Reformed worship the *Nunc dimittis* found a place in the Communion Service after the Post-communion prayer and before the Benediction. Many churches in Scotland still use the metrical version of the *Nunc dimittis* either in the position described or as a recessional, and a few use the prose version. In the Eastern Orthodox Service (*Liturgy of St. Chrysostom*) the *Nunc dimittis* is part of the celebrant's final devotions. If progress is made at last in this generation towards achieving the

Reformers' intention to celebrate the Sacrament of the Lord's Supper weekly, as seems possible, then the *Nunc dimittis* may recover its proper place at the heart of the Reformed Church's devotion. The mastering of one or more of the simple chants set in the book will then prove vastly rewarding. Finally, it will be obvious that this canticle can be said or sung very suitably at a funeral service.

The description of Simeon, to whom Luke ascribes the canticle is full of interest. He is described in the gospel as 'just and devout, waiting for the consolation of Israel'. Scholars have noted that in relation to this man and indeed to the whole incident of the presentation of the child Jesus in the Temple, the attitude to the Temple and to the cult is positive and not negative. They make the point that this positive attitude may reflect the grateful recognition that the Temple and the Jewish cult were gifts of providence and grace and that they pointed to something or Someone coming who would fulfil what they promised. Later in the gospels we find, in what might appear our Lord's most dramatically negative attitude, an underlying positive which ties up well with this earlier regard. For the whole purpose of what we call the cleansing of the Temple was to sanctify the Court of the Gentiles. The Court of the Gentiles had been built as a symbol of Israel's faith that one day she would be 'a light to lighten the Gentiles' and that is the faith which finds lyrical expression in the canticle. It was from this holy ambition that the Jews had defaulted. Our Lord performed His most dramatic-ever miracle to reinstate that holy hope. Now a group of faithful people of the Simeon and Anna type have been identified by scholars and connected with Galilee, as the chosen place of eschatological fulfilment and holiness. It has been suggested that from these pious people of Galilee emanated the new Christian cult, the celebration of the Lord's Supper—a daily meal, a love-feast, and a celebration of the presence of the Lord. The fact that Luke connects this canticle with Simeon and therefore, as we believe, with this Galilee community, must not pass unnoticed for it means that the *Nunc dimittis* belongs, in spirit if not in historical fact, to the very earliest and purest strain of Christian worship and piety.

Te Deum Laudamus (345)

The *Te Deum* as it is commonly called is a Latin hymn of great antiquity written in rhythmical prose. The English version printed in CH3 is the version found in *The Book of Common Prayer*. A tradition dating back to the eighth century assigned the composition of the *Te Deum* to St. Ambrose and St. Augustine at the latter's baptism but this account of its origin is not now accepted by scholars. There seems general agreement that the hymn is the work of Niceta, Bishop of Remesiana (Yugoslavia) (392–414). It has been used in the Church mainly in the West and mainly on festival occasions in one of the daily services. From thence it passed into regular use at Mattins of the *Book of Common Prayer*, where it alternates with the *Benedicite*. It has long been regarded as one of the great hymns of the Church and certainly ought to be in the repertoire of more congregations so that it may be used especially on great occasions, for which the nobility and breadth of its conception are so admirably suited. Its similarity to the Creeds and to the content of the eucharistic prayer makes it undesirable to associate it with them in the same act of worship but if Holy Communion is not being celebrated then it ranks as the Church's greatest hymn of confessional adoration and thanksgiving and naturally stands at the head of its section in CH3.

The *Te Deum* is a composite structure. The first part (verses 1-4 in CH3), the *Te Deum* proper, is praise of the Trinity. This part further subdivides into two parallel divisions, the first being the praise of earth and heaven, including the angels, and concluding with a form of the angelic *Sanctus*. The second division is the praise of the Church on earth and concludes with a trinitarian *Gloria*. This hymn may well have existed earlier as a separate item. Each verse, except the *Gloria*, begins with 'Te' or 'Tibi'. In part two (verses 5-7), which is a hymn to Christ, each verse begins with 'Tu' or 'Te'. It seems likely, therefore, that part two, if belonging to a later time, was written as a continuation of part one. Part two proclaims the Christ-event and passes in the buoyancy of faith to prayer for the sanctification of the redeemed and their entrance into glory. The third part is a prayer of supplication in the form of versicles and responses which draw heavily from the Psalms. With mounting intensity these versicles and responses bring the hymn to its confident conclusion where supplication is shot through with unshakeable Christian trust.

The People's Part in the Liturgy

Hymns in the CH3 have been arranged in liturgical order, that is to say in the order in which they will be used in worship. In the Introduction to CH3 it is clearly stated that the Committee in preparing the book has borne in mind that 'the Order of Holy Communion is normative for worship in the Reformed Church and that, where there is no regular weekly celebration of Holy Communion, the service should still follow the eucharistic pattern'.

Hymns are not, therefore, religio-musical interludes to relieve the tedium of much speaking, but rather in the broadest sense the people's part in the liturgy. This greater liturgical consciousness makes it natural to include in the book the liturgical material which anciently and traditionally has been the people's part. These parts are the spiritual heritage of all congregations, to be spoken by the people and where appropriate, and where there exist the musical resources, sometimes to be sung.

Kyrie eleison (60)

The Greek words mean, 'Lord have mercy'. The tiny trilogy which is found in CH3 under this heading is a relic of a very ancient mode of prayer known as litany whose origins are in the liturgy of the synagogue. Kyrie eleison is a response by the people to each of several petitions and intercessions. It appears in all Eastern liturgies from the latter half of the fourth century onwards. It was apparently new to Egeria, the pilgrim nun, who visited Jerusalem in A.D. 381 and who took the trouble to translate it for her 'sisters' in her letter to them. It may be assumed that through her agency and that of other pilgrims it gradually spread to the West. It is specifically commended by the Synod of Vaison in southern France in 529 which notes that it is already in use in other places, especially in Rome. In the West some churches translated the words into Latin but Rome preserved the original Greek, no doubt on the grounds that the meaning of such a short phrase can be easily learned. Kyrie eleison therefore ranged itself alongside other words in their native form: Alleluia, Amen, etc.

The introduction of Kyrie eleison into the Roman liturgy is now ascribed to Pope Gelasius, bishop of Rome at the end of the fifth century. He found in the Kyrie type of prayer a crisper and preferable alternative to the older indigenous form of the intercessory prayer. The latter was somewhat long drawn-out since for each of a number of subjects of intercession there was a bidding, silent prayer by the congregation, and then a collect. Kyries were obviously much neater though they robbed the congregation of the opportunity to pray silently. At about the same time the prayer for which this Kyrie was adopted was moved from its old position as the beginning of the Mass of the Faithful, or Liturgy of the Upper Room, to the beginning of the Mass of the Catechumens. Later to the words 'Kyrie eleison' there were added the words 'Christe eleison'.

Later still at the end of the sixth century Pope Gregory further abbreviated the Liturgy, and reckoning perhaps that the intercessions within the eucharistic prayer were sufficient he dropped the intercessions of the litany, retaining only the formulae—a repeated 'Kyrie eleison' and 'Christe eleison'.

In English Kyries and a litany are very familiar. The use of Kyries in Divine Service (1972) for the Church of Scotland is in association with prayers of confession to which they form a natural complement. In this way these ancient formulae have recovered a true pastoral function and make a meaningful contribution to the people's part.

Trisagion (61, 240)

This hymn first appears in Eastern Liturgies between 430 and 450 though it may be much older. Its position at first was before lections and it is for use in such a position that it has been brought here for the first time into Reformed worship. It is clear that it will form on occasion a noble complement to the spoken Kyries or to prayers of supplication and an alternative to the *Gloria in excelsis*. Its brevity, the simplicity of its intention—to ask for God's mercy—and its considerable intensity will commend it for those occasions when it is desired to move expeditiously towards the Eucharist yet without making an altogether too slender provision for congregational singing.

The *Trisagion* was also found in Gaul *c.* A.D. 600 and through the Gallican rite passed into the Roman, where it is used as part of the Reproaches on Good Friday. The latter are verses and responses in which God's compassion for Israel is contrasted with the outrages inflicted on Christ in His passion.

Gloria in excelsis (62)

These are again the initial words in Latin and hence the usual designation of the hymn 'Glory be to God on high'. It is also known as the Greater Doxology and the Angelic Hymn. The first line has of course been taken from the angels' song in Luke 2: 14. It is an ancient Greek hymn dating from at least the fourth century, used daily at one of the morning hours and brought to the west by Hilary of Poitiers (d. 367), but the number of local variants in the text already found in the fourth century suggests that it may be of third- or even second-century origin.

In the 1552 *Book of Common Prayer* the *Gloria in excelsis* was placed at the end of the eucharist after the Post Communion prayer. In recent orders this is still offered as an alternative to the ancient position, but it is difficult to see how acclamation can be thought appropriate *after* the eucharistic prayer, in which the Church, with the angels, has as it were sung itself hoarse in adoration and blessing and thanksgiving. In Reformed worship it is in association with supplications that congregations are more likely to want to recapture the ancient gladness of the *Gloria in excelsis* and the assurance of its clamour to Christ.

Alleluia (343)

The inclusion in CH3 of the word *Alleluia* set to music affords congregations the opportunity to respond to the reading of the Gospel briefly and gratefully.

The Hebrew word means 'Praise God' and was used in association with psalms in Jewish worship. In Hellenistic Judaism it seems to have been sung by the people as an acclamation. It is probable that it passed from this latter context into Christian worship. The reference to it in Revelation 19: 6 would suggest that it was already used liturgically when that book was written. Some scholars, indeed, venture to reconstruct a liturgy from the Book of Revelation and find there the *Alleluia* after the Gospel and before the invitation to the 'marriage supper of the Lamb'. This is still its place in eastern liturgies, though in the West, together with a verse from scripture, it followed the gradual psalm immediately preceding the gospel.

The collocation of the ancient Hebrew word and two lines of English set to a bold rhythmic tune should make it possible for many congregations to bring 'Alleluias' into their worship without difficulty and as a festival occasion it may again prove a happy solution to the problem of affording enough congregational participation in the Liturgy of the Word without overloading it and unnecessarily delaying the Liturgy of the Upper Room.

Gloria Patri (344)

The Lesser Doxology is of great antiquity and may go back to apostolic times. Its form was probably influenced by the trinitarian baptismal formula in Matthew 28: 19. Its use from the fourth century onwards in east and west has been as a conclusion sung by the people to a psalm or group of psalms. This ancient practice is reflected in the doxologies which conclude the Psalms in CH3.

Ascriptions of praise to the Trinity are widely used in modern worship and the *Gloria Patri* said or sung ought certainly to retain its ancient status as a people's song.

Nicene Creed (558)

The *Nicene Creed* is of uncertain date in the fourth century. Originally creeds were appropriate to the Sacrament of Baptism but the introduction of the *Nicene Creed* into the eucharistic liturgy in the middle of the fifth century seems to have been for doctrinal rather than pastoral reasons. The practice was not adopted in Rome until the eleventh century. Nevertheless wherever it has existed it has belonged to the people's part. The version in CH3 underlines that it is a people's confession of faith and not an individual's by reverting to the plural 'We believe' of the Greek original.

It can be recited after the gospel or after the sermon or, as in certain Reformation orders, immediately before taking the elements to the

Table. There is an obvious merit in giving the people an opportunity of identifying with the faith that has been or ought to have been proclaimed and of renewing their commitment to the fundamentals of that faith. There is a disadvantage in that it anticipates the confessional sufficiency of the eucharistic prayer which rehearses the mighty acts of God in much the same way as does the Creed. The answer may be to find forms of eucharistic prayer which, reflecting the christological intensity of the earliest eucharistic prayers, form a proper contrast to the trinitarianism of the Creed.

Apostles' Creed (546)

This Creed which can be traced back to at least the early third century has always been associated with baptism and appears in that context in CH3. Although it is expressed in the first person singular the tendency is to use it communally, as in the Church of Scotland's most recent 'Order for Baptism', where the congregation having taken a vow to share responsibility for the Christian upbringing of the child join with the parents, who have answered a brief question on their faith, in saying the Apostles' Creed.

At the Reformation there was also a preference for the Apostles' Creed in eucharistic liturgies, including the Scottish. The preference may have been because of the supposed apostolic authority of this creed or simply because of its being shorter.

Salutation, Sursum Corda, Sanctus, Benedictus Qui Venit, The Lord's Prayer (559-562)

Three of the items named above belong within the eucharistic prayer; the first two form part of the introductory dialogue to it. All of these items traditionally involve the people and the very number of the items indicates how strenuous were the efforts made to make the eucharistic prayer a community exercise and not the monopoly of a clergyman. All should actively co-operate in it. Indeed, in certain places and with a certain treatment of the Lord's Prayer, there was place at the conclusion of the eucharistic prayer for yet another people's part—a great and climactic Amen.

The dialogue which introduces the eucharistic prayer is found in almost exactly the form we have it here in CH3 in Hippolytus' Apostolic Tradition (c. 217) and its use, with minimal variation, is universal. The Salutation was no doubt a common Christian greeting. It was used at various points in worship. Where it is reserved for this position, however, it is perhaps easier for it to carry christological overtones and recall to celebrant and people alike that if they truly give thanks then it is by grace they do it and if they truly worship it is because by grace they are enabled to share in the perfect worship offered to God by Christ.

This is more clearly the implication in the exhortation *Sursum corda*. The worship of the Church on earth is a participation in and an anticipation of the worship of heaven. The eucharist is a foreshadowing of the final consummation of the age to come. The worship-life of the Church is incorporated in that of heaven. Therefore worshippers must *lift up* their hearts. But men are not angels and the mode of worship proper to them still includes proclamation as well as angelic acclamation. Therefore they 'make eucharist' to God. To 'give thanks' is the translation for the Greek word 'eucharistein' here. Thanksgiving is a poor word and wholly inadequate to describe that total adoring acknowledgement of God in His cosmic splendour and in His redemptive mercy and grace. 'Eucharistein' means to bless God as the Jews blessed Him and as Jesus blessed Him at the Last Supper, recalling what God has done in His mighty acts with grateful and confessional devotion. It is to this that the worshipper is summoned in the *Sursum corda*.

The original position of the *Sanctus*, which is a feature of nearly all liturgies, appears to have been at the end of the grateful recital or 'anamnesis' of God's mighty acts. In later liturgies it occurs in the middle. The reasons for this are complicated and beyond the scope of this chapter but wherever it is to be said or sung it is certain that the *Sanctus* was a song for celebrant and people together, uniting them with all the angelic powers and the whole company of the saints. The presence of a form of the *Sanctus* in Revelation 4: 8 and the strongly liturgical character of the passage suggest that the *Sanctus* may be another of those items belonging to the oldest strata of Christian hymns.

Benedictus qui venit with *Hosanna* follows the *Sanctus* in most ancient liturgies from about the eighth century. Where the *Sanctus* is in the middle of the 'anamnesis' of God's mighty acts it serves as a bridge to the commemoration of the Christ-event. Where the *Sanctus* concludes the anamnesis of God's mighty acts the *Benedictus qui venit* with *Hosanna* complements the acclamations of heaven with acclamations of earth recalled from Palm Sunday and at the same time in the verb 'cometh' comprehends for us in one word the three tenses of the mystery of Christ's coming.

Finally, the people join with the celebrant to say *The Lord's Prayer*. Again this practice is general and time-honoured. Its use in the eucharist is first mentioned by St. Cyril of Jerusalem (*c.* 350). This great epitome of the faith follows splendidly on the concluding supplications of the eucharistic prayer and forms a glorious extended *Amen* to them.

Agnus Dei (563)

'Lamb of God, that takest away...'—the formula which is based on St. John 1: 29 is already found in the *Gloria in excelsis*, but its first independent use is ascribed to Pope Sergius I (687–701). It was used in association with the fraction or breaking of the eucharistic bread. The practice of repeating it three times in this position dates from the eleventh century. Said or sung after the fraction it is a people's prayer of great devotional intensity, reverently acknowledging the 'Lamb that was slain' and humbly approaching the communion in bread and wine of the whole congregation. It is widely used in modern Reformed liturgies.

Amen (662)

The last and most obvious and logical of the people's parts in worship is *Amen*. It is their response to prayers, doxologies, benedictions, and other formulae and its use is scripturally attested in 1 Corinthians 14: 16. It is, of course, a Hebrew word signifying assent, but for Christians it has come to have a more profound meaning. Jesus Himself is the *Amen* (Rev. 3: 14) and 'all the promises of God in Him are yea and in Him Amen' (2 Cor. 1: 20). Added to the Hebrew notion of assent or desire therefore is the new Christian dimension of faith and assurance. In the *Amen* of the Christian community there are always overtones of faith in Christ in whom God has *acted*.

Because this eschatological motif in the Christian *Amen* makes it more than a word of assent and more than ever untranslatable it has acquired for many congregations a kind of liturgical independence and for that reason musical settings of the word are also provided in CH3.

All of the items mentioned in this chapter can be said and the mastering of chants and settings for those that can also be sung is not a difficult task. The rewards in using them are found not only in the moving sense of identifying with the saints of all the Christian ages, nor yet only in the satisfaction of good stewardship of the spiritual heritage of the Church, but also in the brave Christian objectivity and assurance and the deeply rooted devotion that is made available through them to modern congregations. They are above all appropriate to that strange interpenetration of the divine and the human which is called worship, because they are at once appropriate to worshipping people and also to the mysterious splendour of Christ in the people's midst.

THE REVISION, 1963-1973

JOHN M. BARKLEY

The Church Hymnary (first edition) was published in 1898, and was authorized for use in public worship by the Church of Scotland, the Free Church of Scotland, the United Presbyterian Church, and the Presbyterian Church in Ireland, having been compiled by a committee appointed by those Churches.

A second edition, commonly referred to as *The Revised Church Hymnary* (RCH), was published in 1927. The task of revision was undertaken by a committee appointed by the Church of Scotland, the United Free Church, and the Presbyterian Church in Ireland. The Presbyterian Churches of England and Wales having expressed a desire to co-operate, the Scottish and Irish General Assemblies approved the addition of representatives from them on the committee. The Presbyterian Churches in South Africa, Australia, and New Zealand also appointed committees to co-operate with the revisers. This also was agreed to, and when the work was completed it was authorized for use by all these Churches.

A third edition (CH3) was published in 1973. The first meeting of the revision committee was held on 24 October 1963, in Edinburgh. Dr. J. M. Hunter, who had been a member of the committee which prepared the 1927 edition, presided and opened the meeting with prayer, after which Dr. Thomas H. Keir was appointed convener, Dr. R. Stuart Louden vice-convener, and Mr. F. N. Davidson Kelly secretary. The committee consisted of representatives from the Church of Scotland, the Presbyterian Churches in Ireland, England, and Wales, and of the Church Hymnary trustees, and the United Free Church were invited to appoint two representatives to its membership. In addition the Presbyterian Churches in Australia, New Zealand, and Southern Africa were requested to nominate consultants from their own membership to work in co-operation with the committee.

During the revision, as well as deciding upon principles of working, the committee had to face several fundamental theological questions. Some of these arose at an early date, others during the committee's work. Sometimes there had to be a re-evaluation, but in what follows they are set out in their final form.

What is a Hymn-book?

The fundamental theological question, 'What is a hymn-book?', was raised at the first meeting of the committee. The decision reached was that *a hymn-book is a book for the use of the people of God in the public worship of God*. The two phrases 'people of God' and 'public worship of God' were basic to the work of the committee throughout its ten years' existence. From this definition of a hymn-book several vital conclusions followed.

(1) The structure of the Hymn-book must be based on The Order of Public Worship. That the central act of worship in the Christian Church is the Eucharist or Lord's Supper was clearly seen by the reformers in Strasbourg, Geneva, and Scotland. Indeed, when Calvin was refused permission by the civil authorities to have a weekly celebration he rubricated the Order for the Supper as to how it should conclude when there was no administration. He did not draw up a Preaching Service and tack on a Communion Service at the end of it. The eucharistic rite was the norm, the absolutely binding. Reformed worship, therefore, is a threefold unity:

Preparation to receive the Gospel: approach to God.
Proclamation of the Gospel: God's mighty acts.
Response to the Gospel: adoration, thanksgiving, etc.

This structure, consequently, was held to be basic to the order in which the hymns were arranged in the new book. So we find:

Approach to God	Hymns	1-134
God's Mighty Acts	Hymns	135-344
Response	Hymns	345-545

CH3, in other words, is not a collection of hymns under various headings, as was the case with RCH, but a hymn-book—a book for the use of the people of God in the public worship of God.

As the committee was representative of the Churches it had to report each year to the various General Assemblies, who in accordance with presbyterian practice and procedure sent the committee's report down to presbyteries for study and comment. On the proposed structure of the book, it is, therefore, interesting to note that it was approved by all the presbyteries in the Church of Scotland who sent in comments except four, that in Ireland 'only one was mildly critical', and in the United Free Church all approved. In England and Wales the General Assemblies gave approval.

(2) This definition of a hymn-book also meant that the content of the book must be decided first, that is, the words and hymns have a priority. When they had been selected, then every effort must be made to find musical settings worthy of the words and faithful to the Divine in public worship.

Who are the Church?

A hymn-book being a book for the public worship of God by the people of God raised the theological question: 'Who are the Church?' In answer it was agreed that membership of the Church of Christ consists of the Church Triumphant, and those who believe in Christ in all lands—the faithful—and their children. This answer influenced the committee in three ways:

(a) It led them to consider the production in co-operation with Churches of other traditions a common hymn-book for all the Churches in the British Isles. However, when the various Churches and Trusts were approached while they were 'sympathetic to the idea of an ecumenical hymn-book' they felt they could not 'at this stage' participate in such a project.

In the light of this, the committee then considered the possibility of preparing a hymn-book for English-speaking presbyterianism throughout the world. This, too, proved to be impossible for a variety of reasons.

(b) The phrase 'in all lands' influenced the approach of the committee as follows. A survey of the RCH revealed that it contained only one hymn by a member of the younger Churches, 'One who is all unfit to count' (RCH 406, CH3 82) by Tilak. If the members of the younger churches are truly our brothers in Christ it was agreed that hymns from this source required greater representation. The result was a detailed study of hymnals like the *East Asia Christian Conference Hymnal, Africa Praise*, and other sources of this type. Here two difficulties were encountered. (i) Many of the hymns in common use in the younger churches are translations of Western hymns. (ii) There was the problem of suitable singable music. While the number of hymns from such sources is smaller than the revision committee would have liked, the new book has been enriched by the introduction of hymns from India (203), China (569), Ceylon (415), Africa (340), and elsewhere.

(c) The phrase 'and their children' also affected the committee's approach. Sometimes it is said, 'The children of today are the Church of tomorrow'. This the committee held to be untrue. The children of today may be the adults of tomorrow, but they are the Church of today. To deny this is to make the Sacrament of Baptism meaningless and to reject the teaching of Reformed theology. So serious consideration had to be given to the meaning and significance of the Sacrament of Baptism, and the situation with regard to hymns for younger children had to be examined.

A survey of RCH showed that (i) the 5–7 age group were inadequately provided for, (ii) that some of the children's hymns used abstract terms whereas children think concretely, (iii) that others were hymns which adults thought children ought to sing rather than children's hymns, and (iv) that children were treated separately rather than as part of the whole people of God, that is, they were confined, broadly speaking, to their 'own small corner' of the hymnary (RCH 653-71).

In dealing with this problem the committee did two things. (i) They held that as the children's thanksgiving or affirmation, etc., is an integral part of the totality of the Church's thanksgiving or affirmation, etc., the hymns for younger children should be placed within the structure of the book as a whole, and that for easy reference it was agreed to order the hymns in each section:

> Hymns,
> Hymns for younger children.

Again, it is interesting to note that while a few presbyteries would have preferred a separate section for children's hymns, 'the majority clearly indicated their preference for these hymns being integrated throughout the book'.

(ii) They gave the structural outline of the book to Miss Carrie M. Barnett, Sunday School Organizer in the Presbyterian Church in Ireland, who prepared a draft of approximately four hymns in each of the sections relevant to the worship of younger children. This was then submitted to a number of Sunday School teachers and Sunday School conferences, to lecturers in Colleges of Education, to Youth Committees in the various churches and in the light of their comments revised.

In this connection one other point must be stressed. The revision committee shares the view of Sunday School organizations and Youth departments in the churches that children should become familiar with the great hymns of the Church. Many of them are suitable for the worship of young people. To neglect them would be to cast a reproach upon our Christian heritage.

Of what does the Church's Praise Consist?

The next theological question faced was, 'Of what does the Church's praise consist?' History shows that it consists of psalms and paraphrases, and canticles and hymns. As the last raised a separate fundamental question, which we will discuss in the next section, let us confine ourselves here to the first three.

Metrical psalmody has always held a prominent and honoured position in the public worship of the Reformed Church. However, an examination of the RCH showed that it contained only one metrical psalm (Ps. 100; RCH 229) and no prose psalms. On the other hand, the RCH was normally bound in one volume with the *Psalter*, whether Scottish or Irish. At the same time, surveys revealed that many congregations used only a very limited number of metrical psalms. The average was somewhere between twenty and twenty-five.

Because of the distinctive position given to metrical psalmody in the Reformed tradition and in the light of the surveys the committee considered how the usage of psalmody might be increased. So it was agreed to include a selection of such psalms in the Hymn-book, placed in their appropriate context of confession, thanksgiving, etc. The intention of the committee was not to reduce the psalter from 150 to 79 (65 metrical) but to increase the usage in public worship from about 23 to 79. Further, they decided to bind the whole *Psalter* along with CH3 in the 'words only' editions, and to publish *The Scottish Psalter*, 1929, and CH3 separately in the music editions.

During the sixteenth and seventeenth centuries many versions of the metrical psalter were published. There is no reason why such a movement should not bring forth rich fruit today so three new metrical versions by Professor Ian Pitt-Watson, Aberdeen, based on the *New English Bible* translation were included (Pss. 19, 51, 139; CH3 126, 64, 68), as well as three Gelineau versions (Pss. 23, 130, 136; CH3 389, 67, 350).

The RCH did not include any prose psalms, but the chanting of these, being an ancient Christian practice followed in some congregations from *The Scottish Psalter*, 1929, it was agreed to include a number of these from Coverdale's version as in *The Book of Common Prayer*, and others from the Authorized Version as in *The Scottish Psalter*, 1929, the latter being designed specifically for seasons of the Christian Year.

Paraphrases of sections of Scripture have formed a part of Reformed worship from the Reformation era. However, following the Westminster Assembly of Divines the practice ceased. It was restored some one hundred and thirty years later, when in 1781 'with tacit consent' the custom arose of printing the paraphrases along with the metrical psalms and so they gradually passed into use. The RCH had included thirteen, and CH3 increases the number to twenty-two.

Canticles are really hymns from Holy Scripture with the addition of the *Te Deum*. An examination of the RCH showed that these were all placed in a block at the end of the book. In other words, they were not placed within the structure of public worship, but were a kind of appendix which presbyterians (with a number of exceptions) never opened. In the hope that it will lead to their wider use, in CH3 the canticles have been placed in their historic and liturgical context, for example, the *Kyrie eleison* under confession and supplication, the *Te Deum* under adoration and thanksgiving, etc.

At this point the full arrangement of the items in each section or subsection can be set out. It is:

> Psalms
> Canticles,
> Hymns and Paraphrases,
> Hymns for younger children.

As there are separate introductory articles on Psalmody and the Canticles by Dr. R. Stuart Louden and the Revd. A. Stewart Todd respectively further comment is unnecessary here.

What is a Hymn?

Having omitted the discussion of hymns in the last section, we must now turn to the theological question, 'What is a hymn?' Augustine described a hymn as 'a song with praise of God'. This is the classical definition, but the term has come to be used in a more general sense. Some hymns are exhortations, such as, 'Workman of God' (670), or 'Courage, brother' (484). Others are prayers, such as, 'Spirit Divine, attend our prayers' (107), or 'O God of Bethel' (72). Because Christ ministers to the whole man and Christianity is a way of life, the revision committee, while always bearing in mind Augustine's definition, accepted the wider connotation. The replies and requests of the presbyteries showed that this was also the viewpoint of the Churches. Dr. T. H. Keir discusses this more fully in his introductory article so it only requires passing mention here. Suffice it to say, therefore, that the revision committee kept the classical definition ever in mind.

Liturgical Material

Early in the worship of the Christian Church there came into being what may be described as 'the people's part', responses, such as, *Kyrie eleison, Amen,* the *Sanctus,* etc. However, by the fifteenth century many of the musical settings had become so elaborate and ornate that the peoples' part had become the trained choir's part with the people as listeners. Luther, at first, attempted to provide chants for the traditional liturgy because he wanted the people to take their part there also. However, it was his hymns that sang themselves into the hearts and worship of the people. The same was true with regard to Genevan psalmody. One result arising from this was the substitution of a psalm or hymn for the traditional canticle, or response. This had both profit and loss. Profit in that the people had an active part. Loss in that roots with the Church Catholic were loosened.

A hymn-book being a book for the use of the people of God in the public worship of God, therefore, raised the theological question, 'What liturgical material (for example, canticles, creeds, and the people's part in the Holy Communion) should be included?' It was agreed that this too should be placed within the structure of public worship and not be a separate section at the end of the book. So the *Apostles' Creed* (without musical setting) was placed first in the section for Holy Baptism, and the *Nicene Creed, Salutation* and *Sursum corda* (without), *Sanctus* and *Benedictus qui venit* (with), *Lord's Prayer* (without), and *Agnus Dei* (with) in the section for Holy Communion. Here, again, reference should be made to the Revd. A. Stewart Todd's introductory article on the Canticles.

The Sacraments

The Reformed Church, being a Church of Word and Sacrament, holds that in Baptism and Holy Communion the people of God meet Christ, their Lord, face to face and are united to him. What is done is done in His name. So a selection had to be made of hymns taking their inspired theme from these mysteries. In the case of Baptism this varies from the Scottish paraphrase of Romans 6: 1-7 (548) to Robertson's 'A little child the Saviour came' (551), to name but two. The same is true in regard to the Lord's Supper. The mystery of the Table of the Lord no words can fully express. The selection varies from the universality of *The Didache* (second century) (586) to the mystical realism of Aquinas's 'Thee we adore' (thirteenth century) (584), from the reverent joy of Franck's 'Deck thyself, my soul, with gladness' (seventeenth century) (567) to the eternity of Briggs's 'Come, risen Lord' (twentieth century) (572).

Such a selection, of course, does not preclude the use of hymns from all sections of the book at a special season or festival, for example, who could celebrate the Lord's Supper at Easter and not sing 'Jesus Christ is risen today. Alleluia' (264), or at Christmas without 'O come, all ye faithful' (191)?

The Reformed rite includes two parts within a unity, and as Lacharet says, 'a service with Holy Communion ought to complete it and to give to it its natural conclusion and true consummation', or, to use the words of Hageman, it is an 'evangelical version of the historic liturgy of western Christendom'. In other words, Hymns 1-590 in CH3 set out the Order of Public Worship in the Reformed Church:

> Liturgy of the Word,
> Liturgy of the Faithful.

Remaining Selections

Of course, the task of the revision committee in its selections did not end at this point. Certain features of the life of the Church and its members remained for which provision had to be made. (i) Hymns had to be provided for Ordinances, such as, Confirmation of Baptized Persons and their Admission to the Lord's Table, for Ordination, for Marriage, for Burial, and the Dedication of Churches, (ii) God is Creator and has appointed times and seasons in His grace and providence, (iii) Reformed hymnals have generally included a selection of hymns suitable for the 'close of services of worship' and eventide, and doxologies, and (iv) there is need for hymns of personal faith and devotion, which speak to the individual rather than to the body corporate, and possess emotional intensity in a right and proper sense. These are covered in the remaining sections of CH3.

Ordinances	Hymns 591-610
Times and Seasons	Hymns 611-633
Close of Worship	Hymns 634-662
Personal faith	Hymns 663-695

Principles of Working

There were two principles of working, (i) that the new book should be a Churches' book, not that of a committee, and (ii) the new book should be rooted in the past while reaching out to fresh fulfilment. These principles are so interdependent that they have to be taken together.

That no revision can be even tolerably good unless it is organically related to, and a natural development of, the custom and practice of the Churches in the past was recognized by the committee. Consequently, having considered some of the theological issues already referred to, it undertook a detailed critical analysis of the RCH in the light of the changes which had taken place in the churches and the world since 1927. Then a draft structure was prepared, which required emendation at various stages during the committee's discussions. Then each member of the committee was asked to make a list of the hymns in the RCH he thought should be retained. These were then co-ordinated and placed in the draft structure. Next, an opportunity was provided for any member to state a case for a particular hymn, which he felt should be included, even though it had received only a few votes. If the reasons stated were adequate, it was then placed in the draft, for example, 'Today I arise' (RCH 505; CH3 401) retained its place following such a discussion. The draft was then sent to the different assemblies and presbyteries, was examined carefully as regards balance, and a survey made of the weaker sections to see how they might be strengthened.

There were two main sources of new material (*a*) other hymn-books, especially those published since 1927, and (*b*) manuscript material. The former proved a rich mine and covered not only British publications, but also those in Europe, America, Canada, Asia, Africa, and Australasia. On this source the committee reported in 1968, 'All published hymn books known to members of the Committee have been examined, together with pamphlets and other publications'. On the other hand, while saying that all hymns submitted in manuscript had been 'meticulously examined', it regretted to report 'that only a few items merit inclusion'. So it proved right to the end of the committee's work as may be seen by consulting Appendix A. Hymns from these two sources were then placed in the draft submitted to the assemblies and presbyteries the following year.

The comments of presbyteries on the contents of the draft were carefully examined. This revealed for the Church of Scotland that presbyteries asked for the restoration of 250 hymns from the RCH and the deletion of 105 hymns from the RCH as well as of seventy-five taken from other hymn-books. An analysis showed that 160 of the 250 had only the support of not more than six of the sixty-five presbyteries and in many cases of only one, that in no instance did more than eight presbyteries ask for a deletion. The comments of the six presbyteries of the United Free Church followed a similar pattern.

An examination of the Irish comments showed that only two presbyteries out of twenty-two and 'two members in another' voted against any hymn in the draft and that this applied to only two hymns, that the restoration of 130 hymns from the RCH was asked for, but of these only eleven received the votes of ten presbyteries, while fifty-nine received the vote of only a single presbytery.

In the Presbyterian Church of England only three of the fifteen presbyteries replied. They asked for the restoration of sixty-eight hymns in the RCH, but only four of these had the support of all three.

Five presbyteries in the Welsh Church sent in comments. They were generally favourable, but requested the committee 'to reconsider more particularly the hymns and tunes associated with Wales'.

The result of this detailed examination led to twenty-three hymns from the RCH being added to the draft list. This procedure was repeated again in 1967 and 1968.

Consultation with the Churches was a fundamental principle. While it involved much work, this was a most necessary task because there is nothing to be achieved by producing a hymn-book which is incapable of being used or is undesired. That the committee may be held to have achieved its objective is evident from the fact that ninety per cent of the book was 'immediately practicable' in the majority of congregations. Of course, while rooted in the past it is only natural that in reaching out to the new there is bound to be material that is fresh and, for a time, unfamiliar. The same was true in 1927 when the RCH was published, and will always continue to be so.

Indeed, if one adds to the consultation with assemblies and presbyteries those with committees of the Churches on Sunday Schools, Youth, Education, Overseas Missions, Evangelism, etc., it means that, at least, four thousand people received an opportunity to comment on the revision committee's work before it was completed and submitted to the Churches for final approval in 1970.

Music

Most of what has been said up to the present refers to the work of hymn-selection. Let us now look at the music. Rather than appoint a single editor, the committee unanimously decided that the music, like the words, should be the responsibility of the committee as a whole. So a music subcommittee, which would contain within itself a panel of skilled consultants, was appointed. The music consultants were Dr. Kenneth Leighton, Mr. Herrick Bunney, Mr. John Currie, Mr. David Murray, and Mr. Guthrie Foote, 'who, in addition to professional competence, had wide experience in the publication of music'. Mr. Ian Barrie also assisted, as did Professor Ian Pitt-Watson.

The same procedure was followed for the music as for the words. The subcommittee presented its proposals to the whole committee, who accepted, rejected, or referred back. When a draft was agreed it was then sent to assemblies and presbyteries for comment. As there is a separate introductory article on the music of CH3 by Professor Ian Pitt-Watson, all that is necessary here is to summarize the committee's principles: (i) 'As the spoken language used in Church must be true and faithful to the Word of Christ, so the musical language also must be true to it', and (ii) 'Tunes must be true to the words to which they are set'.

Based on these two principles three guidelines were followed in selecting the music: (a) 'That the tunes and settings should in general be easily learned and readily singable by the average congregation . . .'; (b) 'That where a familiar tune has to be omitted, it should wherever possible be replaced by another familiar tune, or else a cross-reference given to such a tune occurring elsewhere in the book'; and (c) 'That a fine tune may well be employed more than once, thus bringing into use certain hymns previously unfamiliar because the tune was unknown or uninspiring . . .'.

Hymns in Contemporary Idiom

A critical survey revealed that the provision of hymns in contemporary idiom raised problems, for example, the life-span of the particular idiom or its singability by congregations, no matter how excellent it might be for a group. As two years was the time estimated between the completion of the manuscript of CH3 and publication to include a large number of hymns in contemporary idiom might mean that many of them would have already fallen out of use during the two-year period. In other words, the result would be that a book, which should have a life-span of some twenty to twenty-five years, would include a certain amount of dead wood before it was even available for use.

At the same time, the need to provide such material was realized. So a committee from the Church of Scotland's committees on Public Worship and Aids to Devotion and Religious Instruction of the Young, with representatives from Ireland, England, and Wales as consultants, was appointed with the Revd. John D. Ross as convener, to undertake the task of compiling a selection of hymns in modern idiom. The result was the publication of *Songs for the Seventies*, 1972. Its aim and limitations are clearly set out in the preface:

'The book should not be confined . . . to youth only, but . . . should deal "with the love of God and the need for God in the glories and dilemmas of the contemporary world situation and have a general appeal to the entire membership of the Church".' Its title 'indicates a built-in obsolescence. These are pieces which we believe say something relevant to our time in the language—and this includes the musical language—of our time. Probably most of them will vanish when their relevance ceases. At the same time we believe that there are some in this collection which bear the mark of such quality as will see them into a later Church Hymnary.'

New Music

While music in contemporary idiom created difficulties, as we have seen, it was hoped from the first that CH3 would be enriched by contributions from outstanding composers of church music today. The committee, therefore, commissioned tunes for a number of hymns, and some thirty of these have been included as representative of the best work of modern composers. It is hoped that they will not only prove an important feature of the book, but enrich the public worship of the Churches. Also, some manuscript material was submitted to the committee, but again, as in the case of the words, this proved disappointing in quality. Details of the new music are given in Appendix B.

New music may feel strange when it is first heard, nevertheless congregations and choirs before rejecting it (on one or two hearings) should keep in mind the purpose of the revision committee which may be summarized in the words of William Byrd, 'For even as among artisans it is shameful in a craftsman to make a rude piece of work from some precious material, so indeed to sacred words in which the praises of God . . . are sung, none but some celestial harmony (so far as our powers avail) will be proper'.

Political Decisions

Because the work of the revision was so harmonious members may be surprised to find any reference to 'political decisions'. The committee did have to keep in view the requirements of somewhat differing communities and their specific needs, but 'political decisions' were only called for on two issues. One was in the use of the term 'Confirmation' in the proposed structure of the book. This was unanimously overcome by undertaking to insert in the 'Introduction' to CH3 the sentence, 'In Confirmation Christ strengthens and blesses the baptized, who profess their faith, as members of his Body with both privileges and responsibilities'.

The second was the necessity to include a number of tunes, which are commonly used in Wales, but not elsewhere. Again, there was complete unanimity on the committee's proposals.

Conclusion

A hymn-book is a book for the use of the people of God in the public worship of God. Every age, including that of today, has contributed something new and of value to the rich treasury of the Church's devotion and hymnody. Throughout its work the committee sought to secure a proper balance, not only between the various sections of the book but between the riches of the different centuries. The twentieth century, understandably, was but poorly represented in the RCH. In CH3 a number of hymns and tunes written this century have been introduced. CH3 is rooted in Christian history, and while seeking to enrich fully takes into account the familiar. Five hundred and two of the psalms, canticles, paraphrases, and hymns are taken from *The Scottish Psalter*, 1929, and the RCH, four of the historic canticles (60, 61 and 240, 561, 563) have been restored and given musical settings, and 188 new hymns introduced, of which eight are completely new (see Appendix A) and many of the remaining 180 are already familiar from other hymn-books, or as carols and children's hymns. As regards the music, new settings were commissioned for the canticles to provide simpler forms to enable the people to participate, twenty-six new commissioned tunes and two contributed tunes are introduced, of which ten are in 'irregular metre', seven in metres so uncommon that they also might even be so classified, and eight are provided with alternatives or cross-references. CH3 retains 358 tunes from *The Scottish Psalter*, 1929, and the RCH, and introduces from other hymn-books 124, of which, again, many are well known.

Having completed the task assigned to it by the Churches, the revision committee sent out *The Church Hymnary* (third edition), 1973, as its preface states, 'in the prayerful hope that it may enrich the worship of congregations to the greater glory of God'.

THE MUSIC

IAN PITT-WATSON

THE Church Hymnary Revision Committee, at an early stage in its proceedings, carried out a survey of the approach and method adopted in the compilation of *The Church Hymnary*, first edition, 1898 and the 1927 revision. In the light of this it was decided not to appoint a music editor, but that the music as well as the words should be the responsibility of the committee as a whole. This involved a new approach to the music arrangements. The procedure adopted was parallel to that followed with regard to the words. First a music subcommittee was appointed from its membership, and then, because of the absolute necessity for the best expert and technical advice, a number of Music Consultants. The latter were Mr. Herrick Bunney, Organist and Master of Music at the High Kirk, Edinburgh, St. Giles' Cathedral, Dr. Kenneth Leighton, Reid Professor of Music in the University of Edinburgh, Mr. John Currie, Head of the Department of Music in the University of Leicester (formerly of Glasgow University), Mr. David Murray, Organist and Choirmaster at St. Machar's Cathedral, Aberdeen, and Mr. Guthrie Foote, a member of the Oxford University Press staff and music editor of several important recent hymn-books. At the request of the consultants the writer was appointed to sit and co-operate with them in their work.

To the consultants in particular and the music subcommittee in general fell the arduous task of preparing constructive proposals for submission to the committee as a whole. This involved making a critical assessment of the music of the RCH, the examination of suggested tunes from other hymn-books and an assessment of contributions made in manuscript. Again, should their proposal be rejected by the committee there was the often difficult problem of providing a viable alternative.

The decision to adopt this method in preparing the music had both advantages and disadvantages. On the one hand, it meant that sometimes the book does not follow a consistent policy. For example, a large number of re-harmonizations were commissioned, but many of these were rejected by both the committee and the consultants—and correctly so. The result was that sometimes—and that reluctantly—the committee had to return to the harmonization in the RCH. On the other hand, it prevented the book being based on the views or whims of an individual, or following a rigid stereotyped pattern acceptable to some but unwelcome to others. Having given this all too brief summary of the interrelationship of the revision committee, its music subcommittee and the consultants, let us now turn to the choice of music and the principles governing it.

In preparing a new hymn-book the rewarding task of selecting new tunes must always be preceded by the more hazardous task of rejecting old ones. Selecting new tunes is relatively easy. If the selection is well-judged, the music will be sung and loved—not perhaps at once, but given time—and the skilled selector will have his reward. If the selection is ill-judged, the tune will simply be ignored and the errant selector forgotten. But if the *rejection* of a tune is ill-judged, if music that is sung and loved by many is no longer to be found in a new book and no good reason can be given for its exclusion, then indeed the selector is in dire trouble! And even if good reason *can* be given for the exclusion his critics may still argue that the fact that many people enjoy singing a certain kind of music is in itself sufficient reason for its inclusion. The church musician may sound a little self-righteous (especially in a tradition of worship where joy is at a premium) if he replies that he is not simply a religious entertainer paid to give people what they want. Like the preacher, he must always try to be *intelligible* but he need not always try to be *popular*. Many popular tunes are good tunes, but popularity alone is not a sufficient criterion of a tune's merits. Music is a kind of language that can 'say' things that words alone cannot say. It follows that music can say false things as well as true things. In the visual arts this is self-evident. Anyone who knows his New Testament and who looks at a weak, effeminate representation of Christ in a stained-glass window or an illustrated Bible can immediately recognize that this is not simply bad art; it is bad theology. Weak, effeminate sentimental music can as effectively distort our image of God in Christ as can weak, effeminate, sentimental pictures—or words.

Hence the need to face honestly the awkward and unpopular task of rejecting the tawdry even when the tawdry is popular. The compilers of CH3 did their best, though they were anything but ruthless. It was not merely cowardice, however, that influenced the committee and the consultants to approach this task of rejection with restraint and caution. Some tunes quite unacceptable to contemporary standards of musical judgement have gathered round them precious and sacred associations—especially for older people. Moreover, the words and music of a hymn have sometimes become so interwoven as to be virtually inseparable. In such cases there are no rule of thumb solutions. For example, once the revision committee had decided after long debate not to exclude the words of Hymn 482,

'Yield not to temptation', it was agreed that there was no alternative but to recommend the retention of the original tune FORTITUDE as in the RCH—poor as that tune was musically. The metre of the hymn was irregular, no suitable alternative tune was available, and it was felt that to commission new music for words of questionable value would be pointless. On the other hand, for Hymn 688, 'I need Thee every hour', since a well-wrought contemporary tune was available which strengthened the words, and was in harmony with the author's opposition to a refrain it was decided in this instance to discard the weak tune set to it in the RCH. In many other instances where a familiar and much-used tune was felt by the committee to be less than satisfactory a compromise solution was effected by reprinting the old tune, but offering as a first choice what the committee believed to be a better alternative. For example, the familiar Children's Hymn 'Jesus loves me' (418) is given with its original Victorian setting in spite of the rhythmic difficulty which the chorus presents to very young children and its lack of musical interest. But an alternative is offered as the committee's first choice in which a traditional Gaelic melody of great simplicity and charm is used for the same words, very slightly adapted. Another example of the refusal to recommend the wholesale rejection of familiar and much-sung tunes even when a splendid alternative was available is to be found at Hymn 387, 'The Lord's my Shepherd'. Both WILTSHIRE and CRIMOND are widely used. But the committee believed that in SEARCHING FOR LAMBS they had found a tune ideally worthy for these most precious words. Both the consultants and committee agreed, however, that precisely because these words were so universal in their appeal and the nineteenth-century tunes were so familiar, no violence should be done to the present association of words and music, but rather that the new tune (which is really an old one) should be allowed to make its own way in its own time.

Having dealt with the awkward and sensitive problem of tune rejection, the committee and consultants were then able to turn to the much more rewarding task of tune *selection*. Fine poetry does not necessarily make a fine hymn; nor does fine music necessarily make a fine hymn-tune. A certain basic literacy in both words and music is essential. But the quality which can transform mere literacy and musical competence into great hymnody is hard to define. In a book for public worship, so far as music is concerned, 'singability' must be the first criterion, and was first in the minds of the committee in making their selection. But 'singability' is obviously relative to the resources available to any group of worshippers at any given time. What is singable in one congregation may be unsingable in another. Further, 'singability' is not necessarily the same as simplicity and immediate accessibility. OLD 124TH (Hymn 392) is perhaps the most singable tune in the *Scottish Metrical Psalter*, 1929, but it is certainly not the simplest. The relative 'difficulty' of SINE NOMINE (Hymn 534) and DOWN AMPNEY (Hymn 115) is concealed not only by their familiarity but by their intrinsic 'singability'. This is the quality which made them popular in the first instance and hence familiar. Their intrinsic musicality made them last. By the same token, audiences at the last night of the 'Proms' are not the only people to relish the 'singability' of Parry's JERUSALEM (Hymn 487)—though the tune certainly creates some problems for the average congregation. SINE NOMINE, DOWN AMPNEY, and JERUSALEM represented a tradition of early twentieth-century hymn-tune writing that immensely enriched the RCH. We believe that music of the latter half of the twentieth century will similarly enrich the CH3—not least some of the music published in it for the first time. Thomas Wilson's STONELAW (Hymn 86) and Kenneth Leighton's MAYFIELD (Hymn 672) may one day rival in popularity SINE NOMINE and DOWN AMPNEY; and the austere splendours of Leighton's Communion Music (Hymns 60, 62, 560, 561, 563) may well prove no less rewarding to sing (and certainly no more difficult to learn) than Parry's JERUSALEM. Special attention ought also to be drawn here to the essential 'singability' of the music specially written for this book by other distinguished modern composers.

But exciting and rewarding as these contemporary tunes are, the main strength of CH3 is, of course, drawn from the music of the past. Here the compilers have tried to bring together the best of more than five centuries of the Church's music. The new book is certainly less dependent on the music of the nineteenth century than the RCH was, and much less so than the first edition of *The Church Hymnary*. At the same time, the great tune writers of the nineteenth century retain on merit a substantial and honoured place and at least one splendid period piece 'The Battle Hymn of the Republic' (Hymn 318) has been restored.

The compilers have been at great pains to ensure that congregations should be able to make the transition from the RCH to CH3 with the minimum disruption of their present pattern of worship. It is especially important to recognize that, although everyone can read new words at sight, the majority of people have to learn new tunes by rote. This takes time and patience. During this learning period there is a danger that some may feel that the worship of the Church has been impoverished rather than enriched. For this reason the compilers have tried to ensure that in each section of the book there is still ample familiar material, words and music, for congregational worship to continue undisturbed even before any new tunes are learned. In many instances new words have been set to tunes already familiar, and where a new tune has been set to familiar words, a cross-reference is, given wherever possible to an alternative tune which the congregation may already know. In addition, many fine tunes already familiar to the congregation have been used more than once in the book. In consequence new words can be immediately released for use. For example, OLD 124TH set to Psalm 124 at Hymn 392 may also be used to release three other splendid sets of words at Hymns 84, 507, and 640. By this device new words are released for use more quickly than congregations can be expected to learn new tunes. The use of a fine tune for more than one set of words offers other advantages. Hymns, used only on special occasions are, wherever possible, set to tunes in regular use—for example, the four Marriage Hymns nos. 599-602. Sometimes this borrowing can bring with it enriching associations as in Hymn 606 where the tune VULPIUS with its overtones of Easter (see Hymns 266 and 270) is set to the words of a hymn suitable for use at a funeral service (Hymn 606), the musical association bringing to mind the resurrection.

Indeed, in this connection the work of the committee received an unsolicited tribute to its efforts when an organist of 'over fifty years' experience' wrote to *Life and Work* pointing out that if one omitted the twenty-three psalms and hymns involving chanting, and the thirty-seven hymns set to more difficult and 'ornate' tunes, 635 of the 695 items in CH3 are 'immediately practicable', or 91 per cent of the book.

Perhaps a word should be said about some of the music which has *not* been included in CH3. It may seem surprising and a little depressing to some that a hymn-book, produced at a time when 'popular' religious music is on the crest of a wave and when 'religious musicals' are packing the theatres, should show no hint of these influences anywhere in its pages. There are two main reasons for this. First the style of contemporary popular music changes so rapidly and dates so quickly that its inclusion in a book designed to be used for several decades could hardly be justified. No doubt contemporary popular music includes some material of permanent worth, but only the perspective of time will make it possible to sift the dross from the gold. But, secondly, much of the best contemporary popular religious music cannot in the generally accepted sense of the word be regarded as hymnology. For example, Sydney Carter's 'Lord of the Dance' and 'Friday Morning' (both of which were considered by the revision committee) are religious songs of real distinction and one may reasonably suppose of permanent worth (see *Songs for the Seventies*, nos. 13 and 30). But it must still be asked whether or not they are hymns. 'Lord of the Dance' might reasonably be included in a hymn-book on the grounds that it is a carol using the same kind of imagery as the traditional carol 'My Dancing Day' (which is assumed to be respectable simply because it is old). But 'Friday Morning', though in the present writer's judgement an even better religious song than 'Lord of the Dance', can hardly be regarded as a hymn, containing as it does such lines as 'To Hell with Jehovah to the Carpenter I said'— powerful as these words undoubtedly are in their context. It is for these reasons that the present book offers no contemporary 'popular' hymns of this type in its pages. Meantime the continuing publication of paperback books like *Songs for the Seventies*, which was originally planned as a kind of supplement to CH3, is to be warmly welcomed. No doubt, in due course, *The Church Hymnary*, fourth edition, will richly benefit.

The singing of the Psalms and of other words from Scripture has always had a place of honour in the Church's song. So long as these words are metred, no special problem is posed by their use in congregational singing, though often considerable violence is done to the text of the original prose version. Metring, however, has been the traditional solution of the Churches directly concerned in the compilation of CH3, hence the inclusion of many traditional metrical psalms and paraphrases and the continuance of that tradition by the provision of two new paraphrases and three new metrical psalms all based on the *New English Bible* translation (see Hymns 162, 399, 64, 68, and 126). But the search continues for a practicable way to sing *non-metrical* words congregationally. The classic solutions of plain-chant and Anglican chant, though not ideally adapted to congregational singing, are represented in this book and should certainly be used where choral resources allow of it. But even where such resources are not available the singing of non-metrical words should not be regarded as impossible. In recent years the *Gelineau Psalter* has sought to provide a genuinely *congregational* means of participation in singing prose psalms (see Hymns 350, 389, and 67). An alternative, and even simpler solution to the same problem is offered by John Currie (see Hymns 21 and 66). The Music Edition of CH3 in its 'Introductory Notes' (pp. xiii–xvi) gives some useful guidance on how these various solutions to the singing of non-metrical words work out in practice.

The notation of the music in CH3 is designed to make it as easily read as possible, hence the use of the crotchet as the standard pulse instead of the traditional minim; for example, compare the notation of the familiar tune PRAISE MY SOUL as it appears in the RCH no. 21 and in CH3 no. 360. For the same reason the traditional hymn-book notation was abandoned. It used double bar lines across the stave (often in the middle of 'real' bars) sometimes to indicate the ends of lines, sometimes the ends of half verses (see, for example, IN DULCI

JUBILO and LOVE UNKNOWN in RCH nos. 58 and 76, and compare with CH3 nos. 183 and 207). In CH3 the sign ∥ above the stave indicates where each line ends, without disturbing the sense of the musical notation within the stave itself.

In CH3 many tunes are set a little lower in pitch than in its predecessor and, at the same time, encourages the more extensive use of unison singing. These two things are obviously connected. Part singing is immensely enriching to those who can do it whether in choir or congregation; but it compels a compromise in regard to pitch. Take, for example, Hymn 368 'Now thank we all our God'. The present book agrees with most of its recent predecessors in setting this in a relatively low key, in spite of the fact that the part singers and choir sopranos would prefer to sing it at least a tone higher. The majority of the congregation, however, and especially the men in it, are already strained in the present key by the repeated top C's and D's and would happily sing a semitone lower. But then the part singers would go out of business altogether. Some compromise is inevitable. In the CH3 we have sometimes been able to ease the situation by printing tunes that appear in the book more than once in more than one key, for example, DEUS TUORUM MILITUM (42 and 483), MOVILLE (301 and 317), etc. But the general principle in deciding the key in which tunes are to be set has been that a hymn-book is primarily designed for *congregational* singing, hence the general lowering of the pitch. But if this is not to result in a loss of vigour and incisiveness in the lead that the choir can give to the congregation, the use of unison settings or at least of occasional unison verses must frequently be resorted to. Part singers may at first feel a little frustrated and perhaps a little strained. But they, recognizing that worship is a corporate action of the congregation, will be amply compensated by the knowledge that they are giving the congregation far more help by singing the tune in their middle and upper register than by singing an inaudible bass or alto part. A further advantage of the use of unison singing is that genuinely contemporary music, of which there are some splendid examples in CH3, can use bold and arresting harmonies in the accompaniment while still offering the congregation a relatively simple melodic line—see, for example, Thomas Wilson's HEATON which is a bold and original setting of the 'Aaronic Blessing' (Hymn 556), or Kenneth Leighton's Communion Music (Hymns 560, 561, and 563).

A book like CH3 serving a wide constituency and subject to substantial legitimate pressures from its constituents can, in the nature of the case, never wholly satisfy everyone, or perhaps anyone. The choice of music in the book has, quite properly, been the product of conflicting interests. In consequence some will think it too conservative, some too radical; some will feel we have tried too hard to please, some will feel we have not tried hard enough. Certainly by no means all the music in the book will be of value to everyone using it. That ideal was always impossible and was never attempted, since many minority interests of one kind or another had to be catered for. But it is the belief and prayer of the committee that all who use CH3 will find in it sufficient of splendour, old and new, to nourish and enrich their worship of God in the years to come.

NOTES ON THE HYMNS

JOHN M. BARKLEY

1. All people that on earth do dwell

This version of the 100th psalm appears in 1561 in *The Anglo-Genevan Psalter* and in the *Psalter* published, probably in the same year, by John Daye. It is included in *The Scottish Psalter* of 1564, where it is assigned to William Kethe, who was at Geneva in 1559 and contributed to the Anglo-Genevan version. As to text, *The Scottish Psalter* of 1650 changed 'fear' into 'mirth' in v. 1, and 'The Lord ye know' into 'Know that the Lord' in v. 2, but the mis-spelling of 'folck' (folk) as 'flock' in v. 2 persisted. In v. 4 'for why' means 'because', which was adopted in *The Irish Psalter*, 1880. In the RCH and CH3 'flock' has been changed to 'folk'.

From 1575, or possibly 1567, it became customary to sing a metrical 'Gloria Patri', or Doxology, to the Psalms. Charteris's edition of 1596 provides thirty-two, one for each metre. In 1650, following the Westminster Assembly, the practice ceased. In CH3 they have been restored.

OLD 100TH was composed or adapted by Louis Bourgeois for Ps. 134 in *The French Psalter*, 1551. In the *Psalter*, 1561, it was set to this psalm, and has ever since remained associated with it.

2. Before Jehovah's awesome throne

This version of the 100th psalm is a composition of Isaac Watts in his *Psalms of David*, 1719, as altered by John Wesley in his *Collection of Psalms and Hymns*, 1737. Owing to the connotation of 'awful' having changed this was altered to 'awesome'.

OLD 100th. See 1.

3. O be joyful in the Lord all ye lands

Prose psalm 100, *Jubilate Deo*, in the Great Bible version as in the BCP. Chanting of prose psalms is not a common feature in the worship of the Reformed Church, but several have come to be used regularly in some congregations. See also 20, 21, 67, 349, 598.

A number of prose psalms, suitable for use on occasions of the Christian Year, set to one or other of the eight ancient Gregorian Tones are also provided. These are taken from the A.V. as in *The Scottish Psalter*, 1929. See 63, 158, 166, 231, 232, 239, 262, 284, 310, 326, 349.

CHANTS   Alcock, J. in B flat single.
          Ouseley in E single.

4. How lovely is thy dwelling-place

Metrical psalm 84: 1–5 taken from *The Scottish Psalter*, 1650. No version of this psalm is in the Anglo-Genevan book, 1556. That in *The Scottish Psalter*, 1564, was by John Hopkins.

HARINGTON was originally written as a glee for three voices under the title 'Retirement', to the words 'Beneath the silent rural cell of innocence and peace'. It first appears as a psalm tune in Williams's *Psalmodia Evangelica*, 1789. It is taken from *The Scottish Psalter*, 1929, which preserves the original melody and bass.

5. Within thy tabernacle, Lord

Metrical psalm 15 from *The Scottish Psalter*, 1650. Thomas Sternhold's version appeared in the Anglo-Genevan book, 1556, and was retained in *The Scottish Psalter*, 1564.

NUN DANKET ALL (GRÄFENBERG) is from Crüger's *Praxis Pietatis Melica*, Berlin, 1647, where it is set to the hymn 'Nun danket all' und bringet Ehr'. The present is the original form of the melody.

6. Thy mercy, Lord, is in the heavens

Metrical psalm 36: 5–9 from *The Scottish Psalter*, 1650. William Kethe's version was given in the Anglo-Genevan book, 1561, and the Scottish, 1564.

LONDON NEW is from one of the thirty-one Common Tunes found in *The Psalmes of David*, 1635, where it is named 'Newtoun' with a variation in the third line. This appears to have been its form in the east and north of Scotland. The present form of the melody appears first in Playford's *Psalms*, 1671, and is that found in the west of Scotland and in England. Since R. A. Smith's *Collection*, 1825, this has become universal.

7. O send thy light forth and thy truth

Metrical psalm 43: 3–5 from *The Scottish Psalter*, 1650. Sternhold's version appeared in the Anglo-Genevan book, 1556, and was retained in the Scottish, 1564.

MARTYRS is one of the twelve Common Tunes in *The CL Psalmes of David*, 1615. In Ravenscroft's *Psalter*, 1621, it is classified among 'Scottish Tunes' and is in triple time. Playford follows Ravenscroft. In 1615 the tune is in minims throughout with the exception of the first and last notes of each line. In 1635, semibreves are introduced in the first and last lines. In all the old books, Scottish and English, the tune is in the Dorian mode, but many editors have introduced changes into the tune in order to force it into the modern minor mode.

The story of its being sung by the Covenanters at Drumclog to Ps. 76 is legend. It gets its name probably from its association with Ps. 51, which George Wishart desired to be sung on the evening before his arrest and martyrdom in 1546.

8. I love the Lord, because my voice

Metrical psalm 116: 1–7. V. 1 is from *The Scottish Psalter*, 1650, v. 2 from *The Irish Psalter*, 1880, and vv. 3–5 from the Scottish. Thomas Norton's version appeared in *The English Psalter*, 1562, and was retained in the Scottish, 1564.

ST. FLAVIAN is from *The English Psalter*, 1562. The present version is the first half, slightly altered, of the tune of Ps. 132, where the tune is DCM. This is first found in Redhead's *Ancient Hymn Melodies*, 1853, and ascribed to him. In *Hymns Ancient and Modern*, 1861, it is called 'Redhead', but this is changed to 'St. Flavian' in the 1875 edition.

9. Praise to the Lord, the Almighty, the King of creation

A free paraphrase of Pss. 103: 1–6 and 150, written at Düsseldorf and first published in Joachim Neander's *Glaub- und Liebesübung*, Bremen, 1680. The translation is by Miss Winkworth in her *Chorale Book for England*, 1863.

LOBE DEN HERREN is first found in the *Stralsund Gesangbuch*, 1665, where it is set to the hymn 'Hast du denn, Liebster'. In 1680 Neander set it to this hymn. Later German books show many variations in the form of the melody. The present is that in *The Chorale Book for England*.

10. Christ is made the sure foundation

Four of the five stanzas which were published by Neale in his *Hymnal Noted*, 1852–4, as altered for *Hymns Ancient and Modern*, 1861. The lines are a version of the second part of a Latin hymn, 'Urbs beata Hierusalem', which was in use in the ninth century but may date from the sixth. The first verse echoes Eph. 2: 20–1.

WESTMINSTER ABBEY (BELVILLE) is an adaptation of the 'Alleluias' at the end of Purcell's anthem, 'O God, Thou art my God', which appeared in Boyce's *Cathedral Music*, 1760. The arrangement by Ernest Hawkins first appeared in Novello's *The Psalmist*, 1843, and was included in *Hymns Ancient and Modern*, 1939.

11. Jesus, stand among us

William Pennefather, founder of the Mildmay Conferences, wrote this hymn as it stands, except that in v. 3 'we'll' has been changed to 'we' and 'the' omitted before 'eternal'. His hymns were published posthumously in *Original Hymns and Thoughts in Verse*, 1873, though many of them, including the present one, had already been used at conferences.

ADSIS, JESU was given in manuscript by Mrs. Monk, after the composer's death, to A. H. Mann, musical editor of *The Church of England Hymnal*, and it was published in that work in 1895.

12. Lift up your heads, ye mighty gates

Georg Weissel's hymn is based on Ps. 24 and first appeared in *Preussische Fest Lieder*, Elbing, 1642. Miss Winkworth's translation was published in *Lyra Germanica*, 1855, and her *Chorale Book for England*, 1863.

LOWER MARLWOOD was composed by Basil Harwood for *The BBC Hymn Book*, 1951.

13. Light of the anxious heart

Newman's rendering in *Tracts for the Times*, 1836, of a cento in the Roman

Breviary of 1632 is a free adaptation from the medieval hymn 'Jesu dulcis memoria'. See 377, 378, 571.

RUTHERGLEN was composed for this hymn by Thomas Wilson for CH3.

14. We come unto our fathers' God

This hymn, based on the first verse of Ps. 90, was composed by T. H. Gill on St. Cecilia's Day, 1868, and first appeared in his *Golden Chain of Praise*, 1869. Three stanzas from the middle of the original have been omitted. It 'was inspired', says the author, 'by a lively delight in my Puritan and Presbyterian forefathers of East Worcestershire. Descended from a Moravian martyr and an ejected minister, I rejoice not a little in the godly Protestant stock from which I spring. A staff handed down from him, and inscribed with the date, 1692, was in my hand when I began the hymn.'

NUN FREUT EUCH is from Klug's *Geistliche Lieder*, Wittenberg, 1535, where it is set to the hymn, 'Nun Freut euch lieben Christengemein'. This hymn by Luther appeared first in 1523 or 1524 to a different tune. The present tune came into use in England to the hymn, 'He thinks the last great day has come' in Needham's *Hymns Devotional and Moral on various Subjects*, 1768, and in 1802 to 'Great God, what do I see and hear?' It was popularly known as 'Luther's Hymn', but there is no evidence that it was his composition. The present version is that by J. S. Bach.

15. We love the place, O God

Bullock's hymn is based on Ps. 26: 8 and was composed in 1827 for the dedication of a church, where he was rector, at Trinity Bay, Newfoundland. It is from his *Songs of the Church*, 1854, as revised by Sir H. W. Baker for *Hymns Ancient and Modern*, 1861. The first verse is by Bullock with 'other' altered to 'earthly', v. 2 is rewritten, vv. 3–5 are by Baker.

QUAM DILECTA by H. L. Jenner was composed for this hymn in *Hymns Ancient and Modern*, 1861. The name is the Latin title for Ps. 84.

16. Lord Jesus, be thou with us now

Edith F. B. Macalister's hymn was written for the National Sunday School Union and appeared in *Child Songs*, 1914.

SURREY is among some 'entirely new' pieces in Church's *Introduction to Psalmody*, 1723, where it is headed 'Psalm the 23rd, Paraphrased by Mr Addison, set to Musick by Mr Henry Carey'. The reference is to Addison's 'The Lord my pasture shall prepare', for which Carey composed this tune.

17. Serve the Lord with joy and gladness

This one verse hymn, based on Ps. 100: 2, was written by Mary E. Huey in 1959 and appears in *Songs and Hymns for Primary Children*, 1963.

SHIPSTON by Miss L. E. Broadwood is as arranged by Vaughan Williams in *The English Hymnal*, 1906, from the air of a Warwickshire ballad, 'Bedlam City', which tells of the lament of a young maiden for her lover who has been killed in battle.

18. This is God's holy house

Louise M. Oglevee's hymn appears in *The School Hymn Book of the Methodist Church*, 1950.

MAINZ, also known as MARIA JUNG UND ZART, takes its name from these words for which it is a setting in *Ausserlesene Catholische, Geistliche Kirchengesänge von Pfingsten biss zum Advent*, Cologne, 1623. The present version first appeared in Cologne in *Psalteriolum Harmonicum*, 1642.

19. O come, and let us to the Lord

Metrical psalm 95: 1–6 from *The Irish Psalter*, 1880. The version in the Scottish book, 1564, was by John Hopkins, which was revised in 1650.

IRISH first appears in Powell's *Collection of Hymns and Sacred Poems*, 1749, among the 'Tunes adapted to the foregoing Hymns' at the end of the volume. It is without a name, and seems to have received the name 'Irish' in Ashworth's *Collection*, 1760. Originally it was probably a folk-tune, as it is associated with a Galloway and Antrim folk-song, 'The Cameronian Cat'. It is possibly Jacobite in origin as James Hogg refers to it in his *Jacobite Relics of Scotland*.

20. O come let us sing unto the Lord

Prose psalm 95: 1–7, *Venite exultemus*, as in BCP. See 3.

CHANTS   Macfarren in A single.
          Goss in A single.

21. O come let us sing unto the Lord

Prose psalm 95: 1–7 (A.V.). See 3.

CHANT   This short chant was written for CH3 by John Currie.

22. O sing a new song to the Lord

Metrical psalm 96: 1–2, 6–8 from *The Scottish Psalter*, 1650. John Hopkins's version was given in the Scottish book, 1564.

SOUTHWARK appears in *The Actes of the Apostles, translated into Englyshe Metre, and dedicated to the Kynges moste excellent Maiestye, by Christopher Tye*, 1553, which contains a metrical version of the first fourteen chapters of the Acts of the Apostles, each having set to it a tune in four parts. Southwark is the first half of the tune set to chapter 8.

23. God shall endure for aye; he doth

Metrical psalm 9: 7–11 from *The Scottish Psalter*, 1650. Thomas Sternhold's version in *The Anglo-Genevan Psalter*, 1556, was retained in the Scottish book of 1564.

STROUDWATER, named after the river on which Stroud stands in Gloucestershire, appeared in *A Book of Psalmody, containing some easy instructions for young beginners; to which is added a select number of Psalm-tunes, Hymns, and Anthems. Collected, Printed, Taught, and Sold by Matthew Wilkins of Great*

Milton, near Thame in Oxfordshire, c. 1730. Wilkins was a butcher at Great Milton, and evidently a musical enthusiast. He names the tune 'Stroudwater New Tune' to distinguish it from a 'Stroudwater Old Tune'. The former was set to Ps. 146 and the latter to Ps. 40. While always popular in Scotland, it fell out of use in England until it was revived in *Songs of Praise*, 1925.

24. God is our refuge and our strength

Metrical psalm 46: 1–5 from *The Scottish Psalter*, 1650. John Hopkins's version was that in the Scottish book, 1564.

STROUDWATER. See 23.

25. Only on God do thou, my soul

Metrical psalm 62: 5–8 from *The Irish Psalter*, 1880. William Kethe's version is given in *The Anglo-Genevan Psalter*, 1561, and was included in the Scottish, 1564. In 1595 it was replaced by Hopkins's version but reintroduced in 1611.

HOWARD (DUBLIN) first appears in John Wilson's *A Selection of Psalm Tunes, Sanctuses, Doxologies, &c., for use of the Congregation of St. Mary's Church, Edinburgh*, 1825. No composer's name is given. In works published in 1840 and 1854 it is ascribed to Sir John Andrew Stephenson, but no evidence to support this is given. In Scotland it has been attributed to Samuel Howard, but there is no evidence for this. *The Wesleyan Tune Book*, 1877, attributes it to Stephenson and calls it 'Dublin'.

26. The Lord's my light and saving health

Metrical psalm 27: 1, 3–5, 14 from *The Scottish Psalter*, 1650. Kethe's version was included in *The Anglo-Genevan Psalter*, 1561, and retained in the Scottish book, 1564.

FARRANT is adapted from the anthem 'Lord, for thy tender mercies' sake', usually attributed to Richard Farrant, but by some to John Hilton, by others to William Mundy. Hilton is the most probable. The adaptation to CM first appears in Havergal's *Old Church Psalmody*, 1847, and in an almost identical form by Edward Hodges in *The Bristol Tune Book*, 1863.

27. Ye righteous, in the Lord rejoice

Metrical psalm 33: 1–5 from *The Scottish Psalter*, 1650. Hopkins's version was included in *The Anglo-Genevan Psalter*, 1561, and retained in the Scottish, 1564.

BRISTOL is from Ravenscroft's *Psalter*, 1621, where it is set to Pss. 26 and 64. It is called 'Bristol Tune' and classified amongst the English tunes.

Cross ref. to IRISH. See 19.

28. Praise waits for thee in Zion, Lord

Metrical psalm 65: 1–4 from *The Scottish Psalter*, 1650. Hopkins's version had been that in the Scottish book, 1564.

ST. STEPHEN (ABRIDGE) is from *A Collection of Psalm Tunes in Three Parts...* *by Isaac Smith, c.* 1770. The original name is 'Abridge', by which it continues to be known in England. In *Sacred Harmony for the Use of St George's Church, Edinburgh,* 1820, it is named 'St. Stephen's'. The form given here is in accordance with the original.

29. To render thanks unto the Lord

Metrical psalm 92: 1–4. Verses 1–2 are from *The Scottish Psalter,* 1650, v. 3 from *The Irish Psalter,* 1880, and v. 4 from the Scottish. Hopkins's version was that in the Scottish book, 1564.

ST. FULBERT comes from *The Church Hymn and Tune Book, edited by W. J. Blew and H. J. Gauntlett,* 1852, where it is set to the hymn, 'Now Christ, our Passover, is slain'. The original name of the tune is 'St. Leofred'. In *Hymns Ancient and Modern,* 1861, the tune was set to 'Ye choirs of New Jerusalem', written by St. Fulbert of Chartres.

Cross ref. to HOWARD. See 25.

30. All creatures of our God and King

W. H. Draper's rhymed version of the 'Sun Song' or 'Song About Creatures', 'Cantico di fratre sole, laude della creature', written by St. Francis of Assisi in 1225, when he lay depressed by blindness at San Damiano, tortured by the fierce heat, unable to endure any light on his weak eyes, and plagued by a swarm of field-mice so that he had no peace by day or night. Draper's paraphrase, based on the theme of Ps. 145, was written for a School-children's Whitsuntide Festival at Leeds, when he was rector at Adel.

LASST UNS ERFREUEN in the *Geistliche Kirchengesäng,* Cologne, 1623, is set to an Easter hymn, 'Lasst uns erfreuen herzlich sehr'. Its origins, however, go back beyond this date to possibly *c.* 1525 for its phrases are to be found in German and Genevan tunes for Pss. 22, 68, and 138. This form of the melody is given in *Songs of Syon,* 1910, and *The Westminster Hymnal,* 1940. The harmony is that by Vaughan Williams in *The English Hymnal,* 1906.

31. Father most holy, merciful and loving

The hymn 'O Pater sancte, mitis atque pie' appears in the Sarum, York, Aberdeen, old Roman, and other Breviaries. G. M. Dreves prints it in his *Hymnarius Moissiacensis,* Leipzig, 1888, from a tenth-century manuscript, and Newman included it in his *Hymni Ecclesiae,* 1838. There have been several translations. That given is A. E. Alston's in his *Some Liturgical Hymns,* 1903, which also appeared in *Hymns Ancient and Modern,* 1904.

ISTE CONFESSOR is a French Church melody and comes from the *Chartres Antiphoner,* 1784. The arrangement is that in *The BBC Hymn Book,* 1951.

32. Immortal, invisible, God only wise

From W. C. Smith's *Hymns of Christ and the Christian Life,* 1867, it first appears as a hymn in Horder's *Congregational Hymns,* 1884. It is based on 1 Tim. 1: 17. In v. 1 'and' has been added before 'silent', 'striving' changed to 'wanting', 'high' inserted before 'mountains', and 'mercy' altered to 'good-ness'; in v. 3 'to' added before 'both' and 'the' before 'true' and last two lines rewritten. Verse 4 of the original has been omitted, and the present v. 4 made up of the opening couplets of stanzas five and six as written by Smith.

ST. DENIO (JOANNA) is a Welsh air, probably founded on a folk-melody sung to a ballad about a cuckoo about the beginning of the nineteenth century. It was first printed as a hymn-tune in 1839. Its variants are given in the *Welsh Folk-Song Journal*, 1911.

33. Let us with a gladsome mind

This was first published in Milton's *Poems in English and Latin*, 1645, in twenty-four two-line verses with the refrain as given here. It was written when he was fifteen years old and a schoolboy at St. Paul's. The number of stanzas used varies in different books though most include the six given here.

MONKLAND appeared in *Hymn Tunes of the United Brethren*, 1824, edited by John Lees. No composer's name is given, but in *Hymns Ancient and Modern*, 1861, it was 'arranged by J. Wilkes', who was organist at Monkland. Most of the tunes in Lees's book are arrangements of German chorales and this one is closely related to 'Fahre Fort' in Freylinghausen's *Geistreiches Gesangbuch*, Halle, 1704. There are also similarities to Lübeck. See 38. Probably it was composed by John Antes as it appears in a recently discovered manuscript inscribed 'A Collection of Hymn Tunes chiefly composed for private amusement by John Antes'.

HARTS is from *Sixteen Hymns as they are Sung at the Right Honorable the Countess of Huntingdon's Chapel in Bath. Set to Music by Benjn Milgrove*, *c.* 1769, where it is set to the hymn 'Brethren, let us join to bless', with the addition of a 'Hallelujah', which is now omitted.

34. Lord of all being, throned afar

First printed in *The Atlantic Monthly*, 1859, at the end of Oliver Wendell Holmes's *Professor at the Breakfast Table*, with this introduction, 'Peace to all such as may have been vexed in spirit by any utterance these pages may have repeated'. They will doubtless forget for the moment the difference in the hues of truth we look at through our human prisms, and join in singing (inwardly) this hymn to the source of the light we all need to lead us, and the warmth which alone can make us all brothers.' It was called 'A Sunday Hymn' and entitled 'God's Omnipresence'.

OMBERSLEY is from *The Hymnary*, 1872, where it is set to 'Jesus shall reign where'er the sun'. See 413.

35. O worship the King all-glorious above

A free version of Ps. 104, based on Kethe's version in the *Anglo-Genevan Psalter*, 1561, published in Bickersteth's *Christian Psalmody*, 1833, the year before Sir Robert Grant became governor of Bombay; then in his post-humous *Sacred Poems*, 1839.

HANOVER is from *A Supplement to the New Version of Psalms by Dr. Brady and Mr Tate, &c. The Sixth edition, corrected and much enlarged*, 1708, where it is set to Ps. 67. No name is given, and it is headed 'A New Tune to the 149th

Psalm of the New Version, and the 104th Psalm of the Old'. It was frequently attributed to Handel at the end of the eighteenth century and at the beginning of the nineteenth, but this is highly improbable. In *The People's Music Book*, 1844, edited by J. Turle and E. Taylor, it is credited to Croft on 'satisfactory evidence', but it is not stated what this is. It is probably by him.

36. The Lord is king! lift up thy voice

From Josiah Conder's *Star in the East*, 1824, omitting two stanzas. It is based on Rev. 19: 6.

CHURCH TRIUMPHANT is J. W. Elliott's tune from *Church Hymns with Tunes*, 1874, originally composed for the hymn, 'Again the Lord's own day is here'. It was first set to the above words in the *Congregational Hymnary*, 1916.

37. Praise the Lord! ye heavens, adore him

This hymn is first found, pasted on a leaflet, in *Psalms, Hymns, and Anthems of the Foundling Hospital*, 1798, and headed 'Hymn from Psalm cxlviii, Haydn'. The author is unknown.

AUSTRIAN HYMN, Joseph Haydn's air, was composed for the national hymn by Hauschka, 'Gott erhalte Franz den Kaiser' and first performed on the Emperor's birthday, 12 February 1797. It is based on a Croatian melody. The composer later used the melody as the subject of one of the movements of his *String Quartet, No. 77*. It first appears in an English collection in Edward Miller's *Sacred Music*, 1802.

Cross ref. to LAUS DEO. See 337.

38. Songs of praise the angels sang

Based on Luke 2: 13–14. The allusion in the first verse is to Job 38: 7. It was first published in Cotterill's *Selection of Psalms and Hymns*, 1819, with the heading 'God worthy of all praise', and later in the author's *Christian Psalmist and Original Hymns*, 1825, entitled 'Glory to God in the highest'.

LÜBECK, in *Geistreiches Gesangbuch ... von Anastasio Freylinghausen*, Halle, 1704, was originally set to the hymn 'Gott sei Dank in aller Welt'. Now the passing-notes have been omitted in the melody. In this simplified form it was arranged by Havergal and Monk for *Hymns Ancient and Modern*, 1861.

Cross ref. to MONKLAND. See 33.

39. Stand up, and bless the Lord

Written by James Montgomery for the anniversary service of the Sheffield Red Hill Wesleyan Sunday School, 15 March 1824. With one stanza omitted the text is as in his *Christian Psalmist and Original Hymns*, 1825.

CARLISLE by C. Lockhart was originally set to 'Come, Holy Spirit, come' in the *Lock Hospital Collection, edited by Martin Madan*, 1792, where it is named 'Invocation'. See 104.

40. Worship the Lord in the beauty of holiness

Monsell's hymn for Epiphany first appeared in his *Hymns of Love and Praise*,

1863, where it began 'O worship the Lord'. The form given is that in his *Parish Hymnal*, 1873.

WAS LEBET, WAS SCHWEBET is from a manuscript chorale-book, *Choral-Buch vor Johann Heinrich Reinhardt*, Üttingen, 1754, where it was set in two versions, the first of which is given here. The manuscript contains many melodies not found elsewhere which may be from older sources, now unknown, so the tune may be an arrangement of a traditional song. Its association with this hymn is due to the influence of *The English Hymnal*, 1906.

MOREDUN by Henry Smart was composed for this hymn in *The Presbyterian Hymnal*, 1877.

41. Lord, thee my God, I'll early seek

Metrical psalm 63: 1–4 from *The Scottish Psalter*, 1650. Sternhold's version was given in *The Anglo-Genevan Psalter*, 1556, and retained in the Scottish, 1564.

SONG 67 (ST. MATTHIAS) by Orlando Gibbons was set to a hymn for St. Matthias' Day in Wither's *Hymnes and Songs of the Church*, 1623. The poet obtained from the King a patent authorizing the issue of his book bound up with the Old Version of the Psalter; but the Company of Stationers offered strenuous and successful opposition, and in this form the book never passed into circulation. It contained a number of tunes in two parts, treble and bass, by Orlando Gibbons. This one was set to a metrical version of the passage in Acts referring to St. Matthias. It had appeared two years earlier in Prys's *Llyfr y Psalmau*.

Cross ref. to JACKSON. See 565.

42. Awake, my soul and with the sun

This is the first three, fifth, sixth, and fourteenth stanzas of Ken's 'Morning Hymn' as revised by him in *A Manual of Prayers For the Use of the Scholars in Winchester College, and All Other Devout Christians*, 1709. An earlier version appeared in *A Manual*, 1695.

DEUS TUORUM MILITUM is a Grenoble Church melody from the *Grenoble Antiphoner*, 1752, as in *The English Hymnal*, 1906.

During the sixteenth and seventeenth centuries there came into use, throughout the churches and cathedrals of several dioceses in France, a number of tunes in measured form, taking the place of the older unmeasured plain-song melodies. In many cases these were founded on the plain-song melody, but in others on favourite secular airs. The original sources of the individual tunes have not been ascertained. Their place in continental Roman Catholic hymnody is similar to that which the psalm-tunes occupy in Protestantism. They were introduced to this country by *The English Hymnal*, 1906. This also applies to the following—43, 56, 116, 504, 540, 568, 656.

MORNING HYMN is found in *The Hymns and Psalms used at the Asylum or House of Refuge for Female Orphans. Printed for W. Gawler, Organist to the Asylum*, where it is set to the present hymn and headed 'New Tune. Published by permission of Mr Barthélémon'. While not dated this work was published in 1789. In the edition of 1785 this hymn is set to a different tune. In the *Life of Barthélémon* by his daughter it is stated that 'about the year 1780 an acquaintance commenced between Mr B and the Rev. Jacob Duché, then chaplain to the Asylum . . . One immediate consequence of this acquaintance was an application to Mr B to compose a hymn tune to "Awake, my soul".' The arrangement is by S. S. Wesley.

43. Father, we praise thee, now the night is over

Dearmer's translation was contributed to *The English Hymnal*, 1906. The Latin original, 'Nocte surgentes', has been ascribed to Gregory the Great (540-604); others ascribe it to the reign of Charlemagne.

CHRISTE SANCTORUM is drawn from *La Feillée's Méthode du Plain-Chant*, Paris, 1745. Its original source is the *Paris Antiphoner*, 1681, where it is set to the hymn 'Mille quem stipant' for the festival of St. Michael. See 42.

44. Most glorious Lord of life, that on this day

This is sonnet 68 in *Amoretti and Epithalamion* by Edmund Spenser. It was first used as a hymn in *The English Hymnal*, 1906.

DUNOON was composed for this hymn for CH3 by Kenneth Leighton.

45. Now that the daylight fills the sky

Neale's version, as in the *Hymnal Noted*, 1852-4, of the hymn for Prime (probably seventh century) as it appears in the *French Breviary*, Paris, 1736.

SONG 34 (ANGELS' SONG) by Orlando Gibbons was set to the song, 'Thus angels sung, and thus sing we', from Lam. 1 in *Hymns and Songs of the Church*, 1623. See 41. With two additional lines it was also set to another song in six-line form. The form of the tune, in triple time throughout, seems to have been introduced in the eighteenth century, and is the form usually found in English and Scottish collections. It is written chiefly in the Dorian mode.

46. This is the day of light

Ellerton's hymn is taken from *Hymns for Special Occasions and Festivals*, 1867, in Chester Cathedral, with one stanza omitted.

OLD 134TH (ST. MICHAEL) is an adaptation from a tune in *The French Psalter*, 1551, composed or arranged by Louis Bourgeois for Marot's version of Ps. 101. A variant form appears in *The Anglo-Genevan Psalter*, 1561, to Ps. 134. This form of the melody is retained in all editions of *The Scottish Psalter*. The present form of the tune and also the name 'St. Michael', by which it is usually known in England, are probably due to Crotch, who revived it in his *Psalm Tunes*, 1836.

47. New every morning is the love

A selection from the original sixteen stanzas which Keble composed on 20 September 1822, and published in *The Christian Year*, 1827. Based on Lam. 3: 22-3.

MELCOMBE is found in *An Essay on the Church Plain Chant*, 1782, where it is set to 'O Salutaris hostia', and is headed 'At Exposition, Elevation, or Benediction of the Blessed Sacrament'. No composer's name is given, but in *A Collection of Motetts*, 1792, it is ascribed to Samuel Webbe, the elder. It appears as a hymn tune under the name 'Melcombe' in Harrison's *Sacred Harmony*, 1791, again with Webbe's name as composer.

48. O Lord of life, thy quickening voice

From George Macdonald's *The Disciple, and other Poems*, 1860.

NATIVITY first appeared in the appendix to *The Metrical Psalter*, 1855, of which the musical editor was Henry Lahee, where it is set to Doddridge's 'High let us swell our tuneful notes'.

49. The morning bright, with rosy light

Based on 1 Thess. 5: 10, this hymn was written about the close of 1845 by T. O. Summers for his daughter. It was written on the back of a letter on board a river-steamer in Alabama, U.S.A., and published anonymously in *The Southern Christian Advocate*, of which he was editor.

CHERRY TREE is a traditional melody of the carol known as 'The Cherry Tree Carol'. See 229. It is also known as Rimbault from his arrangement in *Old English Carols*, 1865. The harmonization is by Martin Shaw (adapted).

50. The sun is sinking fast

Caswall's version of the Latin 'Sol praeceps rapitur' was published in his *Masque of Mary*, 1858. It is given here, except for an alteration in the second line of v. 2, as in his *Hymns and Poems*, 1863.

BINHAM was composed by Lennox Berkeley for this hymn for CH3.

ST. COLUMBA, from *Hymns Ancient and Modern*, 1861, was written for this hymn. It is so named from St. Columba's College, Dublin, of which H. S. Irons was for a time organist.

51. As now the day draws near its ending

Winslow's hymn is based on Ellerton's 'Saviour, again to thy dear name we raise' (see 649), and first appeared in *Hymns for Church and School*, 1964.

RENDEZ À DIEU (PSALM 118) is from *La Forme des Prières et Chantz Ecclésiastiques*, Strasbourg, 1545, the second line being altered in *The Genevan Psalter*, 1551. It was composed or adapted by Louis Bourgeois, who set it to Ps. 118. In *The Scottish Psalter*, 1564, it was set to John Craig's version of the same psalm.

52. At even, when the sun was set

Twells says in a letter the hymn was written 'in 1868, at the request of Sir Henry Baker, who said a new evening hymn was wanted for the first edition of *Hymns Ancient and Modern*, and being at that time headmaster of . . . Godolphin School, Hammersmith, I wrote it one afternoon while the boys were under examination, and I was supposed to be seeing "all fair" '. 'Ere' was changed to 'when' in the first line to suit Mark 1: 32, though the author defended his original wording by an appeal to the R.V. of Luke 4: 40. It first appears in the 1868 supplement, not the first edition.

ANGELUS goes back to a melody by Georg Joseph in *Heilige Seelenlust, oder geistliche Hirten-Lieder . . . von Johann Angelo Silesio, und von Herren Georgio Josepho mit aussbundig schönen Melodeyen geziert . . . Breslau,* 1657. But, though this has always been cited as the source, only the first line and half of the second are to be found there. The earliest publication in which the entire tune has been found is *Cantica Spiritualia, oder Auswahl der schönsten geistlichen Lieder älterer Zeit,* Munich, 1847, where it is set to the hymn 'Du meiner Seelen güldne Zier', and the editor gives the 1657 book and Braun's *Echo Hymnodiae Coelestis,* Berlin, 1675, as the sources. Its name is taken from 'Angelus Silesius', the name which Johann Scheffler took after entering the Church of Rome in 1653.

53. Before the day draws near its ending

Written by Ellerton on 22 April 1880, for a festival of choirs at Nantwich, and published in the *Nantwich Festival Book* of that year.

SUNSET was composed by Stocks for this hymn, and it comes from *Repton School: Hymns for Use in Chapel,* 1924.

GOTTLOB, ES GEHT is a melody found in various forms in German music-books from 1742 onwards, when it appears in a manuscript entitled *Sammerlung alter und neuer mit orgelmässigen Bässen versehene Melodien . . . von Johann Gottlieb Wagnern.* It was first printed in Reimanns's *Sammlung alter under neuer Melodien,* 1747. The present form of the melody and harmony are Bach's in his *Choralgesänge,* 1769.

54. Hail, gladdening Light, of his pure glory poured

This Greek hymn is quoted by St. Basil in the fourth century. The Greek Church uses it in the Vesper Service at the lighting of the lamps. Keble's version first appeared in *The British Magazine,* 1834, and then in *Lyra Apostolica,* 1836. See 55.

MELFORT was composed by Lennox Berkeley for this hymn for CH3.

SEBASTE was composed by Stainer for this hymn in *Hymns Ancient and Modern,* 1875.

55. O gladsome Light, O grace

Another version of 54. This translation is by Robert Bridges in *The Yattendon Hymnal,* 1899.

NUNC DIMITTIS is by Louis Bourgeois, harmonized by Claude Goudimel. It derives its name from the fact that it was originally set to the 'Song of Simeon' in *The Genevan Psalter,* 1549.

56. O Trinity, O blessed Light

By the ninth century, the Latin original of this vesper hymn, 'O lux beata Trinitas', had been attributed to Ambrose, but it had no place in the Milanese liturgy. So it is probably an anonymous early Latin composition. It is found for Vespers in the Sarum, York, Paris, and Roman Breviaries. There have been many translations. The present one belongs to a group of nineteen hymns which appeared in an English *Primer or Office of the Blessed Virgin Mary*, 1619, where they were described as 'a new translation done by one most skilful in English poetry'. This was believed to be Drummond of Hawthornden, whose editors included them among his works in 1711.

SOLEMNIS HAEC FESTIVITAS is one of the French melodies referred to in 42. It is from the Sequence for our Lord's ascension in the *Paris Gradual*, 1689, and was first introduced into English usage in *The English Hymnal*, 1906.

57. The duteous day now closeth

Gerhardt's hymn, though appearing in Crüger's *Praxis Pietatis Melica*, Berlin, 1647, failed to win popularity for over two centuries. The present free translation is that of Bridges in *The Yattendon Hymnal*, 1899. The original has nothing corresponding to vv. 3–4.

INNSBRUCK has commonly been attributed to Heinrich Isaak. It first appeared in *Ein ausszug guter alter ün newer Teutscher liedlein*, Nürnberg, 1539, where it is set to the song 'Innsbruck ich muss dich lassen'. Later the melody was adapted to the hymn 'O Welt ich muss dich lassen', and later still to Gerhardt's 'Nun ruhen alle Wälder'. The melody appears in a large variety of forms, and that adopted here is Bach's in his *St. Matthew Passion*.

58. If I come to Jesus

From Mrs. van Alstyne's *Silver Spray*, 1868.

AU CLAIR DE LA LUNE is an old French melody. The harmony was arranged by A. J. Hedges for *Sunday School Praise*, 1958, where it was set to the hymn 'Jesus' hands were kind hands'. See 228.

59. Jesus Christ, our Lord and King

This hymn is based on Emily M. Shapcote's 'Jesus, holy, undefiled', which appeared in *Hymns for Infant Children by A., C., and E.*, 1852. E. is Mrs. Shapcote (then Miss Steward), C. her sister Eleanor, and A. their aunt, Mary Steward.

TRES MAGI DE GENTIBUS is from the Andernach *Catholische Geistliche Gesänge*, 1608. This was a choral book published under the auspices of the Society of St. Cecilia at Andernach.

60. Lord have mercy upon us

Kyrie eleison (Lord, have mercy) occurs several times in the *Septuagint* though more often in the form *eleison me kyrie*. It is used as an address to our Lord (Matt. 17: 15; 20: 30–1). It is also found in nearly all the ancient liturgies. In many of them it is still said in Greek irrespective of the language of the liturgy. The first evidence for it comes from Jerusalem and Antioch in the fourth century as a response to the petitions of a litany. In the West its equivalent was 'Miserere domine'. The introduction of the Eastern response in the West, according to Gregory of Tours, was when Gregory the Great

(590–604) 'ordered litanies to be sung for the removal of the plague, and that choirs should sing *Kyrie eleison*'. The evidence, broadly speaking, points to the *Kyrie eleison* coming into Eastern Services in the fourth century, spreading into Italy in the fifth, and being imported into Gaul from either Constantinople or Rome in the sixth.

About the eighth century, when the litany had disappeared almost completely in the West, the acclamations were arranged — *Kyrie eleison* three times, the variant *Christe eleison* three times, and *Kyrie eleison* three times. This remained the common form for over eleven hundred years. Ninefold and sixfold forms are also provided in the Roman rite.

In some early Reformed rites the *Kyrie eleison* remained for a period, but it was gradually replaced by a psalm because the Reformers desired to use simple music in which all the people, not simply a trained choir, could join.

The first form is the traditional, and the second that in the BCP.

KYRIE ELEISON. This setting was composed by Kenneth Leighton for CH3.

61. Holy God, holy and mighty, holy and immortal

According to legend the *Trisagion* was revealed in Constantinople during the episcopate of Proclus (434–6). It is quoted in a work attributed to Caesarius of Nazianzus (d. 369), but it is not by him. The hymn, however, may date from the fifth century. At the Council of Constantinople in 536 it was sung before the Gospel. It comes before the lections in the Liturgies of St. James and St. Mark and also in the Byzantine and Nestorian rites, although the *Liturgy of St. Chrysostom* does not always use it on festivals, sometimes substituting 'As many as have been baptised unto Christ have put on Christ'.

The *Trisagion* is not in the Roman Mass, but forms part of the Veneration of the Cross on Good Friday, where it had become part of the Good Friday Office by the twelfth century, although not therein in the ninth. It forms part of the response by the deacon in Greek, and by the subdeacon in Latin to the Reproaches. See 240. Bishop thinks it was a revival in the ninth century in France of an old Gallican form, and traces the Reproaches to the *Bobbio Missal*, which had taken them from the Mozarabic rite.

TRISAGION. This setting was composed by George Thalben-Ball for CH3.

62. Glory be to God on high, and in earth peace, good-will towards men

The original form of the *Gloria in excelsis* is given in Luke 2: 14. Later it was expanded into an 'elaborate hymn'. It is found in the *Clementine Liturgy* (fourth century), the *Liturgy of St. James*, and *Codex Alexandrinus* (fifth). The Latin form in the Roman Missal dates from the eighth. There have been numerous translations into English, but the most commonly used is that in the 'Order for Holy Communion' in the BCP, which is based on the Latin text. That in *The Scottish Prayer-Book*, 1929, is based on the Greek.

In the *Apostolic Constitutions* and the Byzantine rite it is a morning prayer. Athanasius, also, mentions it as a part of morning prayer. In the West, on the other hand, while it has been used at Lauds it is chiefly associated with the Mass. Its first appearance in the books is in the Gregorian. It does not appear to have belonged to the Gallican, but the Ambrosian and Mozarabic adopted it from Roman usage. It is probable, therefore, that while it took its use in the Mass from Rome, the text was Eastern and was previously used in morning prayer. Musical settings were provided in the first two editions of *The Church Hymnary*.

GLORIA IN EXCELSIS. This setting was composed by Kenneth Leighton for CH3.

63. Have mercy upon me, O God

Prose psalm 51: 1–4, 6–12 (A.V.), *Miserere mei, Deus*. Suitable for Lent. See 3.

PLAIN-SONG TONE IV, ending 4.

64. O God be gracious to me in thy love

This metrical version of Ps. 51: 1–3, 9–12, based on the NEB translation, was written for CH3 by Professor Ian Pitt Watson, Aberdeen. In *The Anglo-Genevan Psalter*, 1556, the version was that by William Whittingham. This was retained in the Scottish book, 1564, and revised in 1650.

SONG 24 by Orlando Gibbons was set to a paraphrase of Lam. 1 in *Hymnes and Songs of the Church*, 1623. See 41. It is chiefly in the Dorian mode.

Cross ref. to SONG 22. See 108.

65. Lord, from the depths to thee I cried

Metrical psalm 130: 1–7. Verses 1–3 are from *The Scottish Psalter*, 1650, and v. 4 from *The Irish Psalter*, 1880. Whittingham's version was given in *The Anglo-Genevan Psalter*, 1556, and retained in the Scottish book, 1564.

CHESHIRE is set to Ps. 146 in *The Whole Booke of Psalmes with their wonted Tunes, as they are song in Churches, composed into foure parts . . . Compiled by sondry authors*, 1592. In this book of Este's it is named 'Chesshire Tune' and said to be 'newly added in this booke'.

66. Out of the depths have I cried unto thee, O Lord

Prose psalm 130 (A.V.), *De profundis*. See 3.

CHANT. This short chant was written by John Currie for CH3.

67. Out of the depths I cry to you, O Lord

The numbering of the psalms in the Hebrew and *Septuagint* differs. The Hebrew numbering, with the LXX in brackets, is 1–8 (1–8), 9–10 (9), 11–113 (10–112), 114–15 (113), 116 (114–15), 117–46 (116–45), 147 (146–7), and 148–50 (148–50).

This is Ps. 130 (LXX 129) from *The Psalms: A New Translation from the Hebrew arranged for singing to the Psalmody of Joseph Gelineau*. In the *Bible de Jérusalem* the aim was not only to achieve literary fidelity, but also to be faithful to the rhythmic structure of Hebrew poetry. 'This allowed a sung or recited psalmody to be fashioned on the basis of the analogy that exists between the Hebrew tonic rhythm and that of our modern languages.' Since 1953 this way of singing spread rapidly in France, so an English translation, based on the same principles, was undertaken. It began in 1954 with the assistance of Gall Schuon, O.C.S.O., Albert Derzelle, O.C.S.O., and Hubert

Richards, L.S.S., for the translation, of Philippa Craig for literary style, and Dom Gregory Murray, O.S.B., for the music's 'singability'. Twenty-four psalms appeared in 1956, thirty more in 1958, and the whole psalter in 1966.

PSALM 129 appeared in *Formules Psalmodiques pour choeurs à voix égales* and the Gelineau antiphon in *Deux cent six antiennes pour choeurs à voix égales*. This new form of singing first appeared in English in *Six Psalms and Three Canticles to the psalmody of Joseph Gelineau*, 1955-6. Antiphon I is by Gelineau and Antiphon II by Dom Gregory Murray.

68. Thou art before me, Lord, thou art behind

This metrical version of Ps. 139, based on the NEB translation, was written for CH3 by Professor Ian Pitt Watson, Aberdeen.

SURSUM CORDA was composed by A. M. Smith for the hymn 'Lift up your hearts'. It first appeared in *The Hymnal*, 1940, of the Protestant Episcopal Church of America.

69. Come, let us to the Lord our God

This metrical version of Hosea 6: 1–4 by John Morison is in the form in which it first appeared in *The Scottish Paraphrases*, 1781.

ST. FULBERT. See 29.

KILMARNOCK, though circulated in manuscript earlier, first appears in *Parochial Psalmody: A New Collection of the Most Approved Psalm Tunes ... By J. P. Clarke*, 1831.

70. O, hear my prayer, Lord

Metrical psalm 143: 1, 6–8 from the second version in *The Scottish Psalter*, 1650. In the Scottish book, 1564, that included was by John Craig, which was substantially retained in 1650.

LEONI. See 358.

LEUCHARS, composed by T. L. Hately for the second version of Ps. 143, first appeared in *Scottish Psalmody*, 1858.

71. O God, give ear unto my cry

Metrical psalm 61: 1–4 from *The Scottish Psalter*, 1650. Hopkins's version appeared in *The Anglo-Genevan Psalter*, 1561, and was retained in the Scottish book, 1564.

ST. MARY is set to Ps. 2 in Prys's *Llyfr y Psalmau, wedi eu cyfieithu, a'i cyfansoddi ar fesur cerdd, yn Gymraeg*, 1621. It is found in its present form in Playford's *Book of Psalms*, 1677.

Cross ref. to SALZBURG. See 72.

72. O God of Bethel! by whose hand

This paraphrase of Gen. 28: 20–2 is based on a hymn by Doddridge entitled 'Jacob's Vow', written on 16 January 1736. The hymn was used in the 1745 and 1751 editions of *The Scottish Paraphrases*, but extensively revised by John Logan in the 1781 edition.

ST. PAUL first appears, its melody exactly as at present, in a book printed by John Chalmers in Aberdeen in 1749. The title-page is missing, but that in the third edition, 1753, says the tunes are 'collected by Andrew Tait, Organist'. As he was organist in St. Paul's Episcopal Church, it is possible that he was the composer. In Bremner's collection issued in Edinburgh in 1756 it is included under the name 'Aberdeen or St. Paul'.

SALZBURG is an adaptation of Haydn's air in a movement of a Mass 'for the use of country choirs', and is printed in Latrobe's *Selection of Sacred Music*, 1806, where it is in 6–8 time and the key of F major.

73. I waited for the Lord my God

Metrical psalm 40: 1–4 from *The Scottish Psalter*, 1650. That in the 1564 book was by Hopkins.

ABBEY is one of the twelve Common Tunes in *The CL Psalms of David*, 1615.

74. Show me thy ways, O Lord

Metrical psalm 25: 4, 5a, 6–10 from *The Scottish Psalter*, 1650. Thomas Sternhold's version was included in *The Anglo-Genevan Psalter*, 1556, and retained in 1564.

FRANCONIA is from *Harmonischer Lieder-Schatz, oder Allgemeines Evangelisches Choral-Buch . . . gestellet von Johann Balthasar König*, Frankfurt am Main, 1738, where the melody is set to the hymn, 'Was ist, das mich betrübt?'. The present tune was arranged by W. H. Havergal and published in his *Old Church Psalmody*, 1847.

Cross ref. to ST. BRIDE. See 410.

75. Lord, thine heart in love hath yearned

This version of Ps. 85 first appears in Keble's *The Psalter or Psalms of David: In English Verse: by a Member of the University of Oxford, Adapted for the most part, to Tunes in Common Use*, 1839, from which it was taken into *The Irish Psalter*, 1880.

76. Dear Lord and Father of mankind

AUS DER TIEFE (HEINLEIN) is from *Nürnbergisches Gesangbuch*, 1677. Possibly it is by Martin Herbst. Bach used it in his cantata 'Aus der Tiefe'. Monk arranged it for *Hymns Ancient and Modern*, 1861.

ST. DUNSTAN is from Redhead's *Church Hymn Tunes*, 1853.

OLD 18TH was the tune set to Ps. 18 in *The English Psalter*, 1561. The present version is that of Cobbold in Este's *Psalter*, 1592.

REPTON is from C. H. H. Parry's oratorio *Judith*, 1888, in which in the second scene there is a dialogue-duet between Meshollemeth and a Child. The former sings 'Long since in Egypt's plenteous land'. The tune was first used for this hymn in *The Repton School Hymn Book*, 1924, hence its name.

77. Father of heaven, whose love profound

Contributed by E. Cooper to a Staffordshire *Selection of Psalms and Hymns for Public and Private Use*, 1805, and republished in his *Selection of Psalms and Hymns*, 1811.

SONG 5 by Orlando Gibbons is from *Hymnes and Songs of the Church*, 1623. See 41.

RIVAULX was composed by J. B. Dykes for this hymn in *A Hymnal for use in the English Church, with accompanying tunes*, 1866, edited by the Hon. and Revd. J. Grey.

78. Jesus, Lover of my soul

Many stories are told of the origin of this hymn, but they may be dismissed as fancy. It first appears in Wesley's *Hymns and Sacred Poems*, 1740, and the opening line was probably suggested by Wisd. 11: 26. In the first line Wesley wrote 'Jesu', the correct form of the vocative. While many have taken great liberties with the text, that given here is the original with 'Jesu' changed to 'Jesus' and omitting the third verse. Though not included in any official Methodist hymnbook until 1797, it is interesting to note that his great antagonist Toplady inserted it in his *Psalms and Hymns*, 1776.

ABERYSTWYTH was composed by Joseph Parry, Professor of Music in Aberystwyth. It appeared in *Ail Lyfr Tonau ac Emynau*, 1879.

HOLLINGSIDE was composed for this hymn by J. B. Dykes for *Hymns Ancient and Modern*, 1861. It was so named because 'Hollingside Cottage' was where he lived.

79. Just as I am, without one plea

'More than half a century of suffering went to the making of Miss Elliott's hymns.' This one was written for *The Invalid's Hymn Book*, 1841, and based upon John 6: 37. Her brother, Revd. H. V. Elliott, had organized a bazaar; unable to go she wrote this hymn. It was written as a confession of faith in the face of her inability to engage in active work.

SAFFRON WALDEN by A. H. Brown appeared in *The Hymnal Companion to the Book of Common Prayer*, 1890. It was originally composed for Charlotte Elliott's hymn, 'O holy Saviour, Friend unseen', and was first set to the present hymn in *The English Hymnal*, 1906.

80. Lord Jesus, think on me

This is a paraphrase rather than a translation, omitting the first, eighth, and ninth stanzas, of the last of the odes composed by Synesius, Bishop of Cyrene, 375–430. It appears in Chatfield's *Songs and Hymns of the Earliest Greek Christian Poets, Bishops, and others*, 1876.

SOUTHWELL is set to Ps. 45 in Damon's *Psalmes of David*, 1579, and is called by this name in Ravenscroft's *Psalter*, 1621, where it is set to Ps. 70. It was originally in the Dorian mode.

Cross ref. to ST. BRIDE. See 410.

81. My faith looks up to thee

Ray Palmer's hymn was first published in Hastings's *Spiritual Songs for Social Worship*, 1831, where it is entitled 'Self-Consecration'.

OLIVET was composed for this hymn by Lowell Mason for the same publication.

DENBIGH is from *Llyfr Tonau Cynulleidfaol*, 1859, edited by J. Roberts.

82. One who is all unfit to count

Narayan Vaman Tilak was a distinguished poet whose hymns and *Metrical Life of Christ* have had great popularity in India. This translation by Nicol Macnicol was originally contributed to *The Indian Interpreter*, and its first appearance in any collection was in *A Missionary Hymn Book*, 1922.

WIGTOWN is one of the Common Tunes in *The Psalmes of David*, 1635.

Cross ref. to CAITHNESS. See 125.

83. Rock of Ages, cleft for me

Toplady's hymn first appeared in *The Gospel Magazine*, 1776, at the end of an article by him entitled 'A remarkable calculation Introduced here for the sake of the Spiritual Improvements subjoined. Questions and answers relating to the National Debt.' It is designed to show how impossible it is to pay the National Debt, the calculation being made on the basis of how many sins each human being commits in the day, half-day, hour, minute, and second. It ends with 'A living and dying Prayer for the Holiest Believer in the World'. Then follows the hymn as here with two exceptions in v. 4 'whilst' for 'while' and the second line 'When my eye-strings break in death'. There appears to be no foundation for the story of the hymn inspired by the author's finding shelter in a cleft of a rock in the Mendips in 1764. The idea of Christ as a Rock had always fascinated Toplady and in a sermon on Isa. 42: 11 he says, 'Chiefly may they sing who inhabit Christ the Spiritual Rock of Ages. He is a Rock in three ways: as a Foundation to support, a Shelter to screen, a Fortress to protect.' Its inspiration was a sermon by Dr. Brevint, Dean of Durham, which referred to Christ as a Rock 'struck and cleft for me', prefaced to Wesley's *Sacramental Hymns*, 1745. ·

PETRA (REDHEAD No. 76) is from Redhead's *Church Hymn Tunes, Ancient and Modern*, 1853, and was set to this hymn in *Hymns Ancient and Modern*, 1861.

84. Turn back, O man, forswear thy foolish ways

This hymn was written by Clifford Bax in 1916 at the request of Gustav Holst to go to the 'Old 124th', on which the latter had composed a motet. It was published in the League of Art's *Motherland Song Book*, 1919, and in Bax's *Farewell, my Muse*, 1932.

OLD 124TH first appeared in *The Genevan Psalter*, 1551, set to Beza's version of Ps. 124, later put into English by William Whittingham.

85. O for a heart to praise my God

From *Hymns and Sacred Poems*, 1742. Charles Wesley based it on Ps. 51: 10. Originally it had eight stanzas.

SONG 67 (ST. MATTHIAS). See 41.

86. I greet thee, who my sure Redeemer art

John Calvin, unlike Luther, was not a great hymn-writer. In the history of church music his principal significance lies in the encouragement he gave to congregational singing and to authors and composers such as Marot, Goudimel, and Bourgeois. Nevertheless, a few of his compositions are worthy of inclusion in the hymn-book of any church.

'Je Te salue, mon certain Rédempteur', entitled 'Salutation à Jésus-Christ', first appeared in *The French Psalter*, 1545, at Strasbourg. It is attributed to Calvin by Bovet and Reuss, but Douen ascribes it to Jean Gernier. There are two translations. One by Bannerman, 'I greet Thee, my Redeemer sure', was first published in *The Catholic Presbyterian*, 1879. The other, given here, is in the original metre and was made by Mrs. E. L. Smith (*née* Allen) and first appeared in Schaff's *Christ in Song*, 1869.

STONELAW was composed by Thomas Wilson for this hymn for CH3.

87. Be thou my Vision, O Lord of my heart

The original old Irish poem probably dates from the eighth century. Miss Byrne's translation appeared in *Erin*, 1905, and Miss Hull's metrical version in her *Poem-book of the Gael*, 1912.

SLANE is an Irish traditional air from Joyce's *Old Irish Folk Music and Songs*, 1920. It is the melody of a song, 'With my love on the road'.

88. God of grace and God of glory

Fosdick in his autobiography, *The Living of These Days*, says he wrote this hymn for the Dedication Service of the Riverside Church, New York, on 8 February 1931. He writes: 'That was more than a hymn to me when we sang it that day—it was a very urgent personal prayer. For with all my hopeful enthusiasm about the new venture there was inevitably much humble and sometimes fearful apprehension.'

RHUDDLAN is from Edward Jones's *Musical Relicks of the Welsh Bards*, 1800. In Wales it is known as 'Dowch i'r Frwydr' (Come to Battle). The arrangement is from *The English Hymnal*, 1906.

89. Guide me, O thou great Jehovah

Written in Welsh and published by William Williams in his *Alleluia*, 1745. Verse 1 in the English translation is possibly by Peter Williams of Carmarthen and was published in *Hymns on Various Subjects*, 1771. Verses 2–3 were translated either by William Williams himself or his son John Williams, first Principal of Trevecca College. It was published as a leaflet in 1772 with the title, 'A favourite hymn sung by Lady Huntingdon's Young Collegians. Printed by the desire of many Christian friends. Lord, give it Thy blessing.' The 'Collegians' were those of Trevecca.

MANNHEIM is from *Vierstimmiges Choralbuch herausgegeben von Dr. F. Filitz*, Berlin, 1847. The present form of the melody appeared in *Congregational Church Music*, 1853, which is much altered from the original.

CWM RHONDDA was composed by John Hughes for the anniversary at Chapel Rhondda, Pontypridd, in 1907. It was first introduced into English hymnals in 1933 in *The Fellowship Hymn Book* and *The Methodist Hymn Book*.

90. Lead us, heavenly Father, lead us

From Edmeston's *Sacred Lyrics*, 1821, where it is headed 'Hymn written for the Children of the London Orphan Asylum'.

CORINTH comes from *An Essay on the Church Plain Chant*, 1782, where it occurs in 'Part Second, containing several Anthems, Litanies, Proses, and Hymns, as they are sung in the Public Chapels at London'. There it is headed 'The Hymn at Benediction', the words being 'Tantum ergo sacramentum'. No name is attached, but it is probably by Samuel Webbe, the elder, who probably was the editor. In his 'Mass in A' printed in *A Collection of Modern Church Music*, 1791, and in *A Collection of Masses . . . for the use of Small Choirs*, 1792, this setting of 'Tantum ergo' is the closing number. It is also included in *A Collection of Motetts or Antiphons . . . by S. Webbe*, 1792, in which many of the pieces have 'Webbe' printed at the close, but this is not one of them. So it is doubtful whether this is an original composition by Webbe or an older melody arranged by him.

Cross ref. to MANNHEIM. See 89.

91. Defend me, Lord, from hour to hour

George Snow's hymn was written for *Hymns for Church and School*, 1964.

TALLIS ORDINAL occurs in *The whole Psalter translated into English Metre, which contayneth an hundreth and fifty Psalmes, c. 1561.* This work bears neither date nor author's name, but is known to have been the work of Matthew Parker, Archbishop of Canterbury. At the end it includes nine tunes in four parts by Thomas Tallis, of which this is the ninth. Each of the first eight is in one of the ancient ecclesiastical modes. It receives its name from its original association with the 'Veni Creator' (see 118 and 342) in the Anglican *Ordinal*, 1550.

92. Lord of all hopefulness, Lord of all joy

Written at the request of Dearmer for *Songs of Praise*, 1925, of which he was editor, by Jan Struther. This was the pen-name, based on that of her mother, Dame Eva Anstruther, D.B.E., of Mrs. A. K. Placzek.

MINIVER, composed for this hymn, receives its name from Mrs. Placzek's novel, *Mrs. Miniver*. It was composed by Cyril V. Taylor and first appears in *The BBC Hymn Book*, 1951.

Cross ref. to SLANE. See 87.

93. Loving Shepherd of thy sheep

From Miss Leeson's *Hymns and Scenes of Childhood*, 1842, where it is headed with the text John 10: 27. It originally consisted of three eight-line stanzas. The text has been much changed over the years.

BATTISHILL goes back to *Twelve Hymns; the Words by the Rev. Charles Wesley, M.A., late student at Christ Church, Oxford; set to music by Jonathan Battishill,* 1765, where it was set to 'Jesus, Lord, we look to Thee'. It has been much altered.

94. O Jesus, strong and pure and true

Written by W. W. How for the jubilee of Marlborough College in 1893. It first appeared in *Hymns for the Use of Rugby School,* 1896.

ST. FULBERT. See 29.

Cross ref. to PRAETORIUS. See 288.

95. O Light that knew no dawn

A cento from Gregory of Nazianzen's 'Hymn to Christ' as translated in John Brownlie's *Hymns of the Greek Church,* 1900, with the third verse as he recast it for RCH, 1927.

LOVE UNKNOWN was composed by John Ireland for the hymn 'My song is love unknown'. See 224. Donald Ford (*Daily Telegraph,* 5 April, 1950) says that the tune was written on a scrap of paper in a quarter of an hour after Ireland received a request from Geoffrey Shaw for a tune for these words. It first appeared in *The Public School Hymn Book,* 1919, and *Songs of Praise,* 1925.

96. Thou hidden Love of God, whose height

Tersteegen's poem in ten stanzas, based on Gal. 2: 20, appeared in his *Geistliches Blumengärtlein,* Frankfurt am Main, 1729, entitled 'The longing of the Soul quietly to maintain the secret drawings of the Love of God'. See 355. Wesley's translation appeared in *Psalms and Hymns,* 1738, but had been written two years earlier during his stay at Savannah. Verse 1 lines 5–6 are based on Augustine, 'Thou hast made us for Thyself, O Lord, and our heart is restless until it repose in Thee'. There is no allusion to this in Tersteegen's original.

VATER UNSER (OLD 112TH) in V. Schumann's *Geistliche Lieder,* Leipzig, 1539, is set to Luther's version of the Lord's Prayer, 'Vater unser im Himmelreich'. In *The Anglo-Genevan Psalter,* 1558, it is set to Richard Coxe's version of the Lord's Prayer, and was included in many later English and Scottish psalters. In *The Anglo-Genevan Psalter,* 1561, it is set to Kethe's version of Ps. 112, hence it came to be known as the 'Old 112th'. This adaptation was continued in the English and Scottish psalters of 1562 and 1564. It is used by Bach in his *St. John Passion.*

Cross ref. to MELITA. See 527.

97. Father, lead me, day by day

Published by J. P. Hopps in *Hymns, Chants, and Anthems for Public Worship,* 1877, and entitled 'Child's Prayer for Divine Guidance'. One verse has been omitted.

GALLIARD is an adaptation by Martin Shaw of a melody in John Dowland's *The First Booke of Songs or Ayres*, 1597. This first appears in *Songs of Praise*, 1925.

98. Jesus, Saviour ever mild

From *The People's Hymnal*, 1867, edited by R. F. Littledale; then in *Hymns Ancient and Modern*, 1875.

RESONET IN LAUDIBUS is a German carol melody found in a manuscript at Leipzig University *c.* 1500 to the words 'Joseph lieber, Joseph mein' in a mystery play acted round the crib. It also occurs in Johann Walther's *Gesangbuch*, Wittenberg, 1544, to the words 'Resonet in Laudibus'.

99. Father, we thank thee for the night

Rebecca J. Weston's hymn was first published in 1885 in Pennsylvania in *The Tonic Solfa Course* and two years later in *Kindergarten Chimes*, neither of which indicates an author.

SOLOTHURN is a Swiss melody, 'Dursli und Babeli', and appears in *Sammlung von Schweitzer Kükreihen und Volkslieden*, 1826. It is used by Beethoven as a theme for his *Variationen über ein Schweizerlied*. It is taken from *The English Hymnal*, 1906.

100. Jesus, Friend of little children

Composed by W. J. Mathams in May 1882 at the request of the Psalms and Hymns Committee of the Scottish Baptist Union, who published it in their *Psalms and Hymns for School and Home*, 1882.

CUTTLE MILLS by W. Griffith was set to 'Art thou weary?' in *The English Hymnal*, 1906. It was first set to these words in RCH, 1927.

101. Give praise and thanks unto the Lord

Metrical psalm 106: 1–5, 48 from *The Scottish Psalter*, 1650. Thomas Norton's version had appeared in the English book, 1562, and was included in the Scottish, 1564.

DUNFERMLINE is one of the twelve Common Tunes in *The CL Psalms of David*, 1615. It is also in Ravenscroft's *Whole Book of Psalms*, 1621, where it is classified among the Scottish tunes, and set to Ps. 89, and called for the first time 'Dunfermline'.

102. Lord, thou hast been our dwelling-place

Metrical psalm 90: 1–2, 14, 16–17 from *The Scottish Psalter*, 1650. Kethe's version was given in *The Anglo-Genevan Psalter*, 1561, and retained in the Scottish book, 1564.

CULROSS is one of the Common Tunes in *The Psalms of David*, 1635.

103. Breathe on me, Breath of God

First published by Hatch in a pamphlet, *Between Doubt and Prayer*, 1878. It was included in *The Congregational Psalmist*, 1886. Hatch's hymns were published posthumously in *Towards Fields of Light*, 1890.

WIRKSWORTH appeared in *A Book of Psalmody containing Variety of Tunes for all the Common Metres of the Psalms in the Old and New Versions, and others for Particular Measures . . . all set in Four Parts, within such a compass as will most naturally suit the voices in Country Churches, yet may be sung in Three or Two without any Disallowances. By John Chetham, 1718*. Tunes are not named and no composers given. This tune is set to Ps. 50. The present form of the tune appears in *A Book of Psalm Tunes with variety of Anthems in Four Parts . . . By James Green*, 1724.

104. Come, Holy Spirit, come

Hart's hymn originally had nine verses and appeared in *Hymns Composed on Various Subjects*, 1759.

FRANCONIA. See 74.

105. Come, thou Holy Paraclete

This thirteenth-century Latin hymn, 'Veni, sancte Spiritus', has been ascribed to Pope Innocent III and also to his contemporary, Stephen Langton, Archbishop of Canterbury, but its authorship cannot be determined. In the Middle Ages this Sequence for Whitsuntide was often called the 'Golden Sequence'. The immense multiplication of Sequences necessitated reform by the Council of Trent, so in 1570 they were reduced to five—this one, 'Dies Irae', 'Stabat Mater', 'Lauda Sion', and 'Victimae Paschali'. Neale's version first appeared in his *Hymnal Noted*, 1852-4.

JORDAN was composed for this hymn by Donald Swann for CH3.

106. Holy Spirit, Truth Divine

Contributed by Longfellow to *Hymns of the Spirit*, 1864, of which he was editor. Verse 6 alludes to Num. 21: 17.

BUCKLAND by L. G. Hayne is from *The Merton Tune Book*, 1863.

107. Spirit Divine, attend our prayers

Reed's hymn appeared in *The Evangelical Magazine* in June 1829, and had been sung by instruction of the London Board of Congregational Ministers at the services of 'Solemn Prayer and Humiliation in the Eastern district of the metropolis' on Good Friday of that year, services designed 'to promote by the divine blessing, a revival of religion in the British churches'. Each verse is built on a different metaphor—light, fire, dew, dove, and wind.

MARTYRS. See 7.

Cross ref. to GERONTIUS. See 238.

108. Spirit of God, descend upon my heart

Based on Gal. 5: 25, Croly's hymn is from his *Psalms and Hymns for Public Worship*, 1854.

SONG 22 appeared in *Hymnes and Songs of the Church*, 1623. See 41. By Orlando Gibbons, it was set to a paraphrase of Hezekiah's prayer in Isa. 37, hence in some collections it is named 'Hezekiah'.

109. Spirit of God, that moved of old

Mrs. Alexander's hymn is from *Hymns*, 1852, except that in v. 3 'make' has been altered to 'keep' in the third line.

SOLDAU is from Walther's *Geystliche gesangk Buchleyn*, Wittenberg, 1524, where it is set to Luther's hymn, 'Nun bitten wir den heiligen Geist'. It may be a pre-Reformation melody adapted by Walther. The present form of the tune appears in Dibdin's *Standard Psalm Tune Book*, 1851.

110. O thou who camest from above

Wesley's hymn, as in *Short Hymns on Select Passages of Scripture*, 1762, is based on Lev. 6: 13.

FUDGIE first appears in *The English Hymnal Service Book*, 1962, where it is set to these words. It would appear that it was composed specially for them by Arthur Hutchings.

Cross ref. to SONG 34. See 45.

111. Jesus, good above all other

This hymn by Percy Dearmer is based on Neale's 'Jesus, kind above all other', of which two verses appear in *Hymns Ancient and Modern*, 1950. It was first published in *The English Hymnal*, 1906, where it is set to the tune of the German carol 'Quem pastores'.

QUEM PASTORES LAUDAVERE is a fourteenth-century German Christmastide carol. It was first printed in Triller's *Ein Schlesich Singesbuchlein*, Breslau, 1555. The arrangement is that by Vaughan Williams in *The English Hymnal*. A setting to the Latin words appears in *The Oxford Book of Carols*, 1928.

112. Jesus Christ, I look to thee

This is a revision by John M. Barkley of Wesley's 'Gentle Jesus, meek, and mild', which appeared in his *Hymns and Sacred Poems*, 1742, and his *Hymns for Children*, 1763. It is an attempt to minimize abstract terms like 'simplicity' which are meaningless to a child, while in v. 1 seeking to give more concrete expression to Wesley's ideas in vv. 1–2, in v. 2 to his ideas in vv. 3–4, and retaining v. 5 as v. 3.

GENTLE JESUS was composed by Martin Shaw for Wesley's hymn, and appears in *Additional Tunes and Settings in use at St. Mary's, Primrose Hill*, 1915.

113. Blest are the pure in heart

Verse 1 and v. 3 are by Keble from *The Christian Year*, 1827, at 'The Purification' where v. 3 reads 'for His cradle and His throne' in the third line. Verse 2 and v. 4 are from *The New Mitre Hymnbook*, 1836, and were composed by either W. J. Hall or Edward Osler, joint-editors. Keble authorized the text as it stands.

SWABIA comes from *Davids Harpffen Spiel, In hundert und funffzig Psalmen, Auch dreyhundert zwey und vierzig Lieder Melodien ... Aufgestzt von Johann Martin Spiess*, Heidelberg, 1745, where it is set to the hymn 'Ach wachet! wachet auf!' The present arrangement of the melody is by W. H. Havergal and appears in his *Old Church Psalmody*, 1847.

Cross ref. to FRANCONIA. See 74.

114. Christ, whose glory fills the skies

From Wesley's *Hymns and Sacred Poems*, 1740, where it is entitled 'Morning Hymn'. It is based on Mal. 4: 2.

CHRIST, WHOSE GLORY FILLS THE SKIES was composed for these words by Malcolm Williamson, and first appears in *12 New Hymn Tunes*, 1962.

PSALM 135 (MINISTRES DE L'ÉTERNAL) is set to Ps. 135 in *The French Psalter*, 1562. The arrangement is by Kenneth Elliott.

115. Come down, O Love Divine

This is a cento from the original Latin eight stanzas of 'Discendi amor santo' as published in Bianco da Siena's *Laudi Spirituali*, Lucca, 1851. The translation appeared in Littledale's *People's Hymnal*, 1867.

DOWN AMPNEY, composed by Vaughan Williams for this hymn, appeared in *The English Hymnal*, 1906, and is named after his birthplace.

116. Come, gracious Spirit, heavenly Dove

The original hymn in seven stanzas appeared in Browne's *Hymns and Spiritual Songs*, 1720. It was written in the first person and began 'Come, holy Spirit', since when it has been much altered. The last verse comes from Mercer's *Church Psalter and Hymnbook*, 1864.

VERBUM SUPERNUM, as in *The English Hymnal*, 1906, is one of the French tunes referred to under 42. The plain-song melody is from the *Antiphonarium Romanum*, Mechlin, 1848. The setting is that in *Liber Usualis*. The two alternative settings are by Kenneth Elliott.

117. Command thy blessing from above

Written by Montgomery for the Sheffield Sunday School Union on 3 June 1816, and published in the *Evangelical Magazine* for September of that year. The text is as printed in Cotterill's *Selection of Psalms and Hymns*, 1819.

EISENACH was first published on a single sheet entitled 'Trost-Liedlein über den seligen Hintritt der Frawen Margariten, des Herrn Caspar Werners ... Hausfrawen ... Componirt und Musicirt von Johan-Herman Schein, 1628'. Then it was included in Schein's *Cantonal oder Gesangbuch Augsburgischer Confession*, Leipzig, 1645. The hymn for which it was composed was 'Machs mit mir, Gott, nach deiner Güt'. The present arrangement is that by Bach in his *St. John Passion* and *Choralgesänge*, 1769.

118. Creator Spirit! by whose aid

'Veni, Creator Spiritus' cannot be traced earlier than the ninth century, though some threads of evidence seem to connect it with Rabanus Maurus (776–856). Dryden's version, from which fifteen lines have been omitted between lines four and five of v. 3 appeared in his *Miscellaneous Poems*, 1693. It was adapted for congregational use by Wesley in his *Psalms and Hymns*, 1738.

ATTWOOD was published in leaflet form, 'Come Holy Ghost, a Hymn for Four Voices . . . composed by Thomas Attwood, organist of St. Paul's Cathedral', 1831. It was composed in two days at the request of Dr. Blomfield, Bishop of London, for an Ordination Service at St. Paul's on Trinity Sunday, 1831. It was written in F major in anthem form, for a solo voice, a trio, and chorus. He rehearsed the choir-boy on the solo in his gig on the way to the cathedral for the service.

119. Enter thy courts, thou Word of life

Written by Bridges for a tune by Tallis, published in *The Yattendon Hymnal*, 1899.

FIFTH MODE MELODY by Tallis appears in *The whole Psalter translated into English Metre, which contayneth an hundreth and fifty Psalmes*, 1561. See 91.

120. Lord of beauty, thine the splendour

Alington's hymn was written for *Hymns Ancient and Modern*, 1950.

CORINTH (TANTUM ERGO). See 90. This is the tune set to these words in *The BBC Hymn Book*, 1951.

121. Thou art the Way: to thee alone

From Doane's *Songs by the Way*, 1824, based on John 14: 6.

ST. JAMES comes from *Select Psalms and Hymns for the Use of the Parish Church and Tabernacle of St. James's, Westminster*, 1697. The tune is named after the church.

122. Come, Holy Ghost, our hearts inspire

Wesley's version of 'Veni Creator' is not very close to the original. It appears in his *Hymns and Sacred Poems*, 1740, with the title 'Before reading Holy Scripture'.

ST. COLUMBA (ERIN) from *The Church Hymnal*, 1874, of the Church of Ireland. It is one of the traditional airs in George Petrie's *Collection of Irish Melodies*, 1855. The triplet in the second line is not original, but part of Stanford's arrangement.

123. Hushed was the evening hymn

Based on I Sam. 3: 1–10, Burns published his hymn in his *Evening Hymn*, 1857, when he was minister of Hampstead Presbyterian Church, London.

SAMUEL was composed by Sir Arthur Sullivan for this hymn in *Church Hymns with Tunes*, 1874. The original arrangement was for treble voices in unison with organ accompaniment. The four-part arrangement was made by the composer for *The Presbyterian Hymnal*, 1877.

Cross ref. to LOVE UNKNOWN. See 95.

124. Holy Spirit, hear us

Parker's hymn first appeared in *The School Hymnal*, 1880, and *The Children's Book of Praise*, 1881.

GLENFINLAS by K. G. Finlay first appeared in *Songs of Praise*, 1925, to the hymn 'Summer suns are glowing'. See 624. Originally it was in three parts for children, but the four-part setting is the composer's. It is written on the pentatonic scale.

125. God's law is perfect, and converts

Metrical psalm 19: 7–10, 14 from *The Scottish Psalter*, 1650. Sternhold's version had appeared in the Anglo-Genevan book, 1556, and was retained in the Scottish, 1564.

CAITHNESS, from *The Psalmes of David*, 1635, is one of the thirty-one Common Tunes appearing in this edition of the Scottish psalter.

126. God's perfect law revives the soul

This metrical version of Ps. 19: 7–14, based on the NEB translation, was written for CH3 by Professor Ian Pitt-Watson, Aberdeen.

ALLEIN GOTT IN DER HÖH 'SEI EHR' (STETTIN) is from *Geistliche Lieder auffs new gebessert und gemehrt*, Leipzig, 1539, where it is set to Nicolaus Decius's version of the 'Gloria in excelsis', 'Allein Gott in der Höh "sei Ehr"'. The melody is probably an adaptation from a pre-Reformation source. The present form of the tune is that used by Mendelssohn in *St. Paul*.

Cross ref. to NUN FREUT EUCH (LUTHER'S HYMN). See 14.

127. Teach me, O Lord, the perfect way

Metrical psalm 119: 33–40 from *The Scottish Psalter*, 1650. Whittingham's version was that given in *The Scottish Psalter*, 1564.

YORK is one of the twelve Common Tunes in *The CL Psalmes of David*, 1615, where it is named 'The Stilt'. In Ravenscroft's *Whole Book of Psalms*, 1621, it occurs four times, with three different harmonizations, two of them by John Milton, father of the poet. One of these is still used in *The Scottish Psalter*, 1929, and is that given here. Ravenscroft classifies it as a 'Northern Tune', saying it was 'proper for joyful ditties'. It was he who gave up the Scottish name and called it 'Yorke'. The tune may have originated as a church chime for the first and third strains are identical with part of a tune known in Cornwall as 'Stratton Church Chimes'.

128. Book of books, our people's strength

Dearmer's hymn was written 'to express the modern appreciation of the Bible' for *Songs of Praise*, 1925.

LIEBSTER JESU (DESSAU) comes from the *Neue geistliche auf die Sonntage durchs gantze Jahr gerichtete Andachten*, Mühlhausen, 1664, where the original form of Ahle's melody was set to the hymn 'Ja, er ists, das Heil der Welt'. Later German collections contain the same melody with numerous

variations set to Clausnitzer's hymn. See 129. The present form of the tune is
that adopted by Bach in his *Choralgesänge*, 1769.

129. Look upon us, blessèd Lord

The German original, from *Altdorffisches Gesang-Büchlein*, was written in
1663 when Clausnitzer was a minister at Weiden. It was intended to be sung
by the congregation before the Scripture Lesson. The present translation by
Professor R. A. S. Macalister appeared for the first time in RCH, 1927.

LIEBSTER JESU (DESSAU). See 128.

130. Lord, thy word abideth

Written by Baker for *Hymns Ancient and Modern*, 1861, where its caption was
Ps. 119: 105.

RAVENSHAW is from *Ein Neu Gesengbuchlein*, Behmen, 1531, the earliest
German hymnbook of the Bohemian Brethren, edited by Michael Weisse. It
is set to the hymn 'Menschenkind, merk eben'. The melody is of pre-
Reformation origin, and was associated with the Latin hymn 'Ave
Hierarchia, coelestis et pia'. It forms the subject of the Third Prelude in Bach's
Orgelbuchlein, and was set by him to the words 'Gottes Sohn ist Kommen' in
his *Choralgesänge*, 1769. The present arrangement by Monk appeared in
Hymns Ancient and Modern.

131. Light of the world! For ever, ever shining

From Bonar's *Hymns of Faith and Hope*, 1861, omitting three verses.

WILTON was composed by Mann for this hymn in the first edition of *The
Church Hymnary*, 1898.

132. Tell me the old, old story

Published as a leaflet in 1867, entitled 'The Story wanted'. It was written, says
Miss Hankey, on 29 January 1866, 'when I was weak and weary after an
illness, and especially realizing what most of us realize that simple thoughts in
simple words are all we can bear in sickness'. She was absolutely opposed to
the hymn being printed in any other form than that in which she wrote it,
that is, in four-line verses, each complete in itself without any refrain.

TELL ME was composed by W. H. Doane and contributed to *The Silver Spray*,
1868.

133. Break forth, O living light of God

Frank von Christierson's hymn was first published by the Hymn Society of
America in *Ten New Bible Hymns*, 1953.

MONTROSE seems to appear first in Gilmour's *Psalm-singer's Assistant*, 1793,
but it is probably considerably older because it was known as 'The Burghers'
Rant' from the secession split into burghers and antiburghers in 1746.

134. Heavenly Father, may thy blessing

Piggott's hymn first appears in *Songs of Praise*, 1925, for which it was written.

PLEADING SAVIOUR is from the *Plymouth Collection of Hymns and Tunes*, 1855, edited by H. W. Beecher, with John Zundel and C. Beecher as musical editors, and is the tune set to these words in *Songs of Praise*. The arrangement is by Vaughan Williams.

135. The Lord of heaven confess

Metrical psalm 148 from the second version in *The Scottish Psalter*, 1650. John Pullain's version, which appeared in *The Anglo-Genevan Psalter*, 1561, was retained in the Scottish book, 1564.

ST. JOHN is attributed by most modern authorities to J. B. Calkin as written for Barrett's *Congregational Church Hymnal*, 1887. On the other hand, Moffatt attributes it to *The Parish Choir*, 1851, where no information is given as to its source. The latter is probably the original source, later adapted.

136. Praise ye the Lord; for it is good

Metrical psalm 147: 1–5 from *The Scottish Psalter*, 1650. Norton's was the version given in the English book, 1562, and the Scottish, 1564.

DUNFERMLINE. See 101.

137. Praise God, for he is kind

Metrical psalm 136: 1–5, 23–6. Verses 1–2 are from *The Scottish Psalter*, 1650, v. 3 from *The Irish Psalter*, 1880, v. 4 as revised by the compilers, and v. 5 from the Scottish. John Craig's version had been that in *The Scottish Psalter*, 1564. John Marckant's was substituted for it in 1595, but Craig's was restored in 1611.

CROFT'S 136TH first appeared in *The Divine Companion; or, David's Harp new Tun'd*, 1709, by Henry Playford, where it is headed 'A Psalm set by Mr William Crofts. Psalm cxxxvi.'

Cross ref. to DARWALL'S 148TH. See 296.

138. How excellent in all the earth

Metrical psalm 8: 1, 3–5 from *The Scottish Psalter*, 1650. Sternhold's version was given in *The Anglo-Genevan Psalter*, 1556, and retained in the Scottish, 1564.

WINCHESTER OLD is from Este's *The Whole Booke of Psalms*, 1592. There it is set to Ps. 84, the name G. Kirby being attached, meaning that it was arranged by him. In the 1594, 1604, and 1611 editions of this work the tune does not appear, Ps. 84 being set to a tune known as 'Old Common Tune'. Ravenscroft, 1621, and Playford, 1671, 1677, again set Ps. 84 to 'Winchester Old'. The name of the tune first appears in Ravenscroft. It seems to be partly an adaptation from the second half of the melody set to chapter 8 in Tye's *Actes of the Apostles*, the first part being the melody of 'Southwark'. See 22.

139. I to the hills will lift mine eyes

Metrical psalm 121 from *The Scottish Psalter*, 1650. Whittingham's was the version in the Scottish book, 1564.

FRENCH (DUNDEE) is one of the twelve Common Tunes appearing in *The CL Psalmes of David*, 1615. Its first appearance in an English psalter is in Ravenscroft's *Whole Booke of Psalms*, 1621, where it is called 'Dundy' and classified among the 'Scottish Tunes'.

140. The Lord doth reign, and clothed is he

Metrical psalm 93 from *The Scottish Psalter*, 1650. The version in Scottish book, 1564, was by John Hopkins.

PSALM 107 was an air composed or adapted by Louis Bourgeois for Ps. 107 in *The French Psalter*, 1543. In *The Scottish Psalter*, 1564, it was altered to suit Kethe's version of the same psalm. The arrangement is by Kenneth Elliott.

STROUDWATER. See 23.

141. O Lord of every shining constellation

A. F. Bayly's hymn was published by the National Sunday School Union in *Sunday School Praise*, 1958, but had already appeared in his *Rejoice, O People*, 1951.

KILVAREE was composed for this hymn by Sebastian Forbes for CH3.

Cross ref. to DONNE SECOURS (PSALM 12). See 250.

142. Sing praise to God who reigns above

This hymn by Johann Jakob Schultz appears in Freylinghausen's *Geist-reiches Gesangbuch*, Halle, 1704. The English translation first appears in Miss Cox's *Sacred Hymns from the German*, 1841.

MIT FREUDEN ZART is from the *Kirchengesänge*, Berlin, 1566, of the Bohemian Brethren, but is probably older.

NUN FREUT EUCH. See 14.

143. The spacious firmament on high

At the close of an essay on 'Faith and Devotion' in *The Spectator*, 1712, Addison prints these words based on Ps. 19: 1–3. This hymn, along with number 150, gained circulation in a curious way. They were among the hymns added by the University printers to Tate and Brady's version of the psalter, *c.* 1818. In *The Scottish Paraphrases*, 1781, they were also two out of the five 'Hymns' appended. Another was by Watts. See 273.

ST. PATRICK. See 402.

FIRMAMENT was composed for this hymn by Sir Walford Davies for the London Church Choir Association for their Festival in St. Paul's Cathedral in 1908. It was published in *The Fellowship Hymn Book Supplement*, 1920, with the name 'Laudare Domine'.

144. God is Love: his mercy brightens

From Bowring's *Hymns*, 1825.

SUSSEX is a traditional English carol from *The English Hymnal*, 1906, as arranged by Vaughan Williams.

145. O Lord of heaven and earth and sea

From Wordsworth's *Holy Year*, 1863, where it is an Offertory hymn in nine stanzas, of which 1–4 and 6 are given here.

ES IST KEIN TAG is by J. D. Mayer from his *Geistliche Seelenfreud*, Ulm, 1692.

PORTLAND was composed by Cyril V. Taylor, while he was working at the BBC in Portland Place, hence its name. In *The BBC Hymnbook*, 1951, it is set to these words.

146. My God, I thank thee, who hast made

From Miss Procter's *Legends and Lyrics*, 1858, with two verses omitted.

OLDOWN was composed by Basil Harwood for this hymn in the *Public School Hymn-book*, 1919.

SEVERN was composed for this hymn by Herbert Howells in the enlarged *Songs of Praise*, 1931.

147. God moves in a mysterious way

Cowper's hymn appeared anonymously in Newton's *Twenty-six Letters on Religious Subjects; to which are added Hymns*, 1774; then in the *Olney Hymns*, 1779, signed 'C'. Cowper refers to John 13:7 as the origin of the phrase 'blind unbelief'. The hymn was originally entitled 'Light shining out of Darkness'.

LONDON NEW. See 6.

148. A gladsome hymn of praise we sing

Written in 1876 for the Sunday School Anniversary of Ambrose Blatchford's Church at Lewin's Mead, Bristol. It is from his *Songs of Praise for School and Church*, 1897.

ERMUNTRE DICH by J. Schop is set in triple time to a hymn beginning with these words in *Himmlische Lieder*, Lüneburg, 1641. The present form is Bach's in his *Christmas Oratorio*.

149. O God, the joy of heaven above

The hymn 'Rebus creatis nil egens' appears in the *Paris Breviary*, 1736, and is included in Coffin's *Hymni Sacri*, Paris, 1736, Chandler's *Hymns of the Primitive Church*, 1837, and Newman's *Hymni Ecclesiae*, 1838. The present text is an altered form of that by the compilers of *A Plainsong Hymnbook*, 1932.

SOUSTER was composed for this hymn by Martin Dalby for CH3.

150. When all thy mercies, O my God

This hymn comes at the close of an essay on 'Gratitude', in which Addison comments on the failure of Christian poets to give adequate expression to the praise of God. It is stanzas 1, 5, 6, 10, and 11 of the original published by Addison in *The Spectator*, 1712. See also 143.

NATIVITY. See 48.

GODRE'R COED is from *The Welsh Musical Festival Handbook*, 1963–4. It was composed by Matthew W. Davies and first appears in *Hymns and Services for Secondary Schools in Wales*, 1965.

151. God, who made the earth

Written by Mrs. Rhodes for the Whitsuntide Festival of the Sheffield Sunday School Union, 1870, it was first printed in *The Methodist Sunday-School Hymn Book*, 1879.

BEECHWOOD was composed for this hymn by Josiah Booth and published in *The Congregational Sunday School Hymnal*, 1891.

152. How wonderful this world of thine

F. B. Pratt's hymn was written for the Youth Department of the Methodist Church and appears in *The School Hymn Book of the Methodist Church*, 1950, and *Sunday School Praise*, 1958.

FITZWILLIAM is based on a melody by Handel and is that set to these words in both the above publications. See 296.

153. A little child may know

Miss Leeson published *Infant Hymnings* and in 1842 *Hymns and Scenes of Childhood, or A Sponsor's Gift*, in which the former was incorporated. This hymn appears in the latter.

SANDYS is a traditional air set originally to the words 'This day a child is born.' It is from *Christmas Carols Ancient and Modern . . . by William Sandys*, 1833.

154. All things bright and beautiful

From Mrs. Alexander's *Hymns for little Children*, 1848. Several of her hymns were written to illustrate the *Apostles' Creed*, the present being a comment on 'Maker of heaven and earth'.

ROYAL OAK is an English traditional melody said to date from 1667. The arrangement is by Martin Shaw in *Song Time*, 1915.

155. God who put the stars in space

This hymn by Norman and Margaret Mealy, based on a poem by Lucile S. Reid, first appeared in *Sing for Joy*, 1961, and was included in Margaret Kitson's *Infant Praise*, 1964.

MY PLACE by Hubert Grierson was composed for this hymn in *Infant Praise*.

156. I love to think that Jesus saw

This hymn by Ada Skemp appeared in Carey Bonner's *Child Songs*, 1908, and in *School Worship*, 1926.

CHILDHOOD is one of the tunes composed as a corporate effort by the students of the University of Wales, Aberystwyth, under the guidance of the Professor of Music, Sir Walford Davies. It appears in *A Students' Hymnal*, 1923, which they produced. The English section of this work was published separately with the title *Hymns of the Kingdom*, 1923, where the tune is given this name and set to Brooke's poem, 'It fell upon a summer day'.

157. We thank thee, God, for eyes to see

This hymn was written by Jeanette Perkins Brown in 1936, appeared in her *As Children Worship* of the same year, and was included in *Songs and Hymns for Primary Children*, 1963.

FOREST GREEN as in *The English Hymnal*, 1906, arranged by Vaughan Williams from a folk-song called 'The Ploughboy's Dream'.

158. Give the king thy judgments, O God

Prose psalm 72: 1–2, 5, 11, 17–19 (A.V.), *Deus, Judicium*. Suitable for use at Christmastide. See 3.

PLAIN-SONG TONE VIII, ending 2.

159. Behold he comes! your leader comes

Paraphrase 26: 5–10 from *Scottish Paraphrases*, 1781. The original paraphrase was by William Robertson in 1745 and revised by William Cameron in 1781.

FELIX is founded on a phrase in the chorus 'He stirreth up the Jews' in Mendelssohn's unfinished oratorio *Christus*, first performed in 1852. The tune first appeared in Lowell Mason's *The Hallelujah*, 1854, with the name 'Baltic', and may be assumed to be his composition.

160. Hark, the glad sound! the Saviour comes

The original of Paraphrase 39 was written by Doddridge on 28 December 1735, and headed 'Christ's message from Luke iv. 18–19'. It was revised twice in 1745 and 1781, the latter being by William Cameron when it appeared in *Scottish Paraphrases*, 1781. In England, it did not appear in print until 1755, when Orton published Doddridge's hymns.

BRISTOL. See 27.

Cross ref. to CREDITON. See 168.

161. Blessèd be the Lord God of Israel

The *Benedictus* appears in Luke 1: 68–79. The text is that in the *Great Bible*, 1539, as in Morning Prayer in the BCP. At the Council of Constantinople (*sub Menna*, 536) the people sang the *Benedictus* before the Liturgy so it was not part of the rite. As Duchesne shows it appeared for a period in the Gallican Mass and is still sung in the Mozarabic rite on the Festival 'in adventu S. Johannis Baptistae' though it has disappeared completely from the Milanese. Later it became the Breviary canticle for Lauds. Though a metrical version was included in many of the early psalters, including 1564, it fell into disuse following the Westminster Assembly and is omitted in the *Scottish Paraphrases*, 1781. Thereafter the first mention of it in a liturgical text is the sixth edition of the *Euchologion*, 1890, and in the hymnody of the Scottish Church in the first edition of *The Church Hymnary*, 1898.

CHANTS   Robinson in E flat double.
                 Turle in F double.

162. Before all time the Word existed

This hymn, based on John 1: 1–14, was written for CH3 by J. Neil Alexander, lecturer in New Testament, Glasgow.

NEUMARK is adopted by Mendelssohn in the oratorio *St. Paul* from the air originally set to the hymn 'Wer nur den lieben Gott lässt walten' by Neumark in his *Fortgepflanzter Musikalisch-poetischer Lustwald*, Jena, 1657.

163. My soul doth magnify the Lord

The *Magnificat* is from Luke 1: 46–55. The text is that of the *Great Bible*, 1539, as in the BCP. In the Eastern Church it is sung at morning service, but in the West it has been sung at Vespers since the time of St. Benedict, who probably gave it that position.

A metrical version appears in most early psalters including 1564, but like other canticles it fell out of use following the Westminster Assembly. Tate provided a new metrical version, and this, as revised by William Cameron, was included in the *Scottish Paraphrases*, 1781. A prose version is given in *The Church Hymnary*, 1898, to Tone VII ending 1. The first reference to its use in a liturgical text is the sixth edition of the *Euchologion*, 1890.

CHANTS   Goss in E double.
                 Marchant in F double.

164. Tell out, my soul, the greatness of the Lord

T. Dudley-Smith's version of the *Magnificat*, based on the NEB translation, was written in 1961, and was first published by the Church Society in the *Anglican Hymn Book*, 1965.

MAPPERLEY was composed for this hymn by Frank Spedding for CH3.

165. O come, O come, Emmanuel

By the ninth century the Medieval Church had adopted in the Roman rite the custom of singing the Greater Antiphons or short anthem-verses at Vespers from 17 December onwards, before or after the *Magnificat*. Five of them are reproduced in this hymn, which is supposed to date from the twelfth century. They are found in the *Psalteriolum Cantionum Catholicarum*, Cologne, 1710, Neale's version is in his *Mediaeval Hymns*, 1851. He began 'Draw nigh, draw nigh! Immanuel', but two years later in *The Hymnal Noted* altered this to the present form. The text is reproduced as in *Hymns Ancient and Modern*, 1861, where v. 2 is placed last.

VENI EMMANUEL, as in *The Hymnal Noted*, 1856, where the melody is said to be 'from a French Missal in the National Library, Lisbon'. This is possibly a mistake for 'Paris', as it is not to be found in any of the Lisbon manuscripts but occurs in a fifteenth-century manuscript in the Bibliothèque Nationale, Paris. In its present form it cannot be traced to an earlier source than that contributed by Helmore in *The Hymnal Noted*. The likelihood is that the adaptation was made for that book to suit Neale's translation.

166. Why do the heathen rage

Prose psalm 2: 1–2, 6–8, 10–11, 12b (A.V.), *Quare fremuerunt gentes?* Suitable for use at Christmastide. See 3.

PLAIN-SONG TONE V, ending 1.

167. His large and great dominion shall

Metrical psalm 72: 8, 10–11, 17–19 from *The Scottish Psalter*, 1650. Hopkins's version was given in the Scottish book, 1564.

MONTROSE. See 133.

Cross ref. to EFFINGHAM. See 285.

168. The race that long in darkness pined

Watts had also written a hymn on Isa. 9: 2–8, but this paraphrase was composed independently by John Morison. It is printed as it appeared in *Scottish Paraphrases*, 1781.

CREDITON by Thomas Clark is from *A Second Set of Psalm Tunes adapted to the use of Country Choirs, c.* 1810, where it is set to Ps. 8.

169. Hark! the herald angels sing

From Charles Wesley's *Hymns and Sacred Poems*, 1739, the first two lines and the refrain as in Whitefield's *Collection*, 1755. The original hymn had no refrain, and consisted of ten four-line stanzas, of which the first six are here printed.

BETHLEHEM is from Mendelssohn's *Festgesang* for male chorus and orchestra, composed for and first performed at the Leipzig festival in June 1840, to celebrate the invention of printing. The tune is adapted from chorus No. 2 of that work. When W. H. Cummings was organist at Waltham Abbey he copied out the parts and had the tune sung to these words. Finding that it was received with favour he published it in 1856 and it soon found its way into many hymnbooks, the first being Chope's *Congregational Hymn and Tune Book*, 1857, where it is called 'St. Vincent'.

170. It came upon the midnight clear

Sears's hymn first appeared in *The Christian Register*, 1850. Though minister in a Unitarian Church at Wayland, Massachusetts, Sears accepted the divinity of Christ. The hymn was written in a time of upheaval and unrest following the revolution in France and Germany, the Chartist movement in Britain, and the slave laws and Californian gold-rush in America. Reflection on these events comes out in vv. 3–5. It became known in this country through its inclusion in *Hymnal Companion*, 1870, and *Church Hymns*, 1871.

NOEL, a traditional melody adapted and extended by Sir Arthur Sullivan in *Church Hymns with Tunes*, 1874.

171. All my heart this night rejoices

Verses 1, 7, and 8 from Gerhardt's 'Fröhlich soll mein Herze springen' the original had fifteen, and first appeared in Crüger's *Praxis Pietatis Melica*, Berlin, 1653. The translation as in Miss Winkworth's *Lyra Germanica*, 1855.

BONN is from *Geistliche Andacht-Lieder Herrn Paul Gerhardt . . . gesetzt von J. G. Ebeling*, Berlin, 1666, where it is set to Gerhardt's hymn, 'Warum sollt ich mich denn grämen'.

172. O little town of Bethlehem

Written by Phillips Brooks for his Sunday School at Holy Trinity Church, Philadelphia in 1868, after he had visited the Holy Land in 1866. It was included in *The English Hymnal*, 1906.

FOREST GREEN. See 157.

173. The first Nowell the angel did say

'Nowell' is from the French 'Noël', which is commonly identified with the Provençal 'Nadal', that is, the Latin 'Natalis' or 'Birthday'. It came to mean as here a song of the 'Birthday', or 'News' as if from 'Novellare'. Such carols became popular in France and England during the fifteenth century. The present song, a West of England piece, is printed in Sandys's *Christmas Carols*, 1833, in a slightly different form.

THE FIRST NOWELL is a popular carol air in the West of England from the seventeenth century. It is from Sandys's book and the arrangement is by Martin Shaw.

174. While humble shepherds watched their flocks

The original hymn by Tate, based on Luke 2: 8–15, appeared in the *Supplement*, 1708, to the *New Version of the Psalms of David* by Tate and Brady. It was revised in 1781 for *Scottish Paraphrases*.

WINCHESTER OLD. See 138.

175. Angel voices, richly blending

This is a fourteenth-century German carol, of which the first printed version appears to be Triller's *Schlesich Singebüchlein aus Gottlieder Schrifft*, Breslau, 1555. It has been translated many times. That given here is by James Quinn, S. J., which appeared in his *New Hymns for All Seasons*, 1969.

QUEM PASTORES LAUDAVERE. See 111.

176. Still the night, holy the night

'Stille Nacht, heilige Nacht' was first published in the *Leipziger Gesangbuch*, 1838, but had been written in 1818 and was first sung on Christmas Eve of that year in the church of Oberndorf, where Mohr was assistant priest. The translation is based on Stopford Brooke's version in his *Christian Hymns*, 1881, but has been considerably altered in order to render it more faithful to the original.

STILLE NACHT was composed by Franz Gruber, a musical friend of Mohr's, on the day of its first singing. As the organ had become useless, Mohr sang the melody, accompanying himself on a guitar, while the composer sang the bass. A choir of girls from the village joined in the melody, repeating the last two lines of each verse.

177. Gloomy night embraced the place

This hymn is from *The Arundel Hymns*, 1902. It is from a carol in Crashaw's *Steps to the Temple*, 1646, where it consists of eighteen verses and is entitled 'A Hymne of the Nativity, sung by the Shepheards'.

SUMMER IN WINTER was composed for these words by Arthur Oldham for CH3.

178. In the bleak mid-winter

As printed in Christina Rossetti's *Poems*. It is marked as written 'before 1872'. It was first used as a hymn in *The English Hymnal*, 1906.

CRANHAM was composed by Gustav Holst for this hymn for *The English Hymnal*.

179. See! in yonder manger low

This hymn of Caswall's first appears in *Easy Hymn Tunes*, 1851, and in his *Masque of Mary*, 1858. Originally there were seven verses. Some versions begin 'See amid the winter's snow'.

HUMILITY was written by Sir John Goss for this hymn. It appeared first in Bramley and Stainer's *Christmas Carols, New and Old*, 1871.

180. Child in the manger

Verses by Mary (MacDougall) Macdonald, who in the early nineteenth century was a widely recognized poetess in the island of Mull. She named this hymn 'The Child of Aigh', that is, of Happiness, Good Fortune, or Wonder.

BUNESSAN was noted down by Alexander Fraser from the singing of a wandering Highland singer. It is printed in Lachlan Macbean's *Songs and Hymns of the Gael*, 1888.

181. On Christmas night all Christians sing

A traditional carol of which *The Oxford Book of Carols*, 1928, says with regard to the words and melody 'from Mrs Verrall, Monks Gate, Sussex'.

SUSSEX CAROL is a traditional carol tune. The arrangement is that of Vaughan Williams as in the above book. It had, however, been issued earlier in a leaflet, *Eight Traditional English Carols*.

182. Angels from the realms of glory

The original form of Montgomery's hymn as it first appeared in 1816 in *The Sheffield Iris*, a newspaper on whose staff he was then employed. It was entitled 'Nativity'. Later it appeared in his *Christian Psalmist*, 1825. Verse 4 appears to be based on Mal. 3: 1.

IRIS is the melody of a French carol, 'Les anges dans nos campagnes'. Charles Wood arranged it for *Songs of Syon*, 1910. It was set to the present words in *The Oxford Book of Carols*, 1928. The name 'Iris' is derived from the Sheffield newspaper. The arrangement is by Martin Shaw.

183. Good Christian men, rejoice

A patois carol, perhaps of the fourteenth century, from *Carols for Christmastide*, 1853, by Helmore and Neale. It was first translated into English by John Wedderburn in his *Gude and Godly Ballatis, c.* 1540.

IN DULCI JUBILO appears in Klug's *Gesangbuch*, Wittenberg, 1535, where it is set to a hymn consisting of a mixture of Latin and German, beginning 'In dulci jubilo nun singet und seid froh'.

184. God rest you merry, gentlemen

This is an eighteenth-century carol from the *Roxburgh Ballads*, 1770. 'Rest' means 'keep'.

GOD REST YOU MERRY is a carol-tune 'as sung in the streets of London' as arranged by Stainer in Bramley and Stainer's *Christmas Carols New and Old*, 1871.

185. All poor men and humble

The origin of this Welsh traditional carol is unknown. It was translated by K. E. Roberts in 1927, and appears in *The Oxford Book of Carols*, 1928, and *The University of Wales Students' Song Book*, 1937. In some versions there is an additional stanza written by Principal W. T. P. Davies, Brecon.

OLWEN is a Welsh traditional tune. The arrangement is that by Erik Routley in *The Anglican Hymn Book*, 1965.

186. Infant holy, infant lowly

This is a Polish carol, which Miss Reed translated and published in *Music and Youth*, of which she was editor, 1923–6; it is also included in *School Worship*, 1926.

INFANT HOLY is a Polish carol, which was published in *School Worship*. The arrangement is by A. E. Rushbridge.

187. Unto us is born a Son

This is a fifteenth-century Latin carol, 'Puer nobis nascitur'. There have been a number of translations. That given is by G. R. Woodward, editor of the *Cowley Carol Book*, 1901, and *Piae Cantiones* (*1582*), 1910.

PUER NOBIS first appears in *Piae Cantiones*, Nyland, 1582. The arrangement is by G. H. Palmer.

188. Give heed, my heart, lift up thine eyes

While many of Luther's early Christmas hymns had been translations from the Latin, this one is entirely his own. When he wrote it in 1534–5 his children were just old enough to sing it. Some scholars hold that the hymn is a miniature pageant for the family at Christmas, in which in its original form the angel sang vv. 1–5, stanza 6 was sung by the whole group, vv. 7–14 by individual children, and 15 by the group. For his carol Luther originally used the melody of a folk-song. It is found in Klug's *Gesangbuch*, Wittenberg, 1535. We can only surmise that later Luther felt the hymn deserved its own melody. The translation is from Catherine Winkworth's *Lyra Germanica*, 1855.

VOM HIMMEL HOCH comes from Schumann's *Geistliche Lieder*, Leipzig, 1539. The setting is Bach's in his *Christmas Oratorio*.

189. From east to west, from shore to shore

The hymn 'A solis ortus cardine' is attributed to Sedulius, who died *c.* 450. See 209. It is found in many Latin Breviaries. There have been many translations, the text here being an adaptation of that by Ellerton in *Church Hymns*, 1871. VOM HIMMEL HOCH. See 188.

190. Christians, awake, salute the happy morn

From a longer poem by Byrom, written as a Christmas gift for his daughter Dolly in the year 1749. Originally it consisted of forty-eight lines. These were reduced to thirty-six in *Hymns Ancient and Modern*, 1861, and to twenty-four in *Songs of Praise*, 1925. It is from his posthumous *Miscellaneous Poems*, 1773. In Byrom's notebook there is this entry: 'Christmas, 1750. The singing men and boys with Mr. Wainwright came here and sang "Christians awake".'

YORKSHIRE (STOCKPORT) by John Wainwright is said to have been first sung in Stockport parish church on the day of the above entry, but it was not published till ten years later in Ashworth's *Collection*, *c.* 1760. Subsequently it appeared in Wainwright's *Collection of Psalm Tunes*, 1766.

191. O come, all ye faithful

The earliest manuscript copy known of 'Adeste fideles' is in the Wade manuscripts at Stonyhurst, dated *c.* 1750, and it is suggested that it was written by John Francis Wade, a student at the R.C. College at Douai. Some hold that Wade was a layman who copied and sold plain-chant and other music at Douai. Oakeley's translation was made in 1841 for his congregation at Margaret Street Chapel, London. This version appeared in Murray's *Hymnal*, 1852.

ADESTE FIDELES, both words and music, is attributed by Dom John Stephan to Wade and dated between 1740 and 1744, since by the latter date the tune, or something very like it, appears in a comic-opera, *Acajou*, produced in Paris in 1744. Apparently it was originally in triple time. The first appearance of the tune in the rhythm with which we are familiar is in a manuscript dated 1760 in St. Edmund's College, Ware. It was published in this form by Webbe in his *Essay on the Church Plain Chant*, 1782. Its attribution in the past to a Portuguese composer probably arose from the fact that Webbe was organist at the chapel of the Portuguese Embassy in London. The same fact also accounts for its being known as 'Portuguese Tune' in Novello's *The Psalmist*, 1835.

192. A great and mighty wonder

Germanus, to whom this hymn is attributed, was Bishop of Cyzicus and became Patriarch of Constantinople in 715. The translation is by Neale in *Hymns of the Eastern Church*, 1862, as revised by Dearmer and the compilers of *The BBC Hymn Book*, 1951.

ES IST EIN' ROS' ENTSPRUNGEN is a Rhineland carol as found in the *Alte Catholische Geistliche Kirchengesang*, Cologne, 1599. It is a Christmas or Twelfth Night melody used in Trier or Trèves. The name 'A Rose has bloomed' uses the image of a rose come forth from 'the stem of Jessé' and applies it to Mary, the mother of the child Jesus. The harmonization is that by Praetorius in his *Musae Sionae*, Görlitz, 1609.

193. Once in royal David's city

From Mrs. Alexander's *Hymns for Little Children*, 1848, to illustrate the clause in the *Apostles' Creed*, 'Who was conceived by the Holy Ghost, born of the Virgin Mary'.

IRBY was written for this hymn by Gauntlett to be sung by voices in unison with harmonized accompaniment. It appeared in *Hymns for Little Children ... Set to music with piano accompaniment, by H. J. Gauntlett*, 1858. The melody had appeared earlier in his pamphlet, *Christmas Carols, Four Numbers*, 1849.

194. Love came down at Christmas

From Christina Rossetti's *Verses*, 1893. It first appeared in *Time Flies: a Reading Diary*, 1885, where the last line was 'Love the universal sign'.

HERMITAGE was composed by R. O. Morris for this hymn for *Songs of Praise*, 1925.

GARTAN is from Petrie's *Collection of Irish Melodies*, 1855, and is said to be a hymn-tune popular in Co. Donegal. It was harmonized by David Evans for RCH, 1927.

195. Away in a manger, no crib for a bed

Some attribute this hymn to Luther, but there is nothing corresponding to it in any of his writings. The earliest known source is an American Lutheran publication, *Little Children's Book*, 1885. There it is anonymous, but in Murray's *Dainty songs for little lads and lasses*, 1887, it is described as 'Luther's Cradle Hymn. Composed by Martin Luther for his children.' Verse 3 first appears in Gabriel's *Vineyard Songs*, 1892. The hymn is not by Luther, but was probably written in America for the four hundredth anniversary of his birth in 1883.

CRADLE SONG was composed for this hymn by W. J. Kirkpatrick in an American work, *Around the World with Christmas*, 1895.

NORMANDY has been described as an old Normandy carol. It was arranged by Edgar Pettman for *The University Carol Book*, 1923. The present arrangement is by Guthrie Foote.

196. When Christ was born in Bethlehem

Laurence Housman's hymn for Holy Innocents' Day first appears in *The English Hymnal*, 1906.

RODMELL is an English traditional melody. The arrangement, as in *The English Hymnal*, is by Vaughan Williams.

197. Behold the great Creator makes

Thomas Pestel's hymns first appeared in his *Sermons and Devotions old and new*, 1659. One, 'Fairest of Morning Lights appear', entitled 'A Psalm for Christmas Day Morning', was published in *The English Hymnal*, 1906, omitting vv. 1–4, and is that given here.

THIS ENDRIS NYGHT is a fifteenth-century English carol beginning 'Thys endris nyght I saw a syght'. 'Endris' means 'last'. The arrangement is by Vaughan Williams as in *The English Hymnal*.

198. Of the Father's love begotten

The Latin original, 'Corde natus ex parentis', is a cento of eight verses in the *Cathemerinon* of the Spanish poet Prudentius. His idea is that 'at every hour of the day a believer should be mindful of Christ who is Alpha and Omega'. Prudentius therefore praises Him as the creator of all things, as the eternal Son of the Father's love begotten. Verse 5 is a doxology which was added to Prudentius's hymn at a later date. Neale's version in *The Hymnal Noted*, 1856, was altered and adapted by Sir H. W. Baker in *Hymns Ancient and Modern*, 1861. With the omission of four verses this is reproduced here. See 199.

CORDE NATUS (DIVINUM MYSTERIUM) is the air used in the thirteenth century to 'Divinum mysterium' and probably Helmore took it from Petri's *Piae Cantiones*, Nyland, 1582, misreading at some points the melody. The present is the correct form, which was adopted in *Hymns Ancient and Modern*, 1904.

199. Bethlehem, of noblest cities

'Quicumque Christum quaeritis' is the final poem in Prudentius's *Cathemerinon*, and this hymn for the Epiphany begins at line 77. See 198. The translation by Caswall appears in his *Lyra Catholica*, 1849, and then in *The English Hymnal*, 1906.

STUTTGART by C. F. Witt is from *Psalmodia sacra, oder, Andächtige und schöne Gesänge*, Gotha, 1715, where it is set to the hymn 'Sollt es gleich bisweilen scheinen'.

200. As with gladness men of old

Written by W. C. Dix during an illness in 1860 and first published in *Hymns of Love and Joy*, 1861. The text is that in *Hymns Ancient and Modern*, 1861, and approved by the author.

DIX appeared originally in *Stimmen aus dem Reiche Gottes . . . herausgegeben von Conrad Kocher*, Stuttgart, 1838, where it is set to 'Treuer Heiland, wir sind hier'. Dix wrote of the setting of his words to this tune, 'I dislike it, but now nothing will displace it'.

201. Brightest and best of the sons of the morning

First published by Heber in *The Christian Observer*, 1811. It was included in his posthumous *Hymns written and adapted to the Weekly Church Services of the year*, 1827. It was originally written for the Scottish tune 'Wandering Willie'.

CRUDWELL by W. K. Stanton first appeared in *The BBC Hymn Book*, 1951, to the words 'God of eternity, Lord of the ages'. See 517.

202. How brightly beams the morning star

Philipp Nicolai's 'Wie schön leuchtet der Morgenstern' first appeared in an appendix to his *Freudenspiegel*, Frankfurt am Main, 1599. It was re-cast by J. A. Schlegel to such an extent that it could be considered almost a new tune. This appeared in Zollikofer's *Gesang-Buch*, Leipzig, 1766. Miss Winkworth's translation, omitting vv. 4 and 7 of the original, is included in her *Chorale Book for England*, 1863.

WIE SCHÖN LEUCHTET DER MORGENSTERN appears in Nicolai's work of 1599, and so may be by him. *The Oxford Book of Carols*, 1928, gives the harmonizations by Bach and Mendelssohn-Bartholdy, of which the latter is given here. It is from his unfinished oratorio, *Christus*, 1847.

203. King of kings and Lord of lords

This hymn was written in Gujarati by Kahanji Madhavji Ratnagrahi, and was translated by R. H. S. Boyd. It appeared first in *The United Church Review* in India, 1964, and later in the Irish *Teacher's Guide*, 1966. As the metre in the different verses of the translation was not uniform this was revised by J. Neil Alexander, Glasgow.

IN DER WIEGEN appears in Corner's *Geistliche Nachtigall*, Vienna, 1649, and is taken from *The Oxford Book of Carols*, 1928. The arrangement is by Martin Shaw.

204. Lord now lettest thou thy servant depart in peace

The *Nunc dimittis* (Luke 2: 29–32) as in the BCP. For metrical version see 590. It has been used as a canticle at evening worship from the eighth century or earlier. A metrical version appears in most of the early psalters, but it fell out of use following the Westminster Assembly. A metrical version appeared in *Scottish Paraphrases*, 1781, and a prose version in the first edition of *The Church Hymnary*, 1898. In the first edition of the *Euchologion*, 1867, it was suggested as a canticle 'suitable for public worship, in place of or along with the ordinary Psalms, Paraphrases, and Hymns'.

PLAIN-SONG TONUS PEREGRINUS is an ancient plain-song tone associated with Pss. 114–15 in the later Middle Ages, and later still with the *Nunc dimittis*. It was called 'Peregrinus' because it was a 'strange unfamiliar' plain-song tone, added to the existing eight Gregorian Tones, corresponding to the eight ecclesiastical modes.

CHANTS   Ley in C minor single.
          Farrant in F single.

205. 'Jesus!' Name of wondrous love

From *Psalms and Hymns*, 1854, composed by W. W. How on Matt. 1: 21.

PSALM 136 (LOUEZ DIEU) is the tune set to Ps. 136 in *The French Psalter*, 1562. The arrangement is by Kenneth Elliott.

206. When Mary brought her treasure

Jan Struther's Candlemas hymn first appears in *Songs of Praise*, 1936, for which it was written to provide a hymn for Candlemas Day and to 'carry the tune "Ave Maria Klare"'.

AVE MARIA KLARE is from *Psalteriolum Harmonicum*, Cologne, 1642. However, it is first found in Leisentritt's *Catholicum Hymnologium Germanicum*, Cologne, 1587, and *Catholische Kirchen Gesäng*, Cologne, 1619. From the latter it is sometimes called 'Cologne'. Töpler's *Alte Choral-Melodien*, Berlin, 1832, gives a form in common metre, from which Havergal made a four-line adaptation in his *Old Church Psalmody*, 1847, with the name 'Narenza'. See 456.

207. Behold a little Child

The hymn was first published under How's name in *Children's Hymns*, 1873.

LOVE UNKNOWN. See 95.

208. On Jordan's bank the Baptist's cry

Coffin's Latin hymn, 'Iordanis oras praevia', in his *Hymni Sacri*, Paris, 1736, freely translated in Chandler's *Hymns of the Primitive Church*, 1837. It also appears in the *Paris Breviary*, 1736, for Lauds during Advent.

SOLEMNIS HAEC FESTIVITAS. See 56.

209. How vain the cruel Herod's fear

The hymn 'Hostis Herodes impie' is the second part of the poem 'A solis ortus cardine' by Sedulius and dates from the fifth century. See 189. Neale translated it for *The Hymnal Noted*, 1852, 'Why, impious Herod, vainly fear'. The first line has frequently been altered. The present form is that in *Hymns Ancient and Modern*, 1875.

ST. OLAF'S was composed by John Gardner for *The Cambridge Hymnal*, 1967, where it is set to Newton's hymn 'The water stood like walls of brass'.

210. Forty days and forty nights

G. H. Smyttan contributed this hymn to *The Penny Post*, 1856, as 'Poetry for Lent'. Francis Pott reduced the nine verses to six in his *Hymns Fitted to the Order of Common Prayer*, 1861. The text used is Pott's omitting the last stanza.

AUS DER TIEFE (HEINLEIN). See 75.

211. Jesus calls us! O'er the tumult

Mrs. Alexander's hymn on Matt. 4: 18–19 as it appeared in *Hymns*, 1852.

OMNI DIE is from *Gross Catolisch Gesangbuch*, Nürnberg, 1631, compiled by D. G. Corner. The arrangement is Rockstro's, in *The English Hymnal*, 1906.

ST. ANDREW was composed for this hymn by E. H. Thorne in *Hymns Ancient and Modern*, 1875.

212. I heard the voice of Jesus say

Bonar's hymn was written while he was at Kelso and published in *Hymns Original and Selected*, 1846, under the title 'The Voice from Galilee'. It is based on John 1: 16.

KINGSFOLD arranged by Miss L. E. Broadwood from a folk-song called 'The Red Barn', from *The English Hymnal*, 1906, where it is set to these words. It is well known in Ireland as the melody of the ballad 'The Star of the County Down'. The arrangement is by Vaughan Williams.

213. It fell upon a summer day

From Stopford Brooke's *Christian Hymns*, 1881, where it is headed 'Christ blessing little children'. Based on Matt. 19: 13–15, the original had ten verses.

CHILDHOOD. See 156.

214. Thine arm, O Lord, in days of old

Written by Plumptre in 1864 for use in the chapel of King's College Hospital, London. It was first published as a leaflet, and later included in his *Lazarus and Other Poems*, 1865, and the appendix to *Hymns Ancient and Modern*, 1868, where there is a reference to Matt. 14: 35–6.

ST. MATTHEW appeared in *A supplement to the New Version of Psalms by Dr. Brady and Mr Tate . . . The Sixth Edition, corrected and much enlarged*, 1708, under its present name and indexed as a new tune. It is set to Ps. 33, in two parts, treble and bass. No composer's name is given, but it is generally believed to be by Croft.

215. Jesus, whose all-redeeming love

G. W. Briggs's hymn first appears in *Hymns of the Faith*, 1957, published privately for Worcester Cathedral.

CULROSS. See 102.

216. What grace, O Lord, and beauty shone

From Sir Edward Denny's *Selection of Hymns*, 1839, where it is entitled 'The Forgiving One, Psalm xlv. 2'.

ST. BERNARD is from *Neues ... Kirchen und Hauss Gesang der ... Tochter Sion*, Cologne, 1741, where in its original form it is set to a hymn in praise of the Virgin Mary. The melody appears in a different form in *Heil- und Hulfs-Mittel zum thätigen Christenthum*, 1767, and in *Cantica Spiritualia*, Munich, 1767. The present form was arranged from the latter, probably by J. Richardson, and first appeared in *Easy Hymn Tunes with the words in full, adapted for Catholic Schools*, 1851, where it is set to the hymn 'Jesus, the very thought of thee'. See 377.

217. O wondrous type, O vision fair

An anonymous fifteenth-century Latin hymn, 'Caelestis formam gloriae', as translated by Neale in his *Hymnal Noted*, 1852–4, and revised in *Hymns Ancient and Modern*, 1861. Three verses, two of which refer to the presence of Moses and Elijah at the Transfiguration, have been omitted.

EISENACH (LEIPZIG). See 117.

Cross ref. to DAS WALT' GOTT VATER. See 581.

218. There's a wideness in God's mercy

From Faber's hymn of thirteen verses, beginning 'Souls of men, why will ye scatter', in his *Hymns*, 1862. A shorter version of eight verses headed 'Come to Jesus' appeared in his *Oratory Hymns*, 1862. This was included in RCH, 1927, of which vv. 1–2 and 7 have been omitted here.

OMNI DIE. See 211.

Cross ref. to SUSSEX. See 144.

219. Son of the Lord Most High

G. W. Briggs's hymn appears in his *Songs of Faith*, 1945, with the title 'His Ministry'.

DOLGELLEY (DOLGELLAU) first appears in Griffith Harris's *Haleliwiah Drachefn*, 1855.

220. O sing a song of Bethlehem

Contributed by L. F. Benson to the Philadelphia *School Hymnal*, 1899, which he edited for the Presbyterian Church.

KINGSFOLD. See 212.

221. Who is he in yonder stall

From *The Dove: A Collection of Music for Day and Sunday Schools*, 1866, and *Chapel Gems*, 1875, edited by B. R. Hanby and G. F. Root, where it is marked 'B.R.H.'. This means Hanby wrote the tune and possibly also the words.

RESONET IN LAUDIBUS. See 98.

222. Wise men seeking Jesus

J. T. East's hymn is from *The Methodist School Hymnal*, 1910.

CAMBER was composed by Martin Shaw for the hymn 'Little drops of water' for *Songs of Praise*, 1931.

223. O Love, how deep, how broad, how high

This hymn is from a Latin poem on the Incarnation, 'O amor quam ecstaticus', attributed to Thomas à Kempis, but the evidence is far from conclusive. Webb's translation was published in *The Hymnal Noted*, 1854.

EISENACH. See 117.

224. My song is love unknown

Crossman's hymn is from *The Young Man's Meditation*, 1664. It first appeared in a hymn-book in *The Anglican Hymn Book*, 1868.

LOVE UNKNOWN. See 95.

225. Ye who the Name of Jesus bear

Paraphrase 52: 1, 3–6 from *Scottish Paraphrases*, 1781. It is from Phil. 2: 6–12. The author in the 1745 draft is unknown. It was revised by Cameron in 1781

ST. FLAVIAN. See 8.

226. I can picture Jesus toiling

Helen Stone's hymn was published in *Hosanna*, n.d., and is included in *Congregational Praise*, 1951, and *Sunday School Praise*, 1958.

MORGEN, KINDER, WIRD'S WAS GEBEN is a German traditional melody. The arrangement is that of Hedges in *Sunday School Praise*, where it is set to these words.

227. I love to hear the story

Mrs. Miller is said to have composed this hymn in less than a quarter of an hour. It appeared in *The Little Corporal*, 1867, a magazine she edited.

IN DER WIEGEN. See 203.

228. Jesus' hands were kind hands, doing good to all

Margaret Cropper's hymn appears in *The School Hymn Book of the Methodist Church*, 1950 and *Sunday School Praise*, 1958.

AU CLAIR DE LA LUNE. See 58. This is the tune set to these words in *Sunday School Praise*.

229. I like to think of Jesus

Elizabeth Shields's hymn was written for the Presbyterian Board of Education, U.S.A., and appears in *Songs for Early Childhood at Church and Home*, 1958.

CHERRY TREE CAROL is from *The English Carol Book*, 1913. It is a traditional melody of a carol beginning 'Joseph was an old man' and embodying a legend about Joseph, Mary, and a cherry tree. The arrangement is by Martin Shaw.

230. When Jesus saw the fishermen

Edith Agnew's hymn was written in 1953 and included in *Songs and Hymns for Primary Children*, 1963. Lines 1–12 are taken from this, and 13–16 from *The Teachers' Guide Book Revised*.

JOYS SEVEN is an English traditional carol. The melody was published in Bramley and Stainer's *Christmas Carols New and Old*, 1871. The arrangement is by Martin Shaw.

231. As the hart panteth after the water brooks

Prose psalm 42: 1–5, 8–11 (A.V.), *Quemadmodum*. Suitable for use during Passiontide. See 3.

PLAIN-SONG TONE III, ending 4.

232. Open to me the gates of righteousness

Prose psalm 118: 19–29 (A.V.), *Confitemini Domino*. Suitable for use on Palm Sunday. See 3.

PLAIN-SONG TONE VI.

233. All glory, laud, and honour

The Latin original, 'Gloria, laus, et honor tibi sit, rex Christe redemptor', is a cento from the long processional hymn for Palm Sunday commonly attributed to Theodulph, bishop of Orleans. It came into use as a processional on this day in the ninth century in France and England, being found in the rites of Sarum and York. The Scriptures behind the hymn are Pss. 24: 7–10, and 118, Matt. 21: 1–17, and Luke 19: 37–8. Neale's version appeared in *The Hymnal Noted*, 1852–4, and was revised in *Hymns Ancient and Modern*, 1861.

ST. THEODULPH comes from *Ein andächtiges Gebet . . . so wol ein tröstlicher Gesang, darinnen ein frommes Herz dieser Welt Valet gibet*, Leipzig, 1615, a small leaflet containing Herberger's 'Valet will ich dir geben' and two melodies set to it by Teschner, both arranged for five voices. The present is the second of the two.

234. Ride on! ride on in majesty

Milman's hymn first appeared in Heber's posthumous *Hymns*, 1827.

WINCHESTER NEW (CRASSELIUS) comes from *Musikalisch Hand-Buch der Geistlichen Melodien à Cant. et Bass*, Hamburg, 1690, where the melody is set to 'Wer nur den lieben Gott lässt walten'. In Moore's *Psalm-Singer's Delightful Pocket Companion*, 1762, the tune appears in an altered form and is named 'Winchester'. The arrangement is by W. H. Havergal and appeared in his *Old Church Psalmody*, 1847. 'Effingham' is a triple-time version in common metre. See 285.

235. Hosanna, loud hosanna

From Miss Threlfall's *Sunshine and Shadow*, 1873, with 'whilst' in v. 3 altered to 'while'.

ELLACOMBE first appears in *Gesangbuch der Herzöglichen Württembergischen Katholischen Hofkapelle*, 1784, a book used in the private chapel of the Duke of Würtemberg. It was popularized by *Hymns Ancient and Modern*, 1868, where it is set to 'Come, sing with holy gladness'. The setting is taken from the St. Gall *Gesangbuch*, 1863.

236. Children of Jerusalem

This hymn, based on Matt. 21: 15, by John Henley must have been written by him before 1842, the year of his death, but it is first found in Bateman's *Sacred Song Book for Children*, 1843.

HEATHLANDS was composed by Henry Smart for the hymn 'God of mercy, God of grace' (see 497) in *Psalms and Hymns for Divine Worship*, 1867, which he edited.

237. 'Twas on that night when doomed to know

Paraphrase 35 of Matt. 26: 26–9 from *Scottish Paraphrases*, 1781. It is generally attributed to John Morison. Some hold that he must have used William Archibald's translation of Andreas Ellinger's 'Nocte qua Christus rabidis Apellis' when composing it. It first appeared in the 1781 edition.

ROCKINGHAM (COMMUNION) is from *The Psalms of David for the Use of Parish Churches. The Music Selected, Adapted, and Composed by Edward Miller, Mus. Doc.*, 1790, where it is headed 'Part of the melody taken from a hymn tune', and named 'Rockingham'. Miller's adaptation is possibly from 'Tunbridge', which is found in Williams's *Supplement to Psalmody in Miniature*, c. 1780. In Scotland Smith and Wilson in their collections set it to Paraphrase 35, and as this was almost invariably sung on Communion seasons the name 'Communion' became attached to it. Miller gave it the name 'Rockingham . . . in grateful memory of the Marquis of Rockingham, his kind and zealous patron'.

238. Praise to the Holiest in the height

From Newman's *Dream of Gerontius*, 1865, with the first stanza repeated as is usual for the purposes of worship and v. 4 in RCH, 1927, omitted.

GERONTIUS was composed for this hymn by J. B. Dykes for *Hymns Ancient and Modern*, 1868.

CHORUS ANGELORUM by Arthur Somervell first appears in *Arundel Hymns*, 1902, set to Newman's hymn. Another version appears in Somervell's *Passion of Christ*, 1914. It is included in *Hymns Ancient and Modern*, 1950.

239. My God my God why hast thou forsaken me

Prose psalm 22: 1–9, 11, 15–19, 22–4, 27, 30–1, *Deus, Deus meus*. Suitable for use on Good Friday. See 3.

PLAIN-SONG TONE II, ending 1.

240. Holy God, holy and mighty, holy and immortal

For the *Trisagion* see 61. The *Reproaches*, 'improperia', are a part of the Good Friday liturgy in the Roman rite, consisting of 'reproofs' addressed by the crucified to his people, which are chanted by two choirs. They are built up on Old Testament passages, contrasted with the sufferings inflicted on Christ in his Passion. Various versions exist. That given here was prepared by the Revd. John Heron, Stevenston, and approved by the revision committee following a critical examination of existing texts among which, because of its simplicity, the principal was that in Todd's *Prayers and Services for Christian Festivals*, 1951.

TRISAGION AND REPROACHES was composed by Dom Gregory Murray for CH3.

241. There is a green hill far away

From Mrs. Alexander's *Hymns for Little Children*, 1848, written to illustrate 'Suffered under Pontius Pilate, was crucified, dead, and buried'.

HORSLEY is from *Twenty-four Psalm Tunes and Eight Chants, composed by William Horsley*, 1844, where it has no name.

242. Alone thou goest forth, O Lord

Abelard's hymn was written for use in the Abbey of the Paraclete where Héloïse was abbess. F. B. Tucker's translation appears in *The Hymnal*, 1940, of the Protestant Episcopal Church of America.

MARTYRS. See 7.

243. O come and mourn with me awhile

From Faber's poem of twelve stanzas in his *Jesus and Mary*, 1849. Several alterations have been made in the text throughout the years in an attempt to remove Faber's 'unquenchable sentamentalism'. The original refrain was 'Jesus, my love, was crucified'.

ST. CROSS was composed by Dykes for this hymn for *Hymns Ancient and Modern*, 1861.

244. O word of pity, for our pardon pleading

Miss Greenaway's hymn first appeared in *Hymns Ancient and Modern*, 1904. It is based on Luke 23: 34.

INTERCESSOR was composed for this hymn by Hubert Parry for *Hymns Ancient and Modern*.

245. Lord, when thy Kingdom comes, remember me

Written by W. D. Maclagan for *Hymns Ancient and Modern*, 1875. The text given is that as altered and authorized in the 1904 edition.

SONG 24. See 64.

246. At the cross, her station keeping

The Latin original, 'Stabat mater dolorosa', based on John 19: 26–7, has been attributed to Gregory the Great, Bernard of Clairvaux, Innocent III, Bonaventura, Jacobus de Benedictis, John XXII, and others. Though widely used earlier this Sequence was not introduced into the Roman *Breviary* or *Missal* until 1727. Probably it was an anonymous hymn. Numerous translations have been made. The present one is the work of several hands; the first two lines of the first stanza and the first three of the second are practically Caswall's in his *Hymns and Poems*, 1863, and the remainder is drawn mainly from Mant's version as altered in Murray's *Hymnal*, 1852.

STABAT MATER goes back to the *Mainzisch Gesangbuch*, 1661.

247. Throned upon the awesome Tree

Ellerton's hymn, written in 1875, appeared first in *Hymns Ancient and Modern* of that year. For the same reason as in No. 2 'awful' has been altered to 'awesome'.

PETRA. See 83.

248. O perfect God, thy love

Ada R. Greenaway's hymn was written during Lent, 1902, and appears for the first time in *Hymns Ancient and Modern*, 1904.

SOUTHWELL. See 80.

249. O perfect life of love

Written by Sir H. W. Baker in 1875 and first published in *Hymns Ancient and Modern* of that year.

SOUTHWELL. See 80.

250. And now, belovèd Lord, thy soul resigning

Written by Mrs. Alderson in 1868 at the request of her brother, the Revd. J. B. Dykes, omitting two verses. Included in *Hymns Ancient and Modern*, 1875.

PSALM 12 (DONNE SECOURS) was adapted or composed by Louis Bourgeois for Ps. 12 in *The French Psalter*, 1551. The arrangement is by Kenneth Elliott.

251. Ah, holy Jesus, how hast thou offended

Johann Heermann's original hymn, in fifteen verses, appeared in his *Devoti Musica Cordis*, Leipzig, 1630. It was said by him to be 'from Augustine', but it is really from the fifteenth-century *Meditationes*, incorrectly attributed to him. The text here is the free version of Bridges in *The Yattendon Hymnal*, 1899.

HERZLIEBSTER JESU is from Crüger's *Gesangbuch*, Berlin, 1640. Some hold that it is based on 'Geliebter Freund' in Schlein's *Cantonal*, Leipzig, 1627, and that it goes back to 'Psalm 12' in *The Genevan Psalter*, 1551: See 250. Bach used it in both his *St. Matthew Passion* and his *St. John Passion*.

252. O dearest Lord, thy sacred head

From *Poems* by Father Andrew, S.D.C. (Henry Ernest Hardy). It is included in *The BBC Hymn Book*, 1951, and *The Anglican Hymn Book*, 1965.

NUN DANKET ALL (GRÄFENBERG). See 5.

Cross ref. to ST. FLAVIAN. See 8.

253. O sacred Head, sore wounded

The original medieval hymn, 'Salve mundi Salutare', sometimes attributed to Bernard of Clairvaux, was possibly the work of Arnulf von Loewen. The German version is ascribed to Paul Gerhardt in Crüger's *Praxis Pietatis Melica*, Berlin, 1656, and is entitled 'To the suffering Face of Jesus Christ'. The original consists of seven parts on the suffering Saviour the verses beginning 'Salve caput cruentatum' being the seventh section. The present version is based on J. W. Alexander's in his *The Breaking Crucible, and other Translations*, 1861.

PASSION CHORALE goes back to the Middle Ages, and appears in *Lustgarten Neuer Teutscher Gesäng . . . Componirt durch Hanns Leo Hassler von Nürnberg*, 1601, where it is set to a secular song, 'Mein Gmüt ist mir verwirret von einer jungfrau zart'. In *Harmoniae Sacrae*, Görlitz, 1613, it is set to the hymn 'Herzlich thut mich verlangen', and in later books to 'O Haupt voll Blut und Wunden', of which the present hymn is a free translation. Bach used it in his *St. Matthew Passion*. The melody is as used by him and the arrangement is mainly his also.

254. When I survey the wondrous cross

From Watts's *Hymns and Spiritual Songs*, 1707, with 'Where the young Prince' altered to 'On which the Prince of Glory' in v. 2, and 'present' to 'offering' in v. 4. The fourth stanza of the original is omitted. Its original title was 'Crucifixion to the World by the Cross of Christ. Gal. vi. 14'.

ROCKINGHAM (COMMUNION). See 237. It was first set to these words in Godding's *Parochial Psalmist*, 1833.

Cross ref. to LLEFF. See 485.

255. Lord Christ, when first thou cam'st to men

Russell Bowie's hymn was written in 1928 at the request of Dean Dwelly of Liverpool Cathedral, who wanted a new version of the 'Dies irae'. It seeks, to use Bowie's words, 'to express both the solemnity and inspiration of the thought of Christ coming into our modern world in judgment'. It first appeared in *Songs of Praise*, 1931.

WITTENBERG is a melody from *Christliche Lieder*, Wittenberg, 1524, as adapted by Bach. It is also known as 'Reading', 'Spires', and 'Serva nos Domine', the last being the Latin of the opening words of Luther's hymn, 'Erhalt uns, Herr, bei deinem Wort', to which it was set in Klug's *Gesangbuch*, Wittenberg, 1543. There the hymn is headed 'A children's Song, to be sung against the two Arch-enemies of Christ and His holy Church, the Pope and the Turk'. Hence sometimes the tune was popularly referred to as 'the Pope and Turk tune'. It appears in all the early psalters.

256. Sing, my tongue, how glorious battle

This Latin hymn, 'Pange, lingua, gloriosi proelium certaminis', is ascribed to Fortunatus, and tradition associates its composition with 19 November 569. His patroness, Queen Rhadegundis, was held to have secured a fragment of the true cross. She deposited this in the convent which she had founded and over which she presided at Poitiers. To celebrate the occasion Fortunatus wrote his famous poem. See 257. The present version gives four of the original stanzas, together with a doxology which was added when the poet's words passed into church use. Wotherspoon gave this account of it, 'In preparing *The Scottish Mission Hymnbook*, the Committee of the Church of Scotland had before it a collection of some hundred hymns made (and printed) for an important mission-week carried through in Aberdeen under Professor Cooper. I was one of the missioners, and some things of mine were among these hundred hymns. The Committee took a few of them for the first draft of the new book. When we went over those that formed the draft, Dr. Mair was interested in the translation of the hymn of Fortunatus, and as they knew by that time that it was mine, he and I were asked to revise it together ... with the Latin, of course. His suggested changes were all to the good. ... They gave me a large share in the editing and all the arranging of the book, and so I gave myself the pleasure of coupling Dr. Mair's name with mine as translators.'

PANGE LINGUA is the proper plain-song melody of the hymn. It is found in the *Mechlin Gradual*, 1848. The setting is that of Sarum mode iii.

PICARDY is one of the French melodies referred to in No. 42. The arrangement is largely that in *The English Hymnal*, 1906. It is a carol, probably seventeenth century, with the title 'Romancero', from Tiersot's *Mélodies*, Paris, 1887. It is also found in *Chansons populaires des provinces de France*, 1860.

257. The royal banners forward go

The hymn 'Vexilla Regis prodeunt' by Fortunatus was originally in ten verses. It is a song of triumph for Christ's victory on the Cross. It is another section of that given at No. 256. Neale's translation appears first in his *Mediaeval Hymns*, 1851. It has been considerably altered over the years. The present version is that in *The Clarendon Hymn Book*, 1936.

DEUS TUORUM MILITUM. See 42.

Cross ref. to GONFALON ROYAL. See 328.

258. We sing the praise of him who died

From Thomas Kelly's *Hymns*, 1815. The original was headed, 'God forbid that I should glory, save in the Cross. Gal. vi. 14'.

WALTON is from *Sacred Melodies from Haydn, Mozart, and Beethoven, adapted to the best English Poets, and appropriated to the use of the British Church, by William Gardiner*, 1815, where it is headed 'Subject from Beethoven'. This, however, has not been definitely traced though some hold there is a 'marked resemblance' to the first and last lines of 'Walton' in the theme on which the 'Allegretto ma non troppo' movement of Beethoven's *Piano Trio*, Opus 70, No. 2, 1809, is built. Others find a similarity between the first line and the introduction to the solo 'O Isis und Osiris' in Mozart's *Magic Flute*. Consequently some hold it to be from neither Beethoven nor Mozart but to be adapted from a German folk-song, or to be Gardiner's own composition. The tune is also known as 'Fulda'.

Cross ref. to BRESLAU. See 430.

259. In the cross of Christ I glory

Sir John Bowring's hymn, based on Gal. 6: 14, and entitled 'Glorying in the Cross', was published in his *Hymns*, 1825.

STUTTGART. See 199.

260. At eve, when now he breathed no more

John R. Darbyshire's hymn was written for *Songs of Praise*, 1931, 'in order to keep in use the tune "Bohemia", as used in *The English Hymnal*'. See 261.

TRYPHAENA is one of the tunes composed by Frances R. Havergal for words of her own. It first appears in 1871 in an edition she made of her father's hymn-tunes, which included tunes both by him and herself. It also appears in *School Worship*, 1926.

261. By Jesus' grave on either hand

From Gregory Smith's *Hymnbook for the Services of the Church and for Private Reading*, 1855. The compilers of RCH, 1927, included this hymn as 'it is almost alone in commemorating the Saturday evening between Good Friday and Easter Sunday'.

O MENSCH SIEH is from the Bohemian Brethren's *Gesangbuch*, Berlin, 1566, but in the form adopted by *The English Hymnal*, 1906, where the rhythm is altered from the original, and it is called 'Bohemia'.

262. The voice of rejoicing and salvation

Prose psalm 118: 15–24 (A.V.), *Confitemini Domino*. Suitable for use on Easter Day. See 3.

PLAIN-SONG TONE VI.

263. O set ye open unto me

Metrical psalm 118: 19–25, 28–9 from *The Scottish Psalter*, 1650. The version in the 1564 Scottish book was that of John Craig.

SOUTHWARK. See 22.

264. Jesus Christ is risen today

The original Latin Easter carol, 'Surrexit Christus hodie', is from a fourteenth-century manuscript cited by Dreves in his *Cantiones Bohemicae*, Leipzig, 1886. It was often translated into German going back to a broadsheet printed at Nürnberg in 1544, 'Erstanden ist der heilige Christ'. The English form is from *Lyra Davidica: or a collection of Divine Songs and Hymns, partly new composed, partly translated from the high German and Latin hymns; and set to easy and pleasant tunes*, 1708. The modern form is from Arnold's *Compleat Psalmodist*, 1741, from which the present text is taken with 'praises' changed to 'praise' in v. 2. The last verse was added by Charles Wesley.

EASTER HYMN is from *Lyra Davidica*, where the hymn and tune are headed 'The Resurrection'.

265. 'The lord is risen indeed'

From the seven stanzas of the original, based on Luke 24: 34, in Thomas Kelly's *Collection of Psalms and Hymns*, 1802.

ST. MICHAEL (OLD 134TH). See 46.

266. The strife is o'er, the battle done

This anonymous medieval hymn, 'Finita jam sunt proelia', appears first in the Jesuit *Symphonia Sirenum*, Cologne, 1695. Francis Pott's translation was made about 1859 and included in his *Hymns Fitted to the Order of Common Prayer*, 1861, and revised for *Hymns Ancient and Modern*, 1875.

VULPIUS (GELOBT SEI GOTT) is from *Ein schön geistlich Gesangbuch*, Jena, 1609, edited by Melchior Vulpius. The melody was harmonized by Ley for *Songs of Praise*, 1925. The arrangement is that in *The BBC Hymn Book*, 1951.

267. The day of resurrection

This is the first of the eight Odes of the 'Golden Canon' or 'Queen of Canons' by John of Damascus, which is sung in the Eastern Church after midnight on Easter morning, to set forth the fact of the resurrection, its fulfilment of prophecy, and to call the people to thanksgiving and praise. See 269. Neale's translation appears in his *Hymns of the Eastern Church*, 1862. The present form is that in *Hymns Ancient and Modern*, 1904.

CRÜGER appeared originally in Crüger's *Neues vollkomliches Gesangbuch*, Berlin, 1640. Monk's arrangement in *Hymns Ancient and Modern*, 1861, is made from Kühnau's *Vierstimmige alte und neue Choralgesänge*, 1786. The fifth line is Monk's own composition.

268. Christ Jesus lay in death's strong bands

The roots of Luther's hymn go deep into the Middle Ages: for example, *c.* 1050, Vipo, court chaplain to the Emperor Henry III, wrote the Sequence 'Victimae Paschali laudes', which has become part of the Easter Liturgy in the Roman rite. It was first published in *Eyn Encheiridion*, Erfurt, 1524. Massie's translation first appeared in his *Martin Luther's Spiritual Songs*, 1854.

CHRIST LAG IN TODESBANDEN is an old German melody first appearing in its full form in Walther's *Gesangbuchlein*, Wittenberg, 1524. It is based on a thirteenth-century melody.

269. Come, ye faithful, raise the strain

This hymn by John of Damascus was one of the 'odes' for the Sunday after Easter, and is based on the 'Song of Moses' in Exod. 15. See 267. Neale translated it in his *Hymns of the Eastern Church*, 1862, and it was revised in *Hymns Ancient and Modern*, 1868. The latter added the doxology.

AVE VIRGO VIRGINUM is a German traditional melody. It appears in *Ein Gesangbuch der Brüder in Behemen und Merherrn*, Nürnberg, 1544, of the Bohemian Brethren, and in its present form in Laisentritt's *Catholicum Hymnologium Germanicum*, Cologne, 1584. It was first set to these words in *The English Hymnal*, 1906.

270. Good Christian men, rejoice and sing

Written by Alington for *Songs of Praise*, 1925, while he was headmaster of Eton.

VULPIUS. See 266.

271. This joyful Eastertide

From the *Cowley Carol Book*, 1933, of which the author, G. R. Woodward, was editor. It was written to provide words for the tune.

VRUECHTEN is a Dutch tune which in *The Amsterdam Psalter, c.* 1670, was set to J. Oudaen's 'How groot de Vruechten zijh'. The arrangement is by Charles Wood.

272. 'Welcome, happy morning!'—age to age shall say

This is the section for Easter in a long poem by Fortunatus, which begins 'Tempora florigero rutilant distincta sereno', addressed to his friend Felix, Bishop of Nantes, some time before 582. In the poem he dwells on the beauty of spring coming 'in her gayest attire to greet her risen Lord'. The section on the Resurrection opens 'Salve, festa dies'. See 328. Ellerton's free paraphrase first appeared in Borthwick's *Supplementary Hymn and Tune Book*, 1869.

NOUS ALLONS is a French choral melody, found in Grimault's *Noëls Angevins*, 1878, and Rogues's *50 Noëls Anciens*, Paris, 1897. The arrangement is that by Martin Shaw in *Songs of Praise*, 1925, and *The Oxford Book of Carols*, 1928.

273. Blest morning, whose first dawning rays

Watts wrote this in *Hymns and Spiritual Songs*, 1709, and entitled it 'The Lord's Day'. The present version is a revision of this as it appeared in *Scottish Paraphrases*, 1781. See 143.

LANCASTER by Howard is called 'St. Clement's Tune' in *Parochial Harmony: consisting of a Collection of Psalm Tunes in three and four parts, by William Riley*, 1762, where it is set to Ps. 1.

Cross ref. to CREDITON. See 168.

274. The world itself keeps Easter Day

From Neale's *Carols for Eastertide*, 1854. To fit the melody, as in *The Oxford Book of Carols*, 1928, and *The English Hymnal Service Book*, 1962, 'Hosanna in excelsis' has been substituted for the original 'Alleluia'.

O CHRISTE REX is from *Piae Cantiones*, Nyland, 1582. The arrangement is that of Geoffrey Shaw in *The Oxford Book of Carols*, 1928.

275. 'Christ the Lord is risen today'

Charles Wesley's hymn in eleven stanzas and entitled 'Hymn for Easter Day', appeared in *Hymns and Sacred Poems*, 1739. The present version was made by Madan in his *Psalms and Hymns*, 1760.

ORIENTIS PARTIBUS is a medieval French melody. In parts of France, notably at Beauvais, during the Middle Ages there was celebrated on 14 January a church festival known as the Feast of the Ass to commemorate the flight into Egypt. On this occasion a young women holding a child in her arms was seated on an ass, and after a procession through the streets the ass was led into the principal church and took its stand beside the high altar while mass was celebrated. During the service a hymn was sung, written in a mixture of Latin and French, of which the first line was 'Orientis partibus adventavit asinus'. Félix Clément has traced the melody to a manuscript at Sens, entitled 'Office de la Circoncision à l'usage de la ville de Sens', and says this Office was the work of Pierre de Corbeil, Archbishop of Sens, who died in 1222. Nothing in this Office suggests that the ass played a burlesque role. The melody has been preserved and from it the present tune was adapted by Redhead in his *Church Hymn Tunes*, 1853.

276. Easter glory fills the sky

This hymn by Fr. James Quinn, S.J., appears in his *New Hymns for All Seasons*, 1970.

WÜRTEMBERG was set to the hymn 'Straf mich nicht im deinem Zorn' in the *Hundert ahnmuthig und sonderbar geistlicher Arien*, Dresden, 1694. It has been ascribed to Johann Rosenmüller, but this is doubtful. There have been a number of settings, including one by Bach in his *Choralgesänge*, 1759. That given here is Monk's in *Hymns Ancient and Modern*, 1861.

277. O sons and daughters, let us sing

This hymn by Jean Tisserand, a Minorite friar at Paris, has been traced to a booklet published in France *c.* 1520–30, where it consists of nine stanzas. Three were later added, the originals of vv. 4, 5, and 8 in the version in CH3, which corresponds to Neale's in his *Mediaeval Hymns*, 1851, and *Hymnal Noted*, 1852–4 as modified in *Hymns Ancient and Modern*, 1861. The text here therefore incorporates six of Tisserand's stanzas and the three subsequently added.

O FILII ET FILIAE is found in slightly varying forms in seventeenth- and eighteenth-century books, including *Airs sur les hymnes sacrez, odes et noëls*, Paris, 1623, La Feillée's *Méthode Nouvelle pour apprendre . . . les règles du Plain Chant*, Paris, 1748, and the Jesuit *Nordstern's Führers zur Seeligkeit*, 1671. The present form is slightly modified from that found in Webbe's *Essay on the Church Plain Chant*, 1782, and his *Collection of Motetts*, 1792. The harmonization is by Elizabeth Poston in *The Cambridge Hymnal*, 1967.

278. Now the green blade riseth from the buried grain

J. M. C. Crum's hymn was written to provide words for the old French tune associated with 'Noël nouvelet', and first appears in *The Oxford Book of Carols*, 1928.

NOËL NOUVELET is a French traditional carol melody. The harmonization is that by Martin Shaw in *The Oxford Book of Carols*.

279. Thine be the glory, risen, conquering Son

The hymn 'A toi la gloire' was written by Edmond Budry, pastor in Vevey, Switzerland, during the year 1896 after the death of his first wife, Marie de Hayenbourg. It appeared in the Y.M.C.A. *Hymn Book*, Lausanne, 1904, translated by Richard B. Hoyle, editor of the Y.M.C.A. *Red Triangle*.

MACCABAEUS is an arrangement of the chorus 'See the conquering hero comes' in Handel's oratorio *Judas Maccabaeus*, 1746.

280. Good Joseph had a garden

Alda M. Milner-Barry's hymn was written in 1926 for worship in St. Christopher's College, Canterbury. It is included in *The Anglican Hymn Book*, 1965.

CHERRY TREE CAROL. See 229.

281. At Eastertime the lilies fair

Frederick Jackson's hymn was written for the National Sunday School Union and appeared in *Child Songs*, 1908.

HILARITER (DIE GANZE WELT) first appears in the *Cölner Gesangbuch*, 1623, since when it has been associated with various Easter carols. The harmonization is that of Martin Shaw in *Songs of Praise*, 1925.

282. Come, ye children, sing to Jesus

Frederick Smith's Easter hymn for young people appears in *Children Praising*, 1937, and was included in *Infant Praise*, 1964. It has been slightly altered by the revision committee.

IN BABILONE is a Dutch traditional melody collected by Julius Röntgen of which an arrangement was first published in *The English Hymnal*, 1906, and was the tune set to these words in *Children Praising*.

283. Jesus, Lord, Redeemer

P. M. Kirkland's hymn appeared in *Church Praise*, 1907.

KING'S WESTON was composed by Vaughan Williams for this hymn for *Songs of Praise*, 1925.

284. O clap your hands all ye people

Prose psalm 47 (A.V.), *Omnes gentes, plaudite*. Suitable for use for the Festival of the Ascension. See 3.

PLAIN-SONG TONE VIII, ending 2.

285. Thou hast, O Lord, most glorious

Metrical psalm 68: 18a, 19–20 from *The Scottish Psalter*, 1650. The version in *The Anglo-Genevan Psalter*, 1556, was Sternhold's, which was retained in Scotland in 1564.

EFFINGHAM is a derivative from 'Crasselius'. See 234.

286. The Head that once was crowned with thorns

From Thomas Kelly's *Hymns*, 1820. It is based on Heb. 2: 10. The first line and the idea in the second may have been taken from Bunyan's poem on heaven in *One Thing Needful*, 1664.

ST. MAGNUS (NOTTINGHAM) appeared in the *Divine Companion: or David's Harp new tun'd*, 1709, where it is anonymous. In Riley's *Parochial Harmony*, 1762, it is assigned to Jeremiah Clarke. In Gawthorn's *Harmonia Perfecta*, 1730, it is called 'Nottingham'.

287. The Lord ascendeth up on high

A. T. Russell's hymn first appeared in his *Psalms and Hymns, partly selected and partly original, for the use of the Church of England*, 1851. In *The English Hymnal*, 1906, it was altered to suit the melody 'Nun Freut Euch'.

ASCENDIT DEUS appeared in Schicht's *Allgemeines Choralbuch*, Leipzig, 1819, where it is set to 'So hoff ich denn mit festem Mut'.

288. The eternal gates are lifted up

From Mrs. Alexander's *Hymns Descriptive and Devotional*, 1858. In an earlier form in *Hymns*, 1852, the first line read 'eternal gates'. In 1858 this was altered to 'golden gates'. The original form has been here restored.

PRAETORIUS is from *Harmoniae Hymnorum scholiae Gorlicensis*, Görlitz, 1599. It appeared later in Praetorius's *Musae Sionae*, Görlitz, 1609, and was supposed to have been written by him. There it was set to 'In Bethlehem Ein Kindelein'.

IN ARMOUR BRIGHT had its origin at a choir practice in Belmont Presbyterian Church, Belfast, when a member asked Dr. Norman Hay to set out the characteristics of a good psalm-tune. He took a scrap of paper and wrote down both the melody and parts in about five minutes and handed it to J. K. C. Armour as a present, who then asked what its name should be, to which Hay replied 'In Armour Bright'. Mr. Armour was a member of the revision committee which prepared CH3.

289. Look, ye saints! the sight is glorious

From Thomas Kelly's *Hymns*, 1809, where it is headed 'And He shall reign for ever and ever'.

REGENT SQUARE by Henry Smart was composed for Bonar's 'Glory be to God, the Father'. See 354. It first appeared in *Psalms and Hymns for Divine Worship*, 1867, and takes its name from Regent Square Presbyterian Church, London.

290. God is ascended up on high

Henry More's hymn is from his *Divine Dialogues with Divine Hymns*, 1668. The original had twelve stanzas of which 1, 6, and 8 are given here. Verse 1 reproduces part of a German hymn 'Gen Himmel aufgefahren ist', published in 1601. This in turn was a translation of an older Latin hymn, 'Coelos ascendit hodie', which Neale translated as 'Today, above the sky He soared' in *Medieval Hymns*, 1851.

HERMANN is from *Ein Christlicher Abentreien*, Leipzig, 1554, and Hermann's *Die Sontags Evangelia*, Wittenberg, 1560. In the latter it is set to three hymns. Later it became especially associated with the third, an Easter hymn, 'Erschienen ist der herrlich Tag'. Frere suggests it is derived from the French folk-song, 'Quand Jean Renaud de guerre vint'.

291. Again the morn of gladness

Written by Ellerton and appearing in *Children's Hymns*, 1876.

WIR PFLÜGEN (DRESDEN) in *Lieder für Volkschulen*, Hanover, 1800, is set to the third stanza of 'We plough the fields and scatter'. See 620. It is first attributed to Schulz in Lindner's *Jugenfreud*, Berlin, 1812. Its earliest appearance in England was in *The Bible Class Magazine*, 1854.

292. Away with gloom, away with doubt

From Shillito's poems *Jesus of the Scars*, 1919.

BARNTON was composed for this hymn by William Mathias for CH3.

293. The Saviour died, but rose again

Paraphrase 48: 5-9 on Rom. 8: 34-9 as revised and published in *Scottish Paraphrases*, 1781. The original version was by John Logan, Leith.

ST. ANDREW first appeared in Tans'ur's *The New Harmony of Sion*, 1764, in which it is set to Ps. 150 and headed 'Darby Tune, composed in four parts, W.T.' This may only mean that Tans'ur harmonized it.

294. How glorious Zion's courts appear

Paraphrase 20: 1-5 on Isa. 26: 1-7. The original version was by Watts, in his *Hymns*, 1707, 'How honourable is the place'. It was revised by Hugh Blair and issued in this form in *Scottish Paraphrases*, 1781.

IRISH. See 19.

295. Where high the heavenly temple stands

Paraphrase 58 on Heb. 4: 14-16 differs from the hymn printed by Logan in his *Poems*, 1781, in some details. The original was probably written by Michael Bruce though Logan published it as his own. Here it is given in the form in *Scottish Paraphrases*, 1781, where it first appears.

SOLDAU. See 109.

296. Rejoice, the Lord is King

From Wesley's *Hymn for our Lord's Resurrection*, 1746, omitting the sixth verse. It is based on Phil. 4: 4.

DARWALL'S 148TH was composed by John Darwall for the new version of Ps. 148 in Williams's *New Universal Psalmist*, 1770.

GOPSAL by Handel was composed for this hymn, and is one of three tunes composed by him for Wesley hymns. It received its name from Gopsal House, near Ashby de la Zouch, where his friend Charles Jennens, the composer of the libretto for *The Messiah*, resided. The other two were 'Cannons' for 'Sinners, obey the Gospel word', and 'Fitzwilliam' for 'O Love Divine, how sweet thou art'. The last two are also known as 'The Invitation' and 'Desiring to Love', respectively. All three became unknown, but were rediscovered and appeared as *The Fitzwilliam Music, never before published*, 1827. See 152.

297. All praise to thee, for thou, O King divine

Based on Phil. 2: 5–11. Written by F. B. Tucker for *The Hymnal*, 1940, of the Protestant Episcopal Church of America.

ENGELBERG was composed by Sir Charles V. Stanford for the hymn 'For all the saints' (see 534) in *Hymns Ancient and Modern*, 1904. *The Hymnal* and *Congregational Praise*, 1951, set it to these words.

298. Crown him with many crowns

The original, in six stanzas, appeared in Matthew Bridges's *Hymns of the Heart*, 1851, and his *Passion of Jesus*, 1852, under the text Rev. 19: 12. The present text is a rearrangement of Bridges's verses as they appear in *Church Hymns*, 1871, and Thring's *Church of England Hymn Book*, 1880.

DIADEMATA by Sir George Elvey was composed for this hymn in *Hymns Ancient and Modern*, 1868. The name is taken from the Greek word for 'crowns' in Rev. 19: 12.

299. Blessing and honour and glory and power

A cento from Bonar's hymn, 'The Song of the Lamb', in his *Hymns of Faith and Hope*, 1866, which had eight stanzas, and began with the present second verse. The last stanza of the original is given as the first here.

BLESSING AND HONOUR AND GLORY AND POWER is a Scottish traditional melody, 'Bonnie George Campbell'.

300. At the Name of Jesus

Miss Noel's original hymn had seven stanzas, of which the second and fourth are here omitted. It was a processional hymn for Ascension Day, contributed to her *The Name of Jesus, and other Poems*, 1870. It is based on Phil. 2: 9–10.

IN NOMINE JESU was composed by Arthur Oldham for this hymn for CH3.

CUDDESDON by W. H. Ferguson was composed for this hymn in *The Public School Hymnbook*, 1919.

301. Christ is the world's Redeemer

St. Columba's poem 'Altus prosator vetustus dierum et ingenitus' was used as a hymn in Ireland, and when messengers came to Iona from Pope Gregory the Great and presented him with gifts, among which was a book of Hymns for Holy Week, according to tradition Columba gave them his own hymn to take back to the Pope, who said 'the hymn would be the best of all praises if Colum Cille had not too slightly commended the Trinity "per se" as well as in Its creatures'. While Columba, unlike Gregory, would never have referred to the Trinity as 'It', he admitted the validity of the criticism, and wrote a hymn to the glory of the Trinity, 'In Te, Christe, credentium misererais omnium', from which both this hymn and 397 are taken. This is the second section. Both are printed in Duncan Macgregor's *S. Columba*, 1898, where v. 3 line 7 runs 'Whence He had ne'er departed' (ubi nunquam defuerat). This was a medieval way of asserting the full divinity of Jesus, but it has an awkward sound so the compilers of RCH, 1927, substituted 'in glorious dominion' to prevent any misconception.

MOVILLE is a traditional Irish melody adapted from the Petrie–Stanford *Collection of Irish Airs*, 1855. It is entitled 'Scorching is this love'.

302. Jesus, our hope, our heart's desire

The hymn 'Jesu, nostra redemptio' dates from the seventh or eighth century, and occurs in the Roman, Sarum, York, Aberdeen, and other Breviaries. In the revised *Roman Breviary*, 1632, it begins 'Salutis humanae Sator'. This is the form in Chandler's *Hymns of the Primitive Church*, 1837, and Newman's *Hymni Ecclesiae*, 1838. The present text is Chandler's as emended by the compilers of *Hymns Ancient and Modern*, 1904.

METZLER comes from *Ancient Hymn Melodies and other Church Tunes as used at All Saints' Church, Margaret Street, arranged, composed, and harmonized by Richard Redhead, organist*, 1859. It is also known as 'Redhead No. 66' as he did not give names to his tunes.

303. God is working his purpose out

Ainger wrote this hymn at Eton in 1894, dedicating it to Archbishop Benson. It was published as a leaflet set to the tune 'Benson' by Miss Kingham. It is based upon Hab. 2: 14 and Isa. 11: 9. It was first published in *The Church Missionary Hymnbook*, 1899.

PURPOSE was composed for this hymn by Martin Shaw for *Songs of Praise*, 1931.

304. Join all the glorious names

A cento from the original twelve verses in Watts's *Hymns and Spiritual Songs*, 1709, printed exactly as Watts wrote them except that in v. 4 last line 'beneath' has been changed to 'before'. Watts called the hymn 'The same as the 148th psalm'.

CROFT'S 136TH. See 137.

305. Sing we triumphant hymns of praise

'Hymnum canamus gloriae' for Ascension is usually attributed to Bede. It is found in *The York Hymnal*. The Surtees Society published a version from an eleventh-century manuscript in *Latin Hymns of the Anglo-Saxon Church*, 1851. The text given here is Webb's from *The Hymnal Noted*, 1854, emended by the compilers of *The BBC Hymn Book*, 1951.

SOLEMNIS HAEC FESTIVITAS is a French Church melody. See 42. It comes from the Sequence for the Ascension in the *Paris Gradual*, 1689.

Cross ref. to CHURCH TRIUMPHANT. See 56.

306. Immortal Love, for ever full

From Whittier's thirty-five stanza poem, 'Our Master', which appeared in the Boston *Congregationalist*, 1867, and in his *The Tent on the Beach, and other Poems* of the same year. See 439. It was included in *The Hymnal Companion*, 1890.

FINGAL by J. S. Anderson first appeared in *The Scottish Hymnal*, 1885, where it is set to 'I am not worthy, Holy Lord'. See 570.

Cross ref. to ST. PETER. See 376.

307. 'Lift up your hearts': I hear the summons calling

John MacLeod's hymn, slightly altered by the revision committee, comes from *The Hymnal Appendix*, 1874, which he edited for use in his congregation at Duns, as an appendix to *The Scottish Hymnal*, 1872. It was also included in *The Scottish Mission Hymn Book*, 1912.

PSALM 12 (DONNE SECOURS). See 250.

308. Now at last he takes his throne

This Ascension hymn by Fr. James Quinn, S.J., appears in his *New Hymns for All Seasons*, 1969. Here the first verse is omitted.

JOUISSANCE is from a seventeenth-century melody by Pierre Bonnet, who also wrote the bass, as harmonized by Elizabeth Poston in *The Cambridge Hymnal*, 1967.

309. O Son of Man, our Hero strong and tender

Frank Fletcher wrote this hymn *c.* 1924 for use in Charterhouse School, where he was headmaster. It was included in *The Clarendon Hymn Book*, 1936.

DERRY AIR (LONDONDERRY) is an old Irish melody, which was noted down at Limavady by A. P. Groves, who set it to two Irish songs, 'Erin's Farewell' and 'Erin's Apple-blossom'. In 1912, F. E. Weatherly set it to 'Danny Boy'. John Hughes, Dolgelley, arranged it for *The Baptist Hymn Book*, 1962, where it was set to W. Y. Fullerton's 'I cannot tell'. It is also known as 'The Londonderry Air'. The harmony is that of H. G. Ley in *Songs of Praise*, 1931.

Cross ref. to PSALM 12 (DONNE SECOURS). See 250.

310. The mighty God even the Lord hath spoken

Prose psalm 50: 1–6, 14, 23 (A.V.), *Deus deorum*. Suitable for use during Advent. See 3.

PLAIN-SONG TONE III, ending 5.

311. In beauty of his holiness

Metrical psalm 96: 9, 11–13 from *The Irish Psalter*, 1880.

OLD 44TH was set to Ps. 44 in *The Anglo-Genevan Psalter*, 1556, and continued to be so used in the later English and Scottish psalters. The present form is found in Este's *Psalter*, 1592.

Cross ref. to PRAETORIUS. See 288.

312. Behold! the mountain of the Lord

Paraphrase 18 based on Isa. 2: 2–6. It had appeared in *Scottish Paraphrases*, 1745, 'In latter days the mount of God' by an unknown author. It was possibly revised and v. 3 added by Michael Bruce. Logan included it in his *Poems*, 1781, but it is by Bruce. It is given here in the form in which it appeared in *Scottish Paraphrases*, 1781.

GLASGOW appears in *The Psalm Singer's Pocket Companion, containing great variety of the best English Psalm Tunes . . . Likewise all the Tunes that are usually sung in most parts of Scotland*, 1756. This collection was made by a Glasgow publisher, Thomas Moore.

SOUTHWARK. See 22.

313. Christ is coming! let creation

This hymn, based on Rev. 22: 20, is from J. R. Macduff's *Altar Stones*, 1853, published when he was minister of St. Madoes, Perthshire.

NEANDER (UNSER HERRSCHER) is from Neander's *Glaub-und Liebensübung*, Bremen, 1680, where it is set to the hymn 'Unser Herrscher, unser König'. Originally lines 5 and 6 changed into triple time, but since 1698 the form has been common time throughout.

314. Hark what a sound, and too divine for hearing

F. W. H. Myers's hymn first appears in *Songs of Praise*, 1925.

PSALM 12 (DONNE SECOURS). See 250.

315. 'Wake, awake! for night is flying'

In the last six months of 1597 it is said 1,300 of Philipp Nicolai's parishioners died during the plague. His manse overlooked the churchyard, where there were sometimes as many as thirty funerals a day. From such scenes he turned to the contemplation of the eternal life and published a treatise on *The Joyous Mirror of Life Eternal*, in an appendix to which this hymn, 'Wachet auf! ruft uns die Stimme', first appeared, with the title 'Of the Voice at midnight and the wise Virgins who meet their Heavenly Bridegroom: Matthew xxv'. As well as the parable referred to in its title the hymn was also based on the figure of the Watchman in Isa. 52:8 and the Song of Triumph in heaven in Rev. 19: 6–9. Miss Winkworth's translation is from her *Lyra Germanica*, 1855.

WACHET AUF is attributed to Nicolai and appears in *Freuden Spiegel des ewigen Lebens . . . durch Phillippum Nicolai*, Frankfurt am Main, 1599. The present arrangement of melody and harmony is substantially that of Mendelssohn in *St. Paul*, 1836.

316. Lo! he comes, with clouds descending

Verses 1, 2, and 4 go back to Charles Wesley's form in his *Hymns of Intercession for all Mankind*, 1758, and v. 3 to Cennick's in his *Collection of Sacred Hymns*, 1752, as rearranged by Martin Madan in his *Collection of Psalms and Hymns*, 1760, where it had six stanzas of which the third and fifth have been omitted.

HELMSLEY is generally attributed to Thomas Olivers, but its origin has been much discussed. It appears to be an adaptation of the eighteenth-century ballad, variously known as 'De'il tak' the wars that hurried Billy frae me', or 'Guardian Angels', or 'Miss Catley's Hornpipe'. Sheridan used it for his song, 'When sable night each drooping plant restoring'. Olivers is said to have heard it whistled in the street and noted it down. It appears in a different form in Wesley's *Select Hymns*, 1765. The present is practically that in Madan's *Collection*, 1769.

317. Hail to the Lord's Anointed

Written by Montgomery in 1821 for the Christmas worship of a Moravian settlement, probably at Fulneck in Yorkshire. It appears in his *Original Hymns*, 1853, but had been printed earlier in Adam Clarke's *Commentary on the Bible*, 1822, as a paraphrase of Ps. 72.

MOVILLE. See 301.

Cross ref. to CRÜGER. See 267.

318. Mine eyes have seen the glory of the coming of the Lord

Written six months after the outbreak of the American Civil War. Mrs. Howe, on a visit to Washington, heard the Union troops singing 'John Brown's Body'. It was suggested that she should compose new words for the melody. 'I will', she replied, and the words of the hymn came to her that night; she jotted them down before daybreak. They were first published in *The Atlantic Monthly*, 1862.

VISION by Sir Walford Davies was composed for this hymn and first appeared in *In Hoc Signo*, 1915.

BATTLE HYMN OF THE REPUBLIC by William Steffe apparently came into use c. 1855–60 as a hymn-tune in Charleston, South Carolina, where it was used at Methodist meetings to the words 'Say, brother, will you meet us?' John Macgregor of the Temple brought it to England and had it arranged by the organist, E. J. Hopkins. It was published in 1859, and sold for the benefit of the Ragged School Shoe-black Society. During the American Civil War, Captain Hall Green had it taught to his soldiers, among whom grew up the practice of singing it to the words 'John Brown's body lies a-mouldering in the grave' in honour of a Scottish soldier who lost his life fighting for the Republic. Later Mrs. Edna Dean Proctor wrote words in honour of another John Brown of Harper's Ferry who 'tried to free the negro and the slave'. Since being set to Julia W. Howe's 'Mine eyes have seen the glory' it has been included in many hymnals.

319. Ye servants of the Lord

From Orton's posthumous edition of Doddridge's *Hymns*, 1755, where it was entitled 'The active Christian'.

ST. MICHAEL (OLD 134TH). See 46.

320. Come, thou long-expected Jesus

From Wesley's *Hymns for the Nativity of our Lord*, 1744, where Charles had written it in two eight-line stanzas.

STUTTGART. See 199.

321. The Lord will come and not be slow

Based upon Pss. 82, 85, and 86 from Milton's *Nine of the Psalmes done into Metre*, 1648, in which he prints in italics any words to which there is nothing to correspond in the Hebrew, and also in the margin gives some literal renderings of the Hebrew.

PSALM 107. See 140.

MONTROSE. See 133.

322. Thy Kingdom come, O God

From Hensley's *Hymns for the Minor Sundays*, 1867, where it was intended for Advent. Verse 3 line 3 had 'Oppression, lust, and crime'.

ST. CECILIA by Hayne appeared in *The Merton Tune Book: A Collection of Hymn Tunes used in the Church of St. John Baptist, Oxford, Compiled by the Rev. H. W. Sargent, M.A. Edited and Arranged by the Rev. L. G. Hayne*, Oxford, 1863, where it was composed for 'Thy way, not mine, O Lord'.

323. 'Thy Kingdom come!'—on bended knee

Written by F. L. Hosmer on 12 June 1891, for the Commencement of the Meadville Theological School, Pennsylvania. It was entitled 'The Day of God' and first appears in his *Thoughts of God*, 1894, and in Britain in Horder's *Worship Song*, 1905, and *The English Hymnal*, 1906.

IRISH. See 19.

324. Blest is the man, O God

Toplady's hymn, 'Your harps, ye trembling saints' was first printed in *The Gospel Magazine*, 1772, where it consisted of eight eight-line stanzas. A version of seven four-line verses appeared in RCH, 1927. Verses 7, 4–5, and 3 were printed in *Congregational Praise*, 1951. Here the selection is vv. 7, 4–6.

BUCER appeared in *Cantica Laudis, edited by Lowell Mason and G. J. Webb,* 1850, which says it is an adaptation from Robert Schumann. This source has not been traced.

325. From glory to glory advancing, we praise thee, O Lord

This metrical version of the opening words of the Litany of Dismissal in the Greek *Liturgy of St. James* (fifth century) was made for *The English Hymnal,* 1906, by C. W. Humphreys.

LOCHWINNOCH was composed by Robin Orr for this hymn in CH3.

326. Bless the Lord, O my soul

Prose psalm 104: 1–5, 30–4 (A.V.), *Benedic, anima mea.* Suitable for use at Pentecost. See 3.

PLAIN-SONG TONE III, ending 5.

327. O day of joy and wonder

Violet Buchanan's hymn was written in 1957, and first appears in *The Anglican Hymn Book,* 1965.

CRÜGER. See 267.

328. Hail thee, Festival Day!

The line 'Salve festa dies toto venerabilis aevo' comes from a poem by Fortunatus, which begins 'Tempora florigero'. See 272. Many Continental and English Processionals contain hymns taking the opening line from Fortunatus, but are otherwise quite different. This is true here also. It is taken from the fourteenth-century *York Processional.* The translation is by Gabriel Gillett and appears first in *The English Hymnal,* 1906.

SALVE FESTA DIES was composed by Vaughan Williams. It is from *The English Hymnal.*

329. O joy! because the circling year

The hymn 'Beata nobis gaudia Anni reduxit orbita' for Whitsuntide is sometimes ascribed to Hilary of Poitiers. He and his family became Christians in 350, and a few years later he was elected Bishop of Poitiers by popular acclamation. The evidence that he was the author is far from conclusive. Various versions are found in eleventh-century manuscripts. It is also in the Roman *Breviary* and *Latin Hymns of the Anglo Saxon Church,* 1851. The present text is Ellerton's as revised by the compilers of *Hymns Ancient and Modern,* 1904. See 330.

GONFALON ROYAL by Percy Buck was written for Harrow School for the hymn 'Vexilla regis prodeunt'. See 257. From this it received its name. A gonfalon was a banner with streamers. It was first printed in *The Public School Hymnbook,* 1919, where it is set to 'Lord of all being, throned afar'. See 34.

330. Rejoice! the year upon its way

Another version of 329. The translation is that of R. E. Roberts, and appears in *The Baptist Hymn Book*, 1962.

GONFALON ROYAL. See 329.

331. When God of old came down from heaven

From Keble's Whit Sunday poem as it appeared in the *Christian Year*, 1827, omitting the second, fifth, eighth, and tenth stanzas. The text on which it is based is Acts 2: 2–4.

WINCHESTER OLD. See 138.

332. Lord God, the Holy Ghost

From Montgomery's *Original Hymns*, 1853, but it had appeared earlier in Cottrill's *Selection*, 1819, headed 'Whit-Sunday', and in Montgomery's *Christian Psalmist*, 1825.

HAMPTON comes from *Psalmody in Miniature, by Aaron Williams, c.* 1770. There and in a contemporary *Collection of Psalm Tunes in Three Parts ... by Is. Smith* it is named 'Durham'. The present is the original form of the melody.

333. Thou shalt arise, and mercy yet

Metrical psalm 102: 13–18. Verses 1–2 are from the second version in *The Irish Psalter*, 1880, and vv. 3–4 from *The Scottish Psalter*, 1650. The version in the Scottish, 1564, was by John Craig.

DUKE STREET appears first in *A Select Collection of Psalm and Hymn Tunes ... By the late Henry Boyd, Teacher of Psalmody*, 1793, where it is headed 'Addison's 19th Psalm' (see 143) and no composer's name is given. In *Euphonia*, 1805, a collection of tunes, edited by W. Dixon, it is found under its present name and attributed to John Hatton.

334. Holy Spirit, ever living

Timothy Rees's hymn appears first in his *Sermons and Hymns*. It was included in *Hymns for Church and School*, 1964. Here v. 1 has been omitted.

ABBOT'S LEIGH was composed by Cyril Taylor for use in BBC broadcast services. It was printed in leaflet form by the Oxford University Press in 1941 with the words 'Glorious things of thee are spoken'. See 421. It is included in *Hymns Ancient and Modern*, 1950, *Congregational Praise*, 1951, and *The BBC Hymn Book*, 1951.

335. Love of the Father, Love of God the Son

Robert Bridges's hymn is based on the twelfth-century 'Amor Patris et Filii'. It is printed in *Lateinische Hymnen des Mittelalters, aus Handschriften herausgegeben und erklart von F. J. Mone*, Freiburg in Baden, 1853. Bridges's version was published in *The Yattendon Hymnal*, 1899.

MAGDA was composed by Vaughan Williams for the hymn 'Saviour, again to thy dear name we raise' (see 649) in *Songs of Praise*, 1925.

Cross ref. to SONG 22. See 108.

336. Our blest Redeemer, ere he breathed

Six of the seven stanzas in the original form of Miss Auber's hymn as it appeared in her *Spirit of the Psalms*, 1829.

ESSEX was composed by Gustav Holst for this hymn in *The Public School Hymnbook*, 1919.

ST. CUTHBERT was composed for this hymn by J. B. Dykes in *Hymns Ancient and Modern*, 1861.

337. For thy gift of God the Spirit

Edith M. Clarkson's hymn appears in *Hymns of Faith*, 1964.

LAUS DEO (REDHEAD NO. 46) is from *Church Hymn Tunes, ancient and modern, for the several seasons of the Christian Year ... selected, composed, and edited by Richard Redhead*, 1853. Because Redhead did not give names to his tunes but called them by his own name with a number, it is also known as 'Redhead No. 46'. In the *Merton Tune Book*, 1863, it is headed 'German Choral', but no such source has been traced.

338. Spirit of mercy, truth and love

The author is unknown. It comes from *Psalms, Hymns and Anthems sung in the Chapel of the Hospital for the Maintenance and Education of Exposed and Deserted Young Children*, 1774.

HEREFORD, composed by S. S. Wesley, first appeared in his *European Psalmist*, 1872, and receives its name from his being for a period organist of Hereford Cathedral.

339. O breath of life, come sweeping through us

Bessie P. Head's hymn was written *c.* 1914. It was included in *Hymns of Faith*, 1964.

SUNSET by G. G. Stocks was composed for the hymn 'Before the day draws near its ending'. See 53. It first appears in *Repton School: Hymns for Use in Chapel*, 1924.

Cross ref. to LES COMMANDEMENS DE DIEU. See 586.

340. Spirit of Light—Holy

This hymn by A. M. Jones first appears in *Africa Praise*, 1969, where it is set to a Yoruba melody.

MONIKIE was composed by David Dorward for this hymn for CH3.

341. How great the harvest is

This hymn by Percy Dearmer first appears in *The Oxford Book of Carols*, 1928. It also appears in *Songs of Praise*, 1936.

VREUCHTEN. See 271.

342. Come, Holy Ghost, our souls inspire

'Veni, Creator Spiritus' dates from the twelfth century. This is from Cosin's *Collection of Private Devotions in the Practice of the Ancient Church*, 1627. He was one of the revisers of the BCP in 1661–2, and thus his version of the 'Veni Creator' came to be inserted in the Ordinal.

VENI CREATOR is from *Vesperale Romanorum*, Mechlin, 1848. The plain-song melody in its original form is older than the hymn. It was earlier associated with Ambrose's Easter hymn, 'Hic est dies verus Dei'. Mechlin, plain-song having been long forgotten, tried to revive it in France and Belgium in the nineteenth century.

343. Alleluia

The *Alleluia* is derived from two Hebrew words meaning 'Praise the Lord' (Yah(weh)) and occurs frequently in the Book of Psalms. According to tradition, the early Christians on Easter Day saluted each other with the exclamation, 'Alleluia, the Lord is risen'. At an early date the word passed into liturgical use. In the Eastern Church it is closely associated with the Great Entrance. It occurs once at the close of the Cherubic Hymn in the Greek liturgies of St. James and St. Mark, and three times at the same position in the *Liturgy of St. Chrysostom*. It also comes before the Gospel in all the liturgies, except Ethiopic. In the Western Church in the Mozarabic rite and probably the Gallican its normal position is after the Gospel. In the former it was used all the year round until the fourth Council of Toledo ordered its omission during Lent. In Africa use of the Alleluia was confined to Sundays and to Easter and Ascensiontide. In the *Roman Mass* it is used after the Gradual, before the Gospel. Sozomen says *c.* 450 that it was only sung on Easter Day (or perhaps Eastertide). Later it came to be omitted from Septuagesima to Holy Saturday. In the *Breviary* it is said after the opening 'Gloria Patri' at all the Hours except from Septuagesima to Maundy Thursday.

ALLELUIA. The setting for the single 'Alleluia' is sixteenth-century German. The three settings for the threefold 'Alleluia' are (*a*) traditional and (*b*) and (*c*) both sixteenth-century German. The common metre setting is 'Montrose'. See 133.

344. Glory be to the Father, and to the Son, and to the Holy Ghost

Towards the end of the fourth century there was introduced side by side with the 'Psalmus responsorius' another type of psalmody, the antiphon, which consisted of a psalm chanted by two choirs alternately. This practice began at Antioch in the time of Bishop Leontius (344–57). Whatever the form of psalmody might be, it was a general custom for the psalm to end with the doxology, 'Gloria Patri'. While there has been much discussion on the subject it would appear that a metrical 'Gloria Patri' was associated with the metrical psalms from *c.* 1567. In the 1595 edition of *The Scottish Psalter* there are thirty-four, one for each metre, and *The Psalms of David*, 1635, thirty-five. When sympathizers with the English Brownists began to give up using the Lord's Prayer, *Apostles' Creed*, and the 'Gloria Patri', the General Assembly in 1642 denounced the spirit of innovation and commended the 'laudable practices'. With regard to the last, Robert Baillie showed in detail its

Scriptural character, and retorted to those who opposed it as part of the English BCP and the Roman Massbook, 'This proves it not to be any worse than the Lord's Prayer and the Belief (Apostles' Creed) which are both in these evil books too!' However, it was omitted from the Westminster *Directory for the Public Worship of God*, 1645, and fell out of use. Metrical 'Gloria Patri' were printed in *The Irish Psalter*, 1880, and *The Scottish Psalter*, 1929, and prose versions to the Parisian Tone in the first edition of *The Church Hymnary*, 1898, and RCH, 1927. It was also given in *The Scottish Psalter*, 1929. Metrical 'Gloria Patri' are given for each of the psalms in CH3.

PLAIN-SONG TONUS PARISIANUS is a traditional musical phrase, which can 'be regarded as a "leit-motif" of the Genevan Reformation, inasmuch as its shape was practically dictated by the new technique of singing a broad melody in union instead of singing choral polyphony'.

345. We praise thee, O God

Canticles technically are songs from the Bible other than from the Psalms. The term is also applied to the *Te Deum*, which has been described as 'the greatest hymn of the Christian Church outside the Bible'. It has been attributed to Ambrose, Augustine, and Niceta, Bishop of Remesiana at the end of the fourth century, but the evidence while favouring the last is far from conclusive. The earliest versions are found in the *Bangor Antiphonary*, Milan *Breviary*, Bamberg and St. Gall manuscripts. It consists of two separate hymns and a litany—first a hymn of praise to the Trinity, second a hymn in praise of Christ, and third a prayer based on Pss. 28: 9, 31: 1, 33: 22, 123: 3, and 145: 2. Luther ranked it third to the Apostles' and Nicene Creeds, and the English translation in the BCP is probably the work of Cranmer. It was included in both of the earlier editions of *The Church Hymnary*.

CHANTS   Set I   (a)   Boyce in D double.
                      (b)   Cooke in G double.
                      (c)   Soaper in D double.

           Set II   (a)   Stanford in A flat double.
                      (b)   Pye in E flat double.
                      (c)   Goss in A flat double.

346. O Lord, thou art my God and King

Metrical psalm 145: 1–6 from the second version in *The Scottish Psalter*, 1650. That in the Scottish book, 1564, was John Craig's.

DUKE STREET. See 333.

347. Praise ye the Lord. God's praise within

Metrical psalm 150 from *The Scottish Psalter*, 1650. That in the Scottish book, 1564, was Thomas Norton's from the English book, 1562.

CREDITON. See 168.

348. Sing a new song to Jehovah

This version of the 98th Psalm is found in the Free Church's *Paraphrases, Hymns and new Versions of some of the Psalms*, 1871. It also appears in *Scottish*

Psalmody (revised edition, 1873) whence it was taken into *The Irish Psalter*, 1880. In the Free Church, *Report of the Committee on Psalmody* (May 1866) it is stated that this version has been taken from the Psalter of the Associate Synod of America. It has been impossible to trace the name of the author.
STUTTGART. See 199.

349. O sing unto the Lord a new song
Prose psalm 98 (A.V.), *Cantate Domino*. See 3.
CHANTS Thalben-Ball in D double.
Crotch in A double.

350. O give thanks to the Lord for he is good
This is the Gelineau version of Ps. 136 (LXX 135). It first appeared in *Formules Psalmodiques*. The English version was published in *Twenty-four Psalms and a Canticle to the psalmody of Joseph Gelineau*. See 67.

This setting is that given in the above.

351. O thou my soul, bless God the Lord
Metrical psalm 103: 1–5 from *The Scottish Psalter*, 1650. Sternhold's version appeared in *The Anglo-Genevan Psalter*, 1556. It was retained in the Scottish book, 1564, replaced by Kethe's in 1595 and 1611, and reintroduced in 1633.

COLESHILL is not an original tune, but is really a modified form of 'Dundee', which, named 'Windsor', had appeared in Este, 1592, and Ravenscroft, 1621. In Barton's *Book of Psalms in Metre*, 1644, there is a tune headed 'London long tune, proper for solemn ditties and used everywhere', which bears a close resemblance to 'Coleshill'. The earliest appearance of the tune in its present form is in *The Psalms of David in Metre. Newly Translated. With Amendments. By William Barton, M.A. And Set to the best Psalm Tunes, in Two Parts, viz. Treble and Bass*, 1706, by Thomas Smith, where it is named 'Dublin Tune'. The two William Bartons were father and son. The name 'Coleshill' is attached to it in *A Collection of Psalm Tunes in Four Parts. Fitted to the Old and New Versions*, 1711, where it is set to Ps. 116. It first appears in Scotland in Thomas Moore's *Psalm Singer's Delightful Pocket Companion*, 1762, with the note, 'Sing "Dundee" (south of the Border called "Windsor") Bass and Counter to this tune'.

Cross ref. to KILMARNOCK. See 69.

352. Holy, holy, holy, Lord God Almighty
This paraphrase of Rev. 4: 8–11 was written by Heber, but not published till after his death in *A Selection of Psalms and Hymns for the Parish Church of Banbury*, 1826. Heber designed his hymns to be sung 'between the Nicene Creed and the sermon' in Anglican worship.

NICAEA was composed by Dykes for this hymn for *Hymns Ancient and Modern*, 1861. Its name is taken from the Council of Nicaea, 325. Its similarity to 'Wachet auf' may be noted, but probably Dykes and Nicolai were drawing upon and developing traditional material quite independently.

353. Round the Lord in glory seated

From Mant's *Ancient Hymns*, 1837. Originally it consisted of four eight-line stanzas. Here the first four lines of v. 3 and the last four of v. 4 have been omitted. Its basis is Isa. 6: 1–3, which is clearer from the first verse, here omitted, which begins 'Bright the vision that delighted'.

RUSTINGTON by C. H. H. Parry first appears in *The Westminster Abbey Hymn Book*, 1897, and *Hymns Ancient and Modern*, 1904.

Cross ref. to AUSTRIAN HYMN. See 37.

354. Glory be to God the Father

Written specially for *Psalms and Hymns for Divine Worship*, 1867, of the Presbyterian Church of England, though it was included in the author's *Hymns of Faith and Hope*, 1866.

REGENT SQUARE was composed for this hymn. See 289.

355. God reveals his presence

From Tersteegen's *Geistliches Blumengärtlein*, Frankfurt am Main, 1729, entitled 'Remembrance of the glorious and delightful presence of God'. See 96. The English version is from Foster and Miller's English Moravian *Collection of Hymns*, 1789, as revised by Mercer in his *Church Psalter and Hymnbook*, 1854.

GOTT IST GEGENWÄRTIG (GRÖNINGEN) (ARNSBERG) appears in Neander's *Glaub- und Liebesübung*, Bremen, 1680, where it is set to the hymn 'Wunderbarer König, Herrscher von uns allen'. In later German collections it is associated with 'Gott ist gegenwärtig', of which the present hymn is a translation.

356. My God, how wonderful thou art

The original in Faber's *Jesus and Mary*, 1849, had nine stanzas, and was entitled 'The Eternal Father'. In v. 5 line 2 'half so mild' has been changed to 'e'er'.

WESTMINSTER by Turle appeared under the name 'Birmingham' in *The Psalmist: A Collection of Psalm and Hymn Tunes ... edited by Vincent Novello*, 1836.

357. Eternal Light! eternal Light

According to Thomas Binney, writing in 1866, 'this hymn was written about forty years ago, and was set to music and published by Power of the Strand, on behalf of some charitable object to which the profits went'. Its first appearance in a collection appears to have been in *Lyra Britannica*, 1867.

NICOLAUS (LOBT GOTT) by Nicolaus Herman is first found in *Ein Christlicher Abentreien*, Leipzig, 1554, set to the words 'Kommt her, ihr Lieben Schwesterlein', and in *Die Sontags Evangelia*, Wittenberg, 1560, set to Hermann's hymn, 'Lobt Gott, ihr Christen, alle gleich'. Bach, whose version is given here, used the tune in his cantata for the Third Christmas Day, and in his marriage cantata 'Dem Gerechten muss das Licht immer wieder aufgehen'.

358. The God of Abraham praise

Written, probably in 1770, immediately after Olivers had heard Meyer Lyon, a chorister in the Great Synagogue, Duke's Place, London, sing the *Yigdal* or Hebrew Confession of Faith. It is read at the opening of the morning Service, but is sung to traditional tunes on the eve of the Sabbath and on the evenings of the Jewish Festivals. It is believed to have been written by Daniel ben Judah Dayan in 1404 and is based on the thirteen creeds of Moses ben Maimon. Olivers showed the hymn to a friend, saying, 'Look at this—I have rendered it from the Hebrew, giving it as far as I could a Christian character, and I have called on Leoni the Jew who has given me a Synagogue Melody to suit it. Here is the tune, and it is called "Leoni"'. It was first published as a tract entitled 'A Hymn to the God of Abraham', which passed through eight editions. Then it appeared in Wesley's *Pocket Hymnbook for the use of Christians of all Denominations*, 1785. Few hymns are so biblical as this for almost every line contains a reference or allusion to Scripture.

LEONI was the liturgical name for Meyer Lyon.

359. Praise the Lord, his glories show

A version of Ps. 150 from Lyte's *The Spirit of the Psalms*, 1834.

LLANFAIR by Robert Williams is named 'Bethel' in the composer's manuscript book, and dated 14 July 1817. It appeared in Parry's *Peroriaeth Hyfryd*, 1837, harmonized by John Roberts, Henllan.

360. Praise, my soul, the King of heaven

This free paraphrase of Ps. 103 is given in the exact form of the hymn as first published in Lyte's *Spirit of the Psalms*, 1834.

PRAISE, MY SOUL was composed by Goss for this hymn. It first appeared in *The Supplemental Hymn and Tune Book, compiled by the Rev. R. Brown-Borthwick. Third edition, with new Appendix*, 1869.

361. Let all the world in every corner sing

As in *The Temple*, published in 1633, the year after Herbert's death; except that the refrain is repeated at the beginning of the second stanza. It is held that Herbert did not write his hymns for congregational singing. They were meant for reading. The fact that he entitled this one 'Antiphon', however, shows that it ought to be sung, possibly with one voice and a chorus responding, 'Let all the world in every corner sing, my God and King'.

AUGUSTINE by Erik Routley first appears in *Hymns for Church and School*, 1964.

LUCKINGTON by Basil Harwood was composed for this hymn for *The Oxford Hymnbook*, 1908.

362. From all that dwell below the skies

A paraphrase of Ps. 117 from Watts's *Psalms of David*, 1719. The original lacked the Alleluias and had in v. 1 'by every tongue', not 'in every tongue'.

LASST UNS ERFREUEN. See 30.

363. Ye holy angels bright

From 'A Psalm of Praise to the tune of Psalm cxlviii' in sixteen verses, which Baxter appended to *The Poor Man's Family Book*, 1672. It was rewritten by Gurney for his *Collection of Hymns for Public Worship*, 1838, and reshaped by Chope in his *Hymnal*, 1858. It also appears in *Church Hymns*, 1871.

CROFT'S 136TH. See 137.

ST. JOHN. See 135.

364. King of glory, King of peace

From Herbert's *Temple*, 1633, under the heading 'Praise'. It was included in the *Wellington College Hymn Book*, 1902. and *The English Hymnal*, 1906.

GWALCHMAI was composed by Joseph David Jones and first appeared in Stephen's *Llyfr Tonau ac Emynau*, 1868, a collection of hymns adopted by the Welsh Congregational Union.

365. For the might of thine arm we bless thee

Silvester Horne wrote this hymn for use at Whitefield's Tabernacle, London. It was suggested by Mrs. Heman's 'Hymn of the Vaudois Mountaineers' beginning 'For the strength of the hills we bless thee', which was inspired by the thought of the mountains as the defence of God's people. It first appeared in *The Fellowship Hymnbook*, 1909.

CORMAC is a traditional Irish melody from the *Feis Ceoil Collection of Irish Music*. It is the melody of an Irish song, beginning 'Down by the salley gardens'.

366. Sing to the Lord a joyful song

First issued in Monsell's *Hymns of Love and Praise for the Church's Year*, 1863, and later in his *Parish Hymnal*, 1873. It is based on Ps. 145: 1–2.

GONFALON ROYAL. See 329.

367. For the beauty of the earth

The original form of Pierpoint's hymn as it appeared in Shipley's *Lyra Eucharistica*, 1864, omitting the last three stanzas, and with 'brain's delight' altered to 'mind's delight' in v. 3 with the author's approval. It was meant as a Communion hymn and entitled 'The Sacrifice of Praise'.

MOSELEY by John Joubert first appears in *Hymns for Church and School*, 1964, where it is set to these words.

LUCERNA LAUDONIAE was composed for this hymn by David Evans for RCH, 1927.

368. Now thank we all our God

Martin Rinkart's 'Nun danket alle Gott', written *c.* 1630, was a paraphrase of Ecclus. 50: 22–4. It first appeared in *Jesu Herz-büchlein*, Leipzig, 1636. The first two verses were composed as a grace after meals, to be sung by his family, the third was added later as a doxology. The translation is from Catherine Winkworth's *Lyra Germanica*, 1858.

NUN DANKET is from Crüger's *Praxis Pietatis Melica*, Berlin, 1648, where it is set to 'Nun danket alle Gott'. The arrangement here is substantially that by Mendelssohn in his *Lobgesang*, the harmony reduced from six parts to four.

369. God and Father, we adore thee

This hymn is based on v. 1 attributed to John Nelson Darby, the founder of Plymouth Brethrenism. It appeared in Neatby's *History of the Plymouth Brethren*, 1901, and *The British Weekly*, 1901. When the drafting committee of the Presbyterian Church of England were preparing *Church Praise*, 1907, they asked Hugh Falconer to write a Christmas hymn with some reference to 'the family idea' or 'to the forbears who are much in people's minds at this season'. He took this verse as a starting-point altering 'Christ' to 'Son' in the second line. Verse 6 is also a modification of Darby's verse, otherwise the hymn is Falconer's.

LAUS DEO. See 337.

370. When morning gilds the skies

'Beim frühen Morgenlicht' is an anonymous hymn which appears in the *Katholisches Gesangbuch*, Würzburg, 1828. Another form appears in Von Ditfurth's *Fränkische Volkslieder*, Leipzig, 1858. Caswall's translation appears first in Formby's *Catholic Hymns*, 1854. This with an additional eight verses is given in his *Masque of Mary*, 1858, and again in his *Hymns and Poems*, 1873. The present text is by Robert Bridges in *The Yattendon Hymnal*, 1899.

PSALM 3 (O SEIGNEUR) was composed or arranged by Bourgeois for *The French Psalter*, 1551. Slightly altered in *The Anglo-Genevan Psalter*, 1561, it was set to Kethe's version of Ps. 122, both of which were adopted in the complete *English Psalter*, 1562, and *The Scottish Psalter*, 1564. A setting by David Peebles is also given in the *St. Andrews MS. Psalter*, 1566. The arrangement is by Kenneth Elliott.

371. O for a thousand tongues, to sing

A selection from Charles Wesley's original eighteen stanzas in *Hymns and Sacred Poems*, 1740, where it was entitled 'For the Anniversary Day of One's Conversion'. It was written on 21 May 1738, the first anniversary of his great spiritual change, being suggested by the remark of Peter Böhler, the Moravian missionary to whom he owed that change, 'Had I a thousand tongues I would praise Him with them all'. Since John Wesley's arrangement in *The Wesleyan Hymnbook*, 1780, the first stanza has generally been put last as here.

RICHMOND first appeared in Haweis's *Carmina Christo*, 1792, which he edited and to which he contributed some original hymns. It was set to 'O Thou from whom all goodness flows'. The present form is by Samuel Webbe, the younger.

372. Ye servants of God, your Master proclaim

Charles Wesley's original in *Hymns for Times of Trouble and Persecution*, 1744, had six stanzas.

LAUDATE DOMINUM by Sir Hubert Parry was published in *Hymns Ancient and Modern*, 1922. It is an arrangement of one of his own anthems 'Hear my words, O ye people', which he composed for the Festival of the Salisbury Diocesan Festival Association. It was written for Sir Henry Baker's 'O praise ye the Lord, praise Him in the height', which forms the concluding part of the anthem.

373. To the Name of our Salvation

The Latin original, 'Gloriosi Salvatoris', cannot be traced earlier than the fifteenth century. The author is unknown. It is found in the *Meissen Breviary*, 1517, and headed 'In festo S. Nominis Jesu'. Neale's text in his *Hymni Ecclesiae*, 1851, is from the *Liège Breviary*. It is given here as revised in *Hymns Ancient and Modern*, 1861.

TANTUM ERGO SACRAMENTUM is one of the *Chants Ordinaires de l'Office Divin*, Paris, 1881. It is certainly much older, possibly a folk-song, but its source has not been discovered. It was introduced into England by Basil Harwood who arranged it for *The Oxford Hymn Book*, 1908.

374. To God be the glory! great things he hath done

Written by Frances van Alstyne (*née* Crosby), who was born blind. It is from her *Brightest and Best*, 1875.

ST. DENIO (JOANNA). See 32.

375. Fairest Lord Jesus

'Schönster Herr Jesu' first appeared in the *Münster Gesangbuch*, 1677. The author is unknown. Lilian Stevenson's translation first appeared in *Cantate Domino*, Geneva, 1924, the hymn-book of the World Student Christian Federation.

SCHÖNSTER HERR JESU (ST. ELISABETH) is an eighteenth-century Silesian melody. Its history is difficult to disentangle. It is sometimes called 'Crusaders' Melody' or 'Pilgrims' from a tradition associating it with being sung by Westphalian pilgrims on their way to Jerusalem, or from Franz Liszt having in 1862 introduced it into his oratorio, *St. Elisabeth*, as part of the Crusaders' march. All this, however, appears to be imaginary. Baumker calls it a folk-tune which he collected as it was sung by haymakers in the countryside of Silesia in 1836. It then appeared in Hoffmann and Richter's *Schlesicher Volkslieder*, Leipzig, 1842. Its introduction to English-speaking singers was through *Cantate Domino*.

376. How sweet the Name of Jesus sounds

Contributed by Newton to the *Olney Hymns*, 1779, and entitled 'The Name of Jesus'. It is based on Canticles 1. 3. One verse is omitted.

ST. PETER is from Reinagle's *Psalm Tunes for the Voice and the Pianoforte*, 1830, where it is set to Ps. 118. It is named after the church in Oxford of which the composer was organist.

377. Jesus, the very thought of thee

This hymn with 378 and 571 are short centos from a long Latin hymn 'Jesu dulcis memoria' of forty-two stanzas from the eleventh century. It has been attributed to several authors, but commonly to Bernard of Clairvaux. This is extremely doubtful, probably quite inaccurate. Caswall's translation was printed in his *Lyra Catholica*, 1849, then in his *Hymns and Poems*, 1863. Moffatt in the *Handbook to the Church Hymnary, Revised Edition*, 1928, correctly points out, 'Short extracts really give a better impression of the (Latin) hymn than a complete rendering would, for the quatrains circle round the same theme without developing any thought, and they are unequal in quality'.

WINDSOR (DUNDEE) is found in *The Booke of the Musicke of M. William Damon, late one of her maiesties Musitions: conteining all the tunes of David's Psalmes, as they are ordinarily soung in the Church: most excellently by him composed into 4 parts*, 1591. In this book 'Dundee' appears for the first time as a psalm-tune, but it is probably an adaptation from one of the tunes in Tye's *Actes of the Apostles*, 1553. The tune in question is set to chapter 3. See 22. It is next found in *The Whole Booke of Psalmes with their wonted tunes . . . by Thomas Este*, 1592, where it is placed among 'those tunes newly added in this booke', and is set to Ps. 116, the harmony being by G. Kirby. No name is given to the tune, but in three later editions it is called 'Suffolk Tune'. In Ravenscroft's *Psalter*, 1621, it is named 'Windsor or Eaton' and classified among 'English tunes'. Its earliest appearance in Scotland is in *The Scottish Psalter*, 1615, where it is printed among the Common Tunes and headed 'Dundie Tune'.

METZLER (REDHEAD NO. 66). See 302.

378. O Jesus, King most wonderful

This is another section of 'Jesu dulcis memoria' beginning at the ninth stanza, 'Jesu, Rex admirabilis'. The version is from Caswall's *Lyra Catholica*, 1849. See 377, 571.

METZLER (REDHEAD NO. 66). See 302.

379. My God, I love thee; not because

The Latin poem, 'O Deus, ego amo Te', in *Coeleste Palmetum*, Cologne, 1669, is a version of a Spanish sonnet, but there seems to be no valid evidence for the tradition which ascribes the poem to St. Francis Xavier. Caswall's version is from his *Lyra Catholica*, 1849, and his *Hymns and Poems*, 1873.

SONG 67 (ST. MATTHIAS). See 41.

380. Man of Sorrows! wondrous Name

This hymn by P. P. Bliss, as it appeared in *The International Lessons Monthly*, 1875, was entitled 'What a name'. It echoes Isa. 53: 3.

MAN OF SORROWS (GETHSEMANE) by P. P. Bliss as in *Sacred Songs and Solos*, 1883.

381. I will sing the wondrous story

F. H. Rowley, when minister of the First Baptist Church of North Adams, Massachusetts, wrote this hymn on the suggestion of a young singer Peter Bilhorn. The text of the hymn when included in *Sacred Songs and Solos*, 1883, was altered, but the author never sanctioned these changes. The present version, with the exception of the last line, is as in the original manuscript.

HYFRYDOL by R. H. Prichard is from *Cyfaill y Cantorion* and *Haleliwiah Drachefn*, 1855, edited by Griffith Roberts.

382. All hail, the power of Jesus' Name

This is a selection from the original eight stanzas, entitled 'On the Resurrection, the Lord is King', which first appeared anonymously in *The Gospel Magazine*, 1780. Even when Perronet issued his *Occasional Verses*, in which he included it, he did not reveal his authorship directly; the one indication is in some acrostic verses which disclose his name.

MILES LANE was printed in *The Gospel Magazine*, 1779, with one verse of the hymn but without author's or composer's name. Shortly afterwards it appeared in Addington's *Collection of Psalm Tunes*, 1780, under the name 'Miles Lane', which is an abbreviation of St. Michael's Lane, the site in the eighteenth century of both St. Michael's and a Meetinghouse. Shrubsole is named here as the composer.

383. Come, children, join to sing

The original hymn in Bateman's *Sacred Melodies*, 1843, had five stanzas.

MADRID first appeared as a hymn-tune in *The Spanish Hymn, arranged and composed for the Concerts of the Musical Fund Society of Philadelphia, by Benjamin Carr. The Air from an ancient Spanish Melody. Printed from the condensed score of the Society, and presented to the Composer as a tribute of respect and regard by some of the members, his friends. Philadelphia, 1826*, in which the preface states the music was performed on 29 December 1824. Under the name 'Spanish Chant' the tune appears in *A Collection of Metrical Versions . . . by M. Burgoyne*, 1827.

384. Come, let us remember the joys of the town

Doris Gill's hymn appears in *Sunday School Praise*, 1958, where it had five verses. The second and third are here omitted.

TOWN JOYS is an English traditional melody, the arrangement being by Martin Shaw in *Sunday School Praise*.

385. It is a thing most wonderful

How's hymn, based on 1 John 4: 10, first appeared in *Children's Hymns*, 1872. Only the first, second, sixth, and seventh verses are given here.

HERONGATE is an English traditional melody arranged by Vaughan Williams from a folk-song sung in Essex to a ballad about a deserted maiden, called 'Died for love'. It first appeared in *The English Hymnal*, 1906.

Cross ref. to SOLOTHURN. See 99.

386. Praise him, praise him, all ye little children

This hymn, written *c.* 1890, is anonymous and first appears in Carey Bonner's *Child Songs*, 1908.

PRAISE HIM was composed by Carey Bonner for *The Sunday School Hymnary*, 1905.

387. The Lord's my Shepherd, I'll not want

Metrical psalm 23 from *The Scottish Psalter*, 1650. William Whittingham's version to the eight-line tune of Ps. 3 was included in *The Anglo-Genevan Psalter*, 1556, and retained in the Scottish book, 1564.

SEARCHING FOR LAMBS is an English traditional melody. It is taken from *Sunday School Praise*, 1958, where it is called 'Simple Babe'.

WILTSHIRE was long known in Scotland as 'New St. Ann' because it was ascribed to Croft. It first appeared in *Divine Amusement; Being a Selection of the most admired Psalms, Hymns, and Anthems used at St. James's Chapel, c.* 1795. Smart, when organist, set it to Ps. 48. Since then it has been altered considerably, and its present form first appears in Henderson's *Church Melodies*, 1856.

CRIMOND is held by some to have been composed by Jessie S. Irvine and harmonized by David Grant for *The Northern Psalter*, 1872, edited by William Carnie. This psalter began as a series of *Fly Leaves of Psalm and Hymn Tunes* in 1859. Others hold it was composed and harmonized by Grant. The editor thinks the latter to be the more likely. Originally it was set to the hymn 'I am the Way, the Truth, the Life'.

388. The King of Love my Shepherd is

This version of Ps. 23 was written by Sir Henry Baker for *Hymns Ancient and Modern*, 1868.

DOMINUS REGIT ME was composed for this hymn by Dykes for *Hymns Ancient and Modern.*

MARY, composed by John Ambrose Lloyd, is from *Llyfr Tonau Cynulleidfaol*, 1859.

389. The Lord is my shepherd; there is nothing I shall want

This is the Gelineau version of Ps. 23 (LXX 22). It first appeared in French in *Formules Psalmodiques*, and in English in *Twenty-four Psalms and a Canticle to the psalmody of Joseph Gelineau*. See 67.

Setting. The musical setting is from the psalmody of Gelineau. Antiphon I is by Gelineau, Antiphons II and III by Dom Gregory Murray. The setting of Psalm 22 (23) given in *Twenty-four Psalms and a Canticle*, say its editors, 'was a first attempt to provide a musical setting for a psalm, and is not really typical of Gelineau psalmody. It is melodic in character rather than recitative.'

390. O greatly blest the people are

Metrical psalm 89: 15–16, 18 from *The Scottish Psalter*, 1650. The version in the Scottish book, 1564, was by John Hopkins.

NEWINGTON (ST. STEPHEN) is from *Ten Church Pieces for the Organ, with four anthems in score, composed for the use of the Church of Nayland in Suffolk, by William Jones*, 1789, where it occurs at the end of the work set to Pss. 15 and 23 called 'St. Stephen's Tune'. From this source it is sometimes called 'Nayland'. It appears under the name 'Stephen's' in Knott's *Sacred Harmony*, 1815.

391. God will I bless all times; his praise

Metrical psalm 34: 1–2, 7–9, 11, 14–15 from *The Scottish Psalter*, 1650. Sternhold's version had been given in *The Anglo-Genevan Psalter*, 1556, and retained in the Scottish book, 1564.

ST. DAVID is from Ravenscroft's *Psalter*, 1621, where it is set to Pss. 43 and 95, the arrangement being by Ravenscroft. In the Index it is listed under the heading 'Welsh Tunes'. In Playford's *Psalms and Hymns*, 1671, the melody appears in the same form, but in his *Whole Book of Psalms*, 1677, it is found in the present form.

392. Now Israel may say, and that truly

Metrical psalm 124 from the second version in *The Scottish Psalter*, 1650. Whittington's version, based on Beza's French version, had appeared in *The Anglo-Genevan Psalter*, 1561, and was taken over in the Scottish book, 1564. In the 1650 revision this remained practically unaltered.

OLD 124TH. See 84.

393. When Zion's bondage God turned back

Metrical psalm 126 from *The Scottish Psalter*, 1650. Kethe's version was given in *The Anglo-Genevan Psalter*, 1561, and retained in Scotland in 1564.

ABBEY. See 73.

394. Art thou afraid his power shall fail

Paraphrase 22: 3–8, based on Isa. 40: 27–31. Verses 1–2 being omitted the origin of the paraphrase is clearer by quoting the first line, 'Why pour'st thou forth thine anxious plaint'. It is Cameron's revision of Watts's 'Whence do our mournful thoughts arise?' first published in his *Hymns and Spiritual Songs*, 1707. The text is the form in *Scottish Paraphrases*, 1781.

ABRIDGE (ST. STEPHEN). See 28.

395. Father of peace, and God of love

Paraphrase 60 from *Scottish Paraphrases*, 1781. This is a composite hymn. Verse 1 is by Doddridge, vv. 2–3 are revised in *Scottish Paraphrases*, 1781, but based on Doddridge, and v. 4 by William Cameron. Doddridge's original hymn appeared in Orton's posthumous edition of his *Hymns*, 1755, under the title 'The Christian Perfected by the Grace of God in Christ, from Heb. xiii. 20–21'.

CAITHNESS. See 125.

ST. PAUL (ABERDEEN). See 72.

396. Behold the amazing gift of love

Paraphrase 63 from *Scottish Paraphrases*, 1781, based on 1 John 3: 1–4. It is a revision of Watts's 'Behold what wondrous grace', a hymn of six verses in short metre, published in *Hymns and Spiritual Songs*, 1709, where it was entitled 'Adoption'. The text here is William Cameron's revision as in *Scottish Paraphrases*.

ST. STEPHEN (NEWINGTON). See 390.

397. O God, thou art the Father

A free version of part of St. Columba's 'In Te, Christe'. See 301. It is from *Offices for the Commemoration of St. Columba*, 9 June 1897, in Duncan Macgregor's *St. Columba, a Record and a Tribute*, 1897.

DURROW is an Irish folk-song melody, connected with a County Limerick sea-song, 'Captain Thomson'.

398. Alone with none but thee, my God

See 301 and 397. This hymn is attributed to St. Columba. Duncan Macgregor's translation is given in his *St. Columba*, 1897, and *The Irish Church Hymnal*, 1873. The text given here was contributed anonymously to *Life and Work*, the Church of Scotland's journal, in 1963. The author is now known to have been Dr. W. T. Cairns.

EMAIN MACHA was composed by Charles Wood for this hymn in *The Irish Church Hymnal*. According to tradition, when relations between St. Patrick and King Laoghaire became strained, the former moved from Meath to the territory of a king called Daire who dwelt near the historic fort of Emain in Ulster. He was well disposed to Christianity, and gave Patrick permission to form a settlement near Emain at the foot of a hill called Ard Macha. From this tradition the tune receives its name.

399. Though in God's form he was

This paraphrase of Phil. 2: 6–11 was written by Professor A. M. Hunter, Aberdeen, for CH3.

ORB was composed by John Currie for this hymn for CH3.

400. Firmly I believe and truly

This is from Newman's *Dream of Gerontius*, 1866, where it is referred to as 'The Faith of a Christian'. It was included in *The English Hymnal*, 1906.

OTTERY ST. MARY was composed by H. G. Ley and is the tune set to these words in *Hymns for Church and School*, 1964. It was first published in *The Clarendon Hymn Book*, 1936.

401. Today I arise

The *Lorica* or 'Breastplate' of St. Patrick. When Patrick landed in Ireland, *c.* 432, to 'sow the Faith', he made his way to Tara, where the Ard-ri (High King) of Ireland, Laoghaire, held his court. It was the time of the triennial convention of the vassal kings of the land. It was also Easter Eve. Patrick and his company, halting at the Hill of Slane beside the Boyne Water, some ten miles from Tara, and in full view of it, celebrated the Eve of the Feast by lighting a great fire. That same night, at Tara, Laoghaire had issued an edict that no one on pain of death should kindle a fire either in Tara or anywhere on the surrounding plain until the King had lighted the beacon beside the palace. As he went out to do so, far away to the north was seen the gleam of the fire on the Hill of Slane. Laoghaire summoned his Druids and demanded what this meant. They replied, 'O King, unless this fire which you see be quenched this very night, it will never be quenched, and the kindler of it will overcome us all and seduce all the folk of our realm'. Greatly angered, the King declared, 'It shall not be; but we will go to see the issue of the matter, and we will put to death those who do such sin against our kingdom'. Thus saying, he ordered his chariots to be yoked and drove over the plain to the Boyne where they drew rein before they came within the circle of the light of Patrick's fire, lest he should cast his spell on them. But he, when he was summoned and saw their array, lifted up his voice in Ps. 20 from the *Vulgate*, 'Some trust in chariots, and some in horses, but we will remember the name of the Lord our God', and then in the words of the *Lorica* in Irish, which is 'at once an incantation, a war-song, and a creed'. So the 'Day of Tara' was won. The text in Irish with a literal translation is given in the *Irish Liber Hymnorum*, 1898, edited by Bernard and Atkinson. Mrs. Alexander's version (see 402) gained great popularity partly through Stanford's setting of it to old Irish melodies, but the lines with which four of the verses open, 'I bind unto myself today' rest upon a mis-translation. The version 'Today I arise', made by Professor R. A. S. Macalister, is closer to the Irish text, and 'gives a more accurate idea of the picturesque abruptness and nervous vigour of the original'. It was written specially for RCH, 1927, where it first appeared.

EGTON BRIDGE was composed by John Joubert for this hymn for CH3.

RAMELTON (vv. 1–5, 9) and CULRATHAIN (vv. 6–8) based on Irish traditional melodies were composed by James Moore for CH3.

402. I bind unto myself today

See 401. Mrs. Alexander's version of the *Lorica* was first printed in leaflet form for St. Patrick's Day, 1889, and later appeared in Wright's *Writings of St. Patrick* of the same year.

ST. PATRICK is from Petrie's *Irish Melodies*, 1855, arranged by Sir Charles V. Stanford. It is said to be an old Irish setting of 'Jesu dulcis memoria'. See 377, 378, 571.

CLONMACNOISE (v. 5) is an ancient Irish melody, harmonized by Sir Richard R. Terry. It first appears in RCH, 1927.

403. Thee will I love, my God and King

Written by Robert Bridges for *The Yattendon Hymnal*, 1899, for the tune 'Psalm 138' in *The Genevan Psalter*, 1551.

HAMBLEDEN was composed by W. K. Stanton for *The BBC Hymn Book*, 1951.

404. God is my strong salvation

From Montgomery's *Songs of Zion*, 1822. It is a version of Ps. 27.

CHRISTUS DER IST MEIN LEBEN (BREMEN) is from *Ein schön geistlich Gesangbuch ... Durch Melchiorem Vulpium Cantorem zu Weymar*, Jena, 1609, where it is set to the hymn 'Christus der ist mein Leben'. The present form is found in Crüger's *Praxis Pietatis Melica*, Berlin, 1662, which was taken over by Bach in his *Choralgesänge*, 1769.

405. All my hope on God is founded

'Meine Hoffnung stehet feste' is from Neander's *Glaub- und Liebesübung*, Bremen, 1680, with the heading 'Grace after meat'. It is based on 1 Tim. 6: 17. Robert Bridges's version in *The Yattendon Hymnal*, 1899, is not so much a translation as a free paraphrase, the original being merely used for suggestion.

MEINE HOFFNUNG is from Neander's *Glaub- und Liebesübung*, where it is stated to be a melody already known, but it has not been traced to any earlier collection. The present form is that used by Bach in one of his church cantatas.

MICHAEL was composed by Herbert Howells for Charterhouse School, *c.* 1932, at the request of the then Director of Music, T. P. Fielden. It was first published in *The Clarendon Hymn Book*, 1936.

GROESWEN, composed by J. Ambrose Lloyd, is from *Llyfr Tonau · Cynulleidfaol*, 1859.

406. A safe stronghold our God is still

'Ein' feste Burg ist unser Gott' first appeared in Klug's *Gesangbuch*, Wittenberg, 1529. It is a paraphrase of Ps. 46. Attempts to connect this hymn with a specific event in Luther's life have not proved conclusive. The editor rejects the theory associating it with the Diet of Worms, 1521, as there is no valid evidence for the existence of this hymn prior to its publication. If an event has to be found by far the most likely is the Diet of Speier, 1529, when the Evangelical party made their famous 'Protest' that 'in matters relating to the honour of God and the Salvation of our souls, every man must stand alone before God and give account for himself'. But even this cannot be dogmatically asserted though the dates fit. The first translation into English was made in 1539 by Coverdale, 'Our God is a defence and towre'. There is another in *Lyra Davidica*, 1708. But the hymn remained little known in the English-speaking world. Carlyle's translation, while containing defects, is the most widely known and best catches Luther's rugged spirit. His version first appeared in an article on 'Luther's Psalm' in *Fraser's Magazine*, 1831.

EIN' FESTE BURG is first found in the *Kirchen Gesänge*, Nürnberg, 1531, and Klug's *Gesangbuch*, Wittenberg, 1535. Bach squared up the melody into two-bar phrases and the present arrangement is based on his.

407. A fortress sure is God our King

Another version of 406. Thring's translation appears in his *Church of England Hymn Book*, 1882. It omits the third verse and adds a doxology which had been added to the original *c.* 1546 in *Etliche Lieder*, Nürnberg, and later altered in Lobwasser's *Psalmen des Königlichen Propheten Davids*, Leipzig, 1574.

EIN' FESTE BURG. See 406.

408. Happy are they, they that love God

Coffin's 'O quam iuvat fratres, Deus' occurs in the *Paris Breviary*, 1736, as the hymn for Vespers on Tuesdays. Bridges's version in *The Yattendon Hymnal*, 1899, is a free rendering, not a translation. Verses 1–3 are a free version of the original, vv. 4–5 are by the translator. Coffin's fourth verse is left untranslated.

BINCHESTER by Croft is set to Ps. 96 in *The Divine Companion*, 1709. It is first set to these words in *The Yattendon Hymnal*.

409. And can it be, that I should gain

Written by Charles Wesley at 'Little Britain', London, on 23 May 1738. It is based on his conversion experience. It was published in *Psalms and Hymns*, 1738.

SURREY (CAREY'S). See 16.

410. Not what these hands have done

Bonar's hymn first appears in *Hymns of Faith and Hope*, 1861, where it is headed 'Salvation through Christ alone'.

ST. BRIDE comes from *Parochial Harmony; consisting of a Collection of Psalm Tunes in three and four parts . . . by William Riley*, 1762, where it is set to Ps. 130 and headed 'St. Bridget's Tune, by Mr Saml Howard'. St. Bride's is an abbreviation of St. Bridget's, the church in Fleet Street where Howard was organist.

411. My hope is built on nothing less

Edward Mote's hymn was written probably *c.* 1834, and published in *Hymns of Praise. A new Selection of Gospel Hymns combining all the excellencies of our Spiritual Poets, with many Originals*, 1836, where it is entitled 'The immutable Basis of a Sinner's Hope'. The original begins 'Nor earth nor hell my soul can move', and the present first verse was the second.

BUTE was composed by John Currie for this hymn for CH3.

412. Will your anchor hold in the storms of life?

Like most of Priscilla Owens's hymns this was written for a particular occasion, a Youth Service in Baltimore.

WILL YOUR ANCHOR HOLD was composed by W. J. Kirkpatrick of the Methodist Episcopal Church, U.S.A.

413. Jesus shall reign where'er the sun

From Watts's *Psalms of David*, 1719, where it forms the second part of his version of Ps. 72 and is headed 'Christ's Kingdom among the Gentiles'. Three verses are omitted between stanzas 1 and 2, and another between 3 and 4.

WARRINGTON by Ralph Harrison appeared in his *Sacred Harmony*, 1784, which is a collection of psalm-tunes. The tune's name comes from the fact that the composer attended Warrington Academy for a period.

414. We believe in one true God

The hymn 'Wir glauben all' an einen Gott' for Trinity Sunday first appeared in the Culmbach-Bayreuth *Gesangbuch*, 1668, with the initials 'C. A. D'. Then it appears with Clausnitzer's name in the Nürnberg *Gesangbuch*, 1676. Miss Winkworth translated it for her *Chorale Book for England*, 1863, from which it was taken into the U.S.A. *Methodist Episcopal Hymnal*, 1878, and the *Evangelical Association Hymn Book*, 1882. The text consisted of three six-line stanzas. The revision committee altered this by omitting the last two lines of each verse, and then taking those from the third and first and making them into a fourth stanza.

LÜBECK. See 38.

415. The great love of God is revealed in the Son

D. T. Niles's hymn was written for the East Asia Christian Conference and is included in its *Hymnal*, 1964, which he edited.

NORMANDY. See 195.

416. God is love: his the care

This hymn for the young was written by Percy Dearmer for *Songs of Praise*, 1925, and was reprinted in *Songs of Praise for Boys and Girls*, 1930. It was intended to 'set out some fundamental theology in a simple form' and to 'fit the tune "Personent hodie"'.

PERSONENT HODIE is from *Piae Cantiones*, Nyland, 1582. The arrangement is that by Gustav Holst in *Songs of Praise* and *The Oxford Book of Carols*, 1928.

417. God is always near me

Bliss's hymn first appeared in *The Charm*, 1871.

ST. CYRIL, composed by Bliss, appeared along with the words for which he specially composed it.

418. Jesus loves me! this I know

Miss Warner's hymn appeared in her *Say and Seal*, 1859.

GAELIC LULLABY is a traditional Gaelic tune. It is also known as 'Gaelic Fairy Lullaby' and is taken from *The Scottish Students' Hymn Book*.

JESUS LOVES ME was composed for this hymn by Bradbury in *The Golden Chain*, 1861.

419. Lord, I would own thy tender care

Jane Taylor's hymn first appears in *Hymns for Infant Minds*, 1810, which she published in co-operation with her sister.

NEWBURY is a traditional melody arranged by Miss Arkwright from an old Christmas carol beginning, 'There is six good days set in a week'. The harmonization is by Vaughan Williams as in *The English Hymnal*, 1906.

Cross ref. to KINGS LANGLEY. See 618.

420. The Church's one foundation

Written by S. J. Stone in 1866 out of admiration for the opposition shown by Bishop Gray of Capetown to the views of Bishop Colenso. It originally appeared in seven verses in the author's *Lyra Fidelium*, 1866. It was intended to illustrate the phrase in the *Apostles' Creed*, 'I believe in the Holy Catholic Church'. The text here is as in *Hymns Ancient and Modern*, 1868.

AURELIA, from *A Selection of Psalms and Hymns arranged for the Public Services of the Church of England, edited by the Rev. Charles Kemble and S. S. Wesley*, 1864, was originally composed for the hymn, 'Jerusalem the golden'. See 537. It appears to have been set to this hymn first in *Hymns Ancient and Modern*.

421. Glorious things of thee are spoken

Newton's hymn first appeared in the *Olney Hymns*, 1779, where it is said to be based on Ps. 132: 13, Matt. 16: 18, Isa. 26: 1, Ps. 46: 4, and Rev. 1: 6. The present text is the revision in *Hymns Ancient and Modern*, 1875.

AUSTRIAN HYMN. See 37.

422. City of God, how broad and far

Samuel Johnson held that the Church consisted of all men of goodwill without a demand for dogmatic agreement, so he headed this hymn 'The Church, the City of God'. He was minister of a Free Church at Lynn, Mass. It is from *Hymns of the Spirit*, 1864.

RICHMOND. See 371.

423. Through the night of doubt and sorrow

The Danish original 'Igjennem Nat og Traengsel' by Professor B. S. Ingemann was written in 1825, and four years later appeared in *Nyt Tillaeg til Evangelisk-Christelig Psalmebog*, Copenhagen. The present text is from Baring-Gould's version in *The People's Hymnal*, 1867 as revised in *Hymns Ancient and Modern*, 1875.

MARCHING by Martin Shaw was composed for this hymn. It first appeared in *Additional Tunes and settings in use at St. Mary's, Primrose Hill*, 1915.

424. Thy hand, O God, has guided

Plumptre's hymn is taken from the supplement to *Hymns Ancient and Modern*, 1889, omitting two stanzas. It was entitled 'Church Defence'.

THORNBURY by Basil Harwood was composed for the Twenty-fifth Annual Festival of the London Church Choir Association in 1898, and appeared in its Festival Book. Later it was included in the composer's *Hymn Tunes Original and Selected*, 1905.

425. In Christ there is no East or West

From John Oxenham's *The pageant of Darkness and Light*, 1908.

PITYOULISH by R. Barrett-Ayres was composed for this hymn for CH3.

426. A glorious company we sing

A. F. Bayly's hymn was first published by the National Sunday School Union in *Sunday School Praise*, 1958.

ST. MAGNUS (NOTTINGHAM). See 286.

427. The Church is wherever God's people are praising

This hymn by Carol Rose Ikeler was written in 1959 and was inspired by a Presbyterian missionary's address about his work with the emerging indigenous churches in Africa while she was teaching at a Synod Summer Leadership School. It first appeared in *Songs and Hymns for Primary Children*, 1963.

LAREDO appears in *Cowboy Songs and Other Frontier Ballads*, 1938, collected by J. A. Lomax. The tune of 'The Streets of Laredo' went over to America as an unornamented version of 'The Bard of Armagh', which itself is a derivative of 'Príosún Cluain Meala' or 'The Jail of Clonmel'.

428. Lord of creation, to thee be all praise

J. C. Winslow's hymn was first published in his *A Garland of Verse*, 1961, and later in *Hymns for Church and School*, 1964.

SLANE. See 87. The harmonization here is by Erik Routley.

429. My God, accept my heart this day

This hymn is from Matthew Bridges's *Hymns of the Heart*, 1848. It is included in the *Plymouth Collection*, 1855, and *The BBC Hymn Book*, 1951.

ST. JAMES. See 121.

430. 'Take up thy cross,' the Saviour said

From Charles Everest's *Visions of Death, and other Poems*, 1833, published when he was nineteen years old. The original has been much altered through the years, but the text given is the original except for three minor changes.

BRESLAU in *As hymnodus sacer. Zwölff Geistliche anmuhtige und theils newe Gesänge*, Leipzig, 1625, was set to the hymn 'Herr Jesu Christ, meins Lebens Licht'. It is an adaptation of the folk-song 'Ich fahr dahin' from *Locheimer Gesangbuch*, c. 1452. The present form of the melody is that adopted by Mendelssohn in the oratorio, *St. Paul*, 1836.

431. Jesus, Master, whose I am

Miss Havergal's hymn was written in 1865 for her nephew, the Revd. J. H. Shaw, printed as one of a series of leaflets by Messrs. Parlane, Paisley, and then published in *The Ministry of Song*, 1869, under the text Acts 27: 23.

HEATHLANDS. See 236.

432. May the mind of Christ my Saviour

It has proved impossible to trace this hymn, though written *c.* 1912, to an earlier printed source than *Golden Bells*, 1925.

VIGIL by G. T. Thalben-Ball was composed for *The BBC Hymn Book*, 1951, for the hymn 'Soldier go! Thy vow is spoken'. It was called 'Vigil' as it was written while the composer was fire-watching during the Second World War.

433. God be in my head, and in my understanding

Forms of this poem in French go back to the fifteenth century. It is found on the title-page of a *Book of Hours*, 1514, and in a *Sarum Primer*, 1558. It was first printed as a hymn in *The Oxford Hymn Book*, 1908.

PETTRONSEN was composed by Martin Dalby for this hymn for CH3.

GOD BE IN MY HEAD by Walford Davies first appeared as a leaflet in 1910, and two years later in the *Festival Service Book* of the London Church Choir Association.

434. O Jesus, I have promised

Originally printed as a leaflet in 1869, 'A Hymn for the newly confirmed'. It was written by J. E. Bode on the occasion of the confirmation of his daughter and two sons. It was included in *Hymns Ancient and Modern*, 1904.

THORNBURY. See 424.

435. Lord, in the fullness of my might

Written by T. H. Gill in 1855, and published in *The Golden Chain of Praise*, 1869, with the heading 'Early Love. "How good it is to close with Christ betimes!" Oliver Cromwell'. The original had eight stanzas.

UNIVERSITY first appeared in Hellendaal's *Psalms for the Use of Parish Churches*, 1780, where it is attributed to Collignon, Professor of Anatomy in the University of Cambridge. It also appears in *A Collection of Psalm and Hymn Tunes*, 1794, which was edited by Randall, Professor of Music at Cambridge. So the tune has been ascribed to him although it is anonymous. However, there is no adequate reason to reject the attribution to Collignon.

436. O Master, let me walk with thee

Gladden's hymn first appeared in *Sunday Afternoon*, 1870, a magazine of which he was editor, under the title 'Walking with God'.

MELCOMBE. See 47.

437. Love Divine, all loves excelling

Charles Wesley's hymn from *Hymns for those that seek and those that have Redemption in the Blood of Christ*, 1747. The form here is that in Wesley's *Collection of Hymns*, 1780, which omits one verse. It was entitled 'Jesus, show us thy salvation'.

HYFRYDOL. See 381.

Cross ref. to BLAENWERN. See 473.

438. Gracious Spirit, Holy Ghost

From Christopher Wordsworth's *The Holy Year*, 1862, under Quinquagesima for which day the Epistle was 1 Cor. 13, on which the hymn is based.

CAPETOWN comes from *Vierstimmiges Choralbuch herausgegeben von Dr. F. Filitz*, Berlin, 1847, where it was set to 'Morgenglanz der Ewigkeit'.

439. O Lord and Master of us all

This hymn, like 306, is taken from a poem of thirty-five verses by Whittier entitled 'Our Master' which appeared in *The Tent on the Beach and other Poems*, 1867.

FARNHAM is an arrangement by Vaughan Williams of an English traditional melody as in *The English Hymnal*, 1906.

440. 'Lift up your hearts!' We lift them, Lord, to thee

Written by H. M. Butler for the *Harrow School Hymn Book*, 1881, when he was headmaster. It is based on the 'Sursum corda' and was included in *The Public School Hymn Book*, 1903.

WOODLANDS by W. Greatorex was composed for this hymn and contributed to *The Public School Hymn Book*, 1919.

441. Soldiers of Christ! arise

Charles Wesley's hymn from *Hymns and Sacred Poems*, 1749, where it was entitled 'The Whole Armour of God', being based on Eph. 6: 10–17. Originally the hymn consisted of sixteen eight-line verses and is divided into three parts: lines 1–12 and 21–4 are from part i, 13–16 from part ii, and 17–20 from part iii. In the last line 'entire' has been altered to 'complete'. Wiseman suggests that 'the words were set going by the melody' for in the 1761 tune book the hymn is set to one of Handel's marches in the opera, *Richard the First*.

FROM STRENGTH TO STRENGTH was composed by E. W. Naylor *c.* 1902 and issued in sheet form for use in Emmanuel College Chapel, Cambridge, and appears in *The Public School Hymn Book*, 1919.

442. Fight the good fight with all thy might

From Monsell's *Hymns of Love and Praise*, 1863; written for the nineteenth Sunday after Trinity. It is based on 1 Tim. 6: 12.

DUKE STREET. See 333.

CANNOCK by W. K. Stanton first appears in *The BBC Hymn Book*, 1951.

443. Who would true valour see

Valiant's song from Bunyan's *Pilgrim's Progress*. While the compilers of some hymn-books have altered the text considerably, the committee which compiled the RCH, 1927, 'felt that, notwithstanding its ruggedness and occasional quaintness of expression, Bunyan's original is so infinitely superior to any modern version, that it deserves to be sung exactly as it was written'. They, therefore, gave Bunyan's text. This has been continued in CH3. There were many contemporary ballads in this metre. One of these 'The Valiant Sailor's Happy Return to his True Love' may have helped to suggest Bunyan's opening line in Valiant's speech.

MONKS GATE is arranged, as in *The English Hymnal*, 1906, by Vaughan Williams from the melody of a Sussex folk-song, collected by Mrs. Verrall of Monks Gate, Sussex, entitled 'Valiant' or 'Welcome Sailor'. Indeed, it is not impossible that this was the very tune Bunyan had in mind when he wrote his pilgrim's song.

444. I feel the winds of God today

Jessie Adams wrote this hymn in 1907 at a time when long service in certain work was met by seemingly continuous failure. 'If then,' she wrote, 'quitting the labour at the oar, we humbly believe that God's Spirit still leads us aright, we shall pass the point of danger and helplessness. Some little act of kindness may be as the upturned sail which that spirit waits to fill, in spite of past and future.' Verse 3 was added to the original by F. J. Gillman. It appeared in the *Fellowship Hymn Book*, 1910.

PETERSHAM by C. W. Poole appeared in *The Congregational Psalmist*, 1875, where it was set to 'The roseate hues of early dawn'.

445. Make me a captive, Lord

From Matheson's *Sacred Songs*, 1890, written that year at Row, Dunbartonshire, entitled 'Christian Freedom, Paul, the prisoner of Jesus Christ' Eph. 3: 1.

ICH HALTE TREULICH STILL is believed to be an original melody by Bach as found in Schemelli's *Musikalisches Gesangbuch*, Leipzig, 1736. The tune may be Bach's, but there can be no certainty on the point.

446. Land of our Birth, we pledge to thee

'The Children's Hymn' from Kipling's *Puck of Pook's Hill*, 1906. The first work to include it as a hymn was *School Praise*, 1907, issued by the Presbyterian Church of England as a hymn-book for the young.

TRURO is from *Psalmodia Evangelica: A Collection of Psalms and Hymns in Three Parts for Public Worship, by Thos. Williams*, 1790, where it is set to the hymn 'Now to the Lord a noble song'. It is without a composer's name, and although it is assigned to Burney by some there is no evidence for this. On the contrary several tunes have Burney's name attached to them, but this is not one of them.

447. Lord and Master, who hast called us

Florence Smith's hymn was written *c*. 1913 for use in St. Christopher's College, Canterbury. It is included in *Hymns Ancient and Modern*, 1950.

SUSSEX. See 144.

448. Just as I am, thine own to be

Contributed by Miss Farningham to the Sunday School Union of London's *Voice of Praise*, 1887. Two verses have been omitted.

SAFFRON WALDEN. See 79.

449. Looking upward every day

Written by Miss Butler for the confirmation of her niece and god-daughter. It is from Mrs. Brock's *Children's Hymn Book*, 1881.

AVE VIRGO VIRGINUM. See 269.

450. Saviour, teach me, day by day

From Miss Leeson's *Hymns and Scenes of Childhood*, 1842, where it had four eight-line stanzas. Here the second half of vv. 1–2 and the first half of v. 3 have been omitted. The refrain is from 1 John 4: 19.

BUCKLAND. See 106.

451. Almighty Father of all things that be

Dugmore's hymn appears in *Hymns of Adoration for Church Use*, 1900. It was composed for the opening of a small Industrial Exhibition in the author's parish, Parkstone, near Poole, Dorset. The text is as revised in *Hymns Ancient and Modern*, 1904.

CHILTON FOLIAT by Sir G. C. Martin is from *The Westminster Abbey Hymn Book*, 1897, of which he was musical editor. It was set to these words in RCH, 1927.

452. God, who hast given us power to sound

G. W. Briggs's hymn on 'Science' first appeared in the *Sunday Times*, 1954, and then in *Hymns of Faith*, 1957.

BANGOR is from *A Compleat Melody: or, The Harmony of Zion ... By William Tans'ur*, 1734, where it is set to Ps. 12 and headed 'Bangor Tune. Composed in Three Parts. W. T'. It is doubtful whether the tune is an original composition of his or was merely harmonized by him.

453. Behold us, Lord, a little space

Ellerton's hymn 'for use at mid-day service in a London City Church' was first published in *Church Hymns*, 1871. In the RCH, 1927, it consisted of six four-line verses. Here vv. 1 and 3 and 4 and 7 have been combined to make a hymn of two eight-line stanzas.

CARRICK was composed by John Currie for this hymn for CH3.

454. Son of God, eternal Saviour

Written in 1893 at North Holmwood, Surrey, of which S. C. Lowry was then vicar. It was entitled 'For Unity' and was published in *Goodwill*, 1894, and in *The Christian Social Union Hymnbook*, 1895.

PSALM 42 was composed or adapted by Bourgeois for Ps. 42 in *The French Psalter*, 1551. In *The Anglo-Genevan Psalter*, 1561, it was set to Kethe's version of Ps. 27, and this was taken over into *The Scottish Psalter*, 1564. As the scansion of Beza's Ps. 42 and Kethe's Ps. 27 are quite different 'the adaptation is exceedingly bad'. The melody here follows the original.

IN BABILONE. See 282.

455. Angel voices, ever singing

From Francis Pott's *Hymns Fitted to the Order of Common Prayer*, 1866.

ARTHOG by G. T. Thalben-Ball first appears in *The BBC Hymn Book*, 1951, and is the tune set to these words in *Hymns for Church and School*, 1964.

ANGEL VOICES was composed by E. G. Monk for this hymn. Both hymn and tune were written at the request of the Revd. W. K. Macrorie, afterwards Bishop of Maritzburg, for the opening of an organ at Wingate Church, Lancashire, in 1861. Pott, author of the hymn, states that the tune was repeatedly printed in Choral Festival books. It appears in the *Congregational Church Hymnal*, 1887, and the *Supplement*, 1889, to *Hymns Ancient and Modern*.

456. We give thee but thine own

How's hymn was written in 1858 and published in Morrell and How's *Psalms and Hymns*, 1864.

NARENZA is taken from a seven-line melody in Leisentritt's *Catholicum Hymnologium Germanicum*, Cologne, 1584. It was adapted and given the name 'Narenza' by Havergal in his *Old Church Psalmody*, 1847.

457. Fill thou our life, O Lord our God

From Bonar's *Hymns of Faith and Hope*, 1866, where it is headed 'Life's praise'. Originally there were six eight-line verses.

ABBEY. See 73.

Cross ref. to RICHMOND. See 371.

458. Lord of all good, our gifts we bring to thee

A. F. Bayly's hymn is taken from his *Again I say Rejoice*, 1967.

SURSUM CORDA. See 68.

459. Fountain of good, to own thy love

From Doddridge's hymn 'Jesus, my Lord, how rich Thy grace' and headed 'On relieving Christ in the Poor'. The text here is Osler's revision in Hall's *Mitre Hymn Book*, 1836.

PRAETORIUS. See 288.

460. O brother man, fold to thy heart thy brother

From Whittier's poem 'Worship' in fifteen stanzas, published in his *Poems*, 1850, having been written two years earlier. It is prefixed with the text Jas. 1: 27. Verses 1, 3, and 4 of the hymn are the last three stanzas of the poem, v. 2 being the eleventh.

INTERCESSOR. See 244.

461. O God of mercy, God of might

Written in 1877 and published in Thring's *Collection*, 1880. It appeared also in his *Church of England Hymnbook*, 1882, as an Offertory hymn under the text Luke 10: 36–7.

ISLEWORTH by Samuel Howard is from *Melodies of the Psalms of David according to the version by Christopher Smart*, 1765, where it is set to Ps. 6.

Cross ref. to CHILDHOOD. See 156.

462. Take my life, and let it be

From Miss Havergal's *Loyal Responses*, 1878. It was written at Astley House in 1874 following the answer to her prayer 'Lord, give me all in this house'. She wrote, 'It was nearly midnight. I was too happy to sleep, and passed most of the night in praise and renewal of my own consecration; and these little couplets formed themselves, and chimed in my heart one after another till they finished "Ever, only, all for thee".'

LÜBECK. See 38.

463. Forth in thy Name, O Lord, I go

Charles Wesley's hymn from *Hymns and Sacred Poems*, 1749, with the title 'For Believers before Work'.

SONG 34 (ANGELS' SONG). See 45.

464. The wise may bring their learning

This hymn appeared anonymously in *The Book of Praise for Children*, 1881.

TYROLESE is the melody of a Tyrolean carol, 'Ihr Hirten, stehet alle auf'. In *The Oxford Book of Carols*, 1928, it was set to the carol 'Falan-tiding'. It was first set to these words in *The BBC Hymn Book*, 1951.

465. Hands to work and feet to run

Hilda Dodd's hymn was written for the National Sunday School Union and appears in *Child Songs*, 1910.

WINCHMORE by Hilda Dodd is the tune set to these words in *Child Songs* and *The School Hymn Book of the Methodist Church*, 1950.

466. Our thoughts go round the world

Jessie E. Moore's hymn appears in her *Pilgrim Bible Stories for Children*, and is included in *Songs and Hymns for Primary Children*, 1963.

SOUTHWELL. See 80.

467. Take our gifts, O loving Jesus

Margaret Cropper's hymn is taken from *The School Hymn Book of the Methodist Church*, 1950.

EVENING PRAYER was composed by Stainer for the first edition of the *Church Hymnary*, 1898, for the hymn 'Jesus, tender shepherd, hear me'. See 656. According to the composer the tune was based on the opening theme of Beethoven's *Andante in F*.

468. Speak forth thy word, O Father

This hymn was written for a 'Feed the minds campaign' in Glasgow in 1964 by Charles Jeffries and was issued in leaflet form. Here it appears in a hymn-book for the first time.

IST GOTT FÜR MICH is a melody from a Lutheran Chorale in the *Augsburg Gesangbuch*, 1609.

469. God, your glory we have seen in your Son

The French original, 'Dieu, nous avons vu ta gloire', was first sung at the Bible and Liturgy Congress, Strasbourg, in 1957. The English translation, made for the Scottish Churches' Consultation on Music, held at Dunblane, was first sung at St. Columba's College, Edinburgh, in 1964, and was published in *Dunblane Praises No. 1*, 1965. It was written by Didier Rimbaud, the translation of the antiphon being by Roland Johnson and of the verses by Brian Wren.

DIEU, NOUS AVONS VU TA GLOIRE, composed by Jean Langlais, was first sung at the Strasbourg Congress, and is printed in *Dunblane Praises No. 1*.

470. Go ye, said Jesus, and preach the word

George O. Gregory's hymn was written for the East Asia Christian Conference and appears in its *Hymnal*, 1964, edited by D. T. Niles.

ASHTON was composed by R. Barrett-Ayres for this hymn for CH3.

471. Lift up your heads, ye gates of brass

Montgomery's hymn first appeared in *The Evangelical Magazine*, 1843, and ten years later in his *Original Hymns*, where it is extended to nineteen stanzas, and was entitled 'China Evangelized'. It is headed by the text Isa. 13: 4.

WINCHESTER OLD. See 138.

WARWICK by Stanley first appears as a tune 'never before published' in *Sacred Music ... An Appendix to Dr. Watts's Psalms and Hymns, by Edward Miller, Mus.Doc.*, 1802. The same year it appeared in Stanley's own *24 Tunes in four Parts*, where it is set to Ps. 23.

472. Fear not, thou faithful Christian flock

'Verzage nicht, du Häuflein klein', of which the first verse here and it alone, dates from the period of the Thirty Years War, and may have been actually sung on the field of Lützen, where Gustavus Adolphus was killed, 6 November 1632. It was printed in Leipzig in that year as 'Kingly Swan-Song' and was possibly composed by Altenburg, a pastor and musician at Erfurt. It is found in *Epicedion*, Leipzig, late 1632, and Mengering's *Blutige Siegs-Crone*, Leipzig, 1633.

The first version given is Robert Bridges's from *The Yattendon Hymnal*, 1899, which is a free rendering rather than a translation and omits v. 2.

The second version is T. A. Lacey's from *The English Hymnal*, 1906, omitting the first and fourth verses.

PSALM 36 (68) is a version from *The Genevan Psalter*, 1542, of a melody by Matthäus Greiter in *Strassburger Kirchenampt*, 1525, where it was set to Ps. 36. This was retained in all succeeding editions of *The French Psalter*. In the complete psalter, 1562, it is also set to Beza's version of Ps. 68, 'Que dieu se monstre seulement', which became the battle-song of the Huguenots. In *The Anglo-Genevan Psalter*, 1561, it is set to Kethe's version of Ps. 113, and this was continued in *The Scottish Psalter*, 1564. So it is known in England as 'Old 113th'.

473. Lord, who in thy perfect wisdom

This hymn appears in *Sermons and Hymns* by Timothy Rees. It is included in *The Baptist Hymn Book*, 1962.

BLAENWERN by W. P. Rowlands was composed *c.* 1904–5 during the Welsh Revival of those years. It receives its name from a small farm near Tufton in Pembrokeshire where Rowlands had recuperated from a serious illness when a boy. It was first published in Sir Henry Haydn Jones's *Cân a Moliant*, 1916, and later in *Llyfr Emynau a Thonau y Methodistiaid*, 1929, a collection of hymns and tunes published jointly by the Presbyterian and Methodist Churches in Wales.

Cross ref. to HYFRYDOL. See 381.

474. Christ is the King! O friends rejoice

G. K. A. Bell's hymn was written for *Songs of Praise*, 1931. While written to 'carry the tune' 'Llangoedmor', which had been in RCH, 1927 but is omitted in CH3, it reflects the author's concern for Christian unity.

DELHI by E. F. Rimbault was composed in 1857 and first appears in Maurice's *Choral Harmony with Supplement*, 1858.

475. We have heard a joyful sound

Miss Owens wrote this hymn for the mission anniversary of a Sunday School in Baltimore. It was adapted to the chorus of 'Vive le Roi' in Meyerbeer's opera *Les Huguenots*.

LIMPSFIELD was composed by Josiah Booth for this hymn in the first edition of *The Church Hymnary*, 1898.

476. For my sake and the Gospel's, go

Bickersteth wrote this hymn to go to Sullivan's tune 'Bishopgarth', to which it is here set. It first appeared in *The Church Missionary Hymnbook*, 1899.

BISHOPGARTH was composed for How's hymn 'O King of kings, whose reign of old', which was written by Royal Command for the Diamond Jubilee of Queen Victoria in 1897.

477. Rise up, O men of God

This hymn was written for the Brotherhood Movement by W. P. Merrill and was first published in the Presbyterian *Continent*, 1911, entitled 'To the Brotherhood'. It was suggested by G. S. Lee's article 'The Church of the Strong Men', and was included in the University of Wales's *Students' Hymnal*, 1923.

CARLISLE. See 39.

478. Soldiers of the cross, arise

First published by How in Morrell and How's *Psalms and Hymns*, 1864. The text is as revised by the author for *Church Hymns*, 1871. It was intended as a hymn for Home Missions.

ORIENTIS PARTIBUS. See 275.

479. Who is on the Lord's side

Written by Miss Havergal on 13 October 1877, and published in her *Loyal Responses*, 1878. It is based on 1 Chr. 12: 18, and was entitled 'Home Missions'.

ARMAGEDDON was originally set in *The Church Psalter and Hymn Book*, 1872, by W. Mercer to the hymn 'Onward! Christian soldiers'. See 480. The tune appears to be an adaptation by Goss from a melody in Layriz's *Kern des deutschen Kirchengesangs*, Berlin, 1853, set to the hymn 'Wenn ich Ihn nur habe', and ascribed to Luise Reichardt.

BLENCATHRA was composed by Sir Arthur Somervell for the hymn 'Forward! be our watchword' for *Songs of Praise*, 1925.

480. Onward! Christian soldiers

Written in 1864 as a processional hymn for the school children of Horbury Bridge, near Wakefield, Yorkshire, where Baring-Gould was curate in charge of a mission. It was for a school-feast where the children had to march with banners flying from one village to another. It was published in *The Church Times*, 1864, as a 'Hymn for Procession with Cross and Banners'. Originally it was written to be sung to a tune arranged from the slow movement in Haydn's Symphony in D, No. 15, but it derives a great part of its popularity from Sullivan's tune 'St. Gertrude', which has practically superseded all other settings.

ST. GERTRUDE was composed for this hymn by Sir Arthur Sullivan. It appeared in *The Hymnary*, 1872, for which it was written, but first appeared in *The Musical Times*, 1871.

481. Stand up! stand up for Jesus

George Duffield caught the inspiration for this hymn from the dying words of the Revd. Dudley Atkins, rector of the Epiphany Church, Philadelphia. They were, 'Tell them to stand up for Jesus'. As Atkins had been much persecuted for his pleading of the cause of the oppressed and the slave, it was thought that these words had a peculiar significance in his mind. Duffield preached the funeral sermon on Eph. 6: 14, ending with the hymn he had just written. It was first issued as a leaflet for Duffield's Sunday School, and later appeared in the *Church Psalmist*, 1859.

MORNING LIGHT first appeared in *The Odeon: A Collection of Secular Melodies, designed for adult singing schools and for social music parties, by G. J. Webb and Lowell Mason*, 1837, where it is set to '"Tis dawn, the lark is singing'. Its first appearance as a hymn-tune was in *The Wesleyan Psalmist*, 1842, and it is first associated with these words in Bradbury's *Golden Chain*, 1861. It is known as 'Webb' in America.

482. Yield not to temptation, for yielding is sin

Written by H. R. Palmer in 1868 and published in *The National Sunday School Teachers' Magazine* of the same year.

FORTITUDE was the tune composed by Palmer himself for this hymn. It first appears in *Sabbath School Songs*, 1868. It is an adaptation of an earlier tune which had appeared in Bradbury's *Golden Chain*, 1864, and his *New Golden Trio*, 1866.

483. Go, labour on: spend and be spent

Written by Bonar in 1836 to encourage his helpers in a Leith mission district. It was printed in *Songs for the Wilderness*, 1843, and entitled 'Labour for Christ'. Later it was included in his *Hymns of Faith and Hope*, 1857, and headed 'The Useful Life'.

DEUS TUORUM MILITUM. See 42.

484. Courage, brother! do not stumble

Norman Macleod's hymn first appeared in *The Edinburgh Christian Magazine*, 1857, of which he was editor for a period.

NORMAN is from Doles's *Vierstimmiges Choralbuch*, Leipzig, 1785, and Werner's *Choralbuch*, Berlin, 1815. It was set to these words in *The Scottish Hymnal*, 1885.

COURAGE, BROTHER by Sir Arthur Sullivan was the tune to these words in the first edition of *The Church Hymnary*, 1898. In the RCH, 1927, it was omitted and replaced by David Evans's 'Yn y Glyn' and 'Norman', and is here restored.

485. Lord, speak to me, that I may speak

Written by Miss Havergal on 28 April 1872 at Winterdyne and headed 'A Worker's Prayer. None of us liveth unto himself. Rom. xiv. 7'. It first appeared as a leaflet, and later in her *Under the Surface*, 1874.

WARRINGTON. See 413.

LLEF is from *Gemau Mawl*, 1890, edited by D. Jenkins. It is by Griffith Hugh Jones (Gutyn Arfon) and was first sung at the Cymanfa of Dolwyddelen shortly before publication. The composer wrote it in memory of his brother, the Revd. D. H. Jones.

486. Lover of souls and Lord of all the living

The hymn was written by Helen Waddell as a hymn for the Girls' Auxiliary for Foreign Missions of the Presbyterian Church in Ireland. It was issued as a leaflet to a tune by Edith Wilson, and appears here in a hymn-book for the first time.

HEADINGTON was composed by Kenneth Leighton for this hymn for CH3.

487. And did those feet in ancient time

A lyric from Blake's *Milton*, 1804, with the text Num. 11: 29 subjoined. Sir Hubert Parry's music has carried it into wide popularity as a hymn of social hope and economic reconstruction. But originally it had no such outlook; for example, 'satanic mills' had nothing to do with factories, but represent the chopping of logic and science which Blake found and derided in the philosophies of Locke and Bacon. To Blake natural science and ratiocinative philosophy were anti-divine agencies. 'Jerusalem' represents the ideal life of freedom as divine. This liberty was to be built up by the unrestricted activities of the mind in the eyes of this prophet of intuition and imagination. 'I know of no other Christianity', said Blake, 'and of no other gospel than the liberty both of body and mind to exercise the divine arts of imagination.'

JERUSALEM by C. H. H. Parry arose from a conversation with Robert Bridges in which it was suggested that he should write 'suitable simple music to Blake's stanzas, music that an audience could take up and join in'. Parry agreed and gave the manuscript of 'Jerusalem' to Sir Walford Davies, saying, 'Here's a tune for you, old chap. Do what you like with it.' It was first sung in the Albert Hall, and was adopted by the Federation of Music Competition Festivals as the national hymn of that movement. Words and music were first included in a hymn-book in *A Students' Hymnal*, 1923.

488. Jesus bids us shine with a pure, clear light

Miss Warner's hymn first appeared in *The Little Corporal*, 1868.

LUMETTO was written by David Evans for this hymn for RCH, 1927.

489. I joy'd when to the house of God

Metrical psalm 122: 1–2, 6–9 from *The Scottish Psalter*, 1650. Kethe's version appeared in *The Anglo-Genevan Psalter*, 1561, and was retained in the Scottish book, 1564.

ST. PAUL (ABERDEEN). See 72.

490. Jesus, with thy Church abide

One of T. B. Pollock's litanies from his *Metrical Litanies for Special Services and General use*, 1870. For Lent. It is reprinted from the first edition of *The Church Hymnary*, 1898, omitting four verses.

HELFER MEINER ARMEN SEELE by Georg Joseph is from *Heilige Seelenlust, Oder Geistliche Hirtenlieder . . . von Johann Angelo Silesio und von Herren Georgio Josepho mit aussbundig Melodeyen geziert*, Breslau, 1657. The melody here is as adapted in *The English Hymnal*, 1906.

491. Lord of our life, and God of our salvation

'Christe, du Beistand deiner Kreuzgemeine' has been described as a 'sapphic ode for spiritual and temporal peace' by von Löwenstern. It appears in *Geistliche Kirchen und Haus-Musik*, Breslau, 1644. Pusey's version is a free paraphrase and appeared in Reinagle's *Psalm and Hymn Tunes*, 1840. The author writing to his brother says, 'It refers to the state of the Church, that is to say, of the Church of England in 1834 ... assailed from without, enfeebled and distracted within, but on the eve of a great awakening'. Significantly the German original also reflected a disturbed situation arising from the terrors of the Thirty Years War.

ISTE CONFESSOR (POITIERS) is from the *Poitiers Vesperale*, 1746. While it was known earlier in England its use there really dates from its inclusion in Croft's *Collection, c.* 1890, and *The English Hymnal*, 1906.

Cross ref. to DIVA SERVATRIX. See 568.

492. O thou, who at thy Eucharist didst pray

W. H. Turton's hymn, based on John 17: 11, was first used at St. Mary Magdalene's, London, in the Anniversary Service of the English Church Union, 1881. It is a prayer for unity, and is intended to be sung after the *Agnus Dei* at a choral celebration of the Eucharist. It was included in the *Altar Hymnal*, 1884, and the *Supplement*, 1889, to *Hymns Ancient and Modern*, where the first line has 'first' before 'Eucharist'.

SONG 1 by Orlando Gibbons was set to a paraphrase of the 'Song sung by Moses and the people' in Exod. 15 in *The Hymnes and Songs of the Church, by George Wither*, 1623. See 41 and 108.

493. Lord, bless and pity us

Metrical psalm 67 from *The Scottish Psalter*, 1650. Whittingham's version had been given in 1564.

NARENZA. See 456.

494. Thou whose almighty word

Written by John Marriott *c.* 1813, on Gen. 1: 3 and printed first in *The Evangelical Magazine*, 1825, and *The Friendly Visitor* a few weeks later. The reason for its being printed was that it had been quoted at a meeting of the London Missionary Society on 12 May 1825, and had made a deep impression on the audience. It was included in Raffles's *Supplement to Dr. Watts' Psalms and Hymns*, 1853.

MOSCOW comes from *A Collection of Psalm and Hymn Tunes, never published before*, 1769, edited by Madan. It was composed for the hymn 'Come, Thou almighty King' and headed 'Hymn to the Trinity, set by F. G.', the initials of Felice Giardini.

495. O lord our God, arise

Ralph Wardlaw's hymn was first published in *A Collection of Hymns for the use of the Tabernacles in Scotland*, 1800. This book was widely used by Scottish Congregationalists in the nineteenth century.

HAMPTON. See 332.

496. O spirit of the living God

Written by Montgomery in 1823, 'to be sung at the Public Meeting of the Auxiliary Missionary Society for the West Riding of Yorkshire, in Salem Chapel, Leeds, June 4, 1823.' A revised version was published in his *Christian Psalmist*, 1825, entitled 'The Spirit accompanying the Word of God'.

WINCHESTER NEW (CRASSELIUS). See 234.

497. God of mercy, God of grace

First published in Lyte's *The Spirit of the Psalms*, 1834, as a version of Ps. 67. In v. 2 line 5 Lyte wrote 'tributes'. It is not really a paraphrase of the psalm, but rather a hymn based upon it.

RATISBON (JESU, MEINE ZUVERSICHT) appears in Runge's *D. M. Luthers und anderer vornehmen geistreichen und gelehrten Männer Geistliche Lieder und Psalmen*, Berlin, 1653. Variants are found in Crüger's *Praxis Pietatis Melica*, Berlin, 1653, and Neander's *Choralbuch*, Bremen, 1680. Crüger's version is that used by Bach. It is also found in Werner's *Choralbuch*, Berlin, 1815, where it is set to 'Jesu meines Lebens Leben'.

Cross ref. to HEATHLANDS. See 236.

498. Arm of the Lord, awake, awake

This hymn first appeared in *Missionary Hymns*, 1795. In Morison's *Fathers and Founders*, 1844, it is attributed to William Shrubsole, junior, whereas in Rogers's *Lyra Britannica*, 1867, it is attributed to his father. It is impossible to say whether it is by the father or the son, except to note that Rogers's work is usually accurate.

TRURO. See 446.

499. Eternal God, whose power upholds

Henry Tweedy's hymn was awarded first prize out of more than one thousand entries in a contest for modern missionary hymns sponsored by the Hymn Society of America in 1928–9. It was first sung in Riverdale Presbyterian Church, New York, in 1930, and was included in the *Pilgrim Hymnal*, 1931.

DURROW. See 397.

500. Christ for the world we sing

Written by Samuel Wolcott, a Congregationalist minister, in 1869. 'The Young Men's Christian Associations of Ohio', he writes, 'met in one of our churches, with their motto in evergreen letters over the pulpit. "Christ for the World and the World for Christ".' This suggested the hymn which he composed on his way home from the service.

MILTON ABBAS by E. H. Thiman appears for the first time in 1951 in both *Congregational Praise* and *The BBC Hymn Book*, in both of which it is set to these words.

501. Far round the world thy children sing their song

This hymn by Basil Mathews was written in 1909 for a Sunday School Anniversary at Bowes Park, London, and was originally printed in his *The Fascinated Child*. Three years later verses dealing with the peoples of Asia, Africa, and the Islands were added. The whole hymn was included in *School Worship*, 1926.

DUNBLANE CATHEDRAL by A. F. Barnes was composed for this hymn for RCH, 1927.

502. God of heaven, hear our singing

Written by Miss Havergal on 22 October 1869, at Leamington, and published in *Twelve Sacred Songs for Little Singers*, 1870.

SHIPSTON. See 17.

503. Thy love, O God, has all mankind created

Bayly's hymn is from *Rejoice, O People*, 1951, and was included in *Hymns for Church and School*, 1964.

NORTHBROOK by R. S. Thatcher is from *The Clarendon Hymn Book*, 1936, and is the tune set to these words in *Hymns for Church and School*.

504. O God of love, O King of peace

Written by Sir Henry Baker for *Hymns Ancient and Modern*, 1861, where it is headed by the text Ps. 29: 11.

ST. VENANTIUS is generally referred to as a Rouen Church Melody, but comes from the *Paris Antiphoner*, 1681. See 42. It first appeared in its present form in *The English Hymnal*, 1906.

Cross ref. to MELCOMBE. See 47.

505. Christ is the world's true light

G. W. Briggs's advent hymn was written for *Songs of Praise*, 1931.

RINKART (KOMMT SEELEN) is by J. S. Bach and is taken from Schemelli's *Musikalisches Gesangbuch*, Leipzig, 1736, where it is set to 'Kommt Seelen dieser Tag muss heilig sein besungen'. It is first set to this hymn in *Songs of Praise*.

506. O God of our divided world

This hymn was written on 17 September 1965, by A. N. Phillips on returning home from an ecumenical discussion group organized by the Revd. John Williamson, minister of Trinity Presbyterian Church, Birkenhead. It was first sung at the Presbyterian Swanwick Conference in 1966.

O AMOR QUAM EXSTATICUS is an old French melody. It is a mode i melody. The setting is that by Basil Harwood in *The Oxford Hymn Book*, 1908, and *The Anglican Hymn Book*, 1965.

507. Father Eternal, Ruler of Creation

Laurence Housman's poem was written at the request of the Revd. H. R. L. Sheppard, St. Martin-in-the-Fields, London, for the 'Life and Liberty Movement', after the war, with 'their' altered to 'our' in v. 2 line 2. It was included in *Songs of Praise*, 1925.

OLD 124TH. See 84.

508. Almighty Father, who dost give

Masterman's hymn first appeared in *In Hoc Signo*, 1916, and was included in *A Missionary Hymnbook*, 1922.

FINNART by K. G. Finlay first appears and was set to these words in the latter.

509. O Holy City, seen of John

Walter R. Bowie's hymn was suggested by the vision of St. John in Rev. 21. It is from *Hymns of the Kingdom of God*, 1910.

SANCTA CIVITAS by Herbert Howells first appeared in *Hymns for Church and School*, 1964, where it is set to these words.

510. Lord of light, whose Name outshineth

H. E. Lewis's hymn first appears in *The Congregational Hymnary*, 1916. 'This hymn', he says, 'was written to declare that in doing God's will, active co-operation is as much needed as humble resignation.'

RUSTINGTON. See 353.

Cross ref. to BLAENWERN. See 473.

511. O day of God, draw nigh

Based upon 'the Day of Judgment and Salvation' in Isa. 24–7, and written by R. B. Y. Scott for the American Fellowship for a Christian Social Order, and published in *Hymns for Worship*, 1939.

HILLSBOROUGH by John Gardner first appears in *Hymns for Church and School*, 1964, where it is set to these words.

512. Where cross the crowded ways of life

Written by F. M. North on the basis of a translation of Matt. 22: 9, 'Go ye, therefore, unto the parting of the highways'. It was first published in *The Christian City*, 1903, the monthly newsletter of the New York City and Church Extension Society of the Methodist Episcopal Church, but was written for *The Methodist Hymnal*, 1905.

O JESU MI DULCISSIME is first found in the *Clausener Gesangbuch*, 1653.

Cross ref. to BRESLAU. See 430.

513. God of the pastures, hear our prayer

This hymn, written by T. C. Hunter Clare in 1949, first appears as a leaflet and later in *The Anglican Hymn Book*, 1965, of the Church Society.

SEARCHING FOR LAMBS. See 387.

514. Eternal Ruler of the ceaseless round

Written by Chadwick for the graduating class of the Divinity School, Cambridge, Mass., 19 June 1864, shortly before the author's ordination in the Second Unitarian Church, Boston. The date is a few weeks after Grant's desperate battle against Lee in the wilderness, so 'these lines of peace and goodwill', as Reeves says, 'are especially significant as coming at a time so full of hate and slaughter'. It first appeared in his *Book of Poems*, 1876. The text is that in *The Treasury of American Sacred Song*. It was first introduced into England in Horder's *Congregational Hymns*, 1884.

SONG 1. See 492.

515. Father, who on man dost shower

Percy Dearmer's hymn was first published in *The English Hymnal*, 1906, under the heading 'Societies: Temperance'.

QUEM PASTORES LAUDAVERE. See 111.

516. God the Omnipotent! King, who ordainest

The first two verses are from a hymn by Henry Chorley, published originally in Hullah's *Part Music*, 1844. Verses 3–5 are from Ellerton's hymn beginning 'God the Almighty One, wisely ordaining', which had been written by him on 28 August 1870. It appeared in Brown-Borthwick's *Select Hymns for Church and Home*, 1871. Ellerton's hymn was an imitation of Chorley's 'God the all-terrible! King, who ordainest', which he had headed 'In Time of War'. Ellerton's hymn was written during the Franco-German war, four days before the battle of Sedan.

RUSSIA (REPHIDIM) was composed in 1833 for the Russian National Anthem by A. F. Lvov, adjutant to Tsar Nicholas I. He writes, 'In 1833 I accompanied the Emperor Nicholas on his journeys to Prussia and Austria. On returning, I heard that the Emperor had expressed regret that Russia had no national anthem, and as he was tired of the English tune that had been used, I was asked to write a national anthem for Russia.' It was first officially performed and adopted in the autumn of 1833. It was first printed as a hymn-tune in Hullah's *Part Music*.

517. God of Eternity, Lord of the Ages

Written by Merrington in 1912 for the Jubilee of St. Andrew's Presbyterian Church, Brisbane, Queensland, of which the author was then minister. 'The main thought in my heart', he writes, 'was of thankfulness to the Giver of all good for the splendid services rendered in the Colonies of our own blood and creed, and thankfulness for the opening of Emmanuel College during that year.' Emmanuel College was the Presbyterian Theological Seminary in Brisbane.

RUSSIA (REPHIDIM). See 516.

518. Lord, while for all mankind we pray

J. R. Wreford's hymn was contributed to Beard's *Collection of Hymns for Public and Private Worship*, 1837.

ST. PAUL (ABERDEEN). See 72.

519. Judge Eternal, throned in splendour

Scott Holland's hymn first appeared in *The Commonwealth*, 1902, of which he was editor. It was included in *The English Hymnal*, 1906.

RHUDDLAN. See 88.

Cross ref. to PICARDY. See 256.

520. O God of earth and altar

G. K. Chesterton's hymn was first printed in *The Commonwealth*. Scott Holland, the editor, submitted it for inclusion in *The English Hymnal*, 1906, where it duly appeared.

PASSION CHORALE. See 253.

521. God save our gracious Queen

The history of both words and music is very obscure. It is probably Jacobite in origin. In *Harmonia Anglicana*, *c*. 1743, the first line is, 'God save our lord the king', and it consisted of two verses. It is anonymous. Another version in three verses appears in *The Gentleman's Magazine*, 1745, beginning 'God save great George our King'. The third verse is substantially that given in CH3 as the second. The text printed here is the official version.

NATIONAL ANTHEM is alleged to have been sung by Henry Carey *c*. 1740, when it certainly appeared in *Thesaurus Musicus*, *c*. 1743, as later in *The Gentleman's Magazine*, 1745. But in neither is Carey named, and it was not until 1795 that George Carey claimed the authorship for his father. On the other hand, Dr. Arne, who made an arrangement of the anthem for a performance at Drury Lane Theatre on 28 September 1745, says, 'It was a received opinion that it was written for the Catholic Chapel of James II'. This is supported by the discovery of J. A. Fuller-Maitland and W. Barclay Squire. The former writes, 'In editing the catches of Purcell for the Purcell Society, Squire and I found one written to celebrate the return of the Duke of York (James II) from virtual exile in 1680; and that the words "God save the King" which occur in it are set to the very same four notes of the tune ... When the catch was sung at a meeting of the Musical Association at which I reported the discovery, the prominence given to the four notes made it a matter of certainty that the quotation was deliberately made. Before this catch was found, the earliest date for the appearance of the tune we know was 1740 or 1743; as the MS. containing the catch, now in the British Museum, bears a date of ownership 1681, the song is undoubtedly older than that, since it seems to be quoted in the catch as though the allusion would be recognized by those who heard it. Incidentally, the catch proves that the reference of the song was to the house of Stuart, not to that of Hanover.'

522. Our Father, by whose name

F. B. Tucker's hymn is from *The Hymnal*, 1940, of the Protestant Episcopal Church of America. It is included in *The Irish Church Hymnal*, 1960.

RHOSYMEDRE is from *Original Sacred Music, Composed and Arranged by The Revd. John Edwards, B.A., Jesus College, Oxford, c.* 1840, where it is named 'Lovely'.

523. O happy home, where thou art loved the dearest

From Spitta's *Psalter und Harfe*, Leipzig, 1833. This hymn came into common use in Germany following its inclusion in the *Würtemberger Gesangbuch*, 1842. Spitta wrote it in 1826 under the text Luke 19: 9. Mrs. Findlater's translation was adopted in RCH, 1927, 'for musical reasons' though 'it had not the author's approval'. Mrs. Findlater published it in *Hymns from the Land of Luther*, 1858.

NORTHBROOK. See 503.

524. Thy Kingdom come; yea, bid it come

This hymn is taken from the poetical works of the Irish poetess, Katherine Tynan Hinkson. It was included in the *St. Andrew Hymnal*, 1960.

HERONGATE. See 385.

525. From thee all skill and science flow

This hymn consists of stanzas three to six of one beginning 'Accept this building, gracious Lord', which according to Mrs. Kingsley was written for the laying of the foundation-stone of the Working Men's block of the Queen's Hospital, Birmingham, 4 December 1871, and sung on that occasion by a choir of one thousand children. On the other hand, in Kingsley's *Poems* it is dated 'Eversley 1870' and is said to have been sung 'at the opening of the New Wing of the Children's Hospital, Birmingham'.

NUN DANKET ALL (GRÄFENBERG). See 5.

526. Father, whose will is life and good

Rawnsley's hymn for medical missionaries, doctors, and nurses was first published in *A Missionary Hymn Book*, 1922.

TALLIS' ORDINAL. See 91.

527. Eternal Father, strong to save

This hymn was written in 1860, and the text given here is that in *Hymns Ancient and Modern*, 1861. But there are three different versions. The original version was published in *The Anglican Hymn Book*, 1868, that is, seven years after the revised version appeared in *Hymns Ancient and Modern*. A third version, revised by the author, appeared in the appendix to *Psalms and Hymns*, 1869. The hymn was suggested by Ps. 107: 24.

MELITA was composed by Dykes for this hymn for *Hymns Ancient and Modern*. Its name is taken from Acts 28: 1.

528. Thou who dost rule on high

Written by R. W. Littlewood for an Intercession Service in Portstewart Methodist Church in 1939. It first appears in *The School Hymn Book of the Methodist Church*, 1950.

ST. JOHN. See 135.

529. Holy Father, in thy mercy

Written by Isabel Stevenson at Cheltenham on the day her invalid brother sailed for South Africa in 1869. It was printed privately, but a copy came into the hands of an officer on H.M.S. *Bacchante*, the ship on which King George and his brother sailed round the world in 1881–2. There it was used in the ship's worship. The princes sent a copy home to their mother, and it was sung by the Royal Family at home during the cruise. It was included in the *Supplement*, 1889, to *Hymns Ancient and Modern*.

WESTRIDGE by Martin Shaw was composed for *Songs of Praise for Boys and Girls*, 1930, where it was set to 'Jesus, friend of little children'. See· 100.

530. Blest be the everlasting God

Paraphrase 61 from *Scottish Paraphrases*, 1781. It is a paraphrase of 1 Pet. 1: 3–5 and the original was written by Isaac Watts and published in his *Hymns*, 1707, entitled 'Hope of Heaven by the Resurrection of Christ'. It was taken over unaltered into the 1745 and 1751 editions of the *Scottish Paraphrases*, but in the 1781 edition the third stanza of the original was omitted. Verses 1, 2, and 4 are by Watts, v. 3 is attributed to William Cameron.

BISHOPTHORPE first appeared in Gardner's *Select Portions of the Psalms of David*, 1786, and in its present form in *The Psalms of David for the use of Parish Churches. The Music Selected, Adapted, and Composed by Edward Miller, Mus. Doc.*, 1790. There the tune is named 'Bishopthorpe' and assigned to Jeremiah Clarke.

531. Behold what witnesses unseen

Paraphrase 59: 1–4, 13, based on Heb. 12: 1–13, as in *Scottish Paraphrases*, 1781. This is one of the six paraphrases for which no attribution of authorship is given.

ST. NICHOLAS appears in Holdroyd's *Spiritual Man's Companion*, 1753, and the arrangement is that in *Scottish Psalmody*, 1854.

532. Hark how the adoring hosts above

Paraphrase 65: 5, 6, 8, 9, 11 from *Scottish Paraphrases*, 1781. It is based on Rev. 5: 6–14. It is Cameron's arrangement of Watts's 'Behold the glories of the Lamb', said to be his first hymn, which appeared in his *Hymns*, 1707.

ST. MAGNUS (NOTTINGHAM). See 286.

533. How bright these glorious spirits shine

Paraphrase 66 from *Scottish Paraphrases*, 1781, based on Rev. 7: 13–17. It is a revision of Watts's 'These glorious minds, how bright they shine' published in his *Hymns*, 1707, and entitled 'The Martyrs glorified'. It was taken over practically unaltered into the 1745 and 1751 editions of the *Scottish Paraphrases* and re-cast by William Cameron for the 1781 edition.

ST. ASAPH is from *Sacred Music . . . sung in St. George's Church, Edinburgh, edited by R. A. Smith*, 1825, where it is assigned to Giornovichi, but the original has not been traced to any of his works.

NOTES ON THE HYMNS

534. For all the saints who from their labours rest

How's original hymn as published in Nelson's *Hymns for Saints' Days*, 1864, had eleven stanzas. The author approved the alteration of 'Thy' to 'the' in the first line.

SINE NOMINE was composed by Vaughan Williams for this hymn for *The English Hymnal*, 1906.

535. O what their joy and their glory must be

'O quanta, qualia sunt illa sabbata' written by Abelard for the Abbey of the Paraclete at Nogent-sur-Seine over which Héloïse presided. It was the hymn for Saturday evening worship. Neale's version appeared in *The Hymnal Noted*, 1854. It omits two verses. The text is Neale's as revised in *Hymns Ancient and Modern*, 1861.

O QUANTA QUALIA is found in *La Feillée's Méthode du Plain-Chant*, Paris, 1808, where it is set to the hymn 'Regnator orbis'. It was adapted and set to these words by Helmore in *The Hymnal Noted*.

536. There is a land of pure delight

From Watts's *Hymns and Spiritual Songs*, 1707, with the heading 'A prospect of Heaven makes death easy'.

MENDIP from *The English Hymnal*, 1906, is adapted by Cecil Sharp from the melody of an old ballad called 'The Miller's Apprentice' or 'The Oxford Tragedy', familiar in Somerset. The harmonization is by Vaughan Williams.

537. Jerusalem the golden

'Urbs Sion aurea, patria lactea' is a selection from a long poem of almost three thousand lines, entitled 'De Contemptu Mundi' by Bernard of Cluny. The greater part of the poem is a 'savage satire' on the wickedness of the times and is 'full of the fires of hell' though it opens with a description of the peace and glory of heaven. The original is in the 'Leonine metre', that is, 'dactylic hexameter with tailed rhymes'. This was imitated by Gerald Moultrie in his translation in *Lyra Mystica*, 1865. Neale's version is in a different metre, and appeared in *The Rhythm of Bernard de Morlaix, Monk of Cluny on the Celestial Country*, 1858. It was included in *Hymns Ancient and Modern*, 1861.

EWING was published on a single sheet in 1853 as the music for the section 'For thee, O dear, dear country', and was in triple time. It also appears in this form in *A Manual of Psalm and Hymn Tunes ... edited by the Hon. and Rev. J. Grey*, 1857. Its first appearance in the present form is in *Hymns Ancient and Modern*. Ewing never liked it in common time, and said 'It now seems to me a good deal like a polka'.

538. For those we love within the veil

Written by W. C. Piggott for a Commemoration Service in his church during the war, 1915, and published in *Songs of Praise*, 1925, and *Congregational School Worship*, 1926, of which he was one of the editors.

RIPPONDEN by Norman Cocker first appeared in *The BBC Hymn Book*, 1951, where it is set to these words.

Cross ref. to ES IST KEIN TAG (MEYER). See 145.

539. Captains of the saintly band

'Caelestis aulae principes' by Jean Baptiste de Santeüil for the festival of the Apostles appears in the *Cluniac Breviary*, 1686, and in his *Hymni Sacri et Novi*, 1689. The revised *Paris Breviary*, 1736, gives it as the hymn for the 'Common of Apostles at Lauds'. Chandler included it in his *Hymns of the Primitive Church*, 1837, as does Newman in his *Hymni Ecclesiae*, 1838. The text is that by Sir Henry Baker in *Hymns Ancient and Modern*, 1861.

UNIVERSITY COLLEGE by Gauntlett appeared in *The Church Hymn and Tune Book, edited by W. J. Blew and H. J. Gauntlett*, 1852.

540. The eternal gifts of Christ the King

The hymn is attributed to Ambrose (340-97). 'Aeterna Christi munera', originally written for 'martyrs', was later adapted for 'Apostles'. The latter is given here. It appears in the Roman, York, Sarum, and other Breviaries, but there is considerable variations in the texts. The translation here is based on that by Neale in *The Hymnal Noted*, 1852.

AETERNA CHRISTI MUNERA is a Rouen Church-melody from Guidetti's *Directorium Chori*, Rome, 1582. It appears in *The English Hymnal*, 1906. See 42.

541. The Son of God goes forth to war

Written by Heber for St. Stephen's Day and appearing in his *Hymns*, 1827.

ELLACOMBE. See 235.

542. Sing Alleluia forth in duteous praise

The hymn 'Alleluia piis edite laudibus' (possibly fifth century) from the *Mozarabic Breviary* is set for the first Sunday in Lent. Ellerton's translation first appeared in *The Churchman's Family Magazine*, 1865. A freer version, based on Neale, appears in *Songs of Praise*, 1925, from which the text here is taken.

ST. SEBASTIAN was composed specially for this hymn by P. C. Buck. It first appears in his *Fourteen Hymn Tunes*, 1913, and was included in *Hymns Ancient and Modern*, 1916. It is also known as 'Martins'.

543. Let saints on earth in concert sing

The original hymn in Wesley's *Funeral Hymns*, 1759, consisted of five eight-line stanzas, which have been shortened in most hymn-books. The present version first appeared in Murray's *Hymnal for Use in the English Church*, 1852. The first two lines are Murray's, the rest of v. 1 and vv. 2-3 Wesley's, and vv. 4-5 Murray's emendation of Wesley.

FRENCH (DUNDEE). See 139.

544. From heavenly Jerusalem's towers

'O fryniau Caersalem ceir gweled' by David Charles as translated by Lewis Edwards. The probable origin of the hymn was the author's suffering from paralysis in his last years while his intellect was unimpaired, and his 'soul rebelled at the enforced inactivity'. He looks to the day when his frailties would be explained.

CRUGYBAR is from *Moliant Seion*, 1883, edited by J. Cledan Williams, though it was known earlier in the manuscripts of John Jenkins, Ceri, *c.* 1820. It was probably originally a triple-time folk-tune in three-bar phrases, suggesting an origin as a dance-air. It resembles the ballad-tune 'The pretty girl milking her cow', which had been published earlier by Ieuan Gwyllt (John Roberts) as 'Llanarmon'.

545. Far off I see the goal

Written by R. R. Roberts, at the request of the Revd. S. O. Morgan, for the tune 'Moab' for the RCH, 1927, though it first appeared in a small booklet, 'Programme of United Service of Praise, June 29, 1925, held in connexion with the meetings of the Presbyterian Alliance, Cardiff'.

MOAB, composed by Ieuan Gwyllt (John Roberts), is from *Llyfr Tonau Cynulleidfaol*, 1870, the tune book of the Presbyterian Church of Wales, formerly known as the Calvinistic Methodists.

546. I believe in God the Father Almighty

In the early Church the exact wording of the Creed varied in different areas, so there was the Creed of Antioch, of Caesarea, of Rome, and elsewhere. The old Roman Creed, found, for example, in the *Apostolic Tradition* of Hippolytus, developed into the Baptismal Creed of the West, and came to be known as the *Apostles' Creed*. Its final form dates from about the sixth or seventh century. In Scotland it remained part of the Church's heritage after the Reformation, being used at Baptism and each Lord's Day at public worship. Even the Westminster *Confession of Faith* and Catechisms had the *Apostles' Creed* appended to them as 'a brief sum of the Christian faith, agreeable to the Word of God and anciently received in the Churches of Christ'. Its exclusion through English Puritan influence from the Westminster *Directory for the Public Worship of God*, 1645, however, meant that it fell into disuse. Its use as one of the interrogations in the Baptismal Service was restored in the first edition of the *Euchologion*, 1867, and in the Sunday Morning Service in the fifth, 1884. A musical setting by Stainer is provided in both the first edition of *The Church Hymnary*, 1898, and RCH, 1927. Here none is given, as it was held the Creed should be said, but this does not preclude congregations from using a choral version if desired.

547. The praises of the Lord our God

Metrical psalm 78: 4b, 5–7 from *The Scottish Psalter*, 1650. Sternhold's version had been given in *The Anglo-Genevan Psalter*, 1556, and was taken over in the Scottish book, 1564.

CAITHNESS. See 125.

548. When to the sacred font we came

Paraphrase 47 from *Scottish Paraphrases*, 1781, omitting the first verse. The paraphrase 'And shall we then go on to sin' is from Watts's 'Shall we go on to sin?' first published in his *Hymns*, 1709. Only consequential changes occur in the 1745 draft, but in 1781 the whole was rewritten by William Cameron except that the first line was retained. It is a paraphrase of Rom. 6: 1–7.

TALLIS' ORDINAL. See 91.

549. Our children, Lord, in faith and prayer

Part of a baptismal hymn from Haweis's *Carmina Christo*, 1808, as arranged in Nunn's *Psalms and Hymns from the Most Approved Authors*, 1817. In RCH, 1927, three verses were given, but the third is here omitted. To the first two verses have been added two from Heber's 'By cool Siloam's shady rill'. In the first edition of *The Church Hymnary*, 1898, the complete hymn of Heber had been included. In RCH, two verses were omitted which completely altered the 'rationale' of the hymn. Here the compilers of CH3 have made a composite hymn for use at baptism, by adding Heber's last two verses to Haweis's first two. Heber's hymn first appeared in *The Christian Observer*, 1912.

ST. PETER. See 376.

BELMONT has been ascribed to both Samuel Webbes, father and son, and to Mozart, but there are no sufficient grounds for assigning it to any of these. It appears to be an adaptation from a melody in Gardiner's *Sacred Melodies... adapted to the best English Poets*, 1812. No composer is named, but in his *Music and Friends*, 1838, Gardiner cites it as his own. It is given in practically its present form in *A Church Hymn and Tune Book*, 1859, and Routledge's *Church and Home Metrical Psalter and Hymnal*, 1860. In the former it is said to be harmonized by J. Bentley.

550. Lift high the cross, the love of Christ proclaim

This hymn by M. R. Newbolt is based on one having the same first line by G. W. Kitchin, *Supplement* to *Hymns Ancient and Modern*, 1916. Originally it had twelve verses, of which 1–5, 8, and 10 are given here. It first appeared in *Hymns Ancient and Modern*, 1922.

CRUCIFER by Sir S. H. Nicholson first appears in *Hymns Ancient and Modern*, where it is set to these words.

551. A little child the Saviour came

Contributed to the Church of Scotland's *Hymns for Public Worship*, 1861, by William Robertson, minister of Monzievaird, Perthshire.

COMMANDMENTS is a tune adapted from the melody of 'Les Commandemens de Dieu'. See 586.

552. Blessed Jesus, here we stand

Schmolk's 'Liebster Jesu, wir sind hier' first appeared in *Heilige Flammen*, Striegau, 1706, entitled 'Seasonable Reflections of the Sponsors on their way with the child to Baptism'. Miss Winkworth translated six of its seven verses in *Lyra Germanica*, 1856, from which these four stanzas are taken.

LIEBSTER JESU (DESSAU). See 128.

553. O Father, in thy father-heart

Ella S. Armitage's baptismal hymn was written for *The Congregational Church Hymnal*, 1887.

SUSSEX CAROL. See 181.

Cross ref. to SURREY. See 16.

554. O God, thy life-creating love

A. F. Bayly's baptismal hymn is taken from his *Again I say Rejoice*, 1967.

O WALY, WALY is a traditional English melody, which was harmonized by the musical editors of *Sunday School Praise*, 1958.

Cross ref. to COMMANDMENTS. See 551 and 586.

555. O loving Father, to thy care

Alington's baptismal hymn first appears in *Hymns Ancient and Modern*, 1950.

O WALY, WALY. See 554.

Cross ref. to COMMANDMENTS. See 551 and 586.

556. The Lord bless you and keep you

The *Aaronic Blessing* is taken from Num. 6: 24–6 (R.V.) with 'thee' changed to 'you'. Its use in Reformed rites is derived from Strasbourg and Geneva, through Bucer and Calvin, and ultimately from Luther's *Formula Missae*, 1523.

SETTINGS. (i) LILLE is anonymous but was composed specially for CH3; (ii) PLAIN-SONG II, ending 1; (iii) HEATON composed specially for CH3 by Thomas Wilson.

557. Father, hear us as we pray

Edith Macalister's Cradle Roll hymn was written for the National Sunday School Union and appeared first in *Child Songs*, 1914.

BATTISHILL. See 93. This is one of the tunes suggested for these words in *Child Songs*.

558. We believe in one God the Father Almighty

The *Nicene Creed* is not that of the Council of Nicaea, 325, but that of the Council of Constantinople, 381. It is a Confession of the Church's Faith. According to Theodorus Lector, *c.* 528, the Creed was introduced into the Liturgy at Antioch by the Patriarch Peter, the Fuller (470–88) and at Constantinople by the Patriarch Timothy I (511–18). In the West, it was first used in Spain, being ordered to be used before the Lord's Prayer by the third Synod of Toledo, 589. It was introduced into the Roman rite by Benedict VIII in 1014 at the request, or should it be demand, of the Emperor Henry II, who was accustomed to its use in Germany. Its place in the various rites is not uniform. In all the Eastern rites it comes after the Great Entrance. The Roman and Gallican have it after the Gospel, but the Ambrosian after the Offertory.

Originally the text read 'We believe', but later both the Byzantine and
Roman rites changed into the singular, 'I believe'. As it is a confession of the
Church's Faith—not a Baptismal creed—the plural form has been adopted
in CH3. The text, changed into the plural form, is that prepared by Cranmer
for the Communion Service in the BCP, 1549.

In some of the early Reformed rites in Strasbourg, the *Nicene Creed* was
retained, but possibly owing to the influence of Luther's *Formula Missae*,
1523, it was soon replaced by the *Apostles' Creed*. Following the Westminster
Assembly even the latter ceased to be used. See 546. In the first edition of the
Euchologion, 1867, the *Apostles' Creed* is given in the plural, and in the fourth,
1884, the *Nicene Creed* (plural form) is given with the *Apostles'* as an
alternative. In the sixth edition, 1890, the latter is omitted. This remained the
position until 1923, when *Prayers for Divine Service* reverted to the singular
usage. In RCH, 1927, John Merbecke's setting was provided, but here the
intention is that the *Nicene Creed* should be said.

559. The Lord be with you . . . Lift up your hearts . . .

The *Salutation* is found in all the early liturgies. In the Clementine, Syrian,
Nestorian, Byzantine, and Mozarabic rites, with variations in wording, it is:

The grace of our Lord Jesus Christ, and the love of God, and the
communion of the Holy Spirit, be with you all.

℟. And with thy spirit.

In the *Apostolic Tradition*, *Testamentum Domini*, Roman, Ambrosian, and
Ethiopic, it is:

The Lord be with you.
℟. And with thy spirit.

The latter became the general Western usage, and was continued in the
Anglican, Lutheran, and a few early Strasbourg Reformed rites. In the last,
however, it fell out of use at an early date. It does not appear to have been
used in the Reformed rites in Geneva, France, or Scotland.

The *Sursum Corda* is found in all the extant liturgies, Hippolytus' *Apostolic
Tradition* showing that its use dates from at latest the first decade of the third
century. Though there are slight variations in wording it is a universal
practice. This was continued in Lutheranism and Anglicanism. At the
beginning it was found in the German rites in Strasbourg, but not in the
French. However, in the French Strasbourg, Genevan, French, and Scottish
rites the concluding paragraph of the Exhortation before communion was
based upon it. In the third edition of the *Euchologion*, 1874, it was the basis of
the opening words of the Eucharistic prayer, and since the fifth, 1884, it has
been set out responsively.

SETTING. The musical setting for the *Salutation* and *Sursum Corda* was
composed by Kenneth Leighton for CH3.

560. Holy, Holy, Holy, Lord God of Hosts

The *Sanctus* comes from Isa. 6: 3. The Hebrew, LXX, and Vulgate all have
'The earth is full of thy glory', whereas both Eastern and Western liturgies
have 'Heaven and earth'. The praise of God for His creation and providence
in the Eastern rites, and the Roman preface, both lead up to the *Sanctus* as an

act of praise. This continued in the Lutheran and Anglican liturgies. It also continued in some Reformed rites on the Continent. On the other hand, it is missing in the Genevan rites, the Scottish *Book of Common Order*, 1564, and the Westminster *Directory for the Public Worship of God*, 1645. The *Sanctus* was restored in the first edition of the *Euchologion*, 1867. Musical settings for the *Sanctus* by Stainer and Elvey were provided in *The Church Hymnary*, 1898, and in RCH, 1927, the former was omitted and settings by Merbecke and Attwood added.

SETTING. The musical setting for the *Sanctus* was composed by Kenneth Leighton for CH3.

561. Blessed is he that cometh in the Name of the Lord . . . Hosanna . . .

The *Benedictus qui venit* and *Hosanna* come from Ps. 118: 25, 'Give victory now, O Lord; O Lord, send us now prosperity: blessed be he that cometh in the name of the Lord'. In our Lord's time the Hebrew word 'Hoseah-na' (Give victory now) had become 'Hosanna'. The words with which the people greeted Jesus at the triumphal entry were, 'Hosanna to the Son of David: Blessed is he that cometh in the name of the Lord. Hosanna in the highest' (Mark 11: 9–10, Matt. 21: 9, 15, John 12: 13).

While not in the *Clementine Liturgy* (c. 385), it is in the Syrian, Byzantine, and Nestorian rites in the East. Though not in *The Apostolic Tradition*, it is in the Roman, Gallican, and Mozarabic rites in the West. It continued in the Lutheran, some Continental Reformed, and Anglican rites. As in the case of the *Sanctus* (see 560), it fell out of use in Scotland. It was restored in the first edition of the *Euchologion*, 1867. No musical settings were provided in the first and second editions of *The Church Hymnary*.

SETTING. The musical setting for the *Benedictus qui venit* and *Hosanna* were composed by Kenneth Leighton for CH3.

562. Our father which art in heaven

The Lord's Prayer is given in two forms, (i) that in the Gospel according to Matthew 6: 9–13 (A.V.) and (ii) that in the BCP. A setting for singing by Stainer was provided in the first edition of *The Church Hymnary*, 1898, to which was added Merbecke's setting in RCH, 1927. Here it is to be said.

563. O Lamb of God, that takest away the sins of the world

The first known use of the *Agnus Dei*, which consists of two Scriptural verses (John 1: 29 and Matt. 20: 30–1), is in the *Gloria in excelsis*. See 62. Its origin is clearly Eastern where the word 'Lamb' is used to designate both Christ and the consecrated bread and the West Syrian rite contains 'confractoria' which speak of 'the Lamb of God who takes away the sin of the world'. The use of this modified form of part of the *Gloria in excelsis* appears to be referred to in a rubric in the *Gelasian Sacramentary*, 492. It was probably introduced at the Fraction in the Roman rite by Sergius I in the seventh century. Later in the eleventh century with the virtual disappearance of the Fraction it became associated with the Kiss of Peace, hence the change to 'Grant us thy peace'. It was continued in some Lutheran rites and in the BCP, 1549, but was omitted in 1552. It has been restored in the Scottish BCP, 1929. The *Agnus Dei* was used by Schwarz and Bucer in Strasbourg, but apparently not by Calvin. It was re-introduced in the fifth edition of the *Euchologion*, 1884. No musical settings were provided in the first two editions of *The Church Hymnary*.

SETTING. The musical setting for the *Agnus Dei* was composed by Kenneth Leighton for CH3.

564. Mine hands in innocence, O Lord

Metrical psalm 26: 6–8 from *The Scottish Psalter*, 1650. The version in 1564 was by John Hopkins.

ST. JAMES. See 121.

565. I'll of salvation take the cup

Metrical psalm 116: 13–14, 17–19 from *The Scottish Psalter*, 1650. See 8.

JACKSON first appears in *Twelve Psalm Tunes and Eighteen Double and Single Chants . . . composed for Four voices*, 1780, where it is set to Ps. 47. In Miller's *Collection*, 1800, it is called 'Byzantium'.

566. The earth belongs unto the Lord

Metrical psalm 24. Verses 1–4 are from *The Scottish Psalter*, 1650, vv. 5–6 from *The Irish Psalter*, 1880, and vv. 7–10 from the Scottish. The version in the Scottish book, 1564, was by John Craig.

ST. MATTHEW. See 214.

ST. GEORGE'S, EDINBURGH, appeared first in *Sacred Harmony, for the use of St. George's Church, Edinburgh*, 1820, prepared by Andrew Thomson and R. A. Smith. It is often used at the Great Entrance in the Scottish rite.

567. Deck thyself, my soul, with gladness

'Schmücke dich, o liebe Seele' was written by Franck *c.* 1649, and published in *Praxis Pietatis Melica*, Berlin, 1653, where it had nine verses. The version by Miss Winkworth in *Lyra Germanica*, 1858, was rewritten for *The Chorale Book for England*, 1863. In many German churches this hymn is invariably sung at Communion as an expression of the reverent joy which should accompany the sacrament.

SCHMÜCKE DICH by Crüger is from his *Geistliche Kirchen-Melodien*, Berlin, 1649, in which the first verse of the hymn also appears. This tune has always been associated with this hymn in Germany.

568. Father most loving, listen to thy children

This hymn by Fr. James Quinn, S.J. was submitted to the revision committee in manuscript. It appears in a considerably altered form in his *New Hymns for All Seasons*, 1969. Structurally the hymn is a series of verses based on the eucharistic rite: v. 1 Processional, v. 2 Gospel, v. 3 Offertory, v. 4 Communion, and v. 5 Recessional.

DIVA SERVATRIX is from *The English Hymnal*, 1906, and is one of the melodies referred to at No. 42. In *The Hymnal*, 1951, of the Episcopal Church in Scotland it is ascribed to Pierre Daniel Huet, bishop of Avranches, but the evidence for this is inconclusive. It comes from the *Bayeux Antiphoner*, 1739.

569. The bread of life, for all men broken

This hymn by Timothy Tingfang Lew first appears in the *Chinese Union Hymn Book*, 1934. This work is also known in English as *Hymns of Universal Praise*, 1936, where W. R. O. Taylor's translation first appears. It was also included in *The BBC Hymn Book*, 1951.

SHENG EN (GOD'S GRACE) by Su Yin-lan first appears in the *Chinese Union Hymn Book*. It is also given in the other two.

570. I am not worthy, holy Lord

Written by Sir Henry Baker for *Hymns Ancient and Modern*, 1875. It is based on Matt. 8: 8.

WIGTOWN. See 82.

571. Jesus, thou Joy of loving hearts

Ray Palmer's hymn reproduces a different cento of 'Jesu dulcis memoria' from 377 and 378. It begins 'Jesu, dulcedo cordium'. His version first appeared in *The Sabbath Hymnbook*, 1858.

JESU DULCIS MEMORIA is set to the Latin hymn in the *Catholische Geistliche Gesänge*, Andernach, 1608. The setting here is that in *Plainsong for Schools*.

WAREHAM by Knapp comes from *A Sett of New Psalm Tunes and Anthems, in Four Parts by William Knapp*, 1738, where it is set to Ps. 36: 5–10, and headed 'For the Holy Sacrament'. In his *New Church Melody . . . by William Knapp*, 1754, it again appears but now in common time, set to Ps. 139, and called 'Blandford Tune'.

572. Come, risen Lord, and deign to be our guest

Briggs's hymn was first published in *Songs of Praise*, 1925, and also appeared in his *Songs of Faith*, 1945, where it is entitled 'The Upper Room'. The text here is Briggs's original, reading in v. 1 line 4 'thine own sacrament' not 'this our sacrament' as altered by him at Dearmer's request. Verse 4 links the Last Supper with the supper at Emmaus, Luke 24: 28–32.

STONER HILL by William Harris was commissioned for *Hymns for Church and School*, 1964, where it is set to these words.

573. Here, O my Lord, I see thee face to face

Written by Bonar for his elder brother, John James Bonar, Greenock, and read after the Communion in his church, October 1855. The original had ten verses and first appeared in *Hymns of Faith and Hope*, 1857.

SONG 22. See 108.

Cross ref. to STONER HILL. See 572.

574. Bread of the world, in mercy broken

Heber's hymn first appeared the year after his death in *Hymns Written and Adapted for the Weekly Church Service of the Year*, 1827.

PSALM 118 (RENDEZ À DIEU). See 51.

Cross ref. to LES COMMANDEMENS DE DIEU. See 586.

575. Thou standest at the altar

Edward Eddis compiled *Hymns for the Use of the Churches*, 1864, for the Catholic Apostolic Church, and contributed this hymn to it.

CHRISTUS DER IST MEIN LEBEN (BREMEN). See 404.

576. O Christ, who sinless art alone

Wotherspoon's hymn is taken from *The Scottish Mission Hymn Book*, 1912.

COLINTON was composed by Kenneth Leighton for this hymn for CH3.

IONA was composed by Frederick Rimmer for this hymn for CH3.

577. Let all mortal flesh keep silence

This is the Cherubic Hymn from the *Liturgy of St. James* (fifth century). Gerard Moultrie's translation appeared in *Lyra Eucharistica*, 1864, and *The English Hymnal*, 1906.

PICARDY. See 256.

578. Now, my tongue, the mystery telling

Thomas Aquinas wrote the hymn 'Pange lingua gloriosi Corporis mysterium' while he was revising the 'Office for the festival of Corpus Christi' at the request of Pope Urban IV. The version given is that of Caswall in his *Lyra Catholica*, 1849, as revised by the compilers of *Hymns Ancient and Modern*, 1861.

PANGE LINGUA. See 256.

PICARDY. See 256.

Cross ref. to TANTUM ERGO SACRAMENTUM. See 373. This tune may be used for vv. 4–5.

579. Almighty Father, Lord most high

This hymn by V. S. S. Coles for Holy Communion was written for *Hymns Ancient and Modern*, 1904. It was to be sung at the Offertory.

AETERNA CHRISTI MUNERA (GUIDETTI). See 540.

Cross ref. to SOLEMNIS HAEC FESTIVITAS. See 56.

580. And now, O Father, mindful of the love

Bright's hymn based on the 'anamnesis' or 'Unde et memores, Domine, nos servi tui' was first published in *The Monthly Packet*, 1873.

SONG 1. See 492.

581. Forth from on high the Father sends

Thomas Aquinas's hymn 'Verbum supernum prodiens, nec Patris' was probably written *c.* 1263. It is found in the Roman (1478), Mozarabic (1562), Sarum, York, Aberdeen, and other Breviaries. This translation by Fr. James Quinn, S.J., is from his *New Hymns for All Seasons*, 1969.

DAS WALT' GOTT VATER is from Vetter's *Musikalische Kirch- und Hauss-Ergötzlichkeit*, Leipzig, 1713, as arranged by Bach in his *Choralgesänge*, 1769.

Cross ref. to VERBUM SUPERNUM. See 116.

582. In love, from love, thou camest forth, O Lord

John MacLeod's hymn is taken from *The Scottish Mission Hymn Book*, 1912. See 307.

SONG 22. See 108.

583. Lord, enthroned in heavenly splendour

George Bourne's hymn for Holy Communion first appears in his *Post-Communion Hymns*, 1874. In earlier editions of *Hymns Ancient and Modern* v. 5 was omitted, but it was restored in 1904. The text here is taken from *The BBC Hymn Book*, 1951.

TREDEGAR was composed by Guthrie Foote for these words. It appears in *The English Hymnal Service Book*, 1962.

Cross ref. to HELMSLEY. See 316.

584. Thee we adore, O hidden Saviour, thee

Thomas Aquinas's hymn 'Adoro te devote, latens Deitas' was an expression of personal adoration. It has been repeatedly translated, and the present version by J. R. Woodford, written in 1850, appeared in his *Hymns arranged for the Sundays and Holy Days of the Church of England*, 1855, and in *Hymns Ancient and Modern*, 1861. Woodford's followed a version in the *Paris Breviary*, 1736, which substitutes in v. 3 line 1 'Fountain of goodness' for 'Pious Pelican'. Aquinas had used the medieval idea that the pelican fed its young, if need be, with its own blood, an idea which meant that at that time the pelican was seen as a symbol of Christ. The translation also shortens the original; for example, the last two lines of v. 3 summarize three stanzas which have been omitted.

ADORO TE is the proper plain-song melody of this hymn, and is taken from the *Paris Processionale*, 1697, where it was sung at the Eucharist. It has been slightly altered to suit the metre of the translation. Two alternative arrangements by Kenneth Elliott are provided.

585. According to thy gracious word

First published in Montgomery's *Christian Psalmist*, 1825, and entitled 'This do in remembrance of me. St. Luke xxii. 19'. Two stanzas have been omitted here.

ST. FLAVIAN. See 8.

586. Father, we thank thee who hast planted

From *The Didache* (second century). The first three stanzas are a paraphrase of the prayer to be offered at the close of the Lord's Supper, and the last that of the one offered at the distribution of the bread. The text is F. B. Tucker's versification in *The Hymnal*, 1940, of the Protestant Episcopal Church in America.

LES COMMANDEMENS DE DIEU was composed or adapted by Louis Bourgeois, and set in *The French Psalter*, 1549, to the metrical version of the Decalogue by Clement Marot and Ps. 140. The present form of the melody is, with one slight variation, that of the original.

587. Author of life divine

From *Hymns on the Lord's Supper*, 1745, by John and Charles Wesley, where there is no conclusive evidence to show which of the two brothers wrote it. Erik Routley in the *Companion to Congregational Praise*, 1953, attributes it to Charles. This hymn did not come into common usage for over two centuries and was not included in any Methodist Hymnal until *The Methodist Hymn Book*, 1933. It owes its present popularity to its inclusion in *Hymns Ancient and Modern*, 1875.

DOLGELLEY (DOLGELLAU). See 219.

588. Strengthen for service, Lord, the hands

From the *Liturgy of Malabar*, translated by C. W. Humphreys and Percy Dearmer. The former versified this fifth-century prayer of the Church of St. Thomas in South India from Neale's translation in *Liturgies of St. Mark*, 1859, and Dearmer revised it for *The English Hymnal*, 1906.

ACH GOTT UND HERR is an anonymous melody found in Christian Gall's *As Hymnodus sacer*, Leipzig, 1625. Crüger in his *Gesangbuch*, Berlin, 1640, modified the second half of the original tune, and Peter in his *Andachts Zymbeln*, Freiburg, 1655, transposed it into the major key. The form here is Bach's arrangement in his *Choralgesänge*, 1769.

589. Forth in the peace of Christ we go

This hymn by Fr. James Quinn, S.J., appears in his *New Hymns for All Seasons*, 1969.

DANIEL is an Irish traditional melody. It first appeared as 'St. Finian' in *The Church and School Hymnal*, 1926. Martin Shaw arranged it for *Songs of Praise for Boys and Girls*, 1930. The arrangement here is by Erik Routley.

590. Now, Lord! according to thy word

Paraphrase 39: 8, 10–11 from *Scottish Paraphrases*, 1781, is a metrical version of the *Nunc dimittis*. See for prose version 204. It is a revision of Bruce's 'Now let thy servant die in peace', which had appeared in the draft of 1745. In Strasbourg, in Calvin's *La Forme*, 1545, 'Le cantique de Symeon' is sung after the Post-Communion and before the Benediction. An English metrical version appears in *The Anglo-Genevan Psalter*, 1561. This was retained in *The Scottish Psalter*, 1564. In Scotland it became the practice, if there were two Tables at the Lord's Supper, to follow the Genevan *Forme of Prayers*, 1556, and sing Ps. 103 at the end of the morning Table and the *Nunc dimittis* following that in the afternoon.

MORAVIA is derived from Wolder's *Neu Catechismus Gesangbüchlein*, Hamburg, 1598. In Bach's *Choralgesänge*, 1769, it is set to the hymn 'Aus meines Herzens Grunde'.

591. I'm not ashamed to own my Lord

Paraphrase 54 from *Scottish Paraphrases*, 1781. The original by Watts appeared in his *Hymns and Spiritual Songs*, 1707, under the text 1 Tim. 1: 12, and headed 'Not ashamed of the Gospel'. It was retained in the 1745 draft, and revised by Cameron for the 1781 edition.

JACKSON (BYZANTIUM). See 565.

592. We come, O Christ, to thee

Margaret Clarkson's hymn was first sung at the Student Missionary Convention, the precursor to the Urbana Missionary Conventions held every three years since then, held by the Inter-Varsity Christian Fellowship in Toronto in 1946. It was first published in *IVCF Hymns*, 1948, and was included in *Hymns of Faith*, 1964.

CHRISTCHURCH by Charles Steggall is from *Hymns for the Church of England*, 1865.

593. Ye that know the Lord is gracious

Alington's hymn, based on 1 Pet. 2: 3–10, was written for *Hymns Ancient and Modern*, 1950.

ABBOT'S LEIGH. See 334.

Cross ref. to HYFRYDOL. See 381.

594. Witness, ye men and angels, now

From Beddome's *Hymns adapted to the circumstances of Public Worship or Family Devotion*, 1817, entitled 'Joining the Church'.

ARDEN was composed by G. T. Thalben-Ball for the hymn 'O for a thousand tongues to sing' (see 371) in *The BBC Hymn Book*, 1951. It receives its name from the fact that the committee which compiled that hymn-book often met in the district of Arden.

595. We magnify thy Name, O God

Following a discussion on the doctrine of confirmation in Reformed theology during the work of the revision committee, this hymn was written by John M. Barkley in an attempt to give expression to this. Confirmation is an act of God within the context of His covenant and the Household of Faith, and so is linked to baptism and nurture, and to the eucharist and daily living.

ASCENDIT DEUS. See 287.

596. The Lord prepared hath his throne

Metrical psalm 103: 19–22 from *The Scottish Psalter*, 1650. See 351.

PRAETORIUS. See 288.

597. Pour out thy Spirit from on high

Written by Montgomery on 23 January 1833, as a hymn to be sung at a meeting of ministers. The original text had 'assembled servants' in v. 1 line 2, 'we' in v. 2 line 1, and 'our' in v. 3 line 3 and v. 5 lines 1 and 2. It first appeared the year it was written in both Birchell's *Selection of Hymns* and Bickersteth's *Christian Psalmody*.

WINCHESTER NEW (CRASSELIUS). See 234.

598. God be merciful unto us and bless us

Prose psalm 67 (A.V.), *Deus Misereatur*. See 3.

CHANTS   Walford Davies in C double.
          Wesley, S. in G double.

599. O Father, by whose sovereign sway

Alington's hymn was written for *Hymns Ancient and Modern*, 1950.

TALLIS' CANON is the eighth of nine tunes by Tallis in *The Whole Psalter translated into English Metre, which contayneth an hundreth and fifty Psalmes*, 1561, where it is referred to Ps. 67. See 91. The melody in the original is the same as that given here, except that each line is repeated before the next is introduced. The four-line form appears in Ravenscroft's *Whole Book of Psalms*, 1621.

600. O Father, all creating

Written by Ellerton on 29 January 1876, at the request of the Duke of Westminster, for the marriage of his daughter, Lady Elizabeth Harriet Grosvenor, to the Marquis of Ormonde, on 2 February. It was first published in Thring's *Collection*, 1880.

AURELIA. See 420.

601. O God, whose loving hand has led

Written by J. Boyd Moore for a marriage in Mountjoy congregation, Co. Tyrone, and first published here.

MELCOMBE. See 47.

Cross ref. to DANIEL. See 589.

602. O God of love, to thee we bow

Written by W. V. Jenkins for his own wedding. It first appeared in *The Fellowship Hymn Book*, 1909.

CHILDHOOD. See 156.

603. Such pity as a father hath

Metrical psalm 103: 13–17 from *The Scottish Psalter*, 1650. See 351.

KILMARNOCK. See 69.

604. Go, happy soul, thy days are ended

Woodward's hymn appears first in *Songs of Syon*, 1910. The text here is that revised by the compilers of *The BBC Hymn Book*, 1951.

LES COMMANDEMENS DE DIEU. See 586.

605. Jesus lives! thy terrors now

Gellert's Easter hymn, 'Jesus lebt, mit ihm auch ich', appeared in his *Geistliche Oden und Lieder*, Leipzig, 1757. Miss Cox's version in her *Hymns from the*

German, 1841, followed the original six-line form, but the present four-line form of her translation, which first appeared in Rorison's *Hymns and Anthems*, 1851, became very popular owing largely to the tune 'St. Albinus'.

ST. ALBINUS by Gauntlett is from *The Church Hymn and Tune Book*, 1852, edited by W. J. Blew and H. J. Gauntlett. It was composed for the hymn 'Angels to our jubilee'.

606. O lord of life, where'er they be

Composed by F. L. Hosmer in 1888 for the Easter Service in his own church at Cleveland, Ohio. In the original 'Hallelujah' is used at the last verse only. It was published in *The Chicago Unity*, 1888, and *The Thought of God*, 1894.

VULPIUS. See 266.

607. God of the living, in whose eyes

Ellerton's hymn was written for *Hymns for Schools and Bible-Classes*, 1858; then expanded and altered to its present form in *Hymns Original and Translated*, 1867.

VATER UNSER (OLD 112TH). See 96.

608. There is a blessèd home beyond this land of woe

Written by Sir Henry Baker for *Hymns Ancient and Modern*, 1861.

ANNUE CHRISTE is from Aynes's edition of La Feillée's *Nouvelle Méthode du Plain-Chant*, Lyons, 1808. Its source is the *Paris Antiphoner*, 1681. In the *Cluny Antiphoner*, 1686, it is set to the hymn of St. Martin 'Thure sumantes'. It came into use in England through its inclusion in *The Hymnal Noted*, 1852, and *Hymns Ancient and Modern*, 1889.

609. This stone to thee in faith we lay

Montgomery's hymn first appeared in *The Sheffield Iris*, 1822, and then in his *Christian Psalmist*, 1825.

SOLEMNIS HAEC FESTIVITAS. See 56.

610. All things are thine; no gift have we

Written by Whittier for the opening of Plymouth Church, St. Paul's, Minnesota, in 1873, and published in his *Complete Poetical Works*, 1876.

SOLEMNIS HAEC FESTIVITAS. See 56.

611. O God, our help in ages past

Watts's hymn appeared in his *Psalms of David*, 1719, entitled 'Man frail and God eternal'. Wesley in 1737 altered Watts's 'Our God, our help' to the present form. The hymn is based on the first part of Ps. 90.

ST. ANNE appears in *A Supplement to the New Version of Psalms by Dr. Brady and Mr. Tate ... The Sixth Edition, corrected and much enlarged*, 1708, where it is set to the new version of Ps. 42 in two parts, treble and bass, and is called

'St. Anne'. It is marked in the Index as a new tune and no composer's name is given. It is found with Croft's name attached in Hart's *Melodies Proper to be sung to any of ye versions of the Psalms of David*, c. 1720, and Church's *Introduction to Psalmody*, 1723. As both these editors were contemporaries of Croft, and Church was master of the choristers of Westminster Abbey while Croft was organist there, that Croft was the composer may be accepted as accurate.

612. For thy mercy and thy grace

Written by Downton in 1841 and published in *The Church of England Magazine*, 1843. An altered version was printed in *Hymns Ancient and Modern*, 1861, but the original with one verse omitted appeared in *The English Hymnal*, 1906. The latter was followed, omitting a second verse, in *Songs of Praise*, 1925, and is the version given here.

ORIENTIS PARTIBUS. See 275.

613. Great God, we sing that mighty hand

From the posthumous edition of Doddridge's *Hymns Founded on various Texts in the Holy Scriptures*, 1755, where it is headed 'Help obtained from God, Acts xxvi. 22. For the New Year'.

WAREHAM. See 571.

614. March on, my soul, with strength

Wright's hymn first appeared in *The YMCA Hymn Book*, Lausanne, 1904.

RHOSYMEDRE (LOVELY). See 522.

Cross ref. to CHRISTCHURCH. See 592.

615. Heavenly Father, thou hast brought us

Published in *The Home Hymn-book*, 1885, of which Mrs. Hawkins was editor. It was originally written for the golden wedding of her father and mother.

RUSTINGTON. See 353.

Cross ref. to BLAENWERN. See 473.

616. At thy feet, our God and Father

James Burns's hymn first appeared in *The Family Treasury*, 1861, and six years later in his *Psalms and Hymns for Divine Worship*, 1867, an English Presbyterian collection, under the text Ps. 65: 2 as a New Year's hymn.

AUSTRIAN HYMN. See 37.

617. Good unto all men is the Lord

Metrical psalm 145: 9–10, 15–16 from the second version in *The Scottish Psalter*, 1650. The version in the Scottish book, 1564, was by John Craig, which remained substantially the same in 1650.

WINCHESTER NEW (CRASSELIUS). See 234.

Cross ref. to WAREHAM. See 571.

618. The glory of the spring how sweet

Written by Thomas Gill on Whitsunday, 1867, and published in *The Golden Chain of Praise Hymns*, 1869, where it was entitled 'The Divine Redeemer' under the texts Ps. 104: 30 and Eph. 4: 23.

KING'S LANGLEY is a traditional English melody from a Hertfordshire Mayday carol, 'The moon shines bright', collected by Miss L. E. Broadwood. The harmonization is by Vaughan Williams as in *The English Hymnal*, 1906.

619. By the rutted roads we follow

John Arlott's hymn was written for *The BBC Hymn Book*, 1951.

SUSSEX. See 144.

620. We plough the fields, and scatter

This is the 'Peasants' Song' from a sketch by Matthias Claudius, *Paul Erdmann's Fest*, Hamburg, 1782, which depicts a harvest thanksgiving in a North German farmhouse. The original song had seventeen verses of four lines with a refrain. Miss Campbell's translation, though not very literal, preserves the spirit of the original, and first appeared in C. S. Bere's *A Garland of Songs*, 1861.

WIR PFLÜGEN (DRESDEN). See 291.

621. See the farmer sow the seed

Frederick Jackson's hymn was written for the National Sunday School Union and appeared in *Child Songs*, 1908.

SEVEN JOYS OF MARY. See 230.

622. In the lanes and in the parks

M. Temple Frere's hymn was written for the National Society and appeared in *The School Hymn Book of the Methodist Church*, 1950, and *Sunday School Praise*, 1958.

LONGWALL is the tune set to these words in *Sunday School Praise*. It was composed by K. D. Smith, one of the editors of the music.

623. The summer days are come again

Samuel Longfellow intended this hymn to be sung in the open air, and alterations have been made in the text to make it suitable for church services. The original consisted of three eight-line stanzas, each beginning 'The sweet June days are come again'. It was entitled 'Summer Rural Gathering' and appeared in *Hymns and Verses*, 1894. The present hymn consists of vv. 2–3.

FOREST GREEN. See 157.

624. Summer suns are glowing

Written by W. W. How for *Church Hymns*, 1871.

KING'S WESTON. See 283.

625. Let us sing our song of praise

Winifred E. Barnard's hymn first appears in *Nursery Song and Picture Book*, 1947, which she edited.

SAVEZ-VOUS is a French folk melody.

626. Earth thou dost visit, watering it

Metrical psalm 65: 9, 11–13. Verse 1 by the revision committee is based on *The Irish Psalter*, 1880, and vv. 2–4 from *The Scottish Psalter*, 1650.

COLCHESTER (TANS'UR) is one of the tunes in Tans'ur's *Harmony of Zion*, 1734, where it is set to Ps. 150. Whether he was the composer or simply responsible for the harmony is an open question.

627. Come, ye thankful people, come

First published by Alford in his *Psalms and Hymns*, 1844. Various compilers have attempted revisions and that in *Hymns Ancient and Modern*, 1861, was repudiated by him. The hymn here is the author's final revision except that v. 4 line 2 read 'to thy final harvest home' and line 6 'in Thy presence to abide'.

ST. GEORGE'S, WINDSOR by Sir George Elvey first appeared in *A Selection of Psalm and Hymn Tunes, edited and arranged by E. H. Thorne . . . Adapted to Psalms and Hymns compiled by the Rev. T. B. Morrell and the Rev. W. W. How*, 1858, where it was set to the hymn 'Hark! the song of Jubilee'. It was first set to the present words in *Hymns Ancient and Modern*, 1861.

628. Fountain of mercy, God of love

Mrs. Flowerdew's hymn is from her *Poems on Moral and Religious Subjects*, 1803.

UNIVERSITY. See 435.

629. Fair waved the golden corn

Hampden Gurney's hymn first appeared in his *Psalms and Hymns for Public Worship Selected for some of the Churches of Marylebone*, 1851. It applies to harvest festivals the Jewish idea of offering the first-fruits, Exod. 22: 29, 23: 16, Deut. 26: 1–11.

HILLSBOROUGH. See 511.

Cross ref. to SANDYS. See 153.

630. The fields and vales are thick with corn

Frederick Jackson's hymn was written for the National Sunday School Union and appeared in *Child Songs*, 1908.

KING'S LANGLEY. See 618.

631. We thank thee, Lord, for all thy gifts

Miss Macdougall Ferguson's hymn was written for the Religious Education Press and appears in *Sing Praises*, where the first line was 'We thank Thee for Thy loving gifts'.

CHILDHOOD. See 156.

632. 'Tis winter now; the fallen snow

From Samuel Longfellow's *Hymns of the Spirit*, 1864. It was introduced into England in *The English Hymnal*, 1906.

O WALY, WALY. See 554.

633. Little birds in winter time

Frederick Jackson's hymn was written for the National Sunday School Union and appeared in *Child Songs*, 1908.

ST. AIDAN was composed by Herbert Popple for the hymn 'Thine are all the gifts, O God' in *Songs of Praise*, 1931, and is set to the present words in *Sunday School Praise*, 1958.

634. May the grace of Christ our Saviour

John Newton's hymn is from the *Olney Hymns*, 1779, based on 2 Cor. 13: 14.

GOTT DES HIMMELS (WALTHAM) is from a melody by Heinrich Albert, which he wrote for his own hymn 'Gott des Himmels und der Erde' in his *Arien oder Melodeyen*, Königsberg, 1642. The harmonization is that of Bach in his *Christmas Oratorio*.

635. Almighty God, thy word is cast

From Cawood's six stanzas as first published in Cotterill's *Selection of Psalms and Hymns for Public Worship*, 1819, for use 'After Sermon'.

DUNFERMLINE. See 101.

636. And now the wants are told that brought

From Bright's *Hymns*, 1866, entitled 'Hymn for the close of a Service'.

SALISBURY is from Ravenscroft's *Psalter*, 1621, where it is set to Pss. 17 and 54 as 'Salisbury Tune', and classified as an English tune. The melody is exactly as here.

Cross ref. to MARTYRDOM. See 667.

637. Come, dearest Lord, descend and dwell

From Watts's *Hymns and Spiritual Songs*, 1707, with the heading 'The Love of Christ shed abroad in the heart. Ephesians iii. 16'.

WHITEHALL by Henry Lawes is set to Ps. 8 in Sandys's *Paraphrase upon the Divine Poems*, 1638.

Cross ref. to TALLIS' CANON. See 599.

638. Lord, dismiss us with thy blessing

This hymn is ascribed to John Fawcett in the York *Selection of Psalms and Hymns*, 1791, although its earlier appearances in the *Supplement to the*

Shrewsbury Hymnal, 1773, in Conyer's *Collection of Psalms and Hymns*, 1774, and Toplady's *Psalms and Hymns*, 1776, are anonymous.

ORIEL is from *Cantica Sacra in usum Studiosae juventutis. Collegit et edidit J. Michael Hauber . . . Cantui Chorali accomodavit vocem organi Casparus Ett, Regiae Ecclesiae aulicae ad S. Michael Monac. organoedus*, Monachii, 1840, where it is set in four parts to the hymn 'Pange lingua gloriosi'. It is not certain whether Ett composed or arranged it, but it has not been traced to an earlier source. The harmony is by W. H. Monk.

639. Now may he who from the dead

Newton wrote this hymn for *Olney Hymns*, 1779 for use 'after sermon'. It is based on Heb. 13: 20–2.

KEINE SCHÖNHEIT HAT DIE WELT is a melody by Georg Joseph from *Heilige Seelenlust oder Geistliche Hirten-Lieder . . . von Johann Angelo Silesio, Und vom Herren Georgio Josepho mit aussbundig schönen Melodeyen geziert . . . Breslau*, 1657, where it is set to Scheffler's hymn 'Keine Schönheit hat die Welt'.

640. Praise ye the Lord, ye servants of the Lord

From the *Apostolic Constitutions* (fourth century), translated by G. R. Woodward as revised by the compilers of *The BBC Hymn Book*, 1951.

OLD 124TH. See 84.

641. All praise to thee, my God, this night

The text of Ken's hymn is taken from *A Manual of Prayers for the Use of Scholars of Winchester College, and All other Devout Christians*, 1709.

TALLIS' CANON. See 599.

642. Now cheer our hearts this eventide

Selnecker's 'Ach bleib bei uns, Herr Jesu Christ' from *Geistliche Psalmen*, Nürnberg, 1611, has been frequently translated. This version is by Robert Bridges from *The Yattendon Hymnal*, 1899. It was written to suit Bach's setting of the 'Proper tune', and is a free translation of two of the original nine verses.

ACH BLEIB BEI UNS is a melody from the *Geistliche Lieder*, Leipzig, 1589, and Calvisius's *Hymni Sacri Latini et Germanici*, 1594, from which it is sometimes known as 'Calvisius'. The form given here is Bach's in his *Choralgesänge*, 1769.

643. Now God be with us, for the night is closing

Petrus Herbert's hymn, 'Die Nacht ist kommen, drin wir ruhen sollen', was contributed to the *Gesangbuch der Böhmischen Brüder*, Berlin, 1566, which he helped to edit. Miss Winkworth's translation is from her *Chorale Book for England*, 1863.

DIVA SERVATRIX. See 566.

644. Holy Father, cheer our way

Written by Richard Robinson in 1869 for the congregation of St. Paul's, Upper Norwood, London. It was intended to be sung after the third collect at Evensong. The text for the hymn was Zech. 14: 7. It was first published in *Church Hymns*, 1871.

CAPETOWN. See 438.

645. The day is past and over

The Greek original is a cento from anonymous verses used in the Evening Service of the Greek Church, which may date from the sixth or seventh century. Neale's translation first appeared in *The Ecclesiastic and Theologian*, 1853, and a revision in his *Hymns of the Eastern Church*, 1862.

HOMINUM AMATOR by W. H. Ferguson first appeared in *The Public School Hymn Book*, 1919, where it was anonymous. The composer's name was given in the 1949 edition.

646. The day thou gavest, Lord, is ended

The final form of Ellerton's hymn, which was written in 1870 for *A Liturgy for Missionary Meetings*, 1870, appeared in *Church Hymns*, 1871.

LES COMMANDEMENS DE DIEU. See 586.

ST. CLEMENT by C. C. Scholefield appeared in *Church Hymns with Tunes*, 1874, for which it was composed for these words.

647. Sun of my soul, thou Saviour dear

Keble's original poem on 'Evening' in fourteen stanzas appeared in his *Christian Year*, 1827. It was composed on 25 November 1820, and is based on Luke 24: 29.

CONNOLLY was composed by Martin Dalby for this hymn for CH3.

648. Ere I sleep, for every favour

This is the full form of Cennick's hymn as in his *Sacred Hymns for the Children of God*, 1741.

THANET is from Jowett's *Parochial Psalmody*, 1832, where it is set to these words.

649. Saviour, again to thy dear Name we raise

Ellerton's hymn was written in 1866 for a Choral Festival at Nantwich, Cheshire; then revised and abridged for *Hymns Ancient and Modern*, 1868.

FARLEY CASTLE by Henry Lawes was originally set to Ps. 72 in Sandys's *Paraphrase on the Divine Poems*, 1638, in which the music was by Lawes.

ELLERS by E. J. Hopkins comes from *The Supplemental Hymn and Tune Book, Compiled by Rev. R. Brown-Bothwick*, 1869. It was composed for these words, and arranged for voices in unison, with organ accompaniment, the latter being varied in each verse. The present four-part arrangement appeared in the *Appendix to the Bradford Tune Book*, 1872, edited by Samuel Smith, who says it had been 'prepared by the composer, at the request of the editor, specially for this work'.

650. Round me falls the night

William Romanis's hymn first appeared in the *Wigston Magna School Hymns*, 1878. It was included in *The Public School Hymn Book*, 1903, and *The English Hymnal*, 1906.

SEELENBRÄUTIGAM (ARNSTADT) is from *Geistreiches Gesangbuch*, Darmstadt, 1698, and is so called because it was there set to Drese's hymn, 'Seelenbräutigam, Jesu Gottes Lamm'. Zahn holds that Drese composed the tune as well as the hymn. The present form of the melody is almost exactly that of the original.

651. A Sovereign Protector I have

Toplady's hymn was first published in *The Gospel Magazine*, 1774, entitled 'A chamber hymn' and signed 'Minimus'. It was written at Fen Ottery, near Exeter, and is quoted by Toplady in his diary for 1 January 1768.

TREWEN by D. Emlyn Evans comes from *Gemau Mawl*, 1890, edited by D. Jenkins.

652. O Christ, who art the Light and Day

The hymn 'Christe, qui lux es et dies' is quoted by Hincmar, Archbishop of Rheims, in his *Contra Godeschalcum . . . De una et non Trina Deitate*, 857. It is sometimes ascribed to Ambrose, but this is rejected by the Benedictine editors. It is found in the Mozarabic, Sarum, York, and other Breviaries. Copeland's translation, 'O Christ, That art the Light and Day', first appeared in his *Hymns for the Week*, 1848. In *Hymns Ancient and Modern*, 1875, 'That' was altered to 'Who', and to 'Thou' in the *Hymnary*, 1872. Here the text is from *The English Hymnal*, 1906.

JESU NOSTRA REDEMPTIO is a plain-song melody from the *Antiphonale Romanum*.

Cross ref. to TALLIS' CANON. See 599.

653. Now the day is over

Written in 1865 for a Sunday School festival at Horbury Bridge, Yorkshire, Baring-Gould's hymn, based on Prov. 3: 24, was first published without the doxology in *The Church Times*, 1867, and was included in the appendix to *Hymns Ancient and Modern*, 1868.

EUDOXIA was composed for this hymn by Baring-Gould for *Hymns Ancient and Modern*. When he composed it he thought the melody to be original, but afterwards discovered it was reminiscent of a German melody he had heard as a boy. This has never been identified, but it may have been the school song 'The Cricket' by Weber or a children's evening hymn set to this German melody in the *Plymouth Collection*, 1856.

Cross ref. to AU CLAIR DE LA LUNE. See 58.

654. Gentle Jesus, hear our prayer

Miss Macdougall Ferguson's hymn comes from *Children Praising*, c. 1937.

CASSEL first appeared in *Erbaulicher Musicalischer Christen Schatz*, Basle, 1745. Composed by Johann Thommen it was originally an eight-line tune, but was adapted to its present form by H. Parr in his *Church of England Psalmody*, 1889.

655. Into thy loving care

The author is unknown. It appears in *Children Praising*, c. 1937, and was included in *Infant Praise*, 1964.

INTO THY KEEPING was composed by Guthrie Foote for these words for *Infant Praise*.

656. Jesus, tender Shepherd, hear me

Composed by Mrs. Duncan for her infant children in 1839, the year before her death, and published in *Memoir*, 1841, by her mother, where it was entitled 'An evening prayer'. All her hymns were printed in *Hymns for my children*, 1842.

EVENING PRAYER. See 467.

657. Now to him who loved us (doxology)

From Samuel Waring's *Sacred Melodies*, 1826, where it was followed by a second verse. Only the first two and fourth lines are by Waring.

REGENT SQUARE. See 289.

658. Praise God, from whom all blessings flow (doxology)

The last verse of Ken's hymns 42 and 641.

OLD 100TH. See 1.

659. All praise and thanks to God (doxology)

The last verse of Rinkart's hymn 368.

NUN DANKET. See 368.

660. Unto God be praise and honour (doxology)

The last verse of Fortunatus's hymn 256.

TANTUM ERGO SACRAMENTUM. See 373.

661. Laud and honour to the Father (doxology)

The last verse of 'Angularis fundamentum lapis Christus missus est', as translated by Neale 10.

WESTMINSTER ABBEY. See 10.

662. Amen

The response 'Amen' was taken over by the early Church from Jewish worship as a liturgical expression. It is common to Judaism, Christianity, and Islam, always as a response. It pledges the worshipping people to what they have heard or themselves uttered, and is thus a solemn avowal of their faith.

SETTINGS. (i) Perfect cadence, (ii) Plagal cadence, (iii) Inverted-perfect cadence, (iv) Danish, (v) Unison by P. C. Buck, (vi) Dresden by Johann Nauman, and (vii) Threefold by Orlando Gibbons.

663. O for a closer walk with God

Written by Cowper on 9 December 1769 during the illness of his friend Mrs. Unwin. It was first published in Conyer's *Collection of Psalms and Hymns*, 1772, and included in the *Olney Hymns*, 1779, under the title 'Walking with God'. According to tradition Cowper frequently heard an old shoemaker hum the tune 'Ludlow' and was so taken with it that he wrote the hymn to suit it.

WINDSOR (DUNDEE). See 37.

Cross ref. to CAITHNESS. See 125.

664. O for a faith that will not shrink

Bathurst's hymn is from *Psalms and Hymns for Public and Private Use*, 1830, where it was entitled 'The Power of Faith' under the text Luke 17: 5. The text is unaltered except that in v. 5 line 3 he wrote 'e'en here' not 'even now'.

ST. LEONARD by Henry Smart is from *Psalms and Hymns for Divine Worship*, 1867.

665. O God, thou art my God alone

Montgomery's hymn, based on Ps. 63, is from *Songs of Zion*, 1822.

WAINWRIGHT comes from *A Collection of Hymns, with appropriate Symphonies and Accompaniments, as originally composed for the Children of the Liverpool Blue Coat Hospital, c.* 1790, where it is named 'Newmarket' and set to the hymn 'My God, and is Thy table spread'.

666. O thou, my Judge and King

Specially written by MacLean Watt for RCH, 1927, to suit Hugo Nyberg's tune.

HELSINGFORS by Nyberg is taken from *Hengellisiä Lauluja ja Wirsiä*, 1926, the revised edition of the Finnish hymn-book.

667. Approach, my soul, the mercy-seat

Newton's hymn comes from a section headed 'Seeing, Pleading, and Hoping' in *Olney Hymns*, 1779, with one verse omitted.

MARTYRDOM was first printed in sheet form. The original form is in common metre as given here. Its first appearance in triple time appears to have been in Smith's *Sacred Music sung in St. George's Church, Edinburgh*, 1825, where it is designated 'Old Scottish Melody' and the harmony is stated to be 'by Mr. Smith'. It also appeared in triple time in *The Seraph: a selection of Psalms and Hymns*, 1827, edited by J. Robertson, in which a footnote says that 'the above tune "Fenwick" or "Martyrdom", and by some called "Drumclog", was composed by Mr. Hugh Wilson, a native of Fenwick'. While 'Fenwick' referred to Wilson's birthplace, Smith may have thought it referred to James Fenwick, the Scottish martyr, and renamed it 'Martyrdom'. The publication of the tune by Smith was the occasion of a legal dispute, but evidence was produced to show that Wilson was without doubt the composer. The tune may, however, have been suggested to Wilson's mind by a traditional melody, 'Helen of Kirkconnel'.

668. If thou but suffer God to guide thee

Neumark's 'Wer nur den lieben Gott lässt walten' from his *Musikalischpoetischer Lustwald*, Jena, 1657. But it was composed at Kiel in 1641 with the heading 'A Song of Comfort. God will care for and help every one in His own time', under the text Ps. 55: 22. Neumark was robbed by highwaymen near Magdeburg as a student and left destitute with no prospect of earning a living. At last he unexpectedly received an appointment as tutor in the family of a judge in Kiel, 'which good fortune', he says, '... greatly rejoiced me, and on that very day I composed to the honour of my beloved Lord the hymn'. Miss Winkworth first translated this hymn in her *Lyra Germanica*, 1855, under the heading 'Leave God to order all thy ways', and revised it in her *Chorale Book for England*, 1863.

NEUMARK. See 162.

669. Put thou thy trust in God

Paul Gerhardt's hymn 'Befiehl du deine Wege' appeared in the Frankfurt edition of Crüger's *Praxis Pietatis Melica*, 1646. John Wesley's rendering first appears in his *Hymns and Sacred Poems*, 1739. The first stanza comes from an unknown hand.

ICH HALTE TREULICH STILL. See 445.

670. Workman of God! O lose not heart

Stanzas 10, 11, 2, 7, 13, and 18 from Faber's nineteen-verse poem, 'The Right must win', which appeared in his *Jesus and Mary*, 1849.

MARTYRS. See 7.

Cross ref. to LONDON NEW. See 6.

671. O let him whose sorrow

Oswald's 'Wem in Leidenstagen' from his *Letzte Mittheilungen*, Breslau, 1826, entitled 'An exhortation to Tranquillity to the Suffering, Ps. 1. 15'. Miss Cox's translation is from her *Sacred Hymns from the German*, 1841. She sanctioned the present form of v. 4 line 1 where she had written 'When in' not 'If in grief you languish'.

WEM IN LEIDENSTAGEN by Filitz is from *Vierstimmiges Choralbuch heraus-gegeben von Dr. F. Filitz*, Berlin, 1847, where it is set to these words. It is also known as 'Caswall' or 'Bemerton'.

672. Christ who knows all his sheep

From *Additions to the Poetical Fragments of Rich. Baxter, written for himself, and Communicated to such as are more for serious verses than smooth*, 1683. These are the last three of the thirty-one verses of *The Exit*, 1682. The version given here is that in *The BBC Hymn Book*, 1951.

MAYFIELD was composed by Kenneth Leighton for this hymn for CH3.

673. Be still, my soul: the Lord is on thy side

Katharina von Schlegel's 'Stille, mein Wille; dein Jesus hilft siegen' appeared in six stanzas in the *Neue Sammlung Geistlicher Lieder*, Wernigerode, 1752, and was translated by Miss Borthwick in *Hymns from the Land of Luther*, 1855.

FINLANDIA is from Sibelius's Symphonic Poem entitled *Finlandia*, 1899.

674. Jesus, these eyes have never seen

Written by Ray Palmer in 1858 at Albany, N.Y., and published in *The Sabbath Hymn-book* that year. It is based on 1 Pet. 1: 8.

ST. BOTOLPH by Gordon Slater first appeared in *Songs of Praise for Boys and Girls*, 1930.

675. 'Twixt gleams of joy and clouds of doubt

Written by J. C. Shairp in 1871, and published in *Glen Desseray and other Poems*, 1888.

THIRD MODE MELODY is the third of nine tunes by Tallis in *The whole Psalter translated into English Metre, which contayneth an hundreth and fifty Psalmes*, 1561. See 91.

Cross ref. to WINDSOR (DUNDEE). See 377.

676. Hark, my soul! it is the Lord

Cowper's hymn though written a few years earlier was first published in Maxfield's *New Appendix*, 1768. The text in the *Olney Hymns*, 1779, was John 21: 16.

SONG 13 was set to a metrical paraphrase of a portion of the 'Song of Solomon' in Wither's *Hymns and Songs of the Church*, 1623. See 41 and 108.

677. O love that wilt not let me go

Matheson tells us the hymn was written in the Clydeside Manse of Innellan, Argyllshire on 6 June 1882 (this should be 1881). 'It was composed', he says, 'with extreme rapidity: it seemed to me that its construction occupied only a few minutes, and I felt myself rather in the position of one who was being dictated to than of an original artist. I was suffering from extreme mental distress, and the hymn was the fruit of pain.' It first appeared in the January issue of *Life and Work*, 1882, and was included in *The Scottish Hymnal*, 1885, where it was set to 'St. Margaret'.

ST. MARGARET was composed for these words by A. L. Peace in Brodick Manse, Arran, in 1884, at the request of the committee compiling *The Scottish Hymnal*. 'After reading it over carefully', he writes, 'I wrote the music straight off, and I may say that the ink of the first note was hardly dry when I had finished the tune.'

678. Thee will I love, my Strength, my Tower

Johann Scheffler's 'Ich will Dich lieben, meine Stärke' is from his *Heilige Seelenlust*, Breslau, 1657. The present hymn is vv. 1, 4, and 7 from John Wesley's translation, which appeared in his *Hymns and Sacred Poems*, 1759.

KILLINCHY was composed by Sebastian Forbes for this hymn for CH3.

DAS NEUGEBORNE KINDELEIN (JENA) is from Vulpius's *Ein schön geistlich Gesangbuch . . . durch M.V. Cantorem zu Weymar*, Jena, 1609. Bach used the melody in one of his cantatas and the harmony is based chiefly on this.

679. Lord, it belongs not to my care

In his *Poetical Fragments*, 1681, where it first appeared, this hymn was entitled by Baxter, 'Heart Employment with God and itself: The Concordant Discord of a Broken-hearted Heart'. It was dated 'London, at the Door of Eternity: Richard Baxter, Aug. 7, 1681'. A later edition alters the title to 'The Covenant and Confidence of Faith'. The poem begins 'My whole though broken heart, O Lord'. The hymn begins at v. 4 of the original.

ASHWELL, composed by Edric Cundell, is taken from *The Cambridge Hymnal*, 1967, where it is set to these words.

680. My times are in thy hand

From W. Freeman Lloyd's *Hymns for the Poor of the Flock*, 1838.

SWABIA. See 113.

681. In heavenly love abiding

Anna Waring's hymn was first published in *Hymns and Meditations by A. L. W.*, 1850, where it was entitled 'Safety in God'. It is based on Ps. 23: 4.

PENLAN by David Jenkins is from *Gemau Mawl, Ail Attodiad*, 1910.

Cross ref. to DURROW. See 397.

682. Lead, kindly Light, amid the encircling gloom

These verses are marked by Newman as having been composed 'at sea, June 16, 1833'. In the early summer of 1833 Newman was on a voyage home from Sicily to Marseilles, when he fell ill of a fever and was 'aching to get home'. He was held up at Palermo for three weeks owing to a calm, but at last 'got off on an orange-boat bound for Marseilles'. Either at this time, or shortly before it, he wrote this hymn. It was published in *The British Magazine*, 1834, then in

Lyra Apostolica, 1836. Newman entered the Church of Rome in 1848 and was made a Cardinal in 1879. The Revd. James Mearns in *The Catholic World*, 1913, argues that 'kindly Light' originally meant 'the Inward Light of conscience', 'kindly' being used in the Elizabethan sense of 'implanted, innate'.

LUX BENIGNA was composed by Dykes for this hymn and appeared in *Psalms and Hymns for the Church, School, and Home, edited by the Rev. D. T. Barry, B.A. With accompanying Tunes from the Parish Tune Book*, 1867, where it is named 'St. Oswald'. The present version is the revised form in *Hymns Ancient and Modern*, 1868.

683. I hear thy welcome voice

The words and music by Lewis Hartsough were first published in *Guide to Holiness*, 1873, and then in Sankey's *Sacred Songs and Solos*, 1883.

WELCOME VOICE first appeared in *Guide to Holiness*.

684. Beneath the cross of Jesus

Miss Clephane's hymn is taken from a poem in *The Family Treasury*, 1872, where it is anonymous. In v. 2 line 5 'holy' has been changed to 'exiled'.

HELDER (WOHLAUF THUT NICHT VERZAGEN) by B. Helder, first appears in the *Gothaer Cantional*, 1648, set to the hymn 'Wohlauf thut nicht verzagen'. It was included in *The English Hymnal*, 1906.

685. I am trusting thee, Lord Jesus

Written by Miss Havergal in 1874 at Ormont Dessous, Vaud, Switzerland, and published in her *Loyal Responses*, 1878, headed 'Trusting Jesus'.

CUTTLE MILLS. See 100.

686. Jesus, I will trust thee

Mrs. Walker's hymn appeared in her husband's *Psalms and Hymns for Public and Social Worship*, 1864.

NORTH COATES is from *Congregational Melodies: A Collection of Tunes ... by the Rev. T. R. Matthews*, 1862.

687. I am not skilled to understand

From Miss Greenwell's *Songs of Salvation*, 1873.

ACH GOTT UND HERR. See 588.

688. I need thee every hour

Written by Mrs. Hawks in 1872 and published in Lawrie's *Royal Diadem*, 1873, though it had appeared earlier in a small collection, *Gospel Songs*, prepared for the National Baptist Sunday School Association's meetings at Cincinnati, 1872, and was sung there. It was based on John 15: 5.

BREAD OF LIFE by Eric H. Thiman was composed for the hymn 'Break Thou the bread of life' in *Congregational Praise*, 1951.

689. Nearer, my God, to thee

Written by Mrs. Adams in 1840 and based on Gen. 28: 10–22, Jacob at Bethel, it was first published in *Hymns and Anthems*, 1841, compiled by W. J. Fox, of whose congregation in South Place Chapel, Finsbury (Unitarian) she was a member.

WILMINGTON was composed by Erik Routley for this hymn in 1938, and was first published in *Congregational Praise*, 1951.

PROPIOR DEO was composed for this hymn by Sir Arthur Sullivan for *The Hymnary*, 1872.

690. Teach me to serve thee, Lord

This hymn by Edna M. Phillips first appeared in the *Festival Handbook* of the Presbyterian Church of Wales, 1964. It was inspired by the prayer of Ignatius Loyola, 'Teach us, good Lord, to serve Thee as Thou deservest'.

BLACKFORD by Kenneth Leighton was composed for this hymn for CH3.

691. Dear Master, in whose life I see

Originally appeared in *The Monthly Calendar* of Trinity Congregational Church, Glasgow, and later in *Hymns of Faith and Life*, 1896. In the former Dr. Hunter's name is attached to the hymn, but in the latter it is anonymous. The compilers of RCH, 1927, altered 'long' to 'would' in v. 1 line 2, and 'poor' to 'weak' in v. 2. line 2.

DANIEL. See 589.

692. Teach me, my God and King

Herbert's poem 'The Elixir' from *The Temple*, 1633.

SANDYS. See 153.

693. My soul, there is a country

From Vaughan's *Silex Scintillans*, 1650, entitled 'Peace'.

CHERRY TREE CAROL. See 229.

Cross ref. to CHRISTUS DER IST MEIN LEBEN (BREMEN). See 404.

694. The sands of time are sinking

First published by Mrs. Cousins in *The Christian Treasury*, 1857, and later issued as a leaflet 'Last Words of Samuel Rutherford' in nineteen stanzas, which Moffatt describes as 'a beautiful and skilfully constructed mosaic of passages from Rutherford's *Letters and Dying Sayings*'.

RUTHERFORD by Chrétien Urhan comes from *Chants Chrétiens*, Paris, 1834, where it is set to the hymn 'Éternel, O mon Dieu, j'implore ta clémence'. The present form of the melody was made by E. F. Rimbault for *Psalms and Hymns for Divine Worship*, 1867.

695. Abide with me: fast falls the eventide

According to tradition Lyte wrote this hymn on 4 September 1847, just before he left his parish at Brixham, Devon, to go to Nice owing to ill health, dying there on 20 November following. Bindley claimed in the *Spectator*, 1925, that it was written in 1820, after a visit to a dying friend, William Le Hunte, who kept repeating the phrase 'Abide with me'. Conclusive evidence, however, is found in a letter written by Lyte to Julia (Eleanor Julia Bolton), who married his youngest son in 1851. It is dated 25 August 1847, and includes the hymn as 'my latest effusion'. The original had eight stanzas, and appeared in his *Remains*, 1850, and *Miscellaneous Poems*, 1870. The text followed is the latter. It was not meant to be an evening hymn; its outlook is on the closing day of life.

EVENTIDE was composed by W. H. Monk for this hymn for *Hymns Ancient and Modern*, 1861.

BIOGRAPHICAL AND HISTORICAL NOTES
ON AUTHORS AND COMPOSERS

JOHN M. BARKLEY

ABÉLARD, PIERRE (Le Pallet, 1079-1142, St. Marcel), renowned alike for his philosophical ability and his romantic story, was the son of a noble Breton house, and became a lecturer in the Cathedral School at Notre Dame, Paris, where he exercised great influence. Here began, too, his passionate attachment to Héloïse, niece of a canon named Fulbert. The pair fled to Brittany, where a son was born, and they were privately married. In view of the disclosure and catastrophe which followed, Abélard entered the Abbey of St. Denis as a monk, while Héloïse took the veil. Abélard's fame as a teacher increased and, in spite of official condemnation of his doctrines, the hermitage he built himself at Nogent became a noted theological school, which he called the Paraclete. On his taking charge of the Abbey of St. Gildas, the Paraclete was made a religious house for women under the charge of Héloïse. Finally, at the instance of Bernard of Clairvaux, Abélard was found guilty of heresy by a council at Sens and by the Pope. He died on his way to defend himself at Rome and was buried beside Héloïse. Their ashes are now in the Père-Lachaise cemetery in Paris.

As a hymn-writer he was little known until the last century, when several of his poems were discovered in the Vatican and a number of others in the Royal Library at Brussels.

H. 242, 535

ADAMS, JESSIE (Ipswich, 1863-1954, Frimley), was a member of the Society of Friends and leader of the local Adult School at Frimley. She was an ardent advocate of the most advanced progressive causes. She wrote many hymns and verses, which, however, have not been published in a collected form.

H. 444

ADAMS, SARAH FLOWER, née SARAH FULLER FLOWER (Harlow, Essex, 1805-48, London), was the second daughter of Benjamin Flower, editor of *The Cambridge Intelligencer* and, later, of *The Political Review*. For an alleged breach of privilege in criticizing the political action of the Bishop of Llandaff, he was imprisoned in Newgate. There a schoolmistress of South Molton, Devon, one of his ardent political disciples, sought him to tender her sympathy. They were married on his release. Their two daughters were both gifted: the elder, Eliza, in music, Sarah in letters. The latter contributed to *The Repository*, a periodical edited by the Revd. William Johnson Fox, her minister at South Place Religious Society, Finsbury. In 1840-1 he published, for use in his church, a collection of *Hymns and Anthems, the Words chiefly from Holy Scripture and the Writings of the Poets*. The music was edited by Eliza Flower, while Sarah contributed thirteen hymns. In 1834 she married

William Bridges Adams, an engineer and inventor, who was then a contributor of political articles of an advanced type to *The Repository*. She died of consumption in 1848.

H. 689

ADDISON, JOSEPH (Milston, Wiltshire, 1672-1719, London), son of Lancelot Addison, rector of Milston and afterwards Dean of Lichfield, was educated at Charterhouse and at Queen's College and Magdalen, Oxford. Intended for the Church, he turned instead to literature and politics, attached himself to the Whig interest, and found a patron in Charles Montague, afterwards Lord Halifax. The death of William III seemed to threaten his prospects, but in the following reign a laudatory poem on Marlborough's victory at Blenheim brought him preferment to various successive offices of state. His release from public life on the fall of the Godolphin Ministry in 1710 gave him leisure for the composition of the Essays on which his fame mainly rests. Most of these were contributed to the *Tatler*, the *Spectator*, and the *Guardian*. His hymns were all contributed to the *Spectator*.

H. 143, 150

AGNEW, EDITH (Denver, Colorado, 1897), was educated at Park College, Missouri. She taught in mission schools in Utah, New Mexico, and Arizona, before becoming writing assistant to the Board of National Missions, United Presbyterian Church, U.S.A. Later she became assistant editor of Children's Curriculum to the same Church's Board of Christian Education. She contributed to *Hymns for Primary Worship, Songs and Hymns for Primary Children* and the Lutheran *Young Children Sing* (1967). She is now retired and lives at Santa Fe, New Mexico.

H. 230

ÅHLE, JOHANN RUDOLPH (Mühlhausen, Thuringia, 1625-73, Mühlhausen), was educated at the universities of Göttingen and Erfurt. In 1646 he was appointed cantor at St. Andreas's Church, and director of the musical school at Erfurt. Soon he became known as one of the most radical reformers of Church music in his time. In 1649 he accepted the post of organist of St. Blasius's Church, Mühlhausen. He published *Compendium pro tonellis*, a treatise on singing; *Geistliche Dialogen*; *Thüringischen Lust-Gartens*; *Neue Geistliche Chorstücke*; *Neuverfaste Chor-Musik* (motets), etc. He cultivated the simple style of the chorale, avoiding polyphonic counterpoint.

T. 128, 129, 552

AINGER, ARTHUR CAMPBELL, M.A. (Blackheath, 1841-1919, Eton), son of a vicar in Hampstead, was educated at Eton and at Trinity College, Cambridge. From 1864 to 1901 he was an assistant master at Eton.

H. 303

ALBERT, HEINRICH (Lobenstein, Voigtland, 1604-51, Königsberg), attended the Gymnasium at Gera, and afterwards became a pupil of his distinguished uncle Heinrich Schütz at Dresden, later also of Stobäus. At the desire of his parents he abandoned the study of music and went to Leipzig to study law. Thence he set out with an embassy for Warsaw but on the way was taken prisoner by the Swedes, and was not able to return until 1628. The profession of law had little interest for him, and in 1632 he was glad to abandon it on his appointment to the organistship of the cathedral of Königsberg. His chief work was a collection of arias in eight volumes, to many of which he wrote the words. The preface contains an exposition by him of the principles of music.

T. 634

ALCOCK, JOHN, Mus.Doc. (London, 1718-1806, Lichfield), was trained as a chorister in St. Paul's Cathedral and was a pupil of John Stanley, the celebrated blind organist of St. Andrew's, Holborn, and of the Temple Church. He was organist of St. Andrew's, Plymouth, and of St. Lawrence's, Reading, before becoming, in 1749, master of the choristers, lay vicar, and organist of Lichfield Cathedral. Owing to the damp condition of the cathedral he contracted rheumatism, which compelled him to resign his offices, except that of lay vicar, which he retained, while he acted as organist at Sutton Coldfield (1761-6), and St. Editha's, Tamworth (1766-90). He published *Six Lessons for the Harpsichord*; *Twelve Songs*; *Six Concertos*; *A Collection of Psalms, Hymns and Anthems*; *Six and Twenty Select Anthems*; *Divine Harmony, a Collection of Fifty-Five Double and Single Chants*; *The Harmony of Sion* (a collection of Psalms); *Harmonia Festi* (Canons, Glees, and Catches).

C. 3 (i)

ALDERSON, ELIZA SIBBALD, née DYKES (Hull, 1818-89, Heath, near Wakefield, Yorkshire), was a sister of Dr. J. B. Dykes. She had a talent for versification, of which, however, the total published fruit was twelve hymns. These were partly written at Kirkthorpe, where her husband, the Revd. W. T. Alderson, was locum tenens for a time, and partly at Wakefield, where he held the chaplaincy to the West Riding House of Correction from 1832 to 1876. The last years of her life were passed under much suffering. She was buried at Kirkthorpe.

H. 250

ALEXANDER, CECIL FRANCES, née HUMPHREYS (Wicklow, 1818-95, Derry), the daughter of Major Humphreys, married the Revd. William Alexander, who after a stormy youth at Oxford, was then a curate in Londonderry. In 1867 Dr. Alexander's gifts were recognized by his appointment to the Bishopric of Derry and Raphoe; in 1896 he was elected Archbishop of Armagh and Primate of all Ireland. Before her marriage Miss Humphreys published *Verses from Holy Scripture*, and *Hymns for Little Children* (1848) based on the *Church Catechism*. The latter was at once recognized to be of singular excellence. Among her later books were *Moral Songs*; *Narrative Hymns*; *Legend of the Golden Prayer*; *Verses for Holy Seasons*; *Hymns Descriptive and Devotional*; *Poems on Subjects in the Old*

Testament. The best of her work was collected by her husband, after her death, in a single volume, *Poems by Cecil Frances Alexander.*

H. 109, 154, 193, 211, 241, 288, 402

ALEXANDER, James Neil Stewart, B.D., S.T.M., L.R.A.M. (Mount Vernon, Glasgow, 1921), was educated at Glasgow High School and University and Union Theological Seminary, New York. Ordained in 1949, he was minister of St. Paul's, Cambuslang (1949–55), before becoming Assistant (1955–8) and then Lecturer in Biblical Criticism in the University of Aberdeen. He was Lecturer in New Testament Language and Literature (1964–7) in the University of Glasgow, and since then Senior Lecturer. Among his publications are *The Epistles of John; The Way of the Lord and the Way of the World; Life after Easter; The Ante-Nicene Interpretation of Scripture;* and *The United Character of the New Testament Witness to the Christ-Event.* In 1978 he became minister of St. Andrew's Church, Rome.

H. 162, 203

ALEXANDER, James Waddell, D.D. (Hopewell, Louisa County, Virginia, 1804–59, Sweetsprings, Virginia), was of Scottish descent. He was educated at New Jersey College and Princeton Theological Seminary. After pastorates in Charlotte County, Virginia, and Trenton, New Jersey, he occupied for twelve years the Chair of Belles-Lettres and Rhetoric in New Jersey College. After a period of service in the ministry of Duane Street Presbyterian Church, New York, he returned to Princeton as Professor of Ecclesiastical History and Church Government. Finally, in 1851, he returned to the ministry, in Fifth Avenue Presbyterian Church, New York. He was deeply interested in hymnology and issued a small hymn-book containing none but unaltered hymns, about 250. His own contributions to hymnody were translations, which were collected and published under the title, *The Breaking Crucible, and Other Translations.*

H. 253

ALFORD, Henry, D.D. (London, 1810–71, Canterbury), was son of the rector of Aston Sandford. Educated at the Grammar School, Ilminster, and Trinity College, Cambridge, he served as curate to his father at Winkfield, Wiltshire, also at Ampton, became vicar of Wymeswold, Leicestershire, then incumbent of Quebec Chapel, London, and, finally, in 1857, Dean of Canterbury. He was a Fellow of his college and Hulsean Lecturer. *The Contemporary Review* was started and for some time edited by him. He was greatly interested in hymnology and himself wrote and translated many hymns, including a series for Sundays and Holy Days throughout the year. These were published in *Psalms and Hymns* (1844), *The Year of Praise* (1867), *Poetical Works* (1868), and other volumes. His *magnum opus* was his *Greek Testament*, which marked a great advance in the progress of New Testament scholarship in this country.

H. 627

ALINGTON, CYRIL ARGENTINE, D.D., D.C.L. (Ipswich, 1872–1955, Treago, Herefordshire), was educated at Marlborough and Trinity College, Oxford, and became a Fellow of All Souls. He was assistant master at Marlborough and Eton, and became headmaster of Shrewsbury in 1908 and of Eton in 1916. He was Dean of Durham, 1933–51. Among his publications are *Christianity in England*, *Good News* (1945), and *A Dean's Apology* (1952).

H. 120, 270, 555, 593, 599

ALSTON, ALFRED EDWARD (Victoria, British Columbia, 1862–1927, Framingham Earl), was educated at St. Paul's School and Gloucester Theological College. Ordained in 1886, he was appointed rector of Framingham Earl with Bixley in the diocese of Norwich, 1887, where he remained until his death. In 1903 he published *Some Liturgical Hymns, newly rendered from the Latin*.

H. 31

ALSTYNE, FRANCES JANE VAN, *née* CROSBY (South East, Putnam County, New York, 1820–1915, Bridgeport, Connecticut), best known as Fanny Crosby, lost her eyesight when six weeks old. She was educated at the New York (City) Institute for the Blind, and afterwards was a teacher there until, in 1858, she married Alexander van Alstyne, a blind musician. She was a member of the Methodist Episcopal Church. Her first verses were published when she was eight years old and as she continued writing with unfaltering facility until her death in her ninety-fifth year, she produced a vast quantity of verse. Till middle life she wrote songs, principally of a highly sentimental cast; some of them, like 'The Hazel Dell' and 'Rosalie the Prairie Flower', had an enormous popularity. Thereafter she devoted herself to writing hymns. One New York firm salaried her to supply them with three hymns a week all the year round, and she was able to meet the contract. She is said to have written for two firms alone 5,959 hymns, and she wrote about 1,500 more for W. H. Doane, Robert Lawrie, Philip Phillips, Ira D. Sankey, and other editors of evangelistic collections—nearly 8,000 in all. She published under 216 *noms de plume* as well as under her own maiden and married names. About sixty of her hymns are in use.

H. 58, 374

ALTENBURG, JOHANN MICHAEL (Alach, *c.* 1584–1640, Erfurt), was educated at Erfurt, and spent most of his life in the neighbourhood of that town. He was successively pastor of various charges, mostly at or near Erfurt, during the troublous times of the Thirty Years War.

H. 472 (i)

AMBROSE, ST. (Trèves, 340–97, Milan), the greatest bishop in his day of the Western Church, was the son of a prefect of Gaul. He studied law, and was early appointed governor of the district of Northern Italy in which is situated the city of Milan. In the conflict between Catholics and Arians he displayed such courage and wisdom that on the death of the Bishop of Milan in 374 he was elected bishop by acclamation, and, though only a catechumen, was baptized and consecrated forthwith. As bishop he showed himself at once gentle and firm. He was no respecter of persons, as was seen in his long and victorious conflict with the Arian Empress, Justina, and in his refusal to allow the Emperor Theodosius to enter the church till he had done penance for the massacre at Thessalonica. His writings and sermons made a powerful and popular appeal. Ambrose's greatest service to the Church was the improvement he effected in its musical services. He seems to have been the first to introduce in the West the practice of antiphonal singing, besides being himself a hymn-writer of distinction. There is no foundation for the belief (at one time widely accepted) that he was the author or part-author of the *Te Deum*.

H. 56, 540

ANDERSON, JAMES SMITH, Mus.Bac. (Crail, Fife, 1853–1945, Edinburgh), received his musical education in Edinburgh under Sir George Martin, and subsequently in Glasgow under Dr. A. L. Peace. He received the degree of Mus.Bac., Oxon., in 1878, and became F.R.C.O. in the same year. As organist and choirmaster he served in succession Nicolson Square Wesleyan Chapel, Abbey Parish Church, St. Thomas's Episcopal Church, and St. Andrew's Parish Church, all in Edinburgh. He contributed to many hymnals, and revised the harmonies of *The Blackburn Tune Book* and *The Presbyterian Hymnal for the Young* (United Presbyterian). As representing the Society of Organists of Edinburgh, Mr. Anderson acted as an associate member of the revision committee which prepared *The Revised Church Hymnary*, of the Music Sub-Committee, and of the committee of experts who edited the music.

T. 306

ANDREW, FATHER (Kascuili, India, 1869–1946, Bushey Heath, Hertfordshire), is the 'name in religion' of Henry Ernest Hardy. He was educated at Clifton College and later studied theology at Keble College, Oxford. After working for a period at Oxford House, Bethnal Green, with two friends he founded the Society of the Divine Compassion in 1894. For over fifty years he worked in the parish of St. Philip, Plaistow. He published many volumes of poetry and devotional literature, and one of his plays, *The Hope of The World*, was performed at the Old Vic in 1919 and 1920.

H. 252

ANTES, JOHN (Bethlehem, U.S.A., 1740–1811, Bristol), was the son of a German emigrant to America, who had assisted in establishing the first permanent Moravian settlement there at Bethlehem. Here John grew up. He trained in Europe for the Moravian ministry and went to Egypt in 1769 as a missionary. During this time he composed three trios for two violins and cello, said to be the earliest chamber music composed by a musician born in America. He returned to Europe in 1781, and four years later went to the Moravian settlement at Fulneck in Yorkshire. He retired in 1808 and went to live in Bristol. It was during this time at Fulneck he composed his hymn-tunes as well as a number of arias and anthems.

T. 33 (i)

AQUINAS, THOMAS (Aquino, *c.* 1226–74, Fossa Nuova), was the son of a Count of Aquino and was closely related to several of the reigning families of Europe. At an early age and in spite of family opposition he joined the Dominican Order, and studied under Albertus Magnus at Cologne and afterwards at Paris, where at the Pope's request he defended his Order with great success in its controversy with the University on liberty of teaching. His life was one of extraordinary industry. He refused all ecclesiastical preferments and rewards. Summoned by the Pope to attend the Council of Lyons on the differences between the Greek and Latin Churches, he died before reaching the Council. Thomas's philosophy aims at gathering together all known science into a single system, a condensed summary of which is given in his *Summa Theologiae*, still the standard theological textbook of the Roman Church. Though his hymns are not numerous, several of those which he wrote on the Lord's Supper are of great merit. He was canonized in 1323.

H. 578, 581, 584

ARLOTT, LESLIE THOMAS JOHN (Basingstoke, 1914), was educated at Queen Mary School, Basingstoke. He became clerk in a mental hospital and later a police detective (1934–45), before becoming a producer with the B.B.C. (1945–50). After this he became a general instructor in the B.B.C. Staff-training School (1951–3). He is now cricket correspondent for the *Guardian*, a broadcaster, and topographer. Among his publications are *Landmarks* (with G. R. Hamilton), two poetical works *Of Period and Place* (1944) and *Clausentum* (1945), and many books on cricket.

H. 619

ARMITAGE, ELLA SOPHIA, *née* BULLEY, M.A. (Liverpool, 1841–1931, Rawdon, Leeds), a granddaughter of the Revd. Thomas Raffles, D.D., LL.D., of Liverpool, one of the most distinguished figures of English nonconformity. She was one of the first students of Miss Clough at Newnham College. In 1874 she married the Revd. Elkanah Armitage, M.A., afterwards Professor in the (Congregational) Yorkshire United College, Bradford. She served on the West Riding Education Committee: also as an assistant commissioner to the Royal Commission on Secondary Education. For a time she was lecturer on English history in the former Women's Department of Manchester University. Her degree was conferred on her, *honoris causa*, by that university, for her work in archaeology. Her publications include *The Childhood of the English Nation*; *The Connection of England and Scotland*; *A Key to English Antiquities*; *The Education of the Christian Home*; *An Introduction to English Antiquities*; *The Early Norman Castles of the British Isles*; and a Service of Song entitled *The Garden of the Lord*, in which there are sixteen of her hymns.

H. 553

ATTWOOD, THOMAS (London, 1765-1838, Chelsea), was the son of a trumpeter, viola player, and coal merchant. As a chorister in the Chapel Royal, he came under the notice of the Prince of Wales, afterwards George IV, and was sent abroad by him to study, first in Italy, then in Vienna under Mozart. In 1796 he was appointed organist of St. Paul's Cathedral and composer to the Chapel Royal; in 1821, organist of George IV's private chapel in Brighton; in 1823, one of the first professors of the Royal Academy of Music; and in 1836, organist of the Chapel Royal. In early life he was much engaged in dramatic composition, and did not till comparatively late begin to write Church music. In this, however, he showed marked originality. He was one of the first musicians in this country to recognize the genius of Mendelssohn, who dedicated to him his three Preludes and Fugues for the organ. He wrote many songs and glees, one song, 'The Soldier's Dream', long retaining its popularity; many sonatas; and services, anthems, chants. A volume of his Church compositions containing four services, eight anthems, and nine chants, was published about fifteen years after his death.

T. 118

AUBER, HARRIET (London, 1773-1862, Hoddesdon), was one of the daughters of James Auber, whose grandfather, Pierre Auber (Aubert), of Ecquetat in Normandy, came to England in 1685 as a Huguenot refugee after the Revocation of the Edict of Nantes. Most of her life was spent in the quiet villages of Broxbourne and Hoddesdon, Hertfordshire. In *The Spirit of the Psalms* (1829), she endeavoured to put 'elegance' and 'poetic language' into versions of certain selected psalms, hoping that these would displace from use the versions of Sternhold and Hopkins. It also included a number of contributions from her own pen.

H. 336

BACH, JOHANN SEBASTIAN (Eisenach, 1685-1750, Leipzig), was of peasant stock. He was trained in the choir schools of Ohrdruf and Lüneburg, and held official positions at Arnstadt, Mühlhausen, Weimar, and Anhalt Cöthen, before he settled finally in Leipzig as cantor of the famous Thomas School and director of music in the Thomas and Nicholas Churches. His name is held by many to be the greatest of all in the history of music, whether sacred or secular. With the exception of opera he handled every type of musical form with unequalled mastery. He was the greatest organist of all time, both as a player and as a composer for that instrument. His genius was wholly consecrated to the service of God in the Church that held his heart, and what Palestrina was to the Roman Church, Bach became to Protestantism. He had immense physical and mental energy, and poured out works that were prodigal not only in quantity, but in fertility of ideas. He left many vocal works, including motets, masses, about 200 cantatas (verse anthems), and two great Passions, the *St. Matthew* and the *St. John*. He reharmonized the old German chorales, many of which he embodied in his Passions.

T. 53 (ii), 57, 96, 128, 129, 148, 188, 189, 251, 253, 255, 406, 407, 445, 505, 520, 552, 581, 588, 607, 634, 642, 669, 687

BAKER, Sir HENRY WILLIAMS, Bt., M.A. (London, 1821–77, Monkland), was the son of Vice-Admiral Sir Henry Loraine Baker, and was educated at Trinity College, Cambridge. Ordained in 1844, he became vicar of Monkland near Leominster in 1851. In 1859 he succeeded to the baronetcy. He was the chief promoter of *Hymns Ancient and Modern*, and from the first, for twenty years, was chairman and acknowledged leader of the committee responsible for the preparation and development of that book. He contributed translations from the Latin, and many original hymns. He published *Family Prayers for the Use of those who have to work hard*, and a *Daily Text Book* for the same class.

H. 15, 130, 198, 249, 388, 504, 539, 570, 608

BARING-GOULD, SABINE, M.A. (Exeter, 1834–1924, Lew Trenchard), was educated at Clare College, Cambridge, and ordained in 1861. He became curate of Horbury, with special charge of the mission at Horbury Bridge, in 1864; two years later, perpetual curate of Dalton, near Thirsk; in 1871, rector of East Mersea, Colchester; and in 1881, having in the meanwhile succeeded his father in the estate of Lew Trenchard, Devon, he exercised his privilege as squire and patron by presenting himself to the living there as rector. He wrote a long series of *The Lives of the Saints*; *A Study of St. Paul*; *The Origin and Development of Religious Belief*; books of travel; and a very large number of novels. He was a keen collector of folk-songs, of which he edited two valuable collections, *Songs of the West* and *A Garland of Country Song*.

H. 423, 480, 653
T. 653

BARKLEY, JOHN MONTEITH, Ph.D., D.D. (Belfast, 1910), was educated at Magee University College, Derry, Trinity College, Dublin, and the Presbyterian College, Belfast. Ordained in 1935, following pastorates in Drumreagh, Ballybay and Rockcorry, and Cooke Centenary, he was appointed Professor of Church History and Symbolics in the Presbyterian College in 1954. He has published numerous articles on liturgical subjects, and *The Worship of the Reformed Church* (1966). He was editor of *The Book of Public Worship* (1965) of the Presbyterian Church in Ireland.

H. 595

BARNARD, WINIFRED EVA (Twickenham, Middlesex, 1892), was educated at Orme Girls' School, Newcastle (Staffordshire) and Strand Green and Hornsey High School, London. She was assistant head of a children's nursery school in Bow (1928–30), co-head of Kingsley Hall Nursery School, Dagenham (1930–9), and head of the same school when it was evacuated to Gloucestershire during the war years. From 1947 to 1956 she was head of the nursery department attached to a private school at Beckenham, Kent. Among her many publications relevant to the education of beginners and primary children are *Beginners Department Handbook*; *Beginners Work and Worship*; several series of *Tales to Tell Little Children*; and several series of *Song and Picture Book*. She also contributed to *Infant Praise* (1964). Her children's hymns are to be found in the hymnals of nearly all denominations.

H. 625

BARNES, ARCHIE FAIRBAIRN, B.A., Mus.Doc., F.R.C.O., M.C. (Bristol, 1878-1960, Paignton, Devon), was educated at Bristol Grammar School, the Royal College of Music, and Keble College, Oxford. He joined the army in 1914 and served with the British Expeditionary Force in France, was awarded the Military Cross in 1916, and was wounded and captured in 1918. In 1920 he transferred from his regiment, the 2/5th Gloucesters, to the Army Educational Corps. For some time he was headmaster of the Queen Victoria School, Dunblane, and later senior music master at Bishop's Stortford College.

T. 501

BARRETT-AYRES, REGINALD, Mus.Bac. (Aberdeen, 1920), was educated at Banff Academy, Craigmillar School, Edinburgh, and the University of Edinburgh. He was assistant music master at Ackworth School, near Pontefract, Yorkshire (1941) and became Director of Music the following year. He was Director of Music at Glasgow Academy (1945-51), before becoming Lecturer in Music (1951), Senior Lecturer and Head of Department (1955), and Reader and Head of Department in the University of Aberdeen (1968), which post he still holds. He is also Convener of the Scottish Churches' Music Consultation. He has contributed to *Dunblane Praises* (vols. i and ii); *New Songs for the Church* (vols. i and ii); the Supplement to *Hymns Ancient and Modern*; and a number of American hymnals. His main publications and compositions include *Singing for Fun*; *Joseph Haydn and the String Quartet*; a new edition in score and parts of the *Quartets of Joseph Haydn* (with H. C. Robbins Landon); a *Communion Service*; anthems and Church music; a comic opera, *The Proposal*, with script adapted from Chekhov by Alistair Macdonald; *Reveries for Solo Violin and Chorus*; and an opera, *Hugh Miller*, performed in St. Giles Cathedral during the Edinburgh Festival.

T. 425, 470

BARTHÉLÉMON, FRANÇOIS HIPPOLYTE (Bordeaux, 1741-1808, London), was the son of a French Government officer in the colonial department, and an Irish lady of a wealthy Laoghis family. Entering the army, he became an officer in Berwick's Regiment in the Irish Brigade. Here, however, he made the acquaintance of the Earl of Kellie, a musical enthusiast, who induced him to leave the army and adopt music as his profession. He came to England in 1765, and became a distinguished violinist. In that year he was appointed leader of the band at the opera and in 1770 at Marylebone Gardens. He wrote much music for the theatre and the public gardens, but little for the Church. An acquaintance with the Revd. Jacob Duché, the refugee rector of Christ Church, Philadelphia, who became chaplain to the Female Orphan Asylum in 1782, and who is reputed to have edited the 1785 and 1789 editions of *Riley's Psalms and Hymns* for the chapel of that asylum, led to his composing the one tune by which he is known. His works include much music for dramatic pieces, quartets for stringed instruments, and preludes for the organ.

T. 42 (ii)

BARTON, WILLIAM (?1597–1678, Leicester), vicar of Mayfield, Stafford-shire, and afterwards of St. Martin's, Leicester, was a friend of Richard Baxter, and has been described as 'a conforming Puritan'. At Baxter's suggestion, he composed four metrical renderings of the *Te Deum*. He was keenly alive to the defects of the Sternhold and Hopkins version of the psalms, and himself essayed to produce a better, in *The Book of Psalms in Metre* (1644). When, in 1646, the Westminster Assembly of Divines, in their desire to secure uniformity in worship throughout the kingdom, recom-mended for adoption, as the authorized metrical psalter, Francis Rous's version, the House of Lords favoured Barton's in preference to it and submitted his third edition (1646) to the Assembly for approval. They declined to countenance it, and Rous's version was ordered by the House of Commons, 'it and none other . . . to be sung in all the churches and chapels within the kingdom'. The Scots, however, were dissatisfied with it, and in 1647 their Assembly appointed four persons to revise it, enjoining them to compare with it the versions of Zachary Boyd, Sir William Mure of Rowallen, and Barton, as well as *The Scottish Psalter* of 1564–5. Barton always claimed that the resultant version, the Metrical Psalter still in use in Scotland, was 'most-what' composed out of 'mine and Mr. Rous's'. His chief distinction was as a pioneer of modern hymnody. He issued successive 'centuries' of hymns which were finally assembled by his son in *Six Centuries of Select Hymns and Spiritual Songs, collected out of the Bible* (1688). He helped to fix the type and character of English hymns as based upon Scripture and saturated with it.

T. 351

BATEMAN, CHRISTIAN HENRY (Wyke, near Halifax, 1813–89, Carlisle), was first a minister of the Moravian Church; then of Congregational Churches in Edinburgh (Richmond Place), Hopton (Yorkshire), and Reading (Berkshire); then, taking Orders in the Church of England, he served as curate of St. Luke's, Jersey, and chaplain to the Forces; as vicar of All Saints, Childshill, Middlesex; and finally as curate of St. John's, Penymynydd, Hawarden. His latter days were spent at Carlisle, without a charge. A hymn-book for children, edited by him, under the title *Sacred Melodies for Sabbath Schools and Families*, was for many years the book generally used in the Sunday schools of Scotland. After entering the Church of England, he published in London *The Children's Hymnal and Christian Year*.

H. 383

BATHURST, WILLIAM HILEY, M.A. (Cleve Dale, Mangotsfield, near Bristol, 1796–1877, Lydney Park), was son of the Rt. Hon. Charles Bragge, M.P. for Bristol, who assumed the name of Bathurst on succeeding to his uncle's estate of Lydney Park, Gloucestershire. Educated at Winchester and Christ Church, Oxford, he took Orders, and was presented by his kinsman, Earl Bathurst, to the rectory of Barwick-in-Elmet, near Leeds. Doctrinal difficulties arising out of the Prayer Book, and especially the baptismal and burial services, led to his resignation of the living in 1852. He then retired into private life at Darley Dale, near Matlock. In 1863 he succeeded to the family estate. He published *A Translation of the Georgics of Virgil* (1849); *Metrical Musings*; and *Psalms and Hymns for Public and Private Use* (1830).

H. 664

BATTISHILL, JONATHAN (London, 1738-1801, Islington), a chorister of St. Paul's, became deputy to Dr. Boyce as organist of the Chapel Royal, then organist of two city churches, St. Clement, Eastcheap, and Christ Church, Newgate Street. He wrote much music for theatrical and concert platform use; but subsequently he composed almost exclusively for the Church.

T. 93, 557

BAX, CLIFFORD, F.R.S.A., F.S.A. (London, 1886-1962, London), was educated privately and later studied art at the Slade School and at Heatherley's. After living on the Continent for some years, he returned to England, when he gave up art for literature and drama. He published many plays, comedies, and short stories. He published *Twenty-five Chinese Poems* (1910) and his collected poems *My Muse* (1932).

H. 84

BAXTER, RICHARD (Rowton, 1615-91, London), was brought up by his maternal grandfather, and educated at Wroxeter School, but never attended a university. After a short experience of Court life, his strong religious convictions led him to study divinity. Ordained to the ministry, he served successively at Bridgnorth and Kidderminster. Before long he began to distrust episcopacy in its prevalent form, and during the Civil War he attached himself to the Parliamentary army. For a short time after the Restoration he held the office of King's Chaplain, and took part in the abortive Savoy Conference, one result of which was his *Reformed Liturgy*. After the Act of Uniformity he was subjected to much intermittent persecution, culminating in his trial before Judge Jeffreys in 1685. Released after a two years' imprisonment, he passed the remaining four years of his life in peace and honour. Among his 'books enough to fill a cart' (Jeffreys), the three which take first rank are *The Saints' Everlasting Rest* (1650); *The Reformed Pastor* (1656); and *The Call to the Unconverted* (1657). Of great biographical interest are his *Reliquiae*, containing a narrative of his life and times. His poetical works are of less merit.

H. 363, 672, 679

BAYLY, ALBERT FREDERICK (Bexhill-on-sea, 1901), was educated at Mary Magdalen School, St. Leonard's, and Hastings Grammar School. After training as a shipwright, he studied for the ministry of the Congregational Church at Mansfield College, Oxford. He served in Whitley Bay, Morpeth, Burnley, and Swanland, East Yorkshire. He published *God's Building*, *God's Man*, and a collection of hymns in 1951 with the title *Rejoice, O People*.

H. 141, 426, 458, 503, 554

BEDDOME, BENJAMIN (Henley-in-Arden, Warwickshire, 1717-95, Bourton-on-the-Water), was the son of a Baptist minister, the Revd. John Beddome. He was apprenticed to a surgeon, but later entered the ministry of the Baptist Church. In 1740 he was installed in Bourton-on-the-Water, Gloucestershire, where he remained all his life. His hymns were written each week to be sung after his sermon. The Revd. Robert Hall published a collection of them in 1817 with the title *Hymns adapted to Public Worship or Family Devotion*.

H. 594

BEDE, The Venerable (Wearmouth, Co. Durham, 673-735, Jarrow), was the greatest scholar of his time. He is chiefly remembered for his *Ecclesiastical History of the English Nation*, at the end of which he gives a list of his own works including *A Book of Hymns in several sorts of metre or rhyme*. Some ten or twelve of these are thought to be his own.

H. 305

BELL, GEORGE KENNEDY ALLEN, D.D. (Hayling Island, 1883-1958, Canterbury), was educated at Westminster, Christ Church, Oxford, and Wells Theological College. After being a curate in Leeds and a don at Oxford, he was chaplain to Archbishop Davidson. He became Dean of Canterbury in 1924 and Bishop of Chichester in 1929. He was Assistant Secretary of the Lambeth Conference of 1920 and was Episcopal Secretary in 1930. After giving distinguished service to the ecumenical movement, he became a President of the World Council of Churches. Among his publications were *Randall Davidson, Archbishop of Canterbury*, *The Kingship of Christ*, and four series of *Documents on Christian Unity*.

H. 474

BENSON, LOUIS FITZGERALD, D.D. (Philadelphia, 1855-1930, Philadelphia), was educated at the University of Pennsylvania and trained for the Bar, then turned to the Church, and became minister of the Church of the Redeemer, Germanstown, Philadelphia. This charge he resigned to edit the hymnals of the Presbyterian Church. He was lecturer on Liturgics in Auburn Theological Seminary, and on Hymnology in Princeton Seminary. He edited *The Hymnal* (Presbyterian); *The Hymnal for Congregational Churches*; *The Chapel Hymnal*; *The School Hymnal*; and was joint-editor with Dr. Henry Van Dyke of *The Book of Common Worship* of the Presbyterian Church in the United States. He also wrote books on *The Best Church Hymns*; *Best Hymns, a Handbook*; *The English Hymn, its Development and Use in Public Worship*. His collected *Hymns, Original and Translated*, were published in 1925.

H. 220

BERKELEY, Sir LENNOX RANDAL, C.B.E., M.A., Mus.Doc. (Oxford, 1903), was educated at Gresham School, Holt, and Merton College, Oxford. He was on the B.B.C. musical staff (1942-5) and Professor of Composition at the Royal Academy of Music (1946-68). He has contributed to *The Cambridge Hymnal* and *The Catholic Hymn Book*. He collaborated with Benjamin Britten in *Mont Juic*, and has written several operas, including *Nelson* and *A Dinner Engagement*, three symphonies, two concertos for piano, *Four Poems of St. Teresa* for contralto and orchestra, *Stabat Mater* for six voices and orchestra, and much other chamber, orchestral, opera, and piano music.

T. 50 (i), 54 (i)

BERNARD OF CLUNY (twelfth century), sometimes called 'of Morlaix' erroneously, from his supposed birthplace (he was really born at Murles or Morlas), but more commonly 'of Cluny' from the great abbey of which he became a monk, is said to have been of English extraction. Of him, unlike his great contemporary Bernard of Clairvaux, practically nothing is known save his authorship of the poem *De Contemptu Mundi*.

H. 537

BIANCO DA SIENA (Anciolina, ?-1434, Venice). Little is known of his life. In 1367 he joined a religious order founded by John Columbinus of Siena, and is said to have spent the latter part of his life at Venice. His hymns (*Laudi Spirituali*) were published in 1851, and some of them have been translated into English by Dr. Littledale.

H. 115

BICKERSTETH, EDWARD HENRY, D.D. (Islington, London, 1825-1906, London), was a son of the Revd. E. Bickersteth, who was the first secretary of the Church Missionary Society, then rector of Watton, Hertfordshire, a poet, and editor of *Christian Psalmody*. He was educated at Trinity College, Cambridge, and ordained in 1848. After holding curacies at Banningham, Norfolk, and Christ Church, Tunbridge Wells, he was, successively, rector of Hinton Martell; vicar of Christ Church, Hampstead; Dean of Gloucester; and Bishop of Exeter (1885-1900). His best work was probably as editor of *Psalms and Hymns*, based on his father's collection; and of *The Hymnal Companion to the Book of Common Prayer* (1870).

H. 476

BINNEY, THOMAS, D.D., LL.D. (Newcastle upon Tyne, 1798-1874, London), served an apprenticeship to a bookseller. His father was of Scots extraction and a Presbyterian, but the son, for some unknown reason, turned to Congregationalism. Three years in the theological seminary of Coward College, Wymondley, Hertfordshire, prepared him for the ministry. He ministered at the New Meeting, Bedford, St. James's Chapel, Newport, Isle of Wight, and Weigh House Chapel, London. He was a pioneer in the movement towards Nonconformist liturgical services. He edited and published a book by Charles W. Baird, D.D., of New York, on *Historical Sketches of the Liturgical Forms of the Reformed Churches*, with an introduction by himself and an appendix on the question, 'Are Dissenters to have a Liturgy?'.

This book and his own example in the devotional part of his services at the Weigh House Chapel, gave a great impulse to the movement towards improved services in Nonconformist churches. By a published sermon on *The Service of Song in the House of the Lord*, he gave an impetus also to the movement towards better music in such services; he was one of the first Nonconformists to introduce anthems and chanting.

H. 357

BLAKE, WILLIAM (Carnaby Market, London, 1757-1827, Strand, London), was the son of a hosier. An engraver by training and profession, he was also a painter and poet of remarkable individuality and power. Thus his *Poetical Sketches*, begun at 12 and finished at 20, struck an entirely new note in literature, by the freshness of their substance, music, and spirit. His *Songs of Innocence* deal with the homeliest things but the *Songs of Experience* are full of the trouble of the world. Blake was an ardent apostle of liberty, and a rebel against bondage in every form. His passion was to set men free from everything that imposed restraint on thought and conduct, whether in politics, religion, literature, art, or ordinary convention, so that the creative urge of personality, which he regarded as the divine in man, might express itself freely and fully. He was the unsparing enemy, therefore, of all social evils that tended to repress personality or destroy it—poverty, starvation, harlotry, the gambling passion, misery in all forms—at a time when these things stirred in few breasts the spirit of revolt; and he dreamed and sang of a new Jerusalem from which these things should be banished. It was to arise in this present scene; the creative impulse towards it was to be derived from Jesus Christ, who is its centre and its head.

H. 487

BLATCHFORD, AMBROSE NICHOLS (Devonshire, 1842-1925, Bideford, Devon), was educated at Tavistock Grammar School and Manchester New College, London. In 1866 he became assistant minister at Lewin's Mead Unitarian Church, Bristol, and in 1876 succeeded to the full charge, in which he continued until he retired in 1915. He published in 1897 *Songs of Praise for School and Church*.

H. 148

BLISS, PHILIPP (P. P. BLISS) (Clearfield County, Pennsylvania, 1838-76, Ashtabula, Ohio), early in life separated the final p from his Christian name, and made his signature P. P. Bliss. He went to Chicago in 1864 to conduct musical institutes and compose Sunday school melodies, under Dr. G. F. Root. Originally a Methodist, he became in 1871 a choir member and Sunday-school superintendent in the First Congregational Church in that city. In 1874 he joined the evangelist, Major D. W. Whittle, in his campaigning, conducting the music and singing solos, as Sankey did for Moody. He prepared for use in their meetings *Gospel Songs*. On Moody and Sankey's return from their first British evangelistic campaign, it was decided to combine their embryo *Sacred Songs and Solos* with Bliss's collection, and the joint-book was issued as *Gospel Hymns and Sacred Songs*, by P. P. Bliss and I. D. Sankey.

H. 380, 417

T. 380, 417

BODE, JOHN ERNEST, M.A. (London, 1816–74, Castle Camps, Cambridge-shire), was educated at Eton, Charterhouse, and Christ Church, Oxford. He was a Student (Fellow) and Tutor of Christ Church for six years; then, in 1847, became rector of Westwell, Oxfordshire, and, later, of Castle Camps, Cambridgeshire.

H. 434

BONAR, HORATIUS, D.D. (Edinburgh, 1808–89, Edinburgh), was the son of a solicitor of Excise, and was educated at the High School and the University of Edinburgh. He began his ministry in the Church of Scotland as a missionary assistant in Leith, but in 1838 was ordained at Kelso, in charge of the new North Parish there. When the Disruption of the Church of Scotland took place in 1843, he entered the Free Church, and was for a time joint-editor of *The Border Watch*, a newspaper conducted in the interest of that Church. In 1866 he became minister of the Chalmers Memorial Free Church, Grange, Edinburgh, and in 1883 was elected Moderator of the General Assembly of his Church. He loved children, and for them his first hymns were written. His hymns were thrown off in the most casual way; he seemed to attach little importance to them, and was seldom at pains to exercise the artificer's art upon them. Among Dr. Bonar's many books were *Songs for the Wilderness*; *The Bible Hymn Book*; *Hymns Original and Selected*; *The Desert of Sinai*; *Hymns of Faith and Hope*; *The Land of Promise*, etc.

H. 131, 212, 299, 354, 410, 457, 483, 573

BONNER, CAREY (London, 1859–1938, London), was educated at Plaistow School and Rawdon College, Leeds. Ordained to the Baptist ministry in 1884, he ministered at Sale and in Portland Chapel, Southampton. In 1900 he was appointed Secretary of the National Sunday School Union, of which he was President in 1922–3. He was President of the Baptist Union in 1931–2. He edited *The Sunday School Hymnary* and three volumes of *Child Songs*, published *Some Baptist Hymnists* in 1937, and with Dr. W. T. Whitley edited *A Handbook to the Baptist Church Hymnal Revised* in 1935.

T. 386

BONNET, PIERRE (Paris, 1638–1708, Paris), was a French musical historian. He worked on a history of music in collaboration with an uncle, Pierre Bourdelot (real name Michan), but died before it was completed. It was finished by his brother, Jacques, who published *Histoire de la musique et de ses effets* in 1715.

T. 308

BOOTH, JOSIAH (Coventry, 1852–1930, London), was organist at the Wesleyan Chapel, Banbury, and, after study at the Royal Academy of Music, at Park Chapel, Crouch End, London. He edited the music for the chants and anthems in Barrett's *Congregational Church Hymnal* (1887) and acted as principal music adviser for *The Congregational Hymnary* (1916).

T. 151, 475

BORTHWICK, JANE LAURIE (Edinburgh, 1813–97, Edinburgh), was the elder daughter of James Borthwick, manager of the North British Insurance Office, Edinburgh. Along with her sister Sarah (Mrs. Findlater) she published, in four series (1854, 1855, 1858, and 1862), *Hymns from the Land of Luther*, sixty-nine of the translations being from her own pen, and fifty-three from Sarah's. The title of this book supplied the initials—H. L. L.—over which many of her hymns appeared in *The Family Treasury*. These were collected and published in 1857 as *Thoughts for Thoughtful Hours*.

H. 673

BOURGEOIS, LOUIS (Paris, c. 1510–61, Paris), was an adherent of Calvin, and followed him to Geneva in 1541. The Consistory appointed him cantor in one of the churches there, and in 1545 master of the choristers in succession to Guillaume Franc. They also entrusted him with the duty of providing music for the metrical psalter. A partial psalter appeared in 1542. In this Bourgeois made alterations in some of the tunes hitherto in use, and replaced some of the old tunes with others. He seems to have been concerned in the music of all editions of the psalter appearing within the following fifteen years. In 1547, there was printed at Lyons *Pseaulmes cinquante de David Roy et Prophete, traduictz en vers françois par Clement Marot, et mis en musique par Loys Bourgeoys à quatre parties, à voix de contrepoinct égal consonnante au verbe. Tousiours mord envie.* This volume seems to embrace the whole of Bourgeois's work on the psalms to this date. It is not certain whether the melodies were composed by Bourgeois, or merely arranged by him in four-part harmony. Towards the end of 1551 he was thrown into prison for making unauthorized alteration to certain well-known tunes. Calvin, albeit remonstrating with him, secured his release after twenty-four hours. But other troubles followed, and finally, failing to induce his employers to allow the introduction of part-singing into public worship, he left Geneva and returned to Paris. From 1561, when he was still there, he vanishes from history. He had found in use at Geneva a psalter with about thirty tunes; he left one with eighty-five, many of them, probably his own. The alterations for which he was imprisoned ultimately received official sanction and passed into general use.

T. 1, 2, 46, 51, 84, 250, 265, 307, 314, 319, 370, 392, 454 (i), 507, 574, 640, 658

BOURNE, GEORGE HUGH, D.C.L. (St. Paul's Cray, Kent, 1840–1925, Salisbury), was educated at Eton and Corpus Christi, Oxford. He was ordained in 1863, and two years later became headmaster of Chardstock College, which was removed to St. Edmund's College, Salisbury. He became

Sub-Dean of Sarum in 1887, and Treasurer and Prebendary in 1901. In 1874 he published privately *Seven Post-Communion Hymns* for use in the chapel of St. Edmund's.

H. 583

BOWIE, WALTER RUSSELL, D.D. (Richmond, Virginia, 1882–1969, Alexandria, Virginia), was educated at Harvard and Virginia Theological Seminary. Ordained in 1908, he ministered in Emmanuel Church, Greenwood, Virginia, St. Paul's, Richmond, and Grace Church, New York. In 1939 he was appointed Professor of Practical Theology in Union Theological Seminary, New York. He was a member of the committee which prepared the American Revised Standard Version of the Bible.

H. 255, 509

BOWRING, SIR JOHN, LL.D., F.R.S. (Exeter, 1792–1872, Exeter), was trained in his native town for a mercantile career. His friendship with Jeremy Bentham, whose works he afterwards edited, led to his becoming editor of the radical *Westminster Review*. Entering Parliament, he represented the Clyde Burghs, Kilmarnock, and Bolton, took an active share in the agitation for free trade, and was a frequent contributor to debate on fiscal, educational, and commercial problems. In 1847 he was appointed consul at Canton, and subsequently governor of Hong Kong and chief superintendent of trade with China. He was then knighted. A successful vote of censure on him in the House of Commons, because of his policy, led to a General Election and to his resignation. His works, published in thirty-six volumes, are almost forgotten, but some of his hymns survive, and, though he was a Unitarian, are in general Christian use.

H. 144, 259

BOYCE, WILLIAM, Mus.Doc. (London, 1710–79, London), was the son of a cabinet-maker, and became a chorister of St. Paul's. In his youth his hearing became impaired, but he became organist of several London churches; conductor of the Three Choirs of Gloucester, Worcester, and Hereford; composer to the Chapel Royal; Master of the King's Band; one of the organists of the Chapel Royal. His deafness so increased that he had to give up teaching and relinquish some of his offices. He then employed himself in collecting and editing materials for the work by which he is best known, *Cathedral Music, being a Collection in score of the most valuable and useful compositions for that service by the several English masters of the last two hundred years* (1760). He published forty-six anthems, five services, eight symphonies, twelve sonatas, duets and songs, including 'Heart of Oak', and music for the theatre.

C. 345 (a)

BOYD, ROBERT HUGH STEELE, Ph.D., D.D. (Belfast, 1924), was educated at Trinity College, Dublin, New College, Edinburgh, the Presbyterian College, Belfast, and Basle. Ordained in 1951, he acted as Secretary for Theological

Colleges with the S.C.M. before going as a missionary to India in 1954. In 1961 he became a lecturer in Gujurat United School of Theology. He has published *An Introduction to Indian Christian Theology* (1969) and *What is Christianity?* (1970). He now lives in Australia.

H. 203

BRADBURY, WILLIAM BATCHELDER (York, Maine, 1816-68, Montclair, New Jersey), after many struggles, owing to straitened circumstances, succeeded in getting a musical education. He taught singing classes for a time at Machias, Maine, and St. John's, New Brunswick; then obtained appointments as organist, first in the Baptist Church, Brooklyn, and afterwards in the Baptist Tabernacle, New York. Here he organized singing classes for children and juvenile musical festivals, and threw himself into the work of organizing classes and conventions, and editing song-books, sacred and secular. Sunday-school music was at a low ebb then; and his work furnished 'the barrier by which the fearful tide was stopped'.

T. 418 (ii)

BRIDGES, MATTHEW (Maldon, Essex, 1800-94, Sidmouth), the younger son of John Bridges of Wallington House, Surrey, was brought up in the Church of England. He published *Jerusalem regained, a Poem*, in 1825, and in 1828 a book on *The Roman Empire under Constantine the Great*, being moved to this by the desire 'to examine the real origin of certain papal superstitions, whose antiquity has been so often urged against Protestants, with no little triumph and presumption'. Notwithstanding these early Protestant prepossessions, he entered the Roman Church in 1848. The latter part of his life was spent in Canada. His later publications were *Babbicombe or Visions of Memory, and Other Poems* (1842); *Hymns of the Heart* (1847); *The Passion of Jesus* (1852); and *Popular Ancient and Modern Histories*.

H. 298, 429

BRIDGES, ROBERT (SEYMOUR), M.A., M.B., F.R.C.P. (Isle of Thanet, 1844-1930, Boar's Hill, Oxford), son of a Kentish squire, was educated at Eton and Corpus Christi College, Oxford (Hon. Fellow). On leaving the university he travelled on the Continent and in the East, then studied medicine at St. Bartholomew's Hospital, London. On qualifying, he became casualty physician there, and physician at the Great Northern Hospital, and also carried on general practice. He gave up practice in 1882, settled at Yattendon in Berkshire, and devoted himself to literature, in which he had already made his mark as a poet. He was appointed Poet Laureate in 1913. He was a scholar of great learning, both in ancient and modern letters, and a highly skilled and cultivated musician. His *Yattendon Hymnal* is, both in words and music, easily the most distinguished of individual contributions to modern hymnody. After he settled in the Berkshire village of Yattendon, he took charge of the congregational singing in the parish church. With a view to reviving certain old church tunes—set to hymns worthy of them—he published this hymnal containing 100 hymns, with the music, largely from *The Genevan Psalter*, arranged in four parts of unaccompanied singing. Of these hymns, no fewer than forty-four were of his own workmanship as author, translator, or adaptor. Two articles on hymnody are printed in his *Collected Essays* (1935).

H. 55, 57, 119, 251, 335, 370, 403, 405, 408, 472 (i), 642

BRIGGS, GEORGE WALLACE (Kirkby, Northamptonshire, 1875-1959, Worcester), was a scholar of Emmanuel College, Cambridge. He served as a chaplain in the Royal Navy, 1902-9, was vicar of St. Andrew's, Norwich, 1909-18, when he became rector of Loughborough. He was a canon of Leicester, 1927-34, and of Worcester, 1934-56. In 1927 the Leicestershire Education Authority published *Prayers and Hymns for use in Schools*, which was largely his work. From then he acted as adviser to many Education Authorities in connection with worship in schools, and published many books, of which the best known is *The Daily Service*. In 1945 he published a selection of his own hymns entitled *Songs of Faith*. He was one of the founders of the Hymn Society.

H. 215, 219, 452, 505, 572

BRIGHT, WILLIAM, D.D. (Doncaster, 1824-1901, Oxford). was educated at University College, Oxford, and became a Fellow of his college. Ordained in 1848, he became theological tutor at Glenalmond College, Perthshire; Tutor of University College, Oxford; Hon. Canon of Cumbrae Cathedral, 1865-93; Canon of Christ Church, Oxford, and Regius Professor of Ecclesiastical History there, 1868. He published *Ancient Collects, selected from Various Rituals* (1862), *Hymns and Other Poems* (1866), etc.

H. 580, 636

BROADWOOD, LUCY (?, 1858-1929, London), was a collector of folk-songs, especially in Surrey, Sussex, the Scottish highlands, and Ireland. She was one of the founders of the Folk Song Society, and became its Secretary in 1904 and President (1927-9). She edited the *Folk Song Society Journal* from 1904 to 1909 and from 1916 to 1926. She published *English Country Songs* (1893) along with J. A. Fuller-Maitland, and *English Traditional Songs and Carols* (1909).

T. 17, 212, 220, 502, 618, 630

BROOKE, STOPFORD AUGUSTUS, LL.D. (Glendoen, Letterkenny, Donegal, 1832-1916, The Four Winds, Surrey), was educated at Kingstown, Kidderminster, and Trinity College, Dublin. On taking Orders, in London in 1857, he accepted a curacy in St. Matthew's, Marylebone; then another in St. Mary Abbott's, Kensington. From 1862 to 1865 he was chaplain to the British Embassy in Berlin. Returning to London, he took a lease of St. James's (proprietary) Chapel, York Street, then derelict. In 1867 he was appointed chaplain to the Queen. Her Majesty was eager to give him a canonry of Westminster, but his liberal views made the appointment impossible. On the expiry of the lease of St. James's Chapel, his services were transferred to Bedford Chapel, which was proprietary also, and there he ministered till his retirement in 1894. In 1880 his growing restiveness under the doctrinal standards of the Church of England moved him to resign his Orders in that Church, and thenceforward he occupied an independent position, attached to no denomination, retaining in the main the Church of England service, but having close relations with the Unitarians. At this time he prepared for his congregation a collection entitled *Christian Hymns*.

H. 176, 213

BROOKS, PHILLIPS, D.D. (Boston, 1835–93, Boston), studied at Harvard. On graduating he tried teaching in the Boston Latin School. He then studied at the Episcopal Theological Seminary at Alexandria, Virginia. Ordained in 1859, he became rector of the Church of the Advent, Philadelphia; then of Holy Trinity, Philadelphia; then of Trinity Church, Boston; and finally, in 1891, after refusing the office of preacher at Harvard, professorships, and the assistant bishopric of Pennsylvania, he was elected Bishop of Massachusetts.

H. 172

BROWN, ARTHUR HENRY (Brentwood, Essex, 1830–1926, Brentwood), apart from a few organ lessons, was self-taught as a musician. Before he was eleven he was organist of Brentwood Parish Church, and except for five years as organist at Romford, and another brief interval, he continued to hold that office for forty years. Coming under the influence of the Oxford Movement, he threw himself enthusiastically into the furtherance of that Church revival, especially on its musical side. He was a pioneer in the restoration of the ancient plain-chant, and by his *Gregorian Psalter*, and his work in the London Gregorian Association, did much to revive the use of the Gregorian Tones in Anglican worship. He published also *The Altar Hymnal*, designed to enrich with appropriate hymns and introits the Anglican Eucharistic Service; *Metrical Litanies for Use in Church*; *Canticles of Holy Church*; *Accompanying Harmonies for the Gregorian Psalm Tones*; *Hymns of the Eastern Church*; *The Anglican Psalter*; *Divers Carols for Christmas and Other Tydes of Holy Church*. He wrote about 700 hymn-tunes.

T. 79, 448

BROWN, JEANETTE ELOISE PERKINS (Grand Island, Nebraska, 1887–1960, Bennington, Vermont), as Jeanette Perkins, married Edward B. Brown. She was educated at Bradford College for Girls, Boston. She collected and edited *A Little Book of Bed-time Songs*, and published *As Children Worship* (1936), and *A Little Book of Singing Graces* (1946). She also contributed to *Songs for Early Childhood* and *Songs and Hymns for Primary Children*.

H. 157

BROWNE, SIMON (Shepton Mallet, 1686–1732, Shepton Mallet), after studying at the Academy of Mr. Moore, Bridgewater, became Independent minister at Portsmouth, and in 1716 pastor of the important congregation in Old Jewry, London. In 1720 he published *Hymns and Spiritual Songs*.

H. 116

BROWNLIE, JOHN, D.D. (Glasgow, 1859–1925, Crieff), was educated in Glasgow, at the university and the Free Church College. In 1885 he became junior minister of the Free Church, Portpatrick, Wigtownshire, to the full charge of which he succeeded in 1890. His interest in hymnology bore fruit in *Hymns and Hymn-Writers of the Church Hymnary* (1899); and besides publishing many original hymns in *Hymns of our Pilgrimage Zionward*; *Hymns of the Pilgrim Life*; and *Pilgrim Songs*, he diligently cultivated the field of Latin and Greek hymnody. *Hymns of the Early Church*; *Hymns from East and West*; and *Hymns of the Greek Church* (4 series) attested his learning in this field and his gifts as a translator.

H. 95

BUCHANAN, VIOLET NITA (London, 1891), was educated privately. She has contributed hymns to *The Anglican Hymn Book* and *Hymns on the Bible*, the latter at the request of the Hymn Society of America.

H. 327

BUCK, PERCY CARTER, Mus.Doc. (West Ham, Essex, 1871–1947, London), was educated at the Guildhall School of Music and the Royal College of Music. He became organist of Worcester College, Oxford, 1891; of Wells Cathedral, 1895; of Bristol Cathedral, 1900; Musical Director of Harrow School, in succession to Eaton Faning, 1901; Professor of Music, Trinity College, Dublin, 1910-20; first Cramb Lecturer, Glasgow University, 1923; and, from 1925 to 1930, King Edward VII Professor of Music, University of London. He was knighted in 1937. He published three organ sonatas; several choral works and school songs; two organ manuals; *Unfigured Harmony* (1911); *Acoustics for Musicians* (1918). He was editor of *The Oxford Song Book* (1931) and published *The Scope of Music* (1924) and *A History of Music* (1929).

T. 329, 330, 366, 542, 662 (v)

BUDRY (BOUDRY), EDMOND LOUIS (Vevey, Switzerland, 1854-1932, Vevey), was educated at Lausanne where he became a licentiate in theology and philosophy of the theological faculty of the Église Évangélique libre du Canton de Vaud. This Church was an evangelical breakaway from the National Reformed Church of Vaud, but they are now re-united. He was minister at Cully and Sainte Croix from 1886 and at Vevey from 1889. He wrote a vast amount of poetry and many hymns including 'Jésus-Christ est ma sagesse', 'O bonne nouvelle', 'Écoutez le chant des anges', many of which were published in *Chants évangéliques* (Lausanne, 1885).

H. 279

BULLOCK, WILLIAM, D.D. (Prettiwell, Apex, 1798-1874, Halifax, Nova Scotia), was educated at Christ's Hospital, then entered the Royal Navy. On a survey of the coast of Newfoundland, he resolved to take Holy Orders and to become a missionary in that colony. This he did, and served there for thirty-two years under the Society for Propagating the Gospel. He became Dean of Nova Scotia, at Halifax, where he published in 1854 his *Songs of the Church*.

H. 15

BUNYAN, JOHN (Elstow, 1628-88, London), though the son of a tinker, had a fixed residence and was sent to a village school. After a short term of service with the parliamentary army he passed through a period of extreme spiritual ferment and self-distrust. Immediately after the Restoration he was thrown into Bedford gaol, and only fully liberated by the Indulgence of 1671, intended really for the benefit of Roman Catholics. His days in gaol were spent partly in making laces for the support of his family; and partly in writing controversial and other works; but it was during a second and shorter imprisonment in 1675 that *The Pilgrim's Progress* was begun. Perhaps the best lyric from *The Pilgrim's Progress* is that selected for *The Church Hymnary*, depicting the martial aspects of the Christian life.

H. 443

BURNS, JAMES DRUMMOND, M.A. (Edinburgh, 1823-64, Mentone), was educated at Heriot's Hospital, the High School, and the University, Edinburgh. He was studying Divinity when the Disruption took place, and he entered into the Free Church in 1843. He was ordained in Dunblane in 1845. For health reasons, in 1847, he took charge of the Free Church congregation at Funchal, Madeira. In 1855 he undertook the care of a newly formed congregation at Hampstead, and contributed the too brief article on 'Hymns' to the eighth edition of the *Encyclopaedia Britannica*.

H. 123, 616

BUTLER, HENRY MONTAGU (Gayton, Northamptonshire, 1833-1918, Cambridge), was educated at Harrow and Trinity College, Cambridge, of which he became a Fellow in 1855. After travelling in the East, he was appointed headmaster of Harrow in 1859 and remained in this post for twenty-six years. He was Dean of Gloucester, 1885-6, when he became Master of Trinity. He edited the third edition of *Hymns for the Chapel of Harrow School* (1866), in which he included several of his own compositions.

H. 440

BUTLER, MARY (MAY) (Langar, Nottinghamshire, 1841-1916, Shrewsbury), was a granddaughter of Bishop Samuel Butler of Lichfield (1836-9), and daughter of Thomas Butler, M.A., rector of Langar, and Canon of Lincoln. All her life was spent at Langar, until her father retired to Shrewsbury. There she took a deep interest in social work, and founded St. Saviour's Home for Girls. Many of her hymns were written for the inmates.

H. 449

BYRNE, MARY ELIZABETH, M.A. (Dublin, 1880-1931, Dublin)—Maire ni Bhroin—was educated at the Dominican Convent, Eccles Street, Dublin, and the Royal University of Ireland, and was a research worker in Irish to the Board of Intermediate Education. She was awarded the Chancellor's Gold Medal in the Royal University for a treatise on *England in the Age of Chaucer*. She published an edition of *Airec Menman Uraird Maic Coisse*; and Middle Irish religious poems in *Eriù*.

H. 87

BYROM, JOHN (Kersall, near Manchester, 1692–1763, Manchester), son of a Manchester merchant, was educated at Merchant Taylors' School and Trinity College, Cambridge, of which he became a Fellow in 1714. In 1716 he travelled abroad and studied medicine at Montpellier, but never practised or took a medical degree. Until his fortunes improved by succession to the family estates, Byrom maintained himself by teaching a system of shorthand of his own invention. Of strong Jacobite sympathies, he was also greatly interested in philosophical and theological questions. Byrom's poems were first published in 1793.

H. 190

CALVIN, JOHN (Noyon, Picardy, 1509–64, Geneva), studied theology and philosophy at the nominalist College de Montaigu, Paris, but did not enter the Church. Instead, on his father's advice, he went to Orleans to study law. During 1529 he became interested in humanist studies and transferred to Bourges. On his father's death, in 1531, he returned to Noyon, and the following year went again to Paris, but had to flee when a sermon with 'a Lutheran sound' was delivered by Nicholas Cop, the new rector of the University. His *Institutes of the Christian Religion* was published in 1535. Following several years of travel, he was persuaded by Farel to settle in Geneva to assist in the reform of the city. He was expelled in 1538, when he tried to make all the citizens of the city sign the *Genevan Confession*. Urged by Bucer, Calvin went to Strasbourg, but continuing unrest in Geneva led to an official request to him to return. After ten months' hesitation he did so, and remained there until his death. During this time, he made Geneva the Reformed capital of Europe. With regard to worship, Calvin's chief influence is in the field of liturgical reform, his *La Forme des Prières et Chantz Ecclesiastiques auec la manière d'administrer les Sacremens . . . selon la coustume de l'église ancienne*, influencing the whole Reformed Church from that day to this. Calvin was not the musician that Zwingli was, neither was he a hymn-writer of Luther's genius. His chief contribution to the Church's praise rests in the encouragement he gave to writers and musicians like Marot, Goudimel, and Bourgeois.

H. 86

CAMERON, WILLIAM, M.A. (Lochaber, 1751–1811, Kirknewton), studied at Marischal College, Aberdeen. There he became intimate with Dr. Beattie, author of *The Minstrel*. It is believed that Beattie made his poetic talent known to the committee which was then revising the *Scottish Paraphrases*. Cameron, while only a licentiate of the Church received the confidence of the committee, and the chief responsibility for the actual revision was left in his hands. Two paraphrases were written by him—14 and 17; and he revised at least thirty-three, as well as two of the hymns which still appear along with the paraphrases. Not till 1786 did he receive a charge; in that year he was presented by the Duke of Buccleuch to the parish of Kirknewton, where the rest of his years were spent.

H. 530, 533

CAMPBELL, JANE MONTGOMERY (Paddington, London, 1817-78, Bovey Tracey, South Devon), was a daughter of a rector of St. James's, Paddington. She taught singing to the children of her father's parish school. While residing at Bovey Tracey she gave valuable help to the Revd. Charles S. Bere in the compilation of his *Garland of Songs, or an English Liederkranz* (1862), and his *Children's Chorale Book* (1869). To these she contributed a number of translations.

H. 620

CAREY, HENRY (Rothwell, Yorkshire, 1687-1743, Clerkenwell), is said to have been the son of George Saville, Marquis of Halifax, and of a schoolmistress, but this is without foundation. He was a prolific author of burlesques, farces, ballad operas, and vivacious poems and songs, the best known being 'Sally in our Alley'. He was only incidentally a writer of Church music. The authorship of 'God save the King' has been attributed to him, but without sufficient grounds. He collected and published his songs in 1740— *The Musical Century, One Hundred English Ballads on various important Occasions*; and his dramatic works appeared in 1743.

T. 16, 409

CARLYLE, THOMAS (Ecclefechan, 1795-1881, Chelsea), the son of a stonemason who was a member of the Secession Church, was brought up in a frugal and godly household. He was educated first by his parents, then at Annan Academy and the University of Edinburgh. He began, but soon abandoned, study for the ministry of the Church of Scotland; earned a living for some years by teaching in Annan, Kirkcaldy, and Edinburgh. He tried law, with a view to the Scottish Bar, but dropped that also; and finally, after some hack-work, settled down to the serious pursuit of literature. He was an artist, a humorist, and a poet. Passages of *Sartor Resartus* and of *The French Revolution* have been held to rank with the sublimest poetry of the age. In his view of life he was a practical mystic, profoundly religious, though detached from all the official creeds, a sworn foe of atheism. Materialism also he hated. But while powerfully destructive in his criticism, he had few constructive ideas. All he achieved was in the region of thought and imagination. There, however, his teaching did much to kindle other minds to moral enthusiasm and energy. In 1865 he was elected Lord Rector of the University of Edinburgh. Disraeli, in 1874, offered him the G.C.B. or a baronetcy, with a pension, but the offer was declined. When he died, a burial in Westminster Abbey was offered, but, in accordance with his own wish, his body was laid beside the ashes of his kindred in his native village.

H. 406

CASWALL, EDWARD, M.A. (Yately, Hampshire, 1814–78, Edgbaston, Birmingham), son of a vicar of Yately, was educated at Marlborough and Brasenose College, Oxford. Taking Orders in the Church of England, he became perpetual curate of Stratford-sub-Castle, Wiltshire, in 1840. He had been caught, however, in the tide, then running high, of the Tractarian Movement, and in 1847 resigned his living, repaired to Rome, and there was received into the Roman Church. His wife was received a week later. On her death, three years afterwards, he became a priest, and joined the Oratory of St. Philip Neri at Edgbaston, under Newman. Setting himself to translate the ancient Latin hymns in the Roman Breviaries, he enriched English hymnody by many versions second only to Neale's in their high poetic quality; some of them are classics. He published *Lyra Catholica* (197 translations of the Breviary hymns, 1849); *The Masque of Mary, and Other Poems* (1858); *A May Pageant and Other Poems* (1865); *Hymns and Other Poems* (1873).

H. 50, 179, 199, 246, 377, 378, 379, 578

CAWOOD, JOHN, M.A. (Matlock, Derbyshire, 1775–1852, Bewdley), was the son of a farmer and had little education as a boy. But while in the service of a clergyman named Carsham at Sutton-in-Ashfield, Nottinghamshire, he came under decisive religious impressions and was moved to seek Holy Orders. Three years' study enabled him to enter St. Edmund Hall, Oxford, in 1797. Graduating four years later, he became curate of Ribbesford and Dowles; then perpetual curate of St. Anne's Chapel of Ease, Bewdley, Worcestershire. He published two volumes of sermons, but his seventeen hymns were not published by himself.

H. 635

CENNICK, JOHN (Reading, 1718–55, London), belonged to a family of Quakers, but was brought up in the Church of England. His name (originally Cennik) proclaims him of Bohemian stock. He became acquainted with the Wesleys, and was appointed by John Wesley teacher of a school for colliers' children at Kingswood, and subsequently the first lay preacher among the Methodists. Parting from the Wesleys on doctrinal grounds, he came for a time under the influence of Whitefield, but ultimately joined the Moravian brethren, in whose service he spent some time in Germany and Northern Ireland.

H. 316, 648

CHADWICK, JOHN WHITE, M.A. (Marblehead, Massachusetts, 1840–1904, Brooklyn, New York), graduated at the Divinity School, Cambridge, Mass., in 1864, and received the M.A. degree from Harvard in 1888. He was minister of the Second Unitarian Church, Brooklyn, N.Y., from 1864.

H. 514

CHALMERS, JAMES (Aberdeen, *c.* 1700–64, Aberdeen), son of a Professor in Marischal College and University, was printer to the Town Council of

Aberdeen and publisher of *The Aberdeen Journal*. About 1749 he compiled a collection of *Twenty Church Tunes*, containing 'Observations concerning the Tunes and manner of singing them'.

T. 72 (i), 395 (ii), 489, 518

CHANDLER, JOHN, M.A. (Witley, Godalming, Surrey, 1806–76, Putney), was educated at Corpus Christi College, Oxford. Ordained in 1831, he succeeded his father as patron and vicar of Witley. His gifts as a translator were diligently employed on *The Hymns of the Primitive Church, now first Collected, Translated and Arranged* (1837), and *Hymns of the Church most Primitive, Collected, Translated and Arranged for Public Use* (1841)—the previous work revised and altered.

H. 208, 302

CHARLES, DAVID (Pant-dwfn, St. Clears, Carmarthen, 1762–1834, Carmarthen), was the youngest brother of the famous Revd. Thomas Charles, B.A. (Charles o'r Bala), one of the founders of the British and Foreign Bible Society, and a powerful religious and educational force in Wales. The father, a farmer, found himself unable to bear the expense of educating a second son at Oxford. David was therefore apprenticed to a flax-dresser and rope-maker at Carmarthen. He came early under religious impressions, and was brought to final decision in 1777 by reading the sermons of Ralph Erskine. He was made a deacon of Water Street Church in 1788, and acted as such for twenty years. When 46 years of age he was prevailed upon by the Church to enter the ministry, having given proof of his effectiveness as a preacher both in Welsh and in English. He was ordained in 1811. He was perhaps the greatest Church statesman of his time in Wales. He wrote several hymns, one of which is one of the most famous and best-loved hymns in the Welsh language.

H. 544

CHATFIELD, ALLEN WILLIAM, B.A. (Chatteris, 1808–96, Much Marcle), son of a vicar at Chatteris, was educated at Charterhouse and Trinity College, Cambridge, where he graduated in 1831. Ordained in 1832, he became vicar of Stotfold, Bedfordshire, and, in 1848, of Much Marcle, Herefordshire. His most notable work was his rendering into Greek, in various metres, of the *Litany*, the *Te Deum*, and other parts of the Anglican Church Offices. He published also *Songs and Hymns of the Earliest Christian Poets, Bishops and Others, translated into English Verse* (1876).

H. 80

CHESTERTON, GILBERT KEITH (Kensington, 1874–1936, Beaconsfield), was educated at St. Paul's School, London. He attended classes at the Slade School of Art, but, beginning to contribute art criticisms and reviews to *The Bookman* and the *Spectator*, found his way into journalism. Long a pillar of orthodoxy, he became a Roman Catholic under the influence of the ultramontane Hilaire Belloc.

H. 520

CHETHAM, JOHN (?, 16??-*c.* 1746, Skipton), was a schoolmaster at Skipton from *c.* 1725 to 1737, and later curate. He was ordained by the Bishop of Chester in December 1735. *A Book of Psalmody, all set in four parts* was published by him in 1718.

T. 103

CHORLEY, HENRY FOTHERGILL (Blackley, Hurst, Lancashire, 1808-72, London), was intended for a commercial life, but his taste for literature made that career impossible. In 1833 he was given a post on the staff of *The Athenaeum.* His best books were on *Music and Manners in France and Germany* (1841); *Modern German Music* (1854); *Thirty Years' Musical Recollections* (1862); *The National Music of the World* (1880).

H. 516

CHRISTIERSON, FRANK VON, D.D. (Lorisa, Finland, 1900), was taken to America as a boy of four. He was educated at Stanford University and San Francisco Theological Seminary. He served for thirty-seven years as a minister of the United Presbyterian Church in Berkeley, North Holywood, and Sacramento, California. He is now retired and serving as 'interim minister' in the first Presbyterian Church, Roseville, California. He has written six hymns, two of which were published by the Hymn Society of America. He also wrote the hymn sung at the 150th Anniversary celebration of the American Bible Society.

H. 133

CLARK, THOMAS (Canterbury, 1775-1859, London) was a cobbler by trade and a musician by talent. He was leader of psalmody first in the Wesleyan Church, Canterbury, then in a church which was originally Anabaptist, and worshipped in the dilapidated monastery of the Blackfriars, which had been purchased for this purpose by Peter de la Pierre, a surgeon from Flanders. The congregation came to be called General Baptists, but by Clark's time they had drifted into Unitarianism; they were dissolved in 1913. Clark was a prolific composer of hymn-tunes, publishing over twenty sets of them. He reharmonized the second edition of *The Union Tune Book* for the Sunday School Union in 1842.

T. 168, 347

CLARKE, JEREMIAH (London, *c.* 1670-1707, London), was a chorister of the Chapel Royal under Dr. John Blow, and became organist of Winchester College, 1692-5; organist of St. Paul's in 1695, and vicar choral, 1705; joint organist, with Croft, of the Chapel Royal, 1704. He probably officiated at Father Smith's magnificent organ in St. Paul's when that masterpiece of Sir

Christopher Wren was opened on 2 December 1697. Clarke wrote operatic music (Gay used one of his tunes in *The Beggar's Opera*), a cantata, numerous songs, and Church music—anthems and psalm-tunes.

T. 286, 426, 530, 532

CLARKSON, EDITH MARGARET (Melville, Saskatchewan, 1915), was educated at Melville. She taught at Lake of the Woods, Ontario (1935-7), Kirkland Lake (1937-42), and up to 1973, when she retired, in the Toronto area. A member of Knox Presbyterian Church, Toronto, she became active in the work of the Inter-Varsity Christian Fellowship during her student days and has published some ten works on educational and religious subjects, as well as several volumes of poetry.

H. 337, 592

CLAUDIUS, MATTHIAS (Reinfeld, near Lübeck, Holstein, 1740-1815, Hamburg), the son of a Lutheran pastor, was educated at Jena, and lived at Wandsbeck, near Hamburg. An ancestor had latinized his name Claus Paulsen into Claudius Pauli, and his descendants adopted Claudius as their surname. He studied theology with a view to the ministry, but an infection of the chest and the rationalizing influences then dominant at Jena turned him aside to law and languages. He became a journalist, and for some years edited *The Wandsbeck Messenger*. In 1776 he was appointed one of the Commissioners of Agriculture and Manufactures of Hesse Darmstadt, and, a year later, editor of the official newspaper there. In 1788 he was appointed by the Crown Prince of Denmark auditor of the Schleswig Holstein Bank at Altona. In 1815 he retired to his daughter's home at Hamburg, where he died.

H. 620

CLAUSNITZER, TOBIAS (Thurn, near Annaberg, Saxony, 1619-84, Weiden, Upper Palatine), studied at various universities and finally at Leipzig, where he graduated in 1643. In 1644 he became a chaplain in the Swedish army. As such, he preached the thanksgiving sermon in the St. Thomas Church, Leipzig, on the accession of Queen Christina to the Swedish throne, and also the sermon at the peace celebration in General Wrangel's army at Weiden, when the Peace of Westphalia brought the Thirty Years War to an end in 1648. In that year he became first minister at Weiden. Later, he was a member of the Consistory and Inspector of the district.

H. 129, 414

CLEPHANE, ELIZABETH CECILIA DOUGLAS (Edinburgh, 1830-69, Bridgend, Melrose), was a daughter of Andrew Douglas Clephane of Carslogie, Sheriff Principal of Fife and Kinross. After the death of the father, the daughters lived first at Ormiston, East Lothian, and latterly at Bridgend, Melrose. She was known as 'the Sunbeam' among the poor and suffering in Melrose. The sisters spent all their income every year, giving what was not needed for their own maintenance to charity. They were devoted members of the then Free Church of Scotland. Eight of Elizabeth's hymns appeared first under the general title 'Breathings on the Border' in *The Family Treasury*, then edited by the Revd. William Arnot.

H. 684

COCKER, NORMAN (Sowerby Bridge, 1889–1953, Manchester), was organist of St. Philip and St. James, Oxford (1909–13), and in 1912 was appointed music master at Magdalen College School, Oxford. After war service, he became sub-organist in Manchester Cathedral (1919–43) and organist (1943–53).

T. 538

COFFIN, CHARLES (Buzanly, 1676–1749, Paris), a distinguished French ecclesiastic, succeeded Rollin, the historian, in 1712 as principal of the College of Dormans-Beauvais, and in 1718 was rector of the University of Paris. Most of his hymns appeared in *The Paris Breviary* of 1736. In the same year he published a hundred of his hymns as *Hymni Sacri Auctore Carolo Coffin*, with an interesting preface explanatory of their spirit and aim.

H. 149, 208

COLES, VINCENT STUCKEY STRATTON (Shepton Beauchamp, 1845–1929, Shepton Beauchamp), was educated at Balliol College, Oxford. On taking Holy Orders, he became a curate in Wantage and rector of Shepton Beauchamp. In 1884 he became librarian of the Pusey Library, Oxford. He contributed several hymns to *Hymns Ancient and Modern*.

H. 579

COLLIGNON, CHARLES (?London, 1725–85, Cambridge), graduated M.B., and M.D., and from 1753 to 1785 was Professor of Anatomy in the University of Cambridge. His writings were published posthumously. The records of Trinity College, Cambridge, say he was the son of Paul Collignon, London, and was of French origin.

T. 435, 628

COLUMBA, ST. (Gartan, Donegal, *c.* 521–97, Iona) the most renowned of the early saints of Scotland, came of a notable family in Ireland. He studied at the monastic schools of Movilla and Clonard, and was also a pupil of the bard Gemman, whose influence may perhaps be traced in the Latin hymns and Celtic poems ascribed to Columba. The reason for his leaving Ireland is obscure, but most probably it was pastoral. Setting sail from Ireland Columba and his twelve companions landed at Iona, a small island to the west of Scotland, which became the home of the little community, as well as the starting-point for a missionary campaign of extraordinary success on the mainland. Columba's share in the evangelization of Scotland was a great one. A large number of religious houses were founded throughout Scotland by him and his disciples. The *Life* of the Saint by Adamnan, though full of incredible marvels, sheds much light on his career, the account of Columba's last hours being especially graphic and touching. He tells how almost to the end the Saint was engaged in transcribing the Psalter, ending with the words of Psalm 34: 10, 'They that seek the Lord shall not want any good thing'; and how he breathed his last in the church after raising his hand to bless the brethren.

The ecclesiastical buildings of Iona (most of them of considerably later date) were made over in 1899 to the Church of Scotland by the Duke of Argyll.

To Columba is ascribed sacred poetry both in Latin and in his native Gaelic. His hymn known as the *Altus* was translated by the late Marquis of Bute and by the late Bishop Anthony Mitchell of Aberdeen.

H. 301, 397, 398

CONDER, JOSIAH (Aldersgate, London, 1789-1855, St. John's Wood, London), was the son of an engraver and bookseller. At 15 he became assistant in his father's book-store. Among his numerous works were *The Modern Traveller*, a compilation in thirty volumes which cost him seven years' labour; a *Dictionary of Ancient and Modern Geography*; a *Life of Bunyan*; *Protestant Non-conformity*; *Sacred Poems*; *Domestic Poems, Miscellaneous Poems*; *The Choir and the Oratory, or, Praise and Prayer*; *Hymns of Praise, Prayer and Devout Meditation* (a collection of his poems and hymns personally revised, but published after his death). For the Congregational Union he edited their first official hymn-book, *The Congregational Hymn Book, A Supplement to Dr. Watts's Psalms and Hymns*.

H. 36

COOKE, ROBERT (Westminster, 1768-1814, London), son of Dr. Benjamin Cooke, organist of Westminster Abbey and an eminent composer and musical theorist of his day, succeeded his father as organist of St. Martin-in-the-Fields; in 1802 succeeded Dr. Arnold as master of the choristers in Westminster Abbey. He composed an Evening Service in C, anthems, and several songs and glees. He published a *Collection of Eight Glees* of his own (1805) and in 1795 a collection of his father's glees.

C. 345 (b)

COOPER, EDWARD, M.A. (?, 1770-1833, Yoxall, Staffordshire), was educated at Queen's College, and became a Fellow of All Souls, Oxford. He was rector of Hamstall-Ridware, 1788-1809, and of Yoxall, Staffordshire, 1809-33. Cooper was associated with the Revd. Jonathan Stubbs and the Revd. Thomas Cotterill, in the compilation of their *Selection of Psalms and Hymns for Public and Private Use* (1805); and he issued in 1811 for use in his own churches *A Selection of Psalms and Hymns*.

H. 77

COPELAND, WILLIAM JOHN (Chigwell, 1804-85, Farnham), was educated at St. Paul's School and Trinity College, Oxford, and became a Fellow of

Trinity. Ordained in 1827, he was curate in Littlemore, and became rector of Farnham in 1849.

H. 652

CORNER, DAVID GREGOR (Hirschberg, Silesia, 1587-1648, Gottweg), studied probably in Breslau, later in Prague and Gratz. In 1618 he became Pfarrer in Rotz, and later in Maulbronn. When 40 years old he entered the Benedictine Order. From 1638 till his death he was rector of the University of Vienna. It is not claimed that he composed any of the melodies in his *Gesangbuch* (1625); they appear to have been collected from many different sources. His *Geistliche Nachtigall* was published in 1631.

T. 203, 211 (i), 218, 227

COSIN, JOHN (Norwich, 1594-1672, London), was educated at Caius College, Cambridge, took Holy Orders, and was appointed chaplain to the Bishop of Durham. He subsequently became Prebendary of Durham, and Archdeacon of the East Riding of Yorkshire. Other preferments followed, and in 1640 he became Chancellor of the University of Cambridge and Dean of Peterborough. At this point, however, his fortunes suffered eclipse. His *Collection of Private Devotions* had already been criticized by the Puritans, and one of their number whom Cosin had treated with severity succeeded in inducing the Long Parliament to deprive him of his benefices. He retired to France and remained there till the Restoration, when he was restored to his dignities and became Bishop of Durham. A man of profound liturgical knowledge, he took part in the revision of *The Book of Common Prayer* (1662) in which is incorporated his translation of the *Veni, Creator Spiritus*.

H. 342

COURTEVILLE, RAPHAEL (London, c. 1677-1772, London), was son of a chorister of the Chapel Royal who bore the same name, and was trained as one of the children of the Chapel. He became organist of St. James's, Piccadilly, in 1691. According to the church records, he continued in that post for eighty-one years. He wrote *Memoirs of Lord Burleigh*; was associated with Purcell in composing music for D'Urfey's opera *Don Quixote*; and composed songs, sonatas for violins and flutes, and other music.

T. 121, 429, 564

COUSIN, ANNE ROSS, *née* CUNDELL (Hull, 1824-1906, Edinburgh), was the only child of David Ross Cundell, M.D., Leith. She was brought up in the Episcopal Church, but the great ecclesiastical controversy of her youth resulting in the Disruption led her to become a convinced and resolute Presbyterian. She married the Revd. William Cousin. In 1845 she contributed verses anonymously to *The Christian Treasury*, and in 1876 published her collected verses under the title *Immanuel's Land and Other Poems*.

H. 694

COWPER, WILLIAM (Berkhampstead, 1731-1800, East Dereham), was son of a chaplain to George II, whose father was a Judge of Common Pleas, and whose elder brother became Lord Chancellor and first Earl Cowper. The poet's mother, a descendant of Dr. John Donne, died when he was 6 years old. After being articled to an attorney, under whom he worked along with Thurlow, the future Chancellor, he was called to the Bar in 1754. On his being offered, through his kinsman Major Cowper, the post of Clerk to the Journals of the House of Lords, the dread of appearing before the House to stand an examination so affected his reason that he attempted suicide, and was never thereafter entirely free from deep melancholy, often of a religious cast. After undergoing treatment in a private asylum, he found a home at Huntingdon in the family of the Revd. Morley Unwin, whose wife became his lifelong friend and guardian. On the death of Mr. Unwin he removed with the family to Olney, where their friend, the Revd. John Newton, was curate. Here Cowper collaborated with Newton in strenuous parochial and evangelistic work, and also in the production of what became known as the *Olney Hymns*.

H. 147, 663, 676

COX, FRANCES ELIZABETH (Oxford, 1812-97, ?), was one of the most felicitous of translators of German hymns. She was indebted to Baron Bunsen for guidance as to the hymns most worthy of being translated. She published *Sacred Hymns from the German* (1841) and *Hymns from the German* (1864).

H. 142, 605, 671

CRASHAW, RICHARD (London, 1613-49, Loreto), was educated at Charter-house and Pembroke Hall and Peterhouse, Cambridge. For refusing the Covenant he was ejected from his Fellowship. Entering the Church of Rome he went to Paris, but was denied preferment. Under the patronage of Queen Henrietta Maria he became a canon in the Church of Loreto. His *Steps to the Temple* contained versions of two psalms, and his *Carmen Dei Nostro*, published posthumously in 1652, contained a number of hymns both original and translated.

H. 177

CROFT, WILLIAM, Mus.Doc. (Nether Eatington, now Ettington, Warwick-shire, 1678-1727, Bath), was born of good family, became one of the children of the Chapel Royal under Dr. Blow; organist of St. Anne's, Soho, and gentleman extraordinary of the Chapel Royal, 1700; joint organist of the Chapel Royal with Jeremiah Clarke, 1704, and sole organist, 1707; organist of Westminster Abbey and composer to the Chapel Royal, 1708; Mus.Doc., Oxon. 1713. In earlier life he composed for the theatre and also wrote sonatas, songs, and odes; but he became absorbed in sacred music, and made for himself in this field one of the greatest names in English musical history. Many of his fine anthems are still sung; his Service music is of the highest importance; the noble Burial Service of Croft and Purcell especially has never been surpassed for solemn grandeur. It is believed that his Cathedral music was one of the models of Handel's 'high sacred style' in his oratorios. But his tunes give him widest fame. They are 'of importance historically, as they are the earliest examples of the English psalm-tune as distinguished from the Genevan; they require quicker singing, and the glorious rhythmical impulse of "Hanover" and its triple measure marked at once a distinct originality'. In *Divine Harmony* he published a collection of the words of anthems with a brief historical account of English Church music; and in *Musica Sacra*, thirty anthems and a Burial Service of his own composition.

T. 35, 137, 214, 304, 363 (i), 408, 566 (i), 611

CROLY, GEORGE, LL.D. (Dublin, 1780–1860, London), was a graduate of Trinity College, Dublin. Taking orders, he ministered in Ireland till about 1810, when he repaired to London to engage in literary pursuits. In these he displayed great versatility of talent. He was one of the first contributors to *Blackwood's Magazine*, edited *The Universal Review*, and wrote the leading articles of *Britannia*, a conservative newspaper which advocated protection. In 1835 he was presented by Lord Brougham to the united benefices of St. Bene't Sherehog and St. Stephen's, Walbrook. At the request of his people he prepared a collection of *Psalms and Hymns for Public Worship*, containing twenty-five psalms, ten of which were versions by the editor; fifty hymns, ten of which were original; and six longer pieces on Scripture subjects.

H. 108

CROPPER, MARGARET BEATRICE (Kendal, 1886), devoted her life to Sunday school work particularly in the younger grades. She has published several volumes of religious plays, devotional poems, and prayers, many of them designed for use by younger children. She was a contributor to *Sunday School Praise*, *The School Assembly*, and *Infant Praise*.

H. 228, 467

CROSSMAN, SAMUEL (Bradfield Monachorum, Suffolk, 1624–84, Bristol), was educated at Pembroke College, Cambridge. He was vicar of All Saints, Sudbury, where he 'gathered' a Congregational Church. He was a 'messenger' to the Savoy Conference in 1658, and in 1662 was ejected. He conformed in 1665, and became a prebendary of Bristol two years later. In 1682 he became Treasurer of the Cathedral and later Dean.

H. 224

CROTCH, WILLIAM, Mus.Doc. (Norwich, 1775–1847, Taunton), was the son of a carpenter who was an enthusiast for music and built himself a small organ. On this, William was able to play at 2 years old. Sent to Cambridge to study under Randall, he there composed an oratorio, *The Captivity of Judah*, when only 14 years old. Proceeding to Oxford in 1788 to study for Holy Orders, he became organist of Christ Church in 1790, B.Mus. 1794, Mus.Doc. 1797, and in the same year Professor of Music in the University, though only 22 years of age. Ten years later he settled in London. In 1823 he was appointed first Principal of the newly founded R.A.M., but he was no disciplinarian, and resigned in 1832. His oratorio *Palestine*, to Heber's words, was perhaps his most notable achievement; he wrote also a number of anthems, but will be longest remembered by his chants, of which he wrote seventy-four.

C. 349 (ii)

CRÜGER, JOHANN (Grossbriesen, near Guben, Prussia, 1598–1662, Berlin), the celebrated composer of chorales, was educated at the Jesuit College of Olmütz, and at the school of poetry at Regensburg. He travelled through Austria, Hungary, Bohemia, and arrived at Berlin in 1615. There he was tutor in the family of Colonel Christoph von Blumenthal for five years, and then he finished his theological studies at the University of Wittenberg. He became cantor of the Cathedral Church of St. Nicholas, Berlin, in 1622, and founded its celebrated choir. There he continued till his death. He wrote largely on the theory and practice of music, and both as author and composer had a great reputation. He published many concertos and motets, and a collection of Magnificats; but is chiefly known now as composer of some of the most famous and favourite chorales. These appeared in his *Praxis Pietatis Melica*, 1644.

T. 5, 251, 252, 267, 327, 368, 525, 567, 659

CRUM, JOHN MACLEOD CAMPBELL (Knutsford, Cheshire, 1872–1958, Farnham, Surrey), was educated at Eton and New College, Oxford. He was domestic chaplain to the Bishop of Oxford, and later rector of Farnham (1913–28) and a canon of Canterbury (1928–43). His best-known publication is *What mean ye by These Stones?* (1926). He was one of the contributors to *Infant Praise*.

H. 278

CUMMINGS, WILLIAM HAYMAN, Mus.Doc. (Sidbury, Devon, 1831–1915, London), was trained as a chorister at St. Paul's and the Temple Church. In 1847 he became organist at Waltham Abbey. While there he made his adaptation of 'Mendelssohn'. It was first sung there and was published in 1856. He was professor of singing in the Royal College for the Blind (1879–96) and Principal of the Guildhall School of Music (1896–1911). He was one of the founders of the Purcell Society and edited three volumes of its publications. He composed a cantata, *The Fairy Ring*; wrote a *Life of Purcell*; and compiled a *Primer of the Rudiments of Music*.

T. 169

CUNDELL, EDRIC, C.B.E., F.T.C.L., F.G.S.M. (London, 1893–1961, Ashwell, Hertfordshire), was educated at Haberdasher's Aske School and Trinity College, London, in which he was appointed to the teaching staff in 1920. In 1937 he joined the staff of Glyndebourne, and the following year became Principal of the Guildhall School of Music. In 1951 he was appointed chairman of the music panel of the Arts Council of Great Britain. Among his compositions are a String Quartet in C major (1934); a mass for unaccompanied voices, *Hymn to Providence* (chorus and orchestra); Symphony in C minor; a symphonic poem *Serbin*; and some chamber music.

T. 679

CURRIE, JOHN, M.A., Dip.Mus., L.T.C.L. (Prestwick, 1934), was educated at Ayr Academy, the Royal Scottish Academy of Music, and the University of Glasgow. He was Lecturer in Music in Glasgow University (1964-71) and since then has been Director of Music in the University of Leicester. He has been Chorus Master to the Scottish National Orchestra Choir since 1965, and was a music consultant to the revision committee. He composed a *Song Cycle* (for baritone and orchestra), and incidental music for *Phaedra*, films, and plays.

C. 21, 66

T. 399, 411, 453

DALBY, MARTIN, B.Mus., A.R.C.M. (Aberdeen, 1942), was educated at Aberdeen Grammar School, the Royal College of Music, and the University of Durham (external). He was viola player with L'Orchestra dell' Accademia di Napoli (1963-5), music assistant with the B.B.C. (London) (1965-71), Cramb Research Fellow in composition, Glasgow University (1971-2), and is now Head of Music, B.B.C. Scotland. He contributed to *The Faber Catholic Hymnal*, and has composed a symphony, *Concerto Martin Pescatore*, *The Tower of Victory*, etc. Among his choral works are *Orpheus* and *Requiem for Philip Sparrow*.

T. 149, 433 (i), 647

DAMON (or DAMAN), WILLIAM (Liège, c. 1540-c. 1591, London), was organist of the Chapel Royal under Queen Elizabeth. The book by which he is best known, a collection of the Psalms in four parts, which he had prepared for the use of his friend John Bull, citizen and goldsmith of London, was published by John Day under the title: *The Psalmes of David in English meter, with notes of four parts set unto them by Guilielmo Damon* (1579). The tunes used are, with one or two exceptions, those which had appeared in previous books—*The Anglo-Genevan Psalter* of 1556, the English of 1562, and the Scottish of 1564. There are four books, one for each part, and the harmony is simple note against note. In 1591 a second and more elaborate edition was published with this title: *The former (second) Booke of the Musicke of M. William Damon, late one of her majesties Musitions: contayning all the tunes of David's psalms as they are ordinarely soung in the Church, most excellently by him composed into 4 parts*. The work is in eight books, the first four of which have the melody in the tenor, and the second four in the cantus.

T. 80, 248, 249, 377 (i), 466, 663

DARBY, JOHN NELSON (London, 1800-82, Bournemouth), was educated at Westminster School and at Trinity College, Dublin. He graduated there as classical gold medallist in 1819, and was called to the Irish Bar. Conscientious scruples restrained him from practising, and in 1825 he accepted ordination to a curacy in Wicklow. He was at that time a High Churchman. Difficulties about the scriptural basis of Church establishments led him to resign. Just then, Anthony Norris Groves was founding a sect called 'The Brethren' which rejected all ecclesiastical forms and denominational distinctions. This body

Darby joined. From the fact that the meeting of supporters in Plymouth was the first in England to be recognized as a meeting of Brethren, the adherents of the movement became known as Plymouth Brethren, though long called Darbyites in Ireland. He edited the hymnal in general use among the Brethren. His own hymns were collected after his death and published as *Spiritual Songs*.

H. 369

DARBYSHIRE, JOHN RUSSELL, D.D., D.Litt. (Birkenhead, 1880–1948, Claremont, C.P., South Africa), was educated at Dulwich and Emmanuel College, Cambridge. After serving in Cambridge, Liverpool, Manchester, and Sheffield, he was Bishop of Glasgow and Galloway (1931–8), and later Archbishop of Capetown.

H. 260

DARWALL, JOHN, B.A. (Haughton, Staffordshire, 1731–89, Walsall), was educated at Manchester Grammar School and Brasenose College, Oxford. He became curate, and in 1769 vicar, of Walsall, Staffordshire. He wrote hymns and poetical pieces, and was an enthusiastic amateur musician. He composed a tune for each of the 150 metrical psalms. Few of these were published, but some are found in late eighteenth-century tune-books. They were written in two parts only, treble and bass. He published two volumes of pianoforte sonatas, *A Christmas Hymn and Tune*; *A Charity Hymn and Tune*; and *A Hymn*, to which is prefixed a biographical notice.

T. 296 (i)

DAVIES, Sir HENRY WALFORD, Mus.Doc., LL.D. (Oswestry, Shropshire, 1869–1941, Wrington, Somerset), became a chorister of St. George's, Windsor, in 1882; assistant organist to Sir Walter Parratt there, 1885–90; a teacher of counterpoint, Royal College of Music, 1895; conductor, London Bach Choir, 1903–7, and of the London Church Association, 1901–13; organist of the Temple Church, 1890–1919; Professor of Music, University College of Wales, Aberystwyth, from 1919; Chairman, National Council of Music, University of Wales, from 1919; Gresham Professor of Music, 1924; organist of St. George's, Windsor, and master of music to the king, 1927. He was knighted in 1922. He was appointed Master of the King's Music in 1934, and was joint-editor of the *Church Anthem Book*. He was a great inspiring force as director of music in the Welsh University and schools, as adjudicator at musical festivals all over the country, and as a pioneer of community singing. His works include an oratorio, *The Temple*; cantatas, *Three Jovial Huntsmen*; *Everyman*; *Ode on Time*; *Five Sayings of Jesus*; *Song of St. Francis*; *Songs of a Day*; *Noble Numbers*. He was author of *Music and Christian Worship*, and edited *The Fellowship Song Book*, *Fifty-Two Hymn Tunes*, *Hymns of the Kingdom*, and *A Students' Hymnal*.

C. 598 (i)

T. 143 (ii), 156, 213, 318 (i), 433 (ii), 602, 631

DAVIES, MATTHEW WILLIAM, Mus.Bac., B.A. (Neath, 1882–1947, Neath), went to London in 1890 to study under Dr. David Evans. When the latter was appointed to the Chair of Music at the University College of Wales, Cardiff, Davies, who had matriculated in 1897, entered the University at Cardiff. After returning to London for special training, he settled down in his home town and established himself as a teacher of music, and was appointed precentor and organist of Bethlehem Green Presbyterian Church. He conducted the Neath Operatic Society for thirty-six years and also the Neath Male Voice Choir. He wrote many part-songs, anthems, and hymn-tunes.

T. 150 (ii)

DEARMER, PERCY (London, 1867–1936, London), was educated at Westminster School, abroad, and at Christ Church, Oxford. He served as curate in St. Anne's, Lambeth; St. John's, Great Marlborough Street; Berkeley Chapel, Mayfair; St. Mark's, Marylebone Road; then, from 1901 to 1915, was vicar of St. Mary the Virgin, Primrose Hill. He was secretary of the London branch of the Christian Social Union, and chairman of the League of Arts. After service abroad during the war, he became, in 1919, Professor of Ecclesiastical Art in King's College, London. Many books came from his pen, e.g. *The Parson's Handbook*; *The Sanctuary*; *Body and Soul*; *Highways and Byways in Normandy*; *The English Carol Book* (with Martin Shaw); *The Art of Public Worship*; *The Power of the Spirit*; *The Church at Prayer and the World Outside*. He was secretary of the committee that prepared *The English Hymnal*, and acted as editor. He edited also *Songs of Praise* (1925) with the co-operation, in the music, of Dr. R. Vaughan Williams and Martin Shaw. He helped to compile *The Oxford Book of Carols* (1928), *Songs of Praise Enlarged* (1932), which he compiled for *Songs of Praise Discussed* (1933).

H. 43, 111, 128, 341, 416, 515, 588

DENNY, Sir EDWARD, Bt. (Tralee Castle, 1796–1889, London), succeeded his father as 4th Baronet in 1831. Nearly the whole town of Tralee belonged to him, but he lived for the most part at Islington. He was a considerate and popular landlord; the rents on his estate were fixed at so fair a figure that he was almost alone in escaping reductions by the Land Commissioners. With others of the Kerry gentry of his time he joined the Plymouth Brethren. His *Hymns and Poems* (1839; second edition, 1848) contained his published work.

H. 216

DIBDIN, HENRY EDWARD (Sadler's Wells, 1813–66, Edinburgh), was an accomplished harpist, and played at Covent Garden when Paganini made his last appearance there in 1832. In 1833 he moved to Edinburgh where he was organist of Trinity Chapel and a teacher of music. He published *The Standard Psalm Tune Book* (1851) and *The Praise Book* (1865), but these show a lack of critical ability. He also published a few psalm-tunes and pieces for the organ and pianoforte.

T. 109, 295

DIX, WILLIAM CHATTERTON (Bristol, 1837-98, Clifton), was the son of a Bristol surgeon. He was educated at the Grammar School, Bristol, for a mercantile career, and became manager of a marine insurance company in Glasgow. His original hymns were published in *Hymns of Love and Joy* (1861); *Altar Songs, Verses on the Holy Eucharist* (1867); *A Vision of All Saints* (1871); *Seekers of a City* (1878). He wrote also felicitous renderings in metrical form of Littledale's translations from the Greek in his *Offices of the Holy Eastern Church* and of Rodwell's translations of *Abyssinian Hymns*.

H. 200

DOANE, GEORGE WASHINGTON, D.D., LL.D. (Trenton, New Jersey, 1799-1859, Burlington, New Jersey), was educated at Union College, Schenectady, New York, and ordained in the Episcopal Church in 1821. After a time as assistant minister of Trinity Church, New York, he became, in 1824, Professor of Belles-Lettres in Trinity College, Hartford, Connecticut; in 1828, rector of Trinity Church, Boston; and in 1832, Bishop of New Jersey. He was closely in sympathy with the Tractarian movement in England. He edited in 1834 the first American reprint of Keble's *Christian Year*, and published his own *Songs by the Way* in 1824. His *Collected Works* were issued in four volumes the year after his death.

H. 121

DOANE, WILLIAM HOWARD, Mus.Doc. (Preston, New London County, Connecticut, 1832-1916, Cincinnati), was the principal of a firm of manufacturers of woodworking machinery in Cincinnati, Ohio, and for many years superintendent of the Sunday school of the Baptist church there of which he was a member. A musical enthusiast, he acted as conductor of the Norwich (Conn.) Harmonic Society, published thirty-five collections of music for Church and Sunday school, and himself composed numerous hymn-tunes, anthems, and cantatas. The degree of Mus.Doc. was conferred on him by Denison University, Ohio, in 1875.

T. 132

DODD, HILDA MARGARET. The *Companion to the Methodist Hymn Book* says 'It is unfortunate that particulars of this hymn writer are not to hand'. Apart from her contribution to *The School Hymn Book of the Methodist Church* and *Infant Praise* it has proved impossible to get any details.

H. 465

DODDRIDGE, PHILIP, D.D. (London, 1702-51, Lisbon), was the son of a London merchant. His paternal grandfather was a clergyman ejected from his living under the Act of Uniformity, and his mother's father a Lutheran pastor, who fled from Bohemia to England to escape persecution. Philip was the youngest of a family of twenty, most of whom died young. He showed early promise, and is said to have learned the Old Testament history from pictures on Dutch tiles before he could read. Declining an offer from the

Duchess of Bedford to educate him for the Church of England, he studied under Jennings for the Dissenting ministry, and succeeded his preceptor which included the care of a seminary. There he remained for twenty-two years. In 1751, worn down by consumption, he vainly sought health by a voyage to Lisbon, where he died. Doddridge wrote many theological works. He is best remembered, however, by his hymns, first published soon after his death by his friend Orton, and since re-edited. Three of the *Scottish Paraphrases*, No. 2 'O God of Bethel', No. 39 'Hark the glad sound', and No. 60 'Father of peace, and God of Love', owe their original form to him.

H. 319, 459, 613

DOLES, JOHANN FRIEDRICH (Steinbach, Franconia, 1715-97, Leipzig), was a pupil of J. S. Bach at the Thomas Schule, Leipzig. After fourteen years as cantor at Freiburg, he became director of the Thomas Schule himself. Among his publications were: *The Forty-sixth Psalm set to music*; *Melodien zu Gellerts Geistlichen Oden*, for four voices, with accompaniment; *Vierstimmiges Choralbuch, oder harmonische melodien Sammlung für Kirchen* (1785).

T. 484 (i)

DORWARD, DAVID CAMPBELL, M.A., L.R.A.M., G.R.S.M. (Dundee, 1933), was educated at Monikee Primary School, Morgan Academy, Dundee, St. Andrews University, and the Royal Academy of Music. He was a teacher with Middlesex County Council (1960-1) and then freelanced for two years before becoming a music producer with the B.B.C. in 1962. He is at present with the B.B.C. (Edinburgh). Among his compositions are a symphony, Wind concerto, concertos for violin, viola, cello, four string quartets, cantatas, *The Fervent Fire*, *Scots Cantata*, *The Wolf and the Lamb*, *The Goldyn Targe*, as well as chamber and piano music, songs, and music for radio, TV, and documentary films. He has also produced a musical, *A Christmas Carol*.

T. 340

DOUGALL, NEIL (Greenock, 1776-1862, Greenock), was the son of a shipwright, who was impressed into national service and died in Ceylon when Neil was 4 years old. The boy went to school till he was 15, then took to a seafaring life. Three years later, an accident deprived him of his right arm and his eyesight. After some study of music he took up the teaching of singing. For forty-five years he conducted successful singing classes, and for sixty gave an annual concert in Greenock. He published a small volume of poems in 1854, and wrote about a hundred psalm- and hymn-tunes.

T. 69 (ii), 603

DOWLAND (or DOULAND), JOHN, Mus.Bac. (Westminster, 1562-1626, London), graduated with Thomas Morley in 1588. There is evidence that he was of Irish parentage. Dr. Grattan Flood holds that the family name originally was Dolan or O'Dolan. He was a celebrated lutanist. In 1598 he was appointed lutanist to the King of Denmark. In 1612 he received the only appointment he seems to have held in this country, as one of the King's

Musicians for the Lutes. He published three *Bookes of Songs or Ayres*, and a fourth collection under the title *A Pilgrim's Solace*, all with accompaniments for lute and viola da gamba. He harmonized some of the tunes in *Este's Psalter*.

T. 97

DOWNTON, HENRY, M.A. (Pulverbatch, Shropshire, 1818–85, Hopton), was son of the sub-librarian of Trinity College, Cambridge, where he graduated in 1840. Ordained in 1843, he became curate of Bembridge, Isle of Wight, and later, of Holy Trinity, Cambridge; perpetual curate of St. John's, Chatham; and, in 1857, English chaplain at Geneva. Returning to this country in 1873, he became rector of Hopton, Suffolk. His familiarity with the hymnody of the Swiss and French Churches enabled him to render a number of their hymns effectively into English. They are included in his *Hymns and Verses Original and Translated* (1873).

H. 612

DRAPER, WILLIAM HENRY, M.A. (Kenilworth, 1855–1933, Axbridge, Somerset), was educated at Keble College, Oxford. Ordained in 1880, he acted as curate of St. Mary's, Shrewsbury; vicar of Alfreton; vicar of the Abbey Church, Shrewsbury; rector of Adel, Leeds; rural dean of Shrewsbury; and in 1919 was Master of the Temple, London. In 1930 he became vicar of Axbridge. He has published *Hymns for Holy Week*, translations from hymns of the Greek Church; *The Victoria Book of Hymns* (1897); *The Way of the Cross*; translated Petrarch's *Secretum* (1911); and edited *Seven Spiritual Songs by Thomas Campion* (1919) and *Hymns for Tunes by Orlando Gibbons* (1925).

H. 30

DRESE, ADAM (Thuringia, 1620–1701, Arnstadt), was sent by Duke Wilhelm IV of Weimar to Warsaw, to study under the celebrated Kapellmeister Marco Sacchi, and on his return was appointed *Kapellmeister* to the Duke. On the latter's death in 1662, Duke Bernhard took Drese with him to Jena, appointed him his secretary, and in 1672 town mayor. On this Duke's death he lost employment and fell into poverty. The writings of the Pietists, especially of Spener and Luther on Romans, produced profound spiritual impressions on him. He held prayer meetings in his house, which became a meeting-place for the Pietists of the district. His hymns were sung at these meetings before they appeared in print. Later, he became musical director at Arnstadt, and there remained till his death.

T. 650

DRUMMOND, WILLIAM, of Hawthornden (Hawthornden, 1585–1649, Hawthornden), was son of Sir John Drummond, gentleman-usher to King James VI. He graduated at Edinburgh, studied civil law in France, and succeeded his father in 1610 as laird of Hawthornden, near Edinburgh, where he spent most of his life. Throughout his life he was a strong royalist, bitterly resented having to sign the Covenant under compulsion, and felt Charles I's death so keenly that it hastened his own. He wrote verses on the visits of James and Charles to Scotland, and on the death of Prince Henry.

H. 56

DRYDEN, JOHN (Aldwinkle, Northamptonshire, 1631-1700, London), came from an old north-country family, which took the Parliamentary side in the Civil War. The first verses to bring Dryden fame were his *Heroic Stanzas* on the death of Cromwell. Yet he soon afterwards welcomed the royal exile in *Astroea Redux*, and in 1670 was made Poet Laureate. His true genius, however, lay in his use of the heroic couplet for purposes of satire, as shown in *Absalom and Achitophel* and elsewhere. On the accession of James II he became a Roman Catholic, and remained constant to this faith at the Revolution. In addition to his translation of the 'Veni, Creator Spiritus', he is now believed to have been translator of a number of other Latin hymns, which appeared (after his death) in *The Primer or Office of the B.V. Mary, in English* (1706).

H. 118

DUDLEY-SMITH, TIMOTHY, M.A. (Manchester, 1925), was educated at Tonbridge School and Pembroke College and Ridley Hall, Cambridge. After a curacy at St. Paul's, Northumberland Heath, diocese of Rochester (1950-3), he was head of the Cambridge University Mission in Bermondsey (1953-5), chaplain and hon. chaplain to the Bishop of Rochester (1953-60). He was editorial secretary of the Evangelical Alliance and first editor of its magazine *Crusade* (1955-9). Then he became assistant-secretary (1959-65) and secretary (1965-73) of the Church Pastoral Aid Society. He is now Archdeacon of Norwich. He has contributed a number of hymns to Anglican, Presbyterian, Baptist, and youth hymnals in Britain and Canada.

H. 164

DUFFIELD, GEORGE, jun., D.D. (Carlisle, Pennsylvania, 1818-88, Bloomfield, N.J.), son of Dr. Duffield of Detroit, was educated at Yale and Union Seminary, New York, for the Presbyterian ministry. Ordained in 1840, he held charges at Brooklyn; Bloomfield, New Jersey; Philadelphia; Adrian, Michigan; Galesburg, Illinois; Saginaw City, Michigan; Ann Arbor and Lansing, Michigan. His later years were spent at Bloomfield, N.J., with his son, the Revd. Samuel Willoughby Duffield (1843-87), who was a hymnwriter also, a distinguished hymnologist, and author of *English Hymns; their Authors and History* (1886) and *Latin Hymn Writers and their Hymns* (published posthumously, 1889).

H. 481

DUGMORE, ERNEST EDWARD, M.A. (Bayswater, 1843-1925, Salisbury), a son of William Dugmore, K.C., was educated at Bruce Castle School and by private tutors, and at Wadham College, Oxford. He became curate of St. Peter's, Vauxhall; vicar of Parkstone, Dorset; canon of Sarum and prebendary of Gillingham Major, 1900; and in 1910 resigned his living to become

Warden of the College of Missioners, Salisbury, where he became also Succentor of the Cathedral and Vicar of the Close. His published works included *Gospel Idylls, and Other Sacred Verses* and *Hymns of Adoration*.

H. 451

DUNCAN, MARY, *née* LUNDIE (Kelso, 1814–40, Cleish, Kinross-shire), was the daughter of the Revd. Robert Lundie, parish minister of Kelso. Her younger sister became the wife of Horatius Bonar. She went to school in London. In 1836 she married the Revd. William Wallace Duncan, minister of Cleish. Her hymns, written for her own children between July and December 1839, were published in a *Memoir* by her mother in 1841, and in the following year were issued separately—twenty-three in number—as *Rhymes for my Children*.

H. 656

DYKES, JOHN BACCHUS, M.A., Mus.Doc. (Hull, 1823–76, St. Leonards-on-Sea), was son of a banker. 'Bacchus' was the Christian name of his maternal grandfather. John's talent for music developed early, he played the organ in his father's church at the age of 10. Educated at Wakefield and at St. Catharine's College, Cambridge, he helped as an undergraduate, along with William Thompson, afterwards Lord Kelvin, to found the University Musical Society. He was licensed to the curacy of Malton, but two years later proceeded to Durham to be a minor canon, and, soon after, precentor in the cathedral there. In 1861 Durham University conferred on him his doctorate, and a year later he became vicar of St. Oswald's in the same city. During the fourteen years of his ministry in that parish his pastoral devotion won him great influence. He published writings in liturgics, wrote several services and a number of anthems, but his reputation rests on his hymn-tunes, of which he wrote about 300.

T. 77 (ii), 78 (ii), 238 (i), 243, 336 (ii), 352, 388 (i), 527, 682

EAST, JAMES THOMAS (Kettering, Northamptonshire, 1860–1937, Blackburn), was a great-grandson of a sister of John Bunyan. He entered the Wesleyan Methodist ministry in 1886, and after serving in various parts of the country he went in 1922, as a supernumerary, to Blackburn. He contributed to *The Methodist Hymn Book*; *The School Hymn Book of the Methodist Church*; *Wise men seeking Jesus*; and *Sunday School Praise*.

H. 222

EBELING, JOHANN GEORG (Lüneburg, 1637–76, Stettin), in 1662 succeeded Johann Crüger as cantor of St. Nicholas Church, Berlin, and as director of music at the College of St. Charles (Carolinen Gymnasium), Stettin. He published *Archaeologiae Orphicae, sive antiquitates musicae* (1675); *Pauli Gerhardi Geistliche Andachten, bestenhend in 120 Liedern mit 6 Singstimmen, 2 violinen und general-bass* (1666–7).

T. 171

EDDIS, EDWARD WILTON (Islington, London, 1825-1905), Toronto, Canada), was a minister of the Catholic Apostolic Church, the religious communion founded by Edward Irving. He compiled for it, in 1864, *Hymns for the Use of the Churches*, nineteen of which, and two translations, were his own. To the second edition he contributed forty new hymns and one translation. Prior to 1865 he published *The Time of the End, and Other Hymns*.

H. 575

EDMESTON, JAMES (Wapping, London, 1791-1867, Homerton, Surrey), was an eminent London architect and surveyor. Though a grandson of the Revd. Samuel Brewer, minister of an Independent chapel in Stepney, he joined the Church of England early in life, and was latterly churchwarden of St. Barnabas's Church, Homerton. An ardent lover of children, he was a constant visitor and loyal friend of the London Orphan Asylum, and he found there the inspiration for many of his children's hymns. Edmeston wrote over 2,000 hymns, many of which he published in *Sacred Lyrics*, *Infant Breathings*, and numerous other works.

H. 90

EDWARDS, JOHN DAVID, B.A. (Penderlwyn-goch, Cardiganshire, 1805-85, Llanddoget, Denbighshire), was educated at Jesus College, Oxford. He published *Original Sacred Music, Composed and Arranged by The Revd. John Edwards, B.A., Jesus College, Oxford, c.* 1840. Four years later he published a second volume with the same title. He was vicar of Rhosymedre, Ruabon. He composed a considerable quantity of Church music, but is chiefly known for the tune 'Rhosymedre'.

T. 522, 614

EDWARDS, LEWIS, D.D. (Pwllcenawon, near Penllwyn, Cardiganshire, 1809-87, Bala), was educated at schools at Aberystwyth and Llangeitho, and the Universities of London and Edinburgh. He opened a school at Aberystwyth in 1827, became headmaster at Llangeitho in the following year, and entered London University in 1830. Lack of means forced him to return to Wales with his course still incomplete, and for a short time he acted as pastor at Laugharne, Carmarthenshire, then proceeded to Edinburgh University in 1833. Graduating there in 1836, he opened in Bala, in 1837, with the assistance of his brother-in-law David Charles, a school for young preachers, which was adopted a year later by the Countess of Huntingdon's Connexion as a Theological College.

H. 544

ELLERTON, JOHN, M.A. (London, 1826-93, Torquay), was educated at King William's College, Isle of Man, and at Trinity College, Cambridge. Ordained in 1850, he served as curate at Easebourne, Midhurst, Sussex, and at St. Nicholas, then the parish church of Brighton, for the children of which his first hymns were composed. In 1860 he became vicar of Crewe Green and domestic chaplain to Lord Crewe. In 1872 he became rector of Hinstock, Shropshire, and in 1876 of Barnes, Surrey. The heavy burden of this large parish broke him down, but after a year abroad he was able in 1885 to accept the charge of White Roding, Essex. His work as a hymnologist was of the first importance. He was chief compiler and editor of two important hymn-books, *Church Hymns* and *The Children's Hymn Book*, and joint-compiler of the 1875 edition of *Hymns Ancient and Modern*. He edited or assisted in editing *Hymns for Schools and Bible Classes*, *The Temperance Hymn Book*, *The London Mission Hymn Book*. His advice was sought in the compiling of the edition of the *Hymnal Companion to the Book of Common Prayer*. His *Notes and Illustrations of Church Hymns* appeared in the folio edition in 1881. His own hymns were published in 1888 as *Hymns, Original and Translated*. While lying disabled by his last illness he was nominated to a prebendal stall in St. Alban's Cathedral Church, and for the last year of his life received the honorary address of 'Canon' Ellerton; but he was never installed.

H. 46, 53, 189, 247, 272, 291, 329, 453, 516, 542, 600, 607, 646, 649

ELLIOTT, CHARLOTTE (Clapham, 1789-1871, Brighton), in her youth wrote humorous poems, but a grave illness in 1821 which made her permanently an invalid made serious impressions on her which were deepened in the following year by the influence of Cesar Malan, the evangelist of Geneva. He asked her if she was a Christian; she resented the question. He said that he would pray that she might give her heart to Christ and become a worker for Him. This worked on her mind, and finally she asked him how she might find Christ. 'Come to Him just as you are', was the answer. Her hymns appeared in *Psalms and Hymns*, edited by her brother, the Revd. Harry Venn Elliott of Brighton (1835-9); and in her own *Hours of Sorrow cheered and comforted* (1836); *Hymns for a Week* (1839); *The Invalid's Hymn Book* (1834-41); and *Thoughts in Verse on Sacred Subjects* (1869).

H. 79

ELLIOTT, JAMES WILLIAM (Warwick, 1833-1915, London), was trained as a chorister in Leamington Parish Church. He was successively organist in Leamington Chapel; to the Earl of Wilton at Heaton Hall; in the Parish Church, Banbury; St. Mary Bolton's, Brompton; All Saints', St. John's Wood; St. Mark's, Hamilton Terrace, where he served for thirty-six years. His compositions include two operettas, anthems, and many hymn-tunes. He took an active part in the preparation of the musical edition of *Church Hymns* (1874).

T. 36

ELLIOTT, KENNETH, M.A., Mus.B., Ph.D. (Dundee, 1929), was educated at Dundee High School, the University of St. Andrews, and St. John's College, Cambridge. He is a distinguished harpsichordist and pianist. In 1958 he was appointed Assistant in the Department of Music in the University of Glasgow, in 1959 Lecturer, and ten years later Senior Lecturer. He edited 'Music of Scotland, 1500-1700', with Helena M. Shire editing the song texts, in *Musica Britannica*, xv (1957, 1964), which includes sections on 'Latin

Church Music' and the 'Music of the Reformed Church'. The latter section as well as including psalm-settings by Blackhall, Kemp, and Peebles (q.v.) gives a 'Te Deum' by Andro Kemp, who taught in the 'sang-schools' of Dundee, St. Andrews, and Aberdeen, a 'Lord's Prayer' and 'The xii Articles of the Christian Fayth' (Creed) by John Angus of Dunfermline. He edited *Early Scottish Keyboard Music* (1967) and *William Byrd, Consort Music* (1971). With Professor Frederick Rimmer (q.v.) he prepared *A History of Scottish Music* (1973), for the B.B.C. He also edited the musical illustrations in H. M. Shire's *Song, Dance and Poetry of the Court of Scotland under James VI* (1969).

T. 116, 140 (i), 205, 250, 307, 314, 321 (i), 370, 584

ELVEY, Sir GEORGE JOB, Mus.Doc. (Canterbury, 1816–93, Windlesham, Surrey), was baptized in the Presbyterian Chapel, Canterbury (now destroyed), where a congregation worshipped which had been formed by the union, in 1713, of a Presbyterian congregation and a Congregational. He was educated as a chorister in the Cathedral. From 1835 to 1882 he was organist and master of the boys at St. George's Chapel. Much sacred music was composed by him: oratorios, *The Resurrection*, *The Ascension*, *Mount Carmel*; a festival march, etc.; and he contributed tunes to *Hymns Ancient and Modern* and other collections.

T. 298, 627

ESTE (EST, EASTE, EAST), THOMAS (?, 1540?–1608, London), a famous printer and music publisher, appeared first as a music printer in 1587, with *Sonnettes and Songs made into musick of fyve parts. By William Burd*. This is supposed to be identical with the undated edition of Byrd's *Psalmes, Sonnets, and Songs of Sadness and Pietie*. In 1588, Este's *Musica Transalpina*, a collection of Italian madrigals, laid the foundation of the splendid school of English madrigalists. In 1591 he printed the new edition of Damon's *Psalmes*, published by William Swayne. In the edition of the psalter printed by Este in 1592 the tunes were harmonized by ten eminent composers of the time, including Richard Allison, Giles Farnaby, John Dowland, John Farmer, and George Kirbye. This psalter is probably the earliest example in which the parts are printed on opposite pages instead of in separate books.

T. 65, 138, 174, 331, 377 (i), 471 (i), 663

ETT, KASPAR (near Landsberg, 1788–1847, Munich), was a distinguished Bavarian musician who from 1816 onwards was organist of the Michaeliskirche, Munich. He made a special study of Church music from the sixteenth to the eighteenth century, and made large collections of it, which went on his death to the Munich Library. He published in 1840 *Cantica Sacra*, in which were numerous compositions of his own.

T. 638

EVANS, DAVID, Mus.Doc. (Resolven, Glamorganshire, 1874–1948, Rhos-on-sea), was educated at Arnold College, Swansea, and University College, Cardiff, and graduated at Oxford. For a time he was organist and choirmaster of Jewin Street Welsh Presbyterian Church, London. From 1903 he was Professor of Music at University College, Cardiff; then the senior Professor of the University of Wales. At Cardiff he organized a large department of music, in which all branches of the art were taught. He was an adjudicator at the National Eisteddfod, where his compositions constantly appeared as test pieces or as concert items. In spreading enthusiasm for congregational singing he did a great work in the Principality. He was a leading conductor of the great psalmody festivals of which Ieuan Gwyllt was the pioneer, and which have deeply influenced the religious life of Wales. His collection of standard tunes, published as *Moliant Cenedl*, reflects his discrimination and catholicity of taste, and has greatly influenced and enriched subsequent hymn collections. His editorship of *Y Cerddor*, a literary journal devoted to the cause of music in Wales, made a deep and lasting impression upon the life of the Principality. He was a prolific composer of choral and orchestral works, the best known of which are *The Coming of Arthur*, a cantata for chorus and orchestra; *Llawenhewch yn yr Ior* (Rejoice in the Lord); *Deffro mae'n ddydd*, a Welsh choral ballad; *Bro bugeiliaid*, a children's cantata. He wrote a large number of anthems, services, hymntunes, songs, etc. He was one of the representatives of Wales on the Joint Revision Committee of the Revised Church Hymnary, and also chairman of the sub-committee of experts responsible for the editorship of the music.

T. 367 (ii), 488

EVANS, DAVID EMLYN (Penralltwen, Newcastle Emlyn, Cardigan, 1843–1913, Cemmaes, Montgomeryshire), was an amateur composer of distinction. He won seventy Eisteddfod prizes. He composed cantatas, glees, anthems, songs. He was an adjudicator at Eisteddfodau. For over thirty years he was joint-editor of a musical monthly *Y Cerddor*, published at Wrexham (1880–1913), and he was musical editor of the Welsh Congregational *Caniedydd* (1895) and of the Welsh Wesleyan *Llyfr Tonau*. The traditional airs collected by Nicholas Bennett and published as *Alawon fy Ngwlad* (1896) were harmonized by him.

T. 651

EVEREST, CHARLES WILLIAM, M.A. (East Windsor, Connecticut, 1814–77, Waterbury, Connecticut), graduated at Trinity College, Hartford, in 1838, was ordained in 1842, and for thirty-one years thereafter was rector of the Episcopal Church, Hampden, near New Haven.

H. 430

EWING, ALEXANDER (Old Aachar, Aberdeen, 1830–95, Taunton), was the son of Alexander Ewing, M.D., lecturer on surgery at Marischal College, Aberdeen. He studied law at that college with a view to becoming a Writer to the Signet, but was allowed to abandon that aim and to go to Heidelberg to study German and music. He was closely identified with the Haydn Society of Aberdeen, and the Harmonic Choir, which made a speciality of madrigal and anthem singing, under the leadership of William Carnie. One evening, after the practice of this choir, he approached Carnie, told him that he had tried his hand at writing a hymn-tune, and, offering copies of the voice-parts, asked that the choir should sing it over. This was done, and his one tune was launched on its long and honourable career.

T. 537

FABER, FREDERICK WILLIAM, D.D. (Calverley, Yorkshire, 1814-63, London), was educated at Shrewsbury, Harrow, and Balliol and University Colleges, Oxford. He was elected a Fellow of University in 1837. Of Huguenot stock, one of his ancestors having fled from France to England on the Revocation of the Edict of Nantes, he was brought up in the strictest school of Calvinism. In 1838 he published a work on *The Ancient Things of the Church of England*, in which he vindicated the Church of England as against the Roman Church, described the denomination of 'the Archbishop of Rome' as unscriptural and declared that Romanism had added falsehood to the sacraments. At Oxford, however, the potent influence of Newman drew him far towards the other extreme. He took Orders in the Church of England, and was for three years rector of Elton, Huntingdonshire. There by his preaching and influence he effected a moral reformation; but he also introduced auricular confession, penance, and other advanced ritualistic practices, and finally went the whole way to which these practices pointed, abjured Protestantism, and entered the Roman fold. He formed in Birmingham, with eight other young men, a community called 'Brothers of the Will of God', otherwise known as 'the Wilfridians', he himself having been re-baptized under the name of Wilfrid. In 1848, however, he and his companions joined the Oratory of St. Philip Neri, under Newman, and in the following year he established in London a branch of that order, which developed into the present Brompton Oratory. There the rest of his years were spent. He wrote many devotional and theological books, but is best known by his hymns, of which he wrote 150. They were intended primarily for devotional reading, to supply Roman Catholics with an equivalent to the Protestant hymns of Cowper, Newton, and Wesley, the influence of which he knew by personal experience.

H. 218, 243, 356, 670

FALCONER, HUGH, D.D. (Granton, Edinburgh, 1859-1931, Moffat), was educated at the University and New College, Edinburgh. Ordained to the Free Church ministry at Juniper Green in 1882, he passed ten years later to the Presbyterian Church of England, and ministered at Jesmond, Newcastle upon Tyne; Notting Hill, London; Fisher Street, Carlisle, retiring in 1923. He was Moderator of the Presbyterian Church of England in 1919.

H. 369

FARNINGHAM, MARIANNE. See HEARN, MARIANNE.

FARRANT, RICHARD (?, c. 1530-81, Windsor), was a gentleman of the Chapel Royal during the reigns of Edward VI, Mary, and Elizabeth, with an interval of five years (1564–9), during which he was master of the choristers in St. George's Chapel, Windsor, and probably joint-organist with the famous John Merbecke, whose *Book of Common Praier Noted* (1550) is one of the great landmarks in English Church music. Farrant is best remembered by his beautiful Service in G minor, and by two anthems, 'Call to remembrance' and 'Hide not Thou Thy face'. The anthem, 'Lord, for Thy tender mercies' sake', from which the tune that bears his name is taken, is only doubtfully ascribed to him. See note on CH3 No. 26.

C. 204 (iii)

FAWCETT, JOHN, D.D. (Lidget Green, near Bradford, 1740–1817, Hebden Bridge), was deeply impressed at the age of 16 by the preaching of Whitefield, and a few years later joined the Baptist Church at Bradford. He became Baptist minister at Wainsgate, and afterwards at Hebden Bridge, both near Halifax. Invited to become pastor of Carter's Lane Chapel in London, he was induced to remain in Yorkshire by the affectionate regard of his people. Besides a number of books on practical religion, he published a number of hymns, many of which have found a place in Baptist and Congregational hymn-books.

H. 638

FEILLÉE, FRANÇOIS DE LA (*floruit c.* 1750), was a priest attached to the choir of Chartres Cathedral. He wrote an abridgement of the Roman Antiphonary, and a book on plain-song, *Méthode pour apprendre les règles du plain-chant et de la psalmodie* (1745). This work was largely used by Helmore and others who led the way to the revival in the Anglican Church of the ancient psalm-tones which it had abandoned in the seventeenth century.

T. 43, 504, 535, 608

FERGUSON, JESSIE MARGARET MACDOUGALL (Glasgow, 1895–1964, Wallington, Surrey), after taking the Diploma in Religious Education of the Selly Oak Colleges, Birmingham, became a field worker on the staff of the Youth Department of the United Free Church of Scotland. From 1927 to 1934 she was a Sunday School Organizer with the Sabbath School Society in connection with the Presbyterian Church in Ireland. Then she went to work for the Religious Education Press, and in 1960 became Women's Secretary for the British and Foreign Bible Society. She contributed articles on religious education to many journals, was well known as a lecturer and demonstrator of Scripture teaching in schools, and in 1943 published *The School Assembly*, and later *Services of Worship for Schools* and *The Pupils' Service Book*.

H. 631, 654

FERGUSON, WILLIAM HAROLD, M.D. (Leeds, 1874–1950, Littlehampton), was educated first as a chorister of Magdalen College, then at Keble College, and at Cuddesdon College, Oxford. Ordained in 1902, he became assistant master at St. Edward's School, Oxford, then at Bilton Grange, Rugby; next spent eleven years as assistant master, organist, and chaplain at Lancing College, and thereafter eleven as Warden of St. Edward's School, Oxford. From 1927 to 1937 he was Warden of Radley College, Berkshire. During the years 1937-47 he was Canon and Precentor of Salisbury Cathedral. He was a member of the Headmasters' Conference which was responsible for the preparation of *The Public School Hymn Book*, and with Geoffrey Shaw was co-editor of the music of it.

T. 300 (ii), 645

FILITZ (or FIELITZ), FRIEDRICH, Ph.D. (Arnstadt, Thuringia, 1804-76, Bonn), resided in Berlin, 1843-7, and for the rest of his life in Munich. He edited *Vierstimmiges Choralbuch zu Kirchen-und Hausgebrauch*; a book of four-part tunes for the *Allgemeine Gesang und Gebetbuch* of von Bunsen; and collaborated with Erk in bringing out a collection of the chorales of the most distinguished masters of the sixteenth and seventeenth centuries. Later his views seem to have changed, for he published in 1853 a book *Ueber einige Interessen der älteren Kirchenmusik*, in which he asserted the superiority of Roman Catholic over Protestant music in the qualities that touch the heart.

T. 89 (i), 438, 644, 671

FINDLATER, SARAH LAURIE, *née* BORTHWICK (Edinburgh, 1823-1907, Torquay), was the younger daughter of James Borthwick, manager of the North British Insurance Office, Edinburgh, and sister of Jane Borthwick (q.v.). She married the Revd. Eric Findlater, minister of the Free Church of Scotland at Lochearnhead. With her sister she published *Hymns from the Land of Luther*, fifty-three of the 122 translations being from her pen. The hymn which begins 'O happy home', is really an epitome of her home life.

H. 523

FINLAY, KENNETH GEORGE (Aberdeen, 1882-1974, Glasgow), son of Professor D. W. Finlay, Aberdeen University, was educated at Gordon's College, Aberdeen, and Merchiston Castle School, Edinburgh. He was a Member of the Institute of Naval Architects. As an amateur musician, he contributed tunes to *The Missionary Hymn Book* and other collections. In 1928 he decided to give his time wholly to music, and entered the Royal College of Music. After a year at Jordanhill College of Education, he was appointed a teacher of class singing at Irvine, Ayrshire. He composed two cantatas, *The Saviour's Birth* (1928) and *Before the Dawn* (1938).

T. 124, 508

FLETCHER, Sir FRANK, M.A. (Atherton, Manchester, 1870-1954, Hindhead), was educated at Rossall School and Balliol College, Oxford. He was assistant master at Rugby, 1894-1904; master of Marlborough College, 1903-11; and then headmaster of Charterhouse, Godalming. In 1935 he retired to live near Dartmouth and served on the Devonshire Education Committee. He was made an honorary Fellow of Balliol in 1924, was knighted in 1937, and was President of the Classical Association in 1946.

H. 309

FLOWERDEW, ALICE (?, 1759-1830, Whitton, Ipswich), was the wife of Daniel Flowerdew, at one time a Government official in Jamaica. After his death in 1801, she kept a school for young ladies in Islington, and while there was a member of the General Baptist congregation. During this time most of her hymns were written. After a time she removed her school to Bury St. Edmunds, and finally to Ipswich. In 1803 she published *Poems on Moral and Religious Subjects*.

H. 628

FOOTE, GUTHRIE HUBERT (Tunbridge Wells, 1897-1972, Bolney, Haywards Heath), was educated at Skinner's School, Tunbridge Wells, and trained as a violinist at the Royal Academy of Music. After war service he returned to the Royal College of Music and studied conducting under Sir Henry Wood. He conducted the Carl Rosa Opera Company, founded the Tunbridge Wells Symphony Orchestra, and conducted the Wells Choir. He joined the Oxford University Press in 1944, and was first in the music department and later in charge of the Hymn and Service Books department. He retired in 1962, but continued until his death in an advisory capacity. He served as a music consultant for the revision committee. He contributed to *The English Hymnal Service Book*; the *Surrey Hymn Book*; *100 Hymns for Schools*; *Prayers and Hymns for use in Schools*; *Gathered Together*; and made arrangements for *The Scottish School Hymnary*. He published *Merrily on High*—a collection of carols and hymns for Christmas; *Merry Christmas*— carols for young singers; and was musical editor of *Infant Praise*.

T. 155, 195 (ii), 415, 583, 655

FORBES, SEBASTIAN, M.A., Mus.B., L.R.A.M., A.R.C.O., A.R.C.M. (Amersham, Buckinghamshire, 1941), was educated at the Royal Academy of Music and King's College, Cambridge. He was Producer of Music Division (Sound), B.B.C. London (1964-7), Director of Music in Trinity College, Cambridge, during part of 1968, and Lecturer in Music in the University College of North Wales, Bangor (1968-72). His main compositions include nine chamber works, including String Quartet No. 1 and No. 2; seven sets of songs, including *Death's Dominion* for tenor and six instruments; choral works, including *First Sequence of Carols*; five organ works; works for piano and harpsichord; orchestral music, including a symphony in two movements and *Essay* for clarinet and orchestra; and a one-act opera, *Tom Cree*.

T. 141, 678 (i)

FORTUNATUS, VENANTIUS HONORIUS CLEMENTIANUS (c. 530-609), was a native of Italy, though he spent most of his life in Gaul. He lived through the time of the Lombard invasion of Italy. He studied at Milan and Ravenna with the object of excelling as a rhetorician and poet, after which he travelled in various parts of France. Eventually he attached himself to Queen Rhadegundis, who had left her husband, Clothaire II, the Frankish king, to found the nunnery of Ste Croix at Poitiers. Under her influence he took Holy Orders and was afterwards elected Bishop of Poitiers.

H. 256, 257, 272

FOSDICK, HARRY EMERSON (Buffalo, New York, 1878-1969, New York), was educated at Colgate University, Union Theological Seminary, and Columbia University. He was ordained to the Baptist ministry in 1903. He lectured in homiletics (1908-15) and was Professor of Practical Theology (1915-46) in Union. When the First Presbyterian Church of New York was built he became associate minister and preacher. He was challenged by the fundamentalists in the General Assembly and called on to subscribe to the Westminster *Confession of Faith*. He resigned and accepted a call to Park Avenue Baptist Church, which later moved to Morningside Heights. Among his publications are *Christianity and Prayer* (1922); *The Meaning of Prayer* (1919); *The Meaning of Faith*; *The Manhood of the Master* (1925); *The Mind of the Master*; *Adventurous Religion* (1926); and *A Book of Public Prayers* (1960).

H. 88

FOSTER, FREDERICK WILLIAM (Bedford, 1760-1835, Ockbrook, near Derby), was educated at Fulneck, Yorkshire, the educational centre of the Moravian Brotherhood, and at the Moravian College at Barby, near Magdeburg. In 1781 he became assistant master at Fulneck, and, later, minister and provincial superintendent. He edited the 1808 *Supplement to the Moravian Hymnbook* and the 1826 edition of the *Hymnbook* itself. Besides translating from the German, he was the author of a number of hymns in these books.

H. 355

FRANCIS OF ASSISI, ST. (Assisi, 1182-1226, Assisi), son of an Italian trader, spent a youth of self-indulgence and gaiety. A severe illness at the age of 25 changed his view of life, and awoke in him an earnest spirit of self-sacrifice for the good of others. With a few friends he formed at his cell outside the city an order of men sworn to poverty and the renunciation of all worldly goods, and sent them two and two to preach the gospel and relieve distress. The order spread with extraordinary rapidity, and received the sanction of the Pope. An order for women (named 'Poor Clares' from the founder Clara, a pupil of Francis) and a 'third order' of persons of both sexes who were not obliged to forsake social position or worldly employments, were also established. His hymns are among the earliest metrical works in Italian. The best-known is his 'Hymn of the Creation'.

H. 30

FRANCK, JOHANN (Guben, Brandenburg, 1618-77, Guben), the son of an advocate, was educated at Guben, Cottbus, Stettin, and Thorn, and then at Königsberg, the only university not disorganized by the shattering effects of the Thirty Years War. There he was greatly influenced by Simon Dach, Professor of Poetry. After some experience of travel, he settled as an advocate in his native town, where he became a councillor, in 1651 burgomaster, and in 1671 deputy from the town to the Landtag of Lower Lusatia. He marks the transition from the objective form of Church song to the more individual and mystical type: his leading idea is the union of the soul with its Saviour. His 110 hymns were published at Guben in 1674 under the title *Geistliche Sion.*

H. 567

FRERE, TEMPLE, M.A. (Roydon, Norfolk, 1781–1895, Roydon), was the son of John Frere, vicar of Roydon, and Jane Richards, daughter of the Chief Baron of the Exchequer. He was educated at Bury St. Edmunds and Trinity College, Cambridge. He studied divinity at Aberdeen under Bishop Skinner (1802–4). He was curate of Woodbridge, Suffolk (1804–5), and of Royden and Burston and rector of Finningham (1805–15), during which time he became chaplain of Downing College. In 1815 he resigned his curacies and took that of Little Marlow, Buckinghamshire, where he resided until he was presented to Roydon in 1820. In 1825 he was instituted rector of Burston, Norfolk, on the presentation of Lord Chancellor Eldon. He was appointed chaplain to the House of Commons (1833), prebendary of Westminster (1838), and Canon of Westminster under the Cathedral Act of 1840. He contributed to *Sunday School Praise*; *Infant Praise*; and *The Methodist School Hymn Book.*

H. 622

FREYLINGHAUSEN, JOHANN ANASTASIUS (Gandersheim, Brunswick, 1670–1739, Halle), son of the burgomaster of Gandersheim, studied at Jena, but, attracted by the preaching of A. H. Francke and J. J. Breithaupt the Pietist leaders, removed to Erfurt, and then to Halle. There he became colleague to Francke, first in the Glaucha Church, then in St. Ulrich's. Marrying Francke's daughter, he assisted his father-in-law, who was the organizing genius of Pietism, as director of the paedagogium and the orphanage in Halle, and in 1727 succeeded him in that office as well as in full charge of St. Ulrich's. The two hymn-books he published were sources from which later editors drew liberally—*Geist-reiches Gesangbuch den Kern alter und neuer Lieder . . . in sich haltend* (1704) and *Neues Geist-reiches Gesangbuch* (1704). The latter contained 815 hymns and 154 melodies; the former 683 hymns and 173 melodies, and in its complete edition (1741) 1,581 hymns. Freylinghausen was a musician also; he is said to have composed twenty-two melodies.

T. 38, 414, 462

GARDINER, WILLIAM (Leicester, 1770–1853, Leicester), was a stocking manufacturer whose business took him much to the Continent. Both at home and abroad he made acquaintance with musicians of all ranks and with their music. In his youth he published songs and duets of his own composition over the nom de plume of 'W. G. Leicester'. His *Sacred Melodies* (1815), in six volumes, containing tunes by the best masters, adapted to English words, was intended to displace Sternhold and Hopkins, and Tate and Brady, from general use. It did good service in drawing attention to many fine compositions. He compiled an oratorio, *Judah*, on a novel principle, adapting English words to music selected mainly from Haydn, Mozart, and Beethoven, the connecting passages consisting of music of his own.

T. 258, 549 (ii)

GARDNER, JOHN LINTON, B.Mus. (Manchester, 1917), was educated at Wellington College, Berkshire, and Exeter College, Oxford. He was chief music master at Repton School (1939-40), and on the music staff of the Royal Opera House, Covent Garden (1946-52), when he became tutor in Morley College and Director of Music (1965-9). He has been Professor of Harmony and Composition at the Royal Academy of Music since 1966 and Director of Music at St. Paul's Girls School since 1968. His works include *Variations on a theme of C. Neilson*; *Cantiones Sacrae*; an unaccompanied motet *A Latter-Day Athenian Speaks*; two operas, *The Moon and Sixpence* and *The Visitors*; a ballet, *Reflection*; variations for brass quartet; works for military bands; Intermezzo for Organ; cantatas for Christmas and Easter; music for films and plays.

T. 209, 511, 629

GAUNTLETT, HENRY JOHN, Mus.Doc. (Wellington, Shropshire, 1805-76, Kensington), became, at the age of 9, organist of his father's church at Olney, Buckinghamshire. His father destined him for the law, and articled him to a solicitor. This profession he followed till 1844, when he gave it up to devote himself to music. He was organist in turn of St. Olave's, Southwark; Christ Church, Newgate Street; Union Chapel (Dr. Allon's), Islington; and St. Bartholomew the Less, Smithfield. He published in 1844 *The Gregorian Hymnal*, followed by a *Gregorian Psalter* and a *Bible Psalter*.

T. 29, 69 (i), 94, 193, 539, 605

GELINEAU, PERE JOSEPH, S.J. (Champ-sur-Lyon, France, 1920), was educated at the École César-Franck, Paris, the Facultie de Théologie de Lyon/Fourvière, the Institut Catholique, Paris, and the Pontificio Istituto Orientale, Rome. He is a member of the Society of Jesus, and was associated with Father R. Tournay, O.P., R. Schwab, and Father T. G. Chifflot, O.P., for the translation of the Hebrew Psalter in the *Bible de Jerusalem*. In his work of translation Father Gelineau sought to preserve the basic rhythm of the original Hebrew. Once his translation was completed, he studied the religious folk-music of many races, and using these as models he composed simple melodies with a change of pitch on accentuated syllables only. He published *Voices and Instruments in Christian Worship* (1964).

H. 67, 350, 389
T. 67, 350, 389

GELLERT, CHRISTIAN FÜRCHTEGOTT (Haynichen, Saxony, 1715-69, Leipzig), son of a country clergyman, studied at Meissen and Leipzig with some thought of the Church, but experiment proved him too timid for the preacher's calling. He took a degree in the faculty of Belles-Lettres, and became first a lecturer in poetry and then Professor of Philosophy in Leipzig University. He composed comedies; wrote *Consolations for Valetudinarians*; *Didactic Poems*; *Moral Poems*; *Letters*; and, in 1757, *Spiritual Odes and Songs*, which were welcomed with an enthusiasm only less than that which greeted Luther's hymns on their first appearance.

H. 605

GERHARDT, PAUL (Gräfenhainichen, Saxony, 1607-76, Lübben, Saxe Merseburg), son of a burgomaster of his native town, spent most of life amid the distractions and disasters of the Thirty Years War. He studied at Wittenberg for the Lutheran ministry, but was a man of forty-five before he received his first ecclesiastical appointment to the pastorate of a small village called Mittenwalde. Before that, he had been tutor in the household of Andreas Berthold, a Chancery advocate in Berlin, whose daughter he married. From Mittenwalde his hymns began to attract attention, and were quickly adopted into the hymn-books of Brandenburg and Saxony. They had already made him famous when, in 1657, he was called as third 'diaconus' of St. Nicholas Church, Berlin. In 1664, the Great Elector, Friedrich Wilhelm I, in his efforts to make peace between the Lutheran and Reformed Churches in his country, issued an edict restricting freedom of speech on points of disputation between these Churches. Gerhardt, an uncompromising Lutheran, was one of the Berlin clergy who refused obedience. He was in consequence deposed from office and interdicted from performing any function of his office even in private. On the petition of the citizens of Berlin, the Elector absolved him from the obligation of subscription to the edict, but implied a condition that, without signing, he should hold himself bound by its terms. Gerhardt refused to be so bound, and his exclusion from office was made absolute. For more than a year he was without employment. In 1668 he was appointed Archdeacon of Lübben, and the closing years of his life were spent there. His hymns appeared in Crüger's *Geistliche Kirchenmelodien* (1649), and *Praxis Pietatis Melica* (1656). After Luther he was the typical poet of the Lutheran Church, and the first hymn-writer of Germany. His hymns mark the transition from the objective to the subjective in German hymn-writing.

H. 57, 171, 253, 669

GERMANUS (634-732) was Bishop of Cyzicus and became Patriarch of Constantinople in 715. He was driven from office by the Emperor because of his defence of icons. He was noted as a hymn-writer.

H. 192

GIARDINI, FELICE (Turin, Piedmont, 1716-96, Moscow), was trained as a chorister in Milan Cathedral. In 1750 he made his first appearance as a violinist in this country, and took London by storm. He became leader at the Italian Opera in London, and, later, impresario. Most of his life was spent in England, but, having gone to Naples in the train of Sir William Hamilton, British Ambassador to the Sardinian Court, he found on his return, after an absence of five years, that he had lost his place in public appreciation. Russia, to which he betook himself in hope of better fortune, proved as cold to him as London.

T. 494

GIBBONS, ORLANDO, Mus.Doc. (Oxford, 1583-1625, Canterbury), was a son of one of the Cambridge Waits. He joined the choir of King's College,

Cambridge, in 1596; became organist of the Chapel Royal, London, 1604; King's musician for the virginals, 1619; organist, Westminster Abbey, 1623. He was one of the greatest of the polyphonic writers; his madrigals are masterpieces in that kind of composition. Of one of his virginal pieces it is said that it is 'so masterly in design, so finely invented, and so splendidly carried out, that we meet with nothing at all comparable to it until the time of Bach'. Brought up with the strains of Tallis, Byrd, Merbecke, and other worthies of the old school ringing in his ears, he perceived that another world of music was opening; emotion and expression were destined to take the place of orderly, though cold, counterpoint. This new feeling is reflected in his music, sacred and secular. He wrote the tunes for Wither's *Hymns and Songs of the Church* (1623). Commanded by Charles I to attend him to Canterbury Cathedral on the occasion of his marriage with Henrietta Maria of France, Gibbons was seized with apoplexy and died there.

T. 41, 45, 64, 77 (i), 85, 108, 245, 379, 463, 492, 514, 573, 580, 582, 662 (vii), 676

GILL, DORIS, while 'glad if anything of mine serves a useful purpose' wishes to preserve her anonymity. She contributed to *Sunday School Praise* and *The School Assembly*, both published in 1958.

H. 384

GILL, THOMAS HORNBLOWER (Birmingham, 1819-1906, Grove Park, Kent), belonged to a Unitarian family. Educated at King Edward's School, Birmingham, he would have proceeded to Oxford, had not his hereditary Unitarianism, although abandoned by him, made it impossible for him to comply with the condition of admission which then required subscription to the *XXXIX Articles* of the Church of England. He studied alone, principally in history and theology. R. W. Dale, in compiling his hymn-book for Carr's Lane, drew largely on Gill's work, regarding him as the first of living hymn-writers. He published *The Fortunes of Faith* (1841); *The Anniversaries* (1858); and *The Golden Chair of Praise; Hymns* (1869), which Dale found 'a very mine of wealth'. Gill's latter years were spent at Blackheath.

H. 14, 435, 618

GILLETT, GEORGE GABRIEL SCOTT (Hawley, Hampshire, 1873-1948, St. Leonards-on-Sea), was educated at Westminster School and Keble College, Oxford. He was ordained in 1898, and became domestic chaplain to Earl Beauchamp, and later to Viscount Halifax. He worked in South Africa (1913-25), and then became secretary to the Society for the Propagation of the Gospel, after which he was chaplain of St. Peter's Grange, St. Leonards-on-Sea. He wrote the *Claims and Promise of the Church* (1909); *Religion and Politics* (1911); *A Garden of Song* (1922); and contributed a number of hymns to *The English Hymnal* (1906).

H. 328

GIORNOVICHI, GIOVANNI MARIE (Palermo, 1745-1804, St. Petersburg), was a distinguished violinist. On his first appearance in Paris, in 1770, he took that city by storm. Finally he was obliged to leave Paris, and he went successively to Prussia, Vienna, Warsaw, St. Petersburg, Stockholm, and London. Scotland he visited in 1797. His irregular habits continued, and his arrogance frequently embroiled him with his fellow artists.

T. 533

GLADDEN, WASHINGTON, D.D., LL.D. (Pottsgrove, Pennsylvania, 1836–1918, Columbus, Ohio), was educated at Williams College, and ordained to the ministry in the Congregational Communion in 1860. He ministered to congregations in Brooklyn, New York; Morrisania, New York State; North Adams, Massachusetts; and Columbus, Ohio, his last pastorate continuing from 1882 till his death.

H. 436

GLADSTONE, WILLIAM HENRY (Hawarden, 1840–91, London), was the eldest son of the Rt. Hon. William Ewart Gladstone. He was educated at Eton and Christ Church, Oxford. In 1875 he was vested in the ownership of the Hawarden estate, long hereditary in his mother's family, and redeemed from embarrassment by his father's fortune. For twenty years he sat in the House of Commons, representing Chester city for three years, Whitby for twelve, and Eastern Worcestershire for five. He was a fine Greek and Latin scholar, a good singer, and a musician of no mean order, well versed in musical history and with an especial interest in the rich treasures of Anglican Church music. He was himself an accomplished organist. Of a hymn-book which he compiled, Sir Walter Parratt said, 'It is the only one I know in which there are no bad tunes'. His compositions include chants, anthems, introits, organ voluntaries, and ten hymn-tunes.

T. 34

GOSS, Sir JOHN, Mus.Doc. (Fareham, Hampshire, 1800–80, Brixton Rise, London), was the son of the organist of Fareham. He was trained as one of the children of the Chapel Royal. In 1838 he succeeded Attwood as organist of St. Paul's. He was made one of the composers of the Chapel Royal in 1856, was knighted in 1872, and made Mus.Doc. by Cambridge in 1876. He meant every anthem of his to be a sermon in music. Many of the compositions in his sketch-book are prefixed with the letters I.N.D.A., the initial letters of 'In Nomine Domini Amen'. He edited *Parochial Psalmody* (1826); *Chants, Ancient and Modern* (1841); the music of Mercer's *Church Psalter and Hymn Book* (1856); and wrote (1833) *An Introduction to Harmony and Thorough Bass*.

C. 20 (ii), 163 (i), 345 (f)
T. 179, 360, 479 (i)

GOUDIMEL, CLAUDE (Besançon, c. 1505–72, Lyons), first appeared as a composer in Paris, c. 1550. He became a Protestant and joined the Huguenot colony in Metz in 1557. He died in the massacre of the Huguenots at Lyons in

1572. He composed much Church music for the Roman Catholic Church in his earlier years. His chief contribution to the worship of the Reformed Church was his harmonization of the *Genevan Psalter*, first published in 1565.

T. 114 (ii), 205, 250, 307, 314

GRANT, DAVID (Aberdeen, 1833-93, London), was a tobacconist in Union Street, Aberdeen. He had a keen musical interest, and skill, as well, for he scored parts for instrumental bands, and arranged tunes for *The Northern Psalter*. 'Here,' he said one day to William Carnie, then editing that Psalter in parts, 'here, pit that in your bookie'—giving him the manuscript of a new long-metre tune. 'What shall we call it?' 'Anything you like.' 'Well, seeing you deal so successfully in the weed, what do you say to naming it after the introducer of that article?' 'Good,' and so 'Raleigh' the tune became. He was a member of the Footdee (pronounced 'Fittie' in Aberdeen) church and choir. Considerable debate continues as to whether Grant composed the melody 'Crimond' or harmonized a melody by Miss Jessie Irvine. While it must be left an open question, the editor's opinion is that Grant was the composer.

T. 387 (iii)

GRANT, Sir ROBERT (Bengal, 1779-1838, Dalpoorie, Western India), was a son of Charles Grant, sometime M.P. for Inverness, Director of the East India Company, and Indian philanthropist. Educated at Magdalen College, Oxford, of which he became a Fellow, he was called to the Bar in 1807, and became King's Serjeant in the Court of the Duchy of Lancaster. Entering Parliament in 1808, he represented in succession the Elgin Burghs, Inverness Burghs, Norwich, and Finsbury. In 1831 he was made a Privy Councillor. In 1833 he carried through the Commons a Bill for the emancipation of the Jews. He was made Judge Advocate General in 1832, and Governor of Bombay in 1834, being knighted on this occasion. His hymns were contributed to *The Christian Observer* and to H. V. Elliott's *Psalms and Hymns* (1839).

H. 35

GREATOREX, WALTER (Mansfield, 1877-1949, Bournemouth), was educated at Derby School and St. John's, Cambridge. He was a chorister at King's (1888-93). From 1900 to 1911 he was music master at Uppingham School, when he went to Gresham's School, Holt.

T. 440

GREEN, FREDERICK PRATT (Liverpool, 1903), was educated at Rydan School, Colwyn Bay, and Didsbury Theological College, Manchester. He served as a Methodist minister (1927-69) in various circuits, and was Chairman of the York and Hull District (1957-64). In 1969 he retired to Norwich. His hymns are to be found in many books in Britain, America, Canada, including *The Methodist Hymnbook*; *The Sunday School Hymn Book*; *Songs for the Seventies* (published by the Church Hymnary Trustees,

1972); *In Every Corner Sing* (1972); *Praise the Lord* (1972); and *Cantate Domino*.

H. 152

GREENAWAY, ADA RUNDALL (Trivandrum, India, 1861-1937, Guildford), daughter of General Thomas Greenaway of the Indian Army, was brought to England as a child and lived in Guildford. She edited *Songs of Dawn* for Messrs. Mowbray, and wrote occasional verses for their Christmas and Easter publications. She published *A Bunch of Pansies*, a collection of her verses; a booklet for children, *The Story of a Father's Love*; and short manuals for children, *Follow Me* and *Afterwards*, for Lent and Easter. *Hymns Ancient and Modern* contains six of her hymns.

H. 244, 248

GREENWELL, DORA (Greenwell Ford, Durham, 1821-82, London), was the daughter of a country gentleman, who fell into embarrassed circumstances through no fault of his own, and was obliged to sell the family estate when Dora was 27 years old. On the break-up of the home she went to live with her brothers, both clergymen of the Church of England, one at Ovingham, Northumberland, and the other at Golbourne, Lancashire, helping them in their parish work. From 1854 to 1872 her home was with her widowed mother under the shadow of the cathedral at Durham. Her later years were spent at Torquay, Clifton, and London. Her poetical works included *Carmina Crucis* (1869); *Songs of Salvation* (1872); *The Soul's Legend* (1873); *Camera Obscura* (1876).

H. 687

GREGORY, ST. (Rome, 540-604, Rome), surnamed the Great (Pope Gregory I), came of a Roman family distinguished alike for public service and piety. When Gregory became Bishop of Rome, he sent Augustine on his mission to England. Gregory's services to the Church were many. His missionaries reached all parts of the known world. Equally valuable was his work in connection with the liturgy and music of the Church. He founded a school at Rome for singers, and is especially remembered for the reform in ecclesiastical music which made obligatory throughout the Western Church the use of the system of plain-chant which is identified with his name. See Dr. Keir's introductory article pp. 15-17 above.

C. 63, 158, 166, 231, 232, 239, 262, 284, 310, 326, 556 (ii)

GREGORY NAZIANZEN, ST. (Arizanzus, Cappadocia, *c.* 325-90, Arizanzus), one of the three great Cappadocians (the other two being Basil the Great and his brother Gregory of Nyssa), studied at Alexandria and at Athens. His first bishopric was that of Sasima. At Constantinople, where he vigorously defended the Catholic faith against heresy, his influence was such that the Emperor Theodosius made him Patriarch, an appointment, however, which he did not hold long. He retired to Nazianzus and thence to Arizanzus, where he died. His discourses on the Divinity of the Word gained him the title of 'Theologos'. In his retirement he devoted himself to the writing of sacred poetry.

H. 95

GREGORY, George Osborn (Bristol, 1881-1972, Nacton, Ipswich), was educated at Richmond College, and was a Methodist minister. He served in a wide variety of pastorates, and became a supernumerary in 1953. He was a contributor to *The Methodist Hymn Book* and the East Asia *Conference Hymn Book*.

H. 470

GRIERSON, Hubert, was one of the pseudonyms used by Guthrie Foote (q.v.).

T. 155

GRIFFITH, William, Mus.Bac. (Syresham, South Northamptonshire, 1867-1929, Leicester), was educated at Magdalen College School, Brackley, and qualified as a pharmacist in 1888. For a time he was in business in Lancashire, but in 1894 he took the degree of Mus.Bac. at Durham, and, in the following year, gave up business and adopted a musical career. He acted as organist in several English churches, but accepted in 1901 a post in King Street United Free Church, Kilmarnock, and then resided in Scotland. He published anthems, songs, part-songs, hymn-tunes in various collections, etc.

T. 100, 685

GRÜBER, Franz (Hochburg, Upper Austria, 1787-1863, Hallein, near Salzburg), was a member of the Roman Catholic Church. In 1818 he was schoolmaster and organist at Arnsdorf, near Oberndorf, where Joseph Mohr, the writer of the words 'Stille Nacht', was priest.

T. 176

GUIDETTI, Giovanni (Bologna, 1532-92, Rome), was a pupil of Palestrina, who having been commissioned by Pope Gregory XIII to revise the Liturgical Services of the Roman Church, delegated part of the work to his pupil because he had a detailed and intimate knowledge of the manuscripts in St. Peter's and other churches in Rome. Guidetti did all the research and drudgery, leaving to Palestrina the task of revising and finalizing. The work was published in 1582—*Directorium chori . . . opera Joannis Guidetti Bononiensis.*

T. 540, 579

GURNEY, John Hampden, M.A. (London, 1802-62, London), was educated at Trinity College, Cambridge, and after some study of law, turned to the Church. He became curate of Wyclif's old parish of Lutterworth. In 1847 he became rector of St. Mary's, Bryanston Square, Marylebone, London, and in 1857, a prebendary of St. Paul's. Two collections of hymns were made by him—one for Lutterworth in 1838, the other for Marylebone in 1851.

H. 629

GWYLLT, Ieuan. See ROBERTS, John.

HANBY, Benjamin Russell (Rushville, Ohio, 1833–67, Chicago), was co-editor with George Frederick Root of *Chapel Gems* (1866), all the pieces in which were taken from a musical quarterly they had edited. He also contributed to *The Dove, a Collection of Music for Day and Sunday Schools*, published in Chicago in 1866.

H. 221

HANDEL, George Frederick, originally Georg Friedrich Händel (Halle, 1685–1759, London), was son of the surgeon to Duke Augustus of Saxony. His extraordinary musical gifts early made themselves apparent, but the father, intending him for the legal profession, tried to repress them. Ultimately, through the intervention of the Duke of Saxe-Weissenfels, the boy was allowed to take lessons from Zachau, organist of the cathedral. In 1702 he entered the University of Halle, but in the following year repaired to Hamburg. In 1707 he went to Italy. Returning to Germany, he became chapelmaster to the Elector of Hanover, afterwards George I. A first visit to England in 1710 made this country so attractive to him that in 1713 he returned to it finally and made it his home. He was chapelmaster to the Duke of Chandos, who lived in almost royal splendour at Cannons. Here Handel laid the foundation of his future fame, by composing for the duke's private chapel, in which daily cathedral service was maintained, the two Te Deums and the anthems known as the Chandos Te Deums and Anthems, and by writing, in 1720 his first oratorio *Esther*. After *The Messiah*, composed in twenty-four days, swept Dublin with enthusiasm on its first performance there in 1741, the greatness of his genius was fully realized; from that time till blindness befell him in 1753, he lived happily in the sunshine of popular favour. He wrote over forty operas, seven English oratorios, three English serenatas, four odes, besides Psalms, Te Deums, and other works. Most of his instrumental works were for the organ, in the playing of which he was a master, and for the harpsichord, his favourite instrument.

T. 152, 279, 296 (ii)

HANKEY, Arabella Catherine (Clapham, 1834–1911, London), always known as Kate Hankey, was a daughter of Thomas Hankey, senior partner in the banking firm of that name, and a member of the little band of Evangelicals known as the Clapham Sect. While still girls in the school-room, she and her sister began teaching in a Sunday school at Croydon, where their home then was. At 18 she started a Bible Class in London for girl assistants at the big shops in the West End. She published a collection of her hymns under the title of *The Old, Old Story and Other Verses*.

H. 132

HARDY, Henry Ernest. See Father ANDREW.

HARINGTON, HENRY (Kelston, Somerset, 1727-1816, Bath), was educated at Queens' College, Cambridge, graduating in both law and medicine. He practised as a physician at Wells (1753-71) and then at Bath. He composed many glees and catches. The tune 'Harington' is adapted from one of the former. In 1793 he was alderman and mayor of Bath.

T. 4

HARRIS, Sir WILLIAM HENRY (London, 1883-1973, Petersfield), was a chorister at St. David's and studied at the Royal College of Music. He was assistant organist at Lichfield Cathedral and in 1919 was appointed organist to New College, Oxford, and then to Christ Church, Oxford (1928-33), after which he moved to St. George's, Windsor. At Oxford he was also conductor of the Oxford Bach Choir (1926-33). He contributed to *Hymns Ancient and Modern*, composed an unaccompanied eight-part setting for Psalm 103, and was musical editor of *Emynav'r Eglwys* (1952), the hymn-book of the Church in Wales. He was appointed K.C.V.O. in 1954.

T. 572

HARRISON, RALPH (Chinley, Derbyshire, 1748-1810, Manchester), was a member of a family notable in the history of Nonconformity, and son of a minister. Educated at Warrington Academy, he became assistant minister of the Presbyterian Chapel, Shrewsbury, 1769; and minister of Cross Street Chapel, Manchester, 1771. After endeavouring in vain to induce others to undertake the task, he compiled *Sacred Harmony* (1784), and a second edition in 1791, a collection of psalm-tunes, ancient and modern, for use in the Manchester district. Included in it were some tunes of his own composition.

T. 413, 485 (i)

HART, JOSEPH (London, 1712-68, London). Little is known of his early life. He owed his conversion to hearing a sermon on Rev. 3: 10 at the Moravian Chapel in Fetter Lane, London. From 1760 to 1768 he preached regularly at Jewin Street Chapel. Hart was a strong Calvinist, and one of his publications is a criticism of a sermon by John Wesley. He is remembered for his hymns, the first edition of which was published in 1759.

H. 104

HARTSOUGH, LEWIS (Ithaca, New York, 1828-72, Mount Vernon, Iowa), was a minister of the Methodist Episcopal Church. After holding charges at Utica and elsewhere, he was compelled by ill health to retire to the Rocky Mountains. There he organized the Utah Mission, and became its first superintendent. He wrote many hymns and several tunes, and edited the music edition of *The Revivalist* (c. 1868).

H. 683

T. 683

HARWOOD, BASIL, M.A., Mus.Doc. (Woodhouse, Olverston, Gloucestershire, 1859-1949, Woodhouse), was educated at Charterhouse and Trinity College, Oxford. He held posts successively as organist of Trinity College, Oxford; St. Barnabas, Pimlico; Ely Cathedral; Christ Church Cathedral, Oxford; as precentor of Keble College; as conductor of the Oxford Orchestral Association and of the Oxford Bach Choir; and as Choragus of the University of Oxford. He was musical editor of *The Oxford Hymn Book* (1908). His published works include anthems, hymn-tunes, church services, organ works; a cantata, *Song on May Day Morning*; and a motet, *Jesus, Thy boundless love to me.*

T. 12, 146 (i), 361 (ii), 424, 434, 506

HASSLER, HANS LEO (Nürnberg, 1564-1612, Frankfurt), came of a musical family in the Joachimsthal, and studied at Venice under Andrea Gabrieli, organist of St. Mark's. In 1585 he was given a home in the house of the Fuggers, the great merchant princes and art patrons of Augsburg. He was appointed musical director there in 1600, but a year later accepted the post of organist in the Frauenkirche in Nürnberg. In 1608 he entered the service of the Elector of Saxony. Accompanying that prince to the Diet at Frankfurt in 1612, he died there. His works included *XXIV Canzonetti a 4 voci*; *Cantiones Sacrae de praecipuis festis totius anni, 4, 5, 8, et plurium vocum*; *Concentus ecclesiasticae*; *Madrigali*; *Cantiones novae*; *Sacri Concentus* for five to twelve voices; four-part psalms and songs; and five collections of German and Latin secular songs. Many of his chorales were published in the Hizler (Strasbourg) *Chorale Book.*

T. 253, 520

HATCH, EDWIN, D.D. (Derby, 1835-89, Oxford), was educated at King Edward's School, Birmingham, and Pembroke College, Oxford. At the university he was closely associated with Burne-Jones, William Morris, and Swinburne. His parents were Nonconformists, but he took Orders in the Church of England and for a time worked in an East End parish in London. In 1859 he accepted an appointment as Professor of Classics in Trinity College, Toronto. Returning to Oxford in 1867 he became Vice-Principal of St. Mary's Hall; in 1880, Bampton and Grinfield Lecturer; in 1883, rector of Purleigh, Essex; in 1884, University Reader in Ecclesiastical History; in 1888, Hibbert Lecturer.

H. 103

HATELY, THOMAS LEGERWOOD (Greenlaw, Berwickshire, 1815-67, Edinburgh), was by trade a printer. His passion for music, in which he was self-taught, brought him under the influence of R. A. Smith, and led to his becoming precentor in North Leith, and then in St. Mary's Parish Church. He was one of the few precentors who 'came out' at the Disruption, and to him was given the honour, after the first day, of leading the singing at the historic first General Assembly of the Free Church of Scotland, at Tanfield in 1843. Subsequently, he became official precentor of the Free Church Assembly, and of the Free High Church. In 1850 the Assembly sent him forth on a mission of musical instruction over the country among the churches, and from that time he devoted himself entirely to the stimulation of interest in Church music by training teachers and conducting classes. The work of Hately did much to raise the standard of psalmody and to develop congregational singing. He edited many books—*Free Church Psalmody* (1844); *Gaelic Psalm Tunes* (old) taken down by him; *National Psalmody*; *Scottish Psalmody* (1854), etc.; and wrote over forty psalm-tunes.

T. 70 (ii)

HATTON, JOHN (Warrington, ?-1793, St.Helens), resided in St. Helens in the township of Windle, in a street whose name he gave to the tune by which his name is known—'Duke Street'.

T. 333, 346, 442 (i)

HAVERGAL, FRANCES RIDLEY (Astley, 1836–79, Caswall Bay, near Swansea), was the youngest child of the Revd. W. H. Havergal. Her health was delicate but, so far as her strength allowed, she threw herself energetically into religious and philanthropic work; she wrote incessantly, and composed music also. Her collected *Poetical Works* were published in 1884.

H. 431, 462, 479, 485, 502, 685

T. 260

HAVERGAL, WILLIAM HENRY, M.A. (High Wycombe, Buckinghamshire, 1793–1870, Leamington), was educated at the Merchant Taylors' School and St. Edmund Hall, Oxford. Ordained in 1816, he served two curacies in Gloucestershire, and, in 1829, became rector of Astley, near Bewdley. An accident compelled him to resign his living and he devoted his enforced leisure to the pursuit of the study of music, and began publishing anthems and services. He reprinted *Ravenscroft's Psalter* in 1844, and in 1847 issued his best known work, *Old Church Psalmody*. In these works he drew attention to the classical school of English ecclesiastical music, and did much to purify metrical psalmody. In 1842 he was able to resume clerical duty, as rector of St. Nicholas, Worcester, and in 1845 he received an honorary canonry in the cathedral there. Impaired health compelled him to accept in 1860 the quiet living of Shareshill near Wolverhampton, and in 1867 he resigned, and withdrew into retirement at Leamington. Havergal wrote about a hundred hymns, published about fifty musical works including *A History of the Old Hundredth Psalm Tune, with Specimens* (1854); *A Hundred Psalm and Hymn Tunes* (1859), of his own composition; and *Fireside Music*, a collection of songs, rounds, carols, etc.

T. 74, 104, 113, 135, 234, 363 (ii), 456, 493, 496, 497, 528, 597, 617, 680

HAWEIS, THOMAS, LL.B., M.D. (Redruth, 1734–1820, Bath), studied medicine for a time, but eventually resolved to study for Holy Orders, and went to Christ Church, Oxford, subsequently to Magdalen. He held the curacy of St. Mary Magdalen's Church at Oxford. Later he became rector of All Saints, Aldwinkle, Northamptonshire, and chaplain to Lady Huntingdon's chapel at Bath. He published a collection of hymns entitled *Carmina Christo, or Hymns to the Saviour*, a collection which was a companion to the *Select Collection of Hymns* compiled by the Countess of Huntingdon for use in the chapels of her Connexion.

H. 549

T. 371, 422

HAWKINS, ERNEST (Hitchin, 1802–68, London), was educated at Balliol and was for some time a Fellow of Exeter College. After ordination, he was curate of Burwash, sub-librarian of the Bodleian Library, curate of St. George's, Bloomsbury, minister of Curzon Chapel, Mayfair, prebendary of St. Paul's and canon of Westminster. From 1838 to 1868 he was secretary of the Society for the Propagation of the Gospel. In 1851 he published *Verses in commemoration of the Third Jubilee of the S.P.G.* and to it his hymns were contributed.

T. 10, 661

HAWKINS, HESTER PERIAM, *née* LEWIS, F.R.A.S. (Wantage, Berkshire, 1846–1928, Reigate, Surrey), wife of Joshua Hawkins, Bedford, published in 1885 *The Home Hymn Book, a Manual of Sacred Song for the Family Circle*, in which, over her initials, she included seven hymns of her own. She also edited *The Home and Empire Hymn Book*.

H. 615

HAWKS, ANNIE SHERWOOD (Hoosick, New York, 1835–1918, Binnington, Vermont), resided for many years in Brooklyn. Her hymns were contributed to various popular Sunday-school hymn-books. A member of the Baptist Church in Brooklyn of which Dr. Robert Lawrie, the hymn-writer and composer of tunes, was minister, she was encouraged by him to write hymns, and he himself set music to some of them.

H. 688

HAY, EDWARD NORMAN, D.Mus., F.R.C.O. (Faversham, Kent, 1889–1943, Portstewart), was brought to live in Coleraine, Co. Derry, shortly after birth as his mother died while he was still an infant. As he was practically an invalid as a child he was educated privately. He studied music under Dr. Francis Koeller, C. J. Brennan, Dr. E. M. Chaundy, and Dr. Eaglefield Hull, and graduated B.Mus. and D.Mus. at Oxford (1919). He was organist of St. Patrick's, Coleraine (1914–16), and later of Bangor Abbey (Co. Down) and Belmont Presbyterian Church. He was lecturer in music in Queen's University, Belfast (1926–42). He composed *Dunluce* (tone poem), *To wonder* (a choral work), the anthem *Behold! What manner of love*, and orchestral pieces including *Three Irish Sketches*, and songs, with 'Churnin' Day' among the best known.

T. 288 (ii)

HAYDN, FRANZ JOSEPH (Rohrau, Lower Austria, 1732-1809, Gumpendorf, Vienna), was the son of a wheelwright. In later life he cited his own life as 'an example that after all something can be made of nothing'; he had no advantages. At 8 he was taken into the Cantorei of St. Stephen's, the cathedral church of Vienna. When his voice broke, after ten years' faithful service, he was cast out penniless, and for eight years waged a dire struggle with poverty. Some of his works became known, however; Gluck recognized his genius and certain aristocratic patrons gave him his opportunity. For thirty years he was chapelmaster to Prince Anton Paul Esterhazy. The works he now composed spread his fame over Europe. In 1791 he visited England. Oxford gave him its Mus.Doc. degree, and he returned home laden with honours. On a second visit in 1794 he was lionized more than ever. Though 65 on his return home he started, with the inspiration of youth, upon his most important works, the oratorios *The Creation* and *The Seasons*. The inspiration of the oratorios was derived from what he had heard of Handel's oratorios at the Westminster Abbey commemoration and elsewhere. He was a deeply religious man, regarding his talent as a trust given him by God. Every one of his scores, great and small, is prefaced by the words 'In nomine Domini' and closed by the ascription 'Laus Deo'. Religion to him was a wholly cheerful thing. 'When I think of God', he said, 'my heart dances within me, and music has to dance too.' He left over 100 symphonies, 83 instrumental quartets, 44 sonatas, 22 operas, 4 oratorios, and many other works.

T. 37, 421, 616

HAYDN, JOHANN MICHAEL (Rohrau, Lower Austria, 1737-1806, Salzburg), a younger brother of Franz Joseph, was trained as a chorister at St. Stephen's, Vienna. He had a pure soprano voice of unusual compass. He learned to play both violin and organ, but had no formal training in composition. For a time he lived in Hungary. He became Kapelmeister first at Grosswardein to the bishop, Count Firmian; then, in 1762 at Salzburg, to Archbishop Sigismund. He was organist also to the churches of the Holy Trinity and St. Peter in Salzburg. He wrote 114 Graduals, a Mass in D minor, a *Lauda Sion*, Tenebrae in E♭, etc.

T. 72 (ii)

HAYNE, LEIGHTON GEORGE, Mus.Doc. (St. David's Hill, Exeter, 1836-83, Bradfield), son of the Revd. Richard Hayne, D.D., rector of Mistley, Essex, was educated at Eton and Queen's College, Oxford. He took Holy Orders in 1861. In 1863 he was appointed Coryphaeus (conductor of the chorus) of the university, and public examiner in the School of Music. For three years from 1868 he was succentor and organist of Eton College; then, in 1871, became rector of Mistley and vicar of Bradfield, Essex. A large five-manual organ he had built in the music-room at Eton was subsequently divided between his churches of Mistley and Bradfield. He wrote many hymn-tunes and, with the Revd. H. W. Sargeant, edited *The Merton Tune Book*.

T. 106, 322, 450

HEAD, BESSIE PORTER (?, 1850-1936, Wimbledon), as Bessie Porter, went early in life to South Africa to engage in Y.W.C.A. work. There she married A. Head. Her hymns have been included in various books. She also wrote a certain amount of poetry with a spiritual content, but this has never been published.

H. 339

HEARN, MARIANNE, nom de plume MARIANNE FARNINGHAM (Farningham, Kent, 1834-1909, Barmouth), received but a slender education, being early orphaned, and having the care of younger children thrown upon her hands when she herself was little more than a child. She resided for a time in Bristol, taught in a primary school in Gravesend, then also at Northampton, where she settled in 1865. From the start of *The Christian World* newspaper, she was a member of its staff and a regular and popular contributor. She also edited *The Sunday School Times*. Her scattered verses were collected in *Lays and Lyrics of the Blessed Life*; *Poems*; *Morning and Evening Hymns for a Week*; *Songs of Sunshine*; *Leaves from Elim*; *Harvest Gleanings and Gathered Fragments*; and, posthumously, *Songs of Joy and Faith*.

H. 448

HEBER, REGINALD, D.D. (Malpas, Cheshire, 1783-1826, Trichinopoly, India), was a scion of an ancient Yorkshire family. His father inherited the estate of Hodnet, Shropshire, and as lord of the manor presented himself to the living as rector of Hodnet. Educated at the Grammar School, Whitchurch, privately at Neasden, near Willesden, and at Brasenose College, Oxford, Reginald showed brilliant gifts. Having won a Fellowship of All Souls, he devoted two years to travel in Eastern Europe. Taking Orders in 1807, he became rector of the family living at Hodnet. In 1812 he was appointed a prebendary of St. Asaph; in 1822 he was offered the bishopric of Calcutta. His influence did much to popularize the use of hymns in England. In 1811 he began the publication of his own hymns in *The Christian Observer*, and with the help of Dean Milman he made the first attempt to provide a set of hymns adapted to the requirements of the Christian year. These were published in 1827 as *Hymns written and adapted to the Weekly Church Service of the Year*.

H. 201, 352, 541, 549, 574

HEDGES, ANTHONY JOHN, M.A., Mus.B., L.R.A.M. (Bicester, Oxfordshire, 1931), was educated at Bicester Grammar School and Keble College, Oxford. He was Teacher of Counterpoint and Lecturer in Musical History in the Royal Scottish Academy of Music (1957-63) and Senior Lecturer in the University of Hull (1966-8). He edited *Sunday School Praise* (1958), and his compositions include *Cantiones Festivales*; *Sinfonietta*; *Epithalamium*; a string quartet, *Rhapsody for violin and piano*, etc.

T. 226

HEERMANN, JOHANN (Raudten, Silesia, 1585-1647, Lissa, Posen), studied at Fraustadt, Breslau, and Brieg. After teaching at Brieg and Strasbourg, he became pastor of Köben on the Oder in 1611. During his ministry he suffered much during the Thirty Years War, and on several occasions lost all his possessions as Köben was plundered four times.

H. 251

HELDER, BARTHOLOMAEUS (Gotha, 1585-1635, Remstadt, near Gotha), became a teacher at Freimar in 1607, and nine years later pastor of Remstadt. He published *Cymbalum Genethliacum* (1615) and *Cymbalum Davidicum* (1620). The former contains fifteen Christmas and New Year hymns and the latter twenty-five versions of the psalms.

T. 684

HELMORE, THOMAS (Kidderminster, 1811-90, London), was educated at Magdalen Hall, Oxford; became curate of St. Michael's and priest-vicar of the Cathedral, Lichfield, 1840; Vice-Principal and Precentor of St. Mark's College, Chelsea, 1842; Master of the Choristers of the Chapel Royal, 1846; and one of the priests-in-ordinary there, 1847. He was one of the pioneers of the revival of the use of the Gregorian Tones in Anglican services. He translated Fetis's *Treatise on Choir and Chorus Singing*; composed music for some of Neale's translations of *Hymns of the Eastern Church*; and published, as author or editor, *The Psalter Noted*; *The Canticles Noted*; *A Manual of Plain Song*; *A Brief Directory of Plain Song*; *The Hymnal Noted*; *Carols for Christmas*; *Carols for Easter*; *St. Mark's College Chaunt Book*; *The Canticles Accented*; *A Catechism of Music*, etc.

T. 165

HENLEY, JOHN (Torquay, 1800-42, Weymouth), entered the Wesleyan ministry in 1824. He was singularly successful in every circuit in which he served. His spirituality and devotion made a deep impression everywhere.

H. 236

HENSLEY, LEWIS, M.A. (London, 1824-1905, near Great Ryburgh, Norfolk), was educated at Trinity College, Cambridge, where, in 1846, he was Senior Wrangler and Smith's Prizeman. For six years he was a Fellow and Tutor of Trinity. Ordained in 1851, he held the curacy of Upton-with-Chalvey, Buckinghamshire; then was vicar, in succession, of St. Ippolyts-with-Great Wymondley, and of Hitchin, both in Hertfordshire. For a time he was Rural Dean, and latterly an honorary canon of St. Albans. He published *Hymns for the Sundays after Trinity* (1864) and *Hymns for the Minor Sundays from Advent to Whitsuntide* (1867).

H. 322

HERBERT, GEORGE (Montgomery, 1593-1633, Bemerton), was educated at Westminster and at Trinity College, Cambridge. He numbered among his friends the poets Wotton and Donne, and was esteemed by Bacon. As a young courtier he enjoyed the favour of James I, but in the following reign took Holy Orders and in 1630 became rector of Bemerton in Wiltshire, where he spent the remaining three years of his life. His principal work is *The Temple*, singularly attractive in its mingling of the devotional spirit with homely imagery and quaint humour. The same qualities are seen in his hymns.

H. 361, 364, 692

HERBERT, PETRUS (Fulnek, Moravia, ?-1571, Eibenschütz), lived at Fulnek in Moravia, and belonged to the Unity of what were known as the Bohemian Brethren, from which afterwards sprang the Moravian Church. By the Unity Herbert was entrusted with missions to Calvin, the Duke of Würtemberg, the Emperor Maximilian, and other important persons. He helped to compile the Brethren's enlarged hymn-book or *Kirchengeseng* (1566), contributed to it about ninety hymns, some of which are translations from the Bohemian.

H. 643

HERBST, MARTIN (Rothenbach, 1654-81, Eisleben), attended St. Lorenz School at Nürnberg, studied philosophy and theology at Altdorf, and studied at Jena also. In 1680 he became rector of the Gymnasium at Eisleben, and also pastor of the Church of St. Andreas there, but the plague carried him off in the following year.

T. 75 (i), 210

HERMANN, NICOLAUS (Altdorf, Bavaria, 1485-1561, Joachimsthal, Bohemia), came to Joachimsthal *c.* 1518 to teach in the Latin School under Johann Matthesius, pastor of the Lutheran Church. He became organist and choirmaster and wrote many hymns, primarily for the boys and girls in the schools. He published *Die Sonntags-Evangelia über das ganz Jar* (1560) containing 101 hymns and *Die Historien von der Sintflut* (1562) containing seventy-five more. Melodies are provided, but they are not fully harmonized.

T. 290, 357

HILTON, JOHN, B.Mus. (?-1608, Cambridge), may have been a pupil of Tallis. He was organist of Trinity College, Cambridge, in 1594, and earlier was organist and chorister at Lincoln Cathedral. He composed a number of madrigals and anthems.

T. 26

HOLDROYD, ISRAEL (early eighteenth century), used the pseudonym 'Philo-Musicae'. He published *Chants and Anthems* (1733) and *The Spiritual Man's Companion . . . a set of Psalm Tunes* (1753).

T. 531

HOLLAND, HENRY SCOTT, D.D., D.Litt. (Underdown, Ledbury, 1847-1918, Oxford), was educated at Eton and Balliol College, Oxford. He became

Student of Christ Church, and also tutor there. He was ordained in 1872, was Select Preacher at Oxford, 1879-80, and again, 1894-6; Censor of Christ Church, 1882-4; honorary canon of Truro, 1883; canon of St. Paul's, 1884, and precentor there, 1886 to 1910; Romanes Lecturer, Oxford, 1908; Professor of Divinity, Oxford, 1910-18. He was one of the founders of the Christian Social Union, being passionately interested in social questions, and from 1896, when it was founded, to the end of his life, he edited *The Commonwealth*, the organ of the Union. A lover of music, he did much to raise the musical quality of the services in St. Paul's. He was part-editor of *The English Hymnal* and of *The New Cathedral Psalter*.

H. 519

HOLMES, OLIVER WENDELL, M.D., LL.D., D.C.L. (Cambridge, Massachusetts, 1809-94, Boston), son of the Revd. Abel Holmes, D.D., First Congregational Church, Cambridge, was educated at Phillips Academy, New Hampshire, and at Harvard, where he graduated in Arts and Medicine; he studied in Europe also. In 1838 he was appointed Professor of Anatomy and Physiology in Dartmouth College, and in 1847 accepted the Chair of Anatomy at Harvard, where he continued to teach till 1882. *The Autocrat of the Breakfast Table*; *The Professor at the Breakfast Table*; *The Poet at the Breakfast Table*; and *Over the Teacups* contain his most characteristic writings. His poetry was mostly of the occasional order, verses thrown off to mark special events.

H. 34

HOLST, GUSTAV (THEODORE) (Cheltenham, 1874-1934, London), of English blood on his mother's side, was of Swedish extraction on his father's. At the age of 17 he became organist at Wyck Rissington, Gloucestershire. Educated subsequently at the Royal College of Music, London, he served for five years as trombonist in the Scottish Orchestra, and later in the Carl Rosa Opera Company. In 1903 he became a music master in London and Reading, and in 1919 a teacher of composition in the Royal College of Music. In 1918 he went, under the education scheme of the Y.M.C.A., to Salonika, Constantinople, and Asia Minor, as musical organizer in army camps. He was lecturer in Reading University (1919-23). He visited America in 1923, and was Cramb Lecturer in the University of Glasgow, 1925. His works include *The Planets*, a mammoth suite for full orchestra; *The Hymn of Jesus* (two choruses and semi-chorus); *Ode to Death*, to Walt Whitman's words; *Two Hymns* for choir and orchestra ('Lasst uns Erfreuen' and 'Genevan Psalm 86'); an *Ave Maria* for female chorus; a splendid *Hymn to the Unknown*; five operas; *Songs of the West*; *A Somerset Rhapsody*; and many tunes in *Songs of Praise*.

T. 178, 336 (i)

HOPKINS, EDWARD JOHN, Mus.Doc. (Westminster, 1818-1901, London), was trained as a child of the Chapel Royal, played services in Westminster Abbey before he was 16, and at that age was appointed organist of Mitcham Parish Church. Thereafter he was organist successively of St. Peter's, Islington; St. Luke's, Berwick Street; and (1843-98) The Temple Church. He wrote a great deal of Church music, anthems, hymn-tunes, organ pieces. Along with Dr. E. F. Rimbault, he wrote a standard work on *The Organ: its History and Construction*. As musical editor of hymn-books he enjoyed a great reputation. In addition to his own *Temple Choral Service Book*, he edited hymnals for the Wesleyan and the Congregational Churches, the Free Church of Scotland, and the Presbyterian Churches of England and Canada.

T. 649 (ii)

HOPPS, JOHN PAGE (London, 1834-1912, Shepperton), was educated at the Baptist College, Leicester, but after a two years' ministry at Hugglescote and Ibstock, Leicestershire, he became colleague to George Dawson, who had also begun as a Baptist minister, but had broken loose from credal restrictions and exercised in the Church of the Saviour, Birmingham, what was called a 'free', but was virtually a Unitarian, ministry. Between 1860 and 1876 he ministered to congregations of that belief at Sheffield, Dukinfield, and Glasgow; from 1876 to 1892 to the Great Meeting, Leicester; and from 1905 to 1909 to a congregation worshipping first at Little Portland Street Chapel, and then at University Hall, London. He edited *Hymns for Public Worship in the Home* (1858); *Hymns of Faith and Progress* (1865); *Hymns for Public Worship* (1873); *Hymns, Chants, and Anthems for Public Worship* (1877); *The Children's Hymn Book* (1879); *The Young People's Book of Hymns* (1881); and *Hymns for Special Services*.

H. 97

HORN, JOHANN (Domaschitz, Bohemia, ?-1547, Jungbunzlan, Bohemia), is the name taken by Johann Roh when he wrote in German. He took the name 'Cornu' when he wrote in Latin. In 1518 he was ordained and appointed to minister to the Bohemian Brethren's community at Jungbunzlan. The Synod of Brandeis appointed him as one of the three Seniors of the Unity in 1529, and three years later elected him a bishop. He edited the *Bohemian Hymnbook* (1541) and also the second German hymn-book of the Brethren, *Ein Gesangbuch der Bruder in Behemen und Merherrn* (1544). Many of his hymns found their way into Lutheran hymnals.

T. 269, 449

HORNE, CHARLES SILVESTER, M.A. (Cuckfield, Sussex, 1865-1914, Toronto), son of a Congregational minister, was educated at Newport Grammar School, the University of Glasgow, and Mansfield College, Oxford. Ordained in Allen Street Church, Kensington, in 1889, he fulfilled an influential ministry, and continued it when, in 1903, he accepted an invitation to Whitefield's Chapel, Tottenham Court Road. He was chairman of the Congregational Union in 1909; entered Parliament as M.P. for Ipswich in 1910; was elected President of the National Brotherhood Council in 1913; and delivered the Yale Lectures on Preaching in 1914.

H. 365

HORSLEY, WILLIAM, Mus.Bac. (London, 1774-1858, London), was articled to a pianist and composer from whom he received little instruction and much ill-usage. In 1794 he became organist of Ely Chapel, Holborn; in 1802, organist of the Asylum for Female Orphans, in succession to W. H. Callcott, whose daughter he married; in 1812, organist of Belgrave Chapel; and in 1838, organist of the Charterhouse. He was an intimate friend of Mendelssohn. He published five collections of glees, which give him a foremost place among glee composers; many songs, sonatas, etc.; two collections of psalm- and hymn-tunes; and some works on theory. He was one of the founders of the Philharmonic Society.

T. 241

HOSMER, FREDERICK LUCIAN, D.D. (Framingham, Massachusetts, 1840–1929, Berkeley, California), was descended from James Hosmer of Hawkhurst, Kent, one of the first settlers at Concord in 1635. Educated at Harvard, he entered the Unitarian ministry in 1872, and held charges at Northboro, Massachusetts; Quincy, Illinois; Cleveland, Ohio; St. Louis; and Berkeley, California. He was lecturer on hymnody at Harvard in 1908. He published *The Way of Life*; *Prayers and Responsive Service for Sunday Schools*; *University Hymns and Carols*; with W. C. Gannett, *The Thought of God in Hymns and Poems*, containing fifty-six hymns by himself.

H. 323, 606

HOUSMAN, LAURENCE (Bromsgrove, 1865–1959, Glastonbury), was a brother of A. E. Housman. He wrote many books—religious plays, poems, allegorical tales, and several notable novels. As well as his *Little Plays of St. Francis*, his devotional works include *Spikenard* and *Bethlehem*.

H. 196, 507

HOW, WILLIAM WALSHAM, D.D. (Shrewsbury, 1823–97, Dhulough Lodge, Leenane, County Mayo, Ireland), son of William Wybergh How, solicitor, was educated at Shrewsbury School and Wadham College, Oxford, and was ordained in 1846. After curacies at Kidderminster and Holy Cross, Shrewsbury, he became rector of Whittington, 1851; Rural Dean of Oswestry, 1853; Hon. Canon of St. Asaph, 1860; rector of St. Andrew's Undershaft, and Bishop Suffragan, titularly of Bedford, but really of East London, 1879; and Bishop of Wakefield, 1888. He declined the offer of the see of Manchester and also of Durham. In 1854 he collaborated with the Revd. Thomas Baker Morrell in editing a collection of *Psalms and Hymns*; and in 1871 was joint-editor of *Church Hymns*. In 1886 a collected edition of his *Poems and Hymns* was issued.

H. 94, 205, 207, 385, 456, 478, 534, 624

HOWARD, SAMUEL, Mus.Doc. (London, 1710–82, London), was a chorister of the Chapel Royal under Croft; became organist of St. Clement Danes and of St. Bride's, Fleet Street. He wrote for the theatre as well as the Church.

T. 273, 410, 461

HOWE, JULIA WARD, *née* WARD (New York, 1819-1910, Middletown, R.I.), an American poetess and philanthropist, married in 1848 Samuel Gridley Howe. Mrs. Howe was interested in social reform, women's suffrage, and international peace. She published three volumes of verse—*Passion Flowers* (1854), *Words for the Hour* (1856), and *Later Lyrics* (1866); and also books on *Sex in Education*; *Modern Society*; and *Margaret Fuller*.

H. 318

HOWELLS, HERBERT NORMAN (Lydney, Gloucester, 1892), became a pupil of Herbert Brewer and was articled in 1909. Two years later he left Gloucester Cathedral to devote himself to composition. At the Royal College of Music he studied under Stanford, at which, after a short period as sub-organist at Salisbury Cathedral, he was appointed teacher of composition in 1920. His compositions include a Piano Quartet in A minor, *Phantasy String Quartet*, a Sonata in E minor (violin and piano), a Piano Concerto, and choral works to religious texts—*Requiem, Hymnus Paradisi, Missa Sabrinensis*, etc. He was a contributor to *A Garland for the Queen*.

T. 146 (ii), 405 (ii), 509

HOYLE, RICHARD BIRCH (London, 1875-1939, London), was educated for the Baptist ministry. After holding various pastorates, he went to Kingston upon Thames. He worked with the Y.M.C.A., was a distinguished Barthian scholar, and wrote the article on the Holy Spirit in the *Encyclopedia of Religion and Ethics*. From 1934 to 1936 he was a professor in Western Theological Seminary, U.S.A. He translated a number of hymns from various languages.

H. 279

HUEY, MARY ELIZABETH (Leeds, North Dakota, 1916), the maiden name of Mrs. Robert Boshen, was educated at Jamestown College, North Dakota, M'Cormick Seminary, Chicago, and Union Theological Seminary, New York. She was Director of Christian Education and Music in Churches in Chicago, Philadelphia, Fort Worth, and Pasadena. She taught English and music for three years in Sidon Evangelical School for Girls, Sidon, Lebanon. Also, she was a Director with the Board of Christian Education of the United Presbyterian Church, U.S.A. Her hymns for children are found in many publications, including *Songs and Hymns for Primary Children*. She now resides in Santa Fe, New Mexico.

H. 17

HUGHES, JOHN (Dowlais, 1873-1932, Llantwit Fardre), is generally referred to as John Hughes, Pontypridd, to distinguish him from his namesakes of Dolgelley and Glandwr. He began work at Glyn Colliery at the age of 12, and later moved to the traffic department of the Great Western Railway. He was a member of Salem Baptist Church and succeeded his father in the offices of deacon and precentor.

T. 89 (ii)

HULL, ELEANOR HENRIETTA, D.Litt. (Dublin, 1860-1935, Wimbledon), was the founder, and from its beginning in 1899 was the hon. secretary of the Irish Text Society; she was also a President of the Irish Literary Society of London, and a member of the Council of the Folklore Society. She published *The Cuchullin Saga in Irish Literature* (1898, in the Grimm Library); *Pagan and Early Christian Ireland*; *A Text Book of Irish Literature* (2 vols., 1906-7); *The Poem Book of the Gael* (1912); two books for young people on the story of Cuchullin and the Saga Tales of the British Isles, from Norse and Icelandic sources; and *A History of Ireland*. She also was editor of the *Lives of the Celtic Saints* series.

H. 87

HUMPHREYS, CHARLES WILLIAMS (?, 1840-1921, Hastings, Sussex), contributed several translations to *The English Hymnal* (1906). He lived for a period in South America, otherwise nothing is known of him.

H. 325, 588

HUNTER, ARCHIBALD MACBRIDE, Ph.D., D.Phil., D.D. (Kilwinning, Ayrshire, 1906), was educated at Hutcheson's Academy, Glasgow, and the Universities of Glasgow, Marburg, and Oxford. Ordained to the ministry, he was minister at Comrie, Perthshire (1934-7), when he became Professor of New Testament at Mansfield College, Oxford (1937-42). Returning to the pastoral ministry at Kinnoull, Perth (1942-5), he became Professor of New Testament in the University of Aberdeen in 1945 and Master of Christ's College in 1958. In 1971 he retired to Ayr. Among his many publications *Introducing the New Testament*; *Introducing New Testament Theology*; *The Work and Words of Jesus*; *Design for Life*; *Paul and his Predecessors*; *According to John*, may be named.

H. 399

HUNTER, JOHN, D.D. (Aberdeen, 1848-1917, London), was brought up in the Church of Scotland. He left school at 13, and was apprenticed to a draper. Under the influence of the Revival of 1859-61, he felt that his life work must be the ministry. The Scottish Church was barred to him by the long training required for it, and an opportunity of going to Nottingham Congregational Institute was welcomed. There and at Spring Hill College, Birmingham, he spent five years in preparation for the Congregational ministry. Starting with a somewhat crude but intense evangelical faith, he passed at college through an intellectual rebirth which led him to diverge from the teaching in which he had been trained, chiefly in laying dominant emphasis on the Fatherhood of God, in adopting universalist ideas of future destiny, and in treating religious truth in a broader and more liberal way than was at that time common. In 1871 he became minister of Salem Chapel, York; passed in 1882 to Wycliffe Chapel, Hull; and in 1887 to Trinity Church, Glasgow. In 1901 he was persuaded to undertake the pastorate of King's Weigh House Church, London, but his work there was a grim fight against odds, and three years later he accepted a call to return to his Glasgow congregation. A breakdown in health led to his resignation in 1913. Retiring to London, he was able to conduct one service a Sunday in the Æolian Hall, in response to the appeals of a group of affectionate friends, until health finally failed him in 1917. He had an intense desire to raise the standard of public worship, and his pioneer book of *Devotional Services for Public Worship*, by example, inspiration, and suggestion, did much to accomplish this in all the non-episcopal Churches. His *Hymns of Faith and Life* aroused much adverse criticism by the alterations he made, to suit his own ideas, in classic hymns.

H. 691

HUNTER-CLARE, THOMAS CHARLES, B.A. (Leicester, 1910), was educated at Brunswick, Haywards Heath, Sussex, Oakham School, and Selwyn College, Cambridge. He took his theological course at Bishops' College, Cheshunt, and Bede College, Durham. After being assistant curate in Christ Church with St. Andrew, Gateshead, he ministered in Christ Church, Morningside, Buckstone (1943-6), Birstall and Wanlip (1946-8), St. Augustine's, New Batsford, Nottingham (1948-50), and since 1951 in Saxelbye and Shoby. He contributed to *The English Hymn Book*, *The Hymn Book* (Canada), and *Songs for Liturgy* and *More Hymns and Spiritual Songs* of the Episcopal Church, U.S.A. He has published five small books of hymns, now combined in *Songs of Triumph*, and a book of sonnets and other verse, *The Scanty Plot*.

H. 513

HUTCHINGS, ARTHUR JAMES BRAMWELL (Sunbury on Thames, 1906), was an orphan and obtained his academic distinctions externally 'while earning'. After a period as schoolmaster, he became Professor of Music in the University of Durham (1947-67) and in the University of Exeter (1967-71). He was a member of the Board of Governors of Trinity College of Music, and since 1950 has been a member of the editorial board for *The English Hymnal*. He is now retired. He composed works for strings, comic opera, and Church music, and has published works on Schubert, Delius, etc.; *The Invention and Composition of Music* (1954); *The Baroque Concerto* (1966); *Church Music in the 19th century*, etc.

T. 110

INGEMANN, BERNHARD SEVERIN (Thorkildstrup, Island of Falster, Denmark, 1789-1862, Sorö), son of a Lutheran pastor, was intended for the legal profession, but forsook law for letters, and became Lector of Danish Language and Literature at the Academy of Sorö, Zealand. His hymns and songs are sung in every Danish home, and his morning and evening songs in particular are said to have sung the Christian faith into the hearts of many children. On his seventieth birthday the children of Denmark presented him with a beautiful golden horn, ornamented with figures from his poetry. Subscriptions were limited to a halfpenny, and every child in the land contributed, to show gratitude to the man who, next to Hans Andersen, had done most to delight their childhood. In 1825 he published a collection of *High-Mass Hymns*, one for each festival.

H. 423

IKELER, CAROL ROSE, M.A., B.D. (Hartford, Connecticut, 1920), was educated at Mount Holyoke College, Columbia University, Union Theological Seminary, New York, and Yale Divinity School. In 1955 she was ordained at Buckingham Congregational Church, Glastonbury, Connecticut, where her father, Dr. Philip M. Rose, was minister. In 1958 she was the first woman to be received into the Presbytery of Philadelphia when she was appointed to the staff of the Board of Christian Education of the United Presbyterian Church, U.S.A. Prior to her appointment she had lectured in Hawaii, Puerto Rico, Switzerland, and France. She was chairman of the committee responsible for producing *Hymnal for Juniors in Worship and Study* and *Songs and Hymns for Primary Children*, the latter containing eleven of her own compositions. She also contributed to the *Mennonite Children's Hymnary*. She is a regular contributor to *Concern, Presbyterian Life*, and *Christian Faith and Life*.

H. 427

IRELAND, JOHN, Mus.Doc. (Bowden, Cheshire, 1879-1962, Washington, Sussex), came of a Fife family. He was educated at Leeds Grammar School and the R.C.M., where he was a pupil of Stanford. In early life he composed much, but in 1905 he destroyed everything he had written up to then. For a period he was organist at St. Luke's, Chelsea. Durham made him an honorary D.Mus. in 1932. His works include *The Songs of a Wayfarer*; *The Island Spell*; *The Forgotten Rite*; *The Tritons*; a pianoforte Concerto in E♭; *London Pieces*; *These things shall be*; *The Holy Boy*, etc. He contributed to *A Garland for the Queen*.

T. 95, 207, 224

IRONS, HERBERT STEPHEN (Canterbury, 1834-1905, Nottingham), was a chorister in Canterbury Cathedral, of which his father was a lay vicar. He became organist and precentor of St. Columba's College, Rathfarnham; organist and master of the choristers, Southwell Minster; assistant organist, Chester Cathedral; organist of St. Andrew's, Nottingham; and organist and accompanist also to the Sacred Harmonic Society in Nottingham.

T. 50 (ii)

IRVINE, JESSIE SEYMOUR (Dunottar, 1836-87, Crimond), was the daughter of the parish minister at Dunottar, and moved with him to Peterhead and later to Crimond. The tune 'Crimond' is generally attributed to her; see article on David Grant, p. 272 above.

T. 387 (iii)

JACKSON, FREDERICK ARTHUR (London, 1867-1942, Northampton), was educated for the Baptist ministry at Spurgeon's College. Among his pastorates were Campden, Gloucestershire, and Brington, Northamptonshire. Several of his hymns are found in various Sunday-school collections, for example, *The Sunday School Hymnary* (1905); *Sunday School Praise* (1958); *Infant Praise* (1964).

H. 281, 621, 630, 633

JACKSON, THOMAS (?, 1715-81, Newark), was organist of St. Mary's, Newark-on-Trent, and master of the song-school there. He composed *Twelve Psalm Tunes and Eighteen Double and Single Chants . . . composed for four voices* (1780).

T. 565, 591

JEFFRIES, Sir CHARLES JOSEPH, K.C.M.G. (Beckenham, Kent, 1896-1972, Bromley, Kent), was educated at Malvern School and Magdalen College, Oxford. He was Deputy Under-Secretary of State in the Colonial Office (1947-56), was associated with the Feed the Minds Campaign (1954-5) after which he worked with the Society for the Promotion of Christian Knowledge, and in 1966 became secretary of the Ranfurly Library Service.

H. 468

JENKINS, DAVID, Mus.Bac. (Trecastell, Brecon, 1848-1915, Aberystwyth), was at first self-taught, but, later, studied under Dr. Joseph Parry and graduated at Cambridge, 1878. Appointed in 1899 Lecturer in Music (Professor a few years afterwards) and head of the new Department of Music in the University College of Wales, Aberystwyth, he held that post till his death. For many years he acted as precentor to the English Presbyterian Church at Aberystwyth. He was for long a prominent figure at the National and other Eisteddfodau, first as a competitor, and later as adjudicator and as composer. Among his published compositions were: cantatas (*A Psalm of Life, Llyn y Morwynion*); oratorios (*David and Saul, Dewi Sant, Job*); an opera (*The Enchanted Isle*); songs, part-songs, anthems, and hymn-tunes (*Gemau Mawl*).

T. 681

JENKINS, WILLIAM VAUGHAN (Bristol, 1868-1920, Bitton), was educated at Bristol Grammar School, and became a chartered accountant. In his later years he worked with the vicars of Bitton and Oldham Common. He was a leader in the Adult School Movement in Bristol district, and a member of the National Council. He was one of the compilers of *The Fellowship Hymn Book* and of the *Supplement* to it, and contributed two hymns. A collection of his writings, under the title *Grave and Gay*, was published after his death.

H. 602

JENNER, HENRY LASCELLES, D.D., LL.B. (Chislehurst, Kent, 1820-98, Preston-next-Wingham), son of the Right Hon. Sir Herbert Jenner (afterwards Jenner-Fust), Dean of the Arches, was educated at Harrow and Trinity Hall, Cambridge. Ordained in 1843, he was curate successively at Chevening, Kent; St. Columb, Cornwall; Antony, Cornwall; Leigh, Essex; Brasted, Kent. He became vicar of Preston-next-Wingham, near Sandwich, Kent, in 1854; was consecrated first Bishop of Dunedin, New Zealand, 1866; but in 1870 returned to his living at Preston, and resigned his bishopric in the following year. He was one of the Cambridge group who revived interest in ecclesiology, ancient hymnology, plain-song, etc.

T. 15

JOHN, ST., OF DAMASCUS (eighth century), Greek theologian and hymn-writer of the Eastern Church, was born at Damascus, and educated by a learned Italian monk named Cosmas. He and his foster-brother Cosmas the younger (also a hymn-writer and styled 'the Methodist'), retired to the Monastery of St. Sabas near Jerusalem. John was ordained priest late in life, and died at a very advanced age. His fame as a hymn-writer mainly rests on his 'canons'. The canon, in Greek hymnology, was a series of odes, usually eight, sometimes nine, threaded on an acrostic written at the opening of the first of them, and usually founded on one of the canticles of Holy Scripture. John wrote a number of these and arranged them to music, the best known being the Easter canon or 'Golden Canon' from which his hymns are taken.

H. 267, 269

JOHNSON, Sir RONALD ERNEST CHARLES, Kt., C.B., M.A. (Portsmouth, 1913), was educated at Portsmouth Grammar School and St. John's College, Cambridge. By profession he is a civil servant and was Secretary of the Scottish Home and Health Department (1963-72), and is now Secretary of Commissions for Scotland. He has been organist in St. Columba's Episcopal Church, Edinburgh, since 1952. He has composed miscellaneous items of liturgical music, but this has not been published. He contributed to *Dunblane Praises*.

H. 469

JOHNSON, SAMUEL, M.A. (Salem, Massachusetts, 1822-82, North Andover, Massachusetts), studied at Harvard and Cambridge Divinity School. He collaborated with Samuel Longfellow (q.v.) in producing *A Book of Hymns* (1846) and *Hymns of the Spirit* (1864). His radical theology made him unwilling to submit to any credal fetters, and in 1853 he formed a Free Church at Lynn, Massachusetts; there he remained till 1870. Besides many essays on religious, moral, political, and aesthetic subjects, he published a treatise on *The Worship of Jesus, in its Past and Present Aspects* (1868).

H. 422

JONES, ARTHUR MORRIS, M.A., D.Litt. (Islington, 1899), was educated at Keble College, Oxford, and Wells Theological College. Ordained in 1923, he was curate at Ashford (1922-4) and St. Michael and All Angels, Maidstone (1924-8). Then he became Warden to the Universities' Mission to Central Africa in the Teachers' College, Fiwala (1929-32) and Mapanze, Northern Rhodesia (1932-50). He served in St. John the Evangelist, Watford (1952-65), and was Lecturer in African Music in the University of London (1952-66). He has officiated in the Diocese of St. Albans since 1965. He was musical editor of *Africa Praise* (1969), a 'selection of hymns sung in many parts of the world and a collection of hymns set to original African tunes'.

H. 340

JONES, GRIFFITH HUGH (GUTYN ARFON) (Ty Du, Llanberis, 1849-1919, Rhiwddolion), was brought up under the ministry of the Revd. John Roberts

(Ieuan Gwyllt) at Capel Goch, Llanberis, his father being precentor in the church. He was appointed precentor at Capel Goch as assistant to his father at the age of 13, and in his manhood toiled indefatigably in Arfon. A collection of his poetic and musical compositions was published by his son, Owen Arfon Jones of Conway.

T. 485 (ii)

JONES, JOSEPH DAVID (Bryngrygog, Montgomery, 1827–70, Ruthin), published a number of psalm-tunes under the title *Y Pergariedydd* (1847). With the proceeds he went to London for training. He taught music in the British School at Ruthin (1857–66). He published a cantata, *Lys Arthur*, in 1864, and *Llyfr Tonau ac Emynau* four years later.

T. 364

JONES, WILLIAM (Lowick, Northamptonshire, 1726–1800, Hollingbourne), was educated at Charterhouse and University College, Oxford. He became vicar of Bethersden, Kent, 1764; and, in succession, rector of Pluckley, Kent; rector of Paston, Northamptonshire; then perpetual curate of Nayland, Suffolk, from which he came to be known as Jones of Nayland; and, two years before his death, rector of Hollingbourne, Kent. He published *A Treatise on the Art of Music* (1784) and *Ten Church Pieces for the Organ, with Four Anthems in Score* (1789).

T. 390, 396

JOSEPH (or JOSEPHI), GEORG (*c.* 1657), was a musician in the service of the Prince Bishop of Breslau. He edited the music of Scheffler's *Heilige Seelenlust, oder Geistliche Hirtenlieder der in ihren Jesum verliebten Psyche*, three books (Breslau, 1657). Of 123 tunes in these books, 107 are by Joseph; of 32 in a fourth book, subsequently published, 30 were his; and of 50 in a fifth book, 48 were by him—185 in all. Doubtless many of these were adaptations from secular melodies.

T. 52, 490, 639

JOUBERT, JOHN PIERRE HERMAN, B.Mus., F.R.A.M. (Cape Town, South Africa, 1927), was educated at the Diocesan College, Cape Town, and the Royal College of Music. He was Lecturer in Music at the University of Hull (1950–62) and since 1962 in the University of Birmingham, where he is now Reader in Music. He has contributed tunes to *The Cambridge Hymnal* and *Hymns for Church and School*. He has composed several operas including *Silas Marner* and *Under Western Eyes*; two symphonies and a sinfonietta; concertos for violin and orchestra, piano and orchestra, and bassoon and chamber orchestra. Among his choral works with orchestra are *Urbs Beata, The Choir Invisible*, and *The Raising of Lazarus*. In addition he has composed chamber and Church music, songs, and music for solo piano.

T. 367 (i), 401 (i)

JOWETT, JOSEPH (Newington, Surrey, 1784–1856, Silk Willoughby, Lincoln), was the rector of Silk Willoughby. He compiled *Lyra Sacra, Select*

Extracts from the Cathedral Music of the Church of England, for 1, 2, 3, and 4 voices (1825) and *A Manual of Parochial Psalmody, containing 142 Psalm and Hymn Tunes, by various authors* (1832).

T. 648

KEBLE, JOHN, M.A. (Fairford, 1792-1866, Bournemouth), was first educated by his father, the vicar of Coln St. Aldwyn, and at Corpus Christi College, Oxford. He spent nine years at Oxford as tutor and examiner, but having no ambition beyond that of being a faithful parish priest, left Oxford in 1823, and spent the next thirteen years as a curate in Gloucestershire. In 1827, only at the instance of friends he published anonymously the poems of *The Christian Year, or, Thoughts in Verse for the Sundays and Holy Days throughout the Year.* His own plan had been 'to go on improving the series all his life, and leave it to come out, if judged useful, only when he should be fairly out of the way'. The Tractarian Movement made Keble known and attracted people to his ideals. He became vicar of Hursley, near Winchester, in 1833, and in the same year Professor of Poetry at Oxford; he later published *Prelections on Poetry.* The year 1833 also saw the Oxford Movement begin. A sermon of Keble's on National Apostasy was its real inspiration. He became one of its triumvirate of leaders, the others being Newman and Pusey. Some of the most important of the *Tracts for the Times* were written by him. The Anglican Church had an invincible hold on Keble, and he remained steadfastly loyal to it when Newman and others left it for Rome. His *Psalter, or Psalms of David in English Verse* found little favour. His *Letters of Spiritual Counsel*, published after his death, are justly prized. His *Miscellaneous Poems*, including forty-five hymns contributed to *Lyra Apostolica*, and twelve volumes of parochial sermons, were also issued posthumously.

H. 47, 54, 75, 113, 331, 647

KELLY, THOMAS (Kellyville, Athy, Queen's County, Ireland, 1769-1854, Dublin), was educated at Trinity College, Dublin, and intended for the Bar. Coming, however, under evangelical influences, through reading the works of Romaine, which deeply influenced Newman also, he resolved to devote his life to religious work, and was ordained in 1792. The Archbishop of Dublin (Dr. Fowler), disapproving of his 'methodistical' activities, inhibited him from preaching in his diocese. Thereupon Kelly embarked upon an independent course, seceded from the Episcopal Church, founded a new sect, now extinct, and, being a man of means, built places of worship at Athy, Portarlington, Wexford, and other places. His *Hymns on Various Passages of Scripture* (1804) went through several editions, with increasing numbers of hymns included until the 1853 edition contained 765.

H. 258, 265, 286, 289

KEN, THOMAS (Little Berkhampstead, Hertfordshire, 1637-1711, Longleat, Somerset), belonged to a Somerset family. Educated at Winchester and New College, Oxford, he later held several livings, among them that of Brightstone (Brixton), Isle of Wight, where the hymns by which he is best known were written. Returning to Winchester in 1666 as a Fellow of the College, he prepared his *Manual of Prayers* for the scholars there. Appointed in 1679 chaplain to the Princess Mary at The Hague, he incurred her husband's displeasure through his outspokenness, and returned to England. Holding a similar post at the Court of Charles II, his firm refusal to give the use of his house to Nell Gwynn, the King's mistress, is said to have moved the lax but good-natured monarch to appoint him Bishop of Bath and Wells. In the following reign, true to his colours, he was one of the seven bishops sent to the Tower for refusing to read the Declaration; while at the Revolution he was deprived of his see for failure to take the oath of allegiance to the new sovereign. He was given a home by his friend Lord Weymouth at Longleat, where he spent the remainder of his days. His *Hymns and Poems for the Holy Days and Festivals of the Church* were much prized by Keble, who was probably indebted to them for the idea of his *Christian Year*.

H. 42, 641, 658

KETHE, WILLIAM (sixteenth century), is said to have been a native of Scotland, but neither the place nor the date of his birth is known. During the Marian persecution of 1555-8 he lived in exile in Frankfurt and Geneva, and was afterwards employed as an envoy from Geneva to the other English-speaking congregations on the Continent. When the English exiles left Geneva in 1559, Kethe may have been one of the few left behind to 'finish the Bible and the psalms both in metre and prose'. He was chaplain to the forces under the Earl of Warwick in 1563 and again in 1569, and for some time held the living of Childe Okeford in Dorset. He died probably about the end of the century. Twenty-five of his psalm versions are included in *The Anglo-Genevan Psalter* of 1561, and all of these were adopted in *The Scottish Psalter* of 1564-5. The only one transferred to the later *Scottish Psalter* of 1650 is the well-known version of Psalm 100.

KINGSLEY, CHARLES, M.A. (Holne Vicarage, Devonshire, 1819-75, Eversley, Hampshire), son of a country gentleman who became vicar of Clovelly, Devonshire, and rector of St. Luke's, Chelsea, was educated at Clifton; at Helston, under Derwent Coleridge; at King's College, London, and Magdalene College, Cambridge. Ordained in 1842, he became curate of Eversley, on the borders of Windsor Forest, and in 1844 rector. When Kingsley published his two social novels, *Yeast* and *Alton Locke*, violent prejudice was aroused against his supposed sympathy with revolutionary ideas, and the Bishop of London inhibited him from preaching within his diocese. He proved the prejudice groundless, and in 1859 was appointed chaplain to the Queen; in 1860, Professor of Modern History at Cambridge; in 1869, a canon of Chester; and in 1873, a canon of Westminster.

H. 525

KIPLING, RUDYARD (Bombay, 1865-1936, London), was educated at the United Services College, Westward Ho, North Devon, and became a journalist in India. He was assistant editor of *The Civil and Military Gazette* and of *The Pioneer*, Allahabad, from 1882 to 1889. In these papers his first stories were published. Thereafter he published many books that placed him in the first rank of modern writers. *The Jungle Books*; *Just So Stories*; *Puck of Pook's Hill*; *Rewards and Fairies*, have made him beloved of many children. His verse, as in *Recessional* and *The Children's Song*, won him the unofficial title of 'Poet Laureate of the Empire'.

H. 446

KIRKLAND, PATRICK MILLER (Hamilton, 1857–1943, Parkgate, Wirral), studied at Glasgow University and at the Theological Hall of the United Presbyterian Church, in Edinburgh. For a time he was assistant in Highbury, London. Appointed minister-in-charge at West Kirby in the Presbytery of Liverpool, in 1885, he was ordained in 1887, and ministered there continuously until his retirement in 1927, when he went to live at Parkgate.

H. 283

KIRKPATRICK, WILLIAM JAMES (Duncannon, Co. Wexford, 1838–1921, Germantown, Philadelphia), was taken to America as a child, where he was educated at the common schools and studied music while learning his trade of carpenter. He associated himself with the Methodist Episcopal Church. In 1858 he began his editorial work by assisting A. S. Jenks in collecting materials of camp-meeting songs for *Devotional Melodies*. He engaged in business, but his active interest in Church and Sunday-school work led him to begin the composition of Gospel songs. Some forty-seven books were compiled by him in conjunction with J. R. Sweney, and after his colleague's death he published some forty more.

T. 195 (i), 412

KITCHIN, GEORGE WILLIAM, D.D. (Nacton, Suffolk, 1827–1912, Durham), was educated at Ipswich Grammar School, King's College School, London, and Christ Church, Oxford. After several years as tutor in his college and as headmaster of a preparatory school at Twyford, Hampshire, he was appointed Censor of Christ Church, Oxford, and lectured in several colleges on history. He was appointed Dean of Winchester in 1883 and of Durham in 1894. From 1908 he was Chancellor of the University of Durham. He published *A History of France* in three volumes (1877); *A Life of Pope Pius II* (1881); and a *Life of E. B. Browne, Bishop of Winchester*.

H. 550

KNAPP, WILLIAM (Wareham, 1698–1768, Poole), is said to have been the son of a German. He is referred to as 'a country psalm-singer', and is believed to have been organist both at Wareham and at Poole. In 1738 he published *A sett of New Psalms and Anthems in four parts . . . and an Introduction to Psalmody after a plain and familiar manner*; and in 1753 *New Church Melody; a sett of Anthems, Psalms and Hymns, in four parts, with an Imploration wrote by Charles I. during his captivity in Carisbrooke Castle*.

T. 571 (ii), 613

KOCHER, CONRAD, Ph.D. (Ditzingen, Würtemberg, 1786–1872, Stuttgart), was intended for the teaching profession, and at 17 went as a tutor to St. Petersburg; but the impression made on him by hearing there the music of Haydn and Mozart determined him to devote himself to a musical career. After studying in the Russian capital, he returned to Germany and published compositions of such promise that means were found to enable him to proceed to Italy. What he learned there, particularly of the work of Palestrina, made him an enthusiast for Church choral music by popularizing choral singing. From 1827 to 1865 he was organist of the Stiftskirche, Stuttgart, and a school of sacred song (Gesangvereins Liederkranz) founded by him in that city started a movement which spread throughout Würtemberg. He published a large collection of chorales under the title *Zionsharfe* (1854–5); an oratorio *Der Tod Abels*; several operas, sonatas, etc.

T. 200

KÖNIG, JOHANN BALTHASAR (Wattershausen, near Gotha, 1691–1758, Frankfurt am Main), was director of the music in several churches in Frankfurt am Main. He is best known as editor of the most comprehensive chorale book of the eighteenth century, *Harmonischer Lieder Schatz, oder Allgemeines evangelisches Choralbuch* (1738). This collection contains 1,940 tunes, including those to the French Protestant psalms.

T. 74, 104

LACEY, THOMAS ALEXANDER, M.A., D.D., F.S.A. (Nottingham, 1853–1931, Worcester), was educated at Balliol. From 1893 to 1903 he was vicar of Madingley, near Cambridge, after which he became chaplain to the London Diocesan Penitentiary. He was one of the compilers of *The English Hymnal* (1906), to which he contributed twelve translations.

H. 472 (ii)

LAHEE, HENRY (Chelsea, 1826–1912, London), after studying under Sterndale Bennett, Sir John Goss, and Cipriani Potter, became organist of Holy Trinity Church, Brompton, where he remained from 1847 till 1874. Thereafter he resided at Croydon. He produced several cantatas, and numerous madrigals, glees, and part-songs. Several anthems also were written by him, and while at Brompton he compiled *One Hundred Hymn Tunes*, for use along with a collection of hymns edited by the Revd. W. J. Irons, D.D.

T. 48, 150 (i)

LANGLAIS, JEAN (La Fontenelle, Ille-et-Vilaine, 1907), being blind, was sent to the Institution des Jeunes Aveugles, Paris, where he studied pianoforte under Professor M. Blazy, harmony with Professor A. Mahant, and counterpoint, organ, and composition with Professor A. Marchal, and entered the Paris Conservatoire in 1972. After being assistant organist of Saint-Antoine des Quinze Vingts, he became organist of Notre Dame de la Croix in 1932, of Saint Pierre de Montrouge in 1934, and of Sainte Clotilde,

Paris, in 1945. He has published *Trois Poèmes évangéliques* (1932) and *Trois Paraphrases grégoriennes* (1935) for organ, and much incidental, orchestral, and chamber music. His Church music includes motets for two voices and organ (1942); *Tantum ergo* for eight voices and organ (1940); *Mystère du Vendredi-Saint* (1943); *Mass* for four-part chorus and two organs (1949); and *Trois Prières* for solo voice and organ (1949).

T. 469

LAWES, HENRY (Dinton, Wiltshire, 1596-1662, London), was a pupil of John Coperario. He became an epistler of the Chapel Royal, then one of the gentlemen, and later clerk of the cheque there. He composed the music for Milton's *Comus* when it was first presented, at Ludlow Castle, in 1634. He composed the Christmas songs in Herrick's *Hesperides*. Along with his brother William, he published a collection of *Choice Psalms* in 1648. During the Protectorate he lost all his appointments, but was reinstated in them at the Restoration. He was the first musician to use bars in his music to mark the place of the accent and the rhythmical division of the melody.

T. 637, 649 (i)

LEESON, JANE ELIZA (London, 1807-82, London), was a member of the Catholic Apostolic Church, to the hymn-book of which she contributed nine hymns and translations. Some of her hymns were produced as 'prophetical utterances', allegedly under the prompting of the Holy Spirit, at public services. Later in life Miss Leeson entered the Roman communion. She published several books of hymns specially for children—*Infant Hymnings*; *Hymns and Scenes of Childhood*; *The Child's Book of Ballads*; *Songs of Christian Chivalry*; *Paraphrases and Hymns for Congregational Singing*, mostly re-written from the Scottish *Psalms and Paraphrases*.

H. 93, 153, 450

LEIGHTON, KENNETH, M.A., Mus.D., L.R.A.M. (Wakefield, Yorkshire, 1929), was educated at Queen Elizabeth Grammar School and Queen's College, Oxford. He was a pupil of Petrassi in Rome. He was Lecturer in Music Composition, Professor of Theory, and Gregory Fellow in Music in Leeds (1953-6) and has been Reid Professor of Music in Edinburgh University since 1970. His compositions include two piano concertos, concertos for violin, a viola concerto (with harp, strings, and kettledrums), a cello concerto, three piano sonatas, Chorale and Fugue for organ, *Primavera Romana*, *The Birds*, *The Light Invisible*, a number of Services, and incidental music. He was one of the music consultants for the revision committee.

T. 44, 60, 62, 486, 560, 561, 563, 576 (i), 672, 690

LEW, TIMOTHY TINFANG (Shantung, 1891-1947, Tsingtao), was brought up by an aunt following the death of his mother. She was a devoted Buddhist and brought him up in that faith. At 13 he went to live with his father, who was a Christian. He accepted Christianity through family worship and was deeply moved during the Revival of 1908. Having worked as a cook at £4 per year, he entered the Theological College in Fakumen, and was ordained in 1920. The following year he was made travelling secretary for the China for Christ movement. Later he was elected clerk of Synod and a delegate to the National Christian Council in China. In 1925 he was Moderator of Synod. He also ministered in the East Church, Mukden. It was when returning from Shanghai, where he and Professor Ma Ch'ing Hsuan were attending a meeting of the National Christian Council as delegates of the North East Synod, that he was killed when the plane in which they were travelling crashed in fog into a hillside.

H. 569

LEWIS, HOWELL ELVET, D.D. (Conwil Elvet, Caernarvonshire, 1860-1953, Penarth, Glamorgan), was educated at the Presbyterian College, Carmarthen. Entering the Congregational ministry, he held charges at Buckley, Hull, Llanelly, and Harcourt, Canonbury, before becoming minister of the Welsh Tabernacle, King's Cross, London. A poet, he received the bardic crown at the National Eisteddfod of Wales in 1888, and the chair as Arch-Druid, 1924-7. He was created a Companion of Honour in 1948. He published *Sweet Singers of Wales*; *My Christ and Other Poems*; *The Gates of Life*; *By the River Chebar*; *Songs of Victory*; *The Life of Dr. Herbert Evans*; *The Life of Howell Harris*; and *Hymns of Hope and Unity* (1947), besides several Welsh books in verse and prose.

H. 510

LEY, HENRY GEORGE, Mus.Doc., F.R.C.O. (Chagford, Devon, 1887-1962, Ottery St. Mary), was trained as a chorister at St. George's Chapel, Windsor, as a music scholar at Uppingham, at the Royal College of Music, and as an organ scholar at Keble College, Oxford. He was precentor of Radley College; organist of Christ Church Cathedral, Oxford; Choragus of the University, Oxford; and Professor of the Organ at the Royal College of Music, London; and was organist of Eton College, 1926-47. He published much organ music, songs, part-songs, etc. He was joint-editor of *The Oxford Psalter* (1932), *The Church Anthem Book* (1933), and the *Oxford Chant Books* (1933-4).

C. 204 (ii)

T. 266, 270, 309, 400, 606

LITTLEDALE, RICHARD FREDERICK, LL.D., D.C.L. (Dublin, 1833-90, London), was educated at Trinity College, Dublin, where he received the LL.D. degree in 1862, and in the same year received the Oxford D.C.L. *comitatis causa*. He served as curate at St. Matthew's, Thorpe Hamlet, Norfolk, and St. Mary the Virgin, Crown Street, Soho. He was one of the most learned of liturgiologists and a notable translator of hymns—from Greek, Latin, Syriac, German, Italian, Danish, and Swedish. He was joint-editor of *The Priest's Prayer-Book* (1864) and *The People's Hymnal* (1867). He contributed to the Revd. Orby Shipley's *Lyrae*, and published in 1863 *Carols for Christmas and Other Seasons*.

H. 98, 115

LITTLEWOOD, ROBERT WESLEY (Belfast, 1908), is a minister of the Methodist Church in Ireland. As well as serving in several circuits, including both Belfast and Dublin, he was for a period senior secretary of the Church's Board of Examiners and is a governor of Edgehill Theological College, Belfast.

H. 528

LIU HUAI-YI. See LEW, TIMOTHY TINFANG.

LLOYD, JOHN AMBROSE (Mold, Flintshire, 1815-74, Liverpool), founded the Welsh Choral Union of Liverpool, and often acted as adjudicator at the National Eisteddfodau. He composed many hymn-tunes and published two collections of them—the first, *Casgliad o Donau*, in 1843; the second, *Aberth Moliant*, in 1873. His cantata, *The Prayer of Habakkuk*, was the first work of its kind published in Wales. His part-song, *Blodeuyn Olaf*, is regarded as a Welsh classic.

T. 388 (ii), 405 (iii)

LLOYD, WILLIAM FREEMAN (Uley, Gloucestershire, 1791-1853, Stanley Hall, Gloucestershire), was led by his interest in Sunday-school work to become, in 1810, one of the secretaries of the Sunday School Union. *The Sunday School Teachers' Magazine* owed its origin to him. He wrote useful books for Sunday-schools, and a volume of verse, *Thoughts in Rhyme* (1853).

H. 680

LOCKHART, CHARLES (London, 1745-1815, London), was blind from infancy. He became, however, a notable musician, excelling especially in the training of children's choirs. He was organist in succession of the Lock Hospital, where he was associated with Martin Madan; St. Catherine Cree; St. Mary's, Lambeth; Orange Street Chapel; then of the Lock Hospital again. His earliest tunes were published in 1791 on separate sheets. He issued also *A Set of Hymn Tunes and Anthems for Three Voices* (1810); an *Epithalamium, or Nuptial Ode* (1770); and many songs.

T. 39, 477

LOGAN, JOHN (Soutra, 1748-88, London), son of a farmer who belonged to the Burgher section of the Secession Church, was educated at Musselburgh School and at Edinburgh University, where he resolved to enter the ministry of the Church of Scotland. He was appointed in 1771 minister of the second charge of the parish of South Leith. The appointment being disputed, he was not ordained till 1773. In 1775 he was made one of the General Assembly's Committee on the paraphrases, and to him and William Cameron most of the work seems to have been left. Logan's name became prominent in the controversy as to his authorship of certain poems, claimed also on behalf of his fellow student Michael Bruce. Logan admittedly published in 1770 a posthumous volume of Bruce's poems, containing some (unspecified) which he said were by other authors. Eleven years afterwards he published a volume of poems bearing his own name, including some of those in the former book, among them the well-known *Ode to the Cuckoo*. The law courts decided against his claim to be owner of these poems and hymns, holding that they were the work of Michael Bruce. The controversy on the subject still arouses keen partisanship; the fact that instructed opinion is so acutely divided suggests that a final solution is scarcely possible.

H. 72

LOMAX, JOHN AVERY (Goodman, Missouri, 1867-1948, Greenville, Missouri), was educated at Granbury and Weatherford Colleges, University of Texas. He was Registrar of the University of Texas (1897-1903), Instructor in English at Texas Agricultural and Mechanical College (1903-4), a Bond salesman (1917-19), Vice-President of the Republic National Co., Dallas (1925-32), and from 1934 Honorary Curator of Archives of American Folk-song and honorary consultant to the Library of Congress.

T. 427

LONGFELLOW, SAMUEL, M.A. (Portland, Maine, 1819-92, Portland), was a younger brother of Henry Wadsworth Longfellow. He was educated at Harvard for the Unitarian ministry, and served congregations at Fall River, Massachusetts; Brooklyn; and Germantown, Pennsylvania. He resigned this large charge to write his brother's *Life* (1886), and spent the remaining years of his life quietly at Cambridge, Massachusetts. While yet a student of divinity he and his fellow student Samuel Johnson, to provide a young pastor with a better hymn-book than any then available, published *A Book of Hymns* (1846). It had a literary quality and charm of freshness unusual in hymn-books at that time. Two years later a revised edition was issued. In 1853 Longfellow collaborated with Col. T. W. Higginson in editing *Thalatta: A Book for the Seaside*, some of the contents being original. In 1859 he published *Vespers*, and a book of *Hymns and Tunes* primarily for use in Sunday-schools and the home-circle; and then in 1864, again in collaboration with Samuel Johnson, produced *Hymns of the Spirit*, prepared while in Europe, to take the place of *A Book of Hymns*.

H. 106, 623, 632

LÖWENSTERN, MATTHÄUS APELLES VON (Neustadt, 1594-1648, Breslau), was the son of a saddler. His musical proficiency and his business ability were alike recognized by the various princes under whom he successively served, by the Duke of Münsterberg, under whom he became Staatsrath (privy councillor) at Oels, and by the Emperor Ferdinand II and his son Ferdinand · III, who ennobled him. Löwenstern wrote about thirty hymns, originally accompanied with melodies by himself.

H. 491

LOWRY, SOMERSET CORRY (Dublin, 1855-1932, Bournemouth), was educated at Repton and Trinity Hall, Cambridge; ordained 1879, and, after two curacies, was vicar of North Holmwood; St. Augustine's, Bournemouth; Wonston; and St. Bartholomew's, Southsea. He published several devotional books, about sixty hymns in various books and periodicals, and a collection of *Hymns and Spiritual Songs*.

H. 454

LUTHER, Martin (Eisleben, 1483–1546, Eisleben), was the son of a miner at Eisleben. His education, attended with considerable hardship, was mainly at Magdeburg, Eisenach, and the University of Erfurt, where he took his Master's degree in 1505. Embracing the religious life he entered the Augustinian Convent at Erfurt, where he spent three years, being ordained priest in 1507. A visit to Rome in 1511 opened his eyes to the corruptions of the Church, and his opposition to these reached a climax when the Dominican friar Tetzel appeared at Wittenberg selling indulgences. Luther's theses denying the Pope's right to forgive sins were nailed to the church door at Wittenberg, an event which may be called the beginning of the Reformation. Luther was summoned to Rome to answer for his theses, but his university and the Elector of Saxony refused to let him go. His treatise *The Babylonish Captivity of the Church* provoked a papal bull directed against him, which he promptly and publicly burned at Wittenberg. His books were condemned and he was summoned in 1521 before the Diet of Worms, where he insisted on appearing, and refused to retract his doctrines. On his way home he was 'captured' by the Elector who feared for his life, and lodged for a year in the Wartburg, where he translated the Scriptures and wrote various works. He returned to Wittenberg in 1522, his presence being necessary in view of disorders. The latter part of his public life, embracing his controversies with Erasmus, with Henry VIII, and with the Swiss divines, and the part he played in the peasants' war, presents something of an anticlimax. Yet his strong intellect, immense energy, broad sympathies, and loving heart combined to render him one of the greatest spiritual forces in Christian history. He married in 1525 Katherina von Bora, formerly a nun. Popular hymns furnished him with one of the most effective means of propagating the Reformed Faith. Thirty-seven hymns were written by himself. Tradition has credited him also with the composition of a number of original chorales. Exact proof of his authorship is lacking; he himself never advanced any claim to have composed a single air. All his life he studied music diligently, with a passionate love of the art, in the practice of which he found his dearest recreation. In music he recognized one of the most potent means at his command for the development of a more popular form of worship. 'I am strongly persuaded', he wrote, 'that after theology, there is no art that can be placed on a level with music; for besides theology, music is the only art capable of affording peace and joy of the heart, like that induced by the study of the science of divinity. A proof of this is that the devil, the originator of sorrowful anxieties and restless troubles, flees before the sound of music almost as much as before the Word of God.' In preparing melodies for the reformed worship, he found what would serve his purpose in old hymns and chants of the Latin Church, in the tunes of pre-Reformation vernacular sacred songs, and in secular folk-songs.

H. 188, 268, 406, 407

T. 188, 189, 268, 406, 407

LVOV, ALEXIS FEODOROVITCH (Reval, 1799-1871, Kovno), was trained for the army, in which he rose to high rank and imperial favour; he was adjutant to the Tsar Nicholas I. In 1836, however, he left the army to become his father's successor as head of the Imperial Choir at Petrograd. The *Russian National Anthem* was written in 1833. In addition he wrote three operas, a violin concerto, violin fantasias, a *Stabat Mater*, and other Church music. He edited a large collection of old Russian ritual chants, besides writing an essay on their rhythm.

T. 516, 517

LYTE, HENRY FRANCIS, M.A. (Ednam, near Kelso, 1793-1847, Nice), was educated at Portora Royal School, Enniskillen, and at Trinity College, Dublin. He first intended to follow the medical profession, but took Holy Orders and became curate of Taghmon, near Wexford, in 1815. Two years later he removed to Marazion, Cornwall. After serving curacies at Lymington, Hampshire, Charlton, Devonshire, and Dittisham, he was appointed in 1823 perpetual curate of Lower Brixham, Devon. The toils and anxieties of his work there undermined his never robust health. He sought restoration on the Continent, in vain. His works were—*Tales on the Lord's Prayer in Verse* (1826); *Poems, chiefly Religious* (1833); *The Spirit of the Psalms* (1834); and an edition, with a Memoir, of *The Poems of Henry Vaughan* (1846).

H. 359, 360, 497, 695

MACALISTER, EDITH FLORENCE BOYLE (Dublin, 1873-1950, Cambridge), was a daughter of Professor Alexander Macalister of Trinity College, Dublin, and later Professor of Anatomy at Cambridge, and a sister of Professor R. A. S. Macalister (q.v.). In 1895 she married Sir Donald Macalister, Bt., Principal of Glasgow University (1907-29), who on his retirement was unanimously elected Chancellor of the University. She was a Sunday-school teacher (1890-1907). After working in a more general field in primary education, she again took up a Sunday-school class and most of her hymns were written for her Primary department. She wrote three children's books, and her hymns are to be found in *Child Songs, Sunday School Praise, The School Assembly*, and other publications of the National Sunday School Union.

H. 16, 557

MACALISTER, ROBERT ALEXANDER STEWART, A.R.C.O., F.S.A., Litt.D., LL.D. (Dublin, 1870-1950, Cambridge), was educated at Rathmines School, Dublin, in Germany, and at Cambridge University. He became Director of Excavations to the Palestine Exploration Fund, 1900-9, and in 1923-4. On the latter expedition he and his party discovered part of the walls and fortifications of the most ancient Jerusalem, the Jebusite fortress called Millo, which retained its independence until King David stormed it and set up his kingdom in Zion. This discovery settled the site of the city of David as on the eastern hill. He was Professor of Celtic Archaeology in University College, Dublin. He published: *Studies in Irish Epigraphy*; *Excavations in Palestine* (with Dr. F. J. Bliss); *The Vision of Merlino*; *Bible Side-Lights from the Mount of Gezer; Two Irish Arthurian Romances; A History of the Excavation of Gezer; The Philistines, their History and Civilization; A Grammar of the Nuri Language; Muiredach, Abbot of Monasterboice, his Life and Surroundings; The History and Antiquities of Inis Cealtra; Leabhar Gabhala* (with Prof. John MacNeill); *Temair, a Study of the Remains and Traditions of Tara; The Life of Ciaran of Clonmacnoise; A Text-Book of European Archaeology; Ireland in Pre-Celtic Times; A Century of Excavation in Palestine;* and, with J. Garrow Duncan, *Excavations on the Hill of Ophel, Jerusalem* (1923-5). Dr. Macalister was organist and choirmaster of Adelaide Road Presbyterian Church, Dublin, and was throughout a member of the revision committee and the music sub-committee of the *Revised Church Hymnary.*

H. 129, 401

MACBEAN, LACHLAN (Tigh-na-coille, Kiltarlity, Inverness-shire, 1853-1931, Kirkcaldy), at 15 years of age went to Inverness to follow a business career, but his literary proclivities drew him into journalism, first, in 1876, on the staff of *The Highlander*, and in 1877, on that of *The Fifeshire Advertiser* at Kirkcaldy. He has edited the *Kirkcaldy Burgh Records*. His translations of *Dugald Buchanan's Spiritual Songs* in the metres of the originals and his *Songs and Hymns of the Gael*, also in the measures of the originals, and with their traditional tunes, did much to prepare the way for the present vogue of Gaelic songs.

H. 180

MACDONALD, GEORGE, LL.D. (Huntly, Aberdeenshire, 1824-1905, Sagamore, Ashtead, Surrey), the son of a farmer, was educated at King's College, Aberdeen, and Highbury (Congregational) College, London. The only charge he served as a minister was at Arundel, Sussex; his spiritual and intellectual independence displeased his congregation, and he resigned, and turned to literature as a career. He still preached, but as a layman, and without payment. His relations with Nonconformist churches remained cordial, but a friendship with F. D. Maurice led to his becoming a member of the Church of England. He settled in Hammersmith, and devoted himself to writing novels, mystical and historical romances, literary and religious essays, and poetry, all reflecting his spiritual fervour and intellectual sincerity. A long succession of novels won him wide popularity. His poems, appearing in various volumes—*Within and Without; The Disciple, and Other Poems; Exotics; A Threefold Cord,* etc.—were published in a collected form in 1896. Most of his hymns were contributed to *Hymns and Sacred Songs for Sunday Schools* and *School Worship*, edited by his brother and the Revd. G. B. Bubier, and published in Manchester in 1855.

H. 48

MACDONALD, MARY, *née* MACDOUGALL (Ardtun, near Bunessan, Mull, 1789-1872, Mull). She came of a talented family, her brother and a nephew having also written Gaelic poems. She lived all her days in Mull, and married Neill MacDonald, a crofter at Cnocan. She had no English education, but was deeply versed in the Scriptures. She composed several Gaelic songs and hymns, and residents in the island tell of how she sang them while busy at her spinning-wheel. She wrote also a satirical poem on tobacco, of which she thought her husband smoked too much. She was a member of the Baptist communion.

H. 180

MACDUFF, JOHN ROSS, D.D. (Bonhard, Scone, Perthshire, 1818–95, Chislehurst), was educated at the High School and the University, Edinburgh. Ordained in 1842 to the parish of Kettins, Forfarshire, he was translated in 1849 to St. Madoes, Perthshire, and in 1855 to Sandyford Parish, Glasgow. Later, he declined an offer of appointment by the Crown to the Cathedral Church of Glasgow. In 1871 he resigned his charge to devote himself to literary work, and spent the rest of his years at Chislehurst, Kent. For some years he was a member of the Hymnal Committee of the Church of Scotland, and his own thirty-one hymns were published in his *Altar Stones* (1853), and, with other poems, in *The Gates of Praise* (1876).

H. 313

MACFARREN, Sir GEORGE ALEXANDER, Mus.Doc. (London, 1813–87, London), in 1829 entered the R.A.M., and in 1834 became one of its professors. His first work was dramatic; with a series of operas he had marked success. A gradual failure of his sight, ending in total blindness, in no way arrested his industry or impaired his spirit. He continued teaching and lecturing, and dictated his compositions to an amanuensis. In 1875 he became Principal of the R.A.M., and Professor of Music in Cambridge University, and fulfilled the duties of both posts with distinction. He received the degree of Mus.Doc. in 1876, and a knighthood in 1883. Besides operas, cantatas, and oratorios, and much other vocal and instrumental music, he wrote theoretical works on harmony, counterpoint, etc., and edited collections of songs.

C. 20 (i)

MACGREGOR, DUNCAN (Fort Augustus, 1854–1923, Inverallochy), son of a schoolmaster who was a notable Gaelic scholar, was educated at the parish school, Dunnichen, Forfarshire, and the University of Aberdeen. After periods of service as a missionary at Drumoak and Kincardine O'Neill, Aberdeenshire, in the North Isles, Orkney, and at Gardenstown, Banffshire, he was ordained in 1881 at Inverallochy, an Aberdeenshire fishing village, where the rest of his life was spent. He had great learning in liturgiology, and was the leading authority on the worship of the early Scottish Church. Among his published works were—*The Scald, or, The Northern Balladmonger*; *General Principles of Early Scottish Worship*; *Columba*; *The Gospel of the Scots*, a lecture delivered in St. Paul's Cathedral, London; and contributions to the proceedings of learned societies on *The Celtic Inheritance of the Church of Scotland, Internal Furnishings of an Early Scottish Church, An Ancient Gaelic Treatise on the Symbolism of the Eucharist*, etc.

H. 301, 397

MACLAGAN, WILLIAM DALRYMPLE, D.D. (Edinburgh, 1826-1910, London), was a son of David Maclagan, M.D., Edinburgh. He attended the law classes at Edinburgh University, but joined the army as a career. After studying at Peterhouse, Cambridge, he was ordained in 1856. He served in the curacies of St. Saviour's, Paddington, and St. Stephen's, Marylebone. After a time as curate of Enfield, he became rector of Newington; vicar of Kensington; prebendary of Reculverland in St. Paul's Cathedral; in 1878 Bishop of Lichfield; and from 1891 till 1908 when he resigned, Archbishop of York. As such, he crowned Queen Alexandra at the coronation of King Edward VII. Administrative work gave him little leisure for writing, but he wrote a number of hymns and tunes.

H. 245

MACLEOD, JOHN, D.D. (Morven, Argyllshire, 1840-98, Govan), was educated at the University of Glasgow. Ordained in 1861, at Newton-on-Ayr, he was translated in the following year to Duns, and in 1875 to the parish of Govan. He was an ardent advocate of reform in the ordering of public worship. He aimed especially at making the prayers of the sanctuary more congregational by the introduction of responses, at the restoration of the Communion to its place as the central act of Christian worship, and at the observance of the redemptive commemorations of the Christian Year. He was one of the founders of the Scottish Church Society. In 1896 he was appointed convener of the Assembly's Committee on Legislation and Church Reform. Apart from papers contributed to the conferences of the Scottish Church Society, one of them an elaborate treatise on *The Holy Sacrament of Baptism*, he published little except for local use. After his death a collection of his *Poems and Hymns* (1902) was issued, and a volume on *The Gospel in the Institution of the Lord's Supper* (1907).

H. 307, 582

MACLEOD, NORMAN, D.D. (Campbeltown, Argyllshire, 1812-72, Glasgow), was educated at Campbeltown, Morven, Campsie, Glasgow University, and Edinburgh University. After three years of tutoring and Continental travel he was ordained in 1838 to the parish of Loudoun, Ayrshire. At the Disruption he remained in the Church of Scotland. He went to Dalkeith (1843), and was translated to the Barony Parish, Glasgow, in 1851. He was one of the founders of the Evangelical Alliance. The first penny savings bank in Glasgow was founded by him, and he was a leader in many schemes for ameliorating the condition of the people. In 1857 he was appointed chaplain to the Queen. In 1860 *Good Words* was established under his editorship. In 1865 he was the storm-centre of a fierce controversy on the Sabbath question, he taking a liberal view. He visited India in 1867, as Convener of the India Mission Committee of his Church, and was Moderator of Assembly in 1869. His published works included *The Earnest Student*; *Daily Meditations*; *The Old Lieutenant*; *Parish Papers*; *Wee Davie*; *The Starling*; *Reminiscences of a Highland Parish*; *Peeps at the Far East*.

H. 484

MACNICOL, NICOL, D.Litt. (Lochranza, Arran, 1870-1952, Edinburgh), studied at Glasgow University, and at the Free Church College, Glasgow. He was from 1895 till 1927 a missionary of the United Free Church of Scotland, in Poona, India. He was secretary of the National Christian Council of India, Burma, and Ceylon (1926-9), and a member of the Commission on Christian Higher Education in India. He was Wylde lecturer on Comparative Religion in Oxford in 1932. An Indian scholar of the highest standing, he contributed largely to *The International Review of Missions*, and published books on *Indian Theism*; *Psalms of Maratha Saints*; *Tom Dobson, A Champion of the Outcasts*; *The Making of Modern India*; and *What Jesus Means to Men*.

H. 82

MADAN, MARTIN (Hertingfordbury, 1726-90, Epsom), was educated at Westminster School and Christ Church, Oxford, and called to the Bar in 1748. Sent (according to one story) by his fellow members of a convivial club to hear and ridicule the preaching of John Wesley, he became instead deeply impressed, and shortly afterwards took Orders. His preaching as chaplain to the Lock Hospital was so popular that a new chapel had to be opened. In 1780, however, he raised a storm by the publication of a book called *Thelyphthora*, in which he advocated polygamy, defending it by Old Testament examples. A shoal of rejoinders and refutations followed, and Madan resigned his charge and retired into private life at Epsom. Madan is not known to have written any hymns himself, but he had great skill in adapting and piecing together the works of others. In 1760 he published a miscellaneous collection of hymns by various authors which he reissued with an appendix in 1766. It was entitled *Psalms and Hymns extracted from various Authors*. The 1769 edition was called *A Collection of Psalm and Hymn Tunes*. Many of the hymns were retouched by Madan, and it is in this form that many of the great hymns of the eighteenth century are still in use.

H. 316

T. 316, 494

MAIR, WILLIAM, D.D. (Savoch, Aberdeenshire, 1830-1920, Edinburgh), was educated at the Grammar School and Marischal College and University, Aberdeen. He was ordained in 1861, to the parish of Lochgelly. In 1865 he accepted the charge of Ardoch, Perthshire, and in 1869 that of Earlston, Berwickshire, where he remained till his retirement from the active ministry, in 1913. His *Digest of Laws and Decisions Ecclesiastical and Civil, relating to the Constitution, Practice, and Affairs of the Church of Scotland* (1887) is a standard authority on its subject. He published also *The Truth about the Church of Scotland* (1891); *Jurisdiction in Matters Ecclesiastical* (1896); *Speaking* (1900); *My Young Communicant* (1906); *My Life* (1911); and many pamphlets on various phases of the Scottish Church question. The honour in which he was held was marked by his election as Moderator of the General Assembly in 1896. He was an ardent apostle of the cause of the reunion of the Presbyterian Church of Scotland.

H. 256, 660

MANN, ARTHUR HENRY, Mus.Doc. (Norwich, 1850-1929, Cambridge), was
trained as a chorister at Norwich Cathedral. He was organist successively of
St. Peter's, Wolverhampton; Tettenhall Parish Church; Beverley Minster;
King's College, Cambridge. He was also organist to the University of
Cambridge, and music master of the Leys School there. He was a Fellow of
King's College. He composed much church and organ music, and edited
Tallis's famous motet for forty voices. He was musical editor of *The Church of
England Hymnal*.

T. 131, 193

MANT, RICHARD, D.D. (Southampton, 1776-1848, Ballymoney, Co.
Antrim), was educated at Winchester and Trinity College, Oxford. He
became a Fellow of Oriel. After his ordination in 1802 he travelled for a time,
then became curate of Buriton, Hampshire; of Crawley; then of his father's
parish in Southampton. In 1810 he was appointed vicar of Coggeshall, Essex;
in 1811, Bampton Lecturer; in 1815, rector of St. Botolph's, Bishopsgate,
London, and in 1818 rector also of East Horsley, Surrey, these two livings
being held simultaneously. In 1820 he was appointed Bishop of Killaloe and
Kilfenoragh; in 1823 was translated to the see of Down and Connor; and in
1833 the see of Dromore was united with the latter diocese under him. He was
a champion of the interests of his Church, whose history—*The History of the
Church in Ireland*—he wrote (1840). Most of his hymns appeared in *Scripture
Narratives* (1831); and in *Ancient Hymns from the Roman Breviary, with
Original Hymns* (1837).

H. 353

MARCHANT, STANLEY ROBERT, Mus.Doc. (London, 1883-1949, London),
was educated at the Royal Academy of Music. He was sub-organist at St.
Paul's Cathedral (1916-27) and organist (1927-36). He was Warden of the
Royal Academy of Music (1934-6) and Principal from 1936 until his death.
He was also King Edward Professor of Music in the University of London,
and, from 1946, an honorary Fellow of Pembroke College, Oxford. He
published numerous services, anthems, and songs as well as much organ
music.

C. 163 (ii)

MARRIOTT, JOHN, M.A. (Gottesbach, near Lutterworth, 1780-1825,
Broadclyst, near Exeter), was educated at Rugby and Christ Church, Oxford.
Ordained in 1804, he spent four years at Dalkeith Palace as tutor to Lord
George Scott, elder brother of the 5th Duke of Buccleuch. He was also
domestic chaplain to the 4th Duke, who, on the death of Lord George in 1808,
presented him to the living of Church Lawford, Warwickshire. Ill health,
however, made residence there impossible. He had to live in Devonshire,
where he served several curacies—St. James's, Exeter; St. Lawrence, Exeter;
and Broadclyst. He would not allow his hymns to be published in his lifetime,
and would not permit 'Thou whose almighty word' even to be copied by his
friends; but they were made public after his death.

H. 494

MARTIN, Sir GEORGE CLEMENT, M.V.O., Mus.Doc. (Lambourn, Berkshire, 1844–1916, London), gave no evidence as a boy of musical gifts; he was 16 before he could play a note. His awakening came through Sir Herbert Oakeley's playing of Bach's fugues on the parish church organ during a visit. Three months later the novice in music had advanced so far as to be able to play the service in the village church. His first post was as organist to the Duke of Buccleuch at Dalkeith Palace, where a daily cathedral service was maintained. During part of his time there he was organist also of St. Peter's, Lutton Place, Edinburgh. In 1874, Stainer, then organist of St. Paul's Cathedral, called him to London to be master of song under him, and ultimately Martin succeeded his teacher as organist of the Cathedral. He was appointed Professor of the Organ at the R.C.M. in 1883, and at the R.A.M. also in 1895. His primer on *The Art of Training Choir Boys* became a standard work on the subject.

T. 451

MASON, LOWELL, Mus.Doc. (Medfield, Massachusetts, 1792–1872, Orange, New Jersey), became a bank clerk at Savannah. There he conducted the choir of a Presbyterian church and compiled his first collection of Church tunes. He became organist of Dr. Lyman Beecher's church, founded in 1832 the Boston Academy of Music, and did much to extend interest in music and to raise its standard in the United States. Two books of tunes are associated with his name—*The Sabbath Hymn and Tune Book* (1859) and *The Hallelujah*.

T. 81 (i), 159

MASSIE, RICHARD (Chester, 1800–87, Pulford Hall), came of an ancient Cheshire family, and was son of the Revd. R. Massie of Coddington, sometime rector of St. Bride's, Chester, and of Eccleston. A man of wealth and leisure, with two estates—Pulford Hall, Coddington, Cheshire, and another near Wrexham, Denbighshire—he devoted himself to literature. He published a translation of *Martin Luther's Spiritual Songs* (1854); *Lyra Domestica* (2 series); a translation of Spitta's *Psalter und Harfe*; and contributed many similar translations to various collections.

H. 268

MASTERMAN, JOHN HOWARD BERTRAM, D.D. (Tunbridge Wells, 1867–1933, Stoke Damarel), was educated at Weymouth College and St. John's College, Cambridge, of which he became a lecturer. He held the successive posts of University Extension Lecturer; vicar of St. Aubyn's, Devonport; Principal, Midland Clergy College, Birmingham, and Warden of Queen's College there; Canon of Birmingham; Professor of History, University of Birmingham; Hulsean Lecturer, Cambridge; vicar, canon, and Sub-Dean of St. Michael's, Coventry; rector, St. Mary-le-Bow, Cheapside, London; rector of Stoke Damarel, and, from 1923, Suffragan Bishop of Plymouth.

H. 508

MATHAMS, WALTER JOHN (London, 1853-1931, Swanage), spent his early life at sea. He then received training for the Baptist ministry at Regent's Park College, London, held charges in Preston, Falkirk, and Birmingham, and was chaplain to the Forces in Egypt for three years, before, in 1905, he was admitted to the ministry of the Church of Scotland. He served as ordained assistant in Stronsay, Orkney, then from 1909 to 1919 was in charge of Mallaig mission church. He published numerous books—*At Jesus' Feet, Hymns and Poems; Fireside Parables; Rough Sermons; Jack Ahoy; Comrades All; Maxim Shots for Soldiers; A Bowl of Amber; The Day of the Golden Chance; Maxims for Boys,* etc.

H. 100

MATHESON, GEORGE, D.D., LL.D., F.R.S.E. (Glasgow, 1842-1906, North Berwick), was the son of a successful Glasgow merchant. From early years he suffered from impaired vision, and by his eighteenth year he was practically blind. Educated at Glasgow Academy and University, and licensed as a preacher in 1866, he became assistant to Dr. J. R. Macduff in Sandyford Church, Glasgow, and in 1868 minister of the parish of Innellan, Argyllshire. In 1886 he was translated to St. Bernard's Parish Church, Edinburgh. In 1874 he had made his first appearance as a scholar and scientific theologian in his *Aids to the Study of German Theology.* This was followed by the *Growth of the Spirit of Christianity; Natural Elements of Revealed Theology; Landmarks of New Testament Morality;* then by essays in apologetic and books of spiritual meditation and devotion, and *Sacred Songs,* his one volume of verse.

H. 445, 677

MATHEWS, BASIL JOSEPH, M.A. (Oxford, 1879-1951, Oxford), was educated at Oxford High School and University. After five years as private secretary to Principal Fairbairn of Mansfield College, he was for some years on the staff of *The Christian World.* He became director of the Press Bureau of the Conference of British Missionary Societies, and editor of its magazine *Outward Bound* and International Literature Secretary (Boys' Work) of the World's Committee of Y.M.C.A.s, Geneva. He held professorships on Missions and Christian World Relations in Boston, Newtown-Andover, and Vancouver. Among his many publications are *The Splendid Quest* (1911); *Paul the Dauntless* (1916); *A Life of Christ;* and *The Clash of Colour.*

H. 501

MATHIAS, WILLIAM JAMES, D.Mus., F.R.A.M. (Whitland, Carmarthenshire, 1934), was educated at Whitland Grammar School, University College, Aberystwyth, and the Royal Academy of Music. He was lecturer in Bangor, North Wales (1959-68), Senior Lecturer in Music in Edinburgh University (1968-70), and in 1970 became Professor of Music in University College, Bangor, University of Wales. His compositions include a symphonic Concerto for orchestra, two piano concertos, a string quartet, a wind quintet, a sinfonietta, a dramatic cantata, *St. Teilo,* and works for organ, Church music, and incidental music for films, television, and the theatre.

T. 292

MATTHEWS, TIMOTHY RICHARD (Colmworth, Bedford, 1826–1910, Tetney, Lincolnshire), was a son of the Revd. T. R. Matthews. He was educated at Bedford Grammar School and Gonville and Caius College, Cambridge. Ordained in 1853, he was curate at St. Mary's, Nottingham, until 1859, when he accepted the curacy and sole charge of North Coates, Lincolnshire, of which he became rector in 1869. In 1907 he retired and went to live with his eldest son at Tetney Vicarage, where he died. His musical works include over a hundred hymn-tunes, settings of the morning and evening services, two or three songs, and a Christmas carol. He edited *The North Coates Supplemental Tune Book* and *The Village Organist* in its original form. .

T. 686

MEALY, NORMAN and MARGARET. Norman was born in Troy, New York, in 1923. He was Director of Music in St. Mark's Church, Berkeley, and Professor of Music in the University of California. They also contributed to *Infant Praise*. It proved impossible to get further details.

H. 155

MENDELSSOHN-BARTHOLDY, (JAKOB LUDWIG) FELIX (Hamburg, 1809–47, Leipzig), was the son of a Jewish banker. The family settled in his childhood in Berlin, and were baptized into the Lutheran Church, adding Bartholdy to the name on that occasion. At the age of 10 he made his first appearance as a pianist, and while yet a boy composed profusely. In his youth he discovered Bach, and while a student at the University, got together a choir of sixteen voices, and on Saturday evenings practised *The Passion according to St. Matthew*. In 1829 it was performed for the first time since Bach's death, Mendelssohn conducting without a note of the music before him. Bach's influence on him was profound. His overture to *A Midsummer Night's Dream* (1826) had already given him high rank as a composer. In 1829 he visited Great Britain for the first time. His visit to Scotland inspired the overture *Fingal's Cave*. In 1833 he accepted the directorship of concerts at Düsseldorf, where he invented the new form of composition for the pianoforte now familiar in the *Lieder ohne Worte*. From 1835 to 1843 he was director of the Gewandhaus concerts at Leipzig. Reluctantly, in the latter year, at the urgent request of the King of Prussia, he left Leipzig for Berlin, to be the royal Kappelmeister, and director of the musical division of the newly founded Academy of Arts; but in 1845 he was glad to return to Leipzig, to resume the directorship of the Gewandhaus concerts, and to found the Conservatorium. He left great masses of compositions—two oratorios, *St. Paul* and *Elijah*; symphonies, overtures, string quartets, concertos and other pieces for the pianoforte, organ sonatas, much vocal music, secular and sacred.

T. 159, 162, 169, 202, 315, 430, 668

MERCER, WILLIAM, D.D. (Barnard Castle, Durham, 1811–73, Leavy Greave, Sheffield), studied at Trinity College, Cambridge. In 1840 he became incumbent of St. George's, Sheffield. He issued in 1857 *The Church Psalter and Hymn Book, comprising the Psalter, or Psalms of David, together with the*

Canticles, Pointed for Chanting; Four Hundred Metrical Hymns and Six Responses to the Commandments; the whole united to appropriate Chants and Tunes, for the Use of Congregations and Families. Mercer himself contributed to it several translations and paraphrases from Latin and German.

H. 355

MERRILL, WILLIAM PIERSON, D.D. (Orange, New Jersey, 1867-1954, New York), studied at Rutgers College and at Union Theological Seminary, New York. Ordained to the Presbyterian ministry in 1890, he held charges at Philadelphia; Sixth Church, Chicago; and the Brick Church, New York (1911-38). He published several books that have wide acceptance: *Faith Building; Faith and Sight; Footings for Faith; Christian Internationalism; The Common Creed of Christians; The Freedom of the Preacher; Liberal Christianity; We Would See Jesus.*

H. 477

MERRINGTON, ERNEST NORTHCROFT, Ph.D. (Newcastle, New South Wales, 1876-1953, Wellington, New Zealand), was educated at Sydney High School and Sydney University, Edinburgh University and New College, and Harvard University, U.S.A. He was minister of the Presbyterian Church of Australia at Kiama, New South Wales, 1905-8; Haberfield, Sydney, 1908-10; St. Andrew's Church, Brisbane, Queensland, 1910-23; and, from 1923 to 1928 of the First Church of Otago, Dunedin, New Zealand. He lectured on Philosophy to the University of Sydney, 1907-9, and while in Brisbane founded Emmanuel College, under the Presbyterian Church, and from 1912 to 1923 was lecturer in Christian Philosophy and Apologetics there. From 1929 to 1940 he was Master of Knox College, Dunedin, and then Minister of Seatown Parish, Wellington, until his retirement. He published *Casuistry* (1902) and *The Problem of Personality* (1916).

H. 517

MEYER, JOHANN DAVID (c. 1692), was a town councillor at Ulm. He published *Geistliche Seelenfreud, oder Davidische Hauss-Capell* (Ulm, 1692). It contained 111 melodies, of which 54 were his own. His name is also spelt variously Meier, Mayer, or Mejer.

T. 145 (i)

MILGROVE, BENJAMIN (Bath?, 1731-1810, Bath?), was precentor and then organist of the Countess of Huntingdon's Chapel in Bath. He published *Sixteen Hymns as they are sung at the Right Honourable the Countess of Huntingdon's Chapel in Bath. Set to Music (c. 1769).*

T. 33 (ii)

MILLER, EDWARD, Mus.Doc. (Norwich, 1731-1807, Doncaster), was apprenticed to his father's trade of pavior, but ran away to be free to follow his bent towards the study of music. For a time he played the German flute in

Handel's orchestra. For over fifty years (1756-1807), he was organist of Doncaster Parish Church. Dissatisfaction with the existing state of Church music led him to publish an edition of *The Psalms of David, with tunes* in 1790; *Psalms and Hymns set to New Music* (1801); *Sacred Music ... an Appendix to Dr. Watts' Psalms and Hymns* (1802).

T. 237, 254

MILLER, EMILY, *née* HUNTINGTON, M.A. (Brooklyn, Connecticut, 1833-1913, St. Paul, Minnesota), was a daughter of the Revd. Thomas Huntington, D.D. She graduated at Oberlin College in 1857, and in 1860 married Professor John E. Miller. She was Dean of women students in North-Western University, 1891-8. She wrote numerous stories, *Captain Frith, Little Neighbours*, etc., and published in Chicago a volume of poems, *From Avalon, and Other Poems*.

H. 227

MILLER, JOHN—originally JOHANNES MUELLER (Groshennersdorf, near Herrnhut, Saxony, 1756-90, Fulneck, Yorkshire), was of Lutheran parentage, but was educated at the Moravian Grammar School, Niesky, and the Moravian Theological College, Barby, near Magdeburg. In 1781 he came to Fulneck, the educational centre of the Moravians in England, near Leeds. In 1788 he became minister of the neighbouring congregation in Pudsey. The editor of the 1789 edition of *The Moravian Hymnbook* was J. Swertner, but Miller collaborated with F. W. Foster in revising older translations and preparing new ones. At least twelve translations are attributed to them jointly. Miller is not known to have written any original hymns, but several translations are attributed to him.

H. 355

MILMAN, HENRY HART, D.D. (London, 1791-1868, Sunninghill, Ascot), was son of Sir Francis Milman, Bt., physician to the King. He was educated at Greenwich, Eton, and Brasenose College, Oxford, and became a Fellow of his college. Ordained in 1816, he received in 1818 the living of St. Mary's, Reading; in 1821-31 was Professor of Poetry at Oxford and in 1827 was Bampton Lecturer; in 1835 received a canonry of Westminster, with the rectorship of St. Margaret's; and in 1849 accepted the Deanery of St. Paul's. He wrote a number of dramas. In *Nala and Damayanti, and other Poems translated from the Sanskrit* (1834) he was one of the first interpreters of Indian thought and life to the mind of the West. He published translations of Horace, and of the *Agamemnon* and *Bacchae*. His *History of the Jews* and *History of Christianity from the Birth of Christ to the Abolition of Paganism in the Roman Empire* was followed by his *History of Latin Christianity to the Pontificate of Nicholas V* (1856). His *Poetical Works* were collected in three volumes. His *Annals of St. Paul's Cathedral* appeared after his death. His thirteen hymns were written at the instance of his friend Heber, and appeared in *Hymns Adapted to the Weekly Church Service of the Year* and in *Hymns for the Use of St. Margaret's, Westminster* (1837).

H. 234

MILNER-BARRY, ALDA (Scotherne, Lincolnshire, 1877-1941, Weston-super-Mare), was the daughter of the Revd. E. M. Barry. She was a lecturer in St. Christopher's College, Blackheath, and published *Prayers and Praises in the Infant Sunday School* and *The Joyful Life*, and contributed to *Sunday School Praise*.

H. 280

MILTON, JOHN (London, 1608-74, London), was the son of a scrivener. He was educated at St. Paul's School and Christ's College, Cambridge. Milton's literary life falls into three well-marked periods, the first including his earlier and shorter poems, the second almost entirely occupied with controversial and political writings, and the third containing his poems on a grander scale. Much of his best work was produced at a comparatively early age. Thus his paraphrase of Psalm 136 was written before he was 16 years of age. Milton's energies were diverted into the controversies leading to the Civil War and the establishment of the Commonwealth. For many years his chief writings were of a polemical character, on the reform of Church discipline, on divorce, on the liberty of unlicensed printing, and other causes. Having upheld the lawfulness of the King's execution, he was appointed Secretary for foreign tongues to the Council of State, a post which he continued to fill, notwithstanding his blindness (which became total in 1652), until the eve of the Restoration. For some years he lived in close retirement. In spite of the exquisite beauty of his lyrics, Milton's direct influence on hymnology has been slight.

H. 33, 321

MOHR, JOSEPH (Salzburg, 1792-1848, Wagrein), was in 1815 ordained to the priesthood of the Roman Church by the Bishop of Salzburg. He was successively assistant priest at Ramsau and Laufen; then coadjutor at Kuchl, at Golling, Vigann, Adnet, and Authering; then vicar substitute at Hof and at Hintersee—all in the diocese of Salzburg. In 1828 he became vicar at Hintersee, and in 1837 at Wagrein, near St. Johann.

H. 176

MONK, EDWIN GEORGE, Mus.Doc. (Frome, Somerset, 1819-1900, Radley, Berkshire), went early to London, studied singing under Hullah, and was a private pupil of Henry Philips and G. A. Macfarren. After acting as organist of Midsomer Norton Parish Church and of Christ Church, Frome, he was appointed first organist, precentor, and music master of St. Columba's College, Stackallan. After three years he removed to Oxford, and conducted the University Motet and Madrigal Society. For eleven years he was organist and music master of St. Peter's College, Radley. In 1858 he became organist of York Minster, and remained there till 1883. He composed a setting of Milton's *Ode on the Nativity*; numerous songs, anthems, etc.; compiled the libretti for G. A. Macfarren's oratorios *St. John the Baptist, The Resurrection,* and *Joseph*; and edited *The Anglican Chant Book, The Anglican Choral Service Book, Chants for the Daily Psalms as used in York Minster, Unison Chants for the Psalter, The Anglican Hymn Book* (with the Revd. R. C.

Singleton), and (with Sir F. A. Gore Ouseley) *The Psalter and Canticles Pointed for Chanting.*

T. 455 (ii)

MONK, WILLIAM HENRY, Mus.Doc. (Brompton, 1823–89, London), became organist successively of Eaton Chapel, Pimlico; St. George's Chapel, Albemarle Street; Portman Chapel, Marylebone; and St. Matthias, Stoke Newington. Concurrently with this last appointment he held the offices of director of the choir and organist of King's College, London, and from 1874 was professor of vocal music there. In 1876 he was appointed a professor in the National Training School for Music and in Bedford College. His chief title to fame is his identification with *Hymns Ancient and Modern*, of which he was the first musical editor. He published many anthems, Te Deums, Kyries, etc.; and edited *Hymns of the Church*; *The Holy Year*; *Fifty-two Simple Chants*; *The Book of Psalms in Metre*; *The Scottish Hymnal*; and a *Book of Anthems*—the last three for the Church of Scotland.

T. 11, 130, 200, 267, 276, 327, 638, 695

MONSELL, JOHN SAMUEL BEWLEY, LL.D. (Derry, 1811–75, Guildford), was the son of an archdeacon of Londonderry. He was educated at Trinity College, Dublin, and ordained in 1834. He became chaplain to Bishop Mant; Chancellor of the Diocese of Connor; rector of Ramoan; then, proceeding to England, was vicar of Egham, Surrey; and rector of St. Nicholas, Guildford. He published eleven volumes of poetry, including nearly 300 hymns, of which more than seventy are in use: *Hymns and Miscellaneous Poems*; *Parish Musings*; *Spiritual Songs for the Sundays and Holy Days throughout the Year*; *Hymns of Love and Praise for the Church's Year*; *The Passing Bell*; *Litany Hymns*; *The Parish Hymnal after the Order of the Book of Common Prayer*; *Watches by the Cross*; *Simon the Cyrenian*; *Nursery Carols*, etc.

H. 40, 366, 442

MONTGOMERY, JAMES (Irvine, Ayrshire, 1771–1854, Sheffield), was the son of an Ulster Scot of peasant stock who qualified for the ministry of the Moravian Brotherhood, had charge for some years of a congregation in Irvine, then removed to the Moravian Settlement formed in 1746 by John Cennick at Gracehill, Ballymena, Co. Antrim; and finally went as a missionary to the West Indies, where both he and his wife died. He was educated at Fulneck with a view to the ministry, but the Brethren, dissatisfied with his progress, apprenticed him to a baker. He ran away and entered a chandler's shop at Mirfield, near Wakefield. Finding that also uncongenial, he ran away again to Wath-upon-Dearne, near Rotherham. At 18 he repaired to London and spent a year in a vain endeavour to find a publisher for his poems. In 1794 he went to Sheffield to assist a bookseller and printer named Gales on the staff of *The Sheffield Register*. Two years later, Gales had to leave the country to avoid prosecution for the liberal opinions advocated in that newspaper. Montgomery became editor, and conducted the paper, under the name of *The Sheffield Iris*, for thirty-one years. Twice he suffered fine and

316   BIOGRAPHICAL AND HISTORICAL NOTES

imprisonment in York Castle—first for printing a song in celebration of the Fall of the Bastille; and second for giving an account of a political riot in Sheffield.

H. 38, 39, 117, 182, 317, 332, 404, 471, 496, 585, 597, 609, 665

MOORE, JAMES, F.T.C.L., F.T.S.C., A.R.C.O. (Ramelton, Co. Donegal, 1909), studied music with Dr. E. Norman Hay, Dr. Ernest Bullock, John Vine, and had close associations with Sir Hamilton Harty, conductor of the Hallé Orchestra. He was organist in First Ballymoney (1928-34), and in First Coleraine (1934-45 and since 1956), in which congregation he is also an elder. He was Lecturer in Church Music in Magee University College, Derry (1946-62), and is a Past President of the Professional Musicians Society in Ulster. He has published two volumes of pianoforte pieces, *Pupils' Paradise* and *Progressive Piano Pieces*, and also some Irish folk-song arrangements.

T. 401 (ii)

MOORE, JESSIE ELEANOR, M.A., B.Sc., B.D. (Newark, New Jersey, 1886-1969, Ocean Grove, New Jersey), was educated at Teachers' College, Columbia University, and Union Theological Seminary, New York. She taught kindergarten in Newark Public Schools (1907-20), was supervisor of student practice teaching in Teachers' College (1921-3), assistant editor for the Sunday Schools Publications Board of the Methodist Church (1924-9), editor of children's materials for the Pilgrim Press, Boston (1930-47), and from 1947 until her retirement was an editorial consultant for the Board of Education of the Methodist Church, Nashville, Tennessee. She published *Pilgrim Bible Stories for Children* and contributed to *Songs and Hymns for Primary Children*.

H. 466

MOORE, JOHN BOYD, B.A. (Glasleck, Co. Cavan, 1914), was educated at Magee University College, Derry, Trinity College, Dublin, and The Presbyterian College, Belfast. He was ordained in Mountjoy Presbyterian Church, Omagh, Co. Tyrone, in 1939, and has ministered there all his life, except for the years 1942-6 during which he was a chaplain in the Royal Navy.

H. 601

MOORE, THOMAS (Manchester?, c. 1710-c. 1792, Glasgow), was a music teacher in Manchester about 1740-50. In the latter year he published in that city *The Psalm Singer's Divine Companion* (2 vols.), a second edition being issued in the same year as *The Psalm Singer's Compleat Tutor and Divine Companion*. Going to Glasgow, he became, in 1755, precentor in Blackfriars Parish Church. There he published *The Psalm Singer's Pocket Companion, containing great variety of the best English Psalm Tunes, suited to the different metres in the Scotch Version of the Psalms of David, set in three and four parts; likewise all the tunes that are usually sung in most parts of Scotland; with a plain and easy introduction to Musick* (1756); and *The Psalm Singer's Delightful*

Pocket Companion, Containing a Plain and Easy Introduction to Psalmody, and an Introduction explaining more at large the grounds of Music in general. Illustrated with great variety of Tables, Scales, and Initial Lessons (1761).

T. 312 (i)

MORE, HENRY (Grantham, Lincolnshire, 1614-87, Cambridge), was educated at Eton and Christ's College, Cambridge, of which he became a Fellow. Although ordained in 1639, he refused all office in the Church and spent his life as a Fellow of his college. He was a mystic and one of the Cambridge Platonists.

H. 290

MORISON, JOHN, D.D. (Cairnie, Aberdeenshire, 1750-98, Canisbay), studied at King's College, Aberdeen, and after holding several teaching appointments in Caithness, repaired to Edinburgh for further study, especially in Greek. Probably while acting as a master in Thurso school he had become acquainted with John Logan, and on his arrival in Edinburgh Logan introduced him to Dr. Macfarlane of the Canongate Second Charge, who was a member of the Committee of Assembly then engaged on the preparation of the paraphrases. Under encouragement from that quarter, Morison submitted twenty-four pieces to the committee. Seven were accepted—Paraphrases 19, 21, 29, 30, which were but slightly altered; 27 and 28, which were either considerably altered by Logan, or written jointly by Morison and Logan; and 35, which underwent a good deal of alteration. In 1779 Morison was presented to the parish of Canisbay, Caithness, and was ordained nine months later, in September 1780. At the Assembly of the following year he was appointed a member of the committee for revising the collection of *Translations and Paraphrases* to which he had himself contributed.

H. 69, 168, 237

MORRIS, REGINALD OWEN (York, 1886-1948, London), was educated at Harrow and New College, Oxford, and the Royal College of Music. He held a post in America (1929-31) and then was appointed to the teaching staff of the R.C.M. He published *Contrapuntal Technique in the 16th Century* (1922); a *Fantasy for String Quartet*; *Motets for String Quartet*; several symphonies and concertos as well as other music, songs, and part-songs.

T. 194 (i)

MOTE, EDWARD (London, 1797-1874, Horsham, Sussex), became a Baptist minister, and for the last twenty-six years of his life was pastor at Horsham. In 1836 he published *Hymns of Praise, A New Selection of Gospel Hymns, combining all the Excellencies of our spiritual Poets, with many Originals*. The originals number almost one hundred.

H. 411

MOULTRIE, GERARD (Rugby, 1829–85, Southleigh), was educated at Rugby and Exeter College, Oxford. After ordination, he became a master and chaplain at Shrewsbury School (1852–5). In 1869 he became vicar of Southleigh, and in 1873 warden of St. James's College there. He published *Hymns and Lyrics for the Seasons and Saints' Days of the Church* (1867) and the preface to *Cantica Sanctorum* (1880).

H. 577

MURRAY, Dom ANTHONY GREGORY, O.S.B., H.A., F.R.C.O. (London, 1905), was educated at Westminster Cathedral Choir School, where, while still a choir-boy, he acted as assistant organist to Sir Richard Terry and Ealing Priory School. He became F.R.C.O. at the age of 17. After graduating at Christ's College, Cambridge, he was organist and director of music at Downside Abbey (1932–40). He was parish priest of St. Benedict's, Hindley, Wigan (1948–52), and since then of St. Benedict's, Stratton-on-the-Fosse, Bath. He harmonized many tunes in *The Westminster Hymnal* (1940), contributing twenty-two tunes of his own. He also contributed to *Praise the Lord* (1966, rev. 1971) and the *New Catholic Hymnal* (1971). He edited *Music and Liturgy*, and is an authority on Gregorian Chant. His compositions include *Homage to Delius* (orchestra); *Organ Interludes for Liturgical Use*; settings of the Mass for congregations; and several part-songs.

T. 240

MYERS, FREDERICK WILLIAM HENRY (Keswick, 1843–1901, Rome), was educated at Cheltenham and Trinity College, Cambridge. He was a classical lecturer (1865–9), and from 1872 was on the permanent staff of school inspectors. He published many volumes of poems and monographs on Wordsworth and Shelley. He was one of the founders of the Society for Psychical Research, but his *Human Personality and its Survival* was not published till 1903, after his death.

H. 314

NAUMAN, JOHANN GOTTLIEB (Dresden, 1741–1801, Dresden), was educated at the Kreuzschule, Dresden, and studied in Italy under Tartini and G. B. Martini. He is specially known for his operas, which were in Italian, apart from three in Swedish and one in Danish. In 1763 he was appointed Court composer of sacred music. His Church music includes thirteen oratorios and twenty-one masses. He also composed several symphonies.

T. 662 (vi)

NAYLOR, EDWARD WOODALL, Mus.Doc. (Scarborough, 1867–1934, Cambridge), son of Dr. John Naylor, organist of York Minster, was trained as a chorister under his father. After periods of service in St. Michael's, Chester Square, and St. Mary's, Kilburn, London, he became, in 1897, organist of Emmanuel College, Cambridge, of which he became a lecturer and Hon. Fellow. He was also Lecturer in Musical History in the University. His first appearance as a composer was in 1892, in the old St. James's Hall,

London, with *Merlin and the Gleam*. He published *The Angelus*, an opera performed at Covent Garden in 1909; *Arthur the King*; *Pax Dei*, a requiem; anthems, etc. He also published *The Poets and Music* (1928).

T. 441

NAZIANZEN, ST. GREGORY. See GREGORY.

NEALE, JOHN MASON, D.D. (London, 1818-66, East Grinstead), was educated at Sherborne Grammar School and Trinity College, Cambridge. He became a Fellow of Downing College. In 1843 he was presented to the small living of Crawley, Sussex, but he was never instituted to the charge, owing to an attack of lung trouble compelling him to go to Madeira. There he was able to read widely and to store up materials for his subsequent books. In 1846 Earl de la Warr presented him to the wardenship of Sackville College, East Grinstead. There the learned hymnologist and liturgiologist was allowed to remain for the rest of his life. The only preferment ever offered him was the Provostship of St. Ninian's Cathedral, Perth, but the climate was too cold to permit him to reside there. In the face of bitter opposition he instituted a number of beneficent agencies—the sisterhood of St. Margaret's at East Grinstead, an orphanage for girls, and at Aldershot a house for the reclamation of fallen women. This last had to be closed because of the opposition. For fourteen years Neale was inhibited by his bishop. He occupied himself in literary pursuits, producing *A Commentary on the Psalms, from Primitive and Mediaeval Writers* (with Dr. Littledale); *The History of the Holy Eastern Church*; *The Patriarchate of Alexandria*; *Essays on Liturgiology and Church History*. But his chief title to remembrance rests on his translations. He brought to light rich treasures of Greek and Latin hymns, many of which had long been buried in monasteries and cathedral libraries on the Continent and in Asia Minor. He published from the Latin— *Mediaeval Hymns and Sequences*; *The Hymnal Noted* (94 hymns out of 105 translated from Latin are his); *Hymns, chiefly Mediaeval, on the Joys and Glories of Paradise*; and from the Greek, *Hymns of the Eastern Church*. He claimed no rights in his hymns, holding that 'a hymn, whether original or translated, ought, the moment it is published, to become the common property of Christendom, the author retaining no private right in it whatever'.

H. 10, 45, 105, 165, 183, 192, 198, 209, 217, 233, 256, 257, 267, 269, 274, 277, 373, 535, 537, 540, 645, 661

NEANDER, JOACHIM (Bremen, 1650-80, Bremen), whose real name was Neumann, was educated at the Pädagogium and the Gymnasium Illustre in his native city. He associated himself with the Pietists. His zeal, when appointed in 1674 to the headmastership of the Reformed Grammar School at Düsseldorf, induced him to go beyond his official duty and seek, by preaching and private religious meetings, the spiritual good of his fellow townsmen. Opposition was provoked and he was suspended from office and obliged to leave the town. In 1679 he returned to Bremen as second preacher in St. Martin's, but died the following year. He wrote some sixty hymns, many of which are still used in the Reformed and Lutheran Churches there, and composed tunes for them. They were collected and published in 1680 under the curious title *A und Ω, Joachimi Neander Glaub- und Liebes-übung*.

H. 9, 405

T. 313, 355, 405 (i)

NEUMARK, GEORG (Langensalya, Thuringia, 1621–81, Weimar), was the son of a clothier. He was educated at the Gymnasia of Schleusingen and Gotha. On his way to Königsberg to attend the University there, the only one which the Thirty Years War had left undisorganized, he was robbed by highwaymen on the Gardelegen Heath, and stripped of all his possessions but his prayer-book and a little money. The University having been thus made impossible, he tried to find employment, but sought it in town after town in vain. His privations were severe. At last, in Kiel, he succeeded in enlisting the interest of a fellow Thuringian who was chief pastor there, and who got him a tutorship. This sudden relief was the occasion of his composing the hymn and tune in CH3. In Kiel he remained till he had saved enough money to enable him to matriculate at Königsberg (1643). There he studied law, and, under Simon Dach, poetry. On leaving the University he moved about, earning a precarious living, as he could—to Warsaw, Thorn, Danzig, and in 1651 to Hamburg. There again he suffered great poverty through unemployment. When things were at their worst with him, a servant of the Swedish Ambassador, Baron von Rosenkranz, enlisted his master's interest on behalf of this case of suffering genius, and employment was found for him. Afterwards he returned to Thuringia and was appointed Court poet, librarian, and registrar to the administration of Duke Wilhelm II of Saxe-Weimar, and finally custodian of the ducal archives. In 1656 he was made secretary of the Fruit-Bearing Society, the principal German literary union of the seventeenth century. Blindness overtook him in 1681. The hymns of his prosperous years were markedly inferior to those written during his years of hardship.

H. 668

T. 162, 668

NEWBOLT, MICHAEL ROBERT (Dymock, Gloucestershire, 1874–1956, Aylesbury, Buckinghamshire), son of W. C. E. Newbolt, vicar of Dymock, was educated at Radley and St. John's College, Oxford. After ordination and a curacy, he became vicar of Iffley, Oxfordshire, Principal of Dorchester Missionary College, and vicar of St. Michael's, Brighton. He was Canon Residentiary of Chester Cathedral (1927–46). His publications include *The Manifold Wisdom of God*; *Healing*; *The Bible and the Ministry*, etc.

H. 550

NEWMAN, JOHN HENRY, Cardinal, D.D. (London, 1801–90, Edgbaston), son of a banker, had Huguenot blood in him, and was brought up in the evangelical faith. Educated at Trinity College, Oxford, he became a Fellow of Oriel and the vice-president of St. Alban's Hall. From 1828 to 1843 he was vicar of St. Mary the Virgin, the University Church. When he set himself, with others like-minded, to lead the Church of England towards the revival of religion of which they saw its desperate need, the movement he headed turned its face resolutely to the past. It conceived the proper bulwark against the dangers of the time to be a revival of the mystical glories of the Middle Ages. But his idealization of that period was unhistorical; the glories he was fain to lead the Church back to were largely creations of a romantic imagination. A weapon was needed with which to smite the liberal movement; he sought it in a Church whose divinely-given authority would lay under subjection the spirit of free reason in which he saw the root of modern ills. But the notes of authority seemed to him lacking in the Church of England. Driven by his own processes of reason to the conclusion that it was neither apostolic nor catholic, he came to believe that the only Church that answered those requirements was the Church of Rome. Resigning his living, he spent three years in an agony of doubt and hesitation at Littlemore; then, in 1845, he was received into the Roman Communion. His career in that Church was a record of frustration and failure. For nearly forty years he lived a secluded life at the Oratory of St. Philip Neri, Edgbaston, Birmingham. He was intensely unhappy, despite his protestations of having found the haven for his spirit. His *Apologia pro Vita Sua* was at once a powerful defence of the system for which he had left Anglicanism, and a noble vindication of his own sincerity, which Kingsley had impugned. Consolation for long neglect came to him in 1879, in his elevation to the dignity of the cardinalate. This honour, and the veneration felt for his saintly life, made quietly happy the last ten years.

H. 13, 238, 400, 682

NEWTON, JOHN (London, 1725-1807, London), was the son of a ship-master. His mother, a godly and pious woman, died when he was 7 years old. The boy went for some years to sea with his father, was impressed on board a man-of-war, and became a midshipman in the navy. Attempting to desert, he was flogged and degraded, and soon after took service on a slave-trading ship bound for Africa. In 1748 a study of Thomas à Kempis, and a night spent in fear of imminent death, combined to effect his conversion. During the six following years he commanded a slave ship, and felt no scruples as to the lawfulness of his trade, though in after years he was its ardent opponent. His religious convictions deepening, in 1764 he took Orders and accepted the curacy of Olney. With the poet Cowper he produced the *Olney Hymns* (1779), of which he wrote 280 and Cowper sixty-eight. In 1779 Newton became rector of St. Mary Woolnoth, London, where he remained till his death.

H. 376, 421, 634, 639, 667

NICHOLSON, SYDNEY HUGO, D.Mus. (London, 1875-1947, Ashford, Kent), was educated at Rugby, New College, Oxford, and the Royal College of Music. In 1904 he was appointed organist of Carlisle Cathedral; in 1908 of Manchester Cathedral; and in 1918 of Westminster Abbey. In 1927 he resigned to found St. Nicholas College of English Church Music. He published, along with G. L. H. Gardner, *A Manual of English Church Music* (1923), and later *Quires and Places where they Sing*. He was music adviser of

Hymns Ancient and Modern (1916). He composed a number of hymn-tunes and a Service in D♭.

T. 550

NICOLAI, PHILIPP, D.D. (Mengeringhausen, Waldeck, 1556-1608, Hamburg), was the son of a Lutheran pastor who dropped his patronymic of Rafflenböl in favour of an adaptation of his father's Christian name Nicolaus. He studied at the universities of Erfurt and Wittenberg. Ordained at 20 to a pastorate in his native town, he passed in 1583 to Herdecke in the Ruhr, but, most of the town council being Roman Catholics, he found the position one of great difficulty; finally, in 1586, when one of his colleagues, emboldened by the Spanish invasion, reintroducing the mass, he resigned office. For a time he ministered to a secret Lutheran congregation in the Catholic stronghold of Cologne; then held pastorates at Niederwildungen and Altwildungen; was Court preacher to the Dowager Countess of Waldeck and tutor to her son; and after five years of pastorate at Unna, Westphalia, was from 1601 till his death chief pastor of St. Katherine, Hamburg. During his Unna ministry a severe visitation of the plague moved him to write and publish his *Freuden-Spiegel des ewigen Lebens* (Frankfurt, 1599), in which appeared the words and melodies of the two great chorales on which Bach based two of his Church cantatas—*Wachet auf* and *Wie schön leuchtet uns der Morgenstern*.

H. 202, 315

T. 202, 315

NILES, DANIEL THAMBYRAJAH, D.Th., D.D. (Telipallai, Ceylon, 1908-70, Vellore, India), worked with the World Student Christian Federation and the Y.M.C.A. A Methodist minister, he was President of the Ceylon Conference in 1968. Though a world figure, he was concerned that the Asian Churches should make their own impression of the faith meaningful for their own countries, so as General Secretary of the East Asia Christian Conference he prepared an Asian hymn-book, in which Asian music, as well as Asian words, was seen to be important. He also was one of the presidents of the World Council of Churches. His hymns are found in many books in many lands. Among his publications are *Whose I am and Whom I serve*; *That they may have Life*; *Reading the Bible Today*; *Upon the Earth*; *As Seeing the Invisible*, etc.

H. 415

NOEL, CAROLINE MARIA (Teston, Kent, 1817-77, London), was a daughter of the Revd. and Hon. Canon Gerard Thomas Noel, himself a hymn-writer. She wrote her first hymns at 17, but her muse was silent from her twentieth to her fortieth year. Her hymns were published in two volumes, *The Name of Jesus, and Other Verses for the Sick and Lonely* (1861) and *The Name of Jesus, and Other Poems* (1878).

H. 300

NORTH, FRANK MASON, M.A. (New York, 1850-1935, Madison, New Jersey), was a Methodist Episcopal minister. He held several pastorates in Connecticut (1873-92). He was one of the founders and secretary of the New

York City Extension and Missionary Society (1892-1912), of the Methodist Board of Foreign Missions (1912-35), and President of the Federal Council of the Churches of Christ in America (1912-16). He was one of the founders of the Methodist Federation for Social Services. He contributed to *Sursum Corda* (1898) and *The Methodist Hymnal* (U.S.A., 1905).

H. 512

NYBERG, HUGO (Helsingfors, Finland, 1873-1935, Helsingfors), was educated at Helsingfors, ordained in 1898, and became in 1907 a district minister to the deaf and dumb. He founded the Y.M.C.A. choir in Helsingfors. He had no professional music training, and wrote but few tunes.

T. 666

OAKELEY, FREDERICK, D.D. (Shrewsbury, 1802-80, London), son of Sir Charles Oakeley, Bt., was educated at Oxford, where he became a Fellow of Balliol. Under the influence of his brother-in-law, William George Ward, he became deeply interested in the Tractarian Movement, and when, in 1839, he entered upon the incumbency of Margaret Chapel, London (later, All Saints, Margaret Street), he introduced an ultra-ritualistic service. A crisis was precipitated, by his publication of pamphlets, in the controversy about Tract XC, asserting his right 'to hold, as distinct from teaching, all Roman doctrine'. This led to his licence being withdrawn and to his suspension from clerical duty until he retracted his errors. Instead of retracting he resigned his prebendal stall at Lichfield and all appointments in the Church of England, joined Newman at Littlemore, and in the same year (1845) was received into the Church of Rome. He published a preface on antiphonal chanting to Redhead's *Laudes Diurnae*; *Lyra Liturgica* (1865); and many works on Roman doctrine and worship.

H. 191

OGLEVEE, LOUISE M., *née* MCAROY (Chicago, 1872-1953, Rock Island, Illinois), was educated at Geneva High School and the National Kindergarten and Elementary College, now the National College of Education. In 1895 she married the Revd. William G. Oglevee, D.D. As a Director of Education in the Presbyterian Church, U.S., she wrote many books, including *The Beginners Department* (1919); *Cradle Roll Lessons* (1924); *The Child's First Songs in Religious Education* (1927); *Nursery Class Plans and Stories* (1929); as well as contributing articles and stories to educational and religious journals and magazines. She was a contributor to *Songs for Early Childhood* and the *Methodist School Hymn Book*.

H. 18

OLDHAM, ARTHUR WILLIAM (London, 1926), was educated at the County Grammar School, Wallington, Surrey, and the Royal College of Music. He became musical director of the Mercury Theatre in 1949 and of the Ballet Rambert in 1946, and is Chorus Master of the Edinburgh Festival Chorus, the Scottish Opera Chorus, and the London Symphony Orchestra Chorus. He has contributed to the *Cambridge Hymnal* and *Sing Nowell*. Apart from incidental music for theatre and radio, he composed the ballets *Mr. Punch*,

324 BIOGRAPHICAL AND HISTORICAL NOTES

The Sailor's Return, Circus Canteen, Love in a Village, etc., orchestral works, *Divertimento for Strings, The Apotheosis of Lucius,* and a song cycle, *The Commandment of Love.*

T. 177, 300 (i)

OLIVERS, THOMAS (Tregynon, Montgomeryshire, 1725–99, London), was early left an orphan; he grew up uncared for, and had little education. He was apprenticed to a shoemaker, but for a time led a restless life, roaming about and earning a livelihood as a cobbler. He chanced to hear Whitefield preach in Bristol. This changed his life. He became one of Wesley's itinerant preachers, and for twenty-two years travelled through England, Scotland, and Ireland. In 1775 Wesley appointed him supervisor of the Methodist press, but removed him from that post in 1789 because 'the errata were insufferable and pieces were inserted in the magazine without his knowledge'. He spent the rest of his life in retirement in London. He wrote several hymns, and one celebrated tune 'Olivers', now known as 'Helmsley'.

H. 358

T. 316

ORR, ROBIN, C.B.E., M.A., Mus.D., F.R.C.M. (Brechin, Scotland, 1909), was educated at Loretto School, the Royal College of Music, and Cambridge, becoming a Fellow of St. John's College. He also studied in Italy and France. He was Director of Music at Sidcot School (1933–6), Assistant Lecturer in Music at Leeds University (1936–8), and Organist and Director of Music in St. John's College (1938–51). He served in the R.A.F. during the war (1939–45). He was University Lecturer at Cambridge (1947–56), Professor at the R.C.M. (1950–6), and Professor of Music at the University of Glasgow (1956–65). Since 1965 he has been Professor of Music in the University of Cambridge. Since 1962 he has also been Chairman of Scottish Opera. His main compositions include two symphonies and two overtures for full orchestra; *Rhapsody* for strings; incidental music for Greek plays, *Oedipus,* etc.; *Spring Cantata; Philip Sparrow* and *Journey and Places* for mezzo-soprano and strings; Church music, songs, and chamber music; *Full Circle* (one-act opera) and *Hermiston* (three-act opera for 1975 Edinburgh Festival).

T. 325

OSWALD, HEINRICH SIEGMUND (Nimmersatt, near Liegnitz, Silesia, 1751–1834, Breslau), received his education at Schmiedeberg, Silesia, then, in 1765–6, entered the office of his brother Ferdinand, who held a public appointment. Seven years later he became secretary to the Landgrave von Prittwitz at Glatz, but illness lost him this position, and he returned to Schmiedeberg and entered the service of a merchant who sent him on business to Hamburg. Later, he tried business for himself at Breslau, but was not successful, and he took work again as a merchant's clerk. His circumstances subsequently improved; in 1790 King Friedrich Wilhelm II of Prussia appointed him a Court councillor at Potsdam, and in the following year he was made a privy councillor. On the king's death he received a pension, and retired with his family to Hirschberg, and afterwards to Breslau. His years of retirement he devoted to the composition of poetical, musical, and religious works.

H. 671

OUSELEY, Sir FREDERICK ARTHUR GORE, Bt., M.A., Mus.Doc., LL.D. (London, 1825–89, Hereford), was the son of Sir William Gore Ouseley, Bt., a distinguished Oriental scholar who was ambassador to Persia and then at St. Petersburg. He was educated privately and at Christ Church, Oxford. He succeeded to the baronetcy in 1844; received the Mus.Doc. degree from Durham, Oxford, Cambridge, and Dublin; and was made LL.D. by Cambridge and Edinburgh. Taking Holy Orders in 1849 he became curate of St. Barnabas', Pimlico, and St. Paul's, Knightsbridge; precentor of Hereford Cathedral in 1855, in which year also he was appointed Professor of Music in the University of Oxford; and Canon Residentiary of Hereford, 1886. He had shown a remarkable gift for music from infancy; he composed when only 3 years old, and exhibited a marked talent for extemporizing at 5; at 8 he composed an opera to words by Metastasio. His wealth enabled him to amass a unique music library, and to found, build, and partly endow, on an estate of his own near Tenbury, a church and college dedicated to St. Michael and All Angels, 'as a means of promoting the Church services of the Church of England, but also to give at a moderate cost, and in some cases with considerable assistance, to those who need it, a liberal and classical education, to the sons of the clergy and other gentlemen, combined with sound Church teaching'. Of this institution he was first vicar and warden, and John Stainer first organist. Ouseley wrote valuable treatises on harmony, counterpoint, and musical form and composition, and a very large quantity of music— about 100 anthems, church services, hymn-tunes, chants and carols, two oratorios, and much organ music. He was closely associated with *Hymns Ancient and Modern*.

C. 3 (ii)

OWENS, PRISCILLA JANE (Baltimore, 1829–1907, Baltimore), was of Scottish descent. She was engaged in public school work at Baltimore. For fifty years she was active in Sunday-school work, and most of her hymns were written for children's services.

H. 412, 475

OXENHAM, JOHN (Manchester, 1852–1941, London), was educated at Old Trafford School and Victoria University, Manchester. After being engaged in business for some years, and travelling on the Continent and in America, he settled in London and took up writing. During this time he was a deacon in Ealing Congregational Church, where he also conducted a Bible Class. Besides novels he published about twenty volumes of verse and prose.

H. 425

PALMER, GEORGE HERBERT, B.A., D.Mus. (Grantchester, 1846–1926, Oxford), was educated at Trinity College, Cambridge. He began his ministerial career as curate of St. Margaret's, Toxteth Park, Liverpool. His published works include *The Antiphoner and Grail* (1881); *Harmonies of the Office Hymn-Book* (1891); *The Sarum Psalter* (1894). His *magnum opus* was *The Diurnal after the Use of the illustrious Church of Salisbury* and was only completed shortly before his death. It was published in two parts in 1926 and 1929.

T. 187

PALMER, HORATIO RICHMOND, Mus.Doc. (Sherburne, New York, 1834–1907, Yonkers, New York), studied at Berlin and Florence, was an organist at 17, and became director of Rushford Academy of Music, New York, in 1857. In 1861 he settled in Chicago, and established the magazine *Concordia* in 1866. He returned to New York in 1874, and in 1884 took charge of the Church Choral Union for the improvement of Church music. In 1887 he became dean of the school of music at Chautaugua. His choral collections include *The Song Queen, The Song King*, and *The Song Herald*. He also wrote *A Theory of Music* and *A Manual for Teachers*.

H. 482

T. 482

PALMER, RAY, D.D. (Little Compton, Rhode Island, 1808–87, Newark, New Jersey), was the son of a judge. He studied at Phillips' Academy, Andover, and at Yale. He became minister of the Central Congregational Church, Bath, Maine, where the best of his hymns were written; then of the First Congregational Church, Albany, New York; then Corresponding Secretary of the American Congregational Union. In 1879 he retired to Newark. He published *Hymns and Sacred Pieces* (1865) and *Hymns of my Holy Hours* (1867).

H. 81, 571, 674

PARKER, WILLIAM HENRY (New Basford, Nottingham, 1845–1929, Cambridge), the head of an insurance company, was a General Baptist by church affiliation. His active interest in Sunday-school work led him to write hymns for anniversaries. In 1882 he published *The Princess Alice and Other Poems*.

H. 124

PARRY, Sir CHARLES HUBERT HASTINGS, Bt., Mus.Doc. (Bournemouth, 1848–1918, Rustington, Littlehampton), was the son of Thomas Gambier Parry, of Highnam Court, Gloucestershire. He was educated at Twyford, near Winchester, Eton, and Exeter College, Oxford. While still at Eton he took the Oxford Mus.Bac. degree. In 1883 he became Professor of Composition and Lecturer in Musical History in the R.C.M., and also Choragus at Oxford. He was knighted in the same year, and made a baronet in 1905. His books include *The Art of Music*; *The Eighteenth Century* in *The Oxford History of Music*; *Style in Musical Art*; *Bach*; and *College Addresses*.

T. 76 (ii), 244, 353, 372, 460, 487, 510, 615

PARRY, JOSEPH, Mus.Doc. (Merthyr Tydfil, 1841–1903, Penarth), showed marked musical gifts in childhood, but had to begin work at a puddling-furnace when only 10 years old. In 1854 he emigrated to America. On a return visit he won Eisteddfod prizes. He took his Mus.Bac. degree at Cambridge in 1871, and his doctorate seven years later. In 1874 he became Professor of Music in University College, Aberystwyth, and in 1888 Lecturer in Music, University College of South Wales, Cardiff. He wrote oratorios, cantatas, operas, choral works of all kinds, and some instrumental music, as well as anthems and many scores of hymn-tunes. He edited the collection of Welsh songs known as *Cambrian Minstrelsie*.

T. 78 (i)

PATRICK, ST. (Dumbarton?, c. 390–461, Saul), the apostle and patron saint of Ireland, is said to have come of clerical descent, his father having been a deacon and his grandfather a presbyter. At the age of 16 he was carried off to Ireland, where he was sold as a slave. During his captivity he became a Christian. But Ireland's need of the Gospel gave him no rest, and he returned to spend his life in heroic efforts to win its people for Christ. The story of his life is involved in a mass of doubtful legendary matter, but there is no doubt about his apostolic zeal. By the time of his death Ireland had been to a great extent Christianized. Before long the Irish Church was sending missionaries abroad, and Ireland won fame throughout Western Europe as 'the land of Saints and Scholars'.

H. 401, 402

PEACE, ALBERT LISTER, Mus.Doc. (Huddersfield, 1844–1912, Blundell-sands), was a child prodigy in music; at 4 or 5 he could name any note or chord struck on the piano. Yet he had no great education in music; he was practically self-taught. At 9 years of age he was appointed organist of Holmfirth Parish Church, Yorkshire. In rapid succession thereafter he passed through the following appointments—Dewsbury Parish Church; St. Thomas's, Huddersfield; Brunswick Street Chapel, Huddersfield; Providence Place Chapel, Cleckheaton; Trinity Congregational Church, Glasgow; the University, Glasgow; St. John's Episcopal Church, Hillhead Parish Church, St. Andrew's Hall—all in Glasgow; until, in 1879, he was appointed to Glasgow Cathedral. There he remained till 1897, when he went as organist of St. George's Hall, Liverpool, a post which he held till his death.

T. 677

PEARSALL, ROBERT LUCAS DE (Clifton, 1795–1856, Wartensee, Constance), was educated for the Bar. After practising for four years, in 1825 he forsook law for music, studying at Mainz and elsewhere on the Continent. Thereafter most of his life was spent in Germany, first at Carlsruhe (1830–7) and then at the Castle of the Wartensee. An archaeologist, he became a Roman Catholic, and called himself 'de' Pearsall. He wrote and composed madrigals and part-songs. The St. Gall *Catholisches Gesangbuch* of 1863 was partly edited by him.

T. 235, 541

PEEBLES, DAVID (?–1579, St. Andrews, Fife), was a conventual brother of the Abbey of St. Andrews and a distinguished musician. He arranged in four parts the canticle *Si quis diligit me* and presented it to James V, c. 1530. After the Reformation he was invited by the prior, Lord James Stewart, to harmonize the psalms and hymns of the Reformed Church. All the psalms, except two, in the *Scottish Psalter* of Thomas Wood, or *St. Andrews Psalter* of 1566 are from his hand. He also composed a motet in four parts *Quam multi Domine sunt* for 'My Lord Marche'. His name is sometimes spelled Peblis or Pables.

T. 140 (i), 321 (i), 370

PENNEFATHER, WILLIAM, B.A. (Dublin, 1816–73, Muswell Hill, London), was the son of a Baron of the Irish Exchequer. Education at Westbury, near Bristol, and Trinity College, Dublin, was followed by his ordination in 1841. He was curate for a time at Ballymacugh, and vicar of Mellifont, near Drogheda. In 1848 he removed to England, where he held the incumbencies of Trinity Church, Walton, Aylesbury; Christ Church, Barnet; and St. Jude's, Mildmay Park, East London. At Barnet he began a series of conferences which he continued to hold at Mildmay. There he introduced into England the Order of Deaconesses. His hymns, written for his conferences, were collected in *Hymns, Original and Selected* (1872) and *Original Hymns and Thoughts in Verse* (1873).

H. 11

PERKINS, JEANETTE. See BROWN, JEANETTE PERKINS.

PERRONET, EDWARD (Sundridge, Kent, 1726–92, Canterbury), belonged to a family of French refugees who had lived at Chateau d'Oex in Switzerland. His father, Vincent Perronet, vicar of Shoreham, was greatly esteemed by the Wesleys. He became one of Wesley's itinerant preachers. In *The Mitre*, a religious satire published in 1757, he attacked the abuses of the Church in a way which aroused Wesley's anger, and the book was suppressed. He also differed from Wesley in urging separation from the Church of England, and the grant of licence to itinerant preachers to administer the sacraments. By 1771 he had ceased co-operation with the Wesleys, and had joined the Countess of Huntingdon's Connexion. She in turn disagreed with him owing to his violent language about the Church of England, and he ended his days as pastor of a small Independent church at Canterbury.

H. 382

PESTEL, THOMAS (?, 1584–1667, Leicester), was educated at Queens' College, Cambridge. He was vicar of Packington, Leicestershire, but in 1644 resigned his living to his son and became his curate. Both were removed by a county committee in 1646 for observing 'ceremonies'. His hymns are in his *Sermons and Devotions, Old and New* (1659).

H. 197

PETRI, THEODORICUS (DIDRIX) (Borga, Finland, 16th century–?, Poland), was a student at the University of Rostock when he compiled *Piae Cantiones* (1582), desiring to preserve for future use some of the most beautiful psalms, hymns, and school songs of the medieval Church. Most of the contents were doubtless of Suedo-Finnish origin, but some were from pre-Reformation German hymn-books, others, of Hussite parentage, from Bohemia and Moravia, some from Lutheran song-books. The best known of all the melodies is the fourteenth-century spring carol, 'Tempus adest floridum', to which Dr. Neale wrote the famous Christmas carol, 'Good King Wenceslas'.

Petri became secretary to King Sigismund in 1591, but of his later history little is known except that his last years were spent in Poland.

H. 187

T. 187, 198, 274

PETTMAN, CHARLES EDGAR (Faversham, Kent, 1866-1943, Battersea), was a London organist, composer, and editor. He specialized in arranging old French and Spanish carols. He contributed to *The University Carol Book* and *Sunday School Praise*.

T. 195 (ii), 415

PHILLIPS, ALAN NORMAN, M.A., L.R.A.M. (Chatham, Kent, 1910), was educated at Sir Joseph Williamson's Mathematical School, Rochester, Downing College, Cambridge, and Matthay School of Music, Liverpool. He was senior German master at Wirral Grammar School for Boys, Bibington, Wirral, Cheshire (1932-70), part-time music master at Wirral County Grammar School for Girls (1970-1), and is now retired. He has written both poetry and music, but any that has been published has been in leaflet form.

H. 506

PHILLIPS, EDNA MARTHA (Sandycroft, Flintshire, 1904), was educated at Queensferry Council School and Hawarden County School, Flintshire, and was a teacher in the former from 1924 to 1946. Her husband, now retired, was minister of Alpha Presbyterian Church, Builth Wells, Brecon.

H. 690

PIERPOINT, FOLLIOTT SANDFORD, M.A. (Bath, 1835-1917, Bath), was educated at the Grammar School, Bath, and Queens' College, Cambridge. For a time he was classical master at the Somersetshire College. Thereafter he lived at various places, principally at Babbacombe, on a small patrimony, and occasionally doing a little classical teaching. He contributed to *Lyra Eucharistica*, was the author of the Hymns for the Canonical Hours in *The Hymnal Noted*, and published collections of his poems—*The Chalice of Nature and Other Poems*; *Songs of Love*; *Lyra Jesu*.

H. 367

PIGGOTT, WILLIAM CHARTER (Leighton Buzzard, Bedfordshire, 1872-1943, London), was educated at Huddersfield College and Headingley College for the Wesleyan ministry. He entered the Congregational ministry in 1902. After serving charges at Grenville Place, London, and Bunyan Meeting, Bedford, he succeeded the Revd. C. Silvester Horne at Whitefield's, Tottenham Court Road, London, and then at Streatham. He was chairman of The Congregational Union in 1931-2.

H. 134, 538

PITT-WATSON, IAN ROBERTSON, M.A., B.D., L.R.A.M. (Damuir, near Glasgow, 1923), was educated at Dollar Academy and Edinburgh University. Following ordination he was senior assistant minister at St. Giles' Cathedral, Edinburgh (1950-2), chaplain to the University of Aberdeen (1952-8), minister of St. James's Parish Church, Forfar, and Minister of New Kilpatrick Parish Church, Bearsden, Glasgow (1961-72). Since 1972 he has been Professor of Practical Theology at Christ's College, Aberdeen. In 1972-4 he delivered the Warrack Lectures on 'Theology is for Preaching'. He has published *Lively Oracles*; *Letters on Pacifism* with Professor John Ferguson; and *Worship Now*, with Professor David Cairns, Professor James Whyte, and T. B. Honeyman.

H. 64, 68, 126

PLACZEK, Mrs. H. K. See STRUTHER, JAN.

PLAYFORD, JOHN (Norwich, *c.* 1623-86, London), came into prominence as a music publisher in London *c.* 1648, and from 1652 until he retired he kept a shop in the Inner Temple. He virtually had a monopoly of music publishing during the Commonwealth and for some years afterwards. He published *Introduction to the Skill of Musick* (1654); *Cantica Sacra* (1662) with a second set in 1673; *Psalms and Hymns in Solemn Musick* (1671); and *The Whole Booke of Psalms* (1671). In 1658 he invented the 'new ty'd note' in printing music.

T. 6, 147

PLUMPTRE, EDWARD HAYES, D.D. (London, 1821-91, Wells), was educated at King's College, London, and University College, Oxford. He became a Fellow of Brasenose. Ordained in 1846, he was successively chaplain of King's College, London; assistant preacher Lincoln's Inn; Dean of Queen's College, Oxford; prebendary of St. Paul's, and Professor of New Testament Exegesis, King's College, London; rector of Pluckley, Kent; vicar of Bickley, Kent; and in 1881, Dean of Wells.

H. 214, 424

POLLOCK, THOMAS BENSON, M.A. (Strathallan, Isle of Man, 1836-96, Birmingham), was educated at Trinity College, Dublin. He began the study of medicine and walked the London hospitals, but took ordination in 1861. After curacies at St. Luke's, Leek, Staffordshire, and St. Thomas's, Stamford Hill, London, he became, in 1865, curate to his brother, the Revd. J. S. Pollock, vicar of the mission charge of St. Alban's, Bordesley, Birmingham. St. Alban's became the High Church stronghold of Birmingham, and 'Father' Pollock and his brother 'Father Tom' were for a time opposed, but their devotion and self-sacrifice turned all adverse feeling into admiration. After thirty years as curate 'Father Tom' succeeded his brother as vicar, but he died ten months afterwards. He was a member for a time of the committee of *Hymns Ancient and Modern*. He specialized in the metrical litany, and published in 1870 *Metrical Litanies for Special Services and General Use*. He contributed some hymns also to *The Gospeller*, the St. Alban's parish magazine, of which he was editor.

H. 490

POOLE, CLEMENT WILLIAM (Ealing, 1828–1924, Ealing), son of a bencher of Gray's Inn, was appointed at 18 to a junior clerkship in the Audit Office, but relinquished his appointment in the late 1850s to engage in commerce. Music was his chief interest, and being deeply religious, he found happiness in serving the Church with his gifts. He acted as honorary organist of the parish church, Kingston-upon-Thames; Christ Church, Ealing; and Holy Trinity, Ramsgate. He composed over thirty hymn-tunes, a *Magnificat*, several marches, etc.

T. 444

POPPLE, HERBERT (Berkhamsted, 1891–1965, Berkhamsted, Hertfordshire), was educated at Lichfield Theological College and University College, Durham. After war service, he was ordained in 1923, was curate of St. Mary's, Blyth (1923–30), and then of St. Peter's, Streatham. He published a nativity play *The Prince of Peace*, and two masses.

T. 633

POSTON, ELIZABETH (Highfield, Hertfordshire, 1905), was educated at the Royal College of Music. For a period she turned her interest to art. In 1925 she published seven poems, including *Sweet Suffolk Owl*, and later a sonata for violin and pianoforte. The years 1930–9 were spent in foreign travel, and in 1940 she joined the B.B.C. becoming Director of Music in the European Service. She resigned in 1945 to devote herself to composition, and has written the scores for many broadcast plays and programmes, including Milton's *Comus* and *Paradise Lost*, for lives of Suckling, Herrick, and Donne, for *The Elizabethans* and *Twelfth Night*. Her choral works include *Balulalow*, *Carol in Captivity*, *Carol for the Crown*, and many songs. She was music editor for *The Cambridge Hymnal* (1967).

T. 277, 308

POTT, FRANCIS, M.A. (Southwark, 1832–1909, Speldhurst), was educated at Brasenose College, Oxford. Ordained in 1856, he became curate of Bishopsworth, Somerset; of Ardingley, Sussex; and of Ticehurst, Sussex; and was rector of Northill, Bedfordshire, from 1866 to 1891, when he retired owing to increasing deafness, and went to live at Speldhurst, near Tunbridge Wells. He was a member of the original committee that produced *Hymns Ancient and Modern*. In 1861 he published *Hymns fitted to the Order of Common Prayer*. His keen interest in the reform of chanting led him to publish *The Free Rhythm Psalter* (1898). He also wrote a book on the *Te Deum*, and a pamphlet on the Athanasian Creed.

H. 210, 266, 455

PRAETORIUS, MICHAEL (Kreutzburg, Thuringia, 1571–1621, Goslar), whose family name was Schultz, was educated at the University of Frankfurt-on-Oder. He became Kapellmeister at Lüneburg, and later prior of the monastery of Ringelheim, Goslar. He published *Musae Sionae* (1609) and *Syntagma Musicum*, in four parts, the first appearing in 1614, the second and third in 1619. No copy is extant of the fourth.

T. 288 (i), 459, 596

PRICHARD, ROWLAND HUW (Graienyn, near Bala, 1811–87, Holywell), spent most of his life at Bala, but in 1880 moved to Holywell Mill and was given a position as a loom-tender's assistant. He possessed a good voice and acted as a precentor. Many good tunes composed by him appeared in Welsh periodicals; 'Hyfrydol' was a composition of his youth. In 1844 he published *Cyfaill y Cantorion* (the Singer's Friend), mostly made up of his own original tunes.

T. 381, 437

PRITCHARD, THOMAS CUTHBERTSON LEITHEAD, M.A., Mus.Bac., F.R.C.O. (Glasgow, 1885–1960, Glasgow), was educated at the University of Glasgow, and was a graduate in music of Trinity College, Dublin. He studied Church music at York Minster. He was organist and choirmaster of Fullarton Church, Irvine; St. Stephen's United Free Church, Glasgow; North United Free Church, Bearsden; Sherbrook United Free Church, Glasgow; and from 1913 of Belhaven United Free Church, Glasgow. He was a professor in the Athenaeum School of Music; supervisor of music in schools under the Education Authority; lecturer on Church music in a school of training for organists under the Church of Scotland and the United Free Church of Scotland; and was a well-known recitalist. He wrote much music, and a number of articles on musical subjects. As representing the Glasgow Society of Organists, he was an associate member of the revision committee which produced the R.C.H., and a member of the music sub-committee and the editorial committee of musical experts, and was music editor of *The Scottish Psalter*, 1929.

T. 5, 387 (iii), 626

PROCTER, ADELAIDE ANNE (London, 1825–64, London), was the eldest daughter of Bryan Waller Procter (Barry Cornwall), a barrister and commissioner in lunacy, and was an intimate friend of Charles Lamb, Leigh Hunt, and Dickens. Her first poems were sent to Dickens as editor of *Household Words*, under the name of 'Mary Berwick', and were supposed by him to be the work of a governess who had been long in the same family, and had accompanied them to Italy. He had continued publishing her contributions for nearly two years before he discovered through her mother that she was the daughter of his old friends. Two series of her poems were issued under the title *Legends and Lyrics, a Book of Verse*, in 1858 and 1862. In 1851 she entered the Roman Church, but her spirit was in the true sense catholic, and it is difficult to tell from her hymns to which communion she belonged. Some of her songs became popular, such as 'Cleansing Fire', 'The Requital', and 'The Lost Chord'.

H. 146

PRUDENTIUS, AURELIUS CLEMENS (348–c. 413), one of the best and most prolific of early Latin Christian poets, was born in the North of Spain. We know little of his life beyond what he tells us himself. From this it appears that he received a legal training, held a judicial post in two successive cities, and was afterwards promoted to an office of some dignity at the Imperial Court. In his fifty-seventh year he entered a monastery, and began to exercise the talent on which his fame now rests. Centos from his works are freely used in the ancient Breviaries and Hymnaries. His best works are *Liber Cathemerinon*, or hymns for the twelve hours of the day, and *Liber Peristephanon*, hymns of the saints who had won the martyr's crown.

H. 198, 199

PRYS, EDMUND (Maen Twrog, Merionethshire, 1541?–1624, Maen Twrog), after studying at St. John's College, Cambridge, became rector of Festiniog, with the chapelry of Maen Twrog, in 1569; the rectory of Llaneddwyn was added in 1580, with the chapelry of Llanddwywe. In 1567 he became Archdeacon of Merioneth, and chaplain to Sir Henry Sidney, Lord President of Wales, and in 1602 received the second canonry of St. Asaph. He was an accomplished composer in Welsh metres, but did not adopt them when he translated the Psalms into Welsh, his aim being to foster congregational singing. This translation, *Llyfr y Psalmau wedi eu cyfieithu, a'u cyfansoddi ar fesur cerdd, yn gymraeg*, was appended to a new issue of *The Book of Common Prayer* in Welsh, 1621.

T. 41, 71, 85, 379

PURCELL, HENRY (London, 1659–95, London), was a chorister at the Chapel Royal (1667–73) and then was apprenticed to an organ builder called Higston. In 1677 he succeeded Matthew Lock as 'Composer to the King's Violins' and in 1679 John Blow as organist at Westminster Abbey. In 1682 he became organist to the Chapel Royal. He composed many anthems, including 'Thou knowest, Lord' for the funeral of Queen Mary II, a series of *Odes for St. Cecilia's Day*, a *Te Deum*, and *Jubilate*.

T. 10, 661

PUSEY, PHILIP, D.C.L. (Pusey, Berkshire, 1799–1855, Christ Church, Oxford), was a grandson of the 1st Viscount Folkestone and elder brother of Dr. E. B. Pusey. His father changed his name from Bouverie to Pusey on inheriting the estate of the latter name. After education at Eton and Christ Church, Oxford, he settled on his estate, and devoted himself to agriculture and public service. Later he was M.P. for Rye, Chippenham, Cashel, and Berkshire. Among his interests was hymnology; he wished to supplant Sternhold and Hopkins's version of the Psalms by Milman's hymns.

H. 491

334   BIOGRAPHICAL AND HISTORICAL NOTES

PYE, KELLOW JOHN, B.Mus. (Exeter, 1812–1901, Exmouth), studied at the Royal Academy of Music, as one of its original students. In 1842 he graduated B.Mus. at Oxford. Eleven years later he gave up music as a profession and became a wine merchant, but continued it as a leisure-time occupation. He became Director and Chairman of the R.A.M., a council member of the R.C.M., and committee member of the Bach Choir. He published many anthems, madrigals, and songs.

C. 345 (e)

QUINN, JAMES, S.J., M.A. (Glasgow, 1919), was educated at St. Aloysius' College, Glasgow, and the University of Glasgow and Heythrop College. He entered the Society of Jesus, and has been 'consultor' to the Secretariat for Christian Unity since 1968, and is a member of the Advisory Committee of the International Commission on English in the Liturgy. He has published *New Hymns for All Seasons* (1969) and *The Theology of the Eucharist* (1973).

H. 175, 276, 308, 568, 581, 589

RANDALL, JOHN, Mus.Doc. (?, 1715–99, Cambridge), was a chorister of the Chapel Royal. At the age of 17 he sang the part of Esther in Handel's oratorio of that name. He became organist of King's College, Cambridge, in 1743; Professor of Music, Cambridge University, 1755; and later, organist also of Trinity College: all three posts he held simultaneously. In 1794 he published *A Collection of Psalm Tunes, some of which are new, and others by permission of the authors, with six Chants and Te Deums, calculated for the use of Congregations in general.* Six original tunes of his own appeared in this book.

T. 435, 628

RATNAGRAHI, KAHANJI MADHAVJI (Porbandar, India, 1869–1916, Anand, India), whose surname means 'grasper of the precious stone', was a librarian in the then small city-state of Porbandar. He had written several plays and a novel and was a skilled musician. Above all, he was a great searcher after truth and it was this, following the death of his father's sister, to whom he was greatly attached, which led him first to a reforming Hindu sect and later to accept Christianity. He and his wife were baptized in 1892 by Dr. H. R. Scott (Rajkot), a missionary of the Presbyterian Church in Ireland. Later he took the four-year course at the Fleming Stevenson Memorial College, Ahmadabad (now the Gujarat United School of Theology) and finished in 1896. After two years' Bible teaching in a school at Surat, and one year as an evangelist in Brookhill village, he was ordained there in 1899, remaining there until his death in 1916. In the *Gujarati Hymnbook* he contributed some sixty of its 665 hymns. Many were original but others were translations. With regard to the latter a notable feature was that his poetic gifts made the hymns he translated seem not like translations at all.

H. 203

RAVENSCROFT, THOMAS, Mus.Bac. (?, *c.* 1592–1634, Barnet?), was a chorister of St. Paul's Cathedral, and became a Mus.Bac. of Cambridge when only 14 years of age. He edited much music, but is best known by his *Whole*

Booke of Psalmes (1621). This book contains all the psalms and hymns in the version of 'Sternhold and Hopkins'. Ravenscroft adopted practically all the proper tunes which had appeared in previous psalters, and to those psalms that had no such tunes associated with them he set a number of four-line tunes of more recent origin. There is no evidence that any of these melodies were his own. The title says that the tunes are 'composed into 4 parts by Sundry Authors'; which means that the musicians whose names were attached to the tunes were merely the harmonizers. Among these were such men as Thomas and John Tomkins, and John Milton, the father of the poet. A large number of the settings are by Ravenscroft himself. This book became a principal source book for all subsequent compilers of psalmody.

T. 27, 160, 391, 599, 636, 641

RAWNSLEY, HARDWICKE DRUMMOND, M.A. (Shiplake-on-Thames, 1851–1920, Grasmere), son of Canon Drummond Rawnsley, vicar of Shiplake, was educated at Uppingham, and Balliol College, Oxford. In 1875 he was ordained and spent two years as curate of St. Barnabas', Bristol, taking special charge of the Clifton College Mission there. In 1877 he became vicar of Wray, on Windermere, and in 1883 entered upon the incumbency of Crosthwaite, near Keswick. In 1909 he received a canonry in Carlisle Cathedral; he was also a chaplain to the King. Among his published works were *Sonnets at the English Lakes*; *Ruskin and the English Lakes*; *The Literary Associations of the Lake District*; *Valete* (poems); *The Life of Harvey Goodwin, Bishop of Carlisle*; *Memories of the Tennysons*.

H. 526

REDHEAD, RICHARD (Harrow, 1820–94, London), was educated as a chorister of Magdalen College, Oxford. He was organist of Margaret Chapel (subsequently All Saints' Church), Margaret Street, Cavendish Square, London, 1835–64; then, till 1894, of St. Mary Magdalene, Paddington. He and Canon Oakeley edited together the first Gregorian Psalter, with the title *Laudes Diurnae*. Among his many other compositions for the Church were— *Church Music* (chants, sanctuses, responses); *Hymns for Holy Seasons*; *The Celebrant's Office Book*; *The Parish Tune Book*; *The Book of Common Prayer, with Ritual Song*; *Ancient Hymn Melodies and Other Church Tunes*; *The Cathedral and Church Choir Book*. These collections exercised a leading influence on the musical side in the Catholic Revival. His own tunes were so intermingled in them with older compositions that many tunes have been attributed to him which he did not write.

T. 75 (ii), 83, 247, 302, 337, 369, 377 (ii), 378

REED, ANDREW, D.D. (Butcher Row, St. Clement Danes, London, 1787–1862, Hackney), was the son of a watchmaker, and was trained to that trade, but made his way to Hackney College to train for the Congregational ministry. He became minister of New Road Chapel, St. George's-in-the-East, in which he had been brought up; and of Wycliffe Chapel, which he built when New Road Chapel became overcrowded; here he continued from 1831 to 1861. In 1817 he published a *Hymn Book* as a supplement to Dr. Watts's and in 1842 superseded it by *The Hymn Book prepared from Dr. Watts's Psalms and Hymns and Other Authors, with some Originals*. His own twenty-one hymns were contributed to these volumes.

H. 107

REED, EDITH MARGARET GELLIBRAND (Islington, 1885-1935, Barnet), was assistant editor of *Pan Pipes* from the early 1920s until 1930, and editor of *Music and Youth* (1923-6). She was one of the contributors to the *Kingsway Carol Book, Sunday School Praise*, and *The School Assembly*.

H. 186

REES, TIMOTHY, M.C., D.D. (Llanbodarn, Trefeglwys, Cardiganshire, 1874-1939, Llandaff), was educated at Ardwyn School, Aberystwyth, and St. David's College, Lampeter. He was ordained in 1897, and after a few years as lecturer at St. Michael's College he became a member of the Community of the Resurrection. He remained here all his life until he became a bishop in 1931, except during the time he was a chaplain to the Forces (1915-19). He was Bishop of Llandaff (1931-9).

H. 334, 473

REICHARDT, LUISE (Berlin, 1779-1826, Hamburg), was the daughter of the German musician and composer, Johann Freidrich Reichardt, who trained her. She became a well-known writer of popular melodies and songs, and made her début in Berlin in 1794. She accompanied her father on his musical tours, but after his death in 1814 settled in Hamburg. Some of her melodies were published in Layriz's *Kern des deutschen Kirchengesangs* in 1853, and a collection of her melodies and songs was published in 1922.

T. 479 (i)

REINAGLE, ALEXANDER ROBERT (Brighton, 1799-1877, Kidlington, Oxford), was of Austrian extraction. The father was long well known in Scotland as a distinguished violoncellist, and for a time he was leader of the orchestra in the Edinburgh Theatre. Alexander became organist of St. Peter's-in-the-East, Oxford, from 1822 to 1853. He published two books of hymn-tunes, chants, etc.

T. 376, 549 (i)

RHODES, SARAH BETTS (Sheffield, 1829-1904, Worksop), was of humble origin. She married Jehoiada Alsop Rhodes, a manufacturing silversmith and an artist in his craft, and he so devoted himself to educating and refining her that she became a very clever scholar, a good hymn-writer, and a sculptor of very fair credit. On her husband's death she took over a Girls' High School at Worksop and conducted it for the remainder of her life. She was a Congregationalist.

H. 151

RIMAUD, DIDIER, S.J. (Carnac, France, 1922), was educated at the University of Lyons where he became a Licentiate in Letters, and then took the normal course of studies in philosophy and theology required by the Society of Jesus. After ordination he taught French in several colleges. Then he was attached to the Centre National de Pastorale Liturgique where he is responsible for the translation and editing of liturgical texts in the French language.

H. 469

RIMBAULT, EDWARD FRANCIS, Ph.D., LL.D., F.S.A. (London, 1816–76, London), studied under Samuel Wesley and Dr. Crotch and was organist in succession of the Swiss Church, Soho; St. Peter's, Vere Street; St. John's Wood Presbyterian Church; and St. Giles-in-the-Fields. He produced works on the history of the organ and the pianoforte; collections of madrigals, carols, ballads, nursery rhymes; rounds, catches, and canons; anthems and services; psalm-tunes and chants; editions of Tallis's *Cathedral Service* and *Order of Daily Service*; Este's *The Whole Book of Psalms*; Merbecke's *Book of Common Prayer Noted*. His learning brought him honorary degrees.

T. 49, 474

RIMMER, FREDERICK, M.A., B.Mus., F.R.C.O. (Liverpool, 1914), was educated at Quarry Bank High School, Liverpool, Durham University, and Selwyn College, Cambridge. He was Lecturer in Music at Homerton College, Cambridge (1948–51), and organist and Adviser in Musical Studies in Selwyn College (1948–51). From 1951 to 1966 he was Lecturer in Music, and since 1966 has been Gardiner Professor of Music in Glasgow University. He is also Director of Scottish Music Archives, Director of Scottish Opera, and a member of the B.B.C. Scottish Music Advisory Committee. Among his compositions are *Five Tempers* for two violins; *Five Carols of the Nativity*; *Five Preludes for Organ on Scottish Psalm Tunes*; *Pastorale* and *Toccata* for organ, etc. He has published many articles on twentieth-century music and the chapters on the years 1800–1970 in the B.B.C.'s *History of Scottish Music* (1973).

T. 576 (ii)

RINKART, MARTIN (Eilenburg, 1586–1649, Eilenburg), the son of a cooper, was educated at Eilenburg and at Leipzig. After holding various appointments he became, in 1617, Archidiaconus at Eilenburg, where he spent the rest of his life. This period was almost entirely covered by the Thirty Years War, in which the town became a refuge for fugitives from all parts. He was a distinguished poet, dramatist, and musician.

H. 368, 659

ROBERTS, JOHN (IEUAN GWYLLT) (Tanrhiwfelen, near Aberystwyth, 1822–77, Vron, near Caernarvon), was ordained to the ministry of the Calvinistic Methodist Church in 1859, and held pastoral charges first near Merthyr, then at Capel Coch, Llanberis, until 1869, when he retired. He did great work as a reformer of congregational singing. He was the founder of the great institution known in Wales as the Gymanfa ganu, or singing festival, the object of which is to encourage the love for the hymn and the hymn-tune. Ieuan Gwyllt's *Llyfr Tonau Cynulleidfaol* (Book of Congregational Tunes, 1859), the recognized tune-book of the Calvinistic Methodists, was epoch-making. He also edited the monthly musical magazine *Y Cerddor Gymreig*. The tune 'Moab' is held by many to be the best Welsh tune ever written.

T. 545

ROBERTS, KATHARINE EMILY (Leicester, 1877–1962, Peterborough), was the daughter of the Revd. L. Clayton. She studied singing in London and Paris with a view to a professional career. In 1913 she married the Revd. R. E. Roberts (Peterborough), and later was secretary to the Rutland Rural Community Council. She published a history of *Peterborough* (1920) in collaboration with her husband, *Carol Stories* (1923), and contributed to *The School Assembly*.

H. 185

ROBERTS, RICHARD ELLIS (London, 1879–1953, Stroud, Gloucestershire), was educated at St. John's College, Oxford. He worked on the *Pall Mall Gazette* (1903–5). As critic, poet, and essayist he contributed to many journals, becoming in 1930 literary editor of the *New Statesman*, and later of *Time and Tide*. He published several volumes of poems, and *Reading for Pleasure*. Later he went to live in America.

H. 330

ROBERTS, ROBERT ROWLAND, B.A. (Penmaenmawr, 1865–1945, Cardiff), was educated at the University College of Wales, Bangor, and ordained to the ministry of the Presbyterian Church of Wales in 1891, and held pastorates at Aberdare, Cardiff (Cathedral Road), Chester, and Cardiff (Clifton Street). He filled several denominational offices, as Moderator of the South Wales Association, vice-chairman of the South Wales Commission, etc. He delivered the Davies Lecture for 1908, on *The Supreme Experience of Christianity*. He was Moderator of the Presbyterian Church of Wales in 1929 and retired in 1931.

H. 545

ROBERTSON, WILLIAM, M.A. (Cambuslang, 1820–64, Monzievaird, Perth-shire), studied at the University of Glasgow. In 1843 he became minister of the parish of Monzievaird. His interest in hymnody and Scottish psalmody was keen. He was a member of the Hymnal Committee of the Church of Scotland in 1851, 1853, and 1857, and contributed to *Hymns for Public Worship*, issued by that Church, two hymns afterwards included in *The Scottish Hymnal* and *The Church Hymnary*.

H. 551

ROBINSON, JOHN (London, 1682-1762, London), was trained as a chorister of the Chapel Royal under Blow, and was organist of St. Lawrence Jewry, and St. Magnus, London Bridge, before becoming organist of Westminster Abbey in 1727. He was a successful teacher of the harpsichord, and carried the style of playing suited to that instrument into his treatment of the organ. He composed well-known chants, psalm-tunes, etc.

C. 161 (i)

ROBINSON, RICHARD HAYES (?, 1842-92, Bournemouth), was educated at King's College, London. Ordained in 1866, he became curate of St. Paul's, Penge, and of Weston, and afterwards was incumbent of the Octagon Chapel, Bath, and of St. Germain's, Blackheath, then a proprietary chapel. He published *Sermons on Faith and Duty* and *The Creed and the Age*.

H. 644

ROCKSTRO, WILLIAM SMITH (North Cheam, Surrey, 1823-95, London), whose name originally was Rackstraw, studied under Sterndale Bennett and at the Leipzig Conservatorium. He composed a number of songs and madrigals, and published some works on the history and theory of music.

T. 211 (i), 218

ROH, JOHANN. See HORN, JOHANN.

ROMANIS, WILLIAM (London, 1824-99, Southsea, Hampshire), was educated at Emmanuel College, Cambridge. He was classics master at Cheltenham College (1846-56), and after being curate at Axminster and Reading, he was vicar at Wigston Magna, Leicestershire, and Twyford. His hymns appeared in his *Wigston Magna Church Schools* (1878).

H. 650

RÖNTGEN, JULIUS (Leipzig, 1855-1932, Utrecht), was a pupil of Bachner, Hauptmann, Richter, and Reinecke. He became a professor in the Conservatoire at Amsterdam in 1888, and in 1918 its Director. In 1886 he succeeded Verhulst as Conductor of the Society for the Advancement of Musical Art. Among his publications are *Fantasie für Klavier und Violine*; *Nordische Ballade*; *Holländisches Volksleben*; two operas; and shorter works.

T. 282, 454 (ii)

ROSE, BERNARD WILLIAM GEORGE, M.A., D.Mus., F.R.C.O. (Little Hallingbury, Hertfordshire, 1916), was educated at Salisbury Cathedral School, privately, the Royal College of Music, and St. Catharine's College, Cambridge. He was organist and conductor of the Eaglesfield Musical Society, Queen's College, Oxford (1939-57), being a Fellow (1949-57). He has been organist, Fellow, Informator Choristarum, Tutor in Music in Magdalen College, Oxford, since 1957, and University Lecturer in Music since 1948. He has published *Thomas Tomkins*, forty-one verse anthems, and Handel's *Susanna*. His compositions include evening canticles, responses, anthems,

BIOGRAPHICAL AND HISTORICAL NOTES

and *Catharine*, an ode for the quincentenary of St. Catharine's College, Cambridge. He carried out the pointing of the psalms set to plain-song chants in CH3.

·H. 63, 158, 166, 231, 232, 239, 262, 284, 310, 326

ROSSETTI, CHRISTINA GEORGINA (London, 1830-94, London), was the daughter of Gabriele Rossetti, an Italian refugee who became Professor of Italian at King's College, London. She received her education at home. Her face is well known to multitudes who know nothing of her poetry, for she sat as model to several famous artists, such as Holman Hunt, Millais, and Madox Brown, as well as to her brother Gabriel; the face of the Virgin in his *Girlhood of the Virgin* and his *Ecce Ancilla Domini* is hers. Christina broke off an engagement to a man to whom she was deeply attached, because of his having become a Roman Catholic. Disappointed love, and much sorrow and suffering in her later years, intensified her deeply religious temperament. She found relief in befriending the poor children connected with the church where she worshipped. She published a number of devotional books in prose— *Time Flies, a Reading Diary* (1885); *Called to be Saints* (1881); *Seek and Find* (1879); *The Face of the Deep, a Devotional Commentary on the Apocalypse* (1892); and these volumes of poems—*Goblin Market, and Other Poems* (1862); *The Prince's Progress, and Other Poems* (1866); *Poems* (1875); *A Pageant, and Other Poems* (1881); and *Verses* reprinted from her devotional books (1893).

H. 178, 194

ROUTLEY, ERIK REGINALD, D.Phil. (Brighton, 1917), was educated at Fonthill, Lancing, and Magdalen College, Oxford. He studied for the Congregationalist ministry at Mansfield College, Oxford, and ministered in Trinity Congregational Church, Wednesbury, for two years before moving to Dartford, Kent. From 1948 he was lecturer in Church History at Mansfield College, until he resigned to become minister in Augustine-Bristo Congregational Church, Edinburgh. He is now Professor at Westminster Choir College, Princeton, N.J., U.S.A. He has written a number of hymns and hymn-tunes. Among his publications is *Church Music and Theology* (1959). He was secretary to the committee preparing *Congregational Praise* (1951). He wrote the notes on the music in *The Companion to Congregational Praise* (1953).

T. 185, 361 (i), 428, 589, 689 (i), 691

ROWLANDS, WILLIAM PENFRO (Llys-y-frān, Pembrokeshire, 1860-1937, Morriston), was a school-teacher. He conducted the Morriston United Choral Society and later became precentor of the Tabernacle Congregational Church, Morriston. His compositions were confined to anthems and hymn-tunes.

T. 473

ROWLEY, FRANCIS HAROLD, D.D. (Hilton, New York, 1854-1952, Boston), was educated at Rochester University and Theological Seminary, became a Baptist minister, and served charges at Titusville, Pennsylvania; North Adams, Massachusetts; Oak Park, Illinois; Fall River, Massachusetts; and

First Baptist Church, Boston. He was a noted humanitarian. He was president of the Massachusetts Society for the Prevention of Cruelty to Animals, and of the American Humane Education Society, and is associated with much other humanitarian work. He attended his office every afternoon at Angel Memorial Animal Hospital in Boston when he was 93. He published *The Humane Idea, The Horses of Homer*, etc.

H. 381

RUSHBRIDGE, ARTHUR EWART, F.R.C.O. (Reading, 1916-69, Bristol), was educated at Reading School and St. John's College, Oxford. After teaching at Monmouth School (1940-4) he was appointed Director of Music at Mill Hill School, and in 1948 he moved to a similar post at Bristol Grammar School. He was one of the founders of the Baptist Music Society, and a member of the Music Advisory Committee for *The Baptist Hymn Book*.

T. 186

RUSSELL, ARTHUR TOZER, B.C.L. (Northampton, 1806-74, Southwick, near Brighton), was the son of the Revd. Thomas Clout, a Congregational minister who changed his name to Russell and earned some reputation by editing the works of Tyndale, Barnes, Owens, etc. He was educated at St. Saviour's School, Southwark, and the Merchant Taylors' School, London; Manchester College, York; and St. John's College, Cambridge. Ordained in 1829 he became curate of Great Gransden, Huntingdonshire; vicar of Caxton, 1830; of Whaddon, near Royston, Cambridgeshire, 1852; of St. Thomas's, Toxteth Park, Liverpool, 1866; of Wrackwardine Wood, Wellington, Shropshire, 1867; and of Southwick, Brighton, 1874. He published *Hymn Tunes, Original and Selected, from Ravenscroft and Other Musicians*; and in 1851, *Psalms and Hymns, partly Original, partly Selected, for the Use of the Church of England*. In this last collection German hymns were numerous, and the very arrangement was based on the old Lutheran hymn-books. His own hymns number about 140.

H. 287

SANDYS, WILLIAM, F.S.A. (London, 1792-1874, London), was a lawyer by profession, but also a keen amateur musician. He published *Christmas Carols, ancient and modern, including the most popular in the West of England, and the airs to which they are sung; also Specimens of French Provincial Carols, with an Introduction and Notes* (London, 1833); *Christmas-tide, its History, Festivities, and Carols, with their music* (London, 1852); *History of the Violin and other Instruments played on with the Bow, from the remotest times to the present; also an account of the principal makers, English and foreign* (London, 1864).

T. 153, 692

SANTEUIL, JEAN BAPTISTE DE (Paris, 1630-97, Dijon), was educated at the Collège de Sainte Barbe and Louis-le-Grand, and became a canon of St.

Victor's, Paris. He wrote new Latin hymns for a revision of the *Paris Breviary* (1685), and contributed to the *Cluny Breviary* (1686). He published his *Hymni Sacri et Novi* in 1689.

H. 539

SCHEFFLER, JOHANN, M.D. (Breslau, Silesia, 1624–77, Breslau), was the son of Lutheran parents. He studied medicine at the universities of Breslau, Strasbourg, Leyden, and Padua. He early evinced an interest in metaphysical and theological subjects, and fell under the influence of the writings of Jacob Böhme. While in Holland he steeped his mind also in the writings of such mystics as Tauler and Ruysbroeck. On returning to Silesia he was made private physician to the Duke of Württemberg-Oels. His dominant interest in mysticism brought him into controversy with the clergy of the Lutheran Church at Oels. Formalists and dogmatists as they were, they not only refused him sympathy, but assailed his views bitterly, and in the end drove him into the arms of the Roman Church, into which he was received in 1653. He was made imperial Court physician to the Emperor Ferdinand III, but relinquished his profession, took Orders, and in 1671 entered the Jesuit monastery of St. Matthias in Breslau. He adopted the name of Angelus, after Johannes ab Angelis, a Spanish mystic of the sixteenth century, usually adding to it Silesius, to indicate his country. His hymns, almost entirely free from sectarian characteristics, were for the most part included in his *Heilige Seelenlust, oder Geistliche Hirten-Lieder* (1657). Most of these were written while he was still a Lutheran. The music of the book was edited by Georg Joseph.

H. 678

T. 52, 490, 639

SCHEIN, JOHANN HERMANN (Grünhayn, near Zwickau, Saxony, 1586–1630, Leipzig), was for four years a chorister in the chapel of the Elector of Saxony, at Dresden; then he studied theology and philosophy at Leipzig. He was appointed music director at the Court of Duke Johann Ernst of Saxe-Weimar, in 1613. Two years later he was called back to Leipzig, to the office of cantor in St. Thomas's Church and School. He composed many hymn-tunes, and some hymns also. He is best known by the great hymn-book he edited for the Lutheran Church, *Cantional, oder Gesangbuch Augsburgischer Confession* (Leipzig, 1627). He published also *Musica Divina*, a collection of motets for 8, 16, and 24 voices.

T. 117, 217, 223

SCHEMELLI, GEORG CHRISTIAN (Merzberg, *c.* 1678–?), was educated at St. Thomas's School, Leipzig. He published his *Musikalisches Gesangbuch* in 1736. Its musical editor was Bach, who later wrote chorale preludes on some of its hymn-tunes.

T. 445, 669

SCHICHT, JOHANN GOTTFRIED (Reichenau, near Zittau, 1753–1823, Leipzig), succeeded Hiller in the direction of Leipzig Gewandhaus Concerts in 1785, and became organist and cantor of different churches, until he resigned all other work to devote himself entirely to the musical direction of St. Thomas's Church. He wrote many masses, motets, and books of chorales. His *Allgemeines Choralbuch* (1819) contains nearly 300 tunes written by himself.

T. 287, 595

SCHLEGEL, JOHANN ADOLF, D.D. (Meissen, Saxony, 1721–93, Hanover), was educated at the Pforta School, near Naumberg, and at the University of Leipzig. In 1746 he became a private tutor at Strehla, and in 1751 a teacher in his old school at Pforta. In 1754 he became chief pastor of the Holy Trinity Church at Zerbst, and also Professor of Theology and Metaphysics at the academy. He moved to Hanover in 1759 first as pastor of the Markt Kirche, and later of the Neustadt Church and as Consistorialrath and Superintendent. While retaining his pastorate he became General Superintendent of the district of Hoya in 1782, and five years later of the Principality of Kalenberg. At the Jubilee of the University of Göttingen he was awarded the degree of D.D. He contributed hymns to *Sammlung geistlicher Gesänge zur Beförderung der Erbauung* (1766); *Zweite Sammlung* (1769); *Dritte Sammlung* (1772); and *Vermischte Gedichte* (1787–9).

H. 202

SCHLEGEL, KATHARINA AMALIA DOROTHEA VON (1697–?), is said by Koch to have been the head of the Evangelical Lutheran Stift (Protestant nunnery) at Cöthen; but this is unconfirmed. From her extant correspondence with Count Stolberg it seems likelier that she was a lady attached to the ducal court at Cöthen. No details of her life survive.

H. 202

SCHMOLCK, BENJAMIN (Brauchitzchdorf, Silesia, 1672–1737, Schweidnitz), studied at the Gymnasium at Lauban and the University of Leipzig. In 1701 he was ordained as assistant to his father, Lutheran pastor at Brauchitzchdorf, and in the following year was appointed diaconus of the Friedenskirche at Schweidnitz in Silesia. As a result of the terms agreed on at the Peace of Westphalia, the Lutherans were subjected to many restrictions, only one church, with three clergy, being allowed at Schweidnitz to serve a district containing thirty-six villages. Here Schmolck laboured for the rest of his life as preacher, pastor, and organizer. He is credited with the authorship of over 900 hymns.

H. 552

SCHOLEFIELD, CLEMENT COTTERILL, M.A. (Edgbaston, Birmingham, 1839–1904, London), was educated at Pocklington, Yorkshire, and St. John's College, Cambridge. Ordained in 1867, he served curacies at Hove, near Brighton, and St. Luke's, Chelsea; was conduct (chaplain) of Eton College, 1880–90; and from 1890 to 1895 was vicar of Holy Trinity, Knightsbridge. He composed many hymn-tunes.

T. 646 (ii)

SCHOP, JOHANN (Hamburg, 1600–64, Hamburg), entered the Court orchestra at Wolfenbüttel in 1615. In 1644 he became music director at Hamburg, and 'Ratsmusikant' in 1654. Besides much instrumental music, he wrote many hymn-tunes for the hymns of his fellow townsman and friend Johann Rist, and others.

T. 148

SCHULZ, JOHANN ABRAHAM PETER (Lüneburg, 1747–1800, Schwedt), was the son of a baker, and was intended for the Church, but early set his heart on a musical career. An organist who taught him the clavecin told him of the wonderful music to be heard in Berlin and of the greatness of Kirnberger, then at the height of his fame, as a teacher. At 15 years of age he left home, without money and against his family's wishes, to beg Kirnberger to accept him as a pupil. Against all likelihood he succeeded. Later, five years of travel in France, Italy, and Germany, with the Polish Princess Sapieta, formed his taste. On his return he did his generous master great service by assisting him and Sulzer with the musical articles for their *General Theory of the Fine Arts*, and edited Kirnberger's *Treatise on Pure Composition*. In 1776 he became director of the French Theatre in Berlin; in 1780 director of music in the household of Prince Henry of Prussia at Reinsberg; and in 1787 went in the same capacity to the Danish Court at Copenhagen. He published several collections of German songs, sacred and secular, operas, oratorios, and instrumental music.

T. 291, 620

SCHUTZ, JOHANN JAKOB (Frankfurt am Main, 1640–90, Frankfurt am Main), was a lawyer in Frankfurt and joined the pietists. Most of the pietists remained within the Lutheran Church, but a section became what we today know as the Moravians. During a period of persecution some followers of John Hus, the *Unitas Fratrum*, found refuge in Moravia in 1547. After the severe Roman Catholic persecution following 1620 a remnant survived, and Zinzendorf offered them a refuge on his estates. So the Moravian Church was reborn. In later life Schutz left the Lutherans and became a separatist. He published five hymns.

H. 142

SCOTT, ROBERT BALGARNIE YOUNG, D.D. (Toronto, 1899), was educated at the University of Toronto and Knox College. He was professor of Old Testament in the Union College of British Columbia, Vancouver, and later in United Theological College, Montreal, before becoming professor of Religion at Princeton in 1956. He is a Fellow of the Royal Society of Canada, and has written some two dozen hymns. He is author of *The Relevance of the Prophets* (1944); *Treasures from Judaean Caves* (1955); and *Proverbs and Ecclesiasticus* (Anchor Bible, 1965).

H. 511

SEARS, EDMUND HAMILTON, D.D. (Sandisfurt, Berkshire, W. Massachusetts, 1810–76, Weston, Massachusetts), claimed descent from one of the Pilgrim Fathers who emigrated to America in 1620. He was educated at

Union College, Schenectady, New York, and the Theological School, Cambridge. He ministered to Unitarian congregations at the First Church, Wayland, Massachusetts; Lancaster, Massachusetts; then returned to Wayland owing to failure of health, and devoted himself to literature. His later years were spent at Weston. He edited *The Monthly Religious Magazine*, and published among other books, *Regeneration* (1854); *Pictures of the Olden Time* (1857); *Athanasia, or Foregleams of Immortality* (1872); *The Fourth Gospel, the Heart of Christ*; *Sermons and Songs of the Christian Life* (1875).

H. 170

SEDULIUS, CAELIUS (d. *c.* 450) was probably born in Rome and converted to Christianity late in life. His works were collected after his death and include a poem, in which the whole Gospel story is covered.

H. 189, 209

SELNECKER, NICOLAUS (Hersbrück, 1532–92, Leipzig), became organist in the chapel at Nürnberg when only 12 years old. He held successively the positions of lecturer at the University of Wittenberg, Court preacher at Dresden, Professor of Theology at Jena, and pastor of St. Thomas's Church at Leipzig. His frequent movements from one part to another were largely due to the feeling between High Lutherans and those suspected of Calvinism, and Selnecker, as one of the framers of the 'Formula of Concord' designed to unite Lutherans and exclude Romanists and Calvinists, did not escape the abuse that commonly assails a man of moderate views. He helped to build up the famous Motett Choir of St. Thomas's Church at Leipzig, afterwards conducted by Johann Sebastian Bach. He loved the Psalter and was the author of many German hymns.

H. 642

SHAIRP, JOHN CAMPBELL, LL.D. (Houstoun, Linlithgowshire, 1819–85, Ormsary, Argyllshire), was educated at Edinburgh Academy, the University of Glasgow, and Balliol College, Oxford. He considered taking Orders in the Church of England, but took a mastership at Rugby. He spent eleven years at Rugby; acted as deputy Professor of Greek at Glasgow University, 1856; as assistant Professor of Humanity at St. Andrews, 1857–61; was appointed to the Chair of Humanity at St. Andrews in 1861, and to the Principalship of the United College of St. Salvator and St. Leonard there in 1868; concurrently he held the Professorship of Poetry at Oxford from 1877 till 1885. His poems in *Kilmahoe, a Highland Pastoral, with Other Poems* and *Glen Desseray and Other Poems* are full of the spirit of the Scottish scene. In prose he published *Studies in Poetry and Philosophy*; *The Poetic Interpretation of Nature*; *Culture and Religion*; *Aspects of Poetry*; and a volume on *Burns*.

H. 675

SHAPCOTE, EMILY MARY, *née* STEWARD (Liverpool, 1828–1909, Torquay), was one of two sisters who with an aunt published *Hymns for Infant Children* (1852). Hers were marked 'E'. In 1852 she married E. G. Shapcote, curate of

Odiham, Hampshire, and later a missionary in South Africa. She was received into the Church of Rome in 1866, and her husband two years later. She also published *Eucharistic Hours* (1886). In 1906 she retired to Torquay.

H. 59

SHARP, CECIL JAMES, B.Mus. (London, 1859-1924, London), was educated at Uppingham School and Clare College, Cambridge. He went to Australia, where he became Associate to the Lord Chief Justice of Southern Australia, and was organist in Adelaide Cathedral (1889-92). Returning to England he became music master in Ludgrove Preparatory School (1896-1905) and Principal of Hampstead Conservatory. In 1902 he published *A Book of British Song for Home and School*, being a collection of 'national' and folksongs. He was a member of the Folk-song Society and in 1911 founded the English Folk Dance Society. He published *Folk Songs from Somerset* (with C. L. Mason); *Songs of the West*; *English Folk Songs for Schools* (with Baring Gould); *English Folk Carols*; *English Folk Songs from the Appalachian Mountains*; *Morris Dance Tunes*; and a host of other works on similar lines.

T. 536

SHAW, MARTIN EDWARD FALLAS, Mus.Doc. (London, 1875-1958, Southwold, Suffolk), son of an organist of Hampstead Parish Church and elder brother of Geoffrey Shaw, studied at the Royal College of Music. At the end of his time as a student he 'embarked upon a long period of starving along'. He conducted for Ellen Terry and toured Europe as conductor to Isadora Duncan. In later years he held posts as organist and director of music at St. Mary's, Primrose Hill, St. Martin-in-the-Fields, and the Guildhouse, London. He composed from his childhood, and published many songs and much Church music. As a hymn-tune composer he first gained renown when he published *Additional Tunes in use at St. Mary's, Primrose Hill* (1915). He was one of the founders of the Plainsong and Mediaeval Music Society. With Vaughan Williams he was musical editor of *Songs of Praise*. He edited *The English Carol Book* and *The Oxford Book of Carols*.

T. 112, 154, 182, 203, 222, 227, 229, 230, 272, 278, 280, 281, 303, 384, 423, 529, 693

SHIELDS, ELIZABETH MCEWAN (?, 1879-1962, ?), in 1930 was Director of the Children's Division of the Department of Religious Education for the Committee of Publication of the Southern Presbyterian Church, U.S.A. She was a specialist in beginners and primary education. The earliest work of hers the editor has been able to trace is her *Worship and Conduct Songs* (1927). She also published *Guiding the Little Child in the Sunday School* (1936) and *Jesus, our Friend* (1942) for the Sunday School Board of the Southern Baptists, as well as *Happy Times in our Church* (1940); *As the Day Begins* (1944); *Music in the Religious Growth of Children* (1943); *When I Listen to Bible Stories* (1949); and *Guiding Kindergarten Children in the Church School* (1955) for the Presbyterian Committee of Publication.

H. 229

SHILLITO, EDWARD (Hull, 1872-1948, London), was educated at Silcoates School, Yorkshire, and Owens College (now the University), Manchester. He studied for the Congregational ministry at Mansfield College, Oxford, and was ordained at Albion Congregational Church, Ashton-under-Lyne, in 1896. He moved to Albion, Tunbridge Wells, in 1889, to Clifton Road, Brighton, in 1901, to Harlesden, London, in 1906, to be assistant at Lyndhurst Road, Hampstead, in 1909, and to Buckhurst Hill, Essex, in 1918. He was editorial secretary of the London Missionary Society (1920-32). He published many articles, and two volumes of poetry, *The Omega* and *Jesus of the Scars*.

H. 292

SHRUBSOLE, WILLIAM (Canterbury, 1760-1806, London), was the son of a farrier, and was for seven years a chorister in Canterbury Cathedral. In 1782 he was appointed organist of Bangor Cathedral, but within a year got into trouble with the Dean and Chapter because of his unconcealed sympathy with dissenters and his frequenting of 'conventicles'. This led to his being virtually dismissed from his office. Returning to London he became a teacher of music, and from 1784 till his death was organist of Spa Fields Chapel, of Lady Huntingdon's Connexion.

T. 382

SHRUBSOLE, WILLIAM (Sheerness, Kent, 1759-1829, Highbury, London), was the son of a mast-maker in Sheerness dockyard who was also a lay preacher. He was himself in his earlier years a shipwright in the dockyard, and then a clerk. In 1785 he went to London and entered the Bank of England as a clerk. He rose there till he became Secretary to the Committee of the Treasury. For some years he was a member of the Church of England, but for the last twenty years of his life he was a Congregationalist, worshipping in Hoxton Academy Chapel. His hymns, about twenty in number, were contributed to various periodicals.

H. 498

SIBELIUS, JAN (Tavastehus, Finland, 1865-1957, Järvenpää), was a pupil of Helsingfors Music Institute, and afterwards studied at Berlin and Vienna. From 1893 he taught in the Philharmonic Orchestra School, Helsingfors. From 1897 to 1907 he received an annual grant from the Finnish Government, to set him free to devote himself to composition. He produced dramatic works, symphonies, symphonic poems like the famous *Finlandia*, suites, songs, etc. His only religious compositions are *Musique Religieuse* (1927) and *Five Christmas Songs* (1895).

T. 673

SKEMP, ADA (Lockwood, Yorkshire, 1857-1927, ?), was educated at Huddersfield High School, and became a teacher in Gateshead High School. Later she was co-principal of Hale High School, Cheshire (1906-13), and also of Ansdell College, Lytham St. Anne's, Lancashire. She was the wife of a Baptist minister, the Revd. J. G. Skemp.

H. 156

SLATER, GORDON ARCHBOLD (Harrogate, 1896), studied at York Minster (1914-16). Following several minor appointments he was appointed to Leicester Cathedral in 1927, and the same year he founded the Leicester Bach Choir. In 1936 he became organist and master of the choristers at Lincoln.

T. 674

SMART, GEORGE THOMAS (London, 1776-1867, London), was a chorister at the Chapel Royal. When 15 years of age he was appointed organist at St. James's, Hampstead Road. In 1811 he was knighted by the Lord Lieutenant of Ireland following a series of concerts in Dublin. He was an original member of the Philharmonic Society, and its conductor until 1844. In 1822 he became organist to the Chapel Royal, and in 1838 was appointed composer to it. He was musical director of Covent Garden and Grand Organist to the Grand Lodge of Free and Accepted Masons. He composed glees and sacred music, edited Gibbons's first set of madrigals for the Musical Antiquarian Society in 1841, and the *Dettingen Te Deum* for the Handel Society.

T. 387 (ii)

SMART, HENRY (THOMAS) (London, 1813-79, London), was the son of a well-known violinist. He declined the offer of a commission in the Indian Army, and, after four years' trial of law, turned aside from that profession to devote his life to music. In the main, he was self-taught. Organ-playing became his passion and he developed great skill also in the planning and erection of organs. His appointments as organist were at the Parish Church, Blackburn; St. Giles', Cripplegate; St. Philip's, Regent Street; St. Luke's, Old Street; and St. Pancras, London. From 1865 his sight, always defective, failed him altogether; but an extraordinarily retentive memory stood him in good stead, and his rare skill in extempore playing had full scope. He composed a *Credo* and hymn-tunes. He wrote also cantatas—*The Bride of Dunkerron*, *King René's Daughter*; *The Fishermaidens*; an oratorio, *Jacob*; etc. He edited the music of *The Presbyterian Hymnal* (1876) for the United Presbyterian Church.

T. 40 (ii), 236, 289, 354, 431, 657, 664

SMITH, ALFRED MORTON, D.D. (Jenkintown, Pennsylvania, 1879-1971, Brigantine, N.J.), was educated at the University of Pennsylvania and Philadelphia Divinity School. Ordained in 1905, he was rector of St. Matthias' Church, Los Angeles, for ten years and then chaplain to the City Mission there. After acting as a chaplain to the Forces in France and Germany, he was chaplain to the Episcopal City Mission of Philadelphia (1919-55). He composed a number of hymn- and carol-tunes as well as three communion settings.

T. 68, 458

SMITH, FLORENCE MARGARET (Gayton, Norfolk, 1886-1958, Ledbury, Herefordshire). It has been impossible to trace this author. She did have a connection with St. Christopher's College, Canterbury, and so may have been a teacher. She contributed to *Hymns Ancient and Modern* and *The Anglican Hymn Book*.

H. 447

SMITH, FREDERICK (1800-73), cannot be traced. No dictionary refers to him and only one handbook, but it confuses him with his namesake, Frederic Smith (1849-1945). The index at Somerset House includes a 'Frederic Smith', whose death was registered at Beaminster, Dorset, in the first quarter of 1873, 'aged 72', but no works by him are listed in the British Museum catalogue. He may be the author, but without additional evidence this is simply conjecture.

H. 282

SMITH, ISAAC (London, 1734-1805, London), was for a time precentor to the Alie Street Meeting House in Goodman's Fields, London. He composed and published a number of psalm-tunes. About 1770 he published *A Collection of Psalm Tunes in Three Parts: to which are added 2 Anthems and 2 Canons.*

T. 28, 394

SMITH, ISAAC GREGORY, D.D. (Manchester, 1826-1920, Horsell, near Woking), a son of the Revd. Jeremiah Smith, D.D., was educated at Rugby and at Trinity College, Oxford. He gained a Fellowship of Brasenose. He became rector of Tedston-Delamere, Herefordshire, 1854; vicar of Great Malvern, 1872; prebendary of Pratum Minus in Hereford Cathedral, 1870; Rural Dean of Powick; Hon. Canon of Worcester, 1887; rector of Great Shefford, Lambourne, Berkshire, 1896. He retired to Horsell in 1904. He published books on *Monasticism*, *Psychology*, and *The Characteristics of Christian Morality*. With his brother John George Smith, barrister, and the Revd. W. S. Raymond, he edited *A Hymn Book for the Services of the Church and for Private Reading* (1855).

H. 261

SMITH, KENNETH DONALD, M.A. (Manchester, 1928), was educated at Long Eaton Grammar School and Keble College, Oxford. He was assistant director of music at Wrekin College, Shropshire (1953-8) and head of the music department at Sir Thomas Rich's School, Gloucester (1958-63). Since 1964 he has been head of the music department at St. Matthias College of Education, Bristol. He has written articles on music and hymnody for a number of journals, is the composer of numerous items of choral music, but this has not been published, and contributed to *Sunday School Praise* (1958), *The School Assembly* (1958), of both of which he was joint music editor, and to *The Anglican Hymn Book* (1965) and *The New Catholic Hymnal* (1971).

T. 622

SMITH, WALTER CHALMERS, D.D., LL.D. (Aberdeen, 1824-1908, Kinbuck, Perthshire), was educated at the Grammar School and University, Aberdeen, and at New College, Edinburgh. Ordained in 1850 to the charge of a congregation in Chadwell Street, Islington, London, he afterwards became minister of Orwell Free Church, Milnathort; the Free Tron Church, Glasgow; and the Free High Church, Edinburgh (1876-94). He was Moderator of the Assembly of the Free Church of Scotland in its Jubilee year

(1893) and in the following year he retired. His published works were—*The Bishop's Walk* (1860); *Olrig Grange* (1872); *Borland Hall* (1874); *Hilda among the Broken Gods* (1878); *Raban, or Life Splinters* (1881); *North Country Folk* (1883); *Kildrostan* (1884); *Hymns of Christ and the Christian Life* (1886); *Thoughts and Fancies for Sunday Evenings* (1887); *A Heretic, and Other Poems* (1891); *Poetical Works* (1902).

H. 32

SMYTTAN, GEORGE HUNT, B.A. (Hawksworth, Nottinghamshire, 1822–1870, Frankfurt am Main), son of Dr. Smyttan of the Bombay Medical Board, was educated at Corpus Christi College, Cambridge. He was ordained in 1848. In 1850 he became rector of Hawksworth, Nottingham, but resigned in 1859. He died suddenly abroad and being unknown he was interred among the poor in an unpurchased grave. He published *Thoughts in Verse for the Afflicted* (1849); *Mission Songs and Ballads* (1860); *Florum Sacra* (n.d.).

H. 210

SNOW, GEORGE D'OYLY, M.A. (London, 1903), was educated at Winchester College and Oriel College, Oxford. He was headmaster of Ardingly College (1946-61) and Bishop of Whitby (1961-71). Though retired, he is Rural Dean of Purbeck. He contributed to *Hymns for Church and School*.

H. 91

SOAPER, JOHN (London?, 1743-94, London), was a chorister at St. Paul's and became a Gentleman of the Chapel Royal and vicar-choral of St. Paul's.

C. 345 (c)

SOHREN, PETER (Elbing, ?-1693, Elbing), whose name is sometimes given as Sohr, was Kantor in Leichnam's Church in Elbing, 1674-5. Then he went as Kantor to Durschau, but later returned to Elbing. In 1668 he edited Crüger's *Praxis Pietatis Melica*, enlarging it and adding some compositions of his own. In 1683 he published his *Musikalischer Vorschmarck der jauchzenden Seelen im ewigen Leben*, in which were 238 tunes composed by himself.

T. 9

SOMERVELL, Sir ARTHUR, D.Mus. (Windermere, 1863-1937, London), was educated at Uppingham and King's College, Cambridge. In 1885 he went to the Royal College of Music, and later to the Berlin Hochschule. In 1894 he was made a professor at the R.C.M., and in 1901 became an inspector of music in schools, a post he held until 1928. He was knighted in 1929. In later life he was chairman of the council of the School of English Church Music.

T. 238 (ii), 479 (ii)

SPEDDING, FRANK DONALD, D.Mus. (Liverpool, 1929), was educated at Nottingham High School and the Royal College of Music, London. He was music master at Quernmore School, Bromley, Kent (1952-8). At the Royal

Scottish Academy of Music and Drama, Glasgow, he was appointed lecturer in harmony, counterpoint, etc., in 1958, and in 1962 Head of Department. Among his compositions are Cello Concerto, Piano Concerto, Toccata a Tre, Piano Quintet, Eight Impromptus after Paganini for piano, numerous film scores, and various short choral works.

T. 164

SPENSER, EDMUND (East Smithfield, London, c. 1552–99, Westminster), was the son of a cloth maker, and was educated at Merchant Taylors' School and Pembroke Hall, Cambridge. In the Anglican–Puritan controversy he favoured the Puritans. In 1580 he was appointed secretary to Lord Arthur Grey, Lord Deputy of Ireland. After Grey's recall, Spenser remained in Ireland and settled at Kilcolman, Co. Cork. During Tyrone's rebellion in Ulster in 1598, the Munster Irish burned down Kilcolman and Spenser had to flee the country.

H. 44

SPIESS, JOHANN MARTIN (Bavaria, 1715–after 1766, Berne), was professor of music in the Gymnasium at Heidelberg, and organist of St. Peter's Church there; and later settled in Berne. He published *Davids Harpffen Spiel, In hundert und funfzig Psalmen, Auch dreyhundert zwey und vierzig Lieder Melodien* (Heidelberg, 1745); *Geistliche Liebesposaune, in 342 Liedermelodien; Geistliche Arien* (1761).

T. 113, 680

SPITTA, KARL JOHANN PHILIPP, D.D. (Hanover, 1801–59, Burgdorf), was apprenticed to a watchmaker, but his desire was to enter the ministry. He studied at the University of Göttingen, and after four years of a tutorship, was ordained in 1828 as assistant pastor at Sudwalde, near Hoya. At the University he wrote songs and secular poems, and published a number of them anonymously as a *Sangbüchlein der Liebe für Handwerksleute*. He began writing hymns in 1824. In 1830 he was appointed assistant chaplain to the garrison and the prison at Hamelin on the Weser; the report that he was a Pietist and a mystic raised against him a prejudice that lost him the full chaplaincy. After a ten years' pastorate at Wechold, near Hoya, he was successively Lutheran superintendent at Wittingen, at Peine, and at Burdorf, where, soon after his appointment, he died suddenly. His *Psalter und Harfe, Eine Sammlung christlicher Leider zur häuslicher Erbauung* were published in 1833 and 1843.

H. 523

STAINER, Sir JOHN, M.A., Mus.Doc. (London, 1840–1901, Verona), was a chorister of St. Paul's, 1847–56. During this time an anthem and several chants of his composition were sung in the services, and he often acted as organist. He became organist of St. Benet and St. Peter's, Paul's Wharf, at 14, and two years later was appointed first organist of St. Michael's, Tenbury. In

1859 he matriculated at Christ Church, Oxford, and was appointed organist of Magdalen College, and then of the University. In 1872 he succeeded Sir John Goss at St. Paul's Cathedral. Other appointments held by him were those of Professor of the Organ, and then Principal of the National Training School for Music; organist to the Royal Choral Society; Government Inspector of Music in Training Schools; Professor of Music in the University of Oxford. He was knighted in 1888. He wrote a book on *The Music of the Bible*, *A Treatise on Harmony*, several cantatas of which *The Crucifixion* is widely known; many service anthems, hymn-tunes, and other Church music. His editorial work was extensive, among the books the music of which he supervised being the first *Church Hymnary*.

T. 54 (ii), 467, 656

STANFORD, Sir CHARLES VILLIERS, Mus.Doc. (Dublin, 1852–1924, London). At Cambridge—Queens' and Trinity Colleges—he had a classical education. He succeeded Dr. J. L. Hopkins as organist of Trinity College; became leader of the University Musical Society; conductor of the London Bach Choir, 1885; of the R.C.M. orchestra, 1887; of Leeds Festival, 1901; Professor of Music, Cambridge, 1887, and of composition, R.C.M., in the same year. He was a Mus.Doc. of Cambridge and Oxford, and was knighted in 1901. One of the most distinguished figures in the world of music in his time, he appeared as conductor in Berlin, Paris, Amsterdam, Brussels, and America. He did much to help in the revival of interest in folk-music; his settings of Irish airs are singularly fine. He was a prolific composer, producing seven operas, seven symphonies, two cantatas (*Phaudrig Crohoore* and *Revenge*); four *Irish Rhapsodies*; a *Stabat Mater*; *Songs of the Sea*; *Songs of the Fleet*.

C. 345 (d)

T. 122, 143 (i), 297, 402

STANLEY, SAMUEL (Birmingham, 1767–1822, Birmingham), in 1787 became leader of the singing at Carr's Lane Meeting House, Birmingham. He continued with the congregation when it moved in 1818 to a larger chapel in Steelhouse Lane, and served it altogether for thirty-three years. His position in it was not then regarded as inconsistent with his keeping for a time the Crown Tavern in the town. He published *Twenty-four Tunes in Four Parts*; *Nineteen Psalms, Hymns and Charity Hymn Tunes*; *Sacred Music, comprising two new Psalm and Hymn Tunes*; and *Psalm and Hymn Tunes*, in three books.

T. 471 (ii)

STANTON, WALTER KENDALL, M.A., D.Mus. (Dauntsey, Wiltshire, 1891), was a chorister of Salisbury Cathedral. Then he went to Lancing and Merton, Oxford. He was music master at St. Edward's School, Oxford, and then at Wellington College up to 1937. From 1927 to 1937, he was also Director of Music in the University of Reading. Then he became Director of Music to the Midland Region of the B.B.C. (1937–45), and in 1947 the first Professor of Music at Bristol University. He retired in 1957. He composed two motets for double choir, *The Spacious Firmament* and *Sing we triumphant hymns.* He contributed twenty-six hymn-tunes to *The BBC Hymn Book* (1951), of which he was editor-in-chief.

T. 201, 403, 442 (ii)

STEFFE, WILLIAM (*c.* 1852). Nothing is known about him beyond the fact that the tune 'Battle Hymn of the Republic', commonly known as 'John Brown's Body', is attributed to him.

T. 318 (ii)

STEGGALL, CHARLES, Mus.Doc. (London, 1826–1905, London), was educated at the Royal Academy of Music. As organist, he served Christ Church, Maida Hill; Christ Church, Lancaster Gate; and Lincoln's Inn Chapel. For half a century he was chief professor of the organ at the R.A.M. He was one of the founders of the Royal College of Organists, and at its opening gave the inaugural address. He composed anthems and Church music, and had a lifelong interest in hymnology. He succeeded W. H. Monk as musical editor of *Hymns Ancient and Modern.*

T. 592

STEVENSON, ISABEL STEPHANA (Cheltenham, 1843–90, Cheltenham), daughter of an Army officer, spent the whole of an uneventful life in Cheltenham. She was a devoted member of the Church of England. Her one hymn was composed when her faith and affection were under the stress of being an invalid and of the need to find some such mode of expression; that impulse past, she never wrote verse or published either poetry or prose again.

H. 529

STEVENSON, LILIAN (Dublin, 1870–1960, Gerrard's Cross, Buckingham-shire) was a daughter of the Revd. J. Fleming Stevenson, Rathgar Presbyterian Church, Dublin. She studied at the Slade School of Art, and helped to found the Art Students' Christian Union, which became part of the Student Christian Movement. She edited the *Student Volunteer* (1896–7) and *Student Movement* (1898–1900, 1902–3). She was also closely associated with the Fellowship of Reconciliation. In retirement she lived at Gerrard's Cross.

H. 375

STOCKS, GEORGE GILBERT, Mus.Doc. (Huddersfield, 1877–1960, Epsom, Surrey), was first, from 1893, organist at Almondbury, then taught music for ten years in St. Edward's School, Oxford. He was chief music master of Repton School, 1912–34, after which he travelled all over the country as an examiner for the London College of Music. He retired in 1950 and went to live in a home for elderly professional people at Croydon. In *Hymns for Use in Chapel* (1924)—a supplement to *Hymns Ancient and Modern*, for use at Repton—twenty-two tunes specially written by him for unison singing were published, along with five arrangements by him and twenty-two tunes by other composers.

T. 53 (i), 339

STONE, HELEN (?), could not be traced. She contributed to *Hosanna, Sunday School Praise*, and *Congregational Praise*. *The Companion* to the last named says 'We have not been able to obtain any further information about this ... author'.

H. 226

STONE, SAMUEL JOHN, M.A. (Whitmore, Staffordshire, 1839-1900, Charterhouse), was educated at Charterhouse and Pembroke College, Oxford. He was curate, first of Windsor, then of St. Paul's, Haggerston, London. In 1890 he accepted the rectorship of All-Hallows-on-the-Wall, London. He published *Lyra Fidelium* (1866); *The Knight of Intercession, and Other Poems* (1872); *Sonnets of the Christian Year* (1875); *Hymns (Original and Translated)* (1886); *Order of the Consecutive Church Service for Children, with Original Hymns* (1883); and his *Collected Poems and Hymns* were edited, with a memoir, by F. G. Ellerton, after his death. He was a member of the committee of *Hymns Ancient and Modern* in the later stages of that work.

H. 420

STRUTHER, JAN (London, 1901-53, New York), was the pen-name of Mrs. A. K. Placzek, derived from the family name of her mother, the Hon. Dame Eva Anstruther. She was educated privately in London. She contributed numerous poems, articles, and short stories to journals, but was best known for her novel, *Mrs. Miniver* (1939). She also published several volumes of poetry.

H. 92, 206

SU YIN-LAN (Tientsin, China, 1915-37, Tientsin), graduated with honours in music at Yenching University in 1934, where she studied under Dr. Bliss Wiant, who has collected a number of her compositions and describes her as 'a very sweet, very feminine small girl ... She was a Christian in all respects'. After graduating she married and lived in Tientsin, but soon after the birth of her first child, a son, she died as the result of an air raid by the Japanese army of occupation.

T. 569

SULLIVAN, Sir ARTHUR SEYMOUR, Mus.Doc. (London, 1842-1900, London), the son of a player on brass instruments and the clarinet, became a chorister of the Chapel Royal in 1854, and after studying at the R.A.M. and Leipzig Conservatorium was organist of St. Michael's, Chester Square, and St. Peter's, Onslow Gardens; musical director, Royal Aquarium, Principal of the National Training School of Music, and Professor of Composition, 1876; conductor of Glasgow Choral Union, 1875-7; of Covent Garden Promenade Concerts, 1878-9; of Leeds Festival from 1880 onwards; and of the Philharmonic Society, 1885-7. He received the Legion of Honour in 1878, and in 1883 was knighted. He wrote oratorios, *The Light of the World*, *The Prodigal Son*, etc.; a *Festival Te Deum* in 1872; music for *The Tempest* and *The Merchant of Venice*; many songs, much choral and instrumental music, and Church music. But it is by his attractive music for the Savoy Operas, in which he was associated with Sir W. S. Gilbert, that he has international fame. His hymn-tunes were mostly written between 1867 and 1874, and were contributed principally to *The Hymnary* and *Church Hymns*. Of the latter he was musical editor.

T. 123, 170, 476, 480, 484 (ii), 689 (ii)

SUMMERS, THOMAS OSMOND, D.D., LL.D. (near Corfe Castle, Dorset, 1812–82, Nashville, Tennessee), migrated in 1830 to America, and was admitted to the Baltimore Conference of the Methodist Episcopal Church in 1835. He was a missionary in Texas from 1840 to 1843; removed to Tuscaloosa, Alabama, 1844; and to Charlton, South Carolina, 1846. From 1845 he was Book Editor and Secretary of the Conference of the Methodist Episcopal Church, South, when the Southern Conference seceded from the main body of the Church on the issue of slavery; he was chairman also of its Hymn-Book Committee. He edited *Songs of Zion* (1851); also *The Wesleyan Psalter* (1855). In his later years he was Professor of Systematic Theology in Vanderbilt University, Nashville, Tennessee.

H. 49

SWANN, DONALD IBRAHIM, M.A. (Llanelli, Wales, 1923), was educated at Westminster School and Christ Church, Oxford. Although graduating in Modern Languages with honours, since 1948 he has been a freelance composer, singer and pianist. He composed tunes for *Sing True* and published two anthologies of new *Carols*, including some of his own. His works include *Sing round the Year*; *The Rope of Love*; *The Song of Caedmon* (narrative and music); songs from *At the Drop of a Hat*, *The Road goes ever on* (with Professor Tolkien); *A Book of Reflections*; *The Space between the Bars*; *Festival Matins*; and *Requiem for the Living* (words by Day Lewis).

T. 105

SYNESIUS (Cyrene, *c.* 375–430?), after studying at Alexandria under the renowned Hypatia, devoted himself to philosophy and the life of a country gentleman. When his country was attacked by Libyan nomads, he raised a corps of volunteers for the defence of Cyrene. Though he became a Christian in 401, and was consecrated Bishop of Ptolemais in response to the will of the people, there was little of the ecclesiastic in his composition. He was no ascetic, adhered to the married state, and loved sport and open-air life. He wrote a number of odes. Only one, the undernoted, has come into common use.

H. 80

TALLIS (or TALLYS), THOMAS (Leicestershire?, 1510–85, Greenwich), was probably a chorister of a metropolitan choir. He became organist of Waltham Abbey. On the dissolution of the monasteries he was dismissed. Soon afterwards he became a gentleman of the Chapel Royal. In 1575–6, he and William Byrd obtained letters patent, according them the exclusive right to print music and ruled music paper for twenty-one years. The first work printed under the patent was their own *Cantiones quae ab argumento Sacrae vocantur, quinque et sex partium*, containing 34 motets, 16 by Tallis and 18 by Byrd. Outwardly, Tallis conformed to the changes in the forms of worship imposed by the various rulers from Henry VIII to Elizabeth, but the fact that he wrote much before the Reformation and but little for the Reformed Church indicates that his sympathies in the main were with the older faith. His fame rests on the Preces, Responses, and Litany used in the Anglican choral service. His most outstanding composition is his motet *Spem in alium non habui*, written for forty voices, eight choirs of five parts each.

T. 91, 119, 526, 548, 599, 641, 675

TANS'UR, WILLIAM (Dunchurch, Warwickshire, 1706-83, St. Neots), was the son of a labourer, whose name is spelt Tanzer in the parish register. In his youth he became a teacher of psalmody, and in pursuance of this profession appears to have moved about a great deal from town to town conducting psalmody classes; he is found for a time in Barnes, Ewell, Cambridge, Stamford, Boston, Leicester, and other parts of England. Latterly he settled in St. Neots as a bookseller and teacher of music. He described his first book, *A Compleat Melody, or, The Harmony of Sion* (1734), as 'the most curiosest Book that ever was published'. Some of the tunes in it, such as 'Bangor' and 'Colchester', are believed to have been composed by him, but certainty is lacking. He published also *Heaven on Earth, or The Beauty of Holiness* (1738); *Sacred Mirth, or, The Pious Soul's Daily Delight* (1739); *The Universal Harmony, containing the Whole Book of Psalms* (1743); *The Psalm-Singer's Jewel, or Useful Companion to the Book of Psalms* (1760); *Melodia Sacra, or, The Devout Psalmist's Musical Companion* (1771); *A New Musical Grammar, or, The Harmonical Spectator* (1746); *The Elements of Musick Displayed* (1772); *Poetical Meditations* (1740).

T. 293, 452, 626

TATE, NAHUM (Dublin, 1652-1715, London), son of an Irish clergyman, was educated at Trinity College, Dublin. He was, through Court influence, appointed in 1690 Poet Laureate in succession to Shadwell. He also became historiographer-royal in 1702. Tate wrote largely for the stage, besides translating and adapting other men's works. Among his efforts in this field were versions of Shakespeare's *King Lear* and *Richard II*. He also wrote, apparently with Dryden's approval and help, a continuation of *Absalom and Achitophel*. Along with Nicholas Brady, Tate produced in 1696 the '*New Version*' (*metrical*) *of the Psalms*, which gradually supplanted the older version of Sternhold and Hopkins.

H. 174

TAYLOR, CYRIL VINCENT (Wigan, 1907), was educated at Magdalen College School, Oxford, and became a chorister at Magdalen. He went to Christ Church in 1926, and Westcott House in 1930. Ordained in 1931, he held several curacies in the diocese of Leicester before becoming precentor of Bristol Cathedral in 1936. In 1939 he became a member of the staff of the

Religious Broadcasting Department of the B.B.C., and was one of the compilers of *The BBC Hymn Book* (1951), contributing some twenty tunes. From 1953 to 1958 he was a Fellow of St. Michael's College, Tenbury, and warden and chaplain of the Royal School of Church Music. Later he was vicar of Cerne Abbas, and Canon of Salisbury. He is now retired.

T. 92, 145 (ii), 334, 593

TAYLOR, JANE (London, 1783–1824, Ongar, Essex), was the younger daughter of Isaac Taylor who later became a Congregational minister at Colchester and Ongar. She was diffident with others and delayed her acceptance of Church membership until she was 34 years of age. She and her sister Ann, afterwards Mrs. Gilbert, were taught the art of engraving by their father, but their tastes were literary, and they collaborated in producing several volumes of poems and hymns. The nursery rhyme, 'Twinkle, twinkle, little star', was one of Jane's contributions. While resident at Marazion in the interest of the health of her brother Isaac, afterwards well known as the author of *The Natural History of Enthusiasm* and other books of mark and influence in their time, she published *Display, a Tale*, and began a series of contributions to *The Youth's Magazine*, which she continued regularly for seven years. These pieces in prose and verse were collected and published after her death as *The Contributions of Q.Q.* In 1825 her brother issued *A Memoir and Poetical Remains*.

H. 419

TAYLOR, WALTER REGINALD OXENHAM, M.A., L.Th. (Portsmouth, 1889–1973, Sevenoaks, Kent), was educated at the London College of Divinity and St. John's College, Durham. He was ordained in St. James's, Holloway, in 1922, and went under the Church Missionary Society to the Missionary Diocese of West China (1924–9) and to Hangchow (1930–50). He was vicar of St. Margaret's Underriver (1950–60). When he retired he lived at Sevenoaks, Kent.

H. 569

TERRY, Sir RICHARD RUNCIMAN, Mus.Doc. (Ellington, Northumberland, 1865–1938, London), was educated at Oxford and Cambridge (choral scholarship, King's College), held organistships at Elstow School, near Bedford, 1890; St. John's Cathedral, Antigua, West Indies, 1892; Downside Abbey, 1896; and Westminster Cathedral, 1902–24. He was knighted in 1922. He specialized in the revival of the Church music of the polyphonic composers of the sixteenth century; he brought whole schools of this type of composition to light. For a time he was chairman of the Tudor Church Music Publications under the Carnegie Trust. Then he devoted himself to writing and research work. He published: *Downside Masses*; *Downside Motets*; *Motets Ancient and Modern*; *Old Rhymes with New Tunes*; *A Shanty Book*; *A Benediction Manual*; and a book on *Catholic Church Music*; wrote five masses, a requiem, many motets; and edited *The Westminster Hymnal*, the official Roman Catholic hymnal for England.

T. 402

TERSTEEGEN, GERHARD (Mörs, Westphalia, 1697-1769, Mühlheim), was the son of a tradesman, and was apprenticed at 15 to an elder brother, a shopkeeper at Mühlheim. He was of delicate health and scrupulous conscience. He gave up association with the Church, but formed no sect of his own. In 1725 he took a young friend to stay with him. They worked ten hours daily at the loom, and thereafter Tersteegen spent two hours in prayer, and gave two to writing devotional books and addressing private meetings of friends on religion. So many people flocked to him for spiritual fellowship and counsel, that he had to give up weaving and devote himself entirely to an informal ministry. In hymnody he is the chief representative of the mystics, who attached little importance to the ordinary means of grace because they held that the soul may possess an inner light of its own, and enjoy without any mediation direct and intimate fellowship with God. His writings include a collection of hymns, *Geistliches Blumen-Gärtlein* (1729); and a selection of his addresses, taken down in shorthand, *Geistliche Brosamen von des Herrn Tisch gefallen.*

H. 96, 355

TESCHNER, MELCHIOR (Fraustadt, Silesia, 1584-1635, Oberprietschen, Posnania), was Lutheran Cantor at Fraustadt, in Silesia, at the beginning of the seventeenth century, and subsequently was pastor of Oberprietschen, near Fraustadt. The chorale tune which made him famous was composed in 1613 for an acrostic hymn written during a time of pestilence by Valerius Herberger, then pastor at Fraustadt.

T. 233

THALBEN-BALL, GEORGE THOMAS, D.Mus. (Sydney, Australia, 1896) came to England at an early age, and at 14 won an exhibition to the Royal College of Music. A year later he became organist at Whitefield's Tabernacle. After a number of other appointments he became acting organist to the Hon. Societies of the Temple under Walford Davies, and succeeded him in 1923. He still holds this post although the Temple Church was destroyed during an air raid in 1941. Since then he has been consultant and organist to the B.B.C. He also is curator-organist at the Royal Albert Hall, professor at the R.C.M., an examiner and member of Council in the Royal College of Organists, and City and University organist at Birmingham. He is a bard of the Welsh Eisteddfod and a Freeman of the City of London. He edited the music of *School Worship* (1926) and was an editor of *The BBC Hymn Book* (1951).

C. 349 (i)

T. 61, 432, 455 (i), 594

THATCHER, Sir REGINALD SPARSHATT, O.B.E., D.Mus., F.R.C.O. (Salisbury, 1888-1957, Cranleigh, Surrey), was educated at the Royal College of Music and Worcester College, Oxford. He became an assistant music master at Clifton College in 1911, director of music at the Royal Naval College, Osborne, in 1914, director of music at Charterhouse School in 1919, and later at Harrow. In 1928 he was president of the Music Masters Association. He was a member of the editorial committee of *The BBC Hymn Book* (1951). He was principal of the Royal Academy of Music (1949-55) and president of the Royal College of Organists (1954-60). He was knighted in 1952.

T. 503, 523

THEODULPH OF ORLEANS, ST. (*c.* 821), is said to have been born in Italy, where he became abbot of a monastery in Florence. Brought to France by Charlemagne in 821, he was appointed soon afterwards to the bishopric of Orleans. He fell into disfavour with the Emperor Louis (the Pious) and was imprisoned in a monastery at Angers. While in confinement there, according to legend, he composed the original of the undernoted hymn; on Palm Sunday, 821, he sang it at the window of his cell as the King passed the prison on his way to church, and the King was so much impressed that he ordered the bishop's release and restoration to his see. This story is probably untrue. Theodulph appears to have died in prison or very soon after his release.

H. 233

THIMAN, ERIC HARDING, Mus.Doc., F.R.C.O. (Ashford, Kent, 1900-75, London), was educated at Caterham School and the Guildhall School of Music. He was appointed organist at Park Chapel, Crouch End, London, in 1922, and Professor of Harmony at the Royal Academy of Music in 1930. He was also an examiner for the Royal College of Organists. He published several works on the use of varied harmonies in hymn-tunes, and was chairman of the committee which produced *Congregational Praise* (1951). He composed many anthems and organ works, several cantatas including *The Last Supper*, and a number of part-songs.

T. 500, 688

THOMMEN, JOHANN (?-1783, Basel), was from 1738 till his death cantor at St. Peter's, Basel. He published, in 1745, *Erbaulicher musikalischer Schatz*, containing 500 hymns and 257 melodies, arranged for three and four parts.

T. 654

THOMSON, ANDREW MITCHELL, D.D. (Sanquhar, 1778-1831, Edinburgh), was educated at the University of Edinburgh. After a period as school-teacher at Markinch, Fife, he was ordained at Sprouston by the Presbytery of Kelso in 1802. He was translated to the East Church, Perth, in 1808, and to New Greyfriars, Edinburgh, in 1810. In 1814 the Town Council presented him to the newly erected St. George's. He did much to improve psalmody and congregational singing. A major step in this was his inducing R. A. Smith to come in 1823 from Paisley Abbey to be his precentor. They had already collaborated in compiling *Sacred Harmony, Part 1 for the use of St. George's Church, Edinburgh* (1820), to which Thomson contributed thirteen tunes including 'St. George's, Edinburgh'. They also collaborated in producing *Sacred Music, consisting of Tunes, Sanctuses, Doxologies, Thanksgivings, &c., Sung in St. George's Church, Edinburgh* (1825).

T. 566 (ii)

THORNE, EDWARD HENRY, Mus.Doc. (Cranborne, Dorset, 1834-1916, London), was educated at St. George's Chapel, Windsor, under Sir George Elvey, whose assistant he became at the organ at the early age of 12. The churches he served as organist were—Henley-on-Thames Parish Church; Chichester Cathedral; St. Patrick's, Brighton; St. Peter's, Onslow Gardens, South Kensington; St. Michael's, Cornhill; and St. Anne's, Soho. At St. Anne's his enthusiasm for Bach inspired many recitals of that master's organ music, and special performances of the *St. John Passion*. He wrote twenty anthems, eleven services, seven books of original organ music, piano pieces, part-songs, etc.

T. 211 (ii)

THRELFALL, JEANNETTE (Blackburn, Lancashire, 1821-80, Westminster), was the daughter of a wine-merchant, whose marriage to her mother was disapproved of by the latter's family, which was locally of good social standing. She was early left an orphan, and lived with an uncle and aunt at Blackburn, then at Leyland. An accident lamed her for life, and another, later, rendered her a helpless invalid. Her verses, 'thrown off' at intervals in her reading, were published in various periodicals, and were collected for publication in *Woodsorrel, or, Leaves from a Retired Home* (1856) and *Sunshine and Shadow* (1873).

H. 235

THRING, GODFREY, B.A. (Alford, Somerset, 1823-1903, Ploncks Hill, Shamley Green, Guildford), was a son of the rector of Alford. Educated at Shrewsbury and Balliol College, Oxford, he became curate of Stratfield-Turgis; then of Stratfield Saye; and in 1858 succeeded his father as rector of Alford-with-Hornblotton. He was Rural Dean in 1867-76, and in the latter year became prebendary of East Harptree in Wells Cathedral. He resigned his living in 1893. In 1866 he published *Hymns Congregational and Others*; *Hymns and Verses* in 1866; and *Hymns and Sacred Lyrics* in 1874. Impressed by the fact that all the hymn-books in the Church of England were issued by representatives of different parties he prepared and published as a protest 'against this system of party hymn-books', *A Church of England Hymn Book adapted to the daily services of the Church throughout the Year* (1880). An improved edition of it appeared in 1882 under the title *The Church of England Hymn Book*.

H. 298, 407, 461

TILAK, NARAYAN VAMAN (Karazgaon, Ratnagiri District, Bombay Presidency, 1861-1919, Ahmednagar), his father being a government registrar, was 'born in the purple' of Hinduism, steeped in its spirit and tradition, and proud of its history. For a time he taught in school, but, becoming a Christian in 1894, he was baptized the following year in Bombay, and for twenty-one years thereafter worked in connection with the American Marāthi Mission at Ahmednagar, teaching, preaching, doing social work. He was a passionate patriot, and eager for the naturalization of the Christian Church in India.

With this view he used his great poetic gifts to enrich the Marāthi Christian Church with an indigenous hymnody. He produced a great body of spiritual songs, expressive of the Indian Christian heart in its vision of Christ and its worship of God. In 1917 he renounced all means of support, to pursue a new method of evangelism, what he called 'God's Durbar', a brotherhood of the baptized and unbaptized disciples of Christ. His works were: *Tilakāñchi Kavitā*; *Upāsanā Sangīt*; *Bhajan Sañgraha*; *Abhangāñjali*; *Christāyan.*

H. 82

TISSERAND, JEAN (?-1494, Paris), was a Franciscan friar who lived in Paris. He founded an order for penitent women, and was the author of an historical work commemorating some members of his own Order who suffered martyrdom in Morocco in 1220. He also wrote various Latin poems, the most famous of which, 'O filii et filiae', was published shortly after his death in Paris.

H. 277

TOPLADY, AUGUSTUS MONTAGUE (Farnham, 1740-78, London), son of a major who was killed at the siege of Cartagena, was educated at Westminster School, and at Trinity College, Dublin. Ordained to the ministry of the Church of England in 1762, he was some time afterwards appointed vicar of Broadhembury, Devon. In 1775 he was preacher in a chapel of French Calvinists in Leicester Fields, London. Always a strong Calvinist, he wrote various tractates to vindicate the Anglican Church from what he considered the reproach of Arminianism. The controversies on this subject between him and John Wesley show neither disputant at his best. It is charitable to suppose that much of Toplady's bitterness may have been due to the ill health which carried him off at the early age of 38.

H. 83, 324, 651

TUCKER, FRANCIS BLAND (Norfolk, Virginia, 1895), was educated at the University of Virginia and Virginia Theological Seminary. He served as a private during the 1914-18 war. Ordained in 1918, he was rector of Grammer Parish, Brunswick County, Virginia (1920-5), of St. John's, Georgetown, Washington (1925-45), and then of Old Christ Church, Savannah, Georgia. He was a member of the committee which in 1940 revised the *Hymnal* of the Protestant Episcopal Church of America.

H. 242, 297, 522, 586

TURLE, JAMES (Taunton, Somerset, 1802-82, London), was a chorister at Wells (1810-13). Then he was articled to J. J. Goss in London. He was organist at Christ Church, Blackfriars (1819-29) and at St. James's, Bermondsey (1829-31). In 1831 he became organist and master of the choristers at Westminster Abbey. He was joint-editor of the *People's Music Book* (1844), edited *Psalms and Hymns* (1862), and his own tunes were collected and published in 1885.

C. 161 (ii)

T. 356

TURTON, WILLIAM HARRY, D.S.O., B.A. (Peshawur, India, 1856-1938, Oakhampton, Devon), was educated at Clifton College and the Royal Military Academy, Woolwich; gazetted to the Royal Engineers in 1876. He served in the war in South Africa (1900-2) and was mentioned in Dispatches. He published *Hymns written by a Layman between the Festivals of all Saints, 1880 and 1881*. He did the same each of the following two years. He also wrote *The Truth of Christianity*.

H. 492

TWEEDY, HENRY HALLAM (Binghamton, New York, 1868-1953, Brattleboro, Vermont), was educated for the Congregational ministry at Yale, Union Seminary, New York, and the University of Berlin. He was pastor of Plymouth Congregational Church, Utica, New York (1898-1902) and of South Congregational Church, Bridgeport, Connecticut (1902-9). He was Professor of Practical Theology in Yale (1909-37). He published *The Minister and his Hymnal* and edited *Christian Worship and Praise* (1939) as well as several hymnals.

H. 499

TWELLS, HENRY, M.A. (Ashted, Birmingham, 1823-1900, Bournemouth), was educated at King Edward's School, Birmingham, and at Peterhouse, Cambridge. Ordained in 1849, he became curate at Great Berkhampsted; sub-vicar of Stratford-upon-Avon; master of St. Andrew's House School, Wells; headmaster of Godolphin School, Hammersmith. In 1870 he became rector of Baldock, Hertfordshire; in 1871, rector of Waltham-on-the-Wolds, Melton Mowbray; was Select Preacher at Cambridge, 1873-4; and was made Hon. Canon of Peterborough in 1884. He acted as Warden of the Society of Mission Clergy in the Diocese of Peterborough. Owing to failing health he retired to Bournemouth in 1890, but built there and partly endowed the new church of St. Augustine, and, his health improving, served it as priest-in-charge until his death. He took an active part in the preparation of *Hymns Ancient and Modern*, and was on the committee for the *Appendix* of 1889.

H. 52

TYE, CHRISTOPHER, Mus.Doc. (*c.* 1508-72, Doddington?), was a native probably of East Anglia, graduated Mus.Bac., Cambridge, 1536, and Mus.Doc., 1545; and became master of the choristers, Ely Cathedral, 1541-2. In 1560 he was ordained, and presented to the living of Doddington-cum-March, in the Isle of Ely. He held simultaneously the rectorship of two other livings, Newton-cum-Capella and Little Wilbraham or Wilbraham Parva, near Cambridge. In a contemporary document he is described as 'a doctor of music, but not skilful at preaching'. He was a zealous adherent of the Reformed Church, but continued in the service of the Chapel Royal under Edward VI, Mary, and Elizabeth, without any apparent strain on his conscience. The work his name is most associated with appeared in 1553 with this title: *The Actes of the Apostles, translated into Englyshe Metre and dedicated to the Kynge's most excellent Maiestye by Christopher Tye, Doctor in Musyke, and one of the Gentylmen of hys grace's most honourable Chapell, with notes to eche Chapter, to synge, and also to play upon the Lute, very necessarye for studentes after theyr studye, to fyle their wyttes, and also for all*

Christians that cannot synge, to reade the good and Godlye storyes of the lyves of Christ hys Appostles.

T. 22, 263, 312 (ii)

TYNAN-HINKSON, KATHARINE (Dublin, 1861–1931, London), was the daughter of A. C. Tynan, Clandalkin, Dublin. She was educated at the Dominican Convent of St. Catherine of Siena, Drogheda. Her early poems appeared in various Irish journals, and the first collection was published in 1885. After her marriage in 1893 she went to London and there continued journalistic work. She also published several volumes of prose and verse.

H. 524

URHAN, CHRÉTIEN (Montjoie, near Aix-la-Chapelle, 1790–1845, Belleville, near Paris), showed remarkable musical talent from his earliest years, learned without help to play the piano and several other instruments and composed waltzes and violin variations before he reached his teens. The Empress Josephine heard him play in Aix in 1805, and carried him off to Paris to have his talent trained under the best masters. He became a brilliant player, not only on the violin, but on the five- and four-stringed viola and the viole d'amour. He specialized in this last instrument, which had dropped out of use; it was for him that Meyerbeer wrote the solo for that instrument in the first act of *The Huguenots.* Entering the orchestra of the Opera Française in 1816, he became solo violinist in it. During the thirty years he played in it he is said to have never once glanced at the stage, owing to his religious scruples. He was for a long time organist in the Church of St. Vincent de Paul.

T. 694

VAUGHAN, HENRY (Skethiog, Wales, 1621–95, Skethiog), was educated at Jesus College, Oxford. At the age of 24 Henry published a volume of poems. He afterwards became a physician, and practised for some time in Wales, ultimately retiring to his native Skethiog. Vaughan's poems were practically forgotten for two centuries, till Henry Francis Lyte edited them in 1847. They were known, however, to Wordsworth, whose *Intimations of Immortality* owes something to Vaughan's *Retreat.* Apart from this his best-known poems are *The World* and *Beyond the Veil.*

H. 693

VETTER, DANIEL (d. 1730?), was organist of St. Nicholas Church, Leipzig. He is believed to have composed four of the melodies, though he lays claim only to one, in his *Musikalische Kirch- und Hauss-Ergötzlichkeit* (1713).

T. 581

VULPIUS, MELCHIOR (Wasungen, Canton of Henneberg, Thuringia, *c.* 1560–1615, Weimar), became cantor at Weimar about 1600. He composed a number of tunes which were published in two important collections which he edited and issued in 1604 and 1609—*Ein schön geistlich Gesangbuch, &c., durch M. V. Cantorem zu Weymar.* Others were published after his death, in the *Cantional* of Gotha.

T. 266, 270, 404, 575, 606, 678 (ii)

WADDELL, HELEN, M.A., D.Litt., LL.D. (Tokyo, 1889–1965, London), whose father was a distinguished missionary and scholar in China and Japan, returned to Ulster and Kilmacrew House on her father's death in 1900. She was educated at Victoria College and Queen's University, Belfast. She saw her future in creative writing, but the years following Queen's were silent years owing to her stepmother's illness although she did publish *Lyrics from the Chinese* (1915). When her stepmother died she went to Somerville College, Oxford, in 1919, and two years later received a lecturership under the Cassell Trust Fund. Some years later she was appointed by Lady Margaret Hall to a Susette Taylor Travelling Fellowship. Her life was given to research and scholarship, and she received honorary doctorates from Queen's, Durham, St. Andrews, and Columbia universities. Among her works are *The Wandering Scholars* (1927); *Mediaeval Latin Lyrics* (1929); *The History of Chevalier Des Grieux and of Manon Lescaut* (1931); *Peter Abelard: a Novel* (1933); and *The Desert Fathers* (1936).

H. 486

WADE, JOHN FRANCIS (?, c. 1711–86, Douai), was a copyist of plain-chant and other music at Douai for most of his life, and also a teacher of music. The date of his birth is deduced from the inscription on his tombstone.

H. 191

WAINWRIGHT, JOHN (Stockport, 1723–68, Stockport), settled in Manchester in 1746 and was 'singing man' of the Collegiate Church, now the Cathedral, there. In 1750 he appears to have been organist of Stockport Parish Church, his famous tune to Byrom's Christmas carol having been first sung there on Christmas Day of that year, and subsequently, on the same day, by Wainwright and 'his singing men and boys', in Byrom's house in Manchester. He composed anthems and hymn-tunes, and in 1766 published a *Collection of Psalm Tunes, Anthems, Hymns and Chants, for 1, 2, 3, and 4 voices*.

T. 190

WAINWRIGHT, RICHARD (Manchester, 1758–1825, Liverpool), younger son of John, was organist of the Collegiate Church and of St. Ann's, Manchester. In 1782 he succeeded his elder brother Robert in St. Peter's, Liverpool. For a time he officiated in St. James's, Toxteth Park, Liverpool, but afterwards returned to St. Peter's. He wrote the well-known glee, *Life's a Bumper*, and published a *Collection of Hymns* composed for the children of the Liverpool Blue-Coat Hospital.

T. 665

WALKER, MARY JANE, *née* DECK (Bury St. Edmunds, 1816–78, Cheltenham), married in 1848 the Revd. Edward Walker, the first rector of Cheltenham. Dr. Walker, an ardent evangelical, edited *Psalms and Hymns for Public and Social Worship* (1855), which included a number of hymns by members of the then recently formed sect of Plymouth Brethren. It included over thirty by J. G. Deck, and nine by Mrs. Walker.

H. 686

WALTHER, JOHANN (Gotha, near Cola, Thuringia, 1496-1570, Torgau), was in 1524 bass singer in the choir at Torgau, when Luther, knowing his merit, summoned him to Wittenberg to assist in the preparation of the music for the services of the Lutheran Church, and particularly for the new service for Holy Communion. He spent three weeks in Luther's house, helping to adapt the old Church music to the new use, wherever possible, and harmonizing the tunes in five parts. He was present in the Stadtkirche at Wittenberg on 29 October 1525, when the new communion service, arranged by Luther and himself, was first used in German. The Elector Johann of Saxony made him his choir-master in 1526, at Dresden, and took into his pay the choir of eighteen men-singers and twelve boys, which it was his duty to direct. Four years later, on the disbandment of the Electoral Orchestra, it was reconstituted under his leadership by the town of Torgau, and in 1534 he was appointed singing-master also to the school there. In 1548 he accompanied the Elector Moritz to Dresden as his Kapellmeister. Pensioned in 1554, he retired to Torgau. He wrote a number of hymns, but was more notable as a composer. He published *Deutsche Messe und Ordnung Gottes-Dienst*; *Geystliche Gesangk Buchleyn* (Wittenberg); *Wittenbergisch deudsch geistlich Gesangbuchlein*.

T. 268

WARDLAW, RALPH, D.D. (Dalkeith, 1779-1853, Glasgow), was the son of a merchant who became a magistrate of Glasgow, and a mother who was a descendant of Ebenezer Erskine. He studied Arts in Glasgow University, then entered the Theological Hall of the Secession Church, but left it for Congregationalism. His only church was Albion Chapel, Glasgow, which he founded. In 1811 he was appointed Professor of Divinity in the Congregational Theological Hall, Glasgow. Offers of the Principalship of Hoxton Academy, of Spring Hill College, and of Lancashire Independent College, failed to draw him from Glasgow. He was a doughty controversialist on the chief problems of his time, and published a number of theological, expository, and polemical works. To displace the badly edited hymn-book then in use in 'The Tabernacles of Scotland', he published in 1803 *A Selection of Hymns for Public Worship*. It contained eleven hymns of his own.

H. 495

WARING, ANNA LAETITIA (Plas-y-Velin, Neath, Glamorgan, 1820-1910, Bristol), was brought up in the Society of Friends, but was drawn by desire for the sacraments into the Church of England, and baptized in 1842 at St. Martin's, Winnall, Winchester. She began early to write hymns, and contributed to *The Sunday Magazine*. She published *Hymns and Meditations by A. L. W.* (nineteen hymns) in 1850 and in the tenth edition, in 1863, enlarged the number to thirty-nine; also *Days of Remembrance* (1886). She learned Hebrew to be able to study Old Testament poetry in the original, and daily read the Hebrew Psalter.

H. 681

WARING, SAMUEL MILLER (Alton, Hampshire, 1792-1827, Bath), like his niece, Anna Laetitia Waring, was brought up in the Society of Friends, but left it for the Church of England. He published in 1826 *Sacred Melodies*, in which his hymns appeared.

H. 657

WARNER, ANNA BARTLETT (New York, 1827-1915, Highland Falls, New York), was a younger sister of Susan Warner, and was herself a popular authoress. The sisters collaborated in several novels, *Say and Seal*, *Ellen Montgomery's Book-shelf*, etc., and Anna, using the pseudonym of 'Amy Lothrop', wrote *Dollars and Cents*, *My Brother's Keeper*, and other stories. She edited *Hymns of the Church Militant* (1858), and published *Wayfaring Hymns, Original and Translated* (1869).

H. 418

WARNER, SUSAN (New York, 1819-85, Highland Falls, Orange County, New York), was the daughter of a lawyer. Susan's first book, *The Wide Wide World*, was published in 1850 under the pseudonym of 'Elizabeth Wetherell'. Other stories from her pen were *Queechy*; *The Old Helmet*; *The Hills of the Shatemuc*; *Melbourne House*; *Daisy*; and many more. She wrote definitely religious books also, going over the Bible story for children, and illustrating it from manners and customs of Biblical times, and from geography and records of travel—*The Law and the Testimony*; *The Kingdom of Judah*; *The Walls of Jerusalem*; *Standard Bearers of the Old Testament*, etc.

H. 488

WATT, LAUCHLAN MACLEAN, D.D., F.R.S.E., F.S.A. (Grantown, Inverness-shire, 1867-1957, Lochcarron, Ross-shire), came of Isle of Skye stock. He was educated at Edinburgh University, and after mission work and social study in Edinburgh and the Highlands, entered the Church of Scotland ministry in 1896, and was ordained in the following year at Turriff, Aberdeenshire. He was translated to Alloa and Tullibody in 1901; to St. Stephen's, Edinburgh, in 1911; and to Glasgow Cathedral in 1923. He was Moderator of the General Assembly in 1933, and retired the following year. He published *God's Altar Stairs*; *In Love's Garden*; *The Grey Mother*; *The Communion Table*; *By Still Waters*; *The Tryst* (poems); *Edragil, 1745, a Story of the Jacobite Rising*; *The House of Sands*; *Gates of Prayer*; *Green Meadows*; *Scottish Life and Poetry*; *Hills of Home*; *The Saviour of the World*; *In the Land of War*; *The Soldier's Friend*; etc. He was a member of the committee which compiled the RCH.

H. 666

WATTS, ISAAC (Southampton, 1674-1748, Stoke Newington), was the son of an Independent who kept a boarding-house at Southampton, and who suffered imprisonment for his convictions. Isaac was offered an education at one of the universities with a view to ordination in the Church of England, but refused, and entered an Independent academy. In 1702 he became pastor of the Independent congregation in Mark Lane, London. Not long afterwards his health began to fail. From 1712 till his death, thirty-six years afterwards, he lived the quiet life of a semi-invalid as the guest of Sir Thomas

Abney and afterwards of his widow, devoting his time to the production of theological and lyrical works. His *Logic* was for long a textbook at Oxford. Watts wrote about 600 hymns and versions. Watts is also the originator of a number of *The Scottish Paraphrases* though in most cases these have been more or less altered by other hands.

H. 2, 254, 273, 304, 362, 413, 536, 611, 637

WEBB, BENJAMIN (London, 1819–85, London), was educated at St. Paul's School and Trinity College, Cambridge. He became vicar of St. Andrew's, Wells Street, London, in 1862, and prebendary of St. Paul's in 1881. He wrote several works on ecclesiology, and was one of the original editors of *The Hymnal Noted* (1852) and of *The Hymnary* (1872) to which he contributed a number of hymns.

H. 223, 305

WEBB, GEORGE JAMES (Rushmore Lodge, near Salisbury, Wiltshire, 1803–87, Orange, New Jersey), was intended for the ministry, but chose music as his profession. He became organist of a church in Falmouth, but in 1830 emigrated to the United States. For forty years he was organist of the Old South Church in Boston. He acted as Professor in the Boston Academy of Music for many years. In 1870 he left Boston for Orange, New Jersey, and six years later removed to New York, but he settled again in Orange in 1885. A Swedenborgian in religion, he did important work for the Church of the New Jerusalem in arranging its musical service. He published a work on *Vocal Technics*, was part author of another on *Voice Culture*, and, with Lowell Mason and others, edited about a score of volumes of sacred and secular music.

T. 481

WEBBE, SAMUEL (London, 1740–1816, London), was the son of a government official in Minorca. His father died early and left his family unprovided for. Samuel was apprenticed at 11 to a cabinet-maker, but on completing his apprenticeship forsook that calling to copy music and earn enough to obtain music lessons. He received his first instruction from Barbaudt, organist of the Bavarian Chapel, London. He became a prolific composer of unaccompanied vocal music, was secretary to the Catch Club and librarian to the Glee Club, for which he wrote his celebrated glee, *Glorious Apollo*. In religion a Roman Catholic, he was organist of the chapel of the Sardinian Embassy in London, and wrote much religious music—masses, motets, and many hymn-tunes.

T. 47, 90, 120, 436, 601

WEBBE, SAMUEL, jun. (London, 1770–1843, Liverpool), son of Samuel Webbe, sen., studied under his father and Clementi. He became organist successively of the Unitarian Church, Paradise Street, Liverpool; the Spanish Ambassador's Chapel, London; St. Nicholas's Church, and St. Patrick's Roman Catholic Chapel, Liverpool. He was a composer of glees of considerable merit, songs, motets, madrigals, etc. He published a *Collection of*

Psalm Tunes, interspersed with Airs adapted as such, for four voices, in 1808;
Convito Armonico (4 vols.), a collection of madrigals, glees, canons, catches,
etc.; *Harmony epitomized, or Elements of Thoroughbass,* etc.

T. 371, 422

WEISSE (or WEISS), MICHAEL (Neisse, Silesia, *c.* 1480–1534, Landskron,
Bohemia), became a priest, and for a time was a monk at Breslau. Luther's
writings moved him deeply, and with two other monks he left the convent and
took refuge in the Bohemian Brethren's house at Leutomischl, Bohemia. He
joined the Brethren in 1531, and became their preacher at Landskron, and at
Fulnek, Moravia. He was editor of their first hymn-book in German, *Ein Neu
Gesangbuchlein* (1531). This book contained 155 hymns, most, if not all, of
which were either translations by him from Bohemian into German or
originals by himself.

T. 130

WEISSEL, GEORG (Domnau, Prussia, 1590–1635, Königsberg), was the son
of Johann Weissel, Burgomeister of Domnau. He studied at the University of
Königsberg (1608–11), and for a short time in the universities at Wittenberg,
Leipzig, Jena, Strasbourg, Basle, and Marburg. In 1614 he became rector of
the school at Freidland, but resigned three years later to resume his
theological studies. He became pastor of the Altrossgart Church at Königsberg. Most of his hymns appear in various Königsberg hymn-books between
1639 and 1650 and in the *Preussische Fest-Lieder* (1642, 1644).

H. 12

WERNER, JOHANN GOTTLOB (Hayn, 1777–1822, Merseburg), became
organist at Frohburg, Saxony, in 1798. In 1808 he became deputy for
Christian Tag as cantor of Nohenstein, and in 1819 organist and director of
music at Merseburg. His *Choralbuch* was published in 1815.

T. 497

WESLEY, CHARLES (Epworth, 1707–88, London), brother of John Wesley,
was the youngest son of Samuel and Susannah Wesley. He was educated at
Westminster School and at Christ Church, Oxford, where he became a
college tutor. In the same year he became one of the band known as the
'Oxford Methodists'. In 1735, having been ordained, he went with his brother
John to Georgia as secretary to General Oglethorpe, but came back after a
few months' stay. Not long afterwards he came, as did John, under the
influence of Peter Böhler and other Moravians. In 1756 he gave up itinerating
and settled in Bristol, and in 1771 removed to London. Charles was even less
of a separatist than John, disapproved of the latter's ordinations, and
declared that he had lived and would die in the communion of the Church of
England. It was as a hymn-writer that Charles Wesley rendered by far the
greatest service to religion. He is said to have written as many as 6,500 hymns.

H. 78, 85, 110, 112, 114, 122, 169, 275, 296, 316, 320, 371, 372, 409, 437, 441, 463,
543, 587

WESLEY, JOHN (Epworth, 1703-91, London), founder of Methodism, was a son of the Revd. Samuel Wesley, rector of Epworth in Lincolnshire. Educated at Charterhouse and Christ Church, Oxford, he became in 1726 Fellow of Lincoln, and later acted for a time as curate to his father. In 1735 he undertook a mission to Georgia under the Society for the Propagation of the Gospel. There he published the first hymn-book issued in America. Conscious, however, of failure in his mission, he returned to England in 1738. It was at a meeting in Aldersgate Street in May of that year that he felt his heart 'strangely warmed', and experienced the great spiritual change which made him a fervent evangelist. Thenceforward he devoted himself to the work of itinerant evangelism, and, since many of the clergy closed their pulpits against him, took to preaching in the open air. He was no dissenter, however; loved order and good music, and never refused an invitation to preach in church. His marvellous activity is recorded in his famous *Journal*. If he did little in the way of original hymn composition, his fine taste is shown in his translations from the German.

H. 2, 96, 118, 669, 678

T. 316

WESLEY, SAMUEL (Bristol, 1766-1837, London), was a younger son of Charles Wesley, the hymn-writer. He learned to read before he was 5 years old by poring over Handel's *Samson*, and soon after, without instruction, learned how to write. Before he was 8, he composed an oratorio, *Ruth*, which was a really musicianly work. He became a fine classical scholar, a first-rate performer on the violin, the piano, and the harpsichord; but his chief delight was in the organ, on which he was recognized to be the most masterly performer of his time. In 1784 he fell under the influence of the Roman Church, and there is evidence that he joined it, or was regarded as having joined it. This he denied in later life, declaring that the Gregorian music of the Roman Church seduced him to its chapels, but that its tenets never had any influence over his mind. He was more at home in composing for the Roman than for the Anglican service. He wrote four masses and many shorter works for that Church, several Anglican anthems and services, and many glees, songs, symphonies, concertos, etc. His masterpieces are vocal. In 1811 he conducted the Birmingham Festival, and in 1824 was organist of Camden Chapel, now Camden Town Parish Church.

C. 589 (ii)

WESLEY, SAMUEL SEBASTIAN, Mus.Doc. (London, 1810-76, London), was a son of Samuel Wesley, and was named after his father and his father's idol, Bach. He was one of the children of the Chapel Royal, and became an organist at 16. He served five parish churches, including that of Leeds, and four cathedrals—Hereford, Exeter, Winchester, and Gloucester. While at Gloucester he conducted the Three Choirs Festival. In 1844 he was a candidate for the Professorship of Music in Edinburgh University, but Sir Henry Bishop was preferred to him. He 'made a new departure in English service music. Without deserting the stately massiveness of the best of the earlier styles, he introduced some of the freshest and newest forms of modulation and harmonic progression, and movements that were at that time as novel as they were beautiful.' His *Service in E* is one of the finest in English Church music. In 1872 he published *The European Psalmist*, a collection of 733 hymn-tunes, of which 130 were his own.

T. 42 (ii), 338, 420, 600

WESTBROOK, FRANCIS BROTHERTON, B.A., Mus.D., F.R.S.C.M. (Thornton Heath, Croydon, 1903), was educated at Whitgift (now Trinity) Middle School, Croydon, Didsbury Theological College, Manchester, and the universities of Birmingham and Manchester. He has been Ministerial Secretary of the Methodist Church Music Society since 1945, and is Principal of Williams' School of Church Music, Harpenden. He contributed to *Hymns and Songs*; *100 Hymns for Today*; the *Baptist Supplement*; and the *Australian Methodist Hymn Book*. He has published a Passiontide Cantata, *Calvary*; a short *Communion Service*; two works for choir, solo, and orchestra, *The Prophet's Vision* and *Seven Words from the Cross*; an unaccompanied motet, *November*; and a number of anthems.

T. 152

WESTON, REBECCA J. (19th century), cannot be traced. She published a book on Tonic Sol-fa in Pennsylvania in 1885.

H. 99

WHITING, WILLIAM (Kensington, 1825-78, Winchester), was educated at Clapham and Winchester, and was for over twenty years master of the Winchester College Choristers' School. His *Rural Thoughts and Other Poems* (1851) contained no hymns. He is represented in hymnody by a single hymn.

H. 527

WHITTIER, JOHN GREENLEAF (Haverhill, Massachusetts, 1807-92, Hampton Falls, New Hampshire), began life as a farm boy and a slipper-maker. A copy of Burns's poems, bought from a Scots pedlar, whose singing of the Ayrshire poet's songs threw the lad into raptures, first awoke his lyrical genius, and led him to experiment in verse himself. His sister sent some of his verses to a newspaper edited by William Lloyd Garrison who was so much struck by their quality that he sought young Whittier out. The friendship thus begun led the lad to enter the journalistic profession. He became, like Garrison, an ardent abolitionist, and used his pen powerfully in the anti-slavery crusade. In 1828 he became editor of *The American Manufacturer*; in 1830, of *The New England Review*; in 1836, of *The Pennsylvania Freeman*; he was also for some time corresponding editor of *The National Era*. He was a member of the Society of Friends, and to the last wore the distinctive garb of the Quakers and used their mode of speech. He made his home, in 1840, at Amesbury, Massachusetts, but his last years were spent at Oak Knoll, Danvers. He said also that two hundred years of silence had taken all the 'sing' out of the Quakers. None the less, over fifty hymns by him are found in modern hymn-books, most of them being centos from his poems.

H. 76, 306, 439, 460, 610

WILKES, JOHN BERNARD (?, ?-1882, London), was organist at Monkland, near Leominster, about 1860, at the time when *Hymns Ancient and Modern* was about to make its first appearance, and was thus associated with the first edition of that book through his vicar, Sir H. W. Baker.

T. 33 (i)

WILKINS, MATTHEW (Oxford, 1704-72, Great Milton), published his *Psalmody* (c. 1730). He lived most of his life at Thame, Oxfordshire, where he was butcher, teacher, organist, and composer. Nothing more is known of him.

T. 23, 24, 140 (ii)

WILKINSON, KATE BARCLAY (?, 1859-1928, Kensington), was a member of the Church of England and organized work among girls in London. Otherwise nothing is known of her.

H. 432

WILLIAMS. AARON (London, 1731-76, London), was a music engraver and publisher of psalmody, a music teacher also, and he acted as clerk to the Scots Church, London Wall. He compiled and published *The Universal Psalmodist*, containing (i) a *Complete Introduction to Psalmody* ... (ii) a *choice and valuable Collection of Tunes* (1770); *New Universal Psalmodist* (1770); *Harmonia Coelestis, or, the Harmony of Heaven imitated, a Collection of scarce and much-esteemed anthems* (1775); *Psalmody in Miniature* (1778); *Royal Harmony, or the Beauties of Church Music* (1780).

T. 332, 495

WILLIAMS, PETER (Laugharne, Carmarthen, 1722-96, Landyfeilog), was educated at Carmarthen Grammar School. Ordained by the Bishop of St. David's, he held several curacies, but eventually left the Established Church and threw in his lot with the Revivalists. His connection with hymnody is slight, the first stanza only of the undernoted hymn being doubtfully attributed to his translation of one of Williams of Pantycelyn's hymns.

H. 89

WILLIAMS, RALPH VAUGHAN, Mus.Doc., O.M. (Down Ampney, Cirencester, 1872-1958, London), was educated at Trinity College, Cambridge, and at the Royal College of Music under Stanford, Parry, and Charles Wood; also at Paris and Berlin. He was organist of South Lambeth Church, 1896-9; Extension Lecturer for Oxford University; Professor of Composition, Royal College of Music, London. Practically all his music dates after his thirtieth year. He did work of great value in collecting and editing for publication folk-songs and carols, chiefly in East Anglia and Herefordshire; and folk-song music and old English music from the Tudor period to Purcell deeply influenced his own composition. His works include *Towards the Unknown Region* (to Walt Whitman's words); *Willow Wood*; *A London Symphony*; *A Sea Symphony*; *Mystical Songs*; *A Pastoral Symphony*; *Songs of Travel*; *In the Fen Country*; *The Wasps* (overture); *Harnham Down*;

rhapsodies on folk melodies; songs, like 'On Wenlock Edge' and 'Linden Lea'. He composed a *Mass in G Minor, Benedicite, Sancta Civitas, Fantasia on a Theme of Tallis*, and a *Magnificat* and *Dona Nobis Pacem*. He was musical editor of *The English Hymnal*, and, with Martin Shaw, of *Songs of Praise*.

T. 17, 30, 111, 115, 134, 144, 145 (i), 157, 172, 175, 181, 196, 197, 208, 212, 220, 283, 328, 335, 362, 385, 419, 439, 443, 447, 502, 504, 515, 524, 534, 553, 618, 619, 623, 624, 630, 684

WILLIAMS, ROBERT (Mynydd Ithel, Llanfechell, Anglesey, *c.* 1781–1821, Mynydd Ithel), was born blind, but became a skilled basket-maker, so earning his living. A gifted musician, it was said that on hearing a tune once he could write it out without a single mistake.

T. 359

WILLIAMS, THOMAS (18th century), edited *Psalmodia Evangelica, a Complete Set of Psalm and Hymn Tunes for Public Worship* in 1789.

T. 446, 498

WILLIAMS, WILLIAM (Cefn-y-coed, 1717–91, Pantycelyn, near Llandovery), was the son of a well-to-do farmer. He received a good education and was sent to Llwynllwyd Academy (later, the Presbyterian College), Carmarthen, to be trained for the medical profession, but in 1738 decided to enter the ministry, and was licensed to the curacy of Llanwrtyd, Brecon. Being refused priest's orders because of his evangelical views, he withdrew from the Established Church and threw himself into evangelistic work. He composed over 800 hymns in Welsh and over 100 in English, and in addition wrote two long poems, *Theomemphus* and *Golwg ar Deyrnas Crist* (A View of the Kingdom of Christ), several prose treatises, and numerous elegies.

H. 89

WILLIAMSON, MALCOLM BENJAMIN GRAHAM CHRISTOPHER (Sydney, Australia, 1931), was educated at Barker College, Hornsby, New South Wales, and the Sydney Conservatorium, and studied under Lutyens, Sir E. Goossens, and Erwin Stein. He has been resident in England since 1953. He was Composer in Residence in Westminster Choir College, Princeton, New Jersey (1970–1). His works include *Our Man in Havana, The Violins of St. Jacques*, symphonies, string quartets, and organ and piano pieces, as well as film scores and Roman Catholic Church music in popular-song style. He was appointed Master of the Queen's Music in 1975.

T. 114 (i)

WILSON, HUGH (Fenwick, Ayrshire, 1766–1824, Duntocher), was the son of a shoemaker, and was apprenticed to his father's trade. In his spare time he was a diligent student of mathematics and kindred subjects, and qualified himself to add to his income by teaching others. A favourite pastime was the making of sundials. Occasionally he led the psalmody in the Secession

Church. Removing about the end of the eighteenth century to Pollokshaws, he held positions of responsibility in certain mills there, and afterwards at Duntocher. While there he acted as a manager in the Secession Church, and was one of the two founders of the first Sunday school there. He composed many psalm-tunes, but only two—'Martyrdom' and 'Caroline'—appear to have been published.

T. 667

WILSON, JOHN (Edinburgh, 1800–49, Quebec), was apprenticed to a firm of printers in Edinburgh and later became a proof-reader. He was a member of the choir in Duddingston Church, and then precentor in Roxburgh Place Relief Church. In 1825 he became precentor in St. Mary's Parish Church, and the same year edited *A Selection of Psalm Tunes, Sanctuses, Doxologies, &c., for use of the Congregation of St. Mary's Church, Edinburgh.* In 1830 he resigned his precentorship and took to the stage, appearing at Covent Garden and Drury Lane.

T. 25

WILSON, THOMAS BRENDAN, M.A., B.Mus., A.R.C.M. (Colorado, U.S.A., 1927), was educated at the University of Glasgow, where he was appointed Lecturer in Music in 1937 and Reader in 1972. He has published many orchestral works, two symphonies, Concerto for orchestra, Toccata for orchestra, etc., and much chamber music, for example, Piano trio, Violin Sonata, Cello Sonata, Sinfonia for 7 Instruments, as well as several works for brass band. His dramatic works include *Charcoal Burner, Sequentiae Passionis, Te Deum,* and an opera, *Confessions of a Justified Sinner.*

T. 13, 86, 556 (iii)

WINKWORTH, CATHERINE (London, 1827–78, Monnetin, Savoy), was a daughter of Henry Winkworth of Alderley Edge, Cheshire. Her *Lyra Germanica* (two series, 1855 and 1858) ranks with the devotional classics of the nineteenth century. She published also *The Chorale Book for England* (translations with music, 1863), and *Christian Singers of Germany* (1869). During her later years, which she spent at Clifton, Bristol, she took an active interest in the Clifton Association for the Higher Education of Women, and in kindred societies.

H. 9, 12, 171, 188, 202, 315, 368, 414, 552, 567, 643, 659, 668

WINSLOW, JOHN COPLEY, M.A. (Hanworth, Middlesex, 1882–1974, Godalming, Surrey), was educated at Eton and Balliol College, Oxford. After many years as a missionary in India, he became Chaplain to Bryanston School (1942–8), and then to Lee Abbey from which he retired in 1962. He has contributed to various hymn-books in Ireland, Canada, Australia, and New Zealand, including *Hymns for Church and School, Hymns Ancient and Modern,* and *100 Hymns for today.* Among his publications are *When I Awake; The Christian Approach to the Hindu; The Lee Abbey Story; Confession and Absolution; Modern Miracles; The Gate of Life,* etc.

H. 51, 428

WITT (or WITTE), CHRISTIAN FRIEDRICH (Altenburg, c. 1660-1716, Gotha), was Court organist, and, later, Kapellmeister, at Gotha. He composed a number of hymn-tunes, which appeared in his *Psalmodia Sacra* (1715).

T. 199, 259, 320, 348

WOLCOTT, SAMUEL (South Windsor, Connecticut, 1813-86, Longmeadow, Massachusetts), was educated at Yale and Andover. He was a missionary in Syria from 1840-2. On returning to America, he was pastor in several Congregational churches, and was for a period secretary of the Ohio Home Missionary Society. He wrote over two hundred hymns.

H. 500

WOLDER, DAVID (Hamburg, ?-1604, Hamburg), studied at Rostock (1568-73) where he became chaplain and lecturer in theology. In 1577, he was called to preach at St. Peter's, Hamburg, where he remained until his death during the plague. He was a distinguished Biblical scholar, editing a Hebrew Bible in 1587, and a polyglot Bible in 1596. He also compiled the *Neu Catechismus Gesangbüchlein*, Hamburg, 1598. It was dedicated to King Christian IV of Denmark, published by Theodosius Wolder, and contained 250 numbered songs and 178 tunes, which appeared for the first time.

T. 590

WOOD, CHARLES, Mus.Doc. (Armagh, 1866-1926, Cambridge), studied at Armagh, the Royal College of Music, London, and Cambridge, where he became a Fellow of Gonville and Caius College. He became Professor of Harmony at the R.C.M. in 1888; assistant to Villiers Stanford as conductor of the Cambridge University Musical Society, 1888-94; University Lecturer in Harmony and Counterpoint, 1897. He published *Patrick Sarsfield* (symphonic variations); choral works, *Ode to the West Wind*; Milton's *Ode on Time*; *Dirge for Two Veterans*; Swinburne's *Ode on Music*; *Song of the Tempest*; *Ballad of Dundee*; many part-songs, solo songs (e.g. 'Ethiopia saluting the colours'), and Church music. His compositions show great originality. In his treatment of Irish folk-songs he excelled.

T. 271, 341, 398

WOODFORD, JAMES RUSSELL, D.D. (Henley-on-Thames, 1820-85, Ely), was educated at the Merchant Taylors' School, London, and Pembroke College, Cambridge. Ordained in 1843, he was second master for a time in Bishop's College, Bristol, and curate of St. John the Baptist Church in that city. He became incumbent of St. Saviour's, Coalpit Heath, and of St. Mark's, Easton, Bristol; rector of Kempsford, Gloucestershire; vicar of Leeds; honorary chaplain to the Queen; several times Select Preacher at Oxford; and in 1873, Bishop of Ely. His published works included sermons; *Lectures on the Creed*; *Hymns arranged for the Sundays and Holy Days of the Church of England* (1852 and 1855). He was joint-editor of *The Parish Hymn Book* (1863 and 1875), in which his own hymns and translations from the Latin appeared.

H. 584

WOODWARD, George Ratcliffe, D.Mus. (Birkenhead, 1848-1934, West Hill, Highgate), was a scholar of Gonville and Caius College, Cambridge. Ordained in 1874, he became curate of St. Barnabas, Pimlico (1874-82), vicar of Little Walsingham, Norfolk (1882-8), rector of Chelmondiston, Suffolk (1888-94), curate at St. Barnabas again (1894-9), licentiate preacher in the diocese of London (1899-1903), and curate of St. Mark's, Marylebone (1903-6). He edited the first edition of the *Cowley Carol Book* (1901) and *Songs of Syon*. He made an edition of *Piae Cantiones* (1582) for the Plainsong and Early Church Music Society in 1910, and also published *Hymns of the Greek Church* (1922). Much of the musical material introduced to the general public in *The English Hymnal* was based on his researches.

H. 187, 271, 604, 640

WORDSWORTH, Christopher, D.D. (Lambeth, 1807-85, Harewood), was the youngest son of Christopher Wordsworth, in 1807 rector of Lambeth, and afterwards Master of Trinity College, Cambridge. Educated at Winchester and Trinity College, he had a brilliant career, graduating as Senior Classic and Senior Optime in the Mathematical Tripos. He became Fellow and Classical Lecturer in his college, and in 1836 Public Orator of the University. At Harrow, as headmaster, while still under 30, he began in 1836 a great moral reform. In 1844 he was given a canonry at Westminster; in 1848-9 was Hulsean Lecturer at Cambridge; in 1850 began a nineteen years' ministry in the quiet country parish of Stanford-in-the-Vale-cum-Goosey, Berkshire, and in 1868 was appointed Bishop of Lincoln. He was unceasingly diligent as a writer, publishing sermons, addresses, a *Commentary on the whole Bible*, books on *Athens and Attica, Pompeian Inscriptions*, etc., and in 1862, *The Holy Year*, hymns for every season and for every phase of each season in the Christian Year. He held it to be 'the first duty of a hymn to teach sound doctrine, and thus to save souls'.

H. 145, 438

WOTHERSPOON, Arthur Wellesley, M.A. (Kilspindie, Perthshire, 1853-1936, Edinburgh), son of the Revd. W. L. Wotherspoon, D.D., was educated at Perth Academy and St. Andrews University. He acted as assistant at Moulin, Beith, Toward, and Hamilton. In 1883 he was ordained to the parish of Oatlands, Glasgow. He was an active member of the Scottish Church Society; he contributed a number of papers to the proceedings of that Society and to those of the Ecclesiological Society. He acted as sub-editor of *The Scottish Mission Hymn Book* (1912), to which he contributed three hymns and two tunes.

H. 256, 576, 660

WREFORD, John Reynell, D.D. (Barnstaple, 1800-81, Bristol), was educated at Manchester College, York, for the Unitarian ministry. He became colleague-minister of the New Meeting, Birmingham, in 1826, but was compelled to resign in 1831 because of failure of voice. He then withdrew from the ministry and opened a school at Edgbaston. The later years of his life were spent in retirement at Bristol. He wrote *A Sketch of the History of Presbyterian Nonconformity in Birmingham* (the Unitarian variety), and several volumes of devotional verse. In 1837 he contributed fifty-five hymns to the Revd. J. R. Beard's *Collection of Hymns for Public and Private Worship*, which was designed 'as a protest against hymn-tinkering, and as a novel effort to reconstruct Unitarian Hymnody out of materials exclusively Unitarian'. It rejected all Trinitarian and evangelical hymns, and thus sacrificed all the great hymns of the Church, Beard refusing to adapt them to Unitarian use. Even among Unitarians the book had no success.

H. 518

WREN, BRIAN ARTHUR, M.A., D.Phil. (Romford, Essex, 1936), was educated at Romford Royal Liberty Grammar School and New and Mansfield Colleges, Oxford. He was minister of Hockley and Hawkwell Congregational (now United Reformed) Church, Essex (1965-70), and since 1970 has been consultant for Adult Education Churches' Committee on World Development. He has written about thirty hymns, which are to be found in *Dunblane Praises, 100 Hymns for today, Sing* (Lutheran Church in America), *The Hymn Book* (Canada), and various supplements. He has published *Poverty and Hope* (1970), *This We Can Do* (1972), *Nothing to do with Politics*, etc., and contributed to *Contemporary Prayers for Public Worship* (1967).

H. 469

WRIGHT, WILLIAM (Lockerbie, Dumfriesshire, 1859-1924, Belfast), was brought up in the Free Church of Scotland, of which he became an elder at the age of 24. Trained as a pharmacist in Lockerbie, Worthing, and Glasgow, he carried on business as such until invited to join the secretariat of the Scottish Y.M.C.A. After some years spent in this work, he was asked to transfer his service to Ireland, as National Secretary of the Y.M.C.A. there. In that office he did notable work for twenty-four years.

H. 614

ZUNDEL, JOHN (Hockhorf, Germany, 1815-82, Cannstadt, Germany), was educated in Germany. He spent about seven years in St. Petersburg where he was organist of St. Anne's Lutheran Church and bandmaster of the Imperial Horse Guards. He went to America in 1847, where he was successively organist of the First Unitarian Church, Brooklyn, of St. George's Episcopal Church, Manhattan, and Plymouth Congregational Church, Brooklyn. He was musical editor of the *Plymouth Collection* (1855), edited by Henry and Charles Beecher.

T. 134

APPENDIX A

NEW HYMNS

162. *Before all time the Word existed.* James Neil S. Alexander
126. *God's perfect law revives the soul.* Ian Pitt-Watson
203. *King of kings and Lord of lords.* Kahanji Madhavji Ratnagrahi
 64. *O God be gracious to me in thy love.* Ian Pitt-Watson
601. *O God, whose loving hand has led.* J. Boyd Moore
 68. *Thou art before me, Lord, thou art behind.* Ian Pitt-Watson
399. *Though in God's form he was.* A. M. Hunter
595. *We magnify thy Name, O God.* John M. Barkley

APPENDIX B

NEW MUSIC

Commissioned Hymn Tunes

470. *Ashton.* R. Barrett-Ayres
 50. *Binham.* Lennox Berkeley
690. *Blackford.* Kenneth Leighton
292. *Barnton.* William Mathias
411. *Bute.* John Currie
453. *Carrick.* John Currie
576. *Colinton.* Kenneth Leighton
647. *Connolly.* Martin Dalby
 44. *Dunoon.* Kenneth Leighton
401. *Egton Bridge.* John Joubert
486. *Headington.* Kenneth Leighton
576. *Iona.* Frederick Rimmer
678. *Killinchy.* Sebastian Forbes
141. *Kilvaree.* Sebastian Forbes
325. *Lockwinnoch.* Robin Orr
164. *Mapperley.* Frank Spedding
672. *Mayfield.* Kenneth Leighton
 54. *Melfort.* Lennox Berkeley
340. *Monikie.* David Dorward
399. *Orb.* John Currie
433. *Pettronsen.* Martin Dalby
425. *Pityoulish.* R. Barrett-Ayres
 13. *Rutherglen.* Thomas Wilson
149. *Souster.* Martin Dalby
 86. *Stonelaw.* Thomas Wilson
177. *Summer in Winter.* Arthur Oldham

Amens, Chants, Liturgical Settings

 21. *Chant.* John Currie
 60. *Kyrie eleison.* Kenneth Leighton
 61. *Trisagion.* George Thalben-Ball .
 62. *Gloria in excelsis.* Kenneth Leighton
 66. *Chant.* John Currie
240. *Trisagion and Reproaches.* Gregory Murray
556. *Aaronic Blessing.* Anonymous (Lille)

556. *Aaronic Blessing.* Thomas Wilson (Heaton)
560. *Sanctus.* Kenneth Leighton
561. *Benedictus qui venit.* Kenneth Leighton
563. *Agnus Dei.* Kenneth Leighton

Contributed Hymn Tunes

401. *Culrathain.* James Moore
401. *Ramelton.* James Moore

APPENDIX C

CHURCH HYMNARY REVISION COMMITTEE

List of Members, September 1972

THE CHURCH OF SCOTLAND

(a) *Appointed by the Committee on Public Worship and Aids to Devotion*

The Revd. Thomas H. Keir, D.D. (*Convener*)
The Revd. W. H. Rogan, D.D.
The Revd. J. D. Ross, M.A.
The Revd. A. W. Sawyer, O.B.E., M.C., D.D., T.D.
The Revd. A. Stewart Todd, B.D.
Professor Ian Pitt Watson, B.D.
F. N. Davidson Kelly, Esq., LL.B., S.S.C. (*Secretary*)
The Rt. Revd. R. Selby Wright, C.V.O., D.D.
The Revd. R. J. Stewart, B.D.

(b) *Nominated by General Assembly*

The Very Revd. A. C. Craig, D.D.
The Revd. James N. S. Alexander, B.D., S.T.M.
The Revd. Douglas Briggs, M.A.
The Revd. George G. Campbell, M.A.
The Revd. R. A. Fishwick, M.M., B.Mus.
The Revd. John Heron, B.D., S.T.M.
The Revd. T. M. McFarlane, D.D.
The Revd. William Niven, L.T.C.L.
Ian Barrie, Esq., M.A., B.Mus., F.R.C.O.

(c) *Nominated by the Church Hymnary Trustees*

The Revd. R. Stuart Louden, T.D., D.D. (*Vice-Convener*)
The Hon. Lord Strachan, LL.D.

The Revd. John A. Lamb, D.D.
The Revd. Ninian B. Wright, B.D.

THE PRESBYTERIAN CHURCH IN IRELAND

J. K. C. Armour, Esq., M.A.
The Revd. Professor J. M. Barkley, M.A., Ph.D., D.D. (*Editor of Handbook*)
The Revd. Dr. G. T. Lundie, D.D., LL.B.
The Revd. J. T. Carson, B.A.
The Revd. J. Boyd Moore

THE PRESBYTERIAN CHURCH OF ENGLAND

The Revd. R. Aled Davies, M.A.
The Revd. David C. M. Gardner, M.A.
The Revd. E. C. Lane, M.A.
C. E. Strange, Esq., M.B.E., F.R.C.O.

THE PRESBYTERIAN CHURCH OF WALES

The Revd. J. Harries Hughes, B.A.
The Revd. J. W. Phillips, B.A., B.D.
The Revd. J. Price Williams, M.A.

UNITED FREE CHURCH OF SCOTLAND

The Revd. Alex. Ross
The Revd. Elizabeth B. Barr, B.A., B.D.

MUSIC CONSULTANTS

Herrick Bunney, Esq.
Professor Kenneth Leighton
John Currie, Esq.
David Murray, Esq.

ALPHABETICAL INDEX OF TUNES

Brackets round a number indicate words for which the tune is also suitable

INDEX OF
CHANTS, PLAIN-SONG TONES,
PLAIN-SONG MELODIES, AND
SETTINGS OF LITURGICAL ITEMS, ETC.

METRICAL INDEX OF TUNES

Brackets round a number indicate words for which the tune is also suitable

SHORT METRE (S.M.)

Bucer, 324
Carlisle, 39, 477
Franconia, 74, 104, (113)
Hampton, 332, 495
Hillsborough, 511, 629
Narenza, 456, 493
(Old 134th), *see* St. Michael
Rutherglen, 13
St. Bride, (74), (80), 410
St. Michael, 46, 265, 319
Sandys, 153, (629), 692
Southwell, 80, 248, 249, 466
Swabia, 113, 680
Wirksworth, 103

S.M. *and refrain*

Welcome Voice, 683

DOUBLE SHORT METRE (D.S.M.)

Diademata, 298
From strength to strength, 441
Ich halte treulich still, 445, 669

COMMON METRE (C.M.)

Abbey, 73, 393, 457
(Aberdeen), *see* St. Paul
Abridge (St. Stephen), 28, 394
Arden, 594
Ashwell, 679
Bangor (*Tans'ur*), 452
Belmont, 549
Binchester, 408
Bishopthorpe, 530
Bristol, 27, 160
(Byzantium), *see* Jackson
Caithness, (82), 125, 395, 547, (663)
Cherry Tree, 49
Cheshire, 65
Chorus Angelorum, 238
Colchester (*Tans'ur*), 626
Coleshill, 351

Crediton, (160), 168, (273), 347
Crimond, 387
Culross, 102, 215
(Dundee), *see* French *and* Windsor
Dunfermline, 101, 136, 635
Effingham, (167), 285
(Erin), *see* St. Columba
Farnham, 439
Farrant, 26
Felix, 159
Fingal, 306
French, 139, 543
Gerontius, (107), 238
Glasgow, 312
Godre'r Coed, 150
Gräfenberg, 5 (*see also* Nun danket all)
Harington, 4
Horsley, 241
Howard, 25, (29)
In armour bright, 288
Irish, 19, (27), 294, 323
Jackson, (41), 565, 591
Kilmarnock, 69, (351), 603
King's Langley, (419), 618, 630
Lancaster, 273
London New, 6, 147, (670)
Martyrdom, (636), 667
Martyrs, 7, 107, 242, 670
Mendip, 536
Metzler, 302, 377, 378
Miles Lane (irreg.), 382
Montrose, 133, 167, 343
Moravia, 590
Nativity, 48, 150
Newbury, 419
(Newington), *see* St. Stephen
(Nottingham), *see* St. Magnus
Nun danket all, 252, 525 (*see also* Gräfen-
berg)
Pityoulish, 425
Praetorius, (94), 288, (311), 459, 596
(Redhead No. 66), *see* Metzler
(Retirement), *see* Harington

Petra, 83, 247
Psalm 135, 114
Ratisbon, 497
(Redhead No. 76), see Petra

777 777(7)
Jordan, 105

7777. D
Aberystwyth, 78
Hollingside, 78
St. George's, Windsor, 627

7777. D and refrain
Mendelssohn (Bethlehem), 169

7779
Winchmore, 465

7878 and Alleluia
St. Albinus, 605

7878 88
Liebster Jesu (Dessau), 128, 129, 552

8 33 6
Thanet, 648

8484 84
Oldown, 146
Severn, 146

8484 884
Lower Marlwood, 12

8486. D
Fifth Mode Melody, 119

8583
Cuttle Mills, 100, 685
Westridge, 529

8585 843
Angel Voices, 455
Arthog, 455

866. D
Bonn, 171

8684
Essex, 336
St. Cuthbert, 336

8686 7686
Forest Green (irreg.), 172

8686 86
Sancta Civitas, 509

8686 88
Emain Macha, 398

86 886
(Lobt Gott), see Nicolaus
Nicolaus, 357
Old 18th, 76
Repton (86 886(6)), 76

878 and refrain (see also 8787)
Sussex, 144

8785
Vigil, 432

8787
Ach Gott und Herr (Iambic), 588
Dominus regit me (Iambic), 388
Evening Prayer, 467, 656
Gott des Himmels, 634
Laus Deo, (37), 337, 369
Marching, 423
Mary (Iambic), 388
Omni Die, 211, 218
Ottery St. Mary, 400
(Redhead No. 46), see Laus Deo
St. Andrew (Thorne), 211
Shipston, 17, 502
Stuttgart, 199, 259, 320, 348
Sussex, (218), 447, 619
(Waltham), see Gott des Himmels

8787 and refrain
*Where tunes are marked with an asterisk
see also 8787. D*

*Hyfrydol, 381
*In Babilone, 282
Iris, 182
*Rustington, 353

10 10 10 10

Adoro Te (*Plain-song*), 584
Blessing and honour and glory and
    power (*Dactylic*), 299
Chilton Foliat, 451
Dunblane Cathedral, 501
Dunoon (irreg.), 44
Ellers, 649
Eventide, 695
Farley Castle, 649
Magda, 335
Mapperley, 164
O quanta qualia (*Dactylic*), (299), 535
(Regnator orbis), *see* O quanta qualia
Slane (*Dactylic*) (irreg.), 87
Song 22,   (64), 108, (335), (572), 573, 582
Song 24,   64, 245
Stonelaw, 86
Stoner Hill, 572, (573)
Sursum corda, 68, 458
Woodlands, 440

10 10 10 10 10

Old 124th, 84, 392, 640

10 10 10 10   10 10

Finlandia, 673
Song 1, 492, 514, 580
(Stockport), *see* Yorkshire
Yorkshire, 190

10 10 11 11

Hanover, 35
Laudate Dominum (*Parry*), 372

10 11 10 10

Lumetto, 488

10 11 11 11

Slane, 428 (irreg.)

10 11 11 11 *and refrain*

Maccabaeus, 279

10 11 11 12

Miniver, 92
Slane, (92)

11 6 11 6

Headington, 486
Wilton, 131

11 10 10 *and refrain*

Noël Nouvelet, 278

11 10 11 9

Russia (Rephidim), 516 (irreg.), 517

11 10 11 10

Crudwell (*Dactylic*), 201
(Donne secours), *see* Psalm 12
Intercessor, 244, (250), 460
Kilvaree, 141
Northbrook, 503, 523
Psalm 12,   (141), 250, 307, (309), 314

11 10 11 10 *and refrain*

Old 124th, 507

11 10 11 10. D

Derry Air (Londonderry), 309

11 11 11 5

Christe Sanctorum, 43
Diva Servatrix, (491), 568, 643
Herzliebster Jesu, 251
Iste Confessor (*Chartres*), 31
Iste Confessor (*Poitiers*), 491

11 11 11 11

Cradle Song, 195
(Joanna), *see* St. Denio
Normandy, 195, 415
St. Denio, 32, 374
Town Joys, 384

11 11 11 11 (*Trochaic*)

Au clair de la lune, 228
Nous allons, 272

11 11 11 12 *and refrain*

Fortitude, 482

11 12 12 10

Nicaea (irreg.), 352

12 10 12 10

Moredun, 40
Was lebet, was schwebet, 40

12 10 12 11

Laredo (irreg.), 427

INDEX OF FIRST LINES

Hymns for children are marked with an asterisk